SUPPLEMENT XII
Kathy Acker to Richard Russo

American Writers
A Collection of Literary Biographies

JAY PARINI
Editor in Chief

SUPPLEMENT XII
Kathy Acker to Richard Russo

Charles Scribner's Sons
an imprint of the Gale Group
New York • Detroit • San Francisco • London • Boston • Woodbridge, CT

American Writers, Supplement XII

Jay Parini, Editor in Chief

Permissions Department
The Gale Group, Inc.
27500 Drake Rd.
Farmington Hills, MI 48331-3535
Permissions Hotline:
248 699-8006 or 800 877-4253, ext. 8006
Fax: 248 699-8074 or 800 762-4058

Since this page cannot legibly accommodate all copyright notices, the acknowledgments constitute an extension of the copyright notice.

LIBRARY OF CONGRESS CATALOGING-IN-PUBLICATION DATA

American writers : a collection of literary biographies / Leonard Unger
   editor in chief.
      p. cm.
   The 4-vol. main set consists of 97 of the pamphlets originally published as the University of Minnesota pamphlets on American writers; some have been rev. and updated. The supplements cover writers not included in the original series.
   Supplement 2, has editor in chief, A. Walton Litz; Retrospective suppl. 1, c1998, was edited by A. Walton Litz & Molly Weigel; Suppl. 5–7 have as editor-in-chief, Jay Parini.
   Includes bibliographies and index.
   Contents: v. 1. Henry Adams to T.S. Eliot — v. 2. Ralph Waldo Emerson to Carson McCullers — v. 3. Archibald MacLeish to George Santayana — v. 4. Isaac Bashevis Singer to Richard Wright — Supplement[s]: 1, pt. 1. Jane Addams to Sidney Lanier. 1, pt. 2. Vachel Lindsay to Elinor Wylie. 2, pt. 1. W.H. Auden to O. Henry. 2, pt. 2. Robinson Jeffers to Yvor Winters. — 4, pt. 1. Maya Angelou to Linda Hogan. 4, pt. 2. Susan Howe to Gore Vidal — Suppl. 5. Russell Banks to Charles Wright — Suppl. 6. Don DeLillo to W.D. Snodgrass — Suppl. 7. Julia Alvarez to Tobias Wolff — Suppl. 8. T.C. Boyle to August Wilson.
   ISBN 0-684-19785-5 (set) — ISBN 0-684-13662-7
   1. American literature—History and criticism. 2. American literature—Bio-bibliography. 3. Authors, American—Biography. I. Unger, Leonard. II. Litz, A. Walton. III. Weigel, Molly. IV. Parini, Jay. V. University of Minnesota pamphlets on American writers.

PS129 .A55
810'.9
[B]   73-001759

ISBN 0-684-31232-8

Printed in the United States of America
10 9 8 7 6 5 4 3 2

Editorial and Production Staff

Project Editor
ALJA KOOISTRA COLLAR

Assisting Editor
MARK DROUILLARD

Copyeditors
JANET L. BADGLEY
MELISSA A. DOBSON
GRETCHEN GORDON
JEAN KAPLAN

Proofreader
LISA DIXON

Permission Researchers
MARGARET CHAMBERLAIN
JULIE VAN PELT

Indexer
KATHARYN DUNHAM

Compositor
GARY LEACH

Publisher
FRANK MENCHACA

Acknowledgments

Acknowledgment is gratefully made to those publishers and individuals who have permitted the use of the following material in copyright. Every effort has been made to secure permission to reprint copyrighted material.

PAUL AUSTER Excerpts from "Memory's Escape: Inventing the Music of Chance—A Conversation with Paul Auster," by Mark Irwin. *Denver Quarterly* 28 (winter 1994). Reproduced by permission of the author. Excerpts from "Spokes," by Paul Auster. In *Disappearances: Selected Poems, 1970–1979.* Overlook Press, 1988. Copyright © 1987 by Paul Auster. All rights reserved. Reproduced by permission. Excerpts from an interview by Joseph Millia. In *The Art of Hunger: Essays, Prefaces, Interviews.* Sun and Moon Press, 1992. Copyright © 1992 by Paul Auster. All rights reserved. Reproduced by permission. Excerpts from "White Nights," by Paul Auster. In *Wall Writing.* Figures, 1976. Copyright © 1976 by Figures. All rights reserved. Reproduced by permission. Excerpts from "A Dog's Eye View of Life," by Paul Kafka. *Boston Globe,* May 30, 1999. Reproduced by permission of the author.

FREDERICK BUECHNER Excerpts from *The Sacred Journey,* by Frederick Buechner. Harper & Row, 1982. Copyright © 1982 by Frederick Buechner. All rights reserved. Reproduced by permission. Excerpts from an interview by Jean W. Ross. In *Contemporary Authors: New Revision Series,* vol. 11. Gale Research Inc., 1984. Copyright © 1984 by Gale Research Inc. All rights reserved. Reproduced by permission.

ROBERT OLEN BUTLER Excerpts from "Letters from My Father," by Robert Olen Butler. *Cimarron Review* (October 1991). Reproduced by permission. Excerpts from an interview by Kay Bonetti. *Missouri Review* 17 (1994). Reproduced by permission of the author.

PETER CAMERON Excerpts from "Memorial Day," by Peter Cameron. *The New Yorker,* May 30, 1993. Reproduced by permission.

ANNE CARSON Excerpts from "Beauty Prefers an Edge," by Mary Gannon. *Poets and Writers Magazine* 29 (March/April 2001). Reproduced by permission. Excerpts from "Mimnermos: The Brainsex Paintings," "Canicula di Anna," "The Life of Towns," and "The Anthropology of Water," by Anne Carson. In *Plainwater: Essays and Poetry.* Alfred A. Knopf, 1995. Copyright © 1995 by Anne Carson. All rights reserved. Reproduced by permission. Excerpts from "The Glass Essay," "The Truth about God," "TV Men," and "The Gender of Sound," by Anne Carson. In *Glass, Irony and God.* New Directions, 1995. Copyright © 1995 by Anne Carson. Reprinted by permission of New Directions Publishing Corp. Excerpts from *Autobiography of Red: A Novel in Verse,* by Anne Carson. Alfred A. Knopf, 1998. Copyright © 1998 by Anne Carson. All rights reserved. Reproduced by permission. Excerpts from "First Chaldaic Oracle," "Essay on What I Think about Most," "TV Men," and "Irony Is Not Enough: Essay on My Life as Catherine Deneuve," by Anne Carson. In *Men in the Off Hours.* Alfred A. Knopf, 2000. Copyright © 2000 by Anne Carson. All rights reserved. Reproduced by permission. Excerpts from *The Beauty of the Husband: A Fictional Essay in 29 Tangos,* by Anne Carson. Alfred A. Knopf, 2001. Copyright © 2001 by Anne Carson. All rights reserved. Reproduced by permission.

GREGORY CORSO Excerpts from "I Held a Shelley Manuscript," "Marriage," and "Power," by Gregory Corso. In *The Happy Birthday of Death.* New Directions, 1960. Copyright © 1960 by New Directions. All rights reserved. Copyright renewed © 1988 by Gregory Corso. Reproduced by permission of New Directions Publishing Corp. Excerpts from "Man," "Some Greek Writing," and "Writ on the Eve of My 32nd Birthday," by Gregory Corso. In *Long Live Man.* New Directions, 1962. Copyright © 1962 by Gregory Corso. Reprinted by permission of New Directions Publishing Corp. Excerpts from "Elegaic Feelings American," "Mutation of the Spirit," "Eleven Times a Poem," and "The Poor Bustard," by Gregory Corso. In *Elegaic Feelings American.* New Directions, 1970. Copyright © 1970 by Gregory Corso. Reprinted by permission of New Directions Publishing Corp. Excerpts from "Columbia U Poesy Reading—1975," "Return," "For Homer," "Dear Villon," "Getting to the Poem," and "The Whole Mess . . . Almost," by Gregory Corso. In *Herald of the Autochthonic Spirit.* New Directions, 1981. Copyright © 1973, 1975, 1981 by Gregory Corso. Reproduced by permission of New Directions Publishing Corp. Excerpts from "Field Report," by Gregory Corso. In *Mindfield: New and Selected Poems.* Thunder's Mouth Press, 1989. Copyright © 1989 by Gregory Corso. All rights reserved. Reproduced by permission. Excerpts from "The Poet's Theater," by Nora Sayre. *Grand Street* 3 (spring 1984). Reproduced by permission. Excerpts from "Remembering a Poet Gregory Corso, 1930–2001," by Patty Smith. *The Village Voice,* January 24–30, 2001. Reproduced by permission. Excerpts from "Gregory Corso Arrives in Rome," by Massimo De Feo and Corine Young. *Woodstock Journal* 7 (May 11–25, 2001). Reproduced by permission of the authors.

STEPHEN DIXON Excerpts from "Said," by Stephen Dixon. In *Love and Will.* British American Publishing/Paris Review Editions, 1989. Copyright © 1989 by Stephen Dixon. All rights reserved. Reproduced by permission of the author. Excerpts from "Only

Press, 1982. Copyright © 1982 by John Haines. All rights reserved. Reproduced by permission. Excerpts from "Days of Edward Hopper" and "Rain Country," by John Haines. In New Poems 1980–88. Story Line Press, 1990. Copyright © 1990 by John Haines. All rights reserved. Reproduced by permission. Excerpts from "Kent State, May 1970" and "In the Cave at Lone Tree Meadow," by John Haines. In *For the Century's End: Poems 1990–1999.* University of Washington Press, 2001. Copyright © 2001 by John Haines. All rights reserved. Reproduced by permission. Excerpts from "An Interview with John Haines," by Robert Hedin. *Northwest Review* 27 (1989). Reproduced by permission.

JOY HARJO Excerpts from "Finding the Groove," by Joy Harjo. In *Sleeping with One Eye Open: Women Writers and the Art of Survival.* Edited by Marily Kallet and Judith Ortiz Cofer. University of Georgia Press, 1999. Coypright © 1999 by University of Georgia Press. All rights reserved. Reproduced by permission. Excerpts from an interview by Angles Carabi. *Belles Lettres: A Review of Books by Women* 9 (summer 1994). Reproduced by permission. Excerpts from "Origin," "I Am a Dangerous Woman," "Someone Talking," and "Four Horse Songs," by Joy Harjo. In *What Moon Drove Me to This?* I. Reed Books, 1979. Copyright © 1979 by I. Reed Books. All rights reserved. Reproduced by permission. Excerpts from "Anchorage," "The Woman Hanging from the Thirteenth Floor Window," "Kansas City," "She Remembers the Future," "She Had Some Horses," and "I Give You Back," by Joy Harjo. In *She Had Some Horses.* Thunder's Mouth Press, 1983. Copyright © 1983, 1987 by Thunder's Mouth Press. Reproduced by permission of the publisher, Thunder's Mouth Press. Excerpts from "Returning from the Enemy," by Joy Harjo. In *A Map to the Next World: Poems and Tales.* W. W. Norton, 2000. Copyright © 2000 by Joy Harjo. All rights reserved. Reproduced by permission. Excerpts from "Deer Dancer," "For Anna Mae Pictou Aquash, Whose Spirit Is Present Here and in the Dappled Stars (for we remember the story and must tell it again so we may all live)," "The Real Revolution Is Love," "Transformations," and "Eagle Poem," by Joy Harjo. In *In Mad Love and War.* Wesleyan University Press, 1990. Copyright © 1990 by Joy Harjo. All rights reserved. Reproduced by permission. Excerpts from *Secrets from the Center of the World,* by Joy Harjo, photographs by Stephen Strom. Sun Tracks and The University of Arizona Press, 1989. Copyright © 1989 by The Arizona Board of Regents. All rights reserved. Reproduced by permission. Excerpts from "A Postcolonial Tale" and "Perhaps the World Ends Here," by Joy Harjo. In *The Woman Who Fell from the Sky.* W. W. Norton, 1994. Copyright © 1994 by W. W. Norton. All rights reserved. Reproduced by permission. Excerpts from "An Interview with Joy Harjo," by Janice Gould. *Western American Literature* 35 (summer 2000). Reproduced by permission. Excerpts from "I'm Not Ready to Die Yet" and "When the World Ended as We Knew It," by Joy Harjo. In *How We Became Human: New and Selected Poems 1975–2001.* W. W. Norton, 2002. Copyright © 2002 W. W. Norton. All rights reserved. Reproduced by permission.

JOHN KNOWLES Excerpts from "A Naturally Superior School," by John Knowles. *Holiday* 20 (December 1956). Copyright © 1956 by Curtis Publishing Company. Copyright renewed © 1984 by John Knowles. Reproduced by permission of the publisher and the author. Excerpts from "My Separate Peace," by John Knowles. *Esquire,* March 1985. Reproduced by permission. Excerpts from "A Turn with the Sun" and "Phineas," by John Knowles. In *Phineas: Six Stories.* Random House, 1968. Copyright © 1968 by John Knowles. All rights reserved. Reproduced by permission. Excerpts from a letter to John Knowles by Thornton Wilder. In *The Enthusiast: A Life of Thornton Wilder.* Edited by Gilbert A. Harrison. Ticknor & Fields, 1983. Copyright © 1983 by Gilbert A. Harrison. All rights reserved. Reproduced by permission of the Literary Estate of the author. Excerpts from "A Special Time, A Special School," by John Knowles. <http://library.exeter.edu/dept/separate_peace/article.html>. Published by Exeter Bulletin, at exeter.edu. Reproduced by permission of the Estate of John Knowles. Excerpts from *A Separate Peace.* Macmillan, 1960. Copyright © 1959 by John Knowles. All rights reserved. Copyright renewed © 1987 by John Knowles. Reproduced by permission.

J. D. McCLATCHY Excerpts from "At a Reading," "First Steps," and "Ovid's Farewell," by J. D. McClatchy. In *Stars Principal.* Macmillan, 1986. Copyright © 1986 by J. D. McClatchy. All rights reserved. Reproduced by permission. Excerpts from "An Essay on Friendship" and "Kilim," by J. D. McClatchy. In *The Rest of the Way.* Alfred A. Knopf, 1990. Copyright © 1990 by J. D. McClatchy. All rights reserved. Reproduced by permission. Excerpts from "Thou Shalt Have None Other Gods But Me," "Dervish," "After Ovid: Apollo and Hyacinthus," "Stolen Hours," "After Magritte," "Auden's OED," and "Late Night Ode," by J. D. McClatchy. In *Ten Commandments.* Alfred A. Knopf, 1998. Copyright © 1998 by J. D. McClatchy. All rights reserved. Reproduced by permission. Excerpts from "Scenes from Another Life," by J. D. McClatchy. In *Scenes from Another Life.* Braziller, 1981. Copyright © 1981 by Braziller. All rights reserved. Reproduced by permission. Excerpts from "Fado," "Glanum," "Penis," "Feces," "Tattoos," "The News," and "Ouija," by J. D. McClatchy. In *Hazmat.* Alfred A. Knopf, 2002. Copyright © 2002 by Alfred A. Knopf. All rights reserved. Reproduced by permission. Excerpts from "The Art of Poetry," by Daniel Hall. *Paris Review* (2003). Copyright © 2003 by Paris Review. Reproduced by permission of Regal Literary as agent for the author. Excerpts from "My Fountain Pen," by J. D. McClatchy. In *Twenty Questions: (Posed by Poems).* Columbia University Press, 1998. Copyright © 1998 by Columbia University Press. All rights reserved. Reproduced by permission.

FRANK McCOURT Excerpts from *Angela's Ashes.* Scribner, 1996. Copyright © 1996 by Frank McCourt. All rights reserved. Reproduced by permission.

SUE MILLER Excerpt from "Carpe Diem," from *The Poetry of Robert Frost.* Edited by Edward Connery Lathem. Copyright 1942 © 1970 by Lesley Frost Ballantine, © 1969 by Henry Holt and Company. Reproduced by permission of Henry Holt and Company, LLC. Excerpts from "Inventing the Abbotts," by Sue Miller. In *Inventing the Abbotts and Other Stories.* Harper & Row, 1987. Copyright © 1987 by Sue Miller. All rights reserved. Reproduced by permission.

RICHARD RUSSO Excerpts from *The Risk Pool.* Random House, 1988. Copyright © 1988 by Richard Russo. All rights reserved. Reproduced by permission. Excerpts from *Nobody's Fool.* Random House, 1993. Copyright © 1993 by Richard Russo. All

List of Subjects

Introduction

When Shakespeare suggested that "the truest poetry is the most feigning," he put his finger on a complex issue for readers. Truth in literature, whatever forms that literature might take, is difficult to access. When a literary text appears straightforward, it is often quite deceptive or ingeniously constructed. Poets and novelists work hard to create, or discover and embody, what they believe is truth, but they have already decided to use a conventional form of fiction, whether in poetry or prose. A literary text is necessarily woven into complex patterns and uses many different threads. The work of good criticism and close reading is much like unraveling what has been woven. To do this without killing the text under examination is the task of the critic. I suspect that readers of this volume will be delighted by the success of our various authors in unraveling the texts at hand and the lives of the artists who created these texts without killing the life in them.

This supplement of American Writers, our twelfth, is largely concerned with a range of contemporary writers, poets, and novelists, many of whom have won large and enthusiastic audiences for their work, although criticism has yet to catch up with them. The function of these essays is quite simple: to provide introductory criticism that treats the developing career of each writer in the context of his or her life circumstances. While the essays are not necessarily mini-biographies, they all provide key markers in each life, and they suggest ways in which the books produced by each writer might be read in the context of those biographical markers. There is also a concern in all of these essays with close reading; indeed, the writers of

each essay took considerable trouble to examine the most important works of the author under discussion.

American Writers had its origin in a series of monographs that appeared between 1959 and 1972. The Minnesota Pamphlets on American Writers were incisively written and informative, treating ninety-seven American writers in a format and style that attracted a devoted following of readers. The series proved invaluable to a generation of students and teachers, who could depend on these reliable and interesting critiques of major figures. The idea of reprinting these essays occurred to Charles Scribner Jr. (1921–1995). The series appeared in four volumes entitled *American Writers: A Collection of Literary Biographies* (1974).

Since then, a dozen supplements have appeared, treating well over two hundred American writers: poets, novelists, playwrights, essayists, and autobiographers. The idea has been consistent with the original series: to provide clear, informative essays aimed at the general reader. These essays often rise to a high level of craft and critical vision, but they are meant to introduce a writer of some importance in the history of American literature, and to provide a sense of the scope and nature of the career under review. In each case, the critics are asked to avoid using jargon and to write clearly and without pretense.

The authors of these critical essays are mostly teachers, scholars, and writers. Most have published books and articles in their field, and several are well-known writers of poetry or fiction as well as critics. As anyone glancing through this volume will see, they are held to the highest standards of good writing and sound scholarship. The essays each conclude with a select bibliography intended to direct the reading of those who want to pursue the subject further.

The subjects of these eighteen essays have on the whole received little sustained attention from critics. They have been written about in the review pages of newspapers and magazines, and their writing has acquired a substantial readership in many cases, but their work has yet to attract sustained and significant scholarship. That kind of scholarly reading will certainly follow, but the essays included here constitute a beginning.

The poets included here—from Anne Carson, Gregory Corso, and Albert Goldbarth to John Haines, Joy Harjo, and J. D. McClatchy—are well known in the poetry world, and their work has in each case been honored with prizes and fellowships. These poets have been widely anthologized as well. Nevertheless, the real work of assimilation, of discovering the true place of each poet in the larger traditions of American poetry, has only begun. In each case, these poets are written about by critics who are themselves poets, and the depth and eloquence of their essays should be obvious even to casual readers.

The same might be said of the prose writers, from Kathy Acker, Paul Auster, Frederick Buechner, Robert Olen Butler, Stephen Dixon, Peter Cameron, Leslie Epstein, and John Knowles to Frank McCourt (a memoirist, not a novelist), Sue Miller, Ann Patchett, and Richard Russo. Both Butler and Russo have won the Pulitzer Prize in fiction, whereas the others have been written about in the press and honored with various accolades and prizes. John Knowles has become something of a classic author, having sold millions of copies of *A Separate Peace,* whereas McCourt has found a vast audience for his memoirs of life in Ireland and the United States. Yet none of these writers has yet attracted the sustained attention of critics, and these essays should constitute a strong beginning in this direction.

The critics who contributed to this collection represent a wide range of backgrounds and critical approaches, although the baseline for inclusion was that each essay should be accessible to the non-specialist reader or beginning student. The creation of culture involves the continuous reassessment of major texts produced by its writers, and my belief is that this supplement performs a useful service here, providing substantial introductions to American writers who matter, and it will assist readers in the difficult but rewarding work of close reading.

——JAY PARINI

Contributors

Charles R. Baker. Poet, short story writer, and essayist. Published works include "What Miss Johnson Taught," "Christmas Frost," "A Peacock in a Pecan Tree," and "A Fireman's Christmas." Curator of "Mark Twain: Father of Modern American Literature" at Bridwell Library, Southern Methodist University. FREDERICK BUECHNER, JOHN KNOWLES

Jonathan N. Barron. Associate Professor of English, University of Southern Mississippi. Coeditor of *Jewish American Poetry: Poems, Commentary, and Reflections* and of *Roads Not Taken: Rereading Robert Frost.* He also has a forthcoming collection on the poetic movement New Formalism. Editor in chief of *The Robert Frost Review.* GREGORY CORSO, ALBERT GOLDBARTH

Mary Ellen Bertolini. Lecturer at Middlebury College, Vermont. She teaches courses in writing and Jane Austen and nineteen- and twentieth-century fiction. She also is working and publishing in the field of writing and healing and is the author of an essay on Sandra Cisneros for *American Writers Supplement VII.* FRANK MCCOURT

Pegge Bochynski. Visiting Instructor of Creative and Advanced Writing at Salem State College in Salem, Massachusetts. She is the author of reviews and essays on works by William Wordsworth, Nathaniel Hawthorne, Flannery O'Connor, Thomas Sanchez, and Maryse Conde. JOY HARJO

Cornelius Browne. Assistant Professor of English, Oregon State University Cascades. He has published essays on John Steinbeck, Barry Lopez, Rachel Carson, John Muir, and American-Canadian literary relations. He is currently at work on a book about pragmatism, John Dewey, and American environmental writing. JOHN HAINES

Hugh Coyle. Author of both prose and poetry in a number of literary journals. His poem "Love or Nothing" appeared in the Pushcart Prize 2000 anthology. Currently Senior Editor at Macmillan/McGraw-Hill companies while devoting time to his writing in Vermont. PETER CAMERON

Joan Wylie Hall. Teaches American Literature at the University of Mississippi. Author of *Shirley Jackson: A Study of the Short Fiction,* she has published essays on Lee Smith, Ruth McEnery Stuart, William Faulkner, Carolyn Wells, Eudora Welty, Willa Cather, Tennessee Williams, and other writers. ANN PATCHETT

Brian Henry. Assistant Professor of English at the University of Georgia. Author of three books of poetry—*Astronaut, Graft,* and *American Incident*—and editor of *On James Tate* and *The Verse Book of New American Poets.* His criticism has appeared in the *Times Literary Supplement, New York Times Book Review, Yale Review, Kenyon Review,* and many other publications. ANNE CARSON

Jerome Klinkowitz. Professor of English and University Distinguished Scholar at the University of Northern Iowa. He is the author of forty books, including novels, collections of short stories, and studies of literature, philosophy, art, music, sport, and air combat narratives. Recent titles are *Owning a Piece of the Minors* and *Keeping Literary Company.* STEPHEN DIXON

Sanford Pinsker. Shadek Professor of Humanities at Franklin and Marshall College. Writes widely about American literature for journals, such as the *Virginia Quarterly, Sewanee Review, Georgia Review,* and *Partisan Review.* Author of *The Comedy That "Hoits": An Essay on the Fiction of Philip Roth.* LESLIE EPSTEIN

William H. Pritchard. Henry Clay Folger Professor of English at Amherst College. His many books include critical studies of Robert Frost, Randall Jarrell, and John Updike. SUE MILLER

Patrick A. Smith. Faculty member in the Department of English, Bainbridge College, Georgia. Author of *"The True Bones of My Life": Essays on the Fiction of Jim Harrison* and *Thematic Guide to Popular Short Stories.* His essays have appeared in *Studies in Short Fiction, Aethlon: The Journal of Sport Literature,* and previous American Writers volumes, among others. PAUL AUSTER, ROBERT OLEN BUTLER

Julie Sears. Doctoral student in English at the University of California, Davis. She is currently working on her dissertation on contemporary experimental writers. KATHY ACKER

Willard Spiegelman. Hughes Professor of English at Southern Methodist University in Dallas and editor in chief of the *Southwest Review.* His books include *The Didactic Muse: Scenes of Instruction in Contemporary American Poetry* and *Majestic Indolence: English Romantic Poetry and the Work of Art.* J. D. MCCLATCHY

Tricia Welsch. Chair and Associate Professor of Film Studies at Bowdoin College in Maine. Her work has appeared in *Film Quarterly, Cinema Journal, Journal of Film and Video, Film Criticism, Journal of Popular Film and Television, Genre,* and *Griffithiana.* She is currently working on a biography of Gloria Swanson. RICHARD RUSSO

SUPPLEMENT XII
Kathy Acker to Richard Russo

Kathy Acker

1948–1997

*T*HE CHALLENGING SUBJECT matter and demanding style of Kathy Acker's work have elicited considerable debate among critics. Perhaps more striking than their content—which includes sadomasochism, prostitution, incest, terrorism, homosexuality, racism, revolution, abortion, suicide, and murder—are her works' use of a variety of techniques that disrupt novelistic conventions. Acker often interrupts the narrative with anticapitalist and antipatriarchal passages and self-reflexive commentary; combines and alters texts from both pop culture and high art in a collage fashion; introduces historical figures and famous fictional characters; creates surrealistic and apocalyptic scenarios; undermines chronology and consistent characterization; revels in foul language and pornographic imagery; shifts genre; and inserts autobiographical material. Because of its combination of anguish, hope, irony, and rebellious defiance of tradition, her work has been called postmodern, experimental, punk, and postpunk.

Acker considered herself to be part of an alternative tradition of literature; she traced her literary heritage back to Marquis de Sade, Arthur Rimbaud, Jean Genet, Georges Bataille, Gertrude Stein, and William S. Burroughs. Her technique generated contention among critics: whereas some admired her deep enmeshment in textuality—the situation in which every text, for example, a novel, manifests the existence of previous texts and, therefore, is not autonomous and self-contained—others viewed her work as merely plagiaristic. Acker viewed her work as illustrating the relationship between sexuality and power, as foraging into nonrational areas of the mind, and as rejecting the notion that art could or should reflect reality through objective, descriptive narratives.

BIOGRAPHY

The daughter of Donald and Claire (Weill) Lehman, Kathy Acker was born in New York City on April 18, 1948. There is some question as to her year of birth, however: the Library of Congress lists her birth year as 1948, a few sources have listed 1947, but most obituaries state that she was born in 1944. The pregnancy was unplanned, and Donald Lehman abandoned the family before Kathy was born; Acker's relationship with her domineering mother even into adulthood was fraught with hostility and anxiety because Acker felt unloved and unwanted. Her mother soon remarried, a union that Acker later characterized as an essentially passionless marriage to an ineffectual man, and Acker was raised in her mother and stepfather's respectable upper-middle-class Jewish home on New York's Upper East Side.

As a girl, Acker was expected to act with ladylike propriety in this oppressive, well-to-do environment, yet she was fascinated by pirates, a fascination that continued until the end of her life. She wanted to grow up to be a pirate, but she knew that only men could be pirates. Thus Acker experienced early the limitations of gender. However, she found that reading about pirates was a way of running away from home, and she turned to books as her reality. She associated reading and writing with bodily pleasure and remained a voracious reader throughout her life.

Acker acknowledged that she included auto-biographical material in her work, which suggests that her stepfather may have attempted to rape her when she was an adolescent. During her teenage years, Acker managed to escape her family by becoming involved in the New York City art scene. When she was fifteen, Acker's boyfriend, the filmmaker P. Adams Sitney, introduced her to the underground filmmakers Stan Brakhage, Stan Rice, and Gregory Markopoulos; the Fluxus group; and to the work of the Black Mountain poet Charles Olson.

Acker's exposure to the second generation of the Black Mountain poets influenced her first attempts at writing. The Black Mountain School espoused using free-verse forms based on the poet's feelings during the composing process. Olson's theory that the breath and bodily rhythms, rather than set metrical schemes, should create the rhythm of verse inspired Acker's interest in writing to accompany bodily rhythms. However, the advice of poets who emphasized the importance of "finding one's voice" seemed beside the point for Acker personally because she did not believe her work had a particular "voice." She began to search for other ways of writing, principally by improvising from other texts. She would, for example, copy a previous text and then juxtapose it with memories and the experiences of her friends or simply alter the existing text to reflect her own interests. She also rejected the Romantic notion of the artist as a creator of something unique. Her difficulties with these conventional tenets of literature contributed to her experiments with combining different voices in the same text.

During her years in high school, Acker became interested in studying Latin and especially enjoyed reading the works of the Latin poets Catullus and Propertius. In 1963 she left home to attend Brandeis University in the Boston area. At age nineteen she married Robert Acker, a poor friend, and changed her surname from Alexander, her stepfather's last name, to Acker. Acker gave different reasons for her marriage to Robert Acker. She may have been trying to get a scholarship at Brandies or financial support from her parents. In any case, Robert Acker's influence on her life seems minimal, and they soon divorced. No longer supported by her parents, who had wanted her to marry someone wealthy, Acker spent the next years of her life struggling financially.

At Brandeis, Acker studied with Herbert Marcuse, a Marxist and revisionist Freudian whose *Eros and Civilization* (1955) theorized the importance of erotic and economic liberation from powerful capitalist elites; Acker's examination of sexual and political oppression in capitalist society certainly reflects Marcuse's impact. When Marcuse left Brandeis (which was withdrawing support for leftist professors) and moved to the University of California at San Diego, Acker followed him and worked as his teaching assistant. Acker studied Greek and Latin and received a B.A. in classics in 1968.

In college Acker was involved in Students for a Democratic Society, but she considered the student left movement to be too elitist. Acker first heard of feminism while in college; however, her understanding of it did not develop until she left the academic environment. Acker was familiar with the horror stories of women who had self-induced abortions because abortions were illegal at the time. Acker and her friends used to help raise money to enable friends to obtain abortions from a doctor who would perform them more safely. Her participation in feminist politics, thus, was primarily at the personal level. While living in San Diego, Acker also became aware of conceptual art—in which artwork is a realization of a particular concept—and met the poet, artist, and critic David Antin, who introduced her to conceptual artists and taught her about conceptualism's emphasis on artistic creation based on intention rather than "inspiration."

After she finished her bachelor's degree, Acker returned to New York City and began a doctoral program in classics and philosophy at New York University and the City University of New York. Still struggling financially and suffering from an illness, she worked in a variety of jobs, including performing in live sex shows on 42nd Street for six months—an experience that sharply raised her awareness about sexual politics and class differences.

During this time, Acker met the poet Jerome Rothenberg and became involved with the St. Mark's Poetry Project, which was founded in 1966 to promote the development of innovative poetry. Although Acker referred to the poets Olson, Rothenberg, and Antin as her first writing teachers, she preferred to write prose. This put her at odds with the St. Mark's people, who found her writing in prose and engagement with conceptualism strange. For her part, Acker considered the attitudes of the East Village poets toward sexuality hypocritical, for they both embraced "free love" and denounced any deviants such as homosexuals and transvestites. Deemed a freak by the St. Mark's poets because of her involvement with the sex industry, Acker experienced these two worlds—the elite poetry world and the dingy world of the sex industry—as comprising a double life that she could only connect through politics.

When she was twenty-one, she began writing a book of prose poems called *Politics,* which was self-published in 1972. During readings at St. Mark's, she read parts from the lengthy diary section of *Politics,* in which she used what she called "cut-ins"—material, such as dreams, political commentary, and her life as a sex worker, "cut in" abruptly to interrupt one narrative with another, creating a collage effect. With *Politics,* Acker began her conceptualist writing experiments in earnest, imitating William S. Burroughs' innovative work *The Third Mind* (1978) and extensively borrowing his cut-up technique, which is the seemingly haphazard reorganization of sentences and sometimes large passages.

At the time, Acker felt Burroughs was the only prose writer working in a fashion similar to conceptualism. She discovered that his methods allowed her to create "environments," similar to those generated by experimental music, rather than meaningful narratives. Initially she was not aware of how these techniques could be used to undermine language. Later she found his use of language as a method of resisting the control of language germane to her own work. According to Burroughs, conventional language is a method of social control that enforces normative behavior; therefore, to undermine what he considered to be a totalitarian system, one must subvert language itself. In addition, Burroughs' subject matter—his focus on sexuality, violence, and extreme states of consciousness—influenced Acker's content. In this early work, Acker was motivated to perform antinarrative practices primarily out of anger toward male literary authorities and the conventional narrative tradition, although she did not understand the theoretical reasons for her attacks on the sign system (the organization of language according to rules and conventions accepted by a community that reflects the community's interpretation of reality).

Acker discontinued her graduate work after two years, and in the early 1970s she left New York and moved back to San Diego, where she lived with the experimental composer Peter Gordon. In San Diego she adopted the name "Black Tarantula" and apprenticed herself to Antin. When Gordon began his graduate studies at the Center for Contemporary Music at Mills College, Acker and Gordon moved to the Haight Ashbury section of San Francisco. Acker became interested in the androgynous theatrical scene, adopted the name "Rip-off Red," and began to write her first novel, *Rip-off Red, Girl*

Detective (published posthumously, in 2002), a mystery with pornographic elements.

She then became involved in a mail-art network, which allowed her to distribute her works to other members of the network for free. She began the first of her works in which she experimented with the notion of identity, *The Childlike Life of the Black Tarantula* (1973), and sent off the first section, which received a positive response from the network. Encouraged, Acker began to write it as a serial novel. Through the free distribution of her work, Acker gained an audience. In the early 1970s she began to publish her works—*Politics, The Childlike Life of the Black Tarantula,* and *I Dreamt I Became a Nymphomaniac! Imagining* (1974)—with small, independent presses.

Acker and Gordon returned to New York in 1975. This time in New York, Acker did not consort primarily with poets; her newest home was the avant-garde art scene on the Lower East Side. Acker was invigorated by finding people her age, to whom she could relate, who were mixing high culture and pop culture, pornography and art, and she attended gatherings in which cross-dressing and other forms of gender play occurred. Although Acker felt out of place because she was not a visual artist, she discovered in the appropriative artworks of Richard Prince, Sherry Levine, and David Salle visual parallels to her own work.

Not long after she arrived in New York, the punk movement began to develop. Punk particularly attracted Acker because of its emphasis on using a disturbing, anti-art style and abject content to shock people out of their complacency. As a counter to the idealism of the 1960s hippie culture, punk offered a nihilistic alternative that paraded the anguish and disgust of its members. Although anti-utopian, the punk movement did exhibit a profound desire that change could be enacted through extreme measures. In the art world, this meant desecrating sacred texts and shaking up cultural commonplaces through bizarre juxtapositions. Combining punk's celebration of anarchy with her own experimentations with decentralizing and disrupting narrative, Acker found a niche.

Punk's performative aspect also created venues for Acker to read her work. Along with the writers Lynne Tillman and Constance De-Jong, Acker began to perform in bookstores and clubs like the Kitchen, the Mudd Club, and CB-GBs. This group of writers also published their work in the magazines *Bomb* (which Acker's friend Betsy Sussler ran), *Top Stories, Evergreen, Benzene,* and *Between C & D.* Women had a strong role in the punk movement—other notable figures of this major artistic movement included the performance artist Lydia Lunch and the singer Exene Cervenka. Acker's fidelity to this punk aesthetic is evident in the punk personae that she continued to present to her audience long after the movement itself had ended.

During the punk movement, Acker felt her work was at last corresponding with that of others around her; still, she was not able to explain what she was doing in her writing. When Sylvère Lotringer came to New York in 1977, bringing with him French theory, Acker was exposed to the ideas of the French poststructuralists Michel Foucault, Félix Guattari, and Gilles Deleuze. By talking with Lotringer and reading Deleuze and Guattari's *Anti-Oedipus: Capitalism and Schizophrenia,* Acker learned a language with which she could discuss her work, the language of deconstruction. In particular, she could verbalize why she was rejecting linear narrative, why she often changed the genders of her characters, and why she was placing so many disparate texts together. Once exposed to the theories of deconstructionism, Acker began to use them in her novels.

Acker's personal life during the late 1970s was undergoing upheaval. She married Peter Gordon in 1976, but the marriage deteriorated after two years, at which point they divorced,

KATHY ACKER / 5

apparently at Gordon's request. During the same year as her divorce, when Acker was thirty, her mother committed suicide, an event that had a profound emotional impact on Acker and her subsequent work. During the same period, however, Acker continued to publish and develop as a writer. *Florida, Kathy Goes to Haiti,* and *The Adult Life of Toulouse Lautrec by Henri Toulouse Lautrec* all came out from small presses in 1978. In 1981 Acker's short story "New York City in 1979" appeared in *Top Stories* and won the Pushcart Prize for that year. "New York City in 1979" expressed Acker's growing disillusionment with the New York scene. Acker had lost her interest in scrutinizing identity and turned instead to her trademark method, appropriating others' texts. She determined that texts, as products and makers of culture, are just as real as life experiences; therefore, by playing with texts and improvising from them, she could explore and remake culture.

Acker had been honing her craft throughout the 1960s and 1970s; wider success came at last in the 1980s, when she became something akin to a celebrity. After publishing the novel *Great Expectations* (1982), in 1984 Acker had her first work, *Blood and Guts in High School,* published by a major company, the London-based Picador. Launching her career as a writer on the forefront of the avant-garde, *Blood and Guts in High School* was the first book in which Acker used plot, albeit an episodic one, as a structuring device.

Because she felt she could make more money as a literary figure in London than in the United States, Acker left for Britain in the mid-1980s. Acker became a public figure in London; her work was promoted at a show in the South Bank (the art and museum district along the Thames), and she contributed to the *New Statesmen* and made guest appearances on television programs.

Meanwhile, in the United States, Acker's works were being published by Grove Press, which was more prominent than her previous American publishers. As the author became more famous, Grove reissued titles by Acker in editions that often featured full-cover close-up photos of her that emphasized her "tough rebel" image. In these photos, Acker often dressed androgynously, wore her hair very short and bleached, and displayed her tattoos and long earrings. Although the image was self-consciously projected, it was in many ways a genuine reflection of the author: Acker was in fact an avid motorcycle enthusiast, a body builder, and an aficionado of tattooing.

Given this persona, Acker was considered to be something of an American primitive by her British audience. Although Acker believed there were more opportunities for a writer in London and felt accepted as a writer, she thought that her image was obscuring her work because readers and critics tended to fetishize the sexual aspects of her work and overlook the political. Nonetheless, her British critics and readers had forced her to become more politically aware by demanding to know the political reasons for her artistic choices. While in London, Acker produced several of her best-known works, *Don Quixote: Which Was a Dream* (1986), *Empire of the Senseless* (1988), and *In Memoriam to Identity* (1990).

Acker's work went through some changes during her time in England. In the early 1980s Acker had been primarily interested in deconstructing texts; she was intrigued by how texts from different contexts would interact with one another and reveal their assumptions. Acker not only placed these texts together, but she manipulated and dissected them. She mostly experimented with texts that had established cultural currency because these texts reveal much about society's operations. For example, Acker used Miguel de Cervantes' seventeenth-century novel *Don Quixote,* which she took with her to the hospital where she was having an abortion, as a model for her own *Don Quixote.*

After she wrote *Don Quixote,* however, Acker grew tired of her deconstructive techniques; in 1988, with *Empire of the Senseless,* Acker shifted to myth as her primary structuring device. Her shift from deconstruction to myth-making stemmed from Acker's realization that there was nothing left to deconstruct; it was obvious who had power and how that power was maintained. She also felt that deconstruction was too reactionary because it necessitated focusing on and reiterating what one despised. Instead, she wanted to discover a way to get outside of the various power systems—such as sexism, racism, and the class system—her works had revealed. She believed that narrative provided this way out. She found myths useful because they are not personal narratives but rather refer to the story of a culture. Increasingly Acker demonstrated an interest in rituals and rites of passage.

Acker's attitudes toward feminism also shifted while she was in London. In the early and mid-1980s, Acker had attacked feminism for its alliance with conservative positions. Acker considered the feminist anti-pornography movement led by Catharine MacKinnon and Andrea Dworkin, for example, to be counter to the liberationist ideas of feminism. At first Acker's books were generally received unfavorably by feminists; however, more feminist critics began to embrace her work. With the waning influence of the anti-pornography feminists in the late 1980s and the growing number of feminists that supported her work, Acker came to identify herself more with feminism, although she was loath to label herself a feminist. The feminist theorists Acker claimed an affinity with were Luce Irigaray, who critiques Freudian and Lacanian psychoanalysis and the masculine construction of "woman" as a support for Western philosophy; Julia Kristeva, who examines the radical political ramifications of avant-garde literature and whose concept of the "abject" intrigued Acker; and the queer theorist

Judith Butler, who argues that gender is not an inherent quality of male and female bodies but a cultural construct that comes into being through its performance by individuals.

Along with the fame Acker received in Britain and America came notoriety. In 1986 a German court banned *Blood and Guts in High School* for being a threat to minors and objected to the novel's apparently meaningless nature and lack of artistic merit. Acker also faced a plagiarism charge, which motivated her decision to leave London. The British publisher Pandora produced a collection of her earliest works, including *The Adult Life of Toulouse Lautrec by Henri Toulouse Lautrec. The Adult Life of Toulouse Lautrec* has a section, about two thousand words long, taken from Harold Robbins' novel *The Pirate,* a best-selling soft-porn book. Under pressure from Robbins' publisher, Acker's publisher agreed to stop further publication and told Acker to write a public apology. Acker, who had openly discussed her appropriative techniques in interviews and in the introduction of this collection, felt she had not plagiarized. She believed that she was putting a text in a different, ironic context. Although she did write the apology, Acker resented this accusation and later discussed in essays her belief that copyright laws were a relic of bourgeois individualism and capitalism.

When Acker returned to America in the early 1990s, she found that, on a political level, the art scene in New York had turned more commercial and conservative. On a more personal level, many of her friends had died of AIDS. Discouraged, Acker decided to move back to San Francisco. Once in the United States, she published *Hannibal Lecter, My Father* (1991); *Portrait of an Eye: Three Novels* (1992), including *The Childlike Life of the Black Tarantula, I Dreamt I Was a Nymphomaniac: Imagining,* and *The Adult Life of Toulouse Lautrec by Henri Toulouse Lautrec; My Mother: Demonology* (1993); *Pussycat Fever* (1995); *Pussy, King of the Pirates* (1996); *Bodies of Work: Essays* (1997); and *Eurydice in the Underworld* (1997).

Although Acker promoted her work through literary events and readings, she discovered other outlets that would allow her work to be performed. In 1985 she produced (with Richard Foreman) her novel *My Death My Life by Pier Paolo Pasolini* (which had first been published, by Picador, in 1984) as a play at the Theatre de Bastille in Paris, and she wrote the libretto to Peter Gordon's opera *The Birth of the Poet,* which was performed in 1985 at the Brooklyn Academy of Music. Acker wrote the screenplay to the film *Variety,* which was directed by Bette Gordon and released in 1985. In the 1990s, Acker read her work publicly with two rock bands, the Mekons and Tribe 8. With the Mekons she produced a compact disc that included readings of sections from *Pussy, King of the Pirates.* In 1997 Acker wrote the libretto for the three-act opera "Requiem," which was commissioned by the composer Ken Valitsky and the American Opera Project in New York City.

In the early 1990s Acker received some support from academia. Beginning in 1991 she worked as an adjunct professor of writing at the San Francisco Art Institute. She also worked as a visiting professor at the University of California at San Diego, the University of California at Santa Barbara, and the University of Idaho, all in 1994. As academic critics began to view her work more seriously, Acker took advantage of this forum created by academia to discuss her work and ideas.

In 1996 Acker was diagnosed with breast cancer and underwent a double mastectomy. Because her teaching position as adjunct did not provide her with medical insurance, Acker faced exorbitant medical bills if she elected to undergo chemotherapy. Disenchanted with her experience with Western medicine during the diagnosis of her cancer and its removal, Acker opted instead for nontraditional forms of heal-

ing. When Acker wrote about her cancer in newspapers, many of her friends and critics felt that she was setting a bad model for other women facing breast cancer by naively accepting New Age methods of healing, but Acker was firm in her belief in the mind-body relationship and wanted to treat her illness in a holistic fashion. She died on November 29, 1997, at an alternative treatment center in Tijuana, Mexico, still in the prime of her life.

NOVELS OF IDENTITY

In the trilogy of early novels reprinted in the 1992 collection *Portrait of an Eye—The Childlike Life of the Black Tarantula, I Dreamt I Was a Nymphomaniac: Imagining,* and *The Adult Life of Toulouse Lautrec by Henri Toulouse Lautrec*—Acker teases apart the concept of identity. In *The Childlike Life of the Black Tarantula* she plays with first-person narration by combining autobiographical and textual material. At the beginning of this work, the narrator claims that her intention is to become a murderess "by repeating in words the lives of other murderesses." Acker mixes entries from her own diary with accounts from the lives of murderesses and other historical and fictional figures, giving them all the position of first-person narrator. In this manner, Acker demonstrates how texts create identity. Her experiments with "I" also circumvent the notion of art as self-expression because here the "self" is an amalgam of various texts.

In addition, Acker tracks the parallels between her life, the episodes of which are often enclosed in parentheses, and those of these historical and fictional figures to demonstrate the effects of sexism, capitalism, and institutions on women's personal lives; chiefly, her comparisons indicate how various forms of deprivation, such as poverty and discrimination, force destructive countermeasures. The narrator expresses her distaste for the banality of work and her fear that various institutions are attempting to turn her into a robot, that is, a productive member of society. Robert Siegle argues that the "black tarantula" of the title refers to the narrator's voracious sexuality, and, he further argues, the title also suggests the author's appropriation technique, with which the narrator brings all of these characters into her web of shifting identities. The narrator struggles between a desire to escape the "death society" that would make her conform to its strictures and a desire for sexual and social connection, which could compromise her autonomy.

I Dreamt I Was a Nymphomaniac: Imagining again explores the confrontation between the narrator's desires and repressive systems. It also presents autobiographical elements, sometimes blatantly, sometimes in disguised form. *I Dreamt I Was a Nymphomaniac* exhibits Acker's early experimentation with techniques such as repetition, metafictional commentary, and shifting narratives, which allow her to investigate the nature of language and the way in which repetition and memory affect meaning.

Early on, the novel's narrator refers to herself as "Kathy Acker" and tells in pornographic language of her sexual relations with two male artists. Then the narrator recounts a dream that lasts for approximately two pages and is repeated verbatim three times. This repetition technique disrupts the linear narrative and replaces it with a cyclical narrative. A second, longer narrative is repeated, beginning with the narrator's attempts to become a writer and ending with her affair with Peter, a male transvestite that she, disguised as a man, meets at a ball. This section concludes with a discussion of time's relation to identity and of the different narrative possibilities depending upon the configuration of the characters.

At the end of the novel, the narrator expresses her longing for her lover, Peter, who is an anarchistic revolutionary fighting against money and leaders, and she describes her involvement with this fictitious anarchic rebellion, which is taking place in northern California. The chapter catalogs the types of prisoners at Folsom Prison and tells the stories of several of them. Among the prisoners are fictionalized versions of people in Acker's life, including Peter Gordon and David Antin. She also includes her persona, "the Black Tarantula," who has become a Native American imprisoned in solitary confinement apparently without cause.

By making these people in her life, who were experimental artists, into revolutionaries and prisoners of conscience, Acker counters the charge implied in the novel's epigraph that art and personal/sexual experiences do not have political meanings. The epigraph begins with a man's condemnation of a work (perhaps the work it precedes) for being "very nonpolitical, therefore, reactionary," to which the writer/narrator responds, "But what would the world have to be like for these events to exist?" This epigraph introduces Acker's contention that relating one's personal experiences and engaging in formal experimentation can critique society. Her presentation of figures from her life as countercultural revolutionaries operates metaphorically to defend this contention.

In *The Adult Life of Toulouse Lautrec by Henri Toulouse Lautrec,* Acker experiments with genre; by trying on different genres, the novel assumes different identities and frustrates attempts to assign it a label. The novel's epigraph, from the realist novelist Henry Fielding, instructs that the writer should "make sense" and "tell the truth," but the narrator rejects the claim of empiricism that reality can, or should be, objectively recorded and argues that she does not want "to make sense."

In Acker's novel, the French impressionist painter Henri Toulouse-Lautrec is imagined as a deformed woman who craves sex but is denied it because she is ugly. Her need for sex distracts her from her painting. This transformation of Toulouse-Lautrec into a woman allows Acker to point up the even greater degree of marginality that women artists suffer in comparison to male artists. Acker uses the novel to develop a mutation of the murder-mystery genre, in which Toulouse-Lautrec—together with her friend the painter Vincent van Gogh—becomes embroiled in the aftermath of a murder that has taken place in a Paris whorehouse, as the Agatha Christie detective Hercule Poirot attempts to solve the murder of a young girl.

As the novel progresses, Acker continues to experiment with different genres. In the telling of other narratives, Acker borrows generic conventions from beast fables, soft-core porn, and women's "true confessions" magazines from the 1950s. Acker leaps to another cultural artifact, the 1950s Hollywood film *Rebel without a Cause,* when she portrays van Gogh's daughter Marcia as a nine-year-old Janis Joplin who has an affair with James Dean, also known as Scott. The situation of the female artist, the singer Janis Joplin, and the male artist is again compared through the story of their relationship. When they are first dating, they discuss the difficulties of being an artist; James Dean is unable to recognize the added troubles that Janis will face as an "intelligent," independent woman. As well as chronicling this Hollywood affair, Acker intersperses a detailed critique of Henry Kissinger's diplomatic decisions and their relationship to the development of global capitalism. According to Robert Siegle, Acker splices these two apparently disparate textual orders together to illustrate how the operations of global capitalism leave "bums" like Janis/Marcia even poorer and give more power to the already privileged.

The final chapter, titled "The Life of Johnny Rocco," is a deconstruction of the gangster genre that makes the connection between the individual characters and larger sociopolitical events more evident. Johnny Rocco is a mobster helping the CIA. A "dame" tries to infiltrate Johnny's business and claims that she is not a woman; thus, she is attempting to play the man's game rather than being its victim, yet she still gets beaten up by Johnny and murdered by the CIA. A friend of Johnny's explains that America gives him and people like him the privilege to be powerful—hence, to use and abuse others. This, it seems Acker is saying, is both the American way and the man's way. However, Johnny is nearly killed during a government raid. Siegle argues that this situation illustrates how the power of the individual is subsumed by institutional power; thus even male privilege is limited. Nevertheless, in *The Adult Life of Toulouse Lautrec,* Acker consistently stresses the disparity between men and women.

GREAT EXPECTATIONS

Acker's next important work, the novel *Great Expectations,* begins with a section called "Plagiarism," indicating Acker's shift from her emphasis on identity. In addition to the novel by Charles Dickens, Acker also borrows from John Keats's poetry, the Roman poet Sextus Propertius, the pornographic novel *The Story of O* by Pauline Réage, Virginia Woolf's *Orlando,* and Marcel Proust's *Remembrance of Things Past.* Acker starts her novel with the introductory sentences from Dickens' *Great Expectations.* This plagiarism, however, is not exact. Acker alters the protagonist's created name from "Pip" to "Peter," a possible allusion to her former husband. As well, the name of Pip's mother is conspicuously missing, perhaps suggesting, as Martina Sciolino has argued, that the "protagonist's self-naming will occur in a masculine register," referencing the fact that conventional literary texts typically reserve for male characters the position of active, self-creating subject, whereas female characters are merely supporting figures for male protagonists.

Before this male protagonist's bildungsroman can start, Acker presents another protagonist and story, this one of a female. By abruptly cutting off the familiar narrative of a young male protagonist's attempt to establish his identity in the world, and wrenching Dickens' text from him, Acker questions patriarchal modes of self-assertion and the claims of ownership that identity permits. The unnamed female protagonist she introduces here is consulting tarot cards after facing her mother's suicide a year previous. Acker places the young woman in a restricted position; her future seems determined because she is trapped by her mother's influence. Her only escape appears to be working through her mother's legacy.

This narrative is yet again interrupted, this time by various scenes of intercourse amidst the carnage of a battlefield. This imagery implicitly compares war and sex, yet the narrator confesses her "want" that the master-slave dialectic of these scenarios can be overcome through new combinations: "every part changes (the meaning of) every other part so there's no absolute/heroic/dictatorial/S&M meaning." As these two narratives interchange with one another, the narrator slips in commentary on her aesthetic choices: "that's why one text must subvert (the meaning) of another text." These statements introduce this novel's examination of the power of language and the power of memories—whether of mothers or fathers—and the desire to write oneself into existence, despite one's past. This hope forms the essence of the female narrator's "Great Expectations," which she cites at the end of the first chapter. At the same time, the reader's "great expectations"—presumably for a conventional novel—are dashed.

The novel's second section, "The Beginnings of Romance," follows the narratives of the two protagonists, Peter and the female protagonist, now known as either Rosa or Sarah. While the female protagonist is obsessed with her mother, Peter fixates on his father. Sarah attempts to solve the mystery of her mother's death—she believes she was murdered—and to find her real

father. Acker cuts in parallel narratives, including a domestic drama in which a husband and wife bicker, and a plagiarism of the sadomasochistic *The Story of O,* with Anwar Sadat making a brief appearance. Acker relates O's childhood rape by her father and the girl's fear that her father's desire will overcome/become her. As well, Acker interjects a critique of the Seattle Art Society, implicitly comparing the vicious networking that takes place in the art world to the machinations of big business and French court life.

In the final section, "The End," Propertius, who regrets the fact that women have emotions, carries on a tumultuous affair with a woman named Cynthia. Their battles are written as a drama. Acker again depicts the largely unequal yet shifting relations between men and women; eventually, Propertius rejects Cynthia, who gives herself to madness. Although as a male Propertius has power in the personal realm, as an artist whose work is subject to Imperial censure, he is relatively powerless. The Roman Empire, speaking through the voice of Maecenas, criticizes his poetry for being too "emotional" and not fulfilling its role as state propaganda. The narrator compares herself to Propertius; both have their works condemned because they deal with unreasonable topics such as sex and violence. Acker concludes with the female protagonist's agony about her mother's suicide.

Alongside these various stories, the narrator continues her self-reflexive commentary on writing and language. For example, she questions the naming of things because this activity is unable to encompass the changing nature of those same things; she urges herself to "get as deep as possible" in order to create the "least meaning"; and she defines sexuality as "that which can't be satisfied" and is, therefore, comparable to her own writing, which defies conventional expectations. The novel's conclusion comes in medias res with the words "Dear mother," as if to demonstrate that there is no end to the quest for understanding pain or to the mourning that this society engenders, particularly for women. The cycle of expectation continues, as one would expect from a moving language, in which "questioning is our mode."

BLOOD AND GUTS IN HIGH SCHOOL

The 1984 novel *Blood and Guts in High School* may have the most coherent narrative of Acker's works because it recounts the adventures of a single protagonist, Janey Smith, a ten-year-old girl who is having an affair with her father, Johnny. Like *Great Expectations, Blood and Guts* is a bildungsroman that begins with the absence of the mother. After losing her mother when she was one year old, Janey relies on her father for all of her needs. Johnny represents not only a biological father but also the paternal function of society, which dictates the limits of female desire and self-actualization.

Janey's adventures commence when her father rejects her for another woman, a WASP—Janey is a Jew. Acker alternates Janey's conversations with her father and his friend Bill—which are often rendered as portions of a script—with fairly primitive drawings of male and female genitalia accompanied by captions. Acker also uses the repetition technique she deployed in *Nymphomaniac,* but with shorter passages interspersed between a fairly straightforward narrative. Several passages including the word "LASHES" telegraph Janey's masochistic compulsion to torture herself for alienating Johnny. As in previous works, Acker includes passages of cultural and political commentary, mainly critiques of capitalism, and interjects self-reflexive statements.

After Johnny unburdens himself of Janey by sending her from her hometown, Merida, Mexico, to New York City to attend school, she falls in with a gang of disaffected youths, the Scorpions, finds employment at a hippie bakery, leaves high school, and then gets kidnapped by two thugs who are working for a white slaver, Mr. Linker, also known as the Persian slave trader. Mr. Linker is a fervent proponent of Greco-Roman culture and literary classics, no doubt an ironic statement on Acker's part about the relationship between high art and hegemony, a critique that is underlined by a drawing of a headless, naked woman whose feet and hands are bound—the drawing is titled "Ode to a Grecian Urn." Several pages of associational drawings called "dream maps," presumably Janey's, and a beast fable interrupt the narrative of Janey's entrapment and comment upon her obsessions with rejection, being indoctrinated into patriarchal thinking by the overwhelming presence of her incestuous father, and the possibility of freedom.

At a point in the novel where Janey is in prison—where she is being trained to become a prostitute—Acker presents her first significant plagiarism, that of Nathaniel Hawthorne's *The Scarlet Letter,* which Janey revises in a book report. Janey relates her plight to that of *The Scarlet Letter*'s defiant Hester Prynne. Janey views Hester as a fellow "freak," who has also learned self-hatred: "How do you feel about yourself when every human being you hear and see and smell every day of your being thinks you're worse than garbage? Your conception of who you are has always, at least partially, depended on how the people around you behaved towards you." Janey sees the wildness of Hester's daughter Pearl as an alternative to the stifling nature of contemporary culture, particularly its scripts for women.

Janey decides to learn Persian; thus begins "The Persian Poems by Janey Smith." Janey again revises source material, perhaps a grammar text, by turning the Arabic alphabet to her own obsessions; for example, as she demonstrates various grammatical constructions, she refers to herself ("Janey stinks") and creates apparently illogical statements that reflect her understanding of reality ("the peasant is the street"). Janey tries to learn a "new language." In the process of breaking that language down to its grammatical components and then putting it back together so that it reflects her view of life, Janey (and, perhaps, Acker) tries to defy the conventions and assumptions that culture has inculcated in her.

In yet another appropriation and revision of source material, Janey translates the poems of Propertius, rewriting them as poems from herself to the Persian slave trader. Again Janey's version mutates the originals, not only by altering their content but also by distorting their stylistic qualities so that they reflect her own viewpoint. At the same time, Janey's translations demonstrate that "nothing's changed" in the past two thousand years; males and parents still wield power over women and children. Once he discovers she has cancer, Mr. Linker frees Janey; twice rejected (by Linker and her father), she travels to Tangiers.

Acker's second obvious plagiarism, that of the playwright Jean Genet's *The Screens,* begins in this third section, titled "A Journey to the End of the Night." Janey becomes an exploited colonized worker who helps stage a rebellion against the white landowners. Janey meets Genet and begins to prostrate herself to him as literary mentor and man. Genet appears to be a counterpart to Janey: as a gay male artist who consciously adopts a feminine perspective—he enjoys behaving sexually like a woman—he seems a sympathetic figure; however, he only appropriates the female position for his pleasure, and Janey realizes that he does not comprehend women's subjugation in real-world terms. Although he accompanies her through the desert, he too abandons her—he has a staging of one of his plays to attend. Thrice deserted, Janey dies in Egypt. In this section, Acker again contrasts the lot of the female artist with that of the male artist; even the homosexual male artist, however marginalized, fares better than the female artist.

The epilogue of *Blood and Guts* consists of two pictorial series, "The World" and "The Journey," which have been interpreted variously as Janey's dreams, as the split second of consciousness she experiences before her death, and as her afterlife. Like the visionary dream maps, these drawings demonstrate a partial escape from the overdetermined material world and an attempt to reach something akin to the spiritual. "The Journey" concerns a voyage to attain a book that will transform one from a human into a bird (the soul?). The book must be stolen from the Roman poet Catullus; this situation is reminiscent of Acker's and Janey's own "thefts" of culturally valuable texts in order to make personal, artistic, and political transformations.

The novel ends with the statement that "soon many other Janeys were born and these Janeys covered the earth"; at this closing, Acker also offers a short song akin to a high school student's irreverent anthem. The cyclical, rather than linear, structure of the novel suggests that Janey's story is not unique to her and that many versions of her life will surface, as both exemplars of patriarchal culture and evidence of its rejection.

DON QUIXOTE

Of all her works, Acker's novel *Don Quixote* has garnered the most critical commentary. Subtitled *Which Was a Dream, Don Quixote* begins with a woman's preparations for an abortion and her decision to take on a quest: "By loving another person, she would right every manner of political, social, and individual wrong." She adopts the name "Don Quixote," thereby becoming the female version of Miguel de Cervantes' questing hero from the seventeenth-century Spanish novel of the same name.

Several parallels between Acker's Quixote and Cervantes' are apparent. Both are readers of previous texts, both are idealists whose quests appear mad to those around them, and both decide to destroy their enemies, the "evil enchanters" who represent a threat to their causes. Like Cervantes' novel, Acker's work is metafictional in its references to the processes of reading and writing. Unlike the relatively straightforward quest in Cervantes' novel, the female Quixote's quest is cyclical and is continually disrupted by counternarratives. Acker's Quixote dies at the end of the first section yet is once more alive at the beginning of the final section. She dies again in the final section but is still able to write. These deaths and resurrections of the hero defy normal narrative movement.

The novel's first part, "The Beginning of Night," is set in London at the abortion clinic where Quixote "conceive[s]" her quest. On one level, her decision to love is an insane project because reciprocal love is not possible between men and women in a materialistic society in which people treat each other as objects. More specifically, her resolution to love represents her defiance of the literary conventions of novels, which render the female an object rather than a subject; to love is to be an active being, an agent. This quest is "mad" because within the narrative tradition female characters who express their desire and pursue love often come to an end that entails either insanity or death. Indeed, Quixote faces the dilemma of having to choose between two deaths that will symbolically "kill" her subjectivity; she can marry, and therefore no longer be an active being because she would be succumbing to narrative and heterosexual expectations for women, or she can be an outcast and face ostracism from the community. She must also confront the difficulty of expressing female desire without those expressions (which are already largely culturally conditioned) being co-opted by patriarchal notions of desire.

The critics Marjorie Worthington and Nicola Pitchford have each expressed views that Quixote's decision to become a "female-male or a night-knight" is an attempt to straddle both gender roles so as to circumvent the limitations of being either masculine or feminine and, by extension, to defy systems of thinking that divide the world into value-laden binaries, such as black and white. Christopher L. Robinson, however, argues that her position illustrates how becoming male-identified fails to free one from patriarchal models. At the end of the first part, Quixote "dies" because she renounces her visions and her writing, her search for love.

The second part, "Other Texts," represents Quixote's inability to speak her own story because only male textual representations of women are treated as valid and demonstrates Acker/Quixote's interventions into these texts, similar to Janey's revisions. As in Acker's other works, the colonization of the female mind by masculinist representations of women is a key theme. The first section, called "Text 1: Russian Constructivism," is ostensibly a description of St. Petersburg and an allusion to Andrei Biely's pre-revolutionary symbolist novel, *St. Petersburg,* which portrays this city as a kind of character. Acker's rendition of this Russian city is more like a version of New York City. Acker's inclusion of letters to Peter, a possible reference to her former husband Peter Gordon, turns New York City figuratively into "Peter's burg," which may be a testament to her obsession with the end of their marriage. In this section Acker also parses a portion of a love poem by Catullus, printed in its original Latin, and then shifts to commentary and deviant translations of this poem. In the second section, Acker uses Giuseppe Tomasi di Lampedusa's *The Leopard,* a novel about the decline of the aristocracy and the rise of the middle class in Sicily as a result of the unification of Italy, to discuss memory. She concentrates on the death of the principal character, the Prince of Lampedusa, who muses on love, decadence, the pain of memory, and the meaning of his life.

The third section of "Other Texts" is titled "Texts of Wars for Those Who Live in Silence." This section combines a summary of the plot of a Japanese science fiction film with histories of the various wrongs committed by the American government in the name of materialism, whose ultimate realization is multinational capitalism. This situation is discussed in a dialogue between two monsters created by the Western concept of reason, Megalon and Godzilla. For the fourth and final section, Acker combines Frank Wedekind's "Lulu" plays with George Bernard Shaw's play *Pygmalion* to create a drama in which a lower-class Lulu is subjected to patriarchal determination at the hands of adoptive and biological fathers. Lulu, like Shaw's Eliza Doolittle, is a "creation" of male language; her only speech is that which is man-made, yet she manages to escape and become a pirate.

The novel's third part, "The End of the Night," returns to Don Quixote, focusing on her antagonism toward the evil enchanters, Richard Nixon and Henry Kissinger, who are represented in the novel as dogs. Acker explores various myths of America, particularly the myth of freedom, by tracing modern forms of governmental control back to their roots in American history. The political philosopher Thomas Hobbes appears in Nixon's bedroom to announce the logic behind capitalism and materialism; in a dog-eat-dog world, the objectification and exploitation of the less powerful is justified. The third part also examines Quixote's attempts to form a community with a pack of dogs, who appear to represent various marginalized groups. Quixote realizes that communication requires a community—that it requires others who can share its meanings.

One of the dogs, a "bitch" named Villebranche, tells several stories of her sexual adventures and her miserable childhood as a freak. Villebranche's tale of her transgendered and transvestite affair with an effeminate male, De Franville, implies another possibility for heterosexuality. Villebranche also relates her rereading of a scene from Marquis de Sade's *Juliette* in which Juliette is educated into sado-masochistic sexuality. Acker changes Sade's text by removing all of the male figures. Christopher L. Robinson and Richard Walsh have read this section as an indication of the dangers of women appropriating masculinist sexual practices, for this merely helps bolster patriarchy; conversely, Siegle, Pitchford, and Douglas Shields Dix view it as potentially positive, for it demonstrates a more empowering form of education in which the body and its pleasures, rather than the set of knowledge instilled by culture, are privileged. In other words, Villebranche may either represent hopeful alternatives to normative heterosexuality or unsuccessful perversions.

Although the dogs decide to become pirates, Quixote once again wavers between becoming "normal," through marriage, and therefore being accepted into a community, and going mad in her solipsism. She relates the idealistic hopes of the Spanish Republic to her own desire for a community that is not determined by hierarchy. In the midst of Quixote's despair, God intervenes, declaring his/her death to humankind and the necessity of creating one's own meaning despite the fact that there is no source of meaning or ground for asserting one's meaning.

EMPIRE OF THE SENSELESS

Acker's next novel, *Empire of the Senseless,* is considered a departure from the novels of her plagiarism period because Acker endeavors to be more constructive in her approach to narrative. She takes the oedipal myth and attempts to imagine a reality without that myth. Acker primarily employs the works of Sigmund Freud and Marquis de Sade as guides to her understanding of this myth, which she presents as sadistic in its dualistic construction of reality. *Empire of the Senseless* alternates between the experiences of its two first-person narrators and protagonists, one of whom is a female named Abhor who is also "part robot" and "part black," and the other a male named Thivai, who is a psychotic drug addict in need of an enzyme to survive.

Part 1, "Elegy for the World of the Fathers," suggests the end of the oedipal narrative in which the father, or patriarchy, has absolute authority and the language system is intact. In the section called "Rape by the Father," Thivai relates Abhor's childhood, in which her father teaches her to be docile and to find pleasure in her denigration. Abhor's name suggests her situation as an abject being, one who arouses horror and fascination because she does not fit into any clear category. Being a cyborg and of mixed race, Abhor troubles the strict binaries upon which the oedipal narrative depends; for example, the separation of the "natural" from the "manmade." Thivai is also a child of the postmodern era—he is largely apathetic about the lack of meaning in the world—however, he is still affiliated with patriarchal power, as is evident in his attempts to control Abhor. Acker borrows from William Gibson's 1984 cyberpunk novel *Neuromancer* in her depiction of Thivai and his relationship to Abhor. She also clearly references Freud, for example, in her representation of their boss, Dr. Schreber.

Dr. Schreber sends Abhor and Thivai on a mission: they must try to find the code to a "construct" named Kathy. Like their author, they are constructs; that is, their personalities, including their most intimate desires, have been largely determined by society, which disseminates its dictates through various forms of representation, such as literature, language, and the media, and through its institutions, such as the family, religion, and the educational system.

During their search, it becomes apparent that old methods of subverting authority are passé. Thivai explains that the former outlaws, known as the "Moderns," used destructive means to rebel; however, new outlaws must learn the operations of the system. When Abhor and Thivai discover the code, it proclaims: "GET RID OF MEANING. YOUR MIND IS A NIGHTMARE THAT HAS BEEN EATING YOU: NOW EAT YOUR MIND."

Although this code would seem to suggest that one defeats one's societal encoding through self-destruction, Abhor discovers that, in a postmodern world in which the oedipal narrative is no longer operative, the postmodern quest to "get rid of meaning" is moot because meaning has already lost its place. Abhor also realizes that one can no longer point to a central authority, such as the president of the United States or one's father, as the source of all evil because power is dispersed. Hegemony is a transnational, postcolonial empire in which networks of power crisscross.

When Paris is thrown into chaos by an Algerian takeover, the impotence of old methods becomes more apparent. Even after the colonized have been liberated from the colonizer, the conflicting sociopolitical duality of powerful and powerless endures, allowing protean institutions like the CIA to manipulate the situation to their own ends. Although all of the sexual taboos that controlled the oedipal society are broken, gross injustices related to power imbalances thrive. Thivai takes advantage of the mayhem to satisfy his sexual proclivities. In the meantime, Abhor, who has already killed off Dr. Schreber, the last vestige of clear authority, sets off alone on a nomadic quest for "an adequate mode of expression" that can grant the world a provisional sense of meaning.

She decides to adopt the sailor's life, for the sailor rejects the worship of material goods and embraces meaning as an unfolding possibility. Dressed in drag as a navy lieutenant, Abhor finds meaning when she watches a gay Cuban sailor, Agone, receive a new kind of tattoo. The relationship between Agone and his tattoist represents a nonphallocentric form of sexuality, one in which the experience of the whole body is involved and in which the dominant-submissive dynamic is circumvented. The tattoo itself demonstrates an alternative form of knowing, bodily subjectivity, and suggests an embodied writing akin to Acker's. In a monologue on the disruption of hegemonic language, Abhor argues for the significance of the unconscious, albeit a fictional one, which hosts all that is forbidden. She discerns that reactive nonsense, like deconstruction, cannot challenge the empire of the senseless; only taboo knowledge, that which is expressly prohibited, can undermine conventional epistemologies.

"Pirate Night" illustrates the clash between Thivai's patriarchal thinking and Abhor's new knowledge. Acker plagiarizes from Mark Twain's *The Adventures of Huckleberry Finn* and focuses on the myth of freedom that is so prominent in that text and in America. In effect, Abhor's vision of freedom is subjected to the reality of oppression. Thivai takes on the role of Huck, his friend Mark is the mischievous Tom Sawyer, and Abhor suffers as Nigger Jim. Mirroring events in Twain's *Huckleberry Finn,* Thivai and Mark make sport of Abhor's imprisonment through their ludicrous pretensions of freeing her.

Abhor, however, composes a letter in which she denounces Thivai and Mark for their adherence to a system created by Western masculinist thinking, she escapes, and she then tries to form her own motorcycle gang, against protests from Thivai that women cannot be in a motorcycle gang. At first she attempts to follow the rules of the road as designated in the official highway code, but she discovers that they are flawed, like most codes, because they cause her to disregard her instincts. Thivai, Mark, and an Algerian police officer catch up with her, ef-

fectively ending her fantasy of a life as a lonely rebel. This reminder that freedom is contingent upon the behavior of others causes Abhor to wonder if there can ever be a better world.

Acker ends this novel with an illustration, one among several interspersed throughout its text. This final illustration is of a tattoo, a rose pierced by a dagger with the words "Discipline and Anarchy" underneath. According to R. H. W. Dillard, "discipline" symbolizes the fact that the response to hegemony cannot be nonsensical, for communication must take place in order for change to be effective. The writer, therefore, must demonstrate discipline in her craft. Discipline also reminds one of the reality that the self has been disciplined by hegemony. "Anarchy" refers to the hope for freedom that one must pursue despite the fact that one is disciplined.

IN MEMORIAM TO IDENTITY

The 1990 novel *In Memoriam to Identity* demonstrates Acker's continuing interest in myth as a structural device. In this work, she investigates the myth of romance, which promises to bridge the separation between the self and the other through love. This myth, however, often also maintains this separation because romantic partnerships are conventionally divided into unequal roles that make real empathy and mutual understanding between partners difficult. The first part, "Rimbaud," is Acker's rendition of the early life and works of the French symbolist poet Arthur Rimbaud. Part 2, "Airplane," describes the experiences of a woman named Airplane. In her depiction of Airplane, Acker interprets the character Temple Drake from William Faulkner's novel *Sanctuary.* In part 3, "Capitol," Acker again borrows from Faulkner; Capitol is a kind of fusion of Caddie Compson, from *The Sound and the Fury,* and Charlotte Rittenmeyer, from *The Wild Palms.*

The final part, "The Wild Palms," alternates between Capitol's story and Airplane's.

Rather than dissecting her source texts in a deconstructive manner, Acker finds points of connection with them; nevertheless, she initiates a primarily feminist critique of them. In her essay "Poetics of the Periphery: Literary Experimentalism in Kathy Acker's *In Memoriam to Identity,*" Catherine Rock suggests that through her interpretation of Rimbaud's life and works in conjunction with the stories of Airplane and Capitol, Acker demonstrates the limits of his notion of radical alterity, limited because it does not encompass the specific experiences of women. In addition, Rock asserts, Acker revises Faulkner's novels by giving his female protagonists first-person perspectives and substituting his masculinist point of view with a feminist one.

"Rimbaud" begins by examining the destructive nature of the family and education, which collaborate in the project of disciplining the child into the ways of the world. As well as suffering from a mother that resents his existence (yet another nod to Acker's own past), R, as he is known, is molested by his uncle, African Pain, and terrorized by his teacher, Father Fist, who wants to teach him to be a sadist. R contemplates joining a German motorcycle gang. However, when the gang's leader tries to force him to choose between being a victim or a victimizer, R refuses to accept this dualistic choice. Catherine Rock asserts that R, although he may seem to fall into the category of victim, transforms his pain into a method of moving outside himself, of transgressing the self-other binary. Rock further argues that he experiments with bodily and other forms of consciousness that pain grants him in order to write his poetry. The "memoriam to identity" of the novel's title, therefore, implies a departure from identity defined as a stable self to the reformulation of a self as process rather than product and an acknowledgement of the existence in each person of multiple selves.

The remainder of "Rimbaud" traces R's relationship with the French symbolist poet Paul Verlaine, called "V," and shows the conflicts of the bourgeois (V) against the bohemian (R). In his relationship with V, R attempts to recapture a childhood he never had, one in which pure, sensual experience is unmediated by societal formations. However, R's desire to escape his milieu are vexed by his mother, who works with V's wife and mother-in-law to put a stop to their unlawful romance. The siege against the myth of romantic love is manifested in the section titled "R's End as Poet," in which V, assailed by the laws of respectability, ultimately rejects R by choosing normalcy over deviance; as R proclaims, "The nuclear family is now the only reality." At the end of "Rimbaud," R, like Don Quixote, seems to waver in his quest for love and comradeship and to turn against his poetry. Evidently the pressures of the outside world prove too great for him to continue to pursue his heart's desire; he determines to make his inner reality accord with outer reality.

"Airplane" narrates the story of a young woman's "fall" into the sex industry and her attempt to use male power against itself. After she is raped, Airplane allows her rapist to sell her to a sex show called Fun City. A consummate survivor, Airplane uses her sexuality as a means of escape and buys herself out of her position. "Capitol" explores the situation of a young woman overrun by male figures who are scandalized by her sexual promiscuity and who try to define her sexuality and options in life. She is also haunted by a suicidal mother, whose actions seem to predetermine her own. In her incestuous relationship with her brother Quentin, Capitol is subjected to Freudian psychoanalytic moralizing; meanwhile, her other brother, a "reformed" Rimbaud, attempts to profit from her sexuality. Before he can prostitute her, however, Capitol "steals" an inheritance from their mother that Rimbaud had hidden away for his own use, and she escapes from the family home.

"The Wild Palms" shuttles between Airplane's story and Capitol's. Airplane's narrative focuses on her continuing sexual difficulties. At first Airplane lives as an emotional celibate, keeping herself safe from the entanglements and threats to selfhood that romance represents. With a German reporter, however, Airplane reenacts, by choice, what was formerly forced upon her. Through sadomasochism, she finds new levels of self; however, the degree of agency she has is questionable, and it could be argued that loss of identity is a loss of power. Capitol's struggles revolve around her career as a performance artist and her competition with her boyfriend and then husband, Harry. Her provocative work is met with reproach, and at the same time, Capitol grapples with the possibility of giving herself to Harry, for she sees love as a threat to her art. Through these two stories, Acker underlines how women's childhood traumas impinge upon their current lives. The novel's conclusion is ambiguous about the fate of these female characters; however, both Airplane and Capitol appear to be survivors.

CRITICAL RESPONSE

The attention of literary critics has tended to converge upon certain themes and techniques within Acker's oeuvre but diverge in their assessment of the success and value of her work. Many critics disagree about her pornographic representations; although some find her work to be demeaning to women or to reify women's position as object, others regard her work as accurately portraying the effects of patriarchal Western culture on women. The discussion of Acker's treatment of women often revolves around her novels' conclusions. Although most of her female characters seem to "fail," critics differ as to whether or not these largely ambiguous conclusions necessarily deny the possibility of change. Several assert that the works themselves represent the intervention into hegemony that the characters failed to make. Critics also argue about Acker's method of conveying her narratives. Some find her writing to be unreadable or tedious or both. Others contend that she commits the writerly crime of telling rather than showing by dictating to her readers what to think. Favorable critics assert that her techniques of pastiche and literary experimentation allow for an empowered reader, one who must create his or her own meanings. They also maintain that Acker is admirable for continuing and expanding the experimental tradition that she claimed as her literary heritage.

Selected Bibliography

WORKS OF KATHY ACKER

NOVELS

Politics. Papyrus Press, 1972.

The Childlike Life of the Black Tarantula: Some Lives of Murderesses. San Diego: Community Congress Press, 1973. (Reprinted in *Portrait of an Eye.*)

I Dreamt I Became a Nymphomaniac! Imagining. San Francisco: Empty Elevator Shaft Poetry Press, 1974. (Reprinted as *I Dreamt I Was a Nymphomaniac: Imagining* in *Portrait of an Eye.*)

The Adult Life of Toulouse Lautrec by Henri Toulouse Lautrec. New York: Printed Matter, 1978. (Reprinted in *Portrait of an Eye.*)

Florida. Providence, R.I.: Diana's Bimonthly Press, 1978. (Reprinted in *Literal Madness.*)

Kathy Goes to Haiti. Toronto: Rumour Publications, 1978. (Reprinted in *Literal Madness.*)

Great Expectations. San Francisco: Re/Search Productions, 1982; New York: Grove, 1983.

Hello, I'm Erica Jong. New York: Contact II, 1982.

Blood and Guts in High School. New York: Grove, 1984. (First published in London in 1984 by Picador as *Blood and Guts in High School, Plus*

Two, including *Great Expectations* and *My Death My Life by Pier Paolo Pasolini.*)

Algeria: A Series of Invocations because Nothing Else Works. London: Aloes Books, 1984.

Don Quixote: Which Was a Dream. New York: Grove, 1986.

Empire of the Senseless. New York: Grove, 1988.

Literal Madness: Three Novels. New York: Grove, 1988. (Collects *Kathy Goes to Haiti, My Death My Life by Pier Paolo Pasolini,* and *Florida.*)

In Memoriam to Identity. New York: Grove, 1990.

Portrait of an Eye: Three Novels. New York: Pantheon, 1992.

My Mother: Demonology. New York: Pantheon, 1993.

Pussycat Fever. Illustrated by Diane DiMassa and Freddie Baer. San Francisco: AK Press, 1995.

Pussy, King of the Pirates. New York: Grove, 1996.

OTHER WORKS

I Don't Expect You'll Do the Same, by Clay Fear. San Francisco: MusicMusic Corp., 1974.

Persian Poems. 1978; New York: Bozeau of London Press, 1980.

"New York City in 1979." *Top Stories,* no. 9 (1981).

Implosion: Three Short Plays. New York: Wedge, 1983.

The Birth of the Poet. Performed in New York City at Brooklyn Academy of Music, December 3–8, 1985. (Libretto for opera; music by Peter Gordon.)

Variety. Produced by Renée Shafransky. Directed by Bette Gordon. Horizon Films, 1985. (Screenplay.)

Hannibal Lecter, My Father. Edited by Sylvère Lotringer. New York: Semiotext(e), 1991. (Short works. Includes the stories "New York City in 1979," "Lust," "Translations of the Diaries of Laure the Schoolgirl," and "Algeria"; a fragment from *Politics;* the play *The Birth of the Poet;* an interview with Sylvère Lotringer, "Devoured by Myths"; and the text of the German censorship trial of *Blood and Guts in High School.*)

Pussy, King of the Pirates. Quarterstick/Touch and GoRecords, 1996. (Compact disc recorded with Mekons.)

Bodies of Work: Essays. New York: Serpent's Tail Books, 1997.

Eurydice in the Underworld. London: Arcadia Books, 1997. (Short works. Includes the drama *Eurydice in the Underworld;* "New York City in 1979"; the short story "Lust"; *The Birth of the Poet;* the short story "Translations of the Diaries of Laure the Schoolgirl"; *Algeria;* a transcript of the German censorship trial; and "Requiem," a three-act opera commissioned by Ken Valitsky.)

Essential Acker: The Selected Writings of Kathy Acker. Edited by Amy Scholder and Dennis Cooper. New York: Grove, 2002.

Rip-off Red, Girl Detective and the Burning Bombing of America. New York: Grove, 2002.

CRITICAL AND BIOGRAPHICAL STUDIES

Brennan, Karen. "The Geography of Enunciation: Hysterical Pastiche in Kathy Acker's Fiction." In *Gendered Agents: Women and Institutional Knowledge.* Edited by Silvestra Mariniello and Paul A. Bové. Durham, N.C.: Duke University Press, 1998. Pp. 396–422.

Castricano, C. Jodey. "If a Building Is a Sentence, So Is a Body: Kathy Acker and the Postcolonial Gothic." In *American Gothic: New Interventions in a National Narrative.* Edited by Robert K. Martin and Eric Savoy. Iowa City: University of Iowa Press, 1998. Pp. 202–214.

Dillard, R. H. W. "Lesson No. 1: Eat Your Mind." *New York Times Book Review,* October 16, 1988, pp. 9, 11.

Dix, Douglas Shields. "Kathy Acker's *Don Quixote:* Nomad Writing." *Review of Contemporary Fiction* 9, no. 3:56–62 (fall 1989).

———. "'Now Eat Your Mind': An Introduction to the Works of Kathy Acker." *Review of Contemporary Fiction* 9, no. 3:37–49 (fall 1989).

Kennedy, Colleen. "Simulating Sex and Imagining Mothers." *American Literary History* 4, no. 1:165–185 (spring 1992).

McCaffery, Larry. "The Artists of Hell: Kathy Acker and 'Punk' Aesthetics." In *Breaking the Sequence: Women's Experimental Fiction.* Edited by Ellen G. Friedman and Miriam Fuchs. Princeton, N.J.: Princeton University Press, 1989. Pp. 215–230.

Moran, Joe. *Star Authors: Literary Celebrity in America.* London: Pluto Press, 2000.

Pitchford, Nicola. *Tactical Readings: Feminist Postmodernism in the Novels of Kathy Acker and Angela Carter.* Lewisburg, Pa.: Bucknell University Press, 2002.

Redding, Arthur F. "Bruises, Roses: Masochism and the Writing of Kathy Acker." *Contemporary Literature* 35, no. 2:281–304 (summer 1994).

Robinson, Christopher L. "In the Silence of the Knight: Kathy Acker's *Don Quixote* as a Work of Disenchantment." *Yearbook of Contemporary and General Literature* 47:109–123 (1999).

Rock, Catherine. "Poetics of the Periphery: Literary Experimentalism in Kathy Acker's *In Memoriam to Identity.*" *Lit: Literature, Interpretation, Theory* 12:205–233 (June 2001).

Sciolino, Martina. "The 'Mutilating Body' and the Decomposing Text: Recovery in Kathy Acker's *Great Expectations.*" *Textual Bodies: Changing Boundaries of Literary Representation.* Edited by Lori Hope Lefkovitz. Albany: State University of New York Press, 1997. Pp. 245–266.

Siegle, Robert. *Suburban Ambush: Downtown Writing and the Fiction of Insurgency.* Baltimore: Johns Hopkins University Press, 1989.

Walsh, Richard. "The Quest for Love and the Writing of Female Desire in Kathy Acker's *Don Quixote.*" *Critique* 32, no. 3:149–168 (spring 1991).

Worthington, Marjorie. "Posthumous Posturing: The Subversive Power of Death in Contemporary Women's Fiction." *Studies in the Novel* 32, no. 2:243–263 (summer 2000).

INTERVIEWS

Friedman, Ellen G. "A Conversation with Kathy Acker." *Review of Contemporary Fiction* 9, no. 3: 12–22 (fall 1989).

Juno, Andrea. "Kathy Acker." In *Angry Women.* Edited by Andrea Juno and V. Vale. San Francisco: Re/Search, 1991. Pp. 177–185.

McCaffery, Larry. "The Path of Abjection: An Interview with Kathy Acker." In *Some Other Frequency: Interviews with Innovative American Authors.* Edited by Larry McCaffery. Philadelphia: University of Pennsylvania Press, 1996. Pp. 14–35.

Perilli, Paul. "Kathy Acker: An Interview." *Poets and Writers* 21, no. 2:28–33 (March–April 1993).

—JULIE SEARS

Paul Auster

1947–

PAUL AUSTER RARELY shies away from the literary allusion, particularly when it involves a bit of wordplay. As he told Mark Irwin in an interview, "Beckett compared himself to Joyce by saying: 'The more Joyce knew, the more he could. The more I know, the less I can.' As far as I'm concerned, there's an altogether different equation: The less I know, the more I can." While Auster's artistic sensibility is notoriously contradictory and difficult to articulate— Auster's former publisher at Viking, Gerald Howard, posits that "the lack of precise analogies to his work often leaves critics off-center in discussing it and even a little peeved"—his reputation as an iconoclast of American letters was secured by the publication of the component novellas of *The New York Trilogy* in the mid-1980s. Despite the critical success that greeted the *Trilogy,* Auster's popularity in Europe and Japan outstrips his reputation in the United States. A distinctly American writer with one eye always on the giants of European modernism and postmodernism—his literary and philosophical influences include Samuel Beckett, Franz Kafka, Paul Celan, Jorge Luis Borges, Don DeLillo, Knut Hamsun, Ludwig Wittgenstein, and even Jerzy Kosinski, for whom Auster copyedited the manuscript for Kosinski's 1975 novel *Cockpit*—Auster has garnered an international following for his prose and, since the 1990s, his screenplays. The critically acclaimed *Smoke* (1995), a film based on "Auggie Wren's Christmas Story" (a piece that Auster wrote for the *New York Times* op-ed page December 25, 1990), and *Blue in the Face* (1995), a related film—both starring Harvey Keitel and directed by Wayne Wang—attest to Auster's versatility,

as does his 1998 film, *Lulu on the Bridge* (also starring Keitel and Mira Sorvino), which Auster wrote and directed. Auster's novel *The Music of Chance* (1990) was adapted for the screen in 1993 and starred James Spader and Mandy Patinkin as the ill-fated protagonists Pozzi and Nashe.

In his essays, which range from autobiography to critical examinations of the French symbolists, Auster has been honest to the point of confession about his upbringing in the New York suburbs of the 1950s and 1960s. Much of the available biographical information is detailed in *Hand to Mouth* (1997), a collection whose novella-length title essay limns Auster's early life and his obsession with the written word. *Hand to Mouth* also contains three one-act plays Auster wrote in the mid-1970s (the first, *Laurel and Hardy Go to Heaven,* prefigures his novel *The Music of Chance* more than a dozen years later); "Action Baseball," a board game of Auster's invention; and *Squeeze Play,* a traditional and derivative mystery novel written under the pseudonym Paul Benjamin. Auster began the two-part work *The Invention of Solitude* (1982), an exploration of identity in the context of fatherhood, self, and the ever-shifting relationship of truth and fiction, three weeks after his father's unexpected death in 1979. The epigraph to "Portrait of an Invisible Man," the first of the book's two essays, is taken from Heraclitus and offers a glimpse toward the direction that Auster's later fiction would take: "In searching out the truth be ready for the unexpected, for it is difficult to find and puzzling when you find it." "The Book of Memory," the second essay in *The Invention of Solitude,* is an eclectic mix of rumination, literary criticism, and a treatise on the power of memory. *The Art of Hunger,* a hodgepodge of previously uncollected critical pieces and meditation on the nature of writing and art, was originally published in 1982 and has been reissued in expanded form several times since.

Although he is widely regarded in literary circles as an innovative stylist in his fiction, the scope of Auster's work—which includes essays, screenplays, short fiction, the translation of French poetry, and an experiment with the performance artist Sophia Calle that combines art and words to create Calle's *Double Game* (2000)—places him in the ranks of the most versatile American writers of his era. His work has a distinctly "New York" feel—even when his characters manage to escape from the urban environment, they are invariably affected by its irrepressible pull—though his early passion for poetry and his experiences in France both profoundly affect his work as well.

The author's breakthrough into the mainstream of American letters came in 1985, when he published *City of Glass* (1985), the first novella of his *New York Trilogy* (*Ghosts* and *The Locked Room* followed within a year of *City of Glass;* all three were first published in the United States by Sun and Moon Press in Los Angeles). The work effectively overshadowed his early writing, and nearly all of his work since has been in the form of novels that explore the vagaries of chance and the shifting nature of identity and truth in a thick, unmistakably American context. At the same time, Auster's European influences should not be ignored; in an article for the *Review of Contemporary Fiction,* Charles Baxter points out the various contradictory impulses that drive Auster's work: "The achievement of Paul Auster's fiction—and it is considerable—is to combine an American obsession with gaining an identity with the European ability to ask how, and under what conditions, identity is stolen or

lost." The shift from poetry to fiction was a natural artistic progression for Auster, who told Mark Irwin, "What's interesting about fiction is that it can encompass everything. There's nothing in the world that is not fit material for a novel. . . . Everything from the most banal elements of popular culture to the most rigorous, demanding philosophical works."

THE BURGEONING ARTIST

Paul Auster was born in Newark, New Jersey, on February 3, 1947, the son of Samuel and Queenie Auster. He grew up in a solidly middle-class home, although the fact that both of his parents lived through the Great Depression impacted the family's attitudes toward money: "My father was tight; my mother was extravagant," he recounts in the essay "Hand to Mouth." His parents' squabbles over finances were one cause for their divorce during Auster's senior year in high school. As Auster grew into young adulthood, he began to question the value of money; his disillusionment was borne not only of his parents' divorce, but was also a manifest symptom of his generation, that is, of baby boomers whose childhood experiences were similarly shaped by life within disintegrating families in the sprawling American suburbs.

A sister more than three years Auster's junior—and, by the author's account, the more sensitive of the two children—struggled with her parents' relationship and suffered a number of mental collapses. At the age of ten, Auster, the budding iconoclast, hid himself in the pages of *Mad* magazine, and he was positively influenced by an uncle, himself a translator of some note, who gave the boy books that allowed him to hone his autodidactic tendencies (the image would surface in Marco Stanley Fogg's narrative in Auster's 1989 novel *Moon Palace,* when Fogg's Uncle Victor gives him 1,492 books from his collection) and to realize the possibilities of art and language.

Although he matriculated to Columbia in the fall of 1965, having skipped his high school graduation in order to gain passage on a boat to Europe, the restless Auster searched always for an outlet for his artistic yearning. He briefly took a position as a writer for educational filmstrips, a job that ended in his being fired on the first day when he argued a political point of fact with a supervisor. Much more enjoyable was a groundskeeping position at a resort in the Catskill Mountains after the completion of his freshman year in college, where Auster and his friend Bob Perelman "bit by bit covered the walls of our room with poems—crazy doggerel, filthy limericks, flowery quatrains—laughing our heads off as we downed endless bottles of Budweiser chug-a-lug beer." Two characters whom Auster met that summer, Casey and Teddy, inspired the two protagonists of *The Music of Chance;* indeed, the experiences that Auster had during that summer have continued to feed his imagination throughout his career.

In 1967 Auster was accepted into Columbia's Junior Year Abroad program in Paris. Despite having obtained the freedom that might nurture the artist's soul, he despised the curriculum, which he felt insulting to anyone who truly wanted to learn. He dropped out of college for a brief time before being accepted back into the university upon his return to the United States. His experience in Paris fueled a lifelong infatuation with France. During his stay, Auster dedicated himself to the carefree life of the artist, reading, writing, and watching countless movies at two local theaters.

Being sent to fight in the Vietnam War, which Auster in no way supported, was always a distinct possibility for a male of his age who was not enrolled in college. Despite his attitude toward structured education at the time, he did not hesitate to reenroll at Columbia, where he received an M.A. degree in 1970. The ambivalence that Auster felt toward the war—and society in general—was instrumental in forcing him to come to terms with his future: "When I look back on those days now, I see myself in fragments," he has said. Those fragments would find voice in the poetry and fiction that would follow.

After a short stint as a merchant seaman on the *Esso Florence* and a position in the census taking of 1970, Auster returned to France, the place where he felt that he would be most able to write. Auster's three-year stay in France, from 1971 to 1974, nurtured an artistic consciousness that had found its way into the author's early poetry and inspired the first incarnations of his novel *In the Country of Last Things,* published in 1987.

Auster translated French poetry and prose during his time in France, and his own poems, collected in *Disappearances* (1988), detail his fascination with language, which the young writer experienced as a violent and cathartic (albeit ephemeral, as he understood it) release from the penury that he describes in "Hand to Mouth." One of his early long poems, "Spokes," explores the process of creating meaning from the words on the page and prefigures his later obsession with language and meaning in his fiction:

> Picks jot the quarry—eroded marks
> That could not cipher the message.
> The quarrel unleashed its alphabet,
> And the stones, girded by abuse,
> Have memorized the defeat.

Auster's postmodern sensibility (most reminiscent here, perhaps, of Rainer Maria Rilke)—an echo of the fragmentation, alienation, and lack of identity that he felt as a student at Columbia during one of America's most tumultuous times—is also cultivated in the poetry, no more succinctly than in a passage from "White Nights," first published in *Wall Writing* (1976) and written primarily during his time in France:

> The pen
> moves across the earth: it no longer knows

what will happen, and the hand that holds it
has disappeared.

Nevertheless, it writes.
It writes: in the beginning,
among the trees, a body came walking
from the night.
. . . .
I am no longer here.

His poetry is important for establishing
Auster's narrative authority in his fiction; it is a
precursor to the varied and at times bizarre
worlds—where, literally, Black is White—into
which his characters delve. That notion is
echoed by Auster in his interview with Mark Irwin:

This idea of contrasts, contradictions, paradoxes, I
think, gets very much to the heart of what novel
writing is for me. It's a way for me to express my
own contradictions. Unlike poetry, which for me
was always a univocal act—a way of trying to
ground myself in the very substance of my being
and to express, in as articulate, lyrical and intense
form as possible, what I believed at any given
moment. But novel writing is different.

Since those peripatetic early days, Auster's
personal life has taken on the veneer of order
that his characters seek in his fictions. In 1982
he married Siri Hustvedt, whom Auster credits
as a stabilizing influence in his life, and they
have a daughter, Sophie. He also has a son from
a previous marriage to the writer Lydia Davis.
Auster lives and writes in Brooklyn.

THE NEW YORK TRILOGY

The novella trilogy—*City of Glass, Ghosts,* and
The Locked Room—that put Auster on the literary map was also important as a stylistic and
thematic touchstone for much of his later fiction; the detective genre (or in Auster's case, as
some critics have argued, the "anti-detective"
genre) is the superficial guiding force in the

stories and implies a methodical working toward
an understanding of identity—of a suspect, of
the events surrounding the story's center of
gravity, of a life lived always in search of a
context through which to create meaning outside
the self. Despite the novellas' appearance as
separate entities, peopled with characters who
come into contact with one another only through
haphazard meetings, the stories point up the
infinite possibilities for connections in life and
literature and, finally, the integral nature of a
story that can be neither more nor less than the
words on the page. As Auster told Mark Irwin,

Writing isn't mathematics, after all. This doesn't
equal that, one thing can't be substituted for
another. A book is composed of irreducible elements, and I would almost say that to the degree
that the writer does not understand them, that is
the degree to which the book is allowed to become
itself, to become a human being and not just a
literary exercise.

In *City of Glass,* the first of the three novellas, the framework is erected for a final stunning denouement two novellas hence: The
protagonist, a mystery author named Quinn who
writes under the pseudonym William Wilson
(one of many references to authors and literary
figures, in this case Edgar Allan Poe), receives
a wrong-number call from a man looking for a
private investigator named Paul Auster. Quinn,
a thirty-five-year-old widower, is a man whose
free-floating identity in the aftermath of the loss
of his wife and son makes him a perfect subject
for an Austerian odyssey. Realizing that he
likely will never again be anchored to society in
any meaningful way, Quinn seizes the opportunity and claims to be Auster. Quinn's decision sets in motion a series of events that
ultimately drives him to the brink of insanity
and divests him of what little identity he had
before the random call. Quinn is himself a
purveyor of words, and his idea of what it
means to be a "private eye" points up the play

of language that underpins all of Auster's fiction:

> Private eye. The term held a triple meaning for Quinn. Not only was it the letter "I," standing for "investigator," it was "I" in the upper case, the tiny life-bud buried in the body of the breathing self. At the same time, it was also the physical eye of the writer, the eye of the man who looks out from himself into the world and demands that the world reveal itself to him. For five years now, Quinn had been living in the grip of this pun.

Despite having pondered the possibilities of language and its connection to reality, Quinn is unprepared for his meeting with Peter Stillman, the caller, and Virginia, the man's wife. The only means he has of assuring himself that his memories are accurate is to record them in a red notebook (a symbol that becomes vitally important in the trilogy); even then the truth, as Auster readily and so often points out, is negotiable. Stillman's story is both bizarre and captivating: The man who sits before Quinn is clearly well-off, although he was mistreated by his father, an eminent and eccentric psychologist who attempted to erase his son's identity and the very language he used to communicate with the world. The elder Peter Stillman is being released that day from the insane asylum, and Peter Stillman the son assumes that his father will take up where he left off before his incarceration.

After Stillman's release, Quinn shadows the man on his meanderings around the city. Much to Quinn's surprise, the old man's wanderings are not random, but rather spell out "THE TOWER OF BABEL," a reference to the man's fascination with language and his belief, ultimately, that attempts at communicating in modern society are hopelessly muddled. At this point, the narrative begins to mirror Stillman's own views: After several conversations with Peter Stillman the senior, Quinn eventually loses contact with the man. In desperation, he contacts Paul Auster, the detective whom Stillman the

son had sought at the beginning of the narrative. What Quinn finds, not surprisingly, is that Auster, also a writer, is as confused by the whole affair as is the hapless Quinn.

Quinn's lack of ability to shadow Stillman has exposed him as a fraud, and the red notebook that he keeps as witness to the events is the only artifact from which the author of the story at hand (not Auster, as it turns out, but a nameless friend of the author) relates Quinn's narrative. Because he feels that to lose Stillman—or to allow him to exact his revenge on the younger Peter Stillman—would be to fail as a private eye and to eliminate any chance that he may have of establishing an identity outside the tragedy and banality of his previous life, Quinn is compelled to keep watch over the younger Stillman's apartment in the event that the man's father arrives. The elder Stillman, however, does not appear. Quinn later discovers that Stillman committed suicide by jumping off the Brooklyn Bridge.

With Stillman dead and his own life shattered (in fact, Quinn's life had been so completely defined by Stillman that the man's suicide signals Quinn's own symbolic death), Quinn's transformation from a living entity to one of the many "ghosts" that inhabit Auster's fiction is complete. When Quinn passes a shop and does not recognize his own reflection in the mirror, he realizes that he "had been one thing, and now he was another. It was neither better nor worse. It was different, and that was all."

The novella's author has written the story based on Quinn's red notebook, the only record of Quinn's trail aside from his scant contact with Paul Auster. The narrative's title is deceptively simple, though it anticipates the contradictions that Auster explores in later fictions: although everything that happens in the city is transparent, nothing that happens can be accepted as truth, not even by the characters who experience the events recounted in the narrative. As the cautionary tale of Quinn's life makes clear, even a relative truth threatens to destroy the identities of individuals who, like Quinn, wonder "What will happen when there are no more pages in the red notebook?" In an interview with Joseph Mallia, Auster describes the process that Quinn undergoes as "one of stripping away to some barer condition in which we have to face up to who we are. Or who we aren't. It finally comes to the same thing."

Ghosts, the middle and shortest of the three novellas, notably uses colors as analogues for the generic identities of its characters. In an echo of *City of Glass,* a man named Blue, who has been trained by Brown, is hired by White to follow Black. Blue, the pursuer, and Black, the pursued, settle into a routine that will last, unbeknownst to Blue, for many years. In a paradox that becomes commonplace in Auster's work, with its telescoping of time and its shifting between the two-dimensionality of his colorful characters and the infinite regression, repetition, and subtle transformation of those characters and their milieu that recalls the work of M. C. Escher, the narrator states, "The place is New York, the time is the present, and neither one will ever change."

The interweaving of time and text, language and action, is as prevalent in this story as in the first; here, though, Auster uses the characters as tropes for the "ghosts"—people without identity who wander the streets in search of it—who inhabit literature and life. In the beginning, Blue assumes that the case will be simple, involving little more than shadowing Black and recording his own observations. In the course of watching the man, however, Blue surrenders to the ennui of his life (Black does nothing more than sit at a table and read Henry David Thoreau's *Walden*) and begins to create stories about the man in his written reports to White. Paradoxically, the words that he writes on the page undermine his ability to communicate, and "he discovers that words do not necessarily work, that it is pos-

sible for them to obscure the things they are trying to say." The breakdown of communication becomes more profound, until Blue realizes that he knows so much about Black that he does not need to write anymore: in essence Blue and Black, not unlike Stillman and Quinn in the previous novella, have become the same character.

Blue's prolonged absence from his former life causes him to lose his fiancée, and he tracks down White, his ostensible employer, to discover the truth of his hiring. In the process, Blue realizes how desperate his situation is—that is, how close he truly is to having his identity subsumed by Black—and the narrator sums up his predicament in the terse recognition of the fact that "there is no story, no plot, no action—nothing but a man sitting alone in a room and writing a book." In an attempt at reconciling himself to his situation, Blue dresses as an old man and confronts Black, who thinks that Blue looks like Walt Whitman. They discuss the vagaries of identity and writing in terms of the famous writers who have walked the same streets that they now walk, and Black muses on the solitary nature of writing and its power to compromise the writer's identity. As if to prove his point, Black tells the story of Wakefield, a character created by Nathaniel Hawthorne, who disappears from his home only to return decades later as an old man. The parallel to Blue is clear.

In order to bring the case to an end, Blue breaks into Black's apartment and discovers the truth of his predicament, that "to enter Black, then, was the equivalent of entering himself, and once inside himself, he can no longer conceive of being anywhere else." Though he recognizes how truly eccentric the whole affair has become—when Black confesses to having himself hired Blue to follow him, Blue discovers that Black is White (a pun that needs little explanation), the reason for which is never made clear—he also realizes how relevant the observation is to his own life. In one final confrontation, Blue wrests the manuscript that Black has been writing from the man and reads it. Blue realizes that he has known the story all along. In an action that mirrors the very language in the manuscript that he holds in his hands, "Blue stands up from his chair, puts on his hat, and walks through the door. And from this moment on, we know nothing."

The Locked Room, the final installment of the *New York Trilogy,* continues the mystery and wordplay of the first two novellas; taken as a whole, the three stories prefigure the complexities of Auster's later novels. Indeed, *The Locked Room* develops characters who return in spirit, if not in name, in both *Leviathan* (1992) and *Moon Palace.* The story, on the surface, is deceptively simple: The narrator has been contacted by Sophie Fanshawe, the wife of the narrator's oldest and dearest friend, to tell him that her husband has disappeared. In his will, Fanshawe requested that the narrator act as executor of his unpublished literary works. In Fanshawe's absence—everyone, after a time, assumes that he committed suicide—the narrator begins to construct his own identity through the memories and literary remnants of his oldest friend.

Despite their closeness as children and young adults, the two drifted apart later in life. The crux of the narrator's responsibility to Fanshawe revolves, on one superficial level, around the manuscripts that Fanshawe has left behind, the narrator's only way of knowing the man in the years during which the two were estranged. Fanshawe has left directions for the work to be published only if the narrator deems it fit; although the narrator is himself a critic, his own identity is molded by the absent Fanshawe (as Auster suggests it should be, the creator's vision privileged over the critic's retelling), who continues to control his old friend not despite his absence, but because of it. A relationship quickly develops between the narrator and Sophie Fanshawe, which only serves to reinforce the missing man's presence in the lives of those he has left behind.

Once Fanshawe's work is shown to the public, it becomes successful beyond reason, and the narrator is able to live comfortably as a result of his friend's genius. In a narrative move that splits the story into two distinct parts and foreshadows a later confrontation between the narrator and Fanshawe, the narrator muses that "in some sense, this is where the story should end. . . . But it turns out this is only the beginning." The remainder of the novella details the narrator's descent into self-destruction and near-madness and his incessant self-questioning when he realizes that Fanshawe is still alive.

In order to get closer to the reality of Fanshawe's disappearance and to perpetuate the charade of his life as a writer, the narrator purports to write Fanshawe's biography; he has no intention of finishing the book. Instead, he understands that he is entering alien territory—after all, the search for identity in any of Auster's works is neither easy nor enviable for the seeker—though the narrator sees his scheme as his only chance at taking "a living man and put[ting] him in his grave." Still, the narrator has resigned himself to the fact that what he finds in his search for Fanshawe will in no way ameliorate his feelings of inadequacy or mitigate the man's influence in his life. In a brief affair with Fanshawe's mother, the narrator, now married to Sophie Fanshawe and the father of their daughter, makes a desperate and ineffectual attempt at erasing the memory of Fanshawe from his life once and for all. The narrator resolves to track down Fanshawe and kill him. He travels to France on the off chance that he will find him there. Instead, the boundaries of language force the narrator to become more introspective, which only increases his self-loathing.

In a series of encounters with sex and drugs in which the narrator attempts to purge himself of his psychic connection to Fanshawe, the narrator realizes that, ironically, he is increasingly becoming Fanshawe (a notion reiterated in more than one of Auster's fictions), a thought he abhors. The image that occurs to the narrator when he thinks of Fanshawe is that of a locked room, the physical prison of the narrator's old friend and, importantly, the psychic space "located inside my skull." After a period of ravaging his own body and betraying his wife (who is, after all, Fanshawe's former wife) so that he can separate himself from Fanshawe's identity, the narrator makes an astounding declaration: The end of his story is crystal clear to him, perhaps the one image of all those presented in the three narratives that may stand out as the truth. As such,

> The entire story comes down to what happened at the end, and without that end inside me now, I could not have started this book. The same holds for the two books that come before it, *City of Glass* and *Ghosts*. These three stories are finally the same story, but each one represents a different stage in my awareness of what it is about.

In a narrative tour de force, Auster concludes the trilogy: Fanshawe has contacted the narrator again and urges him to come to Boston. When he meets Fanshawe, who claims to have taken a lethal dose of poison several hours before, the narrator takes the notebook from him and reads it. What he finds there does little to clear up the story, obfuscating the language that has been manipulated over the narrative space of the three stories that comprise the *Trilogy:* "If I say nothing about what I found there, it is because I understood very little. All the words were familiar to me, and yet they seemed to have been put together strangely, as though their final purpose was to cancel each other out." The narrator's only response as he reads the notebook—the only key, it would seem, to solving any of the three mysteries presented in the collection—is to tear the pages from the notebook as he waits for the train and to throw the pages in a nearby garbage can.

In one sense, the *Trilogy* remains Auster's most complete fiction to date: the depth of paradox, the push and pull of the competing themes of identity, language, relationships, reality and illusion, and point of view—all of which originate in Auster's profound identification with and questioning of epistemology, the ways in which we know the world around us, the ways in which truth is determined—are separated and explored individually before being pieced back together. The image of the locked door at the end of the third story is indicative of the paradoxes with which Auster works. In the case of the story's narrator, the door represents both the confinement of the narrator within Fanshawe's sphere of influence and the physical door behind which Fanshawe hides from the narrator and from the world. Auster explained to Mark Irwin the writing process in terms of the limited physical space within which he works and the inherent latitude in creating space that such an opportunity affords him:

> There's a curious paradox embedded in all this: when the characters in my books are most confined, they seem to be most free. And when they are free to wander, they are most lost and confused. . . . Every day, I set off on a journey into the unknown and yet the whole time I'm just sitting there in my room. The door is locked, I never budge, and yet that confinement offers me absolute freedom—to be whoever I want to be, to go wherever my thoughts want to take me.

Inherent in the creative process for Auster is the understanding that the work is irreducible from itself; that, in the final analysis, anything written about the work is simply an alternative reality that has little in common with the author's original vision. The paradox of simultaneously reading a story and yet knowing so little about it replays itself repeatedly in Auster's subsequent fiction.

IN THE COUNTRY OF LAST THINGS

Although the *Trilogy* constructs much of the theoretical framework for Auster's fiction, the author begins to narrow his focus from larger epistemological concerns to other subjects more efficiently handled by a "traditional" narrative. To be sure, the works that follow the *Trilogy* retain the stylistic bravado of the earlier work, a combination of intellectual rigor and a narrative that, unlike the work of postmodern predecessors such as John Barth and Donald Barthelme, never devolves into a highly self-reflexive style that excludes many readers.

In the Country of Last Things explores a dystopian society whose protagonist, Anna Blume, searches a dark, violent, and unredeemed wasteland for her missing brother. Auster's title implies the end of time as his characters know it and the physical and psychic stagnation that threatens to annihilate the society. Anna, who writes her own narrative in journal form to an unnamed friend "back home," immediately draws the distinction between her former affluent life and the new reality that haunts her: "I don't expect you to understand," she writes to her friend. "You have seen none of this, and even if you tried, you could not imagine it." Auster told Joseph Mallia that he wrote the book as a catalog of the atrocities that humans were capable of inflicting on one another: "These things actually happened. And in many cases, reality is far more terrible than anything we can imagine. . . . I feel that this is where we live. It could be that we've become so accustomed to it that we no longer see it." In the hell that Anna inhabits, society is a mirror reflection of her former life. Death, not life, is society's art form, "the only way we can express ourselves," and food is so scarce that it has taken on a mythical connection with language: "You must allow your mind to leap into the words coming from the mouths of others. . . . There are even those who say there is nutritional value in these food talks—given the proper concentration and an equal desire to believe in the words among those taking part."

In examining the society in which she finds herself, however, Anna hits upon a notion that reverberates throughout Auster's fiction: the interconnectedness of present reality and memory. As Auster told Irwin,

> A crisis occurs when everything about ourselves is called into question, when the ground drops out from under us. I think it's at those moments when memory becomes a most powerful force in our lives. You begin to explore the past, and invariably you come up with a new reading of the past, a new understanding, and because of that you're able to encounter the present in a new way.

In much the same way, Anna uses the strength of her memories to guide her in a world for which she has no context.

When Anna finds Samuel Farr, a scholar who had known her brother before his disappearance, they fall in love and Anna becomes pregnant, an occurrence that was thought to be impossible in such a place. Anna helps Samuel work on a book that he has been researching and writing, a situation whose irony is not wasted on Anna. While working to complete the book—an improbable assertion of the intellect and a rare creative act, like Anna's own pregnancy—the two must burn other books in order to stay warm. Such are the vagaries of life in the Country of Last Things.

Rebuilding identity in a world where chaos is by far the strongest force that drives the lives of its inhabitants—Anna writes that her experience "is a slow but ineluctable process of erasure. Words tend to last a bit longer than things, but eventually they fade too, along with the pictures they once evoked"—is the greatest frustration for Anna. After manifesting a world where every action is connected to the next in an increasingly tighter web of experience in the *Trilogy,* Auster here examines the nature of entropy. No matter what action Anna undertakes—writing a book with Samuel, becoming pregnant, or helping those less fortunate—the result is bound not to be a coming together, as in the earlier work, but rather a breaking down, a tearing apart. Anna loses track of Samuel for a time, her pregnancy is terminated in an accident, and her attempts at helping the homeless come to naught. Anna's only recourse (in an echo of the actions of more than one character in the *Trilogy*) is "to have my say at last, to get it all down on these pages before it is too late. I tremble when I think how closely everything is connected."

Anna recognizes that "the facts are not reversible. Just because you are able to get in, that does not mean you will be able to get out." That realization reinforces the chaos of the situation; if Anna's predicament were as tidy as a mathematical formula, she would have little trouble reversing the actions that got her there in the first place. The dissipation of society into nothingness, however, does not follow any rules of nature that Anna knows. Her only recourse is, like the characters who use the red notebook in the *New York Trilogy,* to similarly record her observations, which often begin with phrases such as "It happened like this" and "Little by little, I am trying to tell you what happened." The intrusions, acting as they do as signposts signaling section breaks and shifts in narrative direction, give some semblance of coherence to a story that otherwise has little internal cohesiveness. Anna's words, Auster suggests, are her only means of slowing the "ineluctable process of erasure."

That sense of erosion, the immanent destruction that the chaos of her new world engenders, gains momentum as the narrative progresses. Anna realizes that no matter how hard she tries to make a life for herself in society, "there was no chance that you were not going to fail." When Anna accepts a job as an aide in Woburn House, the one place in the city where people could still go to escape the horror of the outside world, Anna realizes that the stories people tell in order to make sense of their lives, different as they are on the surface, are "finally the same. . . . Our lives are no more than the sum of manifold contingencies, and no matter how diverse they might be in their details, they all share an essential randomness in their design: this then that, and because of that, this." The truth of Anna's observation, which bolsters her earlier contention that none of the events that she has experienced are reversible, echoes the author's notions in the *Trilogy* that all stories, finally, are the same.

The small group of pilgrims who make their way into the unknown at the novel's conclusion hit upon the idea of creating a magic show in order to make ends meet along the way. The symbolism of such an act is clear: in a world where reality is dictated always by events outside the protagonists' control, the group will attempt to create their own reality. The contradiction that faces the group is summed up as they survive in a world where "anything is possible, and that is almost the same as nothing, almost the same as being born into a world that has never existed before." Whether or not the characters will succeed is, finally, not relevant in the larger contexts that Auster explores.

MOON PALACE

While Anna Blume's search for her brother is also a search for order in a world defined by its capacity for chaos, Marco Stanley Fogg's movement through time in *Moon Palace* is a haphazard mélange of experiences that has as its focal point the sorts of coincidences and comings-together that become commonplace in Auster's fiction. Fogg's first recollection in a narrative that circumscribes three lives—his own, his grandfather's, and his father's—is, "If not for a girl named Kitty Wu, I probably would have starved to death. I had met her by chance only a short time before." Fogg's focus throughout the narrative, aside from his rather matter-of-fact acceptance of the events that unfold before him, is on the themes that Auster discusses in his autobiographical essay "Hand to Mouth," specifically the notion of penury and its related isolation from society, the question of identity, and the pull of history on the present.

The novel, written in the first person with Fogg as its narrator (Auster employs a pun on his protagonist's initials, M. S., or "manuscript"), implies a certain order that Fogg is able to give his life after the death of his father, whom he meets only toward the end of the narrative, and the loss of his lover, Kitty Wu, who, unlike Anna Blume in *In the Country of Last Things,* willingly terminates a pregnancy in order not to lose her own identity. The intermittent events in Fogg's life are as chaotic as his first recollection implies. Fogg deals with that chaos as logically as he knows how, believing, like an inveterate gambler, that the best way to obtain a desired end is to deny the possibility of its occurrence.

Seemingly, what Fogg wants more than anything else is to establish order in his life. Although he is doomed to fail, except in a final scene in which his demons are kept in abeyance by the rising of the moon—Fogg's constant companion throughout—over the Pacific Ocean, he succeeds for a period of several months in living life in contentment with Kitty Wu. Even after the relationship has begun to sour, the one stabilizing force is the written word. In Fogg's case, though, his life moves too quickly for him to realize the same conjoining of experience and writing that Quinn, Blue, or Paul Aaron (the protagonist of the later *Leviathan*) use to order their own lives. Instead, Fogg writes haltingly, believing that he had "already spent too much of my life living through words," and chooses to live life fully in the present. The idea to write the narrative that has become *Moon Palace* occurs to Fogg only after a chance meeting with an old friend, and even then only when

the man has disappeared down the street and become a ghost alive only in memory. It is not until four years after the novel's action has ended that Fogg gives in to the impulse and writes his story.

That separation of experience from the writer's perception is no more important in Auster's body of fiction than in this, his longest and most complex narrative. In the course of little more than the two years that the novel spans, Fogg moves through history with Kent State, social protest over the Vietnam War, and the moon landing as a backdrop to his experiences. On his journeys, he meets Thomas Effing, an elderly man who takes Fogg on as an aide and asks Fogg to piece together an obituary from the man's bizarre life story. Because of his connection to Effing, Fogg meets the father whom he never knew. In an affirmation of Fogg's earlier assertion regarding the paradoxical control of chaos in his life, he muses,

> It was all a matter of missed connections, bad timing, blundering in the dark. We were always in the right place at the wrong time, the wrong place at the right time. . . . That's what the story boils down to, I think. A series of lost chances. All the pieces were there from the beginning, but no one knew how to put them together.

Hearing the man's life story, despite its tragedy, is a transformational experience for Fogg, who, when forced to describe his surroundings to the blind Effing, must learn to bring objects to life through his words:

> My job was not to exhaust him with lengthy catalogues, but to help him see things for himself. In the end, the words didn't matter. Their task was to enable him to apprehend the objects as quickly as possible, and in order to do that, I had to make them disappear the moment they were pronounced.

Fogg, like Auster, is charged with offering words in place of direct perception in such a way that the words replace the object itself.

When he meets Solomon Barber, Thomas Effing's son, Fogg has no idea that Barber is his father: Fogg was born as the result of Barber's affair with Emily, Fogg's mother, when she was a college student under Barber's tutelage. Barber is an obese academic who has immersed himself in the life of the mind in order to free himself from his grotesque physical being. The relationship between Fogg and Barber becomes clear only when Barber loses a great deal of weight after an accident and Fogg can look into the man's eyes and see the physical resemblance. In one final, halfhearted attempt at discovering the truth of Effing's story, a twisted, improbable tale in which Effing creates and recreates his identity as an artist, a hermit, and an entrepreneur, Fogg heads to the Utah desert in search of a cave that, according to Effing, contains the man's paintings. When he discovers that the area has been submerged under the vast Lake Powell, obliterating any chance that he may discover the truth, the answer to the question of Fogg's life is clear: he walks to the Pacific shore and watches the moon rise. The matter of Effing's claims—and by extension the "truth" of the narrative—remains, like the conclusion of *In the Country of Last Things*, unknowable.

THE MUSIC OF CHANCE

The novel that followed *Moon Palace* continued to draw on Auster's obsession with the vagaries of chance. Of his 1990 novel, *The Music of Chance,* Auster says, "In some sense, *Moon Palace* and *The Music of Chance* are opposite books, mirror reflections of each other," most conspicuously in the ways in which the protagonists meet their fate: Fogg's fate is a heading out, or opening up, the narrative's conclusion suggesting the infinite possibilities that await him, even as the tragic events of his life have sent him to the West Coast; by contrast Nashe, the protagonist of *The Music of Chance,* narrows his peripatetic life to one final point in space and time.

Nashe is a fireman who has been offered a measure of freedom when his father, whom he has not seen in thirty years, dies and leaves Nashe an inheritance of $200,000. Nashe, in language reminiscent of many of Auster's earlier protagonists, relates that the windfall "was one of those random, accidental encounters that seem to materialize out of thin air." He uses his newfound freedom to drive back and forth across the United States. He has saved some of the money in a trust fund for his daughter, who is staying with Nashe's sister in Minnesota, and his wife has left him. When he has only a portion of the inheritance remaining, however, the contradictions of his situation become apparent: "Slowly but surely, the adventure was turning into a paradox. The money was responsible for his freedom, but each time he used it to buy another portion of that freedom, he was denying himself an equal portion of it as well."

The chance meeting that drives Nashe toward his final destination is with Jack Pozzi, a gambler looking for a sponsor. Pozzi convinces Nashe that, with his remaining $10,000, he should stake him to a game with two lottery-rich bachelors in the Pennsylvania countryside; Nashe agrees, and the two set off for what promises to be a lucrative evening. They are surprised at the eccentricities that await them: One of the men, Stone, has created a "City of the World" that foreshadows the fate of Nashe and Pozzi: "It's an artistic vision of mankind. In one way, it's an autobiography, but in another way, it's what you might call a utopia—a place where the past and future come together, where good finally triumphs over evil." Stone's partner, Flower, is obsessed with collecting obscure objects owned by famous people; what strikes Nashe about the collection is the meaninglessness that the objects exude when they are taken out of context.

Nashe and Pozzi are incredulous when they lose the card game and Nashe unsuccessfully stakes his car, the symbol of his freedom, on a last turn of the cards. The two must either stay and face the prospect of building a stone wall from the remnants of a fifteenth-century Irish castle—another of Flower's objects—or flee. They choose to stay, and they are conscripted for the next fifty days to pay off the debt. As they near the end date, Pozzi tries to escape; he is beaten nearly to death, and Nashe disbelieves Murks, the man who has been charged with overseeing the construction, when he tells him that Pozzi has been taken to a local hospital to convalesce. Nashe bides his time building the wall until Murks brings his young grandson to the site. Nashe is filled with hatred for the boy and imagines killing him in retribution for his treatment at the hands of Stone and Flower. The impulse passes, and Nashe completes his duty for the men. Murks invites Nashe to go with them for drinks to celebrate the occasion, and when Murks allows Nashe to drive his old car home from the bar, Nashe steers the car head-on into an oncoming truck, killing them all. Both the forced labor and Nashe's subsequent death are foreshadowed in a passage that Nashe comes upon at random in William Faulkner's *The Sound and the Fury:* "until someday in very disgust he risks everything on the single blind turn of a card."

The passage that gives the novel thematic continuity—the title, after all, suggests that haphazard occurrences within the regular meter and rhythm of the music of everyday life will figure heavily in the story's outcome—is punctuated by Nashe's own response to his final moments. The important distinction between *In the Country of Last Things* and *The Music of Chance* is that Anna Blume survives her nightmare, while Nashe can do little more than meet his end with a dignity that had been stripped from him by Stone, Flower, and the music of chance.

LEVIATHAN

The importance of communication, particularly in the written word, and its connection to identity continues in Auster's fourth novel, *Leviathan.* The narrator, Paul Aaron (who, not coincidentally, bears the same initials as the author), finds himself in the awkward position of having to write a biography of Benjamin Sachs, an old friend whose body has been found mysteriously immolated on a deserted stretch of Wisconsin highway.

The connections between *Leviathan* and the earlier novella *The Locked Room* are worth exploring: Aaron and Sachs struck up their intense friendship many years before at a reading in New York, and Aaron struggles with both his friend's unexplained and bizarre death and the notion that Sachs had always been the better writer. Aaron becomes involved with Fanny, Sachs's wife, an affair that exacerbates Aaron's uncertainty about the "truth" (always a loaded term in Auster's work) and the extent to which his surroundings are knowable.

The accretion of events one upon the other that is key to the structure of *The Locked Room* is also apparent in *Leviathan,* a reference to the eponymous work by Thomas Hobbes and a word taken from the Hebrew *leviath,* meaning "What is joined or tied together." The title implies the relationship between Aaron and Sachs, though it also suggests Sachs's acting on his own to right a perceived wrong, in this case America's venality and its inability to fully appreciate the impact of history on the events that follow. Aaron records the myriad coincidences that compel him to write his estranged friend's life before the police discover the identity of the man's mangled body. At the time, Sachs had been roaming the country as the "Phantom of Liberty," destroying likenesses of the Statue of Liberty along the way; the destructive forces that drive Sachs are linked to his identity as "America's first Hiroshima baby," born on August 6, 1945, at the outset of the atomic age.

Sachs's immersion and participation in American history lends itself to his passion in (re)writing that history. His only published novel, *The New Collosus,* circumscribes American history from 1876 to 1890 and, much as Auster's own work does, interweaves real historical characters and fictive creations who live in the margins of their society. The connection between Sachs's own views on history and Auster's attempts at exploding the "traditional" fictive narrative are clear, expressed both in the narrative at hand and in Auster's later autobiographical essay "Hand to Mouth."

Leviathan, part biography and part mystery, a reworking of the postmodern detective framework of the *Trilogy,* trades on Sachs's nebulous identity to drive the plot. When FBI agents visit Aaron to question him as to why the dead man would have had Aaron's phone number in his pocket, Aaron denies any knowledge of the man's identity. Of the men who interview Aaron, one is young and brash, and the other, Harris, is older, wiser, more circumspect. Harris is the one who finally makes the connection between Aaron and Sachs at the end of the novel, when the various threads that were unwound with the explosion that ended Sachs's life are once again tied. Aaron leads Harris from his house to his writing studio, where the manuscript of *Leviathan,* ostensibly the same work that Auster offers his readers, awaits his perusal.

The novel's key themes—coincidence, memory, language and words, history, and illusion versus reality—are all dependent upon Auster's insistence that life's events are both mystical and inexorable. Once Aaron discovers the truth about Sachs, he is powerless to do anything but write the biography. He writes,

If it still shocks me to report what happened, that is because the real is always ahead of what we can imagine. No matter how wild we think our inventions might be, they can never match the unpredictability of what the real world continually spews forth. This lesson seems inescapable to me now. *Anything can happen.* And one way or another, it always does.

Toward the end of the story—Auster's and Aaron's—the narrator muses, "The book is over because the case is over. If I put in this final page, it is only to record how they found the answer, to note the last little surprise, the ultimate twist that concludes the story." As in *The Locked Room,* the narrative concludes in the intersection of time and space of the physical manuscript and the plot. Only when Aaron knows the final detail of his story—in this case Harris' recognition of the connection between Aaron and Sachs—can he complete Sachs's story.

MR. VERTIGO

Auster's penchant for storytelling, distinct from the stylistic gymnastics that characterize his earlier work, hits its stride in the 1994 novel *Mr. Vertigo* and carries over into his 1999 novel, *Timbuktu. Mr. Vertigo* centers on Walter Claiborne Rawley, a boy of twelve who learns to levitate himself. Master Yehudi, the boy's mentor, has taken him out of adverse conditions (one of the earmarks of Auster's characters, no doubt an homage of sorts to his own beleaguered circumstances in Paris that he details in "Hand to Mouth") and vows to make him a millionaire. The plan would have worked if Rawley had not begun to experience excruciating headaches, the result of his transition from boyhood to manhood. The only remedy (and that, Yehudi tells his young protégé, is no certainty) is to undergo castration. Rawley declines, and without the skill that has made him "Walt the Wonder Boy," he is thrown into a world of thieves and gamblers on the mean streets of Chicago.

Despite the linear plot, Walter's quest is as much a search for identity as it is the retelling, some seven decades after the fact, of the story of a boy who possesses, for a time, an extraordinary talent. The story's setting—amid the heroic acts of Charles Lindbergh, during the heyday of professional baseball, and fraught with villains from the Ku Klux Klan (who lynch Rawley's friend, Aesop, a deformed African American boy headed to Yale on scholarship) to Uncle Slim, the quintessential Dickensian gold-digger—uses history as a backdrop to explore the zeitgeist through the eyes of a boy who is, for much of the narrative, alone in the world. Rawley's realization that "if you look at someone's face long enough, eventually you're going to feel that you're looking at yourself" echoes Fogg's discovery in *Moon Palace* that Solomon Barber is his father, and it connects the two in an important way, as individuals moving through history, subject to its whims, and yet living far enough in the margins to validate their own experiences apart from those events. They are individuals living in times that will be remembered for heroes that have become part of the American psyche.

Although the mystical aspects of experience—the coincidences, the "synchronicities" that pepper Auster's novels—are the author's stock-in-trade, the novel is the first in which the author uses a device such as levitation as the narrative's center of gravity. For the first time, Auster asks the reader not to suspend disbelief, but rather to indulge him in the telling of a story that, while implausible, is too engaging not to join. Memory and the tenuous line between truth and fiction, words whose definitions are nebulous at best in Auster's hands, are blurred even more by the fact that Rawley does not begin his memoir until sixty-eight years after his first meeting with the mysterious Yehudi. Like many of Auster's characters, the act of writing for Rawley performs a much more important function than simple storytelling. In this case, Rawley is unaware that he is capable of such a task (in that sense, perhaps he is not unlike an elderly and ironic Huckleberry Finn), and the

writing becomes an act of memory so intimately connected to the events of the narrator's childhood and early adulthood as to be, finally, inseparable from the events themselves.

Rawley's acquiescence to the movement of time is a departure from the protagonists that have come before him. In fact, no other of Auster's protagonists—Quinn, Blue, Anna Blume, Fogg, Nashe, or Aaron—complete their stories after they have reached early middle age. Perhaps Rawley's acceptance of the life he has lived prefigures Auster's move away from the human protagonist to an entity that is given voice by an author who remains behind the scenes.

TIMBUKTU

The protagonist of Auster's 1999 novel, *Timbuktu,* is Mr. Bones, a mutt whose master, Willy G. Christmas, is dying of cancer in his mid-forties. Christmas, whose real name is William Gurevitch, was a scholarship student at Columbia until he suffered a "schizo flip-out" in 1968. Now, he and Mr. Bones live on the streets. Despite their mean circumstances, the two have been together long enough that Mr. Bones, though he cannot speak "Ingloosh," understands his master's every word. Aware of his own mortality, Christmas has taken Mr. Bones to Baltimore, where he hopes to find Mrs. Swanson, the English teacher who had encouraged his writing more than two decades before. Christmas wants her to have the seventy-four notebooks that he has filled with writing of all kinds.

The story hinges upon Mr. Bones's innocence of the world around him. Auster uses the dog as a tabula rasa to great effect to examine the vagaries of society—homelessness, the all-American family, popular culture (and the baggage that accompanies the term)—that have become commonplace enough to require an outside commentator in order to render them objectively. From a dog's perspective, then (the novel is written in the third-person limited omniscient with the dog as its focus), those aspects of society take on new meaning. Mr. Bones, like Walter Rawley in *Mr. Vertigo,* possesses an understanding of life and truth—perhaps a cynicism borne of continued mistreatment by society—that is absent in the author's earlier protagonists:

> The dog had lived long enough to know that good stories were not necessarily true stories, and whether he chose to believe the stories Willy told him about himself or not was less important than the fact that Willy had done what he had done, and the years had passed. That was the essential thing, wasn't it? The years, the number of years it took to go from being young to not-so-young, and all the while to watch the world change around you.

The story is also an exploration of human nature and the dichotomies that exist in every aspect of life, including the age-old question of whether or not dogs have souls. In the hands of another author, such a question might seem banal or obtuse. Auster, however, treats the question with a whimsy that belies the portentousness of the topic. If dogs have souls, Auster suggests, then what does that say about the rest of our widely held beliefs? If Mr. Bones does possess a special soul, his will is tested when Christmas dies, and he is left on his own in a place that he does not know. Without Christmas, whom the dog loves unconditionally despite the man's shortcomings, Mr. Bones loses his will to live and hopes to join his master in "Timbuktu," the place where all entities go when they die. In a fit of grief, Mr. Bones readies himself for death. Against the odds, however, he is rescued by a young boy, Henry Chow, whose own father beats him. Barely escaping the man's wrath, and leaving the boy to face his own fate, Mr. Bones is adopted by a family with two small children and a wife whose husband, a pilot, is steady but unloving. For a time, Mr. Bones finds life with the Joneses (even the surname is an ironic invocation of the homogenous culture with which Auster takes issue here) perhaps even better than that he had with Christmas. When the family leaves on a vacation without him, however, Mr. Bones dreams of his former master, and, despite Christmas' insistence that he return to the Joneses and live out his life in happiness, he trots onto a highway thick with cars and thinks that "With any luck, he would be with Willy before the day was out."

Timbuktu is, on the whole, a particularly risky book. Eschewing even the improbable human connections that mark his fiction, here the author stakes his narrative success on a nonhuman protagonist. Paul Kafka points to Auster's wide-eyed wonder of the world around him as a complement to his craft:

> There is an innocence in his work that is entirely compatible with the complexity of his artistry. We don't have to notice each time Auster doffs his hat to Cervantes, Edgar Allan Poe, John Berryman, the Dick and Jane books, or television's *Lassie,* but spotting a few of these gestures in no way detracts from the simple pleasures of *Timbuktu.*

CONCLUSION

Although Paul Auster has proven himself over a prolific and wide-ranging creative career, it is his fiction that will perpetuate his reputation as one of America's most capacious talents. The critical reception of Auster's work has been consistent (with the canonists typically questioning what all the hubbub might be about), recognizing the author's contributions to the evolution of the narrative, though reviewers have become more ambivalent with the publication of his last two novels. Those books, not coincidentally, are the two that deviate most from what had popularly been thought of as "Auster's style" (curiously, those two books are probably closest to what critics might consider "mainstream fiction"). Still, Auster's popular appeal seems not to be waning. Not the least reason for the anticipation with which a growing number of readers await future novels is the simultaneous accessibility and complexity of the narratives. As Kafka points out, "Auster's achievement is to balance the literary high jinks of postmodernism with the familiar methods of the popular storyteller. His work can be read by a precocious twelve-year-old, or in a graduate literature seminar on metafiction and narrative theory." The coincidences, philosophical meanderings on the nature of identity and being, and narrative twists and turns that are Auster's stock-in-trade are, like the machinations of Master Yehudi in *Mr. Vertigo,* easily decipherable on one superficial level of meaning.

The importance of Auster's fiction to contemporary American literature, though, is what lies beneath: Subsequent readings of the fiction allow it to blossom under scrutiny, revealing a framework that gives the fiction definition at the same time that the author's imagination is allowed free rein. Such an effect is no doubt the result of Auster's willingness and ability to accept eclectic points of view, beginning with the "univocal" act of poetry and running the gamut of written expression that characterizes his career. The dichotomies that he examines— identity and its absence, freedom and captivity, penury and wealth, solitude and communion, truth and fiction, chance and fate, life and death—finally combine to create narratives that circumscribe the whole of human experience. To attempt to draw more than thematic and stylistic connections from one of Auster's works to the next is tempting in an essay of this scope, though to do so is to impose artificial constraints that, Auster himself has asserted, ignore the status of the narratives as individual entities. Perhaps a fundamental view of Auster's fiction from a reader's perspective should include a variation of his notion in the writing process— "The less I know, the more I can"—as a context for reading work that is as "organic" (a word no

less apt here for its having been overused in discussions of American literature) and experiential as any American fiction of the late twentieth century.

Implicit in the creation of fiction, especially fiction that relies to such a great extent on storytelling, is a strong relationship between the writer and the reader. Auster is careful to nurture that one final connection: "The one thing I try to do in all my books is to leave enough room in the prose for the reader to inhabit it," Auster told Joseph Mallia. "Because I finally believe it's the reader who writes the book and not the writer. . . . In the end, you don't only write the books you need to write, you write the books you would like to read yourself."

Selected Bibliography

WORKS OF PAUL AUSTER

NOVELS AND NOVELLAS
City of Glass. Los Angeles: Sun and Moon Press, 1985.

Ghosts. Los Angeles: Sun and Moon Press, 1986.

The Locked Room. Los Angeles: Sun and Moon Press, 1986.

In the Country of Last Things. New York: Viking, 1987.

The New York Trilogy. London: Faber and Faber, 1987.

Moon Palace. New York: Viking, 1989.

The Music of Chance. New York: Viking, 1990.

Leviathan. New York: Viking, 1992.

Mr. Vertigo. New York: Viking, 1994.

Timbuktu. New York: Henry Holt, 1999.

COLLECTED PROSE
White Spaces. Barrytown, N.Y.: Station Hill, 1980.

The Art of Hunger and Other Essays. London: Menard Press, 1982. Reissued as *The Art of Hunger:*

Essays, Prefaces, Interviews. Los Angeles: Sun and Moon Press, 1992.

The Invention of Solitude. New York: Sun Press, 1982.

Auggie Wren's Christmas Story. New York: William Drenttell, 1992.

Hand to Mouth: A Chronicle of Early Failure. New York: Henry Holt, 1997.

POETRY

Wall Writing. Berkeley, Calif.: Figures, 1976.

Fragments from Cold. Brewster, N.Y.: Parenthèse, 1977.

Facing the Music. Barrytown, N.Y.: Station Hill, 1980.

Disappearances: Selected Poems, 1970–1979. Woodstock, N.Y.: Overlook Press, 1988.

Autobiography of the Eye. Portland, Oreg.: Beaverdam Press, 1993.

EDITED OR TRANSLATED WORKS

A Little Anthology of Surrealist Poems. Translated by Paul Auster. New York: Siamese Banana Press, 1972.

The Random House Book of Twentieth-Century French Poetry. Edited by Paul Auster. New York: Random House, 1982. (Auster also translated forty-two of the anthology's poems.)

The Notebooks of Joseph Joubert: A Selection. Edited and translated by Paul Auster. San Francisco: North Point Press, 1983.

On the High Wire, by Philippe Petit. Translated by Paul Auster. New York: Random House, 1985.

Joan Miró: Selected Writings. Translated by Paul Auster. Edited by Margit Rowell. Boston: G. K. Hall, 1986.

Translations. New York: Marsilio, 1998.

I Thought My Father Was God and Other True Tales from the National Story Project. Edited by Paul Auster. New York: Henry Holt, 2001.

JOURNALS, CORRESPONDENCE, AND MANUSCRIPTS

A collection of Auster's papers are in the Berg Collection at the New York Public Library and at Columbia University Library.

CRITICAL AND BIOGRAPHICAL STUDIES

Alford, Steve E. "Spaced-Out: Signification and Space in Paul Auster's *The New York Trilogy.*" *Contemporary Literature* 36, no. 4:613–632 (1995).

Barone, Dennis, ed. *Beyond the Red Notebook: Essays on Paul Auster.* Philadelphia: University of Pennsylvania Press, 1995.

Baxter, Charles. "The Bureau of Missing Persons: Notes on Paul Auster's Fiction." *Review of Contemporary Fiction* 14, no. 1:40–43 (1994).

Herzogenrath, Bernd. *An Art of Desire: Reading Paul Auster.* Amsterdam: Rodopi, 1999.

Kafka, Paul. "A Dog's Eye View of Life." *Boston Globe,* May 30, 1999, pp. D1, D4. (Review of *Timbuktu.*)

Lavendar, William. "The Novel of Critical Engagement: Paul Auster's *City of Glass.*" *Contemporary Literature* 34, no. 2:219–239 (1993).

Nealon, Jeffrey T. "Work of the Detective, Work of the Writer: Paul Auster's *City of Glass.*" *Modern Fiction Studies* 42, no. 1:91–110 (1996).

Review of Contemporary Fiction 14, no. 1:7–96 (spring 1994). (Special issue on Paul Auster [and Danilo Kis].)

Rowen, Norma. "The Detective in Search of the Lost Tongue of Adam: Paul Auster's *City of Glass.*" *Critique: Studies in Contemporary Fiction* 32, no. 4:224–234 (1991).

Varvolgli, Aliki. *World That Is the Book: Paul Auster's Fiction.* Liverpool: Liverpool University Press, 2002.

INTERVIEWS

Chenétier, Marc. "Around *Moon Palace:* A Conversation with Paul Auster." *Sources* no. 1:5–35 (autumn 1996).

Irwin, Mark. "Memory's Escape: Inventing *The Music of Chance*—A Conversation with Paul Auster." *Denver Quarterly* 28, no. 3:111–122 (winter 1994).

Mallia, Joseph. Interview in Auster, *The Art of Hunger: Essays, Prefaces, Interviews.* Los Angeles: Sun and Moon Press, 1992. Pp. 256–268.

McCaffery, Larry, and Sinda Gregory. Interview in Auster, *The Art of Hunger: Essays, Prefaces, Interviews.* Los Angeles: Sun and Moon Press, 1992. Pp. 269–312.

*FILMS BASED ON THE WORKS OF
PAUL AUSTER*

The Music of Chance. Directed by Philip Haas. Adapted from the novel by Paul Auster. I.R.S. Releasing, 1993.

Smoke. Directed by Wayne Wang. Screenplay by Paul Auster. Miramax, 1995.

Blue in the Face. Directed by Wayne Wang. Screenplay by Paul Auster. Miramax, 1995.

Lulu on the Bridge. Directed by Paul Auster. Screenplay by Paul Auster. Capitol Films, 1998.

—PATRICK A. SMITH

Frederick Buechner

1926–

CARL FREDERICK BUECHNER (BEEK-ner) was born in New York City on July 11, 1926, into a family of wealth, social status, and privilege. His paternal great-grandfather, Hermann Balthazar Scharmann, came to the United States with his family at the age of five in 1843. The Scharmann family, together with several other recent German immigrants, was drawn to California in 1849 by reports of the instant wealth to be found there. Of the seventy-two who attempted the treacherous trip across the country in covered wagons, only eight reached California alive. Among those who died were Scharmann's mother and baby sister. Bad luck followed Scharmann and his father to the mining camps where, instead of the vast fortune about which they had dreamed, they found barely enough gold to keep them alive. Father and son returned to their home in Brooklyn, New York, bereft and disappointed. The dream of wealth, however, remained strong in young Scharmann, and he set about to become the quintessential self-made man. Through shrewd business deals involving real estate and breweries, he amassed the formidable fortune that had eluded the family in California. At the time of his death at the age of eighty-two in 1920, Hermann Scharmann's estate was valued at nearly a half million dollars. This, in addition to some very valuable property holdings in Brooklyn, he left to his five daughters and one son. One daughter, Louise (Grandmother Buechner), remembered her father as a tyrant who was given to terrible fits of rage, but his community standing and keen business sense provided her and her siblings with financial security for the rest of their lives. Louise Scharmann married Carl Frederick Buechner, and it was their son, Carl junior, who would become Buechner's father in 1926.

On his mother's side, Buechner is descended from a Dutch family named Kuhn who settled in North America in the eighteenth century. Adam Kuhn was the president of the Royal College of Physicians and Surgeons in prerevolutionary Philadelphia. Buechner's grandfather Kuhn made his money in the coal mining business and resided with his wife in a mansion on Woodland Road in East Liberty, a wealthy suburb of Pittsburgh. Katherine Kuhn, Buechner's mother, grew up in gracious comfort and was sought after by the sons of such tycoons as Andrew W. Mellon and Henry Clay Frick. Grandfather Kuhn was every bit as tyrannical as Great-grandfather Scharmann, especially when it came to the possible marriage of his children. Indeed when it was announced in the New York papers that his son James had become engaged, Kuhn's anger was such that the engagement was called off and James remained a bachelor for the rest of his life. It is not surprising then that when Katherine Kuhn and Carl Frederick Buechner Jr. decided to marry, they did so quietly on July 17, 1922. Only Katherine's brother James and a friend named Joe Young attended the service at Trinity Episcopal Church in Plattsburgh, New York. True to his nature, Grandfather Kuhn exploded at the news and had all the pictures of Katherine, his first born and favorite child, removed from his sight.

Buechner's recollections of his father, gathered from family members and friends who knew him before the hastily arranged marriage, paint a picture of a young man who could have fit easily into any work by F. Scott Fitzgerald. He was handsome, gentle, kind, and conscientious. He excelled in sports and was the captain of the water polo team at Princeton. He was a good dancer and the family joke was that he could not go anywhere without running into at least six friends, among whom were Zelda and Scott Fitzgerald. If he was as charming, good looking, and brilliant as Jay Gatsby, he was also equally doomed.

The stock market crash of 1929 and the resulting Great Depression of the 1930s ruined many promising young men and destroyed many families. Buechner's father was forced to move his wife and two sons often as he looked for employment. "Virtually every year of my life until I was fourteen," Buechner remembers in *The Sacred Journey* (1982), "I lived in a different place, had different people to take care of me, went to a different school." In 1932 the Buechners were living in the Georgetown section of Washington, D.C., where Buechner's father, through a Princeton roommate, had found a menial job in the circulation department of the *Evening Star* newspaper. It was in Georgetown that Buechner had the good fortune to be cared for by a nurse named Mrs. Taylor: "She cut the pictures of things and the names of things out of magazines for me to paste in a scrapbook and taught me that way how to read and write when I was five." He continues: "She was my mentor, my miracle-worker, and the mother of much that I was and in countless unrecognizable ways probably still am, yet I don't know where she came from or anything about her life apart from the few years of it she spent with us." At this same time Buechner was stricken with what he described as "a glittering combination of pneumonia, tonsillitis, and pleurisy" and spent the better part of a year in bed reading the wondrous Oz books by L. Frank Baum. The stories remained with him throughout his life: "I suppose it is partly because you read so much more slowly as a child that the books you come to then seem as endless as summer and richer, fuller, more inexhaustible than anything you are likely to read later on." One character in particular seized his imagination— King Rinkitink:

> He was a foolish man in many ways who laughed too much and talked too much and at moments of stress was apt to burst into unkingly tears; but beneath all that, he gave the impression of remarkable strength and resilience and courage even, a good man to have around when the chips were down.

An introverted child in love with rainy days and fantasy worlds, Buechner was soon to need all the strength, resilience and courage a young boy could possibly find in himself.

Buechner had begun to see the fine cracks in the foundation of his family's life that would soon expand and bring that life crashing down. The pressures of providing for his family were taking a heavy toll on the dashing Princeton water polo captain. Buechner remembered his father

> coming in to say good-night and standing there at the foot of our beds with his hands on his hips and his face clammy and gray as he threw back his head and laughed in a way that made me know as surely as I knew anything that something had gone terribly wrong with his laughter. Something had gotten broken in it.

There were nights when Buechner's mother gave him the keys to the car and told him to hide them from his father, who had had too much to drink. Accusations and recriminations flew back and forth between Buechner's parents. As his mother's excoriations increased so did his father's abuse of alcohol: "They were married for fourteen years, and there is not a single photograph of my father taken toward the last few of them that shows him smiling. His handsome face has gone hollow-cheeked and skull-like. His deep-set eyes are lost in shadow."

Early one Saturday morning in the fall of 1936 Buechner's father looked in on his sons, who were playing in their room, then went to the garage. He started the engine of his Chevrolet sedan and sat on the running board until the car's exhaust fumes filled his lungs and he could breath no more. He did not leave a will but the family found later that he had left a note written on one of the blank pages at the back of the novel Buechner's mother had been reading, *Gone with the Wind* (1936). The note was addressed to Buechner's mother and read simply, "I adore and love you, and am no good. . . . Give Freddy my watch. Give Jamie my pearl pin. I give you all my love."

LIFE IN OZ

Grandmother Buechner was visiting the family at their home in New Jersey when her son ended his life. Putting her own grief aside, she made sure Buechner, his mother, and his brother had their needs met. She encouraged them to follow her example: be strong and face reality head-on, just like her father had done when tragedy had struck him in 1849. After a brief period of enduring her mother-in-law's well-meant support and advice, Buechner's mother wanted nothing more than to get away from it all. Over Grandmother Buechner's strong objections, she took her sons to live in a place unlike any they had known before.

> My mother took us to Bermuda, of all places, for no motive more profound than simply to get away from things for a while as my grandmother rightly saw; but to get away *from* is also to get away *to,* and that implausible island where we went within a month or two of my father's death turned out to be a place where healing could happen in a way that perhaps would not have been possible anywhere else and to a degree that—even with all the endurance, will, courage we might have been able

to muster had we stayed—I do not think we could ever have achieved on our own.

Despite her objections, Grandmother Buechner provided the family a sizable allowance and, as Buechner remembered, they "lived like kings." They rented a house called The Moorings where Buechner and his brother were able to fish and fly kites from the terrace. The boys attended Warwick Academy, made friends, and for the first time in their lives enjoyed a sense of permanence and stability. There was, however, one brief break in their idyllic life. Grandmother Buechner made a visit to The Moorings and, although she found the island lovely, she declared that living there was unrealistic and extravagant. Therefore in the fall of 1937 the Buechners returned to New York and the boys were enrolled in Trinity School. In his fourth book of memoirs Buechner remembered a fellow student who was a year ahead of him, "a little oddball named Truman Capote." After a few months Grandmother Buechner relented and the family returned to Bermuda. Buechner was surprised to find that she loved them more than she loved her principles.

Two things that occurred while he lived on the island had an inestimable influence on the artist Buechner was to become: first, he had the time and space to reflect on the death of his father and, second, he experienced his first stirrings of erotic desire. Initially Buechner did not grieve over his father's suicide—that was postponed for nearly thirty years—but the event opened his eyes and heart to the reality of the private pains and hidden hurts that are part of the lives of everyone. The somewhat self-absorbed boy was further shaken out of his shell by an attractive thirteen-year-old girl. Buechner grew up, as fortunate children do, accepting the love of his family as something that was his due. Now, presented with the company of a lovely girl, he understood that he was capable of being a source and sharer of love himself.

RETURN AND SEPARATION

After two years, the Buechners' life in Bermuda apart from the troubles of the rest of the world was brought to an end by the savage reality of World War II. There were rumors that the German navy was approaching with the intention of using the island as a submarine base, and all Americans were evacuated. The Buechners returned to the United States and lived with Grandfather and Grandmother Kuhn in Tyron, North Carolina. The Kuhns had moved to this small southern town after losing most of their fortune in Pittsburgh. The situation was far from desperate, however. There was money enough to employ two servants and to send the boys to a private school. Neither the Buechners nor the Kuhns had any church affiliations. Grandmother Kuhn, whom Buechner called Naya, considered herself a Unitarian but rarely attended services. She did, however, enjoy the music at the town's Episcopal church, and it was there she took Buechner from time to time to hear the choir's talented baritone soloist. Something about the Episcopal service appealed to Buechner. When he discovered that neither he nor his brother had been baptized, he arranged with the parish priest to receive that sacrament for himself, his brother, and a cousin.

During this time in Tyron, Buechner was given a copy of Thomas Craven's *A Treasury of Art Masterpieces: From the Renaissance to the Present Day* (1939). The colored reproductions fascinated him; he was especially drawn to the faces in such works as William Hogarth's *Shrimp Girl,* Albrecht Dürer's *Hieronymus Holzschuer,* and Titian's *Man in a Red Cap.* One portrait in particular captured his imagination, a pastel study of the head of Jesus by Leonardo da Vinci.

> I had come across many other representations of Jesus' face in my day, but this was one that I could somehow vouch for, and although I set it aside and gave no special thought to it, somewhere in the back of my mind I seem always to have kept track of it as though to have a way of recognizing him if ever our paths happened to cross again.

He began to draw copies of the faces in this book and others, as well as portraits of live models, and at the age of thirteen decided that painting was his calling.

Whether it was because she noticed how dependent her son had become upon her or how dependent she had become upon him, Buechner's mother decided to send him away to Lawrenceville School in New Jersey. Here Buechner was unfortunate enough to be assigned to an art class that was taught by an uninspiring though talented draftsman. After being drilled on the importance of perspective and drawing countless charcoal sketches of spheres, cubes, and pyramids, Buechner gave up the idea of being a painter. He was extremely fortunate in his assigned English teacher, however. Dick Martin had the gift of making words come alive, the ability to show that words have color, depth, and texture.

> Mr. Martin had us read wonderful things—it was he who gave me my love for *The Tempest,* for instance—but it was a course less in literature than in language and the great power that language has to move and in some measure even to transform the human heart. . . . From that moment on, I knew that what I wanted to be more than anything else was a writer.

Buechner was fortunate too in meeting a fellow classmate who would become his lifelong friend, James Merrill. He and Buechner shared similar backgrounds, likes, dislikes, and—above all—the yearning for transcendence through the written word. The two wrote poetry together and competed in friendly rivalry for prizes and grades. After their graduation from Lawrenceville in 1943, Merrill went on to Amherst and Buechner, who had been awarded a partial scholarship, entered Princeton.

PRINCETON AND THE ARMY

Buechner, like so many other young men of the time, was aware that the war in Europe could claim him at any moment. There was a sense that time was running out, and Buechner chose to fill what was left with intense study. Princeton was brimming with the best and brightest; Buechner often saw Albert Einstein strolling across the campus and attended lectures given by Bertrand Russell. The critic R. P. Blackmur was his creative writing instructor. It was not, however, a time of all work and no play. Buechner put aside his reading of William Blake and T. S. Eliot often enough to enjoy weekends in New York where, as he wrote, there were "the endless parties to get drunk at."

The anticipated interruption in his college career came when the army called him to duty in 1944. Although he had taken German in the hope that he would be eligible for a job in army intelligence, he had done poorly in the class and instead was sent to an infantry training camp in Anniston, Alabama. To his great relief Buechner was declared unqualified for combat duty and spent the majority of his two years in service at a desk compiling statistics.

After he was discharged in 1946 Buechner resumed his studies at Princeton. He became interested in the prose writers of seventeenth-century England and read the works of Sir Thomas Browne, Bishop Jeremy Taylor, and John Donne. He found himself carried away by "the gorgeous latinate words, the stately cadences, the overladen sentences that wound their glittering, labyrinthine way across the page yet always came right at the end." Above all, "the fact that what they were using their extraordinary language to describe was again and again their experience of the Extraordinary itself" intrigued him.

Upon graduation from Princeton in 1948 Buechner rented a house for the summer on an island off the coast of Maine with James Merrill. The two spent their days writing, Merrill his collection titled *First Poems* (1951) and Buechner, who had set poetry aside, a novel he had begun during his senior year at Princeton, *A Long Day's Dying* (1950). At summer's end, the friends went their separate ways again. Merrill set sail for Europe, leaving his old life behind, and Buechner began a job as assistant housemaster and teacher of English at their alma mater, Lawrenceville.

THE FIRST TWO NOVELS

During his second year teaching at Lawrenceville, Buechner's first novel was published. *A Long Day's Dying* takes its title from book ten of Milton's *Paradise Lost* wherein Adam tells Eve that their expulsion from the Garden of Eden "Will prove no sudden, but a slow-paced evil, / A long day's dying to augment our pain." Buechner's story revolves around the actions, interactions, and inactions of six characters: Tristram Bone, George Motley, Elizabeth Poor, her son Leander, Paul Steitler, and Elizabeth's mother, Maroo. Bone, a man of social standing and wealth, and his friend Motley, a novelist, vie for the attentions and affections of Elizabeth, a well-to-do widow. Although the two men are friends, they do not hesitate to use whatever means necessary to overtake each other in their pursuit. Motley has been invited to give a lecture at the university where Leander is a student. Elizabeth, who has not seen her son in months, agrees to join Motley there. Mother and son meet for drinks on the patio of the inn where Elizabeth is staying, and she is introduced to Leander's friend and English teacher, Steitler. Elizabeth is immediately attracted to the man, and the three drink the afternoon away amid the noisy comings and goings of students. Steitler explains to Elizabeth that he considers himself nothing more than "a kind of professional corrupter of the young." Pressed by Elizabeth to explain what he means, he says:

I teach them English is all . . . and the pay-off they finally get to is a kind of corruption, because what they learn, when they've had the full treatment, is nothing about any particular book or any particular author or period so much as something fairly unnerving about life. . . . I mean that what they learn, if nothing worse, is that there's more to it all than this lovely, green place out here, than the society of their kind, these princelings and their young ladies. What they learn from me is that they're never going to have it so good again.

Steitler declares that the students are suffering from "the lovely, giddy, green disease of this place, this sweet and dangerous hospital that nobody wants to leave—ever." Elizabeth, although put off by his cynicism, is excited by his subtly flirtatious interest in her. The threesome attends Motley's lecture and is joined by him afterward. "Almost from the moment they were introduced after the lecture," the narrator tells us, "Motley had taken a dislike to Steitler that was to be reinforced rather than minimized as the evening progressed." The group decides to join a few students for a night of drink and talk beside an artificial lake. Steitler kisses Elizabeth on her temple while everyone's eyes are directed toward a small island in the middle of the lake. Later, when Steitler is escorting her back to her inn, Elizabeth agrees to join him for a drink in his quarters. It is an easy seduction:

There was something in her manner as an attractive, graceful woman with no more than her charm needed to make her significant, that precluded the possibility of any situations but the ones in which she might move effortlessly and without pain. Steitler, returning with a tray, entered one of these.

Chapter 10 begins with some confusion for the reader. Buechner states that Steitler emerges from his rooms in the early afternoon on Sunday to walk across campus in the rain to visit Leander. If that is the case, the reader is left wondering what happened between the time of Elizabeth's seduction, which occurs after Motley's Friday night lecture and concludes

chapter 9, and the Sunday afternoon of chapter 10. Buechner does not explain. However, he does have Bone refer to the time of Motley's lecture as Saturday. It is perhaps simply an error on Buechner's part that has little bearing on the story he is telling. In Leander's dorm room Steitler finds that the boy has not yet quite awakened. He picks up a letter that had been pushed under the door and tells Leander that it is from the boy's grandmother, Maroo. At this news Leander leaps naked from the bed and tears open the envelope. He is reading the letter to Steitler while lying provocatively on the bed when his mother enters to say good-bye. She calmly takes in the scene of her lover sitting at the foot of the bed where her son lies naked. Leander quickly ducks behind a closet door to dress. As the three exchange some small talk about the previous night, Motley arrives. With an almost devilish glee he discerns that Elizabeth and Steitler have spent the night together.

Immediately upon his return to New York, Motley invites himself to Bone's for breakfast and tells the infatuated man of his suspicions. Bone dismisses Motley's report of Elizabeth's escapade as nothing more than the inflated drama that is so much a part of Motley's art. Nevertheless he telephones Elizabeth and invites her to accompany him to visit an aviary in the countryside. There he tells her of Motley's conversation. Elizabeth is outraged and attempts to avoid the truth by suggesting that Steitler is romantically obsessed not with her but with her son. Bone arranges a meeting with Steitler who—once he discovers that Bone is speaking of a romantic entanglement with Leander—firmly tells Bone that it is not true. A letter from Bone to Elizabeth relating his conversation with Steitler pushes Elizabeth further down into the hole of guilt and regret she has dug for herself. In her distress she telephones Maroo for the familiar comfort of her mother's voice. Maroo suspects that there is more behind the telephone call than Elizabeth is willing to admit, and she travels by train from her home in North Carolina to see for herself what the trouble might be.

The trip proves to be too arduous for the frail old woman, and when she arrives at Elizabeth's apartment, she is so ill that she is put to bed and a doctor is called. Before she can resolve the problems of the novel's characters, who have gathered at her bedside, she dies. It is a lonely and isolated crowd she leaves behind, and Buechner gives the reader no hope that all may one day be forgiven and reconciled.

The novel is filled with lush symbolism and imagery, and the Greek myth of Philomela plays an important part; but these are unevenly introduced and sometimes detract from the story. Nevertheless the book was well received and Buechner, like Lord Byron upon publication of *Childe Harold's Pilgrimage,* awoke one morning to find himself famous:

> To my surprise as well as to the publisher's, it was immediately a considerable success both critically and commercially despite the fact that it was very dense, static, psychological, and written in such a mannered, involuted style—the residue of my romance with the seventeenth century—that it seems outrageous when I look at it now.

In 1950, encouraged by the reception of his first book, Buechner took a year off from his teaching duties at Lawrenceville and traveled to England. He settled in Great Milton, a village near Oxford, and began work on his second novel, *The Seasons' Difference* (1951). Although the novel contained some of the same narrative skills displayed in *A Long Day's Dying,* the book was a disappointment to most critics. Set on the country estate of Sam and Sara Dunn, it tells the story of a wealthy family's summer, a lazy summer of outdoor pleasures often interrupted by cocktails. This idyllic existence is suddenly disrupted when the children's tutor, Peter Cowley, claims to have had a mystical experience that proved to him the existence of a loving and caring God. For the remainder of the novel Buechner's characters wrestle with their questions of faith.

Buechner was disappointed that his second novel was not as successful as his first, and he decided to focus all his energies toward honing his craft: "From that day to this I have been driven as a writer, and to a degree as a human being too, to write something, do something, be something to justify the fluke of that early and for the most part undeserved success." To this end he left the position he had held for five years at Lawrenceville and moved to New York City in 1953. In his apartment on Madison Avenue and 74th Street, Buechner found, however, that he was unable to write a word. In his desperation to find a vocation Buechner considered working for an advertising agency but was convinced that he did not have what it took to survive in that business. Likewise he was also dissuaded from pursuing a career in the CIA.

SEMINARY

Finding himself at loose ends, Buechner began attending the Madison Avenue Presbyterian Church for no other reason than to fill the quiet hours of Sunday mornings. There he fell under the spell of the eloquent preacher George Buttrick. One particular Sunday, Buttrick was preaching on Jesus' refusal of the crown Satan offered to him during his forty days in the wilderness. Buechner remembers Buttrick telling his congregation that Jesus "is king nonetheless because again and again he is crowned in the heart of the people who believe in him." That coronation takes place, Buttrick told them, "among confession, and tears, and great laughter."

Buechner wrote,

> It was the phrase *great laughter* that did it, did whatever it was that I believe must have been hiddenly in the doing all the years of my journey up till then. It was not so much that a door opened as

that I suddenly found that a door had been open all along which I had only just then stumbled upon.

The following week Buechner met with Buttrick to discuss the epiphany he had experienced. Buechner asked if entering a seminary might help him find the source of the tearful joy he felt when he heard Buttrick's words. Buttrick answered by immediately driving Buechner to Union Theological Seminary.

Buechner began his studies at Union in the fall of 1954 by means of a Rockefeller Brothers Theological Fellowship. His instructors included the renowned theologians Reinhold Niebuhr, Paul Tillich, and James Muilenburg. For his ministerial training outside the classroom Buechner chose to work part-time for the East Harlem Protestant Parish where he ran an employment clinic that helped African Americans and Puerto Ricans find jobs or training.

As his first year at Union drew to a close, Buechner felt pulled in two directions. He felt he must make a choice between his pursuit of the ministry and his desire to continue his literary career: "At the end of the year, I knew I had been hooked. I had never spent a richer year anywhere, never been so close to total involvement in anything else I had done." However, the inclusion of his short story "The Tiger" in *Prize Stories 1955: The O. Henry Awards* encouraged him to continue writing a novel he had set aside. After consulting with Dr. Muilenburg and spending many nights in anguished prayer for guidance, Buechner decided to leave Union in June 1955 for one year and devote himself to writing his third novel, *The Return of Ansel Gibbs* (1958).

The new novel marked a departure for Buechner. Instead of focusing on the moral and ethical ambiguities of the idle rich, Ansel Gibbs's story is set within the moral and ethical ambiguities of politics. The actions, setting, and narration are tighter and less ornate than in his previous works. And, although his first two novels contained autobiographical material, it is in this novel that Buechner makes an attempt to come to terms with his father's trials and suicide.

Ansel Gibbs, a retired and highly respected public servant, has been called to Washington to serve on the president's cabinet. He makes a stop in New York City to visit his daughter Anne and meets her fiancé, television talk show host Robin Tripp. Years earlier Tripp's father, Rudy, had been Gibbs's closest friend. When the senior Tripp committed suicide, Gibbs felt indirectly responsible. Robin convinces Gibbs to appear on his show and leads him into a discussion of his part in the tragedy. Forced to face his lack of emotion regarding his friend's death, Gibbs decides he is unfit for the cabinet position. Dr. Kuykendall, one of Gibbs's former college professors, helps Gibbs through his identity crisis by persuading him to accept his own flawed human nature. Gibbs is reconciled to Robin and takes the cabinet position. The book received both critical and popular acclaim, and Buechner won the 1959 Rosenthal Award.

During the spring before leaving Union, Buechner was invited to a dance. There he met and fell in love with Judith Friedrike Merck. Dr. Muilenburg married the two on April 7, 1956. After spending two months in England and two in Austria, the couple returned to New York, and Buechner completed the two years he had remaining at Union to earn his bachelor's degree in divinity. On June 1, 1958, Buechner was ordained a Presbyterian minister in the chapel of the Madison Avenue church where he had first heard Buttrick preach nearly five years earlier. At this point in his life Buechner began to understand that there was no longer a need for him to make a choice between the ministry and literature. Indeed he felt that each pursued the same end. To *Contemporary Authors,* Buechner explained his dual calling:

> As a preacher I am trying to do many of the same things I do as a writer. In both I am trying to

explore what I believe life is all about, to get people to stop and listen a little to the mystery of their own lives. The process of telling a story is something like religion if only in the sense of suggesting that life itself has a plot and leads to a conclusion that makes some kind of sense.

TEACHING AND PREACHING AT EXETER

Just before his graduation and ordination Buechner received a letter from Robert Russell Wicks, former dean of the chapel at Princeton and Buechner's colleague at Lawrenceville. Wicks wrote to ask if Buechner would be interested in joining him in his latest venture, organizing a religion program at Phillips Exeter Academy in New Hampshire. Buechner was drawn by the challenge of teaching Christianity to a generation of young men, "negos" he calls them in his journals, who were boldly atheistic and antiestablishment. Buechner and his wife moved to Exeter in September 1958, and the following January their first child, whom they named Katherine after Buechner's mother, was born.

Buechner began the religious studies program at Exeter with a lone teacher, himself, and perhaps twenty students. When he left the school nine years later, the program had grown to include four teachers and three hundred students. Buechner accomplished this success by assigning readings from his mostly jaded students' favorite authors—Albert Camus, Jean-Paul Sartre, Jack Kerouac, Allen Ginsberg, and Ayn Rand—and then comparing their vision of God and man with the visions of Paul Tillich, Karl Barth, C. S. Lewis, Graham Greene, and James Joyce: "I stacked the deck in favor of what I believed in, to be sure, but the game wasn't entirely fixed. I had my students read spokesmen for the other side too." He also incorporated his students' growing fascination with Buddhism into a class in comparative religion that explored the differences and similarities of Hinduism, Judaism, Islam, Buddhism, and Christianity.

As the school's minister after the retirement of Dean Wicks, Buechner conducted communion services, baptisms, weddings, and funerals. Sometimes his Episcopalian upbringing was annoyed by the way rites were observed at Exeter, "with the Pepperidge Farm bread that Judy and I had sliced up into little cubes in the kitchen at home, and the trays full of Welch's grape juice served in little glass thimbles so that everybody could be served separately and antiseptically without leaving their seats." Buechner reflected on the experience in *Now and Then* (1983): "The symbolism couldn't be worse, I thought and still think, and it seemed a wretched way to do it. There should be real wine, of course, to warm the heart and stir the blood. There should be a common cup, germs be damned. People should come up to the table. Together."

In addition to his teaching and sacramental duties, Buechner was required to preach at least one Sunday every month in the school's church. The great responsibility of being God's representative in the pulpit deeply troubled and frightened Buechner. He relied heavily on a short piece of writing by his former teacher Karl Barth to help him through his discomfort. In "The Need for Christian Preaching," Barth cuts to the heart of the matter by stating that the reason both congregation and clergy assemble every Sunday is to search for and discover the truth of the Christian faith. Barth further explains that there is an expectancy that the sermon will answer the question everyone brings to the church: "Is it true?" The discipline of writing on a particular subject and within a time limit for a live audience changed forever the way Buechner wrote his fiction and nonfiction. From this point on, the ornate, serpentine sentences of his earlier works give way to shorter, simpler sentences that speak directly to his reader.

This stylistic change is evident in his next novel, *The Final Beast* (1965), which was written in Vermont during a leave of absence taken from June 1963 until September 1964. The novel's title comes from Stephen Crane's poem "The Black Riders." Theodore Nicolet is a minister in the New England village of Myron. He is also a widower of one year with two young children. His congregation is beset by the beasts of guilt, sin, and desire, and they look to him for deliverance. Nicolet's particular beasts are self-doubt and weak faith. One of his congregants, Rooney Vail, tells him, "There's just one reason, you know, why I come dragging in there every Sunday. I want to find out if the whole thing's true. Just *true*. . . . That's all. Either it is or it isn't, and that's the one question you avoid like death." The novel opens with Nicolet kissing his children good-bye as they lie in their beds. He tells them he needs to go away for a little while and that Irma, his housekeeper, will take care of them. He leaves a note for Irma instructing her to tell anyone seeking him that he has been called away and will be back soon. This haste was precipitated by a phone call from Rooney's husband, Clem, telling Nicolet that Rooney has disappeared. Soon after the telephone call, Nicolet receives a postcard from Rooney sealed in an envelope. The postcard reveals where Rooney has gone, but she warns Nicolet that "no one is to know. No one is to come."

Nicolet manages to catch up with Rooney in the distant town of Muscadine. Rooney explains that she has come there to seek the help of a spiritual healer, Lillian Flagg. She wants the woman to perform a miracle, making it possible for her and Clem to have children. She also wants to be forgiven for an act of infidelity she committed six years earlier. Nicolet tells her, "Cruelty, bitterness, self-pity—they take root in the soul and keep growing. But this, six years ago. . . . It exists only by being remembered. So much better just to forget it now, and better for Clem too. Better for God." However, "even as he spoke, he saw the hopelessness of what he told her—forgetting was a state of grace, after

all, not an act of the will—but he went on with it anyway because the melody if not the meaning of the words seemed right as she touched away the tear with her knuckle." The two agree to stay the night at Lillian's and return to Myron the next morning. Over sherry and while Rooney is out of the room, Lillian finds fault with Nicolet's advice:

> "Forgive her for Christ's sake, little priest!"
> "But she knows I forgive her."
> "She doesn't know God forgives her. That's the only power you have—to tell her that. Not just that he forgives her the poor little adultery. But the faces she can't bear to look at now. The man's. Her husband's. Her own, half the time. Tell her he forgives her for being lonely and bored, for not being full of joy with a houseful of children. That's what sin really is. You know—not being full of joy. Tell her that sin is forgiven because whether she knows it or not, that's what she wants more than anything else—what all of us want. What on earth do you think you were ordained for?"

Before they retire to their separate rooms, Nicolet gives Rooney the blessing she so desperately needs: "The almighty and merciful God pardon and deliver you, forgive you every face you cannot look upon with joy."

The next morning Rooney leaves for Myron but Nicolet decides to pay a visit to his father, who lives only a few hours north of Muscadine, and ponder what Lillian had asked him. The evening he arrives at his father's home he lies down behind the barn and attempts to work on a sermon for the upcoming Pentecost Sunday service. He is so confused by his thoughts of Rooney and Lillian and his father that in despair he fervently calls upon Jesus to come to him with some answers. All he hears is the sound of two branches clacking together on an apple tree.

> Maybe all his journeying, he thought, had been only to bring him here to hear two branches hit each other twice like that, to see nothing cross the threshold but to see the threshold, to hear the dry

clack-clack of the world's tongue at the approach of the approach perhaps of splendor.

He is interrupted by the arrival of his friend Ralph Denbigh, an Episcopal priest, who has learned from Rooney where Nicolet might be found. Denbigh has sought Nicolet out to warn him of some troubling rumors that are being circulated in Myron concerning his and Rooney's disappearances. The chief perpetrator of the viciousness is Will Poteat, owner of the village's newspaper, *The Myron Repository,* and author of the paper's gossip column. It is Poteat, in fact, who shared in the onetime act of adultery with Rooney six years earlier, and he has not quite gotten over her. So far his innuendos about the newly widowed minister and a certain woman have been harmless, but when he learns through tricking Irma that Nicolet and Rooney are staying together in another town, he unleashes his venom in a column that Denbigh now shows to Nicolet. It is a Pauline bit of nastiness that Poteat published the day after Rooney returned to Myron. In "The Epistle to the Myronians," as he calls it, Poteat denounces the young minister and calls upon the villagers to do likewise.

Nicolet returns to find his village split. Some are angry at Poteat and threaten to withdraw advertising money from his newspaper, and others who believe his column avoid Nicolet. When he arrives at his church to deliver the Pentecost sermon, he finds that someone has written "THOU SHALT NOT COMMIT ADULTERY" in chalk on the sidewalk leading to the door. As he steps up to the pulpit he notices that the church is unusually crowded. After he delivers his sermon he calls upon his congregation to join him in the confession. At that moment Irma stands up and cries out in a loud voice that it is she who is responsible for the rumors; that it was she, mad with love for the minister and jealous of his relationship with Rooney, who had told lies to Poteat in order to cause Nicolet pain. She cries, "So you know the truth now,

and you are going to forget all the lies I made. You are going to be good to this pastor again now and not write filth on his sidewalk for children to read." With that she flees from the church and goes into hiding at a friend's house. Some who leave after the service shake hands with Nicolet and pledge their support, but others leave by the side door in order to avoid him.

Word of Irma's confession gets back to Poteat and he is moved to feel a sudden kinship with the woman. He recognizes the similarities in their passions of deep love and deep hatred. When he learns that she has died in a house fire, he feels that the only place for him to be is at her funeral. Nicolet concludes the burial service with these words from Revelation, "And God shall wipe away all tears, and there shall be no more death, neither sorrow, nor crying, neither shall there be any more pain, for the former things have passed away." As the mourners depart in a sudden rainstorm, Poteat walks back to Nicolet, places a hand on his shoulder, and tells him, "Good show, pal." Nicolet's daughters begin to pelt Poteat with wildflowers and he pretends to be a great bear running away, with them in pursuit throwing their flowers, giggling and laughing. Soon Poteat is laughing and so is Nicolet. Reconciliation and forgiveness will conquer isolation and resentment. Jesus has been crowned again in Myron as Buttrick said—amid confession, tears, and great laughter.

Of course, Nicolet's journey is Buechner's journey. His steps away from despair and doubt led him first to Buttrick's church and eventually to a place within himself where his faith is strong and his belief in his ministry through literature is firm. So firm in fact that he decided to leave his position at Exeter and devote himself to a life of writing.

GOD'S MAN IN VERMONT

In 1967 Buechner moved his family to Rupert, Vermont. By that time the family had grown to include two more daughters: Dinah, born in 1960, and Sharman, born in 1964. They moved into a cabin on a farm owned by Buechner's in-laws. It was here that they had spent many summer vacations and holidays, and it was here that they had hoped to settle permanently some day. When that day came, however, it was not what Buechner had hoped for. He suddenly found himself filled with self-doubt—a minister without a church, a teacher without a school, a writer without a subject. He struggled through the first year suffering from loneliness and hypochondria:

> Out of it all, by Caesarian section, I somehow managed to bring a novel forth anyway. *The Entrance to Porlock* I called it in reference to the visitor from Porlock who woke Coleridge out of the visionary trance of *Kubla Khan,* and what it was essentially about, I think, was the tension between everyday reality and the reality of dreams, of imagination. The plot was based loosely on *The Wizard of Oz.*

Buechner goes on to describe the novel as a "symbolic autobiography, a strange, dense, slow-paced book, the labor of writing which was so painful that I find it hard, even now, to see beyond my memory of the pain to whatever merit it may have." He felt caught in a trap of his own making.

As he was finishing the novel, Buechner received an invitation to give the Noble Lectures at Harvard. He decided to use as his topic a single representative day in his own life and what there was of God to be found there. The three lectures were published as *The Alphabet of Grace* (1970). The project opened Buechner's eyes to the holiness of everyday life, and he began to realize that God is present in the darkness as well as in the light: "What I started trying to do as a writer and as a preacher was more and more to draw on my own experience not just as a source of plot, character, illustration, but as a source of truth." Thus began the most prolific period of Buechner's life. For the next

three decades he produced books at the rate of one nearly every year, alternating between fiction and nonfiction. In addition to writing he found the time to maintain an active schedule as a much sought-after preacher and guest lecturer.

All of Buechner's fiction in the 1970s focused on the activities of a spiritual con man who became one of Buechner's best known characters, Leo Bebb. The narrator of the story, which begins with *Lion Country* (1971) and continues through *Open Heart* (1972), *Love Feast* (1974), and *Treasure Hunt* (1977), is Antonio Parr, a thirty-four-year-old former English teacher at a small boarding school who has left his position to be near his dying twin sister. He is a failed novelist and sculptor who lacks any sense of direction and purpose. He has just given up on his fourth attempt at fiction (his previous three manuscripts never got past page thirty-four) when he comes across an advertisement which reads*: "Put yourself on God's payroll—go to work for Jesus* NOW." Parr answers the ad because, as he says, "I hoped that it would provide me with copy. I would set novels aside, I thought, and try my hand at journalistic exposé." In ten days he receives a certificate of ordination from the Church of Holy Love, Inc., in Armadillo, Florida. Included with his certificate is a pamphlet that describes the tax exemptions and discounts he is entitled to as a minister, as well as a catalog of mail-order courses offered by Gospel Faith College. Parr invites the operation's owner and spiritual leader, Leo Bebb, to meet with him the next time Bebb is in New York. After their meeting Parr is convinced that Bebb is a charlatan and later discovers that he is something worse: eleven years earlier Bebb had spent time in jail after being convicted of exposing himself to a group of children at a Miami playground.

The death of his sister frees Parr to descend upon Armadillo, Florida, filled with righteous indignation and a determination to expose the fraudulent Bebb and put an end to his operation. For over five hundred pages, Buechner's tetralogy follows Parr as he becomes a member of the raucous, risqué, Rabelaisian traveling show that surrounds Bebb. Despite their unrestrained humor, the four novels, which were revised and published in one volume, *The Book of Bebb* (1979), manage to explore some of Buechner's most serious beliefs, specifically that life must be lived fully and without fear:

> The trouble with folks like Brownie is they hold their life in like a bakebean fart at a Baptist cookout and only let it slip out sideways a little at a time when they think there's nobody noticing. Now that's the last thing on earth the Almighty intended. He intended all the life a man's got inside him, he should live it out just as free and strong and natural as a bird.

For all his chicanery, Bebb brings people to life and teaches them valuable lessons in what the German theologian Dietrich Bonhoeffer called the cost of discipleship. *Lion Country* received a National Book Award nomination.

In addition to the Bebb works, Buechner produced several collections of nonfiction during this remarkably prolific decade, including books of selected sermons and theological meditations: *Wishful Thinking: A Theological ABC* (1973), *The Faces of Jesus* (1974), *Telling the Truth: The Gospel as Tragedy, Comedy, and Fairy Tale* (1977), and *Peculiar Treasures: A Biblical Who's Who* (1979).

AUTOBIOGRAPHY AND THE LATE NOVELS

The 1980s through the 1990s were a period of autobiographical reflection and recollection for Buechner. In the inviting style of a fireside chat, Buechner writes in *The Sacred Journey* of his family's history and his own life up to the time he entered seminary. He continues the story of his life from ordination to family life in Vermont in *Now and Then*. In *Telling Secrets* (1991) and

The Eyes of the Heart: A Memoir of the Lost and Found (1999), Buechner adds more detail to the story begun in his first autobiographical works. This period also saw the publication of *A Room Called Remember: Uncollected Pieces* (1984), *Whistling in the Dark: An ABC Theologized* (1988), *Listening to Your Life: Daily Meditations with Frederick Buechner* (1992), *The Longing for Home: Recollections and Reflections* (1996), and a collection of literary studies: *The Clown in the Belfry: Writings on Faith and Fiction* (1992).

For his fictional writing of this period Buechner turned to the Bible and lives of the saints for his inspiration. *Godric* (1980) tells the story of a twelfth-century Anglo-Saxon who, after spending the first forty years of his life in a rather unsaintly manner, decided he wanted nothing more to do with the world and so became a hermit, determined to find sanctity and holiness. As the novel begins, Godric, now one hundred years old and expecting death at any moment, is suddenly beset with the annoying presence of a young monk, Reginald, who has been sent by Abbot Ailred to write the story of Godric's life. Despite Godric's determination to tell his life truthfully, Reginald whitewashes or ignores the less seemly episodes and presents to history a rather bloodless saint. *Godric* was nominated for the Pulitzer Prize. It was followed by *Brendan: A Novel* (1987), which is a retelling of the life and adventures of the legendary fifth-century Irish saint through the eyes of Finn, his friend and companion.

In 1990 Buechner turned again to his own life for inspiration. It is important to remember that, despite his literary success and having the gift of a loving wife and three daughters, Buechner remained haunted by his father's failures, alcoholism, and suicide. In the late 1980s Buechner began attending meetings of Al-Anon and Adult Children of Alcoholics. He wrote about these experiences in *Telling Secrets*:

"Adult children" is an odd phrase meaning adults who still carry with them many of the confusions and fears and hurts of their childhood, and one of the luckiest things I ever did, to use one kind of language—one of God's most precious gifts to me, to use another—was to discover that I was one of them and that there were countless others like me who were there when I needed them and by whom I also was needed. I have found more spiritual nourishment and strength and understanding among them than I have found anywhere else for a long time.

The novella that emerged from this period, *The Wizard's Tide: A Story* (1990), concerns just such an adult child, Teddy Schroeder. With great sensitivity and thoughtfulness Buechner shows, through the eyes and heart of a boy who has an infinite capacity for hope, the horror of growing up in an alcoholic household during the Great Depression era of the 1930s.

The Book of Genesis provided Buechner with the material for his next work of fiction, *The Son of Laughter: A Novel* (1993). The well-known story of lies and betrayal, of Abraham and Isaac, of Joseph and his brothers, is told by Jacob, the son of Isaac (whose name means laughter). Next came *On the Road with the Archangel* (1997), another novel that used a biblical source, this time the Book of Tobit, a book found only in Catholic Bibles and in the Apocrypha of Protestant Bibles. Written sometime in the second century B.C., it tells the tale of a pious Jewish family—Tobit, his wife Anna, and their son, Tobias—who were captured when the Assyrians invaded northern Israel and carried off the best and brightest of its inhabitants. In Buechner's version the story is told by the Archangel Raphael, who is sent by God in answer to the prayers of Tobit and a young woman named Sarah. Buechner's thoughts about the nature of God come through in the voice of Raphael. In the following passage, for instance, Tobit is praising God for restoring his sight: "'You afflicted me because my unworthiness deserved affliction,' he said in a voice thick with emotion, 'and now you have restored my sight because your nature is always to be merciful to those who please you.'" Raphael tells the reader, "He was totally wrong on both counts, of course. The Holy One does not go around afflicting people, and although his nature is indeed above all else merciful, Tobit was a good man and in no more need of mercy than a two-year-old child." Raphael finds the human understanding of God a source of endless amusement:

They believed that the One who created time in its goodness and set the world afloat on it like a flowered barge is as ill-tempered and irrational and vengeful as one of their own kings. Yet they never ceased singing his praises even so, adjuring each other to love him with all their might when they had every reason in the world to hide from him in terror. It is no wonder that even in the Presence itself, I find myself shaking with laughter. Unseemly as it may appear, it is surely less so than being perpetually dissolved in tears.

Some acquaintance with Shakespeare's *The Tempest* adds to the understanding and enjoyment of Buechner's fifteenth novel, *The Storm* (1998). Both works deal with the universal themes of betrayal, estrangement, reconciliation, and forgiveness, but *The Storm* is not a retelling or modernization of Shakespeare's play. Kenzie Maxwell is a modestly successful writer who as a young boy wanted to be a magician. Some of his short stories have appeared in *The New Yorker*, and his first book, a collection of these stories, was published with the title *Both, Both, My Girl* (a quotation from act 1, scene 2, line 63 of the play). Kenzie's next book, a study of saints entitled *A Fine Frenzy*, leads him to attend church services, something he has not done since being forced to do so in boarding school. The magic and mystery of the liturgy at a little church known as Smokey Mary's create a desire in the forty-nine-year-old Kenzie to do something that is completely out of character: help those who are less fortunate.

His older brother, Dalton, a law professor at Columbia, suggests that he volunteer at a shelter for young runaways. Dalton is on the board of directors of such a place, the Alodians, in the South Bronx.

Kenzie spends several days a week at the Alodian headquarters listening to the stories of young people for whom life on the streets is a far cry better than the lives of abuse they endured within the walls of their parents' homes. One such victim is a lovely seventeen-year-old graffiti artist named Kia. Kenzie, who is in the middle of a divorce, is using Dalton's apartment while he is away for six months on sabbatical, and on a few nights he has allowed Kia to find shelter there. He offers her the comfort of the bed, but she insists on sleeping on the floor. All is very proper until one rainy night when Kenzie tells Kia how very fond he is of her. Later, long after he has fallen asleep, she slips into bed beside him.

When she discovers that she is pregnant, Kia stops coming to the Alodians. Kenzie tries to find her but is not sure where it is she lives with her grandmother. Some time later the grandmother arrives at the Alodians with a newborn, Kia and Kenzie's daughter. Kia has died shortly after giving birth, and the grandmother wants to know if anyone there can help her find the man responsible. She does not know the man's name, but her description clearly identifies Kenzie. Dalton returns from his sabbatical and confronts his brother with the grandmother's accusations. Kenzie is crushed by the news. Before leaving Dalton's apartment he writes a letter explaining what transpired before the tragic result, accepting full responsibility for his child and enclosing a large check that is to be given to the grandmother.

Rumors begin to circulate and financial supporters of the Alodians want answers. Dalton, with his orderly legal mind, releases an official statement to the press and includes the letter Kenzie wrote. The news media pounces on the story, painting a picture of Kia as nothing more than a child prostitute. Unable to bear the hounding and disgrace, Kenzie leaves the city hoping never to see his brother again. But first he writes a second letter of explanation for Dalton:

> He could forgive Dalton for having exposed him to general opprobrium, he said, because he deserved no better. He could forgive him for having ruined anything he had ever conceived of as his future because it hadn't been much of a future anyway and because he imagined he would eventually be able to make a place for himself somehow in the ruins. But what he could not forgive him for was vilifying the memory and the name of Kia, the name that she had so daringly painted up in so many impossible places like a kind of battle flag whose wild colors and flamboyant curlicues she had hoped might somehow make up for losing the battle itself as she had always known she would lose it. He wrote that it would take a saint as crazy as the ones he had written about to forgive Dalton for that. As for himself, he said, he hoped never to look upon his brother's face again.

In chapter 2 the story jumps ahead twenty years and the similarities to *The Tempest* become obvious. Kenzie (the counterpart of Shakespeare's Prospero) is living on an island on the Atlantic coast of southern Florida with his latest wealthy wife, Willow. Plantation Island is the property of a spinster, Miss Violet Sickert (Sycorax). This bitter, mean-spirited old woman rules the island with an iron hand, deciding who can buy property and what style and color of house can be built there. She knows of Kenzie's fall from grace and allows him on the island only because his wife has owned a house there for years. Two other people live in the house: Willow's forty-ish son by a previous marriage, Averill (Ariel), and their servant, Calvert Sykes (Caliban). Averill is a free-spirited, meditative windsurfer. Calvert is his opposite in every way: a brutish, diminutive drunkard to whom Kenzie offered a job and a room when Miss Sickert banished him from her home.

Calvert is the son of a couple named Sykes who worked for Miss Sickert. She was especially attentive to the boy during his childhood, making sure he had everything he needed and offering to pay for his training in a useful trade. It was rumored that Miss Sickert had born Calvert out of wedlock and had managed to get the Sykes to adopt him. Calvert had begun sneaking drinks of alcohol as a teenager, and when Miss Sickert discovered that he had developed a serious drinking problem, she fired him on the spot. Calvert believes that she turned against him because he knew the truth about her, and while he performs menial tasks for Kenzie he imagines how he will run things on Plantation Island once his "mother" dies and he inherits everything.

Kenzie's seventieth birthday is approaching and a celebration is planned. He sends an e-mail message to his daughter, Bree (Miranda), asking her to fly down from New York for the occasion. Bree has been raised by Kenzie's sister and is now studying ballet. Despite the unusual circumstances of her birth and upbringing, she has a loving bond with her father and gladly accepts his invitation. On her flight she is seated next to a man whom she discovers is her uncle, Dalton Maxwell (Antonio). Dalton, it turns out, is Miss Sickert's lawyer, and she has asked him to come to Plantation Island on the pretext of helping her revise her will. Her real purpose, of course, is to disrupt Kenzie's celebration by bringing the two brothers, who have not seen or spoken to each other for nearly twenty years, face to face.

Kenzie has learned of Miss Sickert's plan, so he is not really surprised to see Dalton at the airport when he arrives to pick up Bree. The two exchange cool, cordial greetings and go their separate ways—Dalton with his stepson Nandy (Ferdinand), and Kenzie with Bree—without any indication that they desire to see

one another again and certainly no sign of any possible reconciliation. Earlier the question of what to do about his brother had puzzled Kenzie: "He could not forgive his brother for what he had done to the memory of Kia because that was not for him to forgive, but he could at least make a path around it somehow." When he tells his wife that he has decided to invite Dalton to the birthday party, she is pleased: "You might as well bury the hatchet, Kenzie," she says. "You're too old to do anything else with it." She sends Averill to Miss Sickert's home with a written invitation.

Miss Sickert is intrigued by Averill and begins to show some signs that perhaps her heart is not as small as everyone suspects. On his way out Averill bumps into Bishop Hazelton (a combination of Trinculo and Stephano). The long-retired bishop has been installed by Miss Sickert to oversee the island's little Episcopal church and shape his sermons to suit her own theology. Hazelton is curious to know more about Averill and engages him in conversation. Averill, who is "struck by the Bishop's purple vest and clerical collar and wondered about the mystery that he officially represented," asks Hazelton if he has ever seen God. Hazelton responds that neither he nor anyone else ever has, but Averill leaves the bishop puzzled by the claim that he, Averill, has.

Dalton and Nandy arrive at Miss Sickert's home, and she is overwhelmed by her strong and immediate feelings of love for the young, handsome stepson: "When he addressed her as Miss Sickert, which was how Dalton had of course introduced her, she told him her name was Violet. It had always seemed to her a foolish sort of name, but on his lips it became the name of a flower." Dalton is anxious to get on with the work that is supposedly the reason he is there, but Miss Sickert puts him off and throws all her attentions toward making Nandy comfortable. She buys him new clothes, introduces him to her friends, gives him a personal tour of her island, and arranges for a large boat from her marina to be at his disposal so he can enjoy some ocean fishing with his stepfather.

On the Sunday of the party Dalton and Kenzie encounter each other at church. Dalton shakes hands with Kenzie and wishes him a happy birthday. He also assures him that he and Nandy will return from their fishing excursion in plenty of time for the festivities. The softening of the two brothers' relationship is matched by the sultry stillness of the air, and one feels that a storm must soon break to relieve the tension.

Nandy and his father are just far enough from shore to be seen from Kenzie's home when the wind suddenly rises and a gale-force storm falls upon them. The boat capsizes and the two men are separated. Watching from the shore in horror, Kenzie's wife accuses him of calling the storm down from the heavens in order to exact revenge upon his brother. She remembers a time when Kenzie, dressed in a blue terry cloth bathrobe covered in moons and stars, had seemingly quelled an oncoming storm that threatened to ruin their cocktail party. "Is this your revenge, Kenzie?" she says. "If you can keep bad weather away, I suppose you can make it happen too." Kenzie wonders if it could be true:

> Had he willed it without knowing that he was doing so? Had he perhaps even known it? When he had thought of the storm making Dalton respond like a human being at last, had he been challenging it to, willing it to make him cry mercy who had never had the faintest idea what it even meant to be merciful?

The storm's power fells trees, knocks out electrical power, and hurls patio furniture through glass windows and doors. Desperate, Kenzie sends Averill and Calvert out to see if perhaps Dalton and Nandy have made it to shore. Calvert finds Dalton alive huddled near some stone steps and brings him back to the house. Averill finds Nandy, who has suffered a head injury, and with Bree's help he is reunited with his stepfather. Miss Sickert and Bishop Hazelton each make the perilous journey from their homes to Kenzie's. She is overwrought with concern for Nandy, and he feels a strong duty to shepherd his flock. All are finally gathered in the storm-damaged home, and the healing that has been long postponed begins among them. The bishop is relieved to see that the young man who claimed to have seen God survived the storm and asks him if he was in earnest when he claimed to have seen God. Reflecting Buechner's belief that we best represent God by our loving actions toward each other, Averill looks at the Bishop and says, "I am seeing him now."

NOW AND TOMORROW

Frederick Buechner had this to say in 1983 regarding his writing:

> I do it because it seems to me that no matter who you are, and no matter how eloquent or otherwise, if you tell your own story with sufficient candor and concreteness, it will be an interesting story and in some sense a universal story. I do it also in the hope of encouraging others to do the same—at least to look back over their lives, as I have looked back over mine, for the certain themes and patterns and signals that are so easy to miss when you're caught up in the process of living them. If God speaks to us at all other than through such official channels as the Bible and the church, then I think that he speaks to us largely through what happens to us.

In 2002 Buechner continues to live with his wife on the Vermont farm they inherited from her parents. He keeps up an active life of teaching, preaching, and traveling and has produced his seventeenth book of nonfiction, *Speak What We Feel (Not What We Ought to Say): Reflections on Literature and Faith* (2001). At age seventy-six Buechner continues to tell his story.

Selected Bibliography

WORKS BY FREDERICK BUECHNER

FICTION

A Long Day's Dying. New York: Knopf, 1950.

The Seasons' Difference. New York: Knopf, 1951.

"The Tiger." In *Prize Stories 1955: The O. Henry Awards.* Edited by Paul Engle, Flannery O'Connor, and Hansford Martin. Garden City, N.Y.: Doubleday, 1955.

The Return of Ansel Gibbs. New York: Knopf, 1958.

The Final Beast. New York: Atheneum, 1965; San Francisco: Harper & Row, 1982.

The Entrance to Porlock. New York: Atheneum, 1970.

Lion Country. New York: Atheneum, 1971.

Open Heart. New York: Atheneum, 1972.

Love Feast. New York: Atheneum, 1974.

Treasure Hunt. New York: Atheneum, 1977.

The Book of Bebb. New York: Atheneum, 1979. (Contains *Lion Country, Open Heart, Love Feast,* and *Treasure Hunt.*)

Godric. New York: Atheneum, 1980.

Brendan: A Novel. New York: Atheneum, 1987.

The Wizard's Tide: A Story. San Francisco: Harper & Row, 1990.

The Son of Laughter: A Novel. San Francisco: HarperCollins, 1993.

On the Road with the Archangel. San Francisco: HarperCollins, 1997.

The Storm. San Francisco: HarperCollins, 1998.

NONFICTION

The Magnificent Defeat. New York: Seabury, 1966.

The Hungering Dark. San Francisco: Harper & Row, 1968.

The Alphabet of Grace. New York: Seabury, 1970.

Wishful Thinking: A Theological ABC. New York: Harper & Row, 1973.

The Faces of Jesus. New York: Riverwood and Simon & Schuster, 1974.

Telling the Truth: The Gospel as Tragedy, Comedy, and Fairy Tale. San Francisco: Harper & Row, 1977.

Peculiar Treasures: A Biblical Who's Who. San Francisco: Harper & Row, 1979.

The Sacred Journey. San Francisco: Harper & Row, 1982.

Now and Then. Cambridge: Harper & Row, 1983.

A Room Called Remember: Uncollected Pieces. San Francisco: Harper & Row, 1984.

Whistling in the Dark: An ABC Theologized. San Francisco: Harper & Row, 1988.

Telling Secrets. San Francisco: HarperCollins, 1991.

The Clown in the Belfry: Writings on Faith and Fiction. San Francisco: HarperCollins, 1992.

Listening to Your Life: Daily Meditations with Frederick Buechner. San Francisco: HarperCollins, 1992.

The Longing for Home: Recollections and Reflections. San Francisco: HarperCollins, 1996.

The Eyes of the Heart: A Memoir of the Lost and Found. San Francisco: HarperCollins, 1999.

Speak What We Feel (Not What We Ought to Say): Reflections on Literature and Faith. San Francisco: HarperCollins, 2001.

CRITICAL AND BIOGRAPHICAL STUDIES

Aldridge, John W. *After the Lost Generation: A Critical Study of the Writers of Two Wars.* New York: McGraw-Hill, 1951.

Davies, Horton. "Frederick Buechner and the Strange Work of Grace." *Theology Today* 36:186–193 (July 1979).

Davies, Horton, and Marie-Hélène Davies. "The God of Storm and Stillness: The Fiction of Flannery O'Connor and Frederick Buechner." *Religion in Life* 48:188–196 (summer 1979).

Davies, Marie-Hélène. *Laughter in a Genevan Gown: The Works of Frederick Buechner, 1970–1980.* Grand Rapids, Mich.: Eerdmans, 1983.

Hassan, Ihab. *Radical Innocence: Studies in the Contemporary American Novel.* Princeton, N.J.: Princeton University Press, 1961.

McCoy, Marjorie Casebier, with Charles S. McCoy. *Frederick Buechner: Novelist/Theologian of the Lost and Found.* San Francisco: Harper & Row, 1988.

Nelson, Shirley, and Rudy Nelson. "Buechner: Novelist to 'Cultural Despisers.'" *Christianity Today* 25:44 [753] (May 29, 1981).

Woelfel, James. "Frederick Buechner: The Novelist as Theologian." *Theology Today* 40:273–291 (October 1983).

INTERVIEWS

Gallagher, Sharon, and Jack Buckley. "A Conscious Remembering: An Interview with Frederick Buechner." *Radix* 15:4–10 (July/August 1983).

Gibble, Kenneth L. "Listening to My Life: An Interview with Frederick Buechner." *The Christian Century* 100:1042–1045 (November 16, 1983).

Ross, Jean W. Interview in *Contemporary Authors, New Revision Series.* Vol. 11. Detroit: Gale, 1984. Pp. 107–109.

—*CHARLES R. BAKER*

Robert Olen Butler

1945–

ROBERT OLEN BUTLER was born on January 20, 1945, in Granite City, Illinois, a small town on the Mississippi River a few miles northeast of St. Louis. The only child of Robert Olen Butler Sr. and Lucille Hall Butler, Robert Jr. spent his youth on the cusp of the Midwest and the South absorbing his mother's stories of the Great Depression and his father's passion for the theater (Butler's father was an actor and the chair of the theater department at Saint Louis University). During his adolescence Butler read the authors who would profoundly influence subsequent generations of American writers— William Faulkner, F. Scott Fitzgerald, James Joyce, Graham Greene, Sherwood Anderson, Flannery O'Connor, Ernest Hemingway ("we all learned to use the word 'and' from Hemingway"). Still, Butler said in a personal interview, "My influences came from elsewhere. I loved music and to this day will put appropriate music on to focus my trance. Given my interest in voice, in the rhythms of prose, and in motif, I think I've been influenced by music as much as I have been by other literature." At Northwestern University, where he began studies in playwriting and acting in 1963, Butler honed his ear and writing style with one eye on the stage, a move that would manifest itself two decades later in the complex human relationships that underpin his novels and short stories. In 1968 he received an M.F.A. in playwriting from the University of Iowa.

Shortly after graduation Butler enlisted for military duty in Vietnam and worked in counterintelligence as a translator and interpreter for the American Foreign Service. His experiences in Vietnam—where from the first day he was fluent in the language—profoundly colored the work that would follow, as he explained succinctly to Kay Bonetti: "I was ravished by the sensuality of Vietnam." Despite Vietnam's influence on the young writer, however, Butler resists being characterized as a "Vietnam novelist," which "is like calling Monet a lily-pad painter. Vietnam for me has always been simply a metaphor, a location, an instigator of action, a source of characters, a matrix of concrete sensual experience that holds the deep universal human issues I'm concerned with." He combines those narrowly focused memories with a far-ranging vision that moves seamlessly from the alleys of Vietnam to the barren landscapes of Alaska to the canyons of New York City to Louisiana's Mississippi Delta to mid-America during the depression. But the sensibility that would carry Butler through all of his fiction was inculcated in him in Granite City, whose duality would inform his life as a writer. During summers he worked at a steel mill and studied the interactions of people from different backgrounds as they carved lives from what was, for many, a hardscrabble existence. Although those experiences would not be directly articulated until his fifth novel, *Wabash* (1987), Butler's sense of what it means to be American is tempered by his formative years in Illinois.

Butler's first work as a writer was not as a playwright or as a novelist, as his background might have predicted, but as a reporter for *Electronic News* in New York City and Chicago. He also spent a brief period as a freelance writer and teacher in the early 1970s, after his return from Vietnam. In the late 1970s at the New School for Social Research, Butler attended creative writing seminars taught by Anatole Broyard, who gave Butler's novel *Countrymen of Bones* (1983) a positive review in the *New York Times.* Butler remembers him fondly as "a wonderful reader. He finally led me to look in the right place in myself." Butler also worked as editor in chief of *Energy User News* for nearly a decade, through the publication in 1985 of his fourth novel, *On Distant Ground* (1985).

Despite a writing career that proceeded in fits and starts until his phenomenal critical success in the early 1990s, Butler was offered a teaching position in creative writing at McNeese State University in Lake Charles, Louisiana, on the strength and generally solid critical reception of his first four novels. *The Alleys of Eden* (1981), his first novel, had been rejected more than a dozen times, though it sold 85,000 copies in paperback upon its publication in 1981. According to Butler, his sixth novel, *The Deuce* (1989), sold 1,086 copies, "which means that it sold nothing, because that many copies fall off trucks and get counted as sales." He held his position at McNeese State University from 1985 until 2000, when he was named Francis Eppes Professor of Creative Writing at Florida State University. He lives outside Tallahassee, Florida, with his wife, the novelist Elizabeth Dewberry. Butler's son, Joshua (from a previous marriage), is himself a writer and director.

In all, Butler has published twelve works of fiction over the past two decades, beginning with *The Alleys of Eden,* a taut psychological exploration of an American deserter and his lover caught between the two worlds they inhabit but from which they are inevitably alienated. The author's early novels show a barely restrained passion for the power of the written word and a fascination with human relationships. Implicit in all Butler's fiction is the notion of "yearning," a word he uses repeatedly in his work:

> You cannot escape the fact that fiction is about human beings and it's about human feelings. . . .

Any Buddhist will tell you—and this is one of the great truths of the religion—that you cannot exist for ten seconds of time on planet Earth as a feeling human being without desiring something. I use "yearning" to get at what art is about, that deepest level of desire. Inescapably, fiction is the art form of human yearning.

That close, nearly obsessive attention to human wants and needs culminated in *A Good Scent from a Strange Mountain* (1992), a short story collection that details the experiences of Vietnamese immigrants in Louisiana and a work that was instrumental, writes Milton J. Bates, in bringing what had previously been "an underground tradition . . . into the full light of day." The collection was awarded the 1993 Pulitzer Prize in fiction, among other notable awards.

Butler last fully explored Vietnam in *Deep Green Sea* (1997). His *Mr. Spaceman* (2000) and *Fair Warning* (2002) are an eclectic mélange of characters who seem far removed from the contradictions and complexities of war. Still, as with the previous ten works, the intense exploration of character is imperative in the narratives, and the articulation of strong relationships that marks Butler's work—replete with many of the contradictions that characterize his war-time relationships—comes to the fore in these books as well. Collectively the body of Butler's fiction employs an impressive range of characterization, point of view, and digression to articulate the "deeper truths" that follow from the author's profound identification with language and its articulation of the everyday experiences that shape the characters' lives and identities.

THE ALLEYS OF EDEN

Butler's first novel, published, according to the author, after "an overextended apprenticeship of writing badly," is presented in two parts—the first during the final days of Saigon before its fall to North Vietnamese troops, the second in post-Vietnam America—that roughly parallel the two parts of the author's life and his own dual identity. Clifford Wilkes, an American deserter, and Lanh, a former prostitute, have fallen in love. Despite the circumstances under which the two have conducted their affair for the better part of four years—neither of the lovers, it seems, will ever be fully accepted by their societies—they cling to each other and to their niche in a squalid apartment in Saigon, framed by the Edenic alleys of the title ("These alleys were once full of deserters but he'd held to this place—and the place had held to him—better than any before."), as if prescient that to move away would mean the end of their relationship.

Intertwined with the search for meaningful human contact that has compelled Cliff to risk his own freedom by deserting from the army are the spirits of the people with whom he has come in contact in the past. Saigon is full of such spirits, and Cliff divulges that one primary influence in his desertion was his participation in an interrogation that resulted in the death of a Vietnamese prisoner. The juxtaposition of life and death for Cliff—in Saigon, the two are practically indistinguishable—is Cliff's guide in his yearning for Lanh, who in her own transformation from prostitute to loving partner symbolizes Cliff's attenuation of guilt and spiritual rebirth after the prisoner's death. Though Cliff and Lanh manage to escape from the city on one of the last helicopters, Cliff would prefer a return to the relative innocence of his life with Lanh. He realizes, however, that such a thing is not possible.

Despite the optimism engendered by their intense love for one another, neither Cliff nor Lanh can imagine what awaits them in America. After all, Cliff is a deserter, and Lanh understands little of the American culture and speaks only the bar-English that reminds Cliff of her previous life as a prostitute. Their reunion in America, however, gives them a brief respite before the reality of their situation signals the end of their relationship. Lanh, despite her love for Cliff, cannot function apart from the language and customs of her country; Cliff, even though he loves Lanh, cannot prevent himself from being re-Americanized upon his return. Cliff admits that his repatriation is forcing him to become "fragments of people myself," and after he searches one last time for his ex-wife he comes to the conclusion that even the banality of the world around him was "imprinted in him—the synapses of culture—the tracks that caught him and pulled him away. . . . He was an American." When reconciliation with Lanh becomes impossible, Cliff leaves, perhaps for Canada, under the impending threat of arrest for his desertion. Lanh joins a family of Vietnamese immigrants who can better understand her own feelings of alienation and fragmentation.

The importance of language as a means of connecting individuals cannot be overstated in Butler's work, a feature of his fiction undoubtedly nurtured by his experiences in Vietnam, when

> every night I'd wander the back alleys of Saigon alone just to talk to people. . . . Knowing the language, everything has been renamed. If you learn a language properly, it's not the learning of equivalencies of words. Instead, you rename the world. And every physical object has a new name. It forces your senses open even further.

Cliff realizes toward the end of their relationship that Lanh "had no language now and her mind, her heart, had been sealed shut—she had no country now and everything was alien to her and turned her into a stranger." Even Cliff, whose identity has been reshaped by years of immersion in another culture and language, "fights to find the markers of a stable identity within language, culture, landscape, custom, architecture, his own body, and can find it in none of these. He is Vietnamese; he is American; he is neither."

That feature of human communication and the profound effects of its absence are intimately intertwined in Butler's fiction with a sense of place and the construction of identity. When he last makes love to Lanh, Cliff imagines "Saigon, their race through the alleyways, he wanted to go back, go back to their alley room, that was their place." Such scenes are important in the body of Butler's work, as Renny Christopher points out, not only in presenting a "nonstereotypical portrait of a Vietnamese character," but by taking seriously "the possibility of an American assuming a Vietnamese identity, the possibility of an American loving the country of Viet Nam."

SUN DOGS

The notion of place—both physical places and the psychological space that nurtures the memories of Butler's characters—would weave its way through the author's work, and no more so than in his second novel. The Vietnam experience is still apparent in this story, though in a much different context from that in *The Alleys of Eden*. Wilson Hand, who appears briefly in the first novel as the man Clifford Wilkes and his compatriots were attempting to free when they killed the Vietnamese, is a private detective coming to terms with a brief imprisonment in Vietnam and his estrangement from his ex-wife, Beth, whose life has been defined, in Wilson's mind, by the superfluous objects with which she surrounds herself. When Beth plummets from the balcony of her apartment shortly after Wilson visits her, the death sets in motion a series of events—all of which are played out in Wilson's mind and remain tangential to the novel's plot—that finally lead him to his own death. Wilson has been hired by an Alaskan-based petroleum firm to investigate the theft of oil-industry data; he takes the opportunity to escape the hustle and bustle of the modern world and to explore his memories of his

relationship with Beth, her suicide, and his own Vietnam experience. On his flight to Alaska he watches two "sun dogs," false images of the sun that appear on the horizon, mirroring the true sun. The image is a metaphor for Wilson's memories as he attempts to piece together his true identity from the remnants of his haunted past.

From his initial firsthand glimpse of the oil company's operation, Wilson "was aware of the oil being pulled from the earth—he was aware of a source of sustenance being drawn down—draining away—he felt the process physically, in his own body—he felt weak, his legs grew weak, he sensed the oil flowing, lost forever." The image recurs in the narrative, calling attention to Wilson's extensive alienation from society and paralleling his relationship with Marta Gregory, a mysterious woman who works for the oil company at the secluded Moonbase operation and who shares Wilson's distaste for the clutter threatening to invade their lives. Wilson's relationship with Marta is as enervating to him as the pull of the oil from the earth, the draining of its lifeblood. When he discovers the truth about the data theft—that Marta and one of her many lovers (in this case, Eli Marcus, an itinerant preacher) have been feeding information to O'Dell, a *New York Times* reporter, that suggests the oil companies have lied about the size of the reserves—the ensuing chaos returns Wilson briefly to New York City and finally forces him back to Alaska, the only place, he understands, that can be restorative for him.

As he follows O'Dell through the canyons of New York City, so much different from the barren Alaskan wilderness he craves, Wilson realizes, in a statement that echoes Cliff's own desire to return to the alleys of Saigon, the necessity that will lead him finally to his death: "He wanted Alaska; he was yearning again now, and he knew that if he used O'Dell in order to find the leaks at Moonbase, his job in Alaska was secure. If he failed, he'd have no way to return to the North Slope." When Wilson gains passage back to Alaska, he meets his pilot friend Clyde Mazer, a drunken, brash Texan who takes Wilson under his wing as they fly some of the most dangerous routes in the world. Wilson repeatedly recalls the series of events that has brought him back to this place—his brief captivity in Vietnam, his estrangement from his wife and her subsequent suicide, his affair with Marta—and he wonders at the way the events have "all kept their shape inside him": "They whispered to him, touched his eyes, and he knew they did not persist on their own, they did not preserve their own lives."

When he and Clyde fly into a whiteout, the two crash far from safety. They are able to dig their way into a snow bank and stay warm for a time, though starvation in the desolate area is imminent. Wilson listens to the elements outside, and his future becomes clear to him: The detritus of his life is cast off; he considers his fate and gives himself up bodily to Clyde, a symbolic gesture that might save Clyde's life, though the implication is that both perish. Even as he dies of his own volition, Wilson has succeeded in removing the clutter from his world.

Though the symbolism of the sun dogs and the significance of Wilson's demise is apparent in the narrative, the events that accrete to form Wilson's worldview are more subtle and thorough in defining Wilson's life. His captivity at the hands of the Vietcong is mentioned repeatedly, though the flashbacks never obtrude fully into the present until his final epiphany in the ice cave when he realizes that his own life is coming to an end. Also, his relationship with Beth, particularly her death, which always threatens to emerge into the narrative's foreground and undermine Wilson's attempt at reordering his life, is held in abeyance for a time by his purely sexual relationship with Marta. Ultimately all relationships, including that with Clyde Mazer, perhaps Wilson's

staunchest ally throughout, fail. Still Wilson is able to reconcile himself, in a final selfless action, to the memories that mediate his yearning for a simpler life, the very reason he has returned to Alaska.

COUNTRYMEN OF BONES

In the first of Butler's novels that explores a topic entirely apart from the Vietnam experience, the author shifts his focus to the advent of the atomic age and the juxtaposition of that irresistible force to an archaeologist's historically important find in the Alamogordo desert. The two principal characters' points of view are rendered in alternating omniscient vignettes: Darrell Reeves, an archaeologist who listens to the B-29s making their practice runs in the days before his site would become ground zero, delves into a five-hundred-year-old history that bears current significance; two hundred miles to the north Lloyd Coulter, the Los Alamos scientist who would become Reeves's competitor for the love of Anna Brown, works with J. Robert Oppenheimer to solve the mystery of the atom.

The novel is as important for the characterization of Darrell and Lloyd as it is for its plot, which interweaves historical fact with the mystery of what lies beneath, a theme that manifests itself often in Butler's fiction, particularly as an exploration of the masked or hidden identities of many of his characters. The two men are the embodiment of the past and the future. Lloyd has been seduced by the bomb's power, by what he has helped to create, and as a result eventually finds himself capable of Anna Brown's rape. Darrell represents the past, which Lloyd hopes to obliterate in one final and decisive show of force. When the two first meet, Lloyd expresses his disdain for Darrell and his work: "Lloyd waited till Oppie and the archaeologist began to move toward the jeep, the archaeologist's two assistants tagging after him. Then Lloyd stepped to the hole and spat on the skull."

Darrell has been given mere weeks to complete his excavation, and the two parallel plots are interwoven in an increasingly tight spiral until they converge, as they must, in one final confrontation between Darrell and Lloyd. As the time for the bomb's trial nears, Darrell scrapes away layers of the desert to gradually reveal a scene of importance exceeding anything he has known. What he thought was a relatively simple "death cult" that was something of an enigma in the desert becomes a link to the events he is about to witness: the Aztecs who had held the Spanish in awe for their power to bring death are now the Americans who are captivated by the power of the atom. As Darrell tells his assistants, thus foreshadowing the events about to unfold at their site, "The death was new and unimaginable and after that the Indians were never the same." In much the same way what Lloyd has wrought will change the world forever, and he becomes as power-hungry as the Spanish; like the Spanish, he is destined to be vanquished by his own overweening pride.

The plot takes on biblical proportions when Darrell and Anna (who returns to the excavation after being raped by Lloyd) escape into the mountains to avoid the explosion. Lloyd, who sees the blast now as an opportunity to redeem himself for giving in to the madness of his power, sacrifices his own life in an attempt to save them. The scene recalls Sodom and Gomorrah—despite what Lloyd has told them of the magnitude of the impending explosion, Anna turns to face the blast—and as the bomb's glare dissipates, Darrell realizes that Anna's existence has been, for a few seconds, "wiped from his mind. . . . She was one person only, as was he. This thing filling the desert comprehended nations, races, worlds. . . . He took her hand and her face turned to him and it was blank, benumbed, as if she'd just been raped."

In drawing one last connection between what they have witnessed and what has gone before in Anna's relationship with Lloyd, Butler privileges the destructive potential of the bomb over even the relationships that exist, both between the men and Anna Brown and between the chief and those who have joined him in death in the desert. Although such a statement might suggest the ultimate ineffectuality of human relationships to slow the pace of history, Anna and Darrell are married, and they listen from their hotel room in New York City to the joyous sounds of the victory brought about by America's bombing of the Japanese in August 1945. The celebration is ambivalent for them, however; though the vision of the greatest destructive force the world has ever known has finally disappeared from their dreams, Darrell feels compelled to apologize to Anna for what she has been forced to witness.

ON DISTANT GROUND

On Distant Ground is the last installment in a trilogy loosely based on the Vietnam experience of Clifford Wilkes (*The Alleys of Eden*), Wilson Hand (*Sun Dogs,* 1982), and David Fleming. The novel details David Fleming's court martial and a search in the hours before the fall of Saigon for the son he never knew he had. Having been instrumental in the rescue of Wilson Hand from the Vietcong, David has gone on trial for impulsively commandeering a military helicopter and freeing Tuyen, a high-ranking Vietcong prisoner, from Con Son Island. His only reason for initiating the act is a graffito scrawled on a prison wall—"hygiene is healthful"—that David had noticed during his visit to the prison where Tuyen had been held captive.

Back in the United States David has a difficult time convincing the court martial that his actions were anything but treasonous. David had been involved in the death of a prisoner who may or may not have had information that would have released Wilson from the Vietcong, yet "now he was a crusader against the dirtiness of the Vietnam war and the faces stuffed tight in the gallery leaned forward and they shouted the silence of an indignant sympathy." Because of the media coverage and public opinion, however, David is given an honorable discharge without prison time.

During the psychologically trying period when his fate is being decided, David's wife, Jennifer, gives birth to a son; at the same time, spawned by incessant broadcasts of stories about the "children of dust" who are being airlifted to safety from Saigon as the North Vietnamese approach, David considers the circumstances surrounding his break from a wealthy, well-placed Vietnamese lover, Suong. In an impulse that David attributes to instinct he realizes that he must have a child—a boy—back in Vietnam. With the help of Trask, a friend in the CIA, David uses a fabricated identity to reenter the besieged Vietnamese city, find the boy, and bring him back to America.

Like many of the relationships Butler draws in his novels, the interaction between David and Tuyen, two men who would otherwise be sworn enemies, is more a result of happenstance and a subsequent exploration of the relationship that ensues rather than a measured, rational response on the part of David. David can little explain his actions to himself—in fact Butler's even-handed presentation of the character neither condemns nor condones the action but rather allows it to stand on its own—let alone to the military board that decides his fate. Still he believes in the goodness of the man he has helped escape.

When David and the boy are about to board a ship for Bangkok, they are captured by the North Vietnamese, who have overtaken Saigon and established their communist government. Tuyen, the man for whom David was a savior, has become Director of Security for Saigon, and their final confrontation fully reveals the absurdity of David's reasoning—Tuyen, it turns out, never wrote the graffito that David attributed to the man and that spawned his action—while also illustrating the essential humanity existing between individuals who must rely on one another for their lives.

The relationship between David and Khai, his son with Suong, who has died a political prisoner, overshadows even the life-and-death struggle he faces upon his capture. As David's own identity is intertwined with that of a man with whom he has exchanged only a few words in his life, so is the identity of the boy in question until David finally accepts the fact that the boy is his son. The important connection for David is not a biological one (in fact David sees no resemblance between the boy and himself and questions throughout whether the child is really his; twice he is determined to leave the boy behind and save himself) but a spiritual bond realized in an epiphany when David finally tells the boy that he is his father:

> For a moment there was nothing. David was conscious of the void about him. Speaking the words brought no feeling to him, nothing at all. . . . Then Khai moved. His arms stretched, his legs hooked themselves around David's waist, the boy pressed himself against David, clung to him, and David was lifted, his body felt light.

As with the body of Butler's fiction about the Vietnam experience, a central fact in the lives of these characters is the tenuous nature of identity and the myriad contexts through which that identity is created. If not for David's court martial, he would have had little reason to return to Vietnam to seek out a son who may or may not exist. The yearning that David feels is not, as he thinks on several occasions, for his relationship with Suong, but rather for the closure that will come when he is able to spiritually connect with the child whose existence came to him as a vision. The quest is not, as Joe Klein points out in a *New York Times* review, to set things right with the war, which will inevitably run its course with or without him; rather, "there is nostalgia here, nostalgia of an unlikely sort: not for innocence or youth, but for the complexity and absurdity, the emotional turbulence and the fractured, almost delirious self-importance of that time."

WABASH

In a retelling of the stories Butler heard from his mother during his post-Depression childhood, Jeremy and Deborah Cole eke out a living in Wabash, Illinois. Jeremy works for a steel-manufacturing plant whose employees are fortunate to have found work just three years removed from Black Tuesday. The town's economy relies solely on the plant, and Hagemeyer, the plant's owner, is seen by the workers as the epitome of the dream-quelling robber baron. To make matters worse, the Coles' relationship has been tested by the death of their three-year-old daughter. Only Deborah's closeness to her mother, four aunts, and a grandmother mitigates the pain and loss she feels in her relationship to Jeremy, although even those relationships are contentious and ultimately provide little comfort for her. In the novel's opening scene, when Deborah's eccentric Aunt Berenice (the woman commits suicide later in the narrative) climbs a tree and refuses to come down, the dichotomy of emotions underpinning the novel comes to the fore as "two opposing feelings that tugged her into silence: she was sad for her aunt, for the fearful impulses that sometimes drove her; and she was happy for her aunt, for her perch there above the hard times."

Berenice's driving impulses are the same ones that allow the sisters to ostracize one of their own, Deborah's Aunt Effie, for having converted to Catholicism. Deborah believes the woman is dead until she discovers otherwise from her grandmother; she now lives in nearby St. Louis as a spinster, though none of the sisters have spoken to her in decades. The only way Deborah's grandmother Birney can cope with the chaos she sees around her is through an eccentric act of her own: writing letters to the rats in her house as if they are villains who make her life difficult and who can be vanquished by language.

Jeremy's increasing interest in the plight of the plant's workers makes a reconciliation with Deborah even more difficult, and both protagonists find themselves focusing not on their relationship—though to be sure Deborah seeks reconciliation much more avidly than Jeremy—but on the problems that assail them from outside their marriage. The workers position themselves to take a stand against management, and when a friend of Jeremy's hangs himself as the only way out of his predicament and another is ferociously beaten, Jeremy decides that he must side with the "Reds."

Jeremy's dilemma is not the first time Butler has explored the political implications of such a stand. Before becoming a soldier in Vietnam, Clifford Wilkes, the army deserter in *The Alleys of Eden*, is drawn into the plight of the individual (in this case a government rather than management) by many of the same arguments that Jeremy hears thirty years before, a result of Butler's ability to work within the political and societal restraints he sees without giving in to the didacticism that might otherwise overwhelm the humanness of his characters. As Butler put it to Bonetti in an interview, "The reason I can be so effective in the realm of ideas and the reason I can be so effective in the realm of politics is that I ignore both of those things when I write." Indeed the historical realities from which Butler takes much of his content are rarely significant, in and of themselves, in the resolution of his relationships.

Understanding the grave danger Jeremy is in from his dealings with the workers' movement, Deborah begins to write her own letters to the rats. In the letters she insists that "you'll have to let go of Jeremy. . . . If I can't have my daughter and I can't have my aunts, I can at least have my husband. Please give him back to me. Please." And even though Jeremy's final act is to be the assassination of Hagemeyer, the reconciliation of Jeremy and Deborah is the primary resolution at the novel's conclusion; Deborah prevents her husband from killing Hagemeyer and the two leave town together to prevent Jeremy from being killed as an instigator.

Philip D. Beidler, the most cogent commentator on Butler's work and its importance in the canon of Vietnam fiction, sees *Wabash* not as a departure from the Vietnam experience but rather as a continuation of the mind-set that allows exploration of such psychically charged subject matter:

> In the self-conscious embrace in his fiction of distinctively American forms of literary-cultural myth, Butler continues in a major way the project of the main body of American writing of Vietnam, a literature that often achieves its finest insights through the calculated fusion of qualities of experiential truth telling with complex and ambitious new strategies of imaginative invention.

In the relationship of Jeremy and Deborah he sees not the overarching influence of history but rather "the old world and holy war of faith and the new world and holy war of labor become co-equal and co-valent, facing worlds of history, connected at their interfluence by the whole human drama of hatreds, violences, pains, lonely exclusions."

THE DEUCE

Despite the close affinity Butler has for his characters in his first five novels, the author moves away from the third-person omniscient point of view and takes on the voice of his protagonist for the first time in *The Deuce.* Butler sees the move as one that reclaimed his roots as an actor and eschewed the more plot-driven narratives that were an analogue to a playwriting career that, the author admits, never took off. The book, he says, "grew out of a curiosity of what might have happened to David Fleming's son (Khai, the son of Fleming and the Vietnamese Suong in *On Distant Ground*) when he came back to the United States. He started shaping himself. I just felt that I needed to hear his voice directly." It was also the first-person narrative in *The Deuce,* Butler recounts, that "convinced me that I could write short stories."

"The Deuce" is Butler's Amerasian protagonist, a seventeen-year-old boy who recounts his tripartite existence—as Võ Đình Thanh, the Vietnamese child; as Anthony James Hatcher, the American whose father has rescued him from a squalid existence in Saigon; and as "The Deuce," the identity fleshed out in the streets of New York—as he lives life always through the lens of the *bui doi,* a "child of dust." His first words in the narrative hint at the difficulty of his situation: "I wish it was simple just to say who I am, just to say my name is so-and-so and that makes you think of a certain kind of person and that would be me." The various names the narrator is given (each symbolic of a different identity) only exacerbate an already confusing existence, although, as Milton J. Bates points out, "The Deuce can always be in two places at once, is always divided, but by the end of the novel he has taken on this duality not as an impediment to his identity, but as his identity."

The narrator's first recollection is as a six year old when Kenneth Hatcher, his American father, appears in his mother's home in Vietnam. The boy's mother, a prostitute, tells him in broken English to leave the room, and the narrator wonders, "If she'd tried as hard as me to learn English, maybe things would've turned out differently that day. Who can love a woman who talks like that?" Later the narrator divulges the irony that it was his mother who had forced him to learn English from her johns, a skill that stands him in good stead when he travels to America. Hatcher, having seen the circumstances under which the boy and his mother live, buys the boy from Nghi, his former lover, and takes him to New Jersey. Hatcher offers the boy a "normal" American life—taking him to Yankee Stadium, Coney Island, the Bronx Zoo—although the young Tony's dual identity forces him away from his father when Hatcher makes a deprecating remark about his Vietnamese mother.

Despite the much different contexts implied by Saigon and New York City, the two worlds the boy has inhabited bear a striking resemblance to one another in their perpetuation of alienation, violence, and chaos: the boy, like his mother, moves out on his own at sixteen; he witnesses a mother selling her young son for drugs; he kills a pederast, Treen, in recompense for the death of his friend Joey Cipriani. But even after these experiences on his odyssey through the streets of New York, the narrator's earlier question regarding his identity carries a haunting echo through to the end of the narrative: "Who do I seem like to you? I listen to myself talk sometimes and I say, Who is this kid?" The question is of the utmost important to "The Deuce," who undergoes a transformation celebrating the two distinct personas that the boy, through no choice of his own, has been given:

> And now I know what voice I have, and who it is I am. A guy on a beach in Vũng Tàu tells me I'm Vietnamese. A civics teacher in Point Pleasant tells me I'm American. Kenneth James Hatcher tells me I'm his son, and I'm the son of a woman named Võ Xuân Nghi who's lost somewhere half a world away. I'm a lot of things but I'm one thing, and I have no doubt about that. I'm The Deuce.

Such a strong statement of identity is engendered by the protagonist's unmediated voice.

For the first time the reader has been invited into the fiction, into the dream space of the first-person narrator. That newfound narrative freedom gave Butler the voice he would need to write his most critically acclaimed work.

A GOOD SCENT FROM A STRANGE MOUNTAIN AND *TABLOID DREAMS*

On the surface Butler's two short story collections have little in common. The first, *A Good Scent from a Strange Mountain,* is a series of fifteen vignettes connected by the Vietnamese characters' displacement from their homeland and their attempts at forging new lives for themselves in an alien culture. *Tabloid Dreams* (1996), a collection that took its ideas from tabloid headlines, resulted from an epiphany Butler had while standing in line at the grocery store. Much more a flight of fancy (the stories' titles include "Woman Uses Glass Eye to Spy on Philandering Husband," "Jealous Husband Returns in Form of Parrot," and "JFK Secretly Attends Jackie Auction"), its characters are, in their way, no less poignant than those drawn in *Good Scent,* a collection that has been recognized as the more serious of the works. Despite their obvious differences, Butler himself sees "a great deal of connection between the two," drawing comparisons that are apt for all of his fiction: "You've got a bunch of voices of people who are exiled, in some way, who are searching for an identity. The yearning for self is in all of those stories, and they are all outsiders trying to find a way back to some kind of sense of belonging and connection and identity."

That identity in *Good Scent* is circumscribed through the lives of people—North and South Vietnamese, Buddhist and Catholic, rich and poor—whose lives are defined by their search for context and wholeness: from "Open Arms," the story of a man who "fought for my country long enough to lose my wife to another man, a cripple," to "Preparation," the poignant tale of a woman who revisits her friendship with a dead woman while preparing the body for burial. In "Crickets," the first story written for the collection (at the request of National Public Radio's Alan Cheuse for the series *The Sound of Writing*), a man who wants to teach his son the art of cricket fighting recalls the conflict that is an inextricable part of the characters' lives. There are two types of crickets, the man explains to his son: the charcoal cricket is large and strong, but slow and easily confused; the fire cricket is small, smart, and quick. As a boy he had cheered for the fire crickets. Despite the man's obvious passion for the Vietnamese folkway, his son is more concerned with a grass stain on his new sneakers than with learning a bit of his father's past.

"Letters from My Father," the story most indicative of Butler's thoroughgoing attention to the plight of the Vietnamese in America, is narrated by a young girl who has been brought to America from Vietnam by her father, a former solider. The story reprises Butler's attention to the "children of dust," the ones who are left behind when their fathers return to their lives in America. The soldier, who struggles with the post-Vietnam bureaucracy to reclaim his daughter, calls the girl Fran, though "I wanted a name for Saigon and Trán was it." Fran recalls looking at a drawing in a bookstall on Nguyen Hue Street, a touching and frightening reminder of the contradictions that guide her life:

> You look once and you see a beautiful woman sitting at her mirror, but then you look again and you see the skull of a dead person, no skin on the face, just the wide eyes of the skull and the bared teeth. We were like that, the children of dust in Saigon. At one look we were Vietnamese and at another look we were American, and after that you couldn't get your eyes to stay still when they turned to us, they kept seeing first one thing and then another.

Despite her father's vehement insistence that she be allowed to immigrate to the United States, the girl notices that when she finally arrives in America her father's passion to be with his daughter has ebbed. She reads the letters he wrote to her and to the government, and she decides as she hides in a storage shack awaiting his return from work that "I will let him see me here, and I will ask him to talk to me like in these letters, like when he was so angry with some stranger that he knew what to say." The girl's struggle for identity, her bittersweet recollection, and the lack of closure provided by her passage to America are themes repeated both throughout the stories in the collection and in the novels.

The title story, in which an old man awaiting death must reconcile himself to the problems his grandson faces, appropriately concludes the collection as the old man recalls his time with Ho Chi Minh in Escoffier's kitchen in London. The seemingly simple connection Butler draws between the two men hints at a much larger truth and becomes the underpinning of the story cycle when the old man dreams of Ho with white powder on his hands, beckoning him to give news of his life. In his final vision the old man realizes what it is that Ho has forgotten in his quest for the perfect glaze fondant: "He should be using granulated sugar. I was only a washer of dishes but I did listen carefully when Monsieur Escoffier spoke. I wanted to understand everything. His kitchen was full of such smells that you knew you had to understand everything or you would be incomplete forever." The passage, like the collection itself, is rendered in fitting understatement, the desires of the characters apparent but held in check by the author's confident rhetorical restraint.

Although *Tabloid Dreams* does not proceed with the continuity that exists in *Good Scent,* the stories are held together by their origin outside the realm of possibility. At the same time, however, the characters are humanized and the situations made plausible through a language that at once asks the reader to suspend disbelief while reveling in the surface absurdity of the plotlines. In "Woman Uses Glass Eye to Spy on Philandering Husband," Loretta is verbally abused by her husband, who has been cheating on her. When she realizes that she can remove her glass eye and still see through it, she takes the opportunity to witness one of her husband's trysts with his lover. Instead of gaining some satisfaction from catching him in the act, Loretta, a court stenographer, is helpless to ignore what she sees. Similarly "Woman Loses Cookie Bake-Off, Sets Self on Fire" and "Woman Struck by Car Turns into Nymphomaniac" explore the human side of pain and loss, the "exile" of characters who are torn from their daily lives by random events sensationalized through the characters' actions. The protagonist who immolates herself in a high-stakes cookie bake-off begins her narrative by recalling without irony or self-indulgent grief that "the day my husband died, I baked a batch of cookies." Despite that loss—and her hope that her husband's death may be in part redeemed by a $100,000 victory in the bake-off—the narrator loses the contest to her best friend. In much the same way, Butler's nymphomaniacal protagonist is an example of the tragicomic impulse that pervades the collection's stories. The narrator, a publisher, offers a self-reflexive narrative that explores the tabloid market and ends with her insistence to a tabloid editor that he make love to her while she embeds a chunk of meteor (a prop from yet another tabloid story) in his skull.

Although separated by four years, a world of sensibility, and another of Butler's experimental novels (*They Whisper,* 1994), the two collections are important in Butler's body of work both for their continued exploration of first-person narration—until *The Deuce,* the novel that preceded *Good Scent,* Butler had written consistently in the third-person omniscient—and for the ways in which the snapshot vignettes that Butler creates in both *Good Scent* and *Tabloid Dreams* influence the later novels. The move was perhaps natural for a writer as introspective as Butler, although he credits his wife, Elizabeth Dewberry, herself a writer, with helping him find a voice, Butler implies, that manifests itself only after a maturation process on the part of the artist:

> Art does not come from the mind; arts does not come from the rational faculties. You do not will a work of art into being. Art comes from the place where you dream. . . . Ikiro Kurosawa, the great Japanese film director, said that to be an artist means never to avert your eyes. Artists struggle all the time not to avert their eyes, not to look into that white-hot center of themselves. . . . I didn't write in a woman's voice until I was forty-six, when I wrote *Good Scent.* So it took a lot of life experience, because you do have to absorb both the outward and the inward.

Both the narrative structure and the voice of these short story collections allow the author even greater latitude in exploring the voices that would come to him during a phase of his writing career that is as rich and varied in its themes and means of expression as it is passionate for the characters who inhabit those stories.

THEY WHISPER

The novel that followed *Good Scent* was as different from Butler's earlier work as the follow-up, *Tabloid Dreams,* would be from the author's seventh novel, a blunt exploration of sexuality and identity. In *They Whisper,* a book that Butler would deem "very risky," Ira Holloway details his life wholly in the context of the women he has known. Surrounding those recollections is the story of his relationship in the present with Fiona Price, a woman he meets in Greenwich Village. Fiona, who would admit to Ira that, for reasons that become apparent in one of Ira's many visions, she has had many sexual experiences of her own, cannot help becoming jealous when she discovers the extent to which Ira worships and defines himself through women. Ira's recollections build on one another, seemingly at random, until they finally drive a wedge between Fiona and himself.

While Ira's days are spent in recollection that is often lugubrious in its longing, Fiona finds that her intense relationship with Ira, including the revelation that she was molested as a child by her father, grounds her in religion, an impulse that deepens with the birth of their son, John. Ira understands Fiona's shame and anger without having heard it explicitly; his preternatural recognition of her pain is a part of the life that Ira creates for himself in the narrative, ostensibly a result of his profound understanding of women: "How is it that I came to know about her father? Most of it flows from her inner voice that I heard in our intimacy, the woman voice whispering to me." Ira's reality is actualized not through language, the touchstone for Butler and his characters throughout the body of his work to this point, but through experience and a quantum leap into the mind of the character. An experience at the altar, mediated by Ira in one of the novel's many interior monologues, gravitates as always toward the sexual. When Fiona takes communion, Ira enters her consciousness and speaks in Fiona's voice: *"I can feel my blood speed up, pounding in my head so hard I am afraid I will faint, but I close my eyes and concentrate on the body of Christ in my mouth and it is as light as a soul and I close my mouth and hold Him inside me."*

The marriage of Ira and Fiona, undermined by Fiona's increasingly negative response to Ira's past and her belief that Ira yearns more for the women of his past than he does for her, disintegrates as Ira's recollections intensify. The narrative is framed, after all its many digressions and salacious vignettes, by Ira's staid recollection of Karen Granger, a young woman whose very bones captured Ira's imagination

twenty-five years before the narrative begins, even before the ten-year-old Ira Holloway "knew there was another part of girls that would one day whisper to me." The young boy is titillated by the thought of seeing Karen's bones light up in an X-ray machine that checks the fit of clients' shoes at his uncle's shoe store. As Ira ruminates at the novel's conclusion on the people who have come and gone from his life, he offers a bittersweet conclusion to his reverie: "I do not know if Karen Granger's lungs now are whole, or if her blood is whole, or if her bones are whole. I only know that, as I stand on the beach at Puerto Vallarta and watch a parasailor glide out over the bay, in some less definable part of me, I am not."

Despite the novel's content, which little resembles anything Butler had written to this point, the narrative does contain certain parallels to the previous work: the protagonist's yearning for something unattainable; the interaction of language and memory in a narrative that creates meaning only through the sum of its components, with plot secondary to the relationships that are articulated; the search for identity by people who share different cultures (in this case, the ideological difference between Ira and Fiona and their son, who, despite being wholly American, is caught between two worlds, like many "children of dust").

Jane Smiley, who reviewed the novel in the *New York Times*, deemed it "a shape-shifting narrative that lingers in the reader's moral consciousness and memory." Yet she also expresses a deep ambivalence for the work that

taught me that it has been the fate of many men of the Vietnam generation to live the realities of imperialism, both abroad and in the home, without conviction, but with seething self-doubt and longing. For that reason and for that reason alone, *They Whisper* is a fully realized and important expression of our era, one that deserves a wide, if unavoidably ambivalent, audience.

THE DEEP GREEN SEA

In what Butler has described as a "Sophoclean tragedy," Ben Cole (the son of Jeremy and Deborah Cole, the protagonists of *Wabash*) returns to Vietnam to confront and to quiet the ghosts that have haunted him since the war. He meets Tien, a beautiful young woman twenty years his junior, and they quickly fall in love. She regales him with stories of the creation of Vietnam, and the legend is played out with Ben's imminent death and Tien's symbolic rebirth. From the outset Ben has a nagging sense, not unlike the prescient vision of David Fleming regarding his own son in *On Distant Ground,* that he could be the woman's father, though he knows that the odds against such a thing are astronomical. There were thousands of prostitutes in that part of Saigon, he reasons; still, he must find out the truth for himself before he can continue to live as Tien's lover.

Although the novel's outcome is apparent from early in the narrative, the story is significant for its two voices—Ben's and Tien's—which interweave and gain strength from one another as they relate a tale of unbearable love at the same time that the unsavory truth unravels before their eyes. Ben, foreshadowing his later discovery, sees in Tien the second chance that he thought he would never be given: "For Christ's sake, to be able to start again from a place where there's nothing to remember, nothing to ask about, nothing but what's there for both of you right in that moment, without any history at all, that's almost too good to be true." Later, as Ben alternately believes the worst and hopes for the best, he thinks, "If there is some higher power in the universe that gives a damn about guilt and shame and forgiveness, then surely . . . I've been forgiven." The passage recalls the naturalistic prose of Stephen Crane (particularly his diatribe against the gods of nature that prevent rescue in "The Open Boat"), and Ben's excessive hope is mingled with a slowly revealed subtext of tragedy. Of course

the story is too good to be true, and Ben's belief in the cleansing power of his love for Tien is an irony that heightens both the tragedy of the novel's conclusion and the miracle of Tien's survival, when she gives birth to the daughter Ben will never know.

Tien relies on her spirituality for survival and to attenuate her feelings of isolation. Her mother, a prostitute, disappeared and insisted that Tien consider her dead, and Tien struggles against the duality of her being even as she manages to deny herself entrance to that identity: "I could keep my American self hidden because it never really existed. It died with my father even before I was born. I had no father." Even in Ben's presence, Tien prays to the spirit of her departed father—whom her mother has told her is dead, effectively orphaning the girl—and discusses her own nebulous history with Ben. Her sole means of constructing identity is through her relationship with Ben; only by his death, it seems, is she able to make peace with her past, present, and future—none of which she can control. Finally she reconciles the contradictions of her relationship with Ben in a prayer that recognizes and embraces the tragedy of her situation. The story has come full circle: Ben is dead—as Tien has been led to believe that he was all along—and Ben has been given a daughter, the result of a loving, doomed relationship with his own daughter.

MR. SPACEMAN

In a novel that is both a sharp departure from the tragedy of *Deep Green Sea* and a continuation of one of the headline-grabbing stories published in *Tabloid Dreams, Mr. Spaceman* details the life and love of Desi, an extraterrestrial whose mission, described in the mock seriousness and stilted language of the science-fiction genre, is to come to Earth on the eve of the new millennium, portentously described as "the end of the revolution of their planet around their star that they have reckoned to be the two thousandth from the birth of a mysterious and influential figure in their history," and to divulge to "the inhabitants of this planet this great and fundamental truth of the cosmos." Despite overtones suggesting both a parody of the science-fiction genre as well as another means of access into the mind of the protagonist, Butler once again tackles serious issues, thus belying the narrative's comedic overtones: Desi yearns to understand the environment into which he is thrown; in the process, he falls in love with Edna Bradshaw, an Alabamian whose country charm melds with Desi's exoticism to create the novel's seriocomic tension; and finally Desi realizes that there is much more to know about humans than he had first supposed.

Desi's contact with humans primarily involves twelve people drawn from all walks of life. The narrative centers on their experiences, to which Desi listens patiently; more importantly, the language he hears washes over him as he prepares himself for his final fate on Earth. One of the travelers, Citrus, assumes that Desi is Christ (certainly the twelve travelers, latter-day disciples, suggest that this could be the case) and that his visitation is the Second Coming, and a soliloquy—through which the stories of all the travelers are told—reveals Citrus as a woman who associates the Bible and religion with sexuality. Desi plays the role of savior haltingly, and only at the novel's conclusion, when the extraterrestrial has appeared in New Orleans at the stroke of midnight and is upstaged by three women dressed as nuns who flash the crowd, does Desi take his rightful place in Jackson Square, sitting at a table next to a sign that reads "TALK WITH A SPACEMAN."

He bides his time on Earth doing

what I have always done. . . . Some people think I really am a spaceman, an incarnate glimpse into the infinite and mysterious elaboration of the universe. Some people think I am just one of them

in costume, an Earthbound creature caught in time and yearning his way along. Look around. Listen to each other. I am both, and so are you.

The scene is surreal, though noticing parallels to other of Butler's fiction, including the Vietnam novels, is unavoidable. Desi, despite his exotic provenance, is simply a character whose life is based on an economy of desire and a quest for identity in the context of human relationships.

FAIR WARNING

Butler's latest effort was conceived when Francis Ford Coppola commissioned a short story for *Zoetrope: All Story* about a female auctioneer after he had seen Sharon Stone perform in the role for a charity auction. The story was part of an entry that won the National Fiction Award in 2001.

Amy Dickerson, the story's forty-year-old protagonist and narrator, is a successful auctioneer at Nichols and Gray, a smallish New York auction house that holds its own against the larger and more recognizable Sotheby's and Christie's. Reflecting on her childhood in Texas, Amy suggests in the novel's opening line that "perhaps my fate was sealed when I sold my three-year-old sister." As innocuous as that simple transaction was, Amy's life has become a series of events characterized by commodities and the cost that the market will bear. She attributes the impulse to collect to "shopping pheromones. They are spoken of in no book, but I know they exist," though the relationships that she develops during the brief span of narrative time behave under disturbingly similar rules of procurement.

Amy is caught between two worlds, one that cherishes valuable objects and one that is wary of the machinations of a system that perpetuates the value of such objects. Though she loves her job and understands the collector's passion for things, she realizes that "my own passion flows both ways—through the objects desired and through the one who desires it. I become part of both. I value and I am valued. I collect and I am collected." In one of her first meetings with Alain Bouchard, the suave Frenchman who would become her suitor, Amy stands on a balcony in Manhattan and cannot help herself from mentally cataloging the objects that surround her.

As passionate as she is about collecting and about the inherent value of things, she seems at times not to gain any pleasure from them. One in particular bothers her a great deal: When she is asked by her mother to appraise and sell her father's belongings shortly after his death, she comes across a portrait of her father. Although it has some value as an art object, the painting takes on a value apart from its "thingness" and becomes a simulacrum for her relationship with her father. He lives (or at least her memories of him live) most strongly through the object. When confronted with memories of her past, Amy the sophisticated New York auctioneer becomes the little girl seeking her father's approval. The language she uses is transformed by the direction the conversation assumes: "I loved Mama. And Daddy, of course. I guess loving Daddy was pretty much what all the crap between Missy and me was about. The crap with Mama, too, though the *loving* part got pretty complicated there."

It seems in fact that all of Amy's relationships with men are beset by some revelation—in Butler's art world, perhaps it would be called an "imperfection"—that undermines Amy's interest. At the outset she is smitten by "Dark Eyes," a man named Trevor Martin, who is himself interested enough in Amy to bid several thousand dollars on a dinner with her after a rather perfunctory affair that reaches its climax in an elevator. Angered by his presumption, Amy dines alone. Similarly her relationship with the stylish Alain, who buys Nichols and Gray

and targets Amy as his lover, reveals itself as nothing more than a collecting expedition for the Frenchman. She realizes that a lute Alain has purchased and then offered to her is nothing more than a prelude to seduction. His gestures become absurd to her, and when, in his upscale Paris apartment, she finds evidence of a catalog of Alain's former lovers, she is finally capable of separating herself from the world of commodity and offering herself to the world, pressing her naked body to the glass in Alain's Paris apartment. Looking at the Venus that adorns Alain's wall, Amy "understood now the look in her upturned face. She was alone in the world, but she was still rapturous with love. Even in the dim light I could see the twinkle in her eyes."

The resolution Amy feels in her identification with the Venus on the wall, one of many objects Alain has collected in his lifetime, is important not only for Butler's character but for the author himself. Devoid of context, art objects—as much as words on a page—lose their meaning; a comparison to Butler's earlier extraterrestrial protagonist, Desi, is apt, as the two much disparate characters face the dilemma of how best to construct one's identity in a world that is or has become alien to them. Butler seizes an image that has been trivialized and deeply inculcated into our society, that of the object for the object's sake, and gives it voice. Amy stands naked before the world declaring her innate value not as object, but as sentient being. The words she speaks are given meaning not merely by their existence, but through their ability to mediate and to communicate the intimate connection between Amy's deepest desires and the outside world.

CONCLUSION

Robert Olen Butler's work is significant in contemporary American literature not only for its passion of expression, but for its eclecticism and the far-ranging sensibility of a versatile author whose writing, despite an often apparent Vietnam context, adamantly defies classification. In twelve works of fiction, plumbing the depths of the "dream space" that is fundamental to his writing process, Butler has written through the minds of men and women, Americans and Vietnamese, extraterrestrials and low-market tabloid fodder. The voices that manifest themselves are a combination of the author's experience and the "yearning that constitutes the center of gravity" of his work. Butler discusses his use in the last decade of the first-person narrator in terms of his increasingly effective response to his unconscious:

> I had written enough books from my unconscious that I was able to get deeper and deeper into my unconscious, and if you do that, finally you break through to a place where you're neither male nor female, black nor white, Jew nor Muslim, Vietnamese or American. You're human. And your authenticity comes from there. You can draw that up through the vessels of characters who, on the surface, seem quite different from one another and from yourself.

When discussing the direction his fiction might take in the future, Butler is noncommittal, pointing to his notion that he will allow the work to come to him. In an attempt at inviting others to view and understand his writing process, in 2001 he undertook an online writing project at Florida State University. The first of its kind, the project allowed the audience to watch a well-known author at work through the lens of technology, illustrating the value Butler places on art and on the writer's inevitable and important connection to other artists and to the reader: "A work of art is not meant to be understood in an analytical or abstract or intellectual way. You are meant to thrum to a work of art. There's a resonance, a harmonics that's set up in you. That's why fiction exists as a necessary mode of discourse unto itself."

Selected Bibliography

WORKS OF ROBERT OLEN BUTLER

FICTION

The Alleys of Eden. New York: Horizon, 1981.

Sun Dogs. New York: Horizon, 1982.

Countrymen of Bones. New York: Horizon, 1983.

On Distant Ground. New York: Knopf, 1985.

Wabash. New York: Knopf, 1987.

The Deuce. New York: Simon & Schuster, 1989.

A Good Scent from a Strange Mountain. New York: Holt, 1992.

They Whisper. New York: Holt, 1994.

Tabloid Dreams. New York: Holt, 1996.

Deep Green Sea. New York: Holt, 1997.

Mr. Spaceman. New York: Grove Press, 2000.

Fair Warning. New York: Atlantic Monthly Press, 2002.

OTHER WORKS

"Moving Day." *Redbook* 143:92–93 (October 1974).

"Upriver to Dexter." *Redbook* 145:92–93 (June 1975).

"At the Sound of the Tone, Charlie." *Cosmopolitan* 186:198, 220, 222 (January 1979).

"Salem." *Mississippi Review* 21:193–201 (spring 1993).

"Three Ways to Die from the Fifties." *Harper's* 287:31–32 (October 1993).

"The Handwriting on the Wall." *Virginia Quarterly Review* 70:51–58 (winter 1994).

"Fair Warning." *Zoetrope: All Story* 4:cover, 5–13 (summer 2000).

"Rafferty and Josephine." *Zoetrope: All Story* 5:37–47 (spring 2001).

CRITICAL AND BIOGRAPHICAL STUDIES

Bates, Milton J. *The Wars We Took to Vietnam: Cultural Conflict and Storytelling.* Berkeley: University of California Press, 1996.

Beidler, Philip D. *Re-Writing America: Vietnam Authors in Their Generation.* Athens, Ga.: University of Georgia Press, 1991.

Christopher, Renny. *The Viet Nam War/The American War: Images and Representations in Euro-American and Vietnamese Exile Narratives.* Amherst, Mass.: University of Massachusetts Press, 1995.

Klein, Joe. "Soldiers and Doctors." *New York Times Book Review,* April 21, 1985, p. 26. (Review of *On Distant Ground.*)

Pratt, John Clark. "Turning the Inner Landscapes of Robert Olen Butler." *Bloomsbury Review* 15:21–22 (January–February 1995).

Smiley, Jane. "Something Is Wrong with This Life." *New York Times Book Review,* February 13, 1994, p. 12. (Review of *They Whisper.*)

INTERVIEWS

Bonetti, Kay. "An Interview with Robert Olen Butler." *Missouri Review* 17, no. 3:83–106 (1994). Reprinted in *Conversations with American Novelists: The Best Interviews from* The Missouri Review *and the American Audio Prose Library.* Edited by Kay Bonetti, Greg Michalson, Speer Morgan, Jo Sapp, and Sam Stowers. Columbia, Mo.: University of Missouri Press, 1997. Pp. 201–216.

Brown, W. Dale. "Robert Olen Butler: On Madness and Longing." In *Of Fiction and Faith: Twelve American Writers Talk about Their Vision and Work.* Edited by Dale W. Brown. Grand Rapids, Mich.: Eerdmans, 1997. Pp. 55–70.

Haydl, Judith. "An Interview with Robert Olen Butler." *Xavier Review* 16, no. 1:5–18 (1996).

Parrill, William. *Louisiana Literature: A Review of Literature and Humanities* 12:69–83 (spring 1995).

Saritsky, Michael. "Robert Olen Butler: A Pulitzer Profile." In *The Future of Southern Letters.* Edited by Jefferson Humphries and John Lowe. New York: Oxford University Press, 1996. Pp. 155–169.

Smith, Patrick A. Unpublished interview. March 3, 2002. Monticello, Florida. (Quotations in this essay not from Butler's works are from this interview unless otherwise indicated.)

—*PATRICK A. SMITH*

Peter Cameron

1959–

FOR THOSE FAMILIAR with Peter Cameron's work, it is no surprise that the author first began writing stories and plays in London, England. His most critically acclaimed work recalls the gentle, character-centered treatments of E. M. Forster and shares both an affinity for and a fascination with the foreign, even when it exists in close proximity to home. At the same time, much of Cameron's shorter work shows the strong influence of American minimalists, such as Raymond Carver. Driven perhaps by Forster's edict to "only connect," Cameron seeks to bridge a number of different cultures in his work. He does this in both literal and metaphorical ways, thereby calling into question the objective truth of "culture." Along the way, he demonstrates how identity can be interpreted as a creative enterprise informed by a myriad of external and internal forces. Perhaps Cameron's greatest achievement is that he can perform this rather postmodern task without sacrificing the essential humanity that informs his characters, adrift and unmoored though they may be.

For many of Cameron's characters, the creation of a stable, desired identity is of paramount concern. This is particularly true in the novel *Andorra* (1997), in which the main character, Alexander Fox, arrives in the title country as a blank slate of sorts. Though we know Fox is in a fugue state, we are kept in quiet suspense for much of the book. This motif of the elusive character finds even more direct treatment in Cameron's novel *The City of Your Final Destination* (2002). Here a graduate student seeks to obtain authorization for a biography of a little-known author. In doing so, he encounters all kinds of obstacles and dif-

ficulties when dealing with the writer's surviving relatives. Facts about the author's actual life remain scarce throughout most of the book, even as readers follow the lives of those who were closest to him. The central irony—that the closer readers get to knowing a character, the further they may veer from the truth—provides one of the postmodern twists central to much of Cameron's work.

With that in mind, the title of Cameron's collected short stories, *The Half You Don't Know: Selected Stories* (1997), seems appropriately cryptic. Throughout his stories, characters are only partially revealed. Cameron's tight control of exposition, dialogue, and descriptive detail owe much to American minimalism. Even so, his evocation of Mary Shelley's *Frankenstein* at the front of the collection establishes a gothic context for the question of identity: "I now hasten to the more moving part of my story. I shall relate events, that impressed me with feelings which, from what I had been, have made me what I am." Are these events the same as those promised by the title of the collection, or is Cameron playing a semantic game with the reader? Which "half" will be revealed in the stories?

If politics exist in the work of Peter Cameron, they are clearly rooted in identity. That said, it is important to note further that they are rooted in individual identity; cultural identity per se does not seem to engage Cameron or his characters, at least not substantively. This may explain why Cameron, despite being both politically and socially active within the gay world, has not achieved more critical success within that culture's literary world. His novel *Leap*

Year (1990), written in the same serialized style as Armistead Maupin's San Francisco–based Tales of the City books, did not attract nearly the same devoted mass-market following on the East Coast. Likewise, his elegiac and critically acclaimed novella *The Weekend* (1994), though similar in tone and sensibility to Michael Cunningham's Pulitzer Prize–winning *The Hours,* did not establish him as a major figure in literary academe. (The temporal similarity between the two titles, it should be noted, seems entirely coincidental.)

Like the actual country of Andorra itself, Cameron's place on the literary map may be small yet significant. As fictionalized by Cameron, however, Andorra provides a backdrop of fantastic potential. There is a sensation of being "on the verge" without its common corollary feeling of marginality. The terraced landscape of Cameron's Andorra offers a literal representation of an author working on many metaphoric levels. What some critics have called "incompleteness" and "alienation" translate into opportunity for many of his characters. As the title *The Half You Don't Know* suggests, there may be much more here than at first meets the eye.

BACKGROUND AND UPBRINGING

Peter Cameron was born into a rather typical suburban American family in Pompton Plains, New Jersey, on November 29, 1959. The third of four children, he had two older sisters and a younger brother. His father, Donald Cameron, worked as an economist with Chase Manhattan Bank, while his mother, Sally Cameron, stayed at home to raise the children. Cameron began his education in the public elementary school system.

At the age of nine, Cameron moved with his family to London, where his father had been transferred to work for an English bank. He was enrolled in the American School, a private school with a more diverse and creatively stimulating curriculum than he had found in the United States. There Cameron began to nurture his creative talents. The city offered him a sense of liberation and constant excitement. He recalls writing a lot of plays during that period, which might have influenced his affinity for dialogue.

By the time he returned to the United States, Cameron had already recognized his love of literature. After graduating from high school in his hometown, Pompton Plains, Cameron pursued undergraduate studies at Hamilton College in New York. Initially, he enrolled in poetry workshops, but he was soon drawn to fiction and the short story format. He majored in English literature, all the while keeping an eye on many of the American writers publishing their work in current magazines, particularly Ann Beattie's work in *The New Yorker.* He began submitting his own fiction to the magazine, recognizing a common undercurrent with the minimalist realism of many stories published there at the time. Though he was still an undergraduate, Cameron's work drew the attention of the prestigious magazine's editors, who tempered their rejection letters with words of encouragement. Wisely, Cameron persevered in his submissions.

In May 1983, one year after graduating from Hamilton, Cameron's short story "Memorial Day" was published in *The New Yorker.* At the time, Cameron was living in New York City and working as a subsidiary rights assistant at St. Martin's Press. Over the course of the next three years, Cameron published seven more short stories in *The New Yorker* and others in *The Kenyon Review, Mademoiselle,* and *Grand Street.* Two of his pieces, "Homework" and "Excerpts from Swan Lake," received the O. Henry Award and were anthologized in 1985 and 1986, respectively.

Cameron left St. Martin's Press after one year of employment, ostensibly so he would have more time to read and less opportunity to become embittered by the publishing industry.

He began work as a word processor for the Trust for Public Land, a nonprofit conservation agency in New York City. After a stay at the MacDowell Colony, a retreat center for artists, he assembled his first collection of short stories, *One Way or Another* (1986). The book received a modest amount of favorable critical attention amid acknowledgement of the author's relatively young age (twenty-six at the time). In 1987 Cameron was awarded a special Ernest Hemingway Foundation/PEN America Award citation for his first book of fiction. Following publication of the book, he also taught for one semester as an assistant professor at Oberlin College in Ohio. He found that teaching, like work in the publishing industry, did not particularly suit him.

Cameron returned to New York City to work on his second book, *Leap Year,* a rambling, plot-driven novel tailored to appear in serialized form throughout 1988 in the New York weekly newspaper *Seven Days.* He also received a grant from the National Endowment for the Arts. The book was something of a recycled effort; Cameron had written a novel featuring similar characters while in college. Aimed toward liberal-minded, alternative audiences, the series attracted a wider audience to Cameron's work and drew the attention of the gay subculture featured in the narrative.

Cameron began to pay more direct attention to the issues affecting the gay and lesbian subculture. He took a part-time job with the Lambda Legal Defense and Education Fund, a nonprofit group that offered legal counsel to gay-related organizations and individuals. Cameron wrote in the morning, then reported to the office for the afternoon. In an interview with Philip Gambone in *Something Inside: Conversations with Gay Fiction Writers* (1999), Cameron stated that through his work for Lambda, "I feel like I'm contributing to something that I believe in that's helping to change the world in a good way."

This deepening awareness of politics informed a number of stories that appeared in *Far-Flung* (1991), Cameron's second short story collection. This book reflected Cameron's development in terms of the length and complexity of his stories. Critics once again offered generous reviews of the work while noting that his characters often appeared to be trapped in their states of disconnection. Verging on disaffectedness, they resembled characters featured in the works of other young writers in the 1980s, most notably Bret Easton Ellis and Jay McInerney. Even so, Cameron's characters were beginning to show a stronger sense of self-awareness. One can also sense that he himself had begun to move beyond the limitations of the short story toward a more complex genre.

One of Cameron's longer stories, "Departing," established the framework for his subsequent novella, *The Weekend.* Cameron was intrigued by the characters and sought to explore their lives more fully after completing the original story. Reviewing *The Weekend,* critics compared Cameron more to Virginia Woolf and E. M. Forster than to his own contemporaries. This follows Cameron's own admission that, at the time, he was reading a great deal of British women's literature from the first half of the century. Perhaps because of that influence, he also did not write short stories at the time. Nevertheless, Cameron published *The Half You Don't Know: Selected Stories* in 1997. The book combined his best work from the two previous short story collections with two new pieces, the aforementioned "Departing" and "Aria."

In the same year, Cameron published *Andorra,* a fully realized novel that expanded on the themes of identity and displacement in unforeseen ways. With its somewhat experimental plot treatment and its surrealistic setting, *Andorra* garnered a great deal of critical praise. The book also moved Cameron a step away from becoming identified mainly as a "gay writer," despite a pivotal homosexual encounter midway through the work. The writer Michael Lowenthal, in defending Cameron's novel as a candidate for a gay literary award, noted in *The Harrington Gay Men's Fiction Quarterly* that, although Cameron had not incorporated more gay characters or gay situations into the book, he had written about a theme quite relevant to the gay community with an unmistakably gay sensibility. Cameron expressed disdain for books or writers that could be categorized too easily. "Everybody's different," Cameron said in his interview with Gambone. "I'm much more interested in looking at what makes people specifically the kind of writer they are."

Though Cameron had not begun work on the novel when he spoke those words, *The City of Your Final Destination* addressed that issue with a philosophical and almost metafictional intensity. Like *Andorra* before it, the setting of the novel is an almost magical-realist fictionalization of an actual country, in this instance Uruguay. As though looking ahead to the legacy his work might leave, Cameron considers the process of writing a literary biography. The main character's failure to write the biography, cast as a victory of sorts in the book, underscores the complexity of creating identity using the written word.

SHORTER WORKS

"Memorial Day," Cameron's first published story, is a relatively slight piece in the minimalist tradition of the early 1980s. Starting off with the first-person present-tense "I am," the main character, a sixteen-year-old boy named Stephen, lists his woes: his father has moved away, his mother has remarried, and he has stopped talking to anyone at home in a gesture of symbolic protest. Such passive aggressive behavior recurs throughout much of Cameron's work; disaffection and apathy become twin siblings in response to life's more challenging circumstances. Cameron amplifies this detachment with another choice detail: Stephen corresponds with prisoners and responds to personal advertisements under false pretenses, "claiming to be whatever it is the placer desires." As Stephen explains, "I like writing letters to people I've never met."

Much of the action of "Memorial Day" takes place on the holiday itself. As the family engages in rather typical suburban activities, Stephen recalls how his mother lost the diamond from her old engagement ring while scrubbing the walls of their swimming pool a year earlier. Obviously distraught, she asked Stephen to dive in after it. For him, the diamond became a symbol of his parents' relationship: "The diamond sitting on the bottom of the pool took on a larger meaning, and I thought that if it was replaced . . . we might live happily ever after." Determined to recover it, to restore what had been lost, Stephen took a brief outing with his father to shop for a diving mask. He then swam along the bottom to find the diamond "glittering in a mess of old leaves and bloated inchworms." The image is neatly evoked again at the close of the piece, when Stephen smells chlorine on his mother's wrist and sees fireflies glinting in the darkness.

Stephen's epiphany in the present-tense story relies more on Cameron's crafted prose than on any actual catalyst. Stephen's mother plainly states that he is breaking her heart. She repeats the line, and then Cameron has him echo a third time, "I look at my mother's chest, as if I could see her heart breaking." It is a small moment, more melodramatic than dramatic, yet Cameron refuses to let it pass unnoticed. He establishes in Stephen a longing for metaphor to become literal, to become real. In so doing, he adds weight to cliché and forces the reader to reexamine the words. Despite the fact that some critics labeled such moments heavy-handed, Cameron continued this stylistic motif in many of his later works, at times establishing an almost poetic intensity to otherwise commonplace dialogue via repetition.

The later story "Not the Point" serves as a prime example of this. Though the perspective has shifted from the young man to the mother, the dynamic is the same—a parent seeks to reconcile a child's psychological defense mechanisms following a displacement within the family. In this instance, Arlene Groener visits the counselor at her son Ellery's school to address his habit of wearing sunglasses throughout the entire day. Arlene does not find her son's behavior troubling. The boy's father has recently taken a new job in the Philippines and expects the family to join him there. As though to stack the psychological deck, we learn that Ellery's twin brother Patrick committed suicide the previous year, precipitating the family's move to a new town. Arlene's behavior is suspect as well; she is in the process of selling off the family's possessions with a rather devil-may-care, take-it-all-away attitude.

Arlene finally decides not to move again, and she relays this information to her husband via telephone near the end of the story. In a subtly revealed triangulation, readers learn that Ellery influenced Arlene's decision to stay and that she had, in turn, influenced her husband Leonard's decision to move away. She confesses as much when she states, "This is true, but it's not the point." A rift has developed between what is real and what is desired, between action and intention. Cameron places great value on bringing the two together. When Arlene goes in to check on her son in bed, he is asleep and finally free of the sunglasses. She reaches down and takes hold of his wrists, moving his hands away from his eyes. She observes that he "assimilates this gesture into the narrative of his dream. His exposed eyelids flicker with secret vision." By invoking the idea of narrative, Cameron places this "secret vision," a sixth sense linked closely with epiphany, firmly within the realm of artistic expression. Creativity and imagination allow one to go beyond the truth, to get to the heart of what really matters.

Cameron finds a unique way to express the value of this elusive knowledge in the story "Homework," which earned him one of his three O. Henry Awards. The protagonist, a high school student named Michael Pechetti, is emotionally unable to attend classes following the death of his dog Keds in the parking lot of the local A&P grocery store. When he finally does return to school, the guidance counselor summons him to her office to discuss the matter of his self-written excuse note. The scene echoes not only one of the settings from "Not the Point" but also the underlying theme as Michael and Mrs. Dietrich discuss the validity of the note. Though his claim to the truth remains unchallenged, the counselor advises him that "it's not the point." She crumples and throws away Michael's note. When he sees it beside the banana peel in the wastebasket, he understand that it is one more sad fact in life, another reminder of the failure of reality to live up to one's dreams.

"Sad facts" pepper the story as Michael learns that the details of life provide ample evidence of disillusionment. The guidance counselor's beautiful handwriting evokes a sense of pathos in Michael, as does most everything else. This empathetic disaffection, confusing and crippling by virtue of its implicit irony, might well be labeled the trademark emotion of many writers in Cameron's generation. For Cameron, however, it becomes the central point, and thus he is able to ask the question directly at the end of the story: "It's all nonsense. I'm working on a new problem: Find the value of n such that n plus everything else in your life makes you feel all right. What would n equal? Solve for n."

The characters in many of Cameron's later stories work toward the solution of that problem, often with equally frustrating results. In "The Secret Dog," for example, an unnamed narrator keeps a dog hidden away in the closet of his home. His wife Miranda, who is allergic to dogs, grows suspicious, particularly when her husband sneaks off late at night (to walk and feed the dog) and begins spinning lies at work to explain his resulting exhaustion. The narrator meets a kindred spirit named Jane at the local A&P, the scene of the dog's death in "Homework." She asks him to assist her with her shopping, all the while pretending that he is her husband. In the nearly vacant parking lot at the end of the excursion, Jane reads the narrator's palm and tells him bluntly that, although he will live a long time, "You will always feel like this," gesturing at the empty lot.

The revelation is one of emotional nihilism, yet this time there is no notion of epiphany attached. The narrator wanders on in his illusory geography, continuing to believe in what the reader must by then realize is a charade. His lack of awareness makes him comic and tragic at the same time. Though seemingly harmless, the notion of the secret dog reveals an underlying cruelty, both to the animal and to the other humans in the narrator's life. Obsessed with his own subjective truth—the desire to own a dog, the narrative overlooks other, real needs in his life. Cameron underscores this blindness by holding back the epiphany. For that reason, the story ends abruptly with the narrator's discovery that the closet is empty and his wife's revelation that "there never was any dog."

In other stories, however, the secret being kept in the euphemistic closet is, in fact, a reality. "Excerpts from Swan Lake" concerns two male lovers, Paul and Neal, who begin the summer having moved temporarily out of New York City to care for Paul's grandmother at her home in Connecticut. Paul's desire to keep their relationship hidden frustrates Neal, who eventually moves back to the city. When he returns for the grandmother's eighty-eighth birthday celebration, Neal confronts Paul on the issue, but Paul once again misses the point, insisting "I don't see the problem in all this." Later that evening, halfway through a ballet performance that the three are attending, Neal leaves.

At the end of the story, Cameron makes his point utilizing something of a reverse epiphany. Paul succumbs to the deceit he is perpetrating, and his inability to see his relationship with Neal for what it is—and to acknowledge that relationship in front of his grandmother—prevents him from seeing any truth in the artistry of the ballet or any beauty in the world in general. He states: "The ballet is such a lie. No one—not my grandmother, not Neal, not I—no one in real life ever moves that beautifully." Paul's failure to love openly leads to a failure to love fully at all. With this, Cameron's story of homosexual love moves beyond its possible cultural confines and speaks to a wider audience. While the personal and the political clash on the page, he sees the aesthetic as a potential secondary victim. In the end readers pity Paul for his inability to embrace beauty, either on the dance stage or in his own life.

"The Meeting and Greeting Area" finds Cameron working more deliberately at the intersection of the personal and political. The story is much longer than many of his earlier works, allowing him to evoke more from a scene than the basic plot elements and one or two telling images. As though preparing himself for his future novels, Cameron takes a more layered approach to narrative. This is reflected literally in the geography of the story. When the two protagonists, the narrator Charles and his ex-lover Tom, wander the city of Kunda, they move "from one terraced level to another." The location is exotic yet nonspecific, an invented yet convincingly rendered third world country. Cameron took even greater geographical liberties in the novels *Andorra* and *The City of Your Final Destination*. In all of these works the local politics intrude only peripherally on the lives of the characters; their personal problems and interactions remain the primary focus.

Even as understated backdrop, however, the politically charged settings exert a strong influence on the narrative. Tom confesses that he is still in love with Charles despite the knowledge that Charles is seeing another man. Tom reveals this information in Kunda as a nationalist rally takes place following a raid by insurgents earlier in the day. The two men, uncomfortable on account of their sexuality, leave the site of the rally to carry on their discussion. Tom asks Charles if anything is a "big deal" to him, and Charles cannot think of anything. At that moment, the two men hear what Charles describes as "a sort of rickety explosion," and then later, "people on the plaza screaming."

In his subsequent phone conversation with Albert, his current lover, Charles hardly registers the fact that a massacre has occurred and that he might have been one of the victims. Instead, he informs Albert rather calmly that Tom has gone back to the United States. The fact of the massacre cannot be erased from the narrative, yet Cameron allows the egocentric Charles to treat it with some indifference. In doing so, the indifference becomes the focal point of the story. In a country rife with border disputes, Charles has yet to reconcile his past with his present. Blindsided by the personal and oblivious to the political, he remains behind in, as he describes it, "the country to which I had been posted." Rather than celebrate his passive fatalism, Cameron calls it into question and challenges the very actions that brought him there.

Cameron's later novels develop these themes in ways that recall the earlier stories. Rather than offer some of the rather pat, imagistic resolutions of his earlier work, the novels explore the subjective lenses of their main characters more scrupulously. At the center of nearly all of Cameron's work is the question of how a life is constructed. What matters? What is the point? What is the big deal? These questions, sprinkled throughout the short stories, weigh heavily on his later novels. Though they may not deal primarily with gay characters, they do show Cameron seeking a way to bridge cultures, either mainstream or marginalized. The degree to which he explores identity politics, one of the more controversial ventures of literary criticism in the late 1980s and the 1990s, establishes him as possessing a "gay aesthetic" despite the absence of explicit homoeroticism in the work.

LONGER WORKS

Before resigning himself completely to the weighty matter of identity politics, however, Cameron published the ostensibly plot-driven *Leap Year*. The novel hurtles from one short chapter to another and never completely breaks free from its serialized structure. While critics came to appreciate the fluid, lyrical style of Cameron's best writing, the frenzied rush of *Leap Year* left some readers underwhelmed. Even so, the novel stands as a representative glimpse of life in New York City during the 1980s. Perhaps more soap opera than authentic social criticism, it allowed Cameron to test the waters outside of the literary marketplace and challenge the mass-market appeal of the similarly structured Tales of the City series.

Leap Year begins and ends in Manhattan on New Year's Eve and spans 1988, the leap year of the title. Its central character, David Parish, ushers in the new year by sleeping with his ex-wife Loren. In so doing, the two cheat on their current boyfriends and shake the foundations of their assumptions about love. David's role as a father likewise complicates his recently discovered homosexuality.

Heath Jackson, the object of David's homosexual affections, finds himself embroiled in an art world scandal and a subsequent courtroom drama. Heath is employed as a bartender at the start of the novel, and his good looks and modest talent as a photographer capture the attention of Amanda Paine, the manager of a prestigious art gallery and mistress of the gallery's owner, Anton Shawangunk. Amanda and Anton concoct a scheme whereby Heath becomes the likely suspect in the shooting and supposed murder of Anton's wife Solange. They play off of Heath's vanity and exploit his own desires to prove his art worthy. The vague nature of his artwork makes this somewhat easy. "In Heath's photographs everything is out of focus," Cameron writes, "but some things are more out of focus than others."

Criminal activity also intrudes on David's life. In a case of mistaken identity, his daughter Kate is kidnapped from the birthday party of another child named Kate. This precipitates a trip to Los Angeles for David and Loren. There, immediately following the recovery of their daughter, a freak accident lands Loren in the hospital. During her stay in the hospital, Loren realizes that her current relationship with Gregory, a media executive hoping to become a big-time producer in Los Angeles, is doomed to fail. She eventually decides to remain in New York, content with the renewal of her sometimes-sexual friendship with David.

The potential significance of David's sexual relationship with Heath provides an interesting psychological counterpoint midway through the novel. Cast by his accusers as the spurned lover of Solange, who is presumed dead, Heath relies on David's testimony to establish that he is, in fact, homosexual. At that time, the two have separated because of David's continuing confusion about his own sexuality. Heath bluntly states to him, "You've renounced your corrupt lifestyle and have returned to the straight and narrow path." The tension seems, in some ways, greater than what the novel can sustain. The fact that David's testimony ultimately has little effect in the courtroom supports this. Cameron rejects the easy opportunity to make a sociopolitical statement and instead embraces a stereotype of another sort. Just after Heath is found guilty of the crime he did not commit, the

"murdered" Solange stands up and removes her disguise in the courtroom to challenge the jury's verdict. Cameron surrenders to the daytime-television-drama structural influence, perhaps for the best.

The novel as a whole becomes a pastiche of styles, from letters to a spooflike transcript of a television talk show, *The Orca Show.* Though entertaining, the structural variety seems to have no substantial rhyme or reason. It as though Cameron has taken one of the definitions of "leap" to heart: "to pass abruptly from one state or topic to another." This desire to wrestle the narrative into a state of thematic unity, to have it conform to its title, might also explain Cameron's need to reconcile each character with his or her fate by the end of the novel. As defined at the start of the book, the purpose of the leap year itself was "to reconcile and harmonize solar and lunar reckonings."

Numerous other characters populate the novel, each with his or her own eccentric story. David's friend Lillian visits a sperm bank and eventually surmises that she has been impregnated with Heath Jackson's semen. Judith, Loren's mother, slips into an extramarital affair with a Vietnamese man named Henry Fank while her own husband is away in India. These tales are only loosely tied to the central narrative as Cameron attempts to evoke the connected chaos that represents urban life in the 1980s. Ultimately, critics noted that the challenge requires a great deal more than could be incorporated in the scope of the novel. As a slice of white, middle-class, urban life, however, the novel suits its purpose.

Such criticism stayed with Cameron after the publication of his second novel, *The Weekend,* in 1994. Though significantly quieter and more contemplative than the relatively boisterous *Leap Year, The Weekend* features a familiar cast of characters. On the anniversary of his lover Tony's death from AIDS, Lyle leaves New York

City to visit Tony's half brother John, his wife Marian, and their infant son at their country home. He brings with him Robert, a much younger aspiring artist with whom he has just started a relationship. The two men had met when Robert attended a series of workshops and lectures Lyle, a notoriously curmudgeonly art critic, delivered at an artists' colony. The plot, expanded from its original short story treatment in "Departing" from *The Half You Don't Know,* consists primarily of the conversations between various characters throughout the course of the weekend.

The novel opens on a scene highly reminiscent of Helen's description of Mrs. Wilcox in Forster's *Howards End.* Marian, one of Lyle's closest friends for many years, walks in the near-dawn stillness of her country estate prior to his visit. In direct contrast to dispositions of several characters in his short stories, her mood is nearly euphoric: "Her house and her garden and the river—they gave her such pleasure; it was all so beautiful, every stone and window and leaf. Her delight was so keen it almost hurt." The moment establishes the style that proceeds in the third-person narrative. Cameron relies on shifting yet intimate points of view while observing the telling gestures and details in the scene with lyrical flourishes.

Such an outlook stands in stark contrast to Lyle's professed views on aesthetic philosophy, published under the witty title *Neo This, Neo That: The Rise and Fall of Contemporary Painting.* As evidence of Cameron's own increasing maturity, the narrative detachment allows him to challenge the still-young Robert's hopeful yet somewhat shallow romanticism. Lyle recalls his time with Tony and realizes he cherished his former lover's simple outlook on life. Caught between the young idealist and the bitter queen he fears he is becoming, Lyle stands at a crossroads near the end of the novel. He can accept the love Robert offers in his new life or

hold fast to the memory of Tony and continue to grieve. Perhaps disastrously, he chooses the latter.

As Tony's life and death are detailed via memorial exposition, Cameron runs the risk of sentimentality and melodrama. Some reviewers point to this as the book's most serious flaw; others portrayed it as a penetrating sensitivity. The book's brevity, which perhaps more accurately defines it as a novella, offsets some charges of authorial indulgence. Cameron seeks a middle ground, mythical though it may be, between the romantic traditions of the past and the critical, postmodern conditions of the present. The country estate, with its archetypal gardens and deep-forest paths, provides a fine microcosmic setting for his experiment. Such a setting returns with even greater effectiveness in both of Cameron's subsequent novels.

Robert's presence—and his relative absence from nearly all past encounters of the characters—is the catalyst for much of the action in *The Weekend.* Lyle questions his motivations for seducing Robert in the first place, and Marian wonders whether Lyle's new lover is an affront to the memory of Tony, whom she also loved, though somewhat secretly. The two confront one another midway through the book, acknowledging the awkwardness of their situation. At the same time, they recognize the wisdom time and age have afforded them, even though they may not have capitalized on it quite fully enough. This underlying awareness lends the novella its tone of simple reflection. Lyle and Marian's conversation does not spark any confrontation, nor does it inspire any of the psychological defense mechanisms so prevalent in Cameron's earlier works. The two remain affectionate companions rather than disaffected individuals. Such a moment demonstrates that Cameron has turned the tide of his earlier work.

To underscore and simultaneously complicate his point, Cameron introduces the character of Laura Ponti, a neighbor of John and Marian who is renting a house for the summer in order to spend time with her daughter Nina and her latest boyfriend Anders. Laura, self-absorbed with her own constructed Italian identity, becomes an ironic catalyst of sorts. With all her fraudulent posturing and clumsy meddling, she manages to elicit some truths out of the others. She and Robert, the two outsiders, find themselves alone together toward the end of the novel. Robert has just had an argument with Lyle while walking in the woods; Laura finds him walking alone in the night in search of the train station. Their observations about the weekend offer the counterpoint the narrative alone could not provide. The truths they exchange, filtered and subjective as they are, simultaneously miss and illuminate the point of all that has happened. "Keep your hope to yourself," Laura advises Robert. "People feel very intimidated by hope. Especially old people like Lyle and me."

Cameron's agility with dialogue allows him to have characters directly address the themes that interest him. *The Weekend* shows a great deal more finesse than some of the awkward expositions of *Leap Year* in this regard. The scriptlike quality of the narrative led more than one reader to see its potential for the silver screen, and in 2000, a feature-length film adaptation of the book arrived in movie theaters. Reviewers criticized its overly literary tone and its reliance on sophisticated dialogue to move the plot forward. In their conversations the characters gain access to the words the author might otherwise have reserved for himself. In the novella this allows Cameron to move away from the first-person perspective and play a seemingly less-forceful role in the lives of his characters. Reviewers of the film found the same strategy somewhat pretentious. Cameron the novelist surpasses Cameron the short story writer, which might explain why the author abandoned the shorter form altogether for some time.

With the publication of *Andorra,* Cameron achieved far greater critical acclaim. Verging on metafiction, the novel explores the notion of invented lives, hazards and all. Without sacrificing the lyrical style of his prose, Cameron began to integrate modernist and postmodernist ideas into his work. Readers question the reliability of the narrator, Alexander Fox, even as he questions himself. Cameron employs a more problematic first-person perspective here, with a narrator unwilling to reveal himself fully. In a review of the book for the *Village Voice,* the author and critic John Weir describes Alex as "a Jamesian figure, a single man alone, shocked into an apparently permanent state of vagueness, perhaps tragically wary of feeling." He is, readers quickly begin to suspect, not as blank a slate as he claims. Cameron's deft narrative twist in the end leads the reader to question all that has come before it, to wonder whether or not a true Alexander Fox ever existed at all.

The very setting of the book, Andorra, is an entirely fabricated and geographically inaccurate portrayal of an actual country. Inspired by chapters from the book *Crewe Train* by Rose Macaulay, Cameron set about transforming the tiny nation into a paradisical microcosm of possibility. The protagonist Alexander Fox has just arrived in the country, ostensibly to begin his life anew. One of his first acts is the purchase of a blank book and a fountain pen, a transaction that fills him "with euphoria and expectation." He sets out to keep a journal of his new life. Cameron immediately establishes a complex connection between the written life and the physical life in his description of Alex's first entry: "And then I opened the book to the first impossibly blank beautiful page . . . and wrote, in ink that glistened and seemed as thick and permeable as blood: *Many years ago I read a book.*"

Shortly after his arrival in Andorra's capital city La Plata, Alex meets the flirtatiously enigmatic Ricky Dent, an Australian expatriate who offers her insider's knowledge of the surroundings. Ricky, or "Mrs. Dent" as Alex continues to call her, finds his hidden past immensely appealing. Her curiosity draws her to him in adulterous fashion. As she explains, "In a country this small, strangers—newcomers— are attractive simply because they're unknown." She elaborates, "That's immensely appealing, because people can imagine all sorts of wonderful things." This schism between "true" and "imagined" identities permeates the novel as Cameron asks which interests us most—if, in fact, we are ever able to discern one from another. We do learn at least one salient fact about Alex: he was once proprietor of a bookstore in San Francisco. Many of Andorra's citizens, we learn as the novel progresses, have come there to disappear or to rebuild their lives, and many are influenced by what they have read. They are outsiders by choice, or so they would have us believe.

Alex learns of an apartment for rent through the former owner of the hotel where he is staying, the Excelsior. This brings him into contact with the women of the Quay family, who inhabit an estate on one of the upper levels of La Plata. Mrs. Quay, the spry matriarch of the family, educates Alex about the history of Andorra and tells him of her family's struggle to bring about some kind of socioeconomic equality there. Mrs. Quay tells Alex, "There is no outside in Andorran society," though she later admits that the country is "divided topographically into the lower and upper berths, as it were." The utopian vision is at last slightly tarnished, though it will still be some time before Alex visits the Vega, the area high above La Plata where the less-fortunate class of Andorrans make their homes.

The two younger Quay women, Jean and Nancy, also live at Quayside. Alex takes an interest in Jean, the more demure and secretive of the two, though he continues to refer to her as "Miss Quay" throughout most of the novel. His later encounter with Nancy provides a stark contrast to her sister. Her brash comments and carefree treatment of her own daughter readily explain the cool tensions between her and the rest of the family. Worldly as she is, Nancy seems the American to Jean's proper English spinster. (It is no coincidence that Jean's favorite authors are Jane Austen and Daphne du Maurier.) Nancy lends a somewhat modern edge to what might otherwise be mistaken for a Victorian period piece, though she might be more at home in a novel like *The Great Gatsby.*

Miss Quay shows Alex the furnished apartment left vacant by her uncle Roddy, who is away in Ceylon on business. While there, she has an explained breakdown of sorts. The two share some champagne as a means of getting beyond the moment, and it becomes quite evident that Alex has fallen for her. He feels something inside himself inflate, and the energy rushes "to the far-flung, impermeable borders of my body. It was the joy that comes from feeling you are where you should be." In that moment Alex's interior state matches his physical location. Andorra, it seems, has found a new and happy citizen, one at peace with the world around him.

Alex's bliss does not last long. He accepts an invitation to dine with Mrs. Dent and her husband, who coincidentally also goes by the name Ricky. This is a clever gimmick on Cameron's part. Mr. Dent is gay, and he is as attracted to the mysterious newcomer as his wife. He suggests to Alex that his homosexuality, in fact, may be the scandal that drove him and his wife from Australia to Andorra. He describes his homosexuality as though it were a condition to suffer, despite the fact that Alex has no problem with the news of Ricky's affection for him. "Other people pursue their lives," Ricky tells Alex. "You're doing that, I can tell. Yet I can't." Alex disagrees, establishing a fleeting bond between the two characters, but the scene, like the consummation of Ricky's passion, is thwarted by its own mysteries.

The next morning, Alex receives a visit from the local police, who ask him to identify a body they believe to be Mr. Dent. Though Alex is convinced it is not, the police continue to pressure him for news of Mr. Dent, who has vanished from La Plata. The scene has the feel of Franz Kafka. Alex's passport is taken away, and he finds Andorra suddenly transformed into something of a prison. The first section of the novel, named for the Hotel Excelsior where Alex begins his stay in Andorra, comes to a close shortly thereafter. The second section, titled with the address of the Dent's subleased apartment, finds Alex no longer a tourist in the magical country. He has become a resident, despite the fact that none of the clothes or furnishings currently in his new home are his.

Perhaps this is why Alex suddenly desires to visit the Vega. As he rides in a cog railway past the various levels of La Plata on his way to Encampo, he reflects on how quickly his life in Andorra has changed: "As I watched La Plata shrink below me, I realized my new life could disappear just as easily, how everything is finally only a matter of perspective." This neatly summarizes Cameron's insistence on the subjectivity of identity. Because of that fact, identity seems to him a poor foundation for political reasoning. When he encounters Mr. Dent in Encampo, Alex sees him as a fugitive, a man running away from his sense of the perceptions of others. Ironically, because of Mr. Dent, Alex is in something of the same position. After he chases after Ricky in the middle of the night, Mrs. St. Pitt, the rather righteous hostess of the rooming house where the two men had been staying, refuses to let him back in, thinking that the two were having a lovers' quarrel. The next morning, Alex smooth-talks his way back into her good graces, explaining along the way, "Traveling gives us an opportunity to reinvent ourselves, to take on new personas." It is a moment of deceit on Alex's part, yet he speaks the truth.

Shortly after Alex's return to La Plata, he becomes involved in an affair with Mrs. Dent, who presses him for more details of his past. Alex tells her of his wife Helen, whose whereabouts throughout the novel have changed from being away on a trip to having committed suicide and infanticide after learning that her husband was unfaithful. Meanwhile, Ricky confides that the accidental death of her son brought the Dents to Andorra and that it subsequently pushed the two of them further apart. The confessions continue when Alex later meets Miss Quay and tells her that he is sleeping with Mrs. Dent. Despite the news, their flirtation continues, though the conversation takes a rather religious turn. Alex tells her, "If we can't explain ourselves, then how do we become understood, and absolved?" He further confesses that he has harmed people in his past, his wife and child in particular. Surprisingly, she remains somewhat smitten with him.

The religious overtones of this scene and several that follow were foreshadowed when Alex sought refuge in a church in Encampo. Alex establishes himself as an atheist, yet throughout the novel he exhibits desperation for some kind of spiritual salvation. By way of describing Alex, Cameron says he "aspires to be religious but he can't make that leap of faith." Instead, Alex believes he will find some sort of divine communion through his relationships with others. He says as much to Miss Quay, stating that love would save him from the fear that he was an awful person. His conceit, while perhaps clear to the reader, catches Miss Quay off guard. She does not recognize his inability to love for what it is; love, instead, draws her further into his trap.

The moment is worth noting, for it reflects Cameron's intentions as the author. As a narrator, Alex Fox has been less than forthcoming about his true identity, and yet readers remain intrigued, just as Mrs. Dent indicated at the beginning. Readers may have even developed an affinity for him, a commentary perhaps on the appeal of unreliable narrators in fiction. Even so, the truth will out. Mrs. Dent confronts Alex with who he really is—sensitive yet egocentric, the perfect unreliable narrator—and calls an end to their relationship. She denies him his identity, the favorable and loved identity he had hoped she would create of him. Alex has no choice but to leave, and so ends the second section of the book.

Alex takes the Quays up on an invitation to sail with them on a friend's yacht for a week or two, to "go neither far nor fast—simply where the wind and our whims carry us." An implicit sense of fatalism is attached to the journey, and the third section is titled after the ship, the *Splendora.* Just prior to the voyage, Alex is introduced to the ship's owner Isolta Fallowfield and her son Vere, who coincidentally had been a lover of Alex's former wife's brother. In fact, Vere had been at Alex and Helen's wedding, though Alex does not remember him. The encounter leaves Alex reeling; memory (and a witness to it) intrudes and disrupts his evening with the Quays and Fallowfields.

Alex's trip is jeopardized when he returns to the police station in La Plata to retrieve his passport. The police, it seems, have grown ever more suspicious of Alex in relation to a series of murders coinciding with his arrival in the city. He attempts to back out of the sea voyage by feigning illness, but Miss Quay insists that he stow away on the *Splendora.* Citing her own father's history with the police and politicians in Andorra, she confirms Alex's paranoid fears of becoming a prisoner in the small country. He begins to accept defeat in the face of reality: "I had been doomed from the very first day; I had arrived in Andorra a failed person and had expected the geography to rehabilitate me."

Pursued by the police, Alex hides in the attic of the Hotel Excelsior. There he finds some solace in reading the Bible, scanning its pages for the phrase "Jesus wept" and expressing surprise when he finds that Jesus wept for Lazarus and not for himself. With his own egocentric enterprise crumbling around him, Alex has a mild epiphany; he even takes the Bible with him as he sneaks off to the *Splendora* with Vere.

Stripping his clothes off and leaving his valise (and the Bible) behind, Alex undergoes a symbolic death as he swims out into the ocean to rendezvous with the anchored *Splendora.* Even the police, alerted by the unsuspecting Mrs. Quay the next morning, assume Alex has killed himself and thus suspend their search for him. On hearing the news, Alex finally confesses to Miss Quay what he had wanted to tell her before: that he had killed his own wife and child and that his reasons for doing so remain unknown or at least uncertain even to him. Vere and Miss Quay bring Alex ashore the next morning, and Alex asks Miss Quay to run off with him. She refuses, unsure if she could ever trust him fully enough to love him. Vere and Miss Quay return to the ship and sail off, leaving Alex to wonder if they were ever there at all. "How quickly things disappear," he thinks to himself.

Cameron ends the novel with an authorial flourish, portraying the narrator living in a prison cell and "having to face the fact that my book is finished and I am not." He finds comfort in the words he sets down on paper and imagines himself in Andorra, having read a book years ago that was set there. The scene, set like a postscript in the final pages of the book, calls into question all that has come before it. In this sense, it recalls some of the more self-reflexive and convoluted works of Latin American writers, such as Jorge Luis Borges and Julio Cortázar, as well as Vladimir Nabokov. Cameron acknowledges those influences and describes the core of the novel as "more informed by the world of books than the world of life."

This conceit is certainly central to Cameron's later novel *The City of Your Final Destination,* which was published in 2002. The book contains many familiar features of Cameron's work: somewhat disaffected characters in an isolated setting, lengthy discourse on philosophical topics, and an obsession with the subjective nature of identity. Cameron trades in one estate for another; Quayside in Andorra becomes Ochos Rios in Uruguay. Cameron has even admitted that his depiction of Uruguay is based mostly on fantasy, since as with Andorra, he has never visited the country himself.

Ochos Rios is the former home of the deceased writer Jules Gund, whose one novel, *The Gondola,* gained him international critical recognition. After spending many years on a second novel that never met his expectations, Gund committed suicide. Though Cameron does not reveal much more about the author or his works, he does acknowledge that they exerted a strong influence on an Iranian-born literary scholar, Omar Razaghi, whose thesis on Gund echoes the title of Lyle's book of art criticism from *The Weekend:* "Remember That? Well Forget It: The Articulation of Cultural Displacement and Linguistic Dismemberment in the Work of Jules Gund." From the outset, Cameron lifts his comic fists, ready to spar with some of the most basic tenets of literary academia. His protagonist, however, encounters an immediate obstacle. The executors of the Gund estate refuse to grant him the authority to complete a biography of the late Mr. Gund—authority to which Omar has laid claim in applying for his already awarded research grant from the University of Kansas.

Jules Gund's executors form a contentious triad. The family, originally from Germany, fled to Uruguay to escape Nazi persecution. Adam, Jules's manipulative brother, now lives with his legally adopted son and his current "companion" Pete, a former prostitute from Thailand whom Adam met while in Germany. Caroline, Jules's wife, is a French artist whose insecurities about her own painting have led her to create renditions of others' works in the attic of the family home. Finally, Arden Langdon, Jules's mistress, speaks of growing up in Wisconsin before returning to boarding school in her native land, England. Arden, who later questions her own claim to Gund's estate, considers Ochos Rios to be a true home for herself and her daughter Portia. She declares to Omar, "I think it's important to be allied with a place: to think you come from someplace specifically."

Omar represents a directionless mix of ethnic influences, a pancultural drifter. He was raised in Iran until he was ten, when his family moved to Toronto, Canada. He later moved to California. At the opening of the novel, Omar is house-sitting in Kansas and doing a bad job of it; he has no true home and is in danger of losing his fellowship at the university. Omar's more assertive girlfriend, Deirdre, challenges him to reject the outcome of his initial request for authorization from the Gunds. An outspoken agent of change, Deirdre seeks to change Omar's drifting ways, to moor him to some purpose in his life. Soon thereafter, he accepts her challenge and flies to Uruguay in hopes of changing the minds of Gund's survivors.

At Ochos Rios, Omar represents the unbidden yet exotic stranger, both naive to the ways of the place and curious about the secrets tucked away there. The characters dance about one another, testing and exploiting each other's strengths and weaknesses, cautious about revealing their true intentions. Adam portrays himself as Omar's greatest ally since he has approved of the biography from the start. Still, he bargains with the young academic, offering to help sway the women's opinions only if Omar will assist him in smuggling the family's rare artwork and jewelry back to the United States. Caroline, whose motives remain as hidden as the canvasses on which she works (turned toward the wall as they are in her tower studio), stands firm on her refusal and tests Omar's resolve with questions of ethics and morality. She bases her refusal to authorize the biography on a fictitious letter given to her by Jules in which he explicitly instructs her to permit no biography.

Most complex of all, Arden rather quickly comes around to Omar's way of thinking, changing her initial refusal to an acceptance of his plans. With her daughter Portia and the attention she pays to the decaying estate, Arden seems the true heir to Jules, even though she has no blood or legal ties to him. Omar's discussions with Arden—and it is, more than anything, a novel of discussions—build up to a passionate kiss just outside the boathouse in which resides the symbolic gondola featured in Jules Gund's book. When Omar goes in to look at the boat, he "felt foolish—or not foolish, he felt wrong, like he was committing a sin." The moment rings hollow for him, superceded as it is by the kiss and the intimacy developing between him and Arden. Omar's own life, it seems, begins to demand more of his attention than does Jules Gund's.

For this reason, Jules Gund is something of a red herring—or, to use the title of one of Cameron's short stories, it is "not the point." Though his story, or at least the felt need to uncover his story, drives the action of the book's first section, Omar's self-discovery drives the second. The break between the two occurs symbolically just after the kiss, when Omar is stung by a bee in the orchard and falls from a ladder. His allergic reaction, complicated by the remote setting, brings him quite close to death.

As he recovers from a coma in a nearby hospital, Arden invites Omar's girlfriend Deirdre to Ochos Rios. Motivated by her own guilt surrounding the kiss, Arden offers her complete hospitality to Deirdre, even after the new outsider continues Omar's campaign for authorization in her own somewhat belligerent manner. Deirdre quickly undoes what Omar has achieved; she alienates Adam and annoys Caroline to the point that she seeks refuge with some friends at a vineyard an hour away. Once he is strong enough, Omar sets about making repara-

tions and eventually sways even the stubborn Caroline. The only problem is that Omar has begun to lose faith in his own project, not only in his own ability to accomplish it (he feels at various times that he is both "doomed" and "foolish" for undertaking it all) but also in the very idea of biography.

Cameron began *The City of Your Final Destination* as an "ambitious intellectual idea." Eventually, the characters began to overwhelm the premise, just as Arden's affection for Omar overwhelms him. The book became more and more complex, and Cameron abandoned it halfway through. The frustration he must have felt is echoed in Caroline's angry reasoning over why she feels compelled to impede Omar's progress: "For there must be an explanation, of course: everything makes sense, or can be made sense of, with people like you around to do that for us." Even Deirdre, in her description of the Ochos Rios inhabitants as "thwarted and poisonous," realizes the dangers that accompany any enterprise dealing with subjective truths.

Ultimately, that is how Cameron characterizes biography: as a subjective truth. Omar subscribes to this notion shortly after his arrival at Ocho Rios, changing the nature of his intended project even before he has secured anyone's authorization: "I came here thinking I would write the standard academic biography, but I see now that it is impossible, even distasteful." When Omar informs his department chair of his decision, he fibs a little, claiming there was not much to tell about Jules Gund in the first place. She readily accepts his position, stating with a certain degree of academic pomp, "That's often the case with writers: the dreariness of their lives! And we critics vainly rooting through things, trying to find something—anything—in the prosaic murk." For Omar, writing a biography, in fact, had become something of an academic exercise, a stepping-stone toward a career he did not necessarily want. He would prefer, at the end, to live more fully in the present and to forget the past, as the title of his previous thesis suggested.

Several critics have noted that *The City of Your Final Destination* reads like a play, though their interpretation of genre ranges from domestic drama to English drawing-room comedy. Elements of both are in the text; the flip title of Omar's thesis, for example, can be taken quite seriously by the end of the novel. Likewise, there are a wink and a nod to Proust as Adam reads his work in bed following Omar's departure. Noting the book's similarities to both Anton Chekhov and George Bernard Shaw, reviewers appreciated its sophisticated dialogue and lofty ideas. Cameron acknowledges that his language often calls attention to itself; in a way, the speech of characters is as creatively imagined as the settings he envisions.

An examined life, in Cameron's world, always risks becoming engulfed in "the prosaic murk." Omar sees this clearly at the end of the novel, realizing that his intention to write Gund's biography will only trouble the waters and stir up memory, not calm the waters and clarify the life of his subject. Though he feels this may be his own failing as a biographer, he appears to understand that any attempt to describe and explain a life is bound to reflect and contain various personal and cultural influences. With that in mind, the reader may not be surprised at all to find Omar stepping in where Jules Gund left off, taking over the household at Ochos Rios and marrying Arden while Caroline ventures off to New York City to find her own fortunes.

In 2002 Cameron still calls New York City his home, so it is fitting that at least one character returns there at the end of the novel. His delight in crossing cultural boundaries no doubt is amplified in the urban environment. While writing, he feels as though he is living in two worlds simultaneously: the real and the imagined. As he plans his next book, he already anticipates traveling, as least fictionally, to another exotic setting. A writer who fully comprehends the imagination's deep influence on the "real" world, he is bound to make himself and his readers feel at home almost anywhere.

Selected Bibliography

WORKS OF PETER CAMERON

NOVELS AND SHORT STORIES

One Way or Another: Stories. New York: Harper & Row, 1986.

Leap Year: A Novel. New York: Harper & Row, 1990.

Far-Flung: Stories. New York: HarperCollins, 1991.

The Weekend. New York: Farrar, Straus and Giroux, 1994.

Andorra. New York: Farrar, Straus and Giroux, 1997.

The Half You Don't Know: Selected Stories. New York: Plume, 1997.

The City of Your Final Destination. New York: Farrar, Straus and Giroux, 2002.

CRITICAL AND BIOGRAPHICAL STUDIES

Budhos, Marina. "The Season of Their Discontent." *Los Angeles Times,* May 19, 2002, p. R7. (Review of *The City of Your Final Destination.*)

Coan, James. "Peter Cameron." In *The Dictionary of Literary Biography.* Vol. 234, *American Short-Story Writers since World War II,* 3d series. Edited by Patrick Meanor and Richard E. Lee. Detroit: Gale Group, 2001. Pp. 64–71.

Dorris, Michael. "A Gripping Tale Suffused with Repressed Emotion, Loneliness." *Los Angeles Times,* July 28, 1994, p. E6. (Review of *The Weekend.*)

Eder, Richard. "Finding New Lives in a Writer's Death." *New York Times,* May 15, 2002, p. E8. (Review of *The City of Your Final Destination.*)

Greenlaw, Lavinia. "Jules and Him: Peter Cameron's Hapless Protagonist Wants to Write a Biography of a Latin American Author." *New York Times Book Review,* May 19, 2002, p. 14.

Leavitt, David. "New Voices and Old Values." *New York Times Book Review,* May 12, 1985, pp. 1, 26.

Livesey, Margot. "The Past Is Another Country." *New York Times Book Review,* December 29, 1996, p. 8. (Review of *Andorra.*)

Lowenthal, Michael. "Wanting It All: The Future of Gay Fiction." *Harrington Gay Men's Fiction Quarterly* 1, no. 1:131–138 (1999).

Mathis, Stephen C. Review of *The Weekend. Lambda Book Report,* September–October 1994, p. 38.

Varner, Greg. Review of *The Half You Don't Know: Selected Stories. Lambda Book Report,* March 1997, p. 18.

Weir, John. "Gilt Trip." *Village Voice,* January 21, 1997, pp. 52–53. (Review of *Andorra.*)

INTERVIEWS

Bahr, David. "Peter Cameron: Yes, Uruguay." *Publishers Weekly,* May 13, 2002, p. 47.

———. "Limning the Elusive: An Interview with Peter Cameron." *Poets and Writers,* July–August 2002, pp. 18–24.

Gambone, Philip. *Something Inside: Conversations with Gay Fiction Writers.* Madison, Wis.: University of Wisconsin Press, 1999.

FILM BASED ON A WORK OF PETER CAMERON

The Weekend. Written and directed by Brian Skeet. Produced by Lunatics and Lovers and Granada Film, 2000.

—*HUGH COYLE*

Anne Carson

1950–

Born in Toronto, in Ontario, Canada, on June 21, 1950, Anne Carson began studying Greek and Latin in high school. After dropping out of college twice (to attend art school and to work), she earned a B.A. (1974), an M.A. (1975), and a Ph.D. (1981) in classics from the University of Toronto. She also studied Greek metrics for a year at the University of St. Andrews in Scotland. Having grown up in small towns in Ontario, Carson married at twenty but divorced eight years later, in 1980. Her father, Robert Carson, was a banker who suffered from Alzheimer's disease before he died; her mother, Margaret Ryerson Carson, died in 1997. In 2002 Carson was a professor of classics in the Department of History at McGill University in Montreal. She has also taught at the California College of Arts and Crafts in Oakland, at the Humanities Institute at the University of Michigan, and in the English Department at the University of California, Berkeley, as well as at Emory University and Princeton University in the 1980s. Publicly reticent about her personal life, Carson has given few interviews and has divulged little about herself: in a 2001 interview with Mary Gannon, she explained, "There has to be a line between my life and art. You don't want to sell the one as the other." In 1997 she told John D'Agata, "I don't like thinking about myself."

Although Carson published a scholarly book, *Eros the Bittersweet,* in 1986, she did not attract the attention of readers and critics of poetry until 1995, when she published two books— *Glass, Irony, and God* and *Plainwater: Essays and Poetry*—which were followed by a 1996 Lannan Literary Award and a Rockefeller Foundation Fellowship. Popular acclaim arrived in 1998 with the publication of *Autobiography of Red: A Novel in Verse,* which was a finalist for the National Book Critics Circle Award in poetry, a *New York Times* Notable Book of the Year, and winner of Quebec's QSPELL poetry award. The book sold more than twenty-five thousand copies in hardcover and was reviewed widely. Since then, Carson has received major awards in the United States, Canada, and England, including the 2001 T. S. Eliot Prize for Poetry, the 2001 Griffin Trust Award for Excellence in Poetry, a 2000 MacArthur Foundation Fellowship, a 1998 Guggenheim Fellowship, and a membership in the American Academy of Arts and Sciences. Her poetry appears regularly in such prestigious magazines as *The New Yorker, American Poetry Review,* and *Raritan,* and has been reprinted in *The Best American Poetry* and *The Best American Essays* annual series.

Highly praised by such critics and writers as Harold Bloom, Susan Sontag, Michael Ondaatje, Alice Munro, and Guy Davenport, Carson has an unusual background and skill set for a poet. Like the modernist poet Ezra Pound, Carson blends the contemporary and the classical (Carson replaces Pound's China with ancient Greece). And like Pound, she has developed a reputation as a fierce innovator; she was quoted in a 2000 profile in the *New York Times Magazine* as saying, "The boundaries people set are both unnecessary and unhelpful." Carson's consistent refusal to conform to traditions of genre has elicited encomiums from many critics. Adam Phillips has called her books "enquiries into the nature of profusion," noting that "one of the many exhilarating things about Carson as a writer is the sheer enigma and momentum of her ambition." In 2001 William Logan wrote that "her poems are full of explanations that aren't quite explanations, of sidelong glances and cul-de-sacs," and in his interview with her D'Agata maintained that Carson is a writer "exploring the outer limits of lyric possibility." Calvin Bedient finds Carson "the most instantly penetrating of contemporary poets" and explains her popularity as a result of her ability to write "in a middle range between philosophy and lyricism, where many can find her." In 1999 Jeffery Beam referred to her as "our new Emerson."

Carson's description of her genre-bending is more self-deprecating, however. In her interview with Gannon she said, "I think the forms are in chaos. I seize upon these generic names like *essay* . . . in despair as I'm sinking under the waves of possible naming for any event that I come up with. I really don't know what to call anything." When speaking with D'Agata, she described her genres as sui generis, or unique: each of her forms "arises out of the thing itself." The fact that Carson uses two desks in two different rooms for her writing—one for "scholarship," the other for "poetry"—helps explain her ability to maintain the highest standards of both scholarship and literature while blending the two fields.

EROS THE BITTERSWEET: AN ESSAY

Part literary theory and part scholarship, *Eros the Bittersweet* (1986) seeks to answer the questions "What does it mean to control another human being? to control oneself? to lose control?" by exploring the complexities of eros. A revision of her doctoral dissertation, the book introduces the theme that appears most frequently in Carson's career, for eros informs, drives, and ruins her protagonists and narrators. Throughout *Eros the Bittersweet* Carson addresses the ambivalence of erotic desire—the necessary presence of both love and hate—and begins with the ancient Greek poet Sappho's own coming to terms with the issue: "It was Sappho who first called eros 'bittersweet.' No one who has been in love disputes her." The book then investigates this quality of bittersweetness with incisiveness and sensitivity while also providing a window onto Carson's later work.

Carson's first task in the book is to describe what Sappho meant by "bittersweet":

Eros seemed to Sappho at once an experience of pleasure and pain. Here is contradiction and perhaps paradox. To perceive this eros can split the mind in two. Why? The components of the contradiction may seem, at first glance, obvious. We take for granted, as did Sappho, the sweetness of erotic desire; its pleasurability smiles out at us. But the bitterness is less obvious. There might be several reasons why what is sweet should also be bitter. There may be various relations between the two savors. Poets have sorted the matter out in different ways.

Carson then charts poetic responses to eros from Homer and Sappho, relying heavily on Socrates' philosophical writings and also making use of Dante, Friedrich Nietzsche, Franz Kafka, Virginia Woolf, Jacques Lacan, and Michel Foucault. The range of references in *Eros the Bittersweet* attests to the breadth of Carson's knowledge, a breadth she also brings to her later poetry and lyric essays.

As Carson explains,

The Greek word *eros* denotes "want," "lack," "desire for that which is missing." The lover wants what he does not have. It is by definition impossible for him to have what he wants if, as soon as it is had, it is no longer wanting. . . . There is a dilemma within eros that has been thought crucial by thinkers from Sappho to the present day.

This dilemma—"All human desire is poised on an axis of paradox, absence and presence its poles, love and hate its motive energies"—makes love bittersweet. The matter of "erotic ambivalence" also becomes a matter of survival when one considers that "Eros is expropriation. He robs the body of limbs, substance, integrity and leaves the lover, essentially, less." Carson's interest in the harmful aspects of erotic desire stems partly from eros's invasion of the lover: "Desire . . . is neither inhabitant nor ally of the desirer. Foreign to her will, it forces itself irresistibly upon her from without. Eros is an enemy." Although an enemy, eros is also impossible to ignore, which creates the difficult situation that Sappho understood so well: "an influx like eros becomes a concrete personal threat. So in the lyric poets, love is something that assaults or invades the body of the lover to wrest control of it from him, a personal struggle of will and physique between the god and his victim."

The notion of eros as both friend and foe emerges repeatedly throughout Carson's writing, linking her to Sappho and the tradition she outlines in *Eros the Bittersweet*. Because "eros is, to some degree, desire *for* desire" and "always a story in which lover, beloved and the difference between them interact," Carson's oeuvre can be considered a multifaceted story of eros and its ramifications—desire, control, and devastation as well as the politics of sexuality and of language.

PLAINWATER: ESSAYS AND POETRY

Plainwater introduced general readers to Carson's idiosyncratic writing and innovative style. Divided into five parts—"Mimnermos: The Brainsex Paintings," "Short Talks," "Canicula di Anna," "The Life of Towns," and "The Anthropology of Water"—the book is Carson's longest and most rewarding work to date. Although initially commercially unsuccessful and largely overlooked by reviewers, *Plainwater* has proved a durable work and continues to

enlighten readers eager to understand the arc of Carson's career.

The first section in *Plainwater,* "Mimnermos: The Brainsex Paintings" consists of fifteen poetic fragments translated from the Greek of Mimnermos, an elegiac poet of the seventh century B.C., a short essay, and three installments of "The Mimnermos Interviews." The piece builds in imaginativeness, as Carson respectively translates, describes, and invents the Greek poet, his work, and his world. Disjunctive, elliptical poems between two and fifteen lines in length, the fragments are free translations of poems by Mimnermos. The first fragment, "What Is Life without Aphrodite?" begins by describing sexual intercourse—"how gentle it is to go swimming inside her"—but Mimnermos undercuts the youthful sexuality of the imagery by negating it:

> . . . but (no) then
> the night hide toughens over it (no) then bandages
> Crusted with old man smell (no) then.

And the poem closes with a list of negatives:

> bowl gone black nor bud nor boys nor women nor
>   sun no
> Spores (no) at (no) all when
> God nor hardstrut nothingness close
> its fist on you.

The sudden rejection of sensuality underscores the violence of Mimnermos's poetic style and Carson's attraction to such disjunction and speed. But, as so often in Carson's work, the poems' status as translations becomes complicated, if not suspect, by anachronistic mentions of Chicago and East Berlin, which would be impossible references in Mimnermos's own work. Carson cannot translate without reinscribing the work in her own time.

The essay "Mimnermos and the Motions of Hedonism" explores the poetry of Mimnermos, particularly its innovations. "A poet intrigued by beginnings and endings, but not in the usual way," Mimnermos experimented with conventions of metrics and syntax to reinvent the poet's treatment of time. Yet he has been considered primarily a hedonist, as the beginning of Carson's essay explains: "Relocation among the substances that have us as humans is his subject. People call it hedonism." Carson proceeds to defend Mimnermos's hedonism, asserting that "the poet's task . . . is to lead the isolated human being into the infinite life, the contingent into the lawful. What streams out of Mimnermos's suns are the laws that attach us to all luminous things." Carson points out the insufficiency of the label "hedonism" as applied to Mimnermos's poetry since "there is no wine in Mimnermos's verse, no warm bath, no running animal, no cherries or silk or pale blue bones, no dice, no slapstick nights of song." Rather, "his hedonism seems to have struck a vein that was running through the times in which he lived—a kind of hunger for the motions of the self."

According to Carson, Mimnermos's hedonism is "haunted from two directions at once . . . Sex and light," which fragment 5 ("A Sudden Unspeakable Sweat Floweth Down My Skin") makes evident:

Sweat. It's just sweat. But I do like to look at them.
Youth is a dream where I go every night
and wake with just this little jumping bunch of arteries
in my hand.

But Mimnermos has even darker concerns, as Carson explains: "The fact that we are no longer in the light (by the time we look for it) is his subject. Insofar as we speak of Mimnermos's hedonism, we can refer to the subject as knowledge." Almost any consideration of knowledge entails a consideration of death: "When Mimnermos *sees the light,* he sees it gone." Thus, when he writes about life, he writes about death, as in fragment 11 ("Would That Death Might Overtake Me"): "No disease no dreamflat famine fields just a knock on the door / at the age of threescore: done."

"The Mimnermos Interviews" simultaneously parody the standard author interview and unearth emotional truths about their purported subject. The absurdity of the interview itself—a Canadian writer in the 1990s interviewing a Greek poet from antiquity—occasionally gives way to revelation, the ultimate goal of such interviews. Yet the fact that these interviews are Carson's own inventions makes their discoveries her own inventions as well. Anachronism figures here, too, as when Mimnermos says, in the first interview, "Well I don't know what you're reading over there nowadays those American distributors get some crazy ideas." Mimnermos is silent through most of the third interview and bursts into eloquence only near the end:

I'm not angry I am a liar only now I begin to understand what my dishonesty is what abhorrence is the closer I get there is no hope for a person of my sort I can't give you facts I can't distill my history into this or that home truth and go plunging ahead composing miniature versions of the cosmos to fill the slots in your question and answer period it's not that I don't pity you it's not that I don't understand your human face is smiling at me for some reason it's not that I don't know there is an act of interpretation demanded now by which we could all move to the limits of the logic inherent in this activity and peer over the edge but everytime I start in everytime I everytime you see I would have to tell the whole story all over again or else lie so I lie I just lie who are they who are the storytellers who can put an end to stories.

The interviews end with the interviewer saying "I wanted to know you" and Mimnermos responding, "I wanted far more." Though seemingly a breakdown in the interview process, Mimnermos's statements in his outburst about being a liar capture the central truth of any act of communication—that is, that one must "tell the whole story all over again or else lie."

In the thirty-two intensely lyrical paragraphs that make up *Plainwater*'s second section, "Short Talks," Carson ranges across such subjects as trout, Ovid, the *Mona Lisa,* hedonism, penal servitude, and "chromoluminism," offering a cornucopia of arcane knowledge and fancy. She welcomes such writers and artists as Rembrandt, Georges Braque, Georges Seurat, Camille Claudel, the Brontë sisters, Emily Dickinson, Fyodor Dostoyevsky, Franz Kafka, Gertrude Stein, Sylvia Plath, and Sergey Prokofiev into her "talks," which remain enigmatic and haunting despite their parading of the intellect. The end of the first piece ("Introduction") makes explicit Carson's *ars poetica* in *Plainwater:* "I will do anything to avoid boredom. It is the task of a lifetime. You can never know enough, never work enough, never use the infinitives and participles oddly enough, never impede the movement harshly enough, never leave the mind quickly enough." This emphasis on quickness, harshness, and busyness is relevant to much of Carson's writing, in *Plainwater* and afterward.

Divided into "What Do We Have Here?"—a sequence of fifty-three poems in free verse—and the prose epilogue "Afterword," the third section of *Plainwater,* "Canicula di Anna," creates a narrative around a painting by the Renaissance artist Pietro di Cristoforo Vannucci, who was known as Perugino, "a contemporary of Michelangelo / and teacher of Raphael" in Perugia, Italy. Carson begins the poetic sequence in "Canicula di Anna" by answering the question in her title: "What we have here / is the story of a painter." Perugino has received a commission from a group of philosophers but is conflicted because of his love for a woman who

. . . has a face
and a past
worth painting.

Perugino has inserted his beloved into the painting:

he applied
the novel rule
of two centers of vision

which allowed him to focus the painting's perspective on his beloved as well as on the philosophers. This fascinates Carson and compels her to become Perugino in the poem; looking at the painting, she places herself in the scene from the painter's point of view. Considering Perugino's skill as

. . . one of the earliest Italian painters
to practice oil painting, in which he
evinced a depth and smoothness
of tint, which elicited much remark

the poem also becomes a celebration of painting itself—as a mechanical act, as an art, and as a mode of creation.

Barking dogs, Italian phenomenologists, and the colors blue and red establish the backdrop of Carson's narrative, which ultimately emerges as a search not only for Perugino's beloved but also for a story. Carson's digressions, though compelling as images or facts, highlight the paucity of narrative detail in the poem. The identity of the narrator itself is in flux, with no clear indication that the narrator has shifted. Sometimes Carson, at other times Perugino, the narrator changes continually throughout the poem, and sometimes appears to be both Carson and Perugino, both of whom are searching for the beloved. At times, Carson seems to project herself imaginatively into Perugino's state of mind as he painted the philosophers, which makes the poem more plausible given the presence of modern details such as the telephone and airplane. The violence that Carson inflicts on linearity and narrative becomes the poem's primary achievement, as the narrative itself is less compelling than Carson's unorthodox presentation of it, which forces the reader to ask, in the afterword, "What is so terrible about stepping off the end of a story?"

The prose afterword explicitly addresses the reader, specifically the reader's expectations and desire for a "story": "After a story is told there are some moments of silence. Then words begin again. Because you would always like to know a little more. Not exactly more story. Not necessarily, on the other hand, an exegesis. Just something to go on with." Though her voice and stance seem direct, Carson actually complicates her position as the narrator of "Canicula di Anna" in the afterword. She seeks to explain not her own position, but the reader's, which results in a delicate equilibrium between arrogance and clairvoyance:

> Let us look more closely at this moment that gathers at the place called the end. Up until this time, you have been fairly successful at holding back your tears, and suddenly you feel brokenhearted. It is not that you loved Anna, or look upon me as a friend, or hate your own life particularly. But there is a moment of uncovering, and of covering, which happens very fast and you seem to be losing track of something. It is almost as if you hear a key turn in the lock. Which side of the door are you on? You do not know. Which side am I on?

The narrator of the book's next section, "The Life of Towns," is similarly problematic, asserting, "I am a scholar of towns" and further defining "a scholar" as "someone who takes a position . . . someone who knows how to limit himself to the matter at hand." But because "Matter which has painted itself within lines constitutes a town," Carson has embedded the reader in a dense network of metaphor. Although most of the "towns" in "The Life of Towns" occupy the names of individuals—as in "Lear Town" and "Pushkin Town"—and abstractions—"Luck Town," "Love Town," "Tolerance Town"—there are no true points of reference, thus leading the reader back to "the matter at hand," or the concept of "town."

The most striking element of the poems in "The Life of Towns" is that every line is end-stopped. This gives the poems a staccato rhythm and multiple levels of interpretation; the punctuation encourages the reader to stop at the end of each line but also, because of the ubiquity of the end punctuation, to ignore it and continue to the next line without stopping. Furthermore, Carson does not include punctuation within the lines, even when convention requires it. Such ambiguity allows for multiple readings of each poem and supports rereadings, recalling Carson's question in her introduction, "But what about variant readings?"

Carson's style here adds friction to the act of reading itself, reinforcing the undercurrent of violence that runs throughout the poems, as in "Town of the Sound of a Twig Breaking":

> A hunter is someone who listens.
> So hard to his prey it pulls the weapon.
> Out of his hand and impales.
> Itself.

The possibilities of multiple meanings created by the punctuation is perhaps most breathtaking in "Wolf Town":

> Let tigers.
> Kill them let bears.
> Kill them let tapeworms and roundworms and
>   heartworms.
> Kill them let them.
> Kill each other let porcupine quills.
> Kill them let salmon poisoning.
> Kill them let them cut their tongues on a bone and
>   bleed.
> To death let them. . . .

What is technically anaphora—the repetition of a phrase at the beginning of a series of lines—becomes not the beginning but the continuation of a thought when one ignores the punctuation, which one must do to understand the poem's literal meaning. Few poems, much less an entire suite of poems, face the issues of meaning, interpretation, and reading so explicitly and forcefully.

"The Anthropology of Water," which comprises more than half of *Plainwater*, begins with an introduction ("Diving: Introduction to the Anthropology of Water") that opens with a statement that resonates throughout the entire work: "Water is something you cannot hold. Like men. I have tried." The men emerge in the essays as her father, her lover, and her brother, all of whom leave her in one way or another.

"Thirst: Introduction to Kinds of Water" explains the reasons for the narrator's pilgrimage to Compostela—the site of Santiago de Compostela, a revered cathedral to which pilgrims journey to pray—which is described in the piece that follows, "Kinds of Water: An Essay on the Road to Compostela." Having watched her father's mind deteriorate until he suffers from dementia—"now his mind was a sacred area where no one could enter or ask the way"—the narrator turns to spirituality for solace: "I prayed and fasted. I read the mystics. I studied the martyrs. I began to think I was someone thirsting for God. And then I met a man who told me about the pilgrimage to Compostela." Being a "young, strong, stingy person of no particular gender," the narrator discovers she is well-suited to being a pilgrim and leaves home with "the only rule of travel" in mind: "Don't come back the way you went. Come a new way."

The road to Compostela runs from St. Jean Pied de Port, France, near the Pyrenees, to Compostela, a city in western Spain. "Kinds of Water" seems like a travelogue: each entry is marked with a place and a date, with roughly one prose entry per day (she skips several days and writes multiple entries on other days), and an excerpt from a poem by a Spanish or classical Chinese poet (such as Machado or Basho) precedes Carson's prose. But in Carson's hands, the travelogue documents the pilgrimage through poetry and mental photographs. The pilgrimage allows for meditations on landscape, penance, loneliness, shame, and madness, but it is complicated by eros because she falls in love with her traveling companion, a man she calls "My Cid," who does not return her love. Though often excruciating, the pilgrimage becomes a way of life: "It is an open secret among pilgrims and other theoreticians of this traveling life that you become addicted to the horizon. There is a momentum of walking, hunger, roads, empty bowl of thoughts that is more luxurious—more civil than any city." Despite her narrative, Carson asserts, "I am a pilgrim (not a novelist) and the only story I have to tell is the road itself."

"Just for the Thrill: An Essay on the Difference Between Women and Men," presents a different kind of pilgrimage—one made by automobile across the United States, not on foot through Europe. In "Very Narrow: Introduction to Just for the Thrill," Carson describes her attempts to become androgynous in order to avoid displeasing her father with her womanliness. Unfortunately, she eventually falls in love—"a harrowing event." Because she takes "an anthropological approach" to love and has "no talent for lyrical outpourings," Carson fills "many notebooks with data" about her new relationship: "I traveled into it like a foreign country, noted its behaviors, transcribed its idioms." But love remains a strange object for Carson, who pretends to offer no wisdom on the subject: "Man is this and woman is that, men do this and women do different things, woman wants one thing and man wants something else and nobody down the centuries appears to understand how this should work."

Narrated during a trip from Quebec to Los Angeles with her lover, "Just for the Thrill" is a deeply moving exploration of the ambivalence of erotic desire as well as a narrative of the end of a relationship. Her lover claims to be "using this trip across America to study up on classical Chinese. A language consisting, so far as I can judge, entirely of wisdom." This "classical Chinese wisdom" provides Carson with numerous quotes, as do lines from blues songs, both of which offer their own kind of counsel. With "enlightenment is useless" as her mantra, she admits, "I came on this trek to videotape desire." But desire has its own plans for her, and only toward the end of the essay does Carson reveal, "We are driving to Los Angeles because he wants to live there. When the ritual is over, campers go their separate ways." When they arrive in Los Angeles, "the void opens"; he ends the relationship, and she must return to Quebec alone. With its double edge, language itself becomes like a lover: "Language is what eases the pain of living with other people, language is what makes the wounds come open again."

GLASS, IRONY, AND GOD

Published the same year as *Plainwater, Glass, Irony, and God* (1995) also investigates how language and desire can save and destroy a person. The most notable piece in the book, "The Glass Essay" explores the aftermath of a love affair in a sequence of nine poems ("I," "She," "Three," "Whacher," "Kitchen," "Liberty," "Hero," "Hot," "Thou") that employs strategies of the essay without being traditionally discursive. The first poem in "The Glass Essay," "I," begins with Carson

. . . Thinking

of the man who
left in September.
His name was Law.

This overt emphasis on the first-person narrative works against the notion of a "glass essay," which implies detachment—"an atmosphere of glass," a subject considered in a traditionally rational form. But Carson then shifts to "She" and therefore to the third person, who here appears as her mother, whom she visits and who lives alone "on a moor in the north." Carson brings *The Collected Works of Emily Brontë*

with her because Brontë is her "favourite author" as well as her "main fear" because of her "sad stunted life." Brontë "never made a friend in her life," and her poetry

. . . from beginning to end is concerned with prisons,
vaults, cages, bars, curbs, bits, bolts, fetters,
locked windows, narrow frames, aching walls.

The problem for the narrator is that

Whenever I visit my mother
I feel I am turning into Emily Brontë
my lonely life around me like a moor.

Throughout "The Glass Essay," she juxtaposes the melodrama of Brontë's *Wuthering Heights* with the melodrama of her recently ended love affair: "When Law left I felt so bad I thought I would die." Law emerges as cruel and unfeeling:

. . . Not enough spin on it,
he said of our five years of love.
Inside my chest I felt my heart snap into two pieces

which floated apart. By now I was so cold
it was like burning.

Yet Carson finds herself unable to resist throwing herself at him:

Everything I know about love and its necessities
I learned in that one moment
when I found myself

thrusting my little burning red backside like a baboon
at a man who no longer cherished me.
There was no area of my mind

not appalled by this action, no part of my body
that could have done otherwise.

This humiliation recalls the bittersweetness of eros as explored in Carson's first book. The poem ultimately becomes an attempt to rid herself of "love and its necessities," and Carson explains that

> Each morning a vision came to me.
> Gradually I understood that these were naked
>   glimpses of my soul.
>
> I called them Nudes.

The Nudes, thirteen in number, portray the narrator in painful or harrowing situations—caught in thorns, without flesh, buffeted by winds. Because of the Nudes, Carson becomes "entirely fascinated with [her] spiritual melodrama," but then the images stop, and for months she sees nothing despite her determination "to peer and glance," her "nerves open to the air like something skinned." Eventually she "stopped watching" and "forgot about Nudes" and proceeded to live her life, "which felt like a switched-off TV." The thirteenth, and final, Nude "arrived when [Carson] was not watching for it":

> I saw a high hill and on it a form shaped against
>   hard air.
>
> It could have been just a pole with some old
>   cloth attached,
> but as I came closer
> I saw it was a human body
>
> trying to stand against winds so terrible that the
>   flesh was blowing off the bones.
> And there was no pain.

Thus the poem, and Carson's "spiritual melodrama," ends positively, or at least painlessly.

Yet the pain that resonates through most of "The Glass Essay" appears elsewhere in *Glass, Irony, and God.* In "TV Men," another significant piece in the book, Carson treats literary and mythological figures—Hektor, Sappho, Socrates, Antonin Artaud, and "The Sleeper"—as actors for television scripts. Specifically, the

"TV Men" poems address the possibility of agency in a media culture: despite the illusion of agency, the actors are always acted upon. The centerpiece of the "TV Men" suite is the first poem in the series, "TV Men: Hektor." The poem begins with statements about television that combine the literal and the figurative:

> TV is ugly, like the future.
> TV is a classic example.
>
> Hektor's family members found themselves
>   engaged in exciting acts,
> and using excited language, which they knew
>   derived from TV.
>
> A classic example of what.
>
> A classic example of a strain of cruelty.

A recurrent topic for Carson, cruelty here emerges as the constant spectacle that television has created and continues to promote. The "TV Men" poems can be humorous, as when they contrast the nobility of figures like Hektor with the crassness of the medium—"Wrong people look good on TV, they are so obviously / *a soul divided* / and we all enjoy the pathos of that." But the triviality with which television approaches its subjects, the ways in which television appropriates pain, and the incongruence of substance and the medium preclude enjoyment.

Each section of "TV Men: Hektor" begins or ends with a statement about television: "TV is dull, like the block of self in each of us"; "TV is presocial, like Man"; "TV is made of light, like shame." The combination of the declarative ("TV is") with the figurative ("like") creates an ambivalently authoritative voice, which, when it crosses from the literal to the poetic, attempts to relinquish its authority. Such an approach to authority also appears in "The Truth about God," a series of eighteen short poems that addresses Carson's conceptions of God. The first, "My Religion," presents religion as a conundrum:

My religion makes no sense
and does not help me
therefore I pursue it.

Throughout the poems, God emerges as an entity who wants only "some simple thing"; the dilemma for human beings arises from the difficulty of finding that thing. In "God's Christ Theory," Carson posits a rationale for the birth of Jesus Christ:

God had no emotions but wished temporarily
to move in man's mind
as if He did: Christ.

The poems also forward a feminist argument; "God Stiff" addresses the politics of gendered language:

God gave an onomatopoeic quality to women's
     language.
These eternally blundering sounds eternally
blundering down

into the real words of what they are
like feet dropped into bone shoes.
"Treachery" (she notices) sounds just like His
     zipper going down.

This focus on the politics of language looks forward to "The Gender of Sound," the essay that closes *Glass, Irony, and God.*

"The Gender of Sound," the only prose work in the book, discusses how the sounds women make have led men to rationalize the subjugation of women: "It is in large part according to the sounds people make that we judge them sane or insane, male or female, good, evil, trustworthy, depressive, marriageable, moribund, likely or unlikely to make war on us, little better than animals, inspired by God." Female sounds have long been viewed negatively; according to Aristotle, a woman's voice is a sign of woman's "evil disposition" in general. Carson explains that "High vocal pitch goes together with talkativeness to characterize a person who is deviant from or deficient in the masculine ideal of self-control. Women, catamites, eunuchs and androgynes fall into this category." She traces examples from classical literature of women whose voices indicate their deviant natures—the Gorgons, the Sirens, the Furies, Artemis, Kassandra—and goes on to demonstrate the political ramifications of these portrayals: "In general the women of classical literature are a species given to disorderly and uncontrolled outflow of sound—to shrieking, wailing, sobbing, shrill lament, loud laughter, screams of pain or of pleasure and eruptions of raw emotion in general." Thus, "Putting a door on the female mouth has been an important project of patriarchal culture from antiquity to the present day. Its chief tactic is an ideological association of female sound with monstrosity, disorder and death" as well as "with wild space, with savagery and the supernatural." Because "Female sound was judged to arise in craziness and to generate craziness," women could not be trusted to keep secrets. These beliefs led to the subjugation of women in the political and social arenas, and patriarchal culture devised ways to control what women said and where they could speak. After presenting the evidence, Carson offers a tentatively hopeful wish: "I wonder if there might not be another idea of human order than repression, another notion of human virtue than self-control." Freedom from repression and lack of self-control emerge as central themes in her next book, *Autobiography of Red* (1998).

AUTOBIOGRAPHY OF RED: A NOVEL IN VERSE

Because of its subject matter and form, *Autobiography of Red* achieved a critical and popular success rare for a book of poetry. The verse novel balances, and benefits from, the narrative drive of fiction and the lyric power of poetry. Critics, many of them poets themselves, were largely enthusiastic about this novel in verse.

Ruth Padel described the book as "a profound love story," and William Logan praised Carson for her "exact eye for the travails of childhood—the longings, disappointments, thwarted triumphs, and hot disasters that make childhood . . . both mystery religion and failed quest." Geraldine McKenzie, writing for the online journal *Jacket,* voiced one of the few primarily negative reviews of the book: "The rewrite of the Geryon myth, while it begins promisingly enough, declines into a dull narrative with few of the excitements poetry should offer." McKenzie further criticized the verse novel for not constructing "a paradigm of invasion and colonisation." Most critics, however, considered Carson's personalization of a distant myth more refreshing than problematic and her language more lyrical than prosaic.

Set in the second half of the twentieth century, the verse novel presents a variation on the portrait of the artist as a young man. But before Carson introduces readers to Geryon, she offers a medley of delay tactics, beginning with a short essay, "Red Meat: What Difference Did Stesichoros Make?" in which Carson explains that the Greek poet Stesichoros "came after Homer and before Gertrude Stein, a difficult interval for a poet." Popular during the seventh century B.C., Stesichoros, Carson tells us, wrote twenty-six books, of which "a dozen or so titles and several collections of fragments" remain. According to Carson, Stesichoros's poetic legacies are his use of adjectives and his poem about Geryon. "Nouns name the world. Verbs activate the names. Adjectives come from somewhere else." They "seem fairly innocent additions but look again. These small imported mechanisms are in charge of attaching everything in the world to its place in particularity. They are the latches of being." After "studying the surface restlessly," Stesichoros, "for no reason that anyone can name, . . . began to undo the latches" by rejecting the Homeric epithet as primary descriptor. The result is that he "re-leased being" and "all the substances in the world went floating up."

Stesichoros applied this process of unlatching to Geryon in the *Geryoneis* (The Geryon Matter), which Carson describes as "a very long lyric poem in dactylo-epitrite meter and triadic structure." A red monster with wings who is responsible for guarding a herd of red cows, Geryon is killed by Herakles (the Greek name for Hercules, the hero of exceptional strength who undertakes twelve "labors" to gain immortality), who must steal the cattle as his tenth labor. In placing Geryon, not Herakles, at the center of the poem, Stesichoros subverts the tradition of heroic poetry. But the *Geryoneis* does not exist in its original form. Rather, it has been found in various fragments, none longer than thirty lines. Thus, "the fragments of the *Geryoneis* itself read as if Stesichoros had composed a substantial narrative poem then ripped it to pieces and buried the pieces in a box with some song lyrics and lecture notes and scraps of meat." Carson reproduces sixteen of these fragments in "Red Meat: Fragments of Stesichoros," her second delay tactic, which she follows with three appendices.

Appendix A, "Testimonia on the Question of Stesichoros' Blinding by Helen," offers three views on the question, citing Suidas' definition of *palinodia,* or palinode—"for writing abuse of Helen Stesichoros was struck blind but then he wrote for her an encomium and got his sight back"—as well as Isokrates' *Helen* and Plato's *Phaedrus.* Appendix B is "The Palinode of Stesichoros by Stesichoros," of which only three lines exist:

> No it is not the true story.
> No you never went on the benched ships.
> No you never came to the towers of Troy.

The third and final appendix, "Clearing Up the Question of Stesichoros' Blinding by Helen," is a series of twenty-one either/or propositions about the issue. Carson pursues the first half of each syllogism ostensibly to arrive at a "clearing up" of "the question of Stesichoros' blinding":

1. Either Stesichoros was a blind man or he was not.

2. If Stesichoros was a blind man either his blindness was a temporary condition or it was permanent.

3. If Stesichoros' blindness was a temporary condition this condition either had a contingent ause or it had none.

4. If this condition had a contingent cause that cause was Helen or the cause was not Helen.

Halfway through the appendix, the argument turns on itself and ends questioning whether or not "we," who still do not know the cause of Stesichoros's blinding, will lie about his blindness. Thus, Carson leaves open the question and her delay tactics seem to have produced more questions than answers. And in the "interview" with Stesichoros at the end of the book, Stesichoros obliquely discusses blindness, "seeing," and description in a way that seems designed to obfuscate the verse novel. Although Logan considered the book "top-heavy with its absurd apparatus," Jed Rasula viewed these "genre-expanding supplements to the story" not as "paraphernalia, but incubators of the uncanny atmosphere in which the story is germinated."

When this story begins, in the title section of the book ("Autobiography of Red: A Romance"), Carson immediately introduces Geryon—specifically his unusual appearance, shyness, sensitivity, and devotion to his mother. Described by Rasula as "a nearly eventless narrative," the verse novel contains little in plot and much in emotional, psychological, and visual exploration. *Autobiography of Red* is divided into forty-seven parts, each with its own title, and each part begins with a one-line statement—such as "Tuesdays were best," "Some-how Geryon made it to adolescence," and "Under the seams runs the pain"—that encapsulates or otherwise introduces what follows.

Sexually abused by his older brother, "Geryon learned about justice . . . quite early." When Geryon's grandmother stayed with his family for several months, he moved into his brother's room, and "So began Geryon's nightlife." He and his brother "developed an economy of sex" for marbles, and "voyaging into the rotten ruby of the night became a contest of freedom / and bad logic." Sex therefore becomes problematic for Geryon, who already feels uneasy in the world because of his appearance. Geryon's wings are a clear indication of his monstrousness—his alien status in relation to other people—which is further compounded by his red skin and homosexuality.

Geryon begins his autobiography, which he "worked on from the age of five to the age of forty-four," before he can write:

In this work Geryon set down all inside things
particularly his own heroism
and early death.

His preliterate autobiography consists mainly of works of visual art, such as sculpture; but when he learns to write, he decides to "set down the facts":

Total Facts Known About Geryon.
Geryon was a monster everything about him was
  red. Geryon lived
on an island in the Atlantic called the Red Place.
  Geryon's mother
was a river that runs to the sea the Red Joy River
  Geryon's father
was gold. Some say Geryon had six hands six feet
  some say wings.
Geryon was red so were his strange red cattle.
  Herakles came one
day killed Geryon got the cattle.

He followed Facts with Questions and Answers.

QUESTIONS Why did Herakles kill Geryon?
1. Just violent.

2. Had to it was one of His Labors (10th).
3. Got the idea that Geryon was Death otherwise he could live forever.

FINALLY
Geryon had a little red dog Herakles killed that too.

When Geryon meets Herakles during adolescence, Herakles does not kill him or steal his cattle; he seduces Geryon instead. Carson's description of their first encounter is simultaneously impressionistic and emotionally accurate: "The world poured back and forth between their eyes once or twice." Only through Herakles does Geryon attain self-awareness: "Up against another human being one's own procedures take on definition." Hopelessly in love with Herakles, Geryon lacks the maturity or experience to understand the possibly damaging effects of his devotion. Sex inevitably becomes an issue for the new lovers; and though only fourteen, Geryon "understood / that people need / acts of attention from one another," but wonders "Does it really matter which acts?" Herakles, two years older than Geryon and far more confident, explains that "*Sex is a way of getting to know someone.*"

Geryon then goes with Herakles to Herakles' "hometown," Hades, which is "at the other end of the island about four hours by car, a town / of moderate size and little importance / except for [its volcano]." With its potential for violence and dormant exterior, the volcano emerges as a metaphor for sexual desire, specifically Geryon's volatile emotional state. Geryon's love for Herakles is total, but Herakles' hedonism compels him to be more cavalier; unwilling to commit to Geryon, he breaks off their relationship by saying, "*Geryon you know / we'll always be friends,*" after which Geryon returns to his family's house to endure "a numb time, caught between the tongue and the taste." Although Herakles does not literally kill Geryon in *Autobiography of Red,* this rejection, through its emotional violence, symbolizes the physical violence that appears in one of the fragments of Stesichoros that Carson has translated: "Arrow means kill It parted Geryon's skull like a comb."

The narrative skips ahead eight years to Geryon's third year as a university student studying German philosophy. Still interested in photography ("the autobiography / . . . had recently taken the form / of a photographic essay"), Geryon travels to Argentina, where he attends a philosophy conference at the University of Buenos Aires. Later that night, Geryon awakes from a nightmare and wanders the city until he happens upon a tango bar, where he has a discussion with the tango singer, who is also a psychoanalyst. During another peregrination, Geryon literally bumps into Herakles at a bookstore. Herakles and his lover Ancash, who is "as beautiful as a live feather," are traveling in South America to record volcanoes for a video documentary on Emily Dickinson. Herakles and Ancash invite Geryon to join them on a trip to Lima, Peru, to visit Ancash's mother. When Ancash discovers Geryon's wings, he tells Geryon about the Yazcamac, "holy men" from a volcanic area in Peru. According to Ancash, "*In ancient times they worshipped / the volcano as a god and even / threw people into it*"; those who emerged were called "*the Ones Who Went and Saw and Came Back,*" and "*the Yazcamac return as red people with wings, / all their weaknesses burned away— / and their mortality.*" A volatile ménage à trois emerges, and when Ancash discovers that Geryon and Herakles have just had sexual intercourse, Ancash attacks Geryon in a quick yet ultimately harmless burst of temper. But Geryon is no longer sure he loves Herakles, and admits to Ancash that he now considers sex with Herakles "degrading," which signals Geryon's emergence into adulthood and the end of his emotional development within the book. Before leaving Lima, Geryon records himself flying around a volcano—"the bitter red drumming of wing muscle on air"—and leaves the recording with Ancash. The verse novel ends immediately before Geryon leaves, with Herakles, Ancash, and Geryon standing "side by side with arms touching, immortality on their faces, / night at their back," and with Geryon thinking, "We are amazing beings, / . . . We are neighbors of fire." This realization signals his decision and ability to endure the pain that almost ruined him, and he, not Herakles, emerges as the hero of the book.

ECONOMY OF THE UNLOST

Recommended by the *Library Journal* reviewer David Kirby "for academic collections only," *Economy of the Unlost: Reading Simonides of Keos with Paul Celan* (1999) is a dense, complicated work that has little in common with Carson's other books except for its primary method: juxtaposing the classical and the contemporary. Originally delivered as lectures in the Martin Classical Lectures series at Oberlin College, *Economy of the Unlost* places the ancient Greek poet Simonides in conversation with Paul Celan, a twentieth-century German poet who committed suicide. Carson discusses Simonides and Celan together because, as she writes in the book's preface, "they keep each other from settling" and therefore "keep [the reader's] attention strong"; "each is placed like a surface on which the other may come into focus." Thus, the relationship between Simonides and Celan remains oblique throughout the book, and her individual observations about each poet seem more convincing than her comparisons, and Celan emerges more as a curiosity than a focal point of the book.

The lack of an explicit link between Simonides and Celan has troubled some critics. Ethan Paquin claims that "Carson's are tenuous links at best" and "nowhere is it explicitly claimed that Celan was influenced by Simonides, or that Simonides provides the ultimate model for a poet of 'economy' and 'negation' and that Celan can be seen as his modern-day counterpart for

adhering so closely to said model." Danielle Allen's assessment is more generous when she writes, "This is a book about nothing: about the poetry of vanishing points, epitaphs, and absences, about parents taken away by Nazis one Friday night." But such a book clearly would be difficult to hold together, and Carson does not maintain an overarching argument throughout the book; nevertheless, her attempt sometimes makes for fascinating reading.

Carson's assertion in *Economy of the Unlost* that "Facts live in their relation to one another" illuminates not only her primary strategy in the book but also her decision to connect Simonides and Celan. According to Carson, Simonides and Celan are linked by "negation": "words for 'no,' 'not,' 'never,' 'nowhere,' 'nobody,' 'nothing' dominate their poems." They are also linked by death: one of Simonides' epitaphs—"We are all debts owed to Death"—resonates with Celan's poetry, which attempts to destroy and then rebuild the German language after the Holocaust. But economy, not death, emerges as the book's main focus, and Celan's only contribution to this aspect of the discussion is his determination to coin new words in German. Relying heavily on Marxist thought, Carson investigates "the poetic life of an economy of loss" through discussions of coinage (economic and linguistic), gift exchange, charity, wage labor, and inscription. Carson explores the evolution of poetry as a system of exchange, tracing its existence in the public sphere from the aesthetic to the economic realm.

Poetry is frequently referred to as a gift economy, which presents a paradox because only through *charis* (charity) is a gift economy possible. Poetry, then, emerges as an act of charity. The ancient Greeks' version of gift exchange, *xenia*, was based on the assumptions of "reciprocation" and "perpetuity," and as such established "a texture of personal alliances that held the ancient world together." Because he charged money for his verse, Simonides transformed the economy of poetry and disregarded the "deep mistrust of money, trade, profit, commerce and commercial persons pervading Greek socioeconomic attitudes from Homer's time through Aristotle's." Charging a fee for poetry undermines the foundation of the gift economy of poetry; and money

> ruptures continuity and stalls objects at the borders of themselves. Abstracted from space and time as bits of saleable value, they become commodities and lose their life as objects. . . . In commodification [an object's] natural properties are extinguished. Extinguished also is its power to connect the people who give and receive it: they become like commodities themselves.

Simonides' "professionalization of poetry," then, represented "the commodification of a previously reciprocal and ritual activity, the exchange of gifts between friends." Carson herself views writing as a means of conveying a gift—the gift being the facts related by the writer.

MEN IN THE OFF HOURS

A collection of epitaphs, poems, short verse essays, poems in prose, and a scholarly essay called "Dirt and Desire: Essay on the Phenomenology of Female Pollution in Antiquity," *Men in the Off Hours* (2000) emerges as a brilliantly intricate response to grief. Throughout the book, Carson inhabits the lives of Lazarus, Sappho, Catullus, Hokusai, John James Audubon, Emily Dickinson, Leo Tolstoy, Sigmund Freud, Anna Akhmatova, Artaud, and "the flat man" at the circus; the figures become subjects as well as personae, and death is their most common concern.

Continuing her tradition of mixing the classical and the modern, Carson begins *Men in the Off Hours* with the short essay "Ordinary Time: Virginia Woolf and Thucydides on War." The Greek historian of the Peloponnesian War,

Thucydides marks time by military campaigns and reports on events from various time references; Woolf, writing at the beginning of World War I, "stays in her own time." Both writers feel "it is important to mark the beginning of war," "when rules and time and freedom are just starting to slip." Because war entails deaths and deaths entail commemoration, this essay serves as an apt beginning to *Men in the Off Hours,* which remembers and reflects on various figures from history, literature, and mythology.

The epitaph becomes Carson's central means of commemoration in *Men in the Off Hours.* A form perfected by Simonides, the epitaph is generally short and concise. But Carson complicates any form she uses, and by the end of the book the traditional epitaph becomes "No Epitaph," a poem about a Chinese poet living through the Communist revolution, and "Appendix to Ordinary Time," a prose elegy for Carson's mother, who "died the autumn I was writing this." Thus, death not only runs through the book but frames it.

Because of death's presence in *Men in the Off Hours,* abstract thought frequently emerges as a way of understanding. For example, in "First Chaldaic Oracle," Carson writes:

> There is something you should know.
> And the right way to know it
> is by a cherrying of your mind.
>
> Because if you press your mind towards it
> and try to know
> that thing
>
> as you know a thing,
> you will not know it.

The means of knowledge—of death and therefore of life—occupy Carson throughout the book, and in "Lazarus (1st draft)," she admits, "Actions go on in us, / nothing else goes on."

This question of going on establishes another level of inquiry in *Men in the Off Hours.* "Essay on What I Think About Most" concerns "Error. / And its emotions." The most common emotions arising from error—"shame and remorse"—do not allow for the pleasures of error, especially those created by error in poetry. Carson believes "Metaphors teach the mind / to enjoy error" and asserts, "what we are engaged in when we do poetry is error, / the willful creation of error." Error emerges as a primary component of "Catullus: *Carmina*," a series of fifteen translations of the Roman poet Catullus that revel in Catullus's biting wit as well as in anachronism. References to the Chinese Communist leader Deng Xiaoping, the Red Cross, a refrigerator, and an ambulance place the poems hundreds of years later than the originals, and the friction between emotional truth and historical fact highlights Carson's determination to "enjoy error."

A comparable kind of error appears in the book's "TV Men" sequence, an expansion of the same series from *Glass, Irony, and God.* With Sappho, Artaud, Tolstoy, Lazarus, Antigone, and Akhmatova at the center of her "scripts," Carson explores how "TV makes things disappear." "TV Men: Artaud," for example, begins "They gave me a week to 'get' Artaud and come up with a script," which presents Artaud's madness as "Teeming with emptiness. Knotted on emptiness. Immodest in its / emptiness." Similarly, Lazarus's resurrection and marketability depend upon his insignificance, as the "director of photography" explains:

Lazarus, a man of no
particular importance,
on whom God bestows
the ultimate benevolence, without explanation,
 then abandons
him again to his nonentity.

We are left wondering, *Why Lazarus?*
My theory is
God wants us to wonder this.
After all, if there were some quality that Lazarus
 possessed,
some criterion of excellence

by which he was chosen to be called
back
from death,
then we would all start competing to achieve this.
But if

God's gift is simply random, well
for one thing
it makes a
more interesting TV show.

The pressures of commerce appear throughout the "TV Men" poems, most poignantly when Antigone's script is cut "from 42 seconds to 7" and the director still feels "we got her 'take' right" even though "substantial changes of wording were involved." And when Carson presents Sappho "smearing on her makeup at 5 A.M. in the woods by the hotel," "He She Me You Thou disappears." Television becomes the ultimate form of erasure.

Television and film are less damaging in "Irony Is Not Enough: Essay on My Life as Catherine Deneuve," which is narrated by a classics professor self-consciously play-acting the French actress Deneuve: "Seminar students are writing everything down carefully, one is asleep, Deneuve continues to talk about money and surfaces." Irony itself becomes a surface— "Deneuve sits in her office looking at the word *irony* on a page. Half-burnt"—and Carson explores its ability to serve as a mask—to present a false surface—by discussing Socrates and Sappho. "Sokrates is ironical about two things. His beauty (which he calls ugliness) and his knowledge (ignorance). . . . Just before going to jail Sokrates had a conversation with his prosecutors about irony, for this was the real source of their unease." For Sappho, "irony is a verb," and she claims that "in time . . . one's mask becomes one's face." Infatuated with one of her female students, Deneuve loses the ability to distinguish between irony and earnestness, between her mask and her self. This loss parallels the reader's experience with *Men in the Off Hours:* poised between poetry and prose, between imagination and scholarship, the writing in the book never settles into a form or genre, yet grief holds together all of Carson's masks.

THE BEAUTY OF THE HUSBAND: A FICTIONAL ESSAY IN TWENTY-NINE TANGOS

Carson continues to demonstrate a lively disregard for generic conventions in *The Beauty of the Husband* (2001). The book's subtitle calls attention to itself because of the unlikelihood of an "essay" being fictional—the essay is a form traditionally based on analysis more than on imagination—and the uniqueness of "tango" being applied to a form of writing. A Latin American ballroom dance, the tango is "characterized by graceful posturing, frequent pointing positions, and a great variety of steps" (*Webster's Revised Unabridged Dictionary,* 1998) and is an appropriate analogy for Carson's complex poetic style in the book. Carson explained in her interview with Gannon that she happened upon the tango because she was intrigued by "the idea of how it works as an emotional history, and it seems like it's a form—just like marriage—where there's a prescription to the steps, and once you get into the dance you have to dance it to the end. There's no way out." The tango is also considered difficult, which calls attention to the other meaning of "essay," namely its verb form, which means "to attempt." Carson's subtitle might signal an effort to write a work of fiction—"a fictional essay" as an essay, or attempt, at fiction—but because *The Beauty of the Husband* emerges as her most autobiographical work to date, the essay seems to fail in its aspirations in this regard.

The book itself, however, is no failure. Richard Bernstein praised it for "its moral ambiguity, its absence of rancor or preachment," and William Logan considered the book "a sublimely funny improvisation, a cracked and updated version of George Meredith's *Modern Love.*" Because the reader knows from the beginning of the book that Carson's marriage has ended years before, the book never allows for optimism about their relationship—the marriage is already over before the book begins, and Carson's reconstruction of her marriage in the book becomes its primary task.

Given her focus on beauty here, Carson's decision to intersperse her twenty-nine tangos with quotes from John Keats's poetry—mainly "Ode on Indolence," the unfinished verse play *Otho the Great: A Tragedy in Five Acts,* and *The Jealousies: A Faery Tale, by Lucy Vaughan Lloyd of China Walk, Lambeth*—and from his notes in his copy of Milton's *Paradise Lost* seems fitting. Carson chose Keats, she explained to Gannon, because he "thought intelligently" about beauty, most famously at the end of "Ode on a Grecian Urn," where he writes, "Beauty is truth, truth beauty." Because each of the tangos has a comically long title, often only tangentially related to the poem that follows, the reader must consider the titles alongside the excerpts from Keats for the fullest possible understanding of *The Beauty of the Husband.*

Carson begins the book with an unflattering view of the husband. In the second tango she writes,

> You know I was married years ago and when he
> left my husband took my notebooks.
> . . . .
> . . . He liked writing, disliked having to start
> each thought himself.
> Used my starts to various ends.

"Loyal to nothing," Carson's husband is a plagiarist as well as an adulterer; during their marriage, he pilfered her writing for letters to his mistress, and once published her writing as his own. He failed to show up at their wedding and sent a five-word telegram to her the next day. Thus, her question "So why did I love him from early girlhood to late middle age?" seems inevitable, as does her answer: "Beauty. No great secret. Not ashamed to say I loved him for his beauty." Asserting that "Beauty convinces" and "Beauty makes sex sex," *The Beauty of the Husband* emerges as a meditation on the power and danger of beauty and, like most of Carson's writing, seeks to answer the question posed in the third tango as to "how . . . people get power over one another." And because Carson associates the husband with beauty and falsehood, the husband becomes an anti-Keats.

Carson directly addresses the issue of truth and language in the seventh tango:

> My husband lied about everything.
> . . . .
> He lied when it was not necessary to lie.
> He lied when it wasn't even convenient.

In one of the book's more inventive tangos, the twelfth, Carson narrates an altercation between her and her husband from his point of view after explaining this perspectival shift:

> let's go round the back,
> there stands the wife
> gripping herself at the elbows and facing the
>   husband.

As *Autobiography of Red* deviates from the traditional focus of the Herakles/Geryon tale, Carson's shift to the husband's point of view in one-fourth of the book undermines the authority of the first person while appearing to offer a fuller accounting of the marriage. Similarly, the twenty-seventh tango, "Husband: I Am," is narrated by the husband. By allowing him speech, Carson shows an empathy reminiscent of, and probably inspired by, Keats's poems. Through Carson, he seems puzzled by the dissolution of their marriage, which to him was a kind of war game:

> She fought me. She lost.
> . . . .

> . . . How could I know. How could I
> know she would lose.

This seems to echo Carson's own observation, in the eighteenth tango, that they were "embedded in the destiny of husband and wife as firmly / as any two contiguous molecules in a chain reaction." But because "she lost," Carson must fashion memory and event into a container she herself can control: "I work at correcting the past," she writes in the twenty-eighth tango. Nevertheless, she is unable to "just finish it. / . . . To say Beauty is Truth and stop"; and the final tango, the twenty-ninth, ends with the imperative "Hold beauty," leaving truth in abeyance.

Surprisingly, Carson gives the husband—not herself or even Keats—the final word in the last poem in the book, which is unnumbered and therefore technically not a tango:

> Some tangos pretend to be about women but look
>   at this.
> Who is it you see
> reflected small
> in each of her tears.
>
> Watch me fold this page now so you think it is
>   you.

Although such sleights of hand typify the husband's untrustworthiness, Carson's own uncommonly dexterous writing reveals a thinker of profound empathy, invention, and analytical power.

Selected Bibliography

WORKS OF ANNE CARSON

BOOKS
Eros the Bittersweet: An Essay. Princeton, N.J.: Princeton University Press, 1986.
Short Talks. London, Ontario: Brick Books, 1992.

Glass, Irony, and God. New York: New Directions, 1995.

Plainwater: Essays and Poetry. New York: Knopf, 1995.

Autobiography of Red: A Novel in Verse. New York: Knopf, 1998.

Economy of the Unlost: Reading Simonides of Keos with Paul Celan. Princeton, N.J.: Princeton University Press, 1999.

Men in the Off Hours. New York: Knopf, 2000.

The Beauty of the Husband: A Fictional Essay in Twenty-nine Tangos. New York: Knopf, 2001.

TRANSLATIONS

Sophocles, *Electra.* Translation from the Greek. New York: Oxford University Press, 2001.

CRITICAL AND BIOGRAPHICAL STUDIES

Burt, Stephen. "Poetry without Borders." *Publishers Weekly,* April 3, 2000, pp. 56–57.

Martin, Sandra. "Who's Afraid of Anne Carson?" *The Globe and Mail,* February 2, 2002, p. R3.

Rae, Ian. "'Dazzling Hybrids': The Poetry of Anne Carson." *Canadian Literature* 166:17–41 (autumn 2000).

Rehak, Melanie. "Things Fall Together." *New York Times Magazine,* March 26, 2000, pp. 36–39.

BOOK REVIEWS

Allen, Danielle. Review of *Economy of the Unlost.* *Chicago Review* 46, no. 1:162–164 (2000).

Beam, Jeffery. Review of *Autobiography of Red* and *Eros the Bittersweet. Oyster Boy Review* 9 (http://www.levee67.com/obr/09/beam.html), 1999.

Bedient, Calvin. "Celebrating Imperfection." *New York Times Book Review,* May 14, 2000, p. 44. (Review of *Men in the Off Hours.*)

Bernstein, Richard. "Beauty Is Truth, and Sometimes Betrayal." *New York Times,* February 14, 2001, p. E13. (Review of *The Beauty of the Husband.*)

D'Agata, John. Review of *Men in the Off Hours. Boston Review* 25, no. 3:60–62 (summer 2000).

Fischer, Barbara. Review of *The Beauty of the Husband. Boston Review* 26, no. 5:54–57 (October/November 2001).

Kirby, David. Review of *Economy of the Unlost. Library Journal* 124, no. 14:190 (September 1, 1999).

Kirsch, Adam. "All Mere Complexities." *New Republic,* May 18, 1998, pp. 37–41. (Review of *Autobiography of Red.*)

Knox, Bernard. "Under the Volcano." *New York Review of Books,* November 19, 1998, pp. 57–60. (Review of *Autobiography of Red.*)

Logan, William. "Vanity Fair." *New Criterion,* June 1999, pp. 66–67. (Review of *Autobiography of Red.*)

————. "Folk Tales." *New Criterion,* June 2001, pp. 69–70. (Review of *The Beauty of the Husband.*)

Marlatt, Daphne. "A Poignant Critique in a Playful Mixing of Genres." *Canadian Forum* 78, no. 881:41–43 (September 1999). (Review of *Autobiography of Red.*)

McKenzie, Geraldine. Review of *Autobiography of Red. Jacket* 11 (http://www.jacket.zip.com.au/jacket11/mckenzie-on-carson.html), April 2000.

Merkin, Daphne. "'The Beauty of the Husband': Anne Carson's Elusive Tangos." *New York Times Book Review,* September 30, 2001, pp. 12–13.

Padel, Ruth. "Seeing Red." *New York Times,* May 3, 1998, p. 23. (Review of *Autobiography of Red.*)

Paquin, Ethan. "Mixed Economy." *Contemporary Poetry Review* (http://www.cprw.com/Paquin/Carson.htm), February 2002. (Review of *Economy of the Unlost.*)

Phillips, Adam. "Fickle Constructs: The Poetry of Anne Carson." *Raritan* 16, no. 2:112–119 (fall 1996). (Review of *Plainwater* and *Glass, Irony, and God.*)

Rae, Ian. "Flights of Verse." *Canadian Literature* 169:186–187 (summer 2001). (Review of *Autobiography of Red.*)

Rasula, Jed. "A Gift of Prophecy." *Canadian Literature* 161/162:187–189 (1999). (Review of *Autobiography of Red.*)

Reynolds, Oliver. "After Homer, Before Stein." *Times Literary Supplement,* December 3, 1999, p. 24. (Review of *Autobiography of Red.*)

INTERVIEWS

D'Agata, John. "A _____ with Anne Carson." *Iowa Review* 27, no. 2:1–22 (summer/fall 1997).

Gannon, Mary. "Beauty Prefers an Edge." *Poets and Writers Magazine* 29, no. 2:26–33 (March/April 2001).

—BRIAN HENRY

Gregory Corso

1930–2001

In "ODE TO the West Wind" the great English Romantic poet Percy Bysshe Shelley called on the "Wild Spirit" of imagination, fertility, life, and love, the forces of poetry itself, which he called both a "destroyer and preserver." Speaking to that force, Shelley famously cries, "Be thou me!" And when that connection initially fails, Shelley laments, "I fall upon the thorns of life! I bleed!" By the poem's end, however, Shelley *has* forged a connection; the wind, he says, will "drive my dead thoughts over the universe / Like withered leaves to quicken a new birth!"

In reading the work of the American Beat poet Gregory Corso, who admired Shelley above all other poets, one is made witness to just such a new birth: Corso's is a distinctive poetry forged specifically for a postindustrial age. In works such as "Bomb," "Power," "Police," "Army," "Hair," "Marriage," and other poems, Corso, in both comic and deadly serious terms, combines beauty and truth to explore the topic at hand, investigating the possibility of redemption and even finding grace in a postmodern world. Like Shelley, he fuses his own desire with that of his art and so in a new era invokes the old Romantic concerns.

EARLY LIFE AND FIRST POEMS

Born on March 26, 1930, in a small apartment on top of a funeral home on the corner of Bleecker and MacDougal Streets in Greenwich Village, New York City, Corso entered a world of poverty and despair. His mother, Michelina Colonni Corso, was sixteen and his father, Fortunato Samuel, a mere seventeen years old when

their son Gregory Nunzio was born. Shortly after his birth, his parents separated. His mother returned to Italy and his father gave Gregory up to foster care. In 1940, when his father remarried, the ten year old returned home. Later, when the United States entered World War II, Corso's father was among the first to be drafted into the navy. By then, Corso, an unusual child, and blessed with an unusually active imagination, had begun having visions. In his poem "Youthful Religious Experiences" he describes some of these early memories: "When I was five / I saw God in the sky." While this visionary impulse may have been a reaction to early trauma, it did not salve his pain. After living with his stepmother for a short time, Corso ran away, beginning a life on the streets that soon led to a series of arrests.

At age twelve Corso was held as a material witness in a larceny case, which led to a term in "the Tombs," a notorious New York City jail where he was routinely beaten and abused by the older prisoners. At one point, he was sent to the children's observation ward of Bellevue Hospital, where, within days of his arrival, he was placed in a straitjacket and sent for three months to the ward for the seriously demented. At age sixteen, he was arrested for stealing a suit from the window of a tailor's shop: "the tailor spotted me wearing the crime."

Reflecting on this childhood, most biographers agree that abandonment by his mother was the central fact of Corso's early life. In a 1972 interview with Michael Andre, Corso affirmed this view, acknowledging, "You can't get away from it, no way, if you are one year old and your mother leaves you." By age fifteen and essentially living on his own, Corso was also a budding artist with a raging curiosity. He found his way to the New York Public Library, where he began not only to read but also to write poems. He dates his first poetry to this period, and he included one of his first poems, "Sea Chanty," in his first book. With his biography in mind, the poem becomes particularly poignant:

> My mother hates the sea,
> my sea especially,
> I warned her not to;
> it was all I could do.
> Two years later
> the sea ate her.

For all his literary investigations, however, Corso still continued his life of crime. At age seventeen, he masterminded a robbery, using walkie-talkies to avoid the security system. With his cut of seven thousand dollars, Corso went to Florida, but he was soon arrested after one of the gang informed on him. That arrest led to a sentence at Clinton State Prison in Dannemora, in upstate New York.

As the saying goes, Clinton State was his Oxford and Cambridge, where he received his real education and where, as he said, "I had the best teachers." His second book, *Gasoline* (1958), is dedicated "to the angels of Clinton Prison who, in my 17th year, handed me, from all the cells surrounding me, books of illumination." Years later, he told his friend and biographer Neeli Cherkovski, "You know what I got in Dannemora? Stendhal's *The Red and the Black* and my Shelley. That's a good thing in life to find Shelley when you're a kid, when they got you locked away for being a menace." He adds that in jail he used his time "to get the literary gems. I even read the dictionary in jail and learned all the words." In fact, those words were the fabulous, crazy, archaic words of a 1905 English dictionary, and they ultimately infused his poetry with a unique blend of streetwise and stentorian diction.

EARLY LITERARY INFLUENCES

When Corso came out of prison at age nineteen, he went back to lower Manhattan's bohemian artist scene of coffeehouses, bars, and literary bookstores. There he met the poet Allen Ginsberg, an encounter that fundamentally shaped Corso's literary career. At the time, Ginsberg was the center of a vibrant group of young writers that came to be known as the Beat Generation. Named by the novelist Jack Kerouac, the Beat Generation of writers meant to return literature to "beatific," fundamentally spiritual concerns. At the same time, they cultivated a beaten, hipster demeanor, even taking the epithet "beat" from a local New York thug and friend, Herbert Huncke. Intensely antimaterialistic, the Beat Generation were thorns in the side of conventional America: advocates of drug use, uninhibited about sexuality, and deeply in thrall to the music of jazz, the Beat writers provoked numerous outraged responses, particularly in the mass media. They also sparked a number of notorious censorship trials, including the famous court case over Ginsberg's book of poems, *Howl.* Through Ginsberg, Corso met Kerouac, William S. Burroughs, and John Clellon Holmes. So close were Corso's ties to the Beat Generation that for a while he was treated by the media as the epitome of that literary and cultural phenomenon.

In his study of the Beats the literary scholar Warren French argues that they hoped to make art "innocent and pure," free not only from the materialism of contemporary American life but also from all forms of systematic thought. According to French, Beat literature's distinguishing characteristic was a shared value system based on pure, fundamental, unencumbered innocence and vision. The Beats called this vision a "new consciousness" and hoped, through it, to break free of all mental and social restraints. But this intellectual link did not mean they shared similar stylistic ideas. In fact, Beat writers did not have many formal technical ideas in common with one another. Of the major poets, for example, Ginsberg's work bears little stylistic resemblance to Corso's. But this stylistic difference, says French, reflects the Beat emphasis on individuality. Each writer had to find his or her own inner soul—what they described as the pure "unconditioned mind." Their search for purity and their desire to free themselves from all encumbrances—social, economic, and political—led them to experiment with a variety of what they termed "liberating" agents: drugs, automatic writing, even the sound of bebop jazz, which they felt expressed the naked soul in its purest form.

Their interest in a new consciousness did not take the Beats away from mainstream literary society. Quite the contrary—the Beat writers fought to enter the mainstream citadel, hoping to persuade serious writers everywhere to adopt their ideas. Corso once noted that Ginsberg had to teach him how to live even in bohemian literary society because, as he said, he had spent so much of his youth immersed in institutional life he did not know how to live an uninstitutional life.

Two years after meeting one another, the Beat Generation of New York City—Ginsberg, Kerouac, Burroughs, and Corso—had left town. By 1952 Corso had found a job in Los Angeles as a reporter for the *Los Angeles Examiner,* but after only a few months he left to work in the merchant marine (a job also held by both Ginsberg and Kerouac). While aboard ship he traveled to South America and Africa, eventually returning once more to Greenwich Village. There, in 1954, he met a young poet, Violet (Bunny) Lang from Radcliffe College.

In her day Lang was a well-known member of a poetry scene in Cambridge and Boston loosely associated with Harvard University. In particular she had been instrumental in the Poet's Theater, a group that included such well-known poets as John Ciardi and Richard Eberhart. It was as different a crowd as one could

imagine from the hipster, beatnik life of New York. As it happened, says Nora Sayre, a member of the Poet's Theater in these years, Bunny Lang had found Corso "destitute in New York . . . brought him to Cambridge and passed the hat among the cast and crew." Sayre speculates that there was an ulterior motive to Lang's behavior: "Planting Corso in Cambridge was probably a deliberate act of sedition. No one at Harvard—not even the New Yorkers—had met anyone like him, and she took him to starchy gatherings and urged him to be insolent."

Altogether, Corso lived in Cambridge for two years, sitting in on classes, sneaking into the library, and generally enjoying his role as, in Sayre's words, "an explosive device that might fragment custom and usage: the hipster language that he imported was utterly new to Harvard Square." Second only to meeting Ginsberg, this Cambridge interlude of 1954 and 1955 inaugurated his career as a poet.

His first collection of poems, *The Vestal Lady on Brattle* (a reference to Brattle Street, one of the main roads in Cambridge), appeared in 1955 and bears the influence of Corso's immersion in a new literary milieu outside of the Beat circle. Corso also experimented with writing drama during this "Harvard Square" period: in 1954 he wrote a play titled *In This Hung-up Age,* which was produced by the Poet's Theater in 1955.

The play is entirely symbolic, an allegory with characters named Beauty, Hipster, Tourist, Mrs Kindhead, Poetman, College Girl, and Apache. Beauty, according to the stage directions, is "dressed in a white gown, she never says anything, takes sleeping pills, occasionally blows the saxophone." She is the personification of the Beat ideal of art, and one can see how the play, in effect, was intended to educate the Cambridge poets into the hipster ethos of Beat artistic ideals. The play's action occurs on a bus that has just broken down on its way to San Francisco. Apache—a stereotype of the infinitely wise Native American—laments the sad condition of both Poetman and Beauty. Hipster, speaking for Poetman and Beauty, then says, "In this hung-up age what's the sense of the guy writing all that boid and tree stuff where there aint nobody to listen?" The characters then debate the various uses of poetry in a comic exchange that plays wonderfully off the cultural stereotypes of that era. In one of the plot threads, meanwhile, it turns out that Poetman's pursuit of Beauty is all but hopeless because she always escapes his grasp. Eventually, Poetman says, "My poems will renew hope, and more! Only a poet can renew hope."

As the characters wait for the bus driver to fix the bus, they continue their debate about the purpose of poetry. Suddenly, however, the driver runs back into the bus; a bison has attacked. Then, an entire herd of buffalo charges through, and all of the characters are killed except for one. In the play's last image one sees Beauty on the stage, "untouched." She "blows her saxophone low, soft, and beautifully."

At the outset of his career, in this his first serious literary work, Corso at once promotes the various types, figures, and themes of Beat literature and mocks them with his own unique blend of satirical humor and hipster wit. In 1964, when Corso published the play, he chose in his introduction to comment only on its sociological truth: "I can safely claim that this play, indeed document, predates anything ever written about the Hipster and hip-talk."

The year his play was produced, 1955, was also the year his first collection of poems was published. Few first books have had such inauspicious beginnings. In fact, *The Vestal Lady on Brattle* was not a commercial venture at all but was, instead, privately printed by Richard Brukenfeld in an edition of 500 copies, 250 copies of which, says the Corso scholar Gregory Stephenson, were almost immediately lost. The whole operation was financed by selling subscriptions to the membership and friends of the Poet's Theater.

The book's thirty-six poems were strikingly original in their blend of surreal imagery; archaic, hipster, and romantic diction; and explosive rhythms. The title poem introduces readers to the Vestal Lady:

> Despaired, she ripples a sunless finger
> across the liquid eyes; in darkness
> the child spirals down; drowns.

According to the Beat scholar Edward Halsey Foster, "the subject matter is often terrifying but it is seen with a child's clear vision and innocence." Interpreting the title poem, he says it "concerns an aged woman who each morning creates a child, drowns him, and then 'drinks' his body."

In addition to the poems about childlike innocence destroyed, one also finds a singular ambivalence about Cambridge in such poems as "In the Tunnel Bone of Cambridge":

> So now I'm stuck here—
> a subterranean
> lashed to a pinnacle

This hipster in the ivory tower admits, "I don't know the better things that people know / All I know is the deserter condemned me to black." From this admission, the poem then develops a surreal scene in which the poetic character of "the deserter" speaks to the poet:

> He said: Gregory, here's two boxes of night
> one tube of moon
> And twenty capsules of starlight, go an' have a
> ball—

For all of his ambivalence, however, throughout the rest of his life Corso looked back on his two years in Cambridge as a golden age. When, for example, at a public symposium in 1965 it was suggested that he was antiacademic, he responded, "How can you put down teachers? My greatest time of life was two years on campus. What more could you want?" And to the biographer and literary historian Bruce Cook he added, "It was a great ball. My friends would get me into classes or the library by day and I would write by night."

While in Cambridge Corso not only printed his first book but also, despite the book's meager press run, made his first mark on the literary establishment. According to the biographer Brad Gooch, up-and-coming young poets like Frank O'Hara praised Corso's ability to adopt "successfully the rhythms and figures of speech of the jazz musicians' world without embarrassment." More significantly, the grande dame of poetry magazines, *Poetry,* also saw fit to review the book as part of a roundup of first books by such then equally unknown poets, such as A. R. Ammons, Lawrence Ferlinghetti, and the Canadian poet Irving Layton. The reviewer, Reuel Denney, focused on the problem of audience faced by these new young poets and suggested that Gregory Corso's language was not welcoming to "outsiders." Corso, said Denney, "cannot balance the richness of the be-bop group jargon from which his manner cleverly derives with the clarity he needs to make his work meaningful to a wider-than-clique audience." In conclusion, Denney sniffed that the poems' "one-man-Calypso of jive goes 'far out' to work that interjectional, parenthetical, real-crazy style associated with bop discourse." In effect, Corso was condemned for being too hip.

The most prominent poet-critic of the era, however, was Randall Jarrell, a man whose book reviews could make or break a reputation. An admirer of Jarrell's work, Corso had sent Jarrell a copy of his first book. The gambit paid off handsomely. Jarrell, who was then the consultant in poetry to the Library of Congress (today the post is called poet laureate), admired the energy, imagery, and compression of Corso's

lyrics, and he invited the young poet to Washington, D.C., for a visit. As Foster explains, "Jarrell's work showed Corso how to write poems in terms of specifics rather than general ideas or emotions." Foster adds, "Much of Jarrell's poetry is concerned with innocence and youth in a world of war and death. In these poems young men who wish no harm are trapped in situations where survival means being decisive and cruel." As a result, says Foster, it was only natural that Corso should have turned to Jarrell in the first place. Although little is known of their actual meeting, Corso referred to it often throughout his life as one of the highlights of his early years, his literary apprenticeship.

THE PARIS YEARS

After publishing his first book, Corso spent two years traveling, first to San Francisco, in 1956, and then to Mexico City, before going to Europe, always in the company of his Beat Generation friends: Ginsberg, Ginsberg's new lover Peter Orlovsky, Kerouac, and William S. Burroughs. By 1957 Corso was in Paris, where he soon entered the most productive period of his literary life. Between 1958 and 1962 he published six books, numerous essays, and poems still uncollected. The Paris years began romantically enough when, with a French girlfriend, he discovered a run-down mess of a hotel, graded thirteen on a scale of one to thirteen in the French hotel evaluation system. He named the hotel, at 9, rue Git-le-Couer, the Beat Hotel and took up residence in a small triangular attic room, sporting a cape and occasionally carrying a cane that looked remarkably like a scepter.

When Corso arrived in Paris most of the poems for *Gasoline* were already written. But they were not shaped into book form until Allen Ginsberg took charge of the manuscript. Under Ginsberg's tutelage, the negotiations, revisions, and work began in Amsterdam and continued in the Parisian Beat Hotel, their new home. Released by the San Francisco publisher City Lights as number eight in its Pocket Poets series, *Gasoline* was published with Ginsberg's introduction warning readers to open the book as they would "a box of crazy toys." On the back cover, readers found a blurb from the now-famous Jack Kerouac: "I think that Gregory Corso and Allen Ginsberg are the two best poets in America. . . . Read slowly and see." Opening the book, readers encountered not only the dedication to the "angels" of Clinton State Prison but also an epigraph from one of Corso's essays, "How Poetry Comes to Me": "It comes, I tell you, immense with gasolined rags and bits of wire and old bent nails, a dark arriviste, from a dark river within."

In thirty-two poems that move from darkness to light, from cruelty to pleasure, from hell to heaven, and that range from New York, to Mexico City, to Rotterdam, and to Paris, Corso brought his unique blend of surreal imagery, comic timing, and hipster lingo mixed with archaic diction to a far wider public than he had yet had. The book's first poem, and also its most recent in terms of composition, "Ode to Coit Tower," is, in essence, an introduction to the symbolic life of the poet. Composed as a poetic address to San Francisco's famous landmark, the poem reveals Corso's poetic intentions through a complex system of symbols. Dramatically, the poem is an apostrophe to the tower as well as a meditation on Alcatraz Prison on Alcatraz Island, visible just beyond the tower in San Francisco Bay. Written in the same verse paragraphs as Ginsberg's "Howl," "Ode to Coit Tower" has been criticized for being too wordy and imitative but it also has been praised for its unusual imagery and diction, hallmarks of Corso's style:

> Ah tower from thy berryless head I'd a vision in
>   common with myself the proximity of Alcatraz
>   and not the hip volley of white jazz & verse or

> verse & jazz embraced but a real heart-rending
>   constant vision of Alcatraz marshalled before
>   my eyes
> Stocky Alcatraz weeping on Neptune's table
>   whose petrific bondage crushes the dreamless
>   seaharp gasping for song O that that piece of
>   sea fails to dream

In these lines Corso turns his gaze from the energy and enthusiasm of Kerouac and the Beat idea of jazz to a harsher reality represented by the prison that lies just beyond in the bay. The tower, a phallic symbol of regeneration and life, is here juxtaposed with a symbol of social and internal psychological, mental strictures, and the island, an otherwise unfettered element of nature, is bound by the "dreamless" fact of a prison. The poem celebrates the Beat faith in dreams and the imagination and recognizes just how hopeless such a faith might be in the modern world.

At the end of this long poem, Corso, alluding to his beloved Shelley, laments,

> Though the West Wind seemed to harbor there
>   not one
>   pure Shelleyian dream of let's say hay-
>   like universe
>   golden heap on a wall of fire
>   sprinting toward gauzy eradication of
>   Swindleresque Ink

In this passage the West Wind fans all that is genuine and best in the world, what Corso calls the true "world of fire." That fire burns away, purges the "Swindleresque Ink" of an overripe, overdeveloped "gauzy" poetry that never quite expresses the truth of the West Wind.

In the collection's shorter poems, such as "In the Fleeting Hand of Time," autobiography is also rendered in mythic, visionary terms:

> born March 26 1930 I am led 100 mph o'er the
>   vast market of choice
> what to choose? what to Choose?

This poem recalls an image of his own mother: "A baby mother stuffs my mouth with a pale

Milanese breast / I suck I struggle I cry O Olympian mother."

Elsewhere, such as in the ten-line "Birthplace Revisited," he recalls a visit back to the apartment where he was born: "I stand in the dark light in the dark street / and look up at my window, I was born there." What begins in realism becomes surreal:

I walk up the first flight; Dirty Ears
aims a knife at me . . .
I pump him full of lost watches.

In fact, all of the poems have an autobiographical referent (in the poem "Zizi's Lament," for example, Zizi turns out to be the person from whom the poets of the Beat Hotel bought their marijuana), but their major impulse is toward large, visionary statements and declarations of belief.

Of all the poems in this collection, "Don't Shoot the Warthog" best captures the spirit of comic play, the abusive, violent imagery, and the theme of innocence brutalized by a cruel world that are typical in Corso's poetry. Making use of a strong rhythmic sensibility and obvious rhyme scheme, Corso's lyric begins,

A child came to me
swinging an ocean on a stick.
He told me his sister was dead,
I pulled down his pants
and gave him a kick.
I drove him down the streets
down the night of my generation
I screamed his name, his cursed name,
down the streets of my generation

By the poem's end, Corso has reiterated several times that he "screamed the [child's] name," which, readers learn, is "Beauty." The scream attracts more and more people, who "gnawed the child's bones." It is a bleak vision that has been interpreted by one critic, Marilyn Schwartz, as representing Corso's attitude toward Romantic poetry's ideal of beauty. She reads the final moment as an analogue "to the passion of Christ," calling it a "contemporary communion banquet" in which the mob sacrifices the child and eats its flesh. Edward Halsey Foster praised the poem's many "startling images and bizarre juxtapositions."

In the contemporary reviews of the book, perhaps the most significant was Rosalind Levine's in *Poetry*. Levine declared that wherever in the book one turned "the reader will experience a sense of discovery." She added that the poems "shine with far-eastern myth" and that Corso "has a way of relating the mystic to the commonplace." Gregory Stephenson has described *Gasoline* as "a seminal work of what has been called 'the new American poetry,' interjecting a spirit of wild, improvisatory freedom of creation and unbridled vision into the literature."

The success of the collection is in no small part due to the care and attention that went into crafting both the manuscript as a whole and each poem, an attention to revision that sparked an intense debate between Corso and Kerouac. Advocating what he called "spontaneous bop prosody," Kerouac argued that a writer had to allow for the uninhibited flow of language and should, therefore, never falsify the soul's expression by revising after the fact. Corso at times violently disagreed. In a letter to Kerouac cited by Barry Miles, Corso defends his artistic methods: "All I can say is that if beauty were to pass my window I would her to move slow slow slow, not shot, whiz, tennis ball, was that beauty? O why didn't she linger? . . . no, I'm sorry Jack, but poetry is Ode to the West Wind."

Even as *Gasoline* was published in the United States, Corso continued his peripatetic European life. He sold encyclopedias to GIs in Frankfurt and traveled to Italy, where, Barry Miles recounts, "Gregory was renowned for a remarkable ability to rub people the wrong way. The first night he was in Venice he was thrown out of Harry's Bar because some Americans at the bar took exception to his long hair and sneakers." Back in Paris, in April 1958, Corso participated in a poetry reading, together with Ginsberg and Burroughs, at the English-language bookshop Le Mistral. Corso later recalled (quoted in Miles's *The Beat Hotel,* 2000) that when another poet read from work that he did not think legitimate, "I protested it was not real poetry. Someone asked me what I meant by real poetry. So I took off all my clothes and read my poems naked. I had two big bearded friends of mine as bodyguards and they threatened they'd beat up anybody who left while I was reciting. I was a big success."

That spring Corso wrote two of his most celebrated poems, "Bomb" and "Marriage." In fact, "Marriage" came to be so frequently anthologized that Corso later joked about it, in the poem "Field Report" (1989), as his big moneymaker:

> . . . so far I've earned 30,000
> from 1958 to 1988
> for my MARRIAGE poem
> and to think I wanted to call it
> EPITHALAMIUM.

If "Marriage" proved to be his most well-known poem, "Bomb" was his most influential. Affected by the rallies in both Paris and London against atomic weapons and influenced by the work of the French poet Guillaume Apollinaire, who had written "concrete" poems in the shape of their subjects, Corso composed "Bomb" in the shape of a mushroom cloud. To achieve the effect he actually pasted the typed text onto construction paper.

Not long after he finished both poems, Corso joined Ginsberg in England and was invited to give a reading at New College in Oxford. When he read "Bomb" to his British audience, which included members of the Campaign for Nuclear Disarmament, he was heckled for being a fascist, and one member of the crowd even threw a shoe at him. While in one of the Oxford dormitories, Corso asked a poet friend where his hero, Shelley, had lived. His friend, having no idea, simply pointed to the nearest room. Corso reportedly crawled through the room on all fours, kissing the floor from one end to the other, as the bemused occupant looked on. After Oxford, Corso and Ginsberg—both riding a crest of publicity as representatives of the new Beat poetry—were invited to record their poetry for the British Broadcasting Corporation.

Returning to Paris, Corso entered a period of renewed creativity, cultivating not just his poetic but also his artistic talents, specifically in drawings. He met French avant-garde writers of an earlier generation and was invited to gatherings such as one where he met the surrealist artists Marcel Duchamp and Man Ray. At that party, Ginsberg and Corso, in an effort to be Dada-surrealists of a new age, crawled around the room after Duchamp, and Corso cut Duchamp's tie off with a pair of scissors. Far from being disgusted with the antics of the young American poets, the older artists seemingly admired the young poets and often asked for them in the weeks following.

As the "beatnik" phenomenon raged in the American mass media during this year, the humor columnist Art Buchwald, in the Paris office of the *New York Herald Tribune,* found the poets at the Beat Hotel and introduced their crazy world to a wide public in the June 26, 1958, edition of that paper. After the article was published, Corso, in a letter to Ginsberg cited by Miles, lamented how ridiculous his words, when in print, seemed to be. Of Buchwald, he said, "he's all right but this 'beat generation' nonsense lessens the poetic intent, no wonder the academy of poets keep aloft, poetry is not for public humor make-fun-kicks, ridiculous, the whole thing, sardine salesmen, I've been failing my Shelley." Depressed about his portrayal, Corso concluded that the article "showed me as a talkative idiot" and admitted,

"I, as a poet, least of all people, should not go novelty on the thing I will die for."

Not long after the Buchwald article, Corso's new publisher, Lawrence Ferlinghetti of City Lights, came to Paris. Corso showed him the manuscript of "Bomb," and Ferlinghetti offered to publish it as a separate poster, or broadside. Corso tinkered some more with the poem, finishing it after a brief trip to Sweden in August on the thirteenth anniversary of the atomic blast over Japan. It was his second major publication within six months and it began:

> Budger of history Brake of time You Bomb
> Toy of universe Grandest of all snatched-sky I
> cannot hate you

Admitting at the outset that it would be an act of bad faith to hate something so powerful, Corso's poem, for all of its visual audacity, is in fact a rather traditional meditative ode on the most traditional of poetic subjects: death. Imagining all the varieties of death—"Scarey deaths like Boris Karloff" and "sadless deaths like old pain Bowery" and even "unthinkable deaths like Harpo Marx girls on Vogue covers my own"—he then has the poetic hubris to declare an atomic death "so laughable a preview I scope / a city New York City streaming star-keyed." He envisions buildings and landmarks sent flying across the globe as so much shrapnel. This apocalypse does not provoke a lament but rather a song of praise. In the language of the classical Greek poets, he exalts something so mighty that it could be an analogue to the ancient Greek gods:

> Electrons Protons Neutrons
> gathering Hesperean hair
> walking the dolorous golf of Arcady
> joining marble helmsmen
> entering the final amphitheater
> with a hymnody feeling of all Troys
> . . . .
> and yet knowing Homer with a step of grace

After comparing the bomb to the ancient powers of the classical age, he next invokes the language of praise from Christian liturgy:

> From thy nimbled matted spastic eye
> exhaust deluges of celestial ghouls
> From thy appellational womb.

In Corso's theological vision the bomb is a challenge to God, not a creation of God; it makes of "His Kingdom an eternity of crude wax."

For all of its apocalyptic imagery, "Bomb" is also a funny poem. At one point Corso creates a surreal baseball game:

> Hermes racing Owens
> The Spitball of Buddha
> Christ striking out
> Luther stealing third

In this scene Greek gods like Hermes and Olympic athletes like Jesse Owens compete with religious figures like Martin Luther, Jesus Christ, and the Buddha. The oppositions in play throughout the poem are here brought to comic and ridiculous allegorical fruition.

Ultimately, this poem encapsulates the Beat ethos of detachment, of purity. In it Corso refuses all political interpretations of the bomb, all religious interpretations, all cultural interpretations: in his eyes the bomb is simply negation itself—raw power that can literally obliterate everything organic and artificial. "I am able to laugh at all things," says Corso in his persona as the visionary poet. This laughter is the only human response when faced with such destructive potential.

Since its publication in 1958, "Bomb" has been hotly debated. Among the scholarly views, Thomas McClanahan, author of one of the first overviews of Corso's work, argues that it is "at once a protest against the violence and certain annihilation brought on by nuclear warfare and a philosophic statement about the need to restructure the value system of America." The powerful forces symbolized by the bomb, he says, "provide the elemental energy that transforms human consciousness." Similarly, Marilyn Schwartz argues that, in the poem, "the world is poetically restructured to become the Divine Kingdom." By contrast, the literary critic Catherine Seigel finds an almost unprecedented nihilism in this poem. Corso, she says, is one of few American poets ever to glorify the full destructive potential, the apocalyptic end of all things represented by the bomb.

THE HAPPY BIRTHDAY OF DEATH, MINUTES TO GO, THE AMERICAN EXPRESS

Not long after City Lights published its broadside edition of "Bomb," Corso returned to the United States, where he quickly became a notorious public figure. Beat writing had been subjected to tremendous media attention due to the *Howl* trial in 1957; in 1959 Beat literature was again in the news after two young editors of the *Chicago Review* decided to devote a year of issues to Beat writing and were subsequently vilified in the *Chicago Daily News* for publishing "filthy writing." Annoyed at the publicity, the administrators at the University of Chicago, which published the magazine, refused to publish the fourth and final Beat issue even though it had already been typeset. That volume was to include Corso's poem "Power," which his publisher, Ferlinghetti, had earlier refused to publish in *Gasoline,* arguing that it was a fascist poem.

Unwilling to be silenced, the editors founded a new, independent magazine, *Big Table,* named by Jack Kerouac. In order to help finance the new magazine, which would print the suppressed issue of the *Chicago Review,* Corso, along with Peter Orlovsky and Allen Ginsberg, gave a fund-raising reading in Chicago. The fund-raiser, held in the Lake Shore Drive apartment of a prominent socialite and banker, became a news event with a story in the *Chicago Sun Times.* The story was picked up by *Time*

magazine, which ran a story about the Chicago poetry reading in its February 9, 1959, issue. A photograph of Corso, Ginsberg, and Orlovsky identified them as "the pack of oddballs who celebrate booze, dope, sex and despair and who go by the name of Beatniks." Corso, says the article, is "a shaggy, dark little man who boasts that he has never combed his hair." The article quotes from Corso's poem "Hair" and concludes with the *Time* reporter asking the poet if he would like to make any comment. "Yes," replied Corso. "Fried shoes." The article was headlined "Fried Shoes." On February 28, in the intellectual weekly *The Nation,* Nelson Algren reacted to the event with a screed against what he saw as the latest example of American moral and cultural decline: "In gaining an affluence so great that we can afford to support infantilism as a trade followed by professional infants, we score another first."

After Chicago the poets went to New York, where the three gave a reading at Columbia University. The crowd was so large that the university had to hire police in order to control it. Among those in the audience was the essayist Diana Trilling (the wife of Ginsberg's former Columbia professor Lionel Trilling). Her lively account of the evening, in a critical essay titled "The Other Night at Columbia," published in the spring 1959 issue of the prestigious literary quarterly *Partisan Review,* further fanned the flames of publicity for Corso. On June 29, 1959, *Newsweek* magazine ran a story about the beatnik appeal to college students, particularly those at elite private colleges, and illustrated the article with a photograph of Corso eating an ice cream bar. The Beat Generation, said the reporter, is "the happy birthday of death," and Corso's photograph bore the corresponding caption: "Gloomy Corso: Birthday of Death."

On that New York trip, Corso and his Beat friends also made a feature-length film, *Pull My Daisy* (1959), in which Corso played the parts of both Kerouac and himself. Based on a script written by Kerouac and directed and produced by Alfred Leslie and Robert Frank, the movie is a comprehensive document of the Beat movement. The social historian James Campbell describes it as "the emblematic Beat generation film" with its elements of "anti-authoritarianism, jazz, bop-prose narration, girls-in-dresses-better-left-at-home spilling into misogyny, boys' adventure spilling into homosexuality. . . . At the close, Kerouac even has them all going on the road again."

By the summer of 1959, Corso was back in Europe. One famous anecdote from this period takes place while Corso was in Venice, where he used the better part of a handsome royalty check that he had received for *Gasoline* to buy a white alpaca suit. Corso reportedly was given to shouting with glee, "Look at my suit! No more of this Lower East Side . . . I'm a prince!" After a commotion one night, however, a woman pushed Corso into a canal, suit and all. Corso, who by this time was thoroughly absorbed by his role as "The Poet," a public figure making serious money from his art, could disregard the ruined suit, but complained indignantly, "You don't throw poets in canals."

On September 7, *Time* ran a story, "Bang Bong Bing," that again used a photograph of Corso to make its point. The reporter asks, "Why the popularity? The beat blather certainly is not literature. But it can be amusing." The article also reported that after less than a year *Gasoline* had gone into three printings and sold six thousand copies, while the broadside "Bomb" had four thousand copies in print. Giving that poem its widest audience to date, the article concluded with an extensive thirty-line excerpt.

By 1960 Corso had compiled enough poetry and enough of a public reputation to warrant a new volume of poems, *The Happy Birthday of Death*. One biographer claims that Corso completed the manuscript on the anniversary of the dropping of the atomic bombs on Japan, which gave him the idea for his title. But one suspects that *Newsweek*'s earlier photo caption of him as the "gloomy birthday of death" also had something to do with the title. In fact, in the front of the book, Corso included a comic list of "saleable titles," of which the first was "Fried Shoes," used earlier by *Time* as a headline for the article on Corso and the Beats.

The fact that this new collection incorporates the world of mass media and popular culture and contrasts it to poetry and its search for beauty marks but one of the many shifts between its poetry and that of *Gasoline*. More notable is the fact that fully half of the new collection consisted of long poems, in long lines. By 1960 many of those poems had already received a great deal of attention: "Marriage," "Bomb," "Hair," and, from *Big Table,* "Power," "Army," and "Police." Among those less known but soon to make their mark as well were the long poems "Clown" and "Death." The most unusual feature of the book, however, was "Bomb," because it was reproduced as a center-fold printed in the shape of a mushroom cloud with text on both sides. Another notable feature was that Corso had a new publisher, New Directions Press. Biographers say the change from City Lights was Corso's revenge for Ferlinghetti's refusal to publish "Power." But if "Power" had proved itself to be the most controversial of the book's poems, and "Hair," the most comic, by far "Marriage" became the most famous.

Beginning "Should I get married? Should I be good?" "Marriage" explores, critiques, mocks, and takes seriously the institution of marriage, asking if one's moral being depends on this institution. In the first stanza the poet imagines wooing his potential bride, dressed in his "velvet suit and faustus hood." On their dates, he says, he would take the intended to graveyards and talk about "werewolf bathtubs and forked clarinets." These surreal images tell just how far from institutional norms is the poet's idea of courtship. And in the second stanza, Corso comically envisions himself—his "hair finally combed, strangled by a tie"—meeting his future in-laws, sitting with his knees together on their "3rd degree sofa," wanting to ask where the bathroom is. He imagines the wedding ceremony in the fourth stanza: "I trembling what to say say Pie Glue." Later he pictures himself as a husband, rising from his comfy chair to shout: "Christmas teeth! Radiant brains! Apple deaf!" As if with a sigh, he laments, "God what a husband I'd make! Yes, I should get married." And in the next quirky stanzas Corso lays out just what sort of husband he would be, with

> So much to do! like sneaking into Mr Jones'
>   house late at night
> and cover his golf clubs with 1920 Norwegian
>   books
> Like hanging a picture of Rimbaud on the lawn-
>   mower
> like pasting Tannu Tuva postage stamps all over
>   the picket fence

To his suburban neighborhood, he would bring the consciousness of the counterculture, transforming the conventional symbols of middle-class life into celebrations of nonconformity (represented by the modernist writer Knut Hamsun, bohemian French poets like Arthur Rimbaud, and postimpressionist visionary painters like Paul Gauguin who moved to Tannu Tuva in the Pacific islands). By the end of the poem, after exploring the various permutations of marriage, he asks, "O but what about love? I forget love." This poetic turn questions the moral association of marriage with goodness and asks, instead, that one consider marriage not as a moral institution but as an emotional one.

Ultimately, Corso's poem, as with the poem "Bomb," reverses the traditional cultural interpretation of his subject. Much the same strategy occurs in the controversial "Power." Despite Ferlinghetti's claims, it is not fascist, but rather a call for an end to ideological thinking as such:

> I am a creature of Power
> With me there is no ferocity
> I am fair careful wise and laughable
> . . . .
> Know my Power
> I resemble fifty miles of Power
> I cut my fingernails with a red Power
> In buses I stand on huge volumes of Spanish
>   Power
> The girl I love is like a goat splashing golden
>   cream Power
> Throughout the Spring I carried no Power

Marilyn Schwartz says that "what 'Power' discovers and 'Bomb' manifests is Corso's essentially moral view of poetry." In this poem, says Schwartz, "Corso found that the poet can rechannel harmful energies by destroying and rebuilding the meanings of words."

Altogether, this third collection of poetry contained fifty-one poems and overwhelmed its readers. G. S. Fraser wrote in the *Partisan Review*, "I feel that full surrender to Mr. Corso would leave you flat on your back waiting for elephants to trample on you." This was not necessarily a condemnation. To emphasize the book's poetic qualities, Fraser quoted an extensive portion of "I Held a Shelley Manuscript," singling out the lines:

> Often, in some steep ancestral book,
>   when I find myself entangled with leopard-apples
>   and torched-mushrooms,
> my cypressean skein outreachs the recorded age
> and I, as though tipping a pitcher of milk,
> pour secrecy upon the dying page.

Other critics, however, weary of Beat writing and its public image in the media, were quick to condemn the book. In the *Minnesota Review* the critic and poet Irvin Ehrenpreis contended that the book was just "a bundle of disconnected perceptions in a perpetual flux." *Poetry* magazine, too, had also had enough of such work; the reviewer Henry Birnbaum declared the book "dull," condemning Corso as "a verbose and exaggerated preacher in verse."

With time, however, the critical and scholarly assessment of the book became generally more favorable. Edward Halsey Foster argued in 1992 that the collection's best poems "tend to be more discursive and less imagistic." This, said Foster, allowed Corso to expand into newer, more topical, themes "in which subconscious revelation is replaced by politics and social observation." Michael Skau, writing in 1999, extolled this collection because of the "sudden strength of the long poems, the extended 'probes' into particular topics." Commenting on the poetic style, Skau wrote, "Corso can provide harmonic variations on the iambic pattern, reinforcing them with such standard devices as alliteration and assonance to generate mellifluous rhythms." Added to this rhythmic originality is the particular use of rhyme. Although often dismissed as too easy or simplistic, Corso's rhymes always call attention to the rhythms he develops. Another hallmark of his new mature style is the consistent use of surreal imagery: surprising, often impossible juxtapositions. Said Skau, "Devoid of gory details, Corso's surrealism is primarily of the humorous stamp. Seldom does a brutal image appear unrelieved by comedy."

In addition to publishing this collection, Corso also wrote many essays, continued to travel through Europe, particularly in Greece, and published a collaborative anthology of "cut-up poetry"—*Minutes to Go* (1960)—with the poets Brion Gysin, Sinclair Beiles, and William S. Burroughs. According to Barry Miles, Corso was unhappy with the experimental methods employed by that book, and for years he refused to sign copies of it. In 1961 Corso published his one and only novel: *The American Express,* in the notorious Traveler's Companion series of the Paris-based English-language Olympia Press.

With *American Express,* Corso joined an elite group of writers—D. H. Lawrence, Vladimir Nabakov, and Henry Miller—who, because of censorship in Great Britain and the United States, had been required to publish in Paris with a press best known for English-language pornography. Corso's novel, however, is in no way pornographic; he had approached the press out of expediency rather than necessity. Olympia Press happened to be located only a few blocks from the Beat Hotel, and it was already a source of ready cash for his friends who wrote pseudonymous pornographic novels for it.

Corso's novel, like his earlier play, "In This Hung-Up Age," is an allegory, and its principal action is a journey to and from a strange land in which the central landmark is an American Express office. Throughout, the book is illustrated with the author's witty pen-and-ink drawings. Skau describes the novel "as a qualified endorsement of the need for society change." He argues that it "portrays and critiques the ideals and tactics of . . . self-proclaimed saviors, providing parallels both to the dangers inherent in the approaches of the rebels and to the concerns of the Beats about how to use their talents to improve humanity." Skau argues that the novel is as much an allegory of Corso's specific Beat friends as it is a generic fable about individuality and the human need to do good on earth, and that it "questions the tactical goals of protagonists representing Beat values." In the 1972 interview with Michael Andre, Corso said he had written the book too quickly—in but one month's time—and that of all his books, "It's the one I hate."

THE DECLINE OF A POET

In 1962, the year the Beat Hotel closed its doors, Corso also published, in London, his first *Selected Poems,* which contained work from his previous three collections of poetry and new work from *Long Live Man* (1962). The latter volume, published in New York, also marked a poetic change. Acknowledging the change in "Writ on the Eve of My 32nd Birthday," Corso writes, "I don't act silly anymore." And in the concluding lines he explains,

I love poetry because it makes me love
    and presents me life.
And of all the fires that die in me,
there's one burns like the sun

In what Schwartz calls the collection's keynote poem, "Man," Corso defies his own title and wonders if devolution on a spiritual plane echoes evolution on a biological one:

Cell, fish, apeman, Adam;
How was the first man born?
And why has he ceased being born that way?

The poem meditates on its own question and has provoked Schwartz to read it not as a despondent poem but rather as a fundamental testament of faith.

Overall, however, the book was not well received either in contemporary reviews or in subsequent criticism. Writing in the *Kenyon Review,* Geoffrey Hartman complained that too many of the poems in *Long Live Man* were "trivial or not sustained." Nonetheless, said Hartman, "He is an authentic sayer, not afraid of palpable statement." He then singled out the poem "Some Greek Writings," which describes Corso's travels and friendships in Greece and concludes:

Thus out into the pitch dark we staggered
behind the taverna we went
where
beneath the starriest sky I ever saw
we all did wonderously pee

Said Hartman, "The unity of man is affirmed by the most universal and reconciling act in the world." In the *Hudson Review,* by contrast, the poet Louis Simpson, noting a variety of allusions to Robert Frost and even a poem, "After Reading 'In the Clearing' for the Author, Robert Frost," could not contain his surprise: "Who could have foreseen that the beats would become academic?" He then mocks Corso's use of archaic language as a reflection not of Romantic wildness but rather as an imitation of the most genteel and polite poetry of society: "The spectacle of Mr. Corso discovering that Robert Frost is an author is funny enough; but the language is funnier."

Two decades later, the critic and academic Marilyn Schwartz said that although too many of the poems "droop toward verse statement," the book was fundamentally religious. She argued that the poems mean to "reconstruct a definition of humanity and build an image of the Divine Kingdom." By contrast, Michael Skau viewed the book as "the most strained of Corso's volumes. . . . The poems are frequently repetitious and prosaic," while Edward Halsey Foster argued the middle ground: "If nothing in *Long Live Man* is as strong as the best of the earlier work, the poems can be joyful, celebrating life in ways the others had rarely done."

After publishing *Long Live Man,* Corso returned to the United States and in 1963 married Sally November, a schoolteacher. Although the American press savored the humor in reporting the wedding and honeymoon of America's famous nonconformist poet (*Newsweek* covered the event with a story titled "Bye Bye Beatnik"), Corso defended to the Beat biographer Bruce Cook his embrace of marriage: "Getting married means having a child. I have never denied life. One falls in love. Is that conforming?" Following the marriage, Corso took a number of odd jobs, including working in his father-in-law's flower shop.

By 1964 American poetry was essentially divided into two distinct camps: the "academics" and the "Beats." In theory, academics were interested in the autonomy and integrity of the individual poem exclusive of the poet, whereas the Beats required one also to read the poet in the poem. As Ginsberg had phrased it: "Mind is shapely poem is shapely." Every poem, said Ginsberg, was but the final product of the poet's own consciousness. Hoping to bring this schism to an open forum for a literary public, the Young Men's Hebrew Association in New York held a symposium inviting a wide range of notable poets, including Corso. Perhaps realizing that he was the one Beat on the panel, Corso chose the occasion to be his more typically rambunctious, loudmouthed, wisecracking self.

James Scully, reporting on the event for the March 9, 1964, issue of the *Nation,* quoted Corso as saying that he wrote poetry "to explain some horrors to myself" and that the task was daunting: "I've got a wife and kid coming and all that jazz. How does a poet like me make it in America?" Punctuating such serious concerns, however, was his almost constant flow of heckling; Corso's demeanor eventually drove one audience member to stand and shout, "Gregory drop dead!" By the end of the evening, the moderator concluded, "The state of contemporary poetry is war." Said Scully, "Gregory Corso alone prevailed—a refreshingly elementary medium in which the moderator, the panel, and the audience swam for their lives."

Shortly after this symposium, Corso was hired by the State University of New York's Buffalo campus to teach in the English department. He began in January 1965, assigned to teach a course on Shelley. As part of the job requirement, however, he was asked to sign a loyalty oath to the United States. Rebelling against this state law—as he said to Cook, "Of all the people who wouldn't sign a loyalty oath it's Shelley!"—he was summarily fired. Not long thereafter the oath requirement was withdrawn, but Corso did not return to teaching for years. Instead, he went back to Europe on what the biographer Bruce Cook calls "his longest ramble . . . favoring the eastern Mediterranean, the Aegean islands, and Greece." By then he had a child, a daughter named Miranda, but his marriage was ending. In 1968 Corso married his second wife, Belle Carpenter, with whom he had two children.

THE POET REBORN: *ELEGIAC FEELINGS AMERICAN*

In a 1968 assessment of Corso's career the poet Richard Howard declared that Corso's work had little craft, that Corso did not select, emphasize, or reject elements from his work. Michael Skau, however, suggests that this was rarely true— correspondence makes clear that Corso's commitment to craft and his rigorous drafting process was a source of long-standing disagreement with both Jack Kerouac and William S. Burroughs. But for Howard, the poetry *seemed* to be without craft, and that was enough for him to condemn it: "All of Corso's poems are hasty productions, untimely ripped and never quite free of the shreds and shrieks of selfhood." Meanwhile, by 1968, Corso had gone six years without publishing any major work. Noting the long silence, Howard speculated that the advocate of youth now found he was too old: "The capacity to project himself alive and kicking and screaming into every and any possibility is being leached out of Gregory by living, or by *having* lived." Although first published in a literary journal, this assessment was republished in Howard's hugely influential collection of essays *Alone with America* (1969), where it had the effect of convincing a generation of more academically inclined poets to dismiss Corso's work. Indeed, when a new edition was published in 1980 the Corso chapter was left unrevised.

Corso defended the fundamentally Romantic premise that the poet and his poetry are inseparable, and he resented the suggestion that he was anti-intellectual: "Well, he's crazy man. Anti-intellectual?" As if to prove just how intellectual his poetics could be, Corso's next volume, *Elegiac Feelings American* (1970), included numerous allusions to mysticism, gnosticism, ancient Greece, and Egypt. Why, one wonders, did Corso wait eight years before publishing? Generally, biographers point to the catastrophic effect of drugs on Corso's life. Corso himself, in the 1972 interview with Michael Andre, said his previous books did not rely on drugs for inspiration but that, by 1964, "everybody was jumping on the bandwagon taking drugs, and so it was like awkward and I said, 'what the Hell, poets do have some kind of old tradition that they can fuck around with this stuff and know how to handle it.'" Of all the poems in *Elegaic Feelings American,* said Corso, "Mutation of the Spirit" is the one that first charts the meaning and potential of the altered consciousness drugs provoke—and it does so, interestingly enough, in conjunction with a series of elegies.

In fact, *Elegaic Feelings American* very much lives up to its title as a lament for the dead. As a whole, the book is not only Corso's longest collection of poems but also his most innovative. Essentially, the book divides into three sections. The first section, consisting of five poems, is elegiac; the second is prophetic and mystical; and the third is plainspoken, located very much in the here and now. The first section includes, as the first and title poem, an elegy to Jack Kerouac, who had died in 1969, as well as an elegy to Native American civilization and an elegy for the assassinated president John F. Kennedy. It also includes "Mutation of the Spirit," which, in this context, is an elegy for the poet himself. Also among these first poems is the sequence "Eleven Times a Poem," a visionary work exploring the meaning of the zodiac and written in the spirit of William Butler Yeats's *A Vision.* That poem is, in this context, an elegy for human civilization, which, according to astrological calendars, will one day vanish as a new age is born in its place.

After these initial five poems there follows, in what amounts to a second section of the book, "The Geometric Poem," a thirty-page exploration of Egyptian mythology reproduced in Corso's handwriting. Following "The Geometric Poem" are twenty-nine more poems ranging from the impressionist plainspoken anecdotes familiar from *Long Live Man* to poems loaded with the surreal imagery and arch wit familiar from his first three collections.

Of all this book's poems, however, the first five, and especially the title poem, have received, by far, the bulk of critical attention. Michael Skau has observed that the title poem, an elegy for Kerouac, is in fact modeled after such famous elegies as Walt Whitman's "When Lilacs Last in the Dooryard Bloomed" (for Abraham Lincoln) and Shelley's "Adonais" (for John Keats): the poem even alludes to both. Marilyn Schwartz read the poem as an elegy for American culture itself, while Gregory Stephenson focused on the way the poem moves from "lamentation to celebration." In the first section Corso writes,

> . . . The American
> alien in America is a bitter truncation; and even
> this elegy, dear Jack, shall have a butchered
> tree, a tree beaten to a pulp, upon which it'll be
> contained—no wonder no good news can be
> written on such bad news—

That lamentation vanishes, however, by the final section of the poem:

> And you were flashed upon the old and darkling
> day
> a Beat Christ-boy . . . bearing the gentle round-
> ness of things
> insisting the soul was round not square
> And soon . . . behind thee
> there came a-following
> the children of flowers

In a conversation with Neeli Cherkovski, Corso glossed these lines, saying of himself, Kerouac, and Ginsberg, "We're the daddies of the hippies and that's a big one. If we hadn't been there before them, nothing would have happened. There wouldn't have been any flower children."

"Mutation of the Spirit," which can be read as an elegy for the poet himself, or for his soul, was, said Corso, meant to chart the death of one consciousness and the birth of another under the influence of heroin and speed. He told Michael Andre, "I started writing when I sensed the change. Something was going. I was no longer this." So profound was the change he experienced that the very idea of narrative continuity seemed ridiculous. Consequently, Corso refers to this poem as a random sequence, what he calls "a shuffle poem": "I don't know where you begin or end with this thing and you can read any page, but it is one poem nonetheless." Speaking of the era in which he wrote the poem, during his fall into serious drug use, around 1964 and 1965, Corso also recalls the pain of world events at the time as "one big suck": "The bombs were falling down, the whole thing with Vietnam was starting, Kennedy was dead."

Virtually all the major critics of Corso's work point to "Mutation of the Spirit" as one of his major poetic statements. As is typical of his best poetry, one finds in this poem a blend of surreal imagery, dark ideas, and comic tones:

> Barbs and Vandals axed whatever light remained
> It was a time of paganblack candles
> and they glowed only when it rained

In the book's next sequence, "Eleven Times a Poem," Corso uses the zodiac as a starting point for a meditation on violence and power in terms of an anticipated messianic future; the poem describes Corso's conception of the Second Coming and is an elegy of sorts for the premessianic age. At one point, he declares,

> I would a tinkler of dreams be
> deluded in zodiacal pretence
> than have to wonder such reality
> as human violence

This sequence uses simple and often excessive rhymes, most obviously in the eighth poem:

> War
> is to deplore
> when peace generates hate
> between the infernal patriot
> and those who demonstrate
> Yet war is hard to deplore
> a great part of life for man throughout history
> has been the times of war—O how real and hard
> a thing!

In his interview with Michael Andre, Corso defended the use of commonplace rhymes in his poetry. Andre had noted these rhymes in the margins of his copy of *Long Live Man,* penciling in the phrase: "usual cheap commonplace rhymes." During the interview, however, Corso grabbed Andre's copy to look up something and saw the marginal comment: "What!?" he yelled. Andre, taken aback and much embarrassed, eventually asks, "Do you ever think you use easy rhymes?" To which Corso replies, "If I use some hard ones, why can't I use the easy ones?"

Of the entire range of hard rhymes, easy rhymes, and unusual poetry Corso had produced thus far, however, nothing in his career was as strange as "The Geometric Poem," a mélange of holographic poems, sketches, notes, graphs, and other working papers abundantly illustrated not only with drawings but also with hieroglyphics and a wide array of symbols, all in Corso's handwriting. "I was in Paris in 1965, and in a beautiful room . . . where Rimbaud lived," Corso told Andre. "I had a big book on hieroglyphics and I studied geometry; I had a compass. I put the two together. . . . As you can see they are mostly just work papers. I never thought to put it in any kind of form as in a poem." To Bruce Cook, he explained, "That's why I've been doing all this traveling. I've spent four years thinking, trying to get right back to the source of things. I had this scary feeling that all I know about is writing and poetry, and so I made up my mind to learn. I stayed in Europe—in Greece and Crete—and I read the oldest books—*Gilgamesh,* the Bible, the Book of the Dead, all the Greek literature—just trying to put it together for myself."

Among scholars, the sequence comprising "The Geometric Poem" is taken quite seriously. Stephenson claims that the poem, in which "portents of evil and prophecies of redemption are reconciled and unified," is meant to "revive the tradition of the sacred scroll, the magical text or the illuminated manuscript, by means of an integration of written word and visual image." The poem is rich with such vivid lines as "The cosmic exterminator skips / down the algebraic void" and "Osiris! I would show visionary children / how to bamboozle the light."

In the twenty-nine poems that constitute the third section of *Elegaic Feelings American,* Corso uses striking and original language. In "The Poor Bustard" he writes,

> But I am the craftsman who carves the words
> At the mouth of shooting arrows;
> The hammered voice of the drawn bowstring.

Corso scholars have argued that the mystic depths plumbed by Corso's imagination in this collection richly reward continued reading and reflection. The book was universally praised as a far more lively, finished, and exciting collection than *Long Live Man.* But, as Michael Skau points out, part of this is due to the fact that almost all of the collection's poems had been written (and many even published) years earlier, between 1956 and 1963.

HERALD AND A *MINDFIELD*

After publishing *Elegaic Feelings American,* Corso once more lapsed into silence. In 1974 he did complete a new manuscript, "Who Am I—Who I Am," but the only copy was stolen, and it was never published. In 1976 City Lights produced a new edition of *Gasoline,* adding to it the complete edition of *The Vestal Lady on Brattle.* This combined edition remained in print and continued to be a strong seller in subsequent decades. Aside from these events, however, Corso did not publish a new book in the years from 1970 through 1981.

Herald of the Autochthonic Spirit, published in 1981, was a surprisingly slim book after so long a silence, consisting of fifty poems in just fifty-seven pages. And rather than follow from the mystical energy and insight of *Elegaic Feelings American,* it followed instead from the plainspoken descriptive poetry of *Long Live Man.* Many of the book's poems are "confessional," openly autobiographical works. Several years before this collection was published Corso told Neeli Cherkovski that he had a new book he intended to call "Heirlooms." But a number of competing ideas sparked a change of title. Cherkovski explains that because Corso's middle name, Nunzio, meant "herald" and so linked him in name to all the mythic and historical heralds of the past, he had decided that he was himself destined to be a herald of the spirit like his great mentor, Shelley. Corso chose to call his spirit "autochthonic," meaning "springs of itself out of the earth," because, as he said to his friend, "I come from the earth, and my hands are always dirty."

In the book's most representative poem, "Columbia U Poesy Reading—1975," Corso recalls the last time he was at Columbia for a poetry reading, at the height of his fame in 1959. In the "Prologue" he sums up his public persona: "16 years ago we were put down / for being filthy beatnik sex commie dope fiends." Having returned to Columbia in 1975 for a poetry reading, he looks back over his iconoclastic literary career and admits, "Me, I'm still considered an unwashed beatnik sex commie dope fiend." Corso declaims his pride in this identity:

> we early heads of present style & consciousness
> (with Kerouac in spirit)
> are the Daddies of the Age

16 years ago, born of ourselves,
ours was a history with a future
. . . .
a subterranean poesy of the streets
enhanced by the divine butcher: humor,
did climb the towers of the Big Lie
and boot the ivory apple-cart of tyrannical values
into illusory oblivion
without spilling a drop of blood
. . . blessed be Revolutionaries of the Spirit!

In the second section of the poem Corso summons three muses to guide him. But instead they turn against him, condemning him for abandoning poetry for drugs. By the end of the poem he cries,

"I swear to you there is in me yet time
to run back through life and expiate
all that's been sadly done . . . sadly neglected . . ."

Ultimately, this urge to self-criticism is the most surprising and also the saddest element of the collection. It occurs over and again. In "Return," writing in the past tense, Corso says,

The days of my poems
were unlimited joys
of blue Phoenician sails
and Zeusian toys

The phrases are made poignant by their tense. That Corso sees himself as having no poetic future is made clear in the final lines:

Of poesy and children have I sung
Father of both
The future is my past
the past my future

This negative self-assessment is also part of the poem "For Homer," in which Corso paints a pathetic self-portrait:

I've no steady income
No home

And because my hands are autochthonic
I can never wash them enough
I feel dumb
I feel like an old mangy bull
crashing through the red rag
of an alcoholic day
Yet it's all so beautiful
isn't it?

Rather than pity, however, Corso finds, in the end, pride in his new condition. In the poem "Dear Villon" he writes,

. . . Nothing is mine, a Prince of Poetry
made to roam the outskirts of society
taking, if I needed a coat, what was taken
from the lamb

This ability to survive, however, does not release him from real guilt at a certain measure of betrayal. For in terms of his own art he is, he admits in "Getting to the Poem," fundamentally bankrupt:

A drunk dreamer in reality
is an awful contradiction
Loved ones fall away from me
and I am become wanting

Not all of the poems sing this particular note. There is, as well, an abundance of humor and irony perhaps nowhere better evident than in the poem "The Whole Mess . . . Almost," which Edward Halsey Foster believes to be among the book's best poems. There, Corso recalls when he ran up to a sixth-floor apartment and "began throwing out / those things most important in life." Out the window go Truth, God, Faith, Hope, Charity, and "Then Beauty . . . ah, Beauty—" In the drama of the poem, after he throws Beauty out the window, he runs down the stairs: "getting there just in time to catch her / 'You saved me!' she cried." Beauty is not the only one to survive; so too does humor: "All I could do with Humor was to say: / 'Out the window with the window!'"

From 1981 to 1989 there followed another silence. Then, in 1989, after changing publishers again, Corso released *Mindfield: New and Selected Poems,* a book that contained selections from each of his previous collections as well as a substantial number of previously uncollected poems, many dating from the later 1980s. Of them, one, an extended meditation titled "Field Report," is a stroll through memories and ideas that, for some critics, fundamentally lacks any coherent narrative structure. Corso himself seems to agree, saying in the middle of the poem:

> I'm tired of this report
> I'd rather be playing black jack
> but I'm a devout sort
> devoted to Mercurio
> the greatest messenger of them all

By the end of this thirty-page poetic ramble, Corso, in the final stanza, reflects on his son:

> My son in my dreams is me
> the dark nurseless room
> the quick shadow
> the small innocent head safe under the blanket
> I am a father far away from his children
> but like Holderlin sayeth I am closer to god
> away from Him . . .

STOP

The poem's final line, "STOP," is at once a plea, a command, and a lament. In this last word Corso tells himself that he has had enough, even as he tells his readers that there can be no end to a poem that is, finally, a reflection of his life: the poet may stop, but life, like the poem, continues. In an extended analysis of the book, and this particular poem, Jim Philip—perhaps one of the collection's most forgiving critics—sees in Corso's writing "the restlessness of the older man who has found that age has brought with it not settled wisdom, but rather, as he puts it earlier . . . 'a multitude of variable thought.'"

This collection, at 268 pages and peppered with his drawings, marks Corso's final legacy. In a foreword, "On Corso's Virtues," Allen Ginsberg argues on behalf of Corso's aphoristic power: "As poetic craftsman, Corso is impeccable. His revision process, which he calls 'tailoring,' generally elision and condensation, yields gist-phrasing, extraordinary mind-jump humor." He also lauds Corso's meditations on American culture's most fundamental ideas, singling out poems such as "Power," "Bomb," "Marriage," "Army," "Police," "Hair," "Death," "Clown," and "Friend" to make his case. Following Ginsberg's essay one finds a set of "Introductory Notes" by William S. Burroughs, who declares, "Gregory's voice . . . will be heard so long as there is anyone there to listen."

THE LEGACY

On January 17, 2001, in Robbinsdale, Minnesota, attended by his daughter Sheri Langerman, a nurse, Gregory Corso died of prostate cancer. He was seventy. In Corso's *New York Times* obituary the Columbia University English professor Ann Douglas suggested that "Corso's early work helped pave the way for the feminists of a later generation" because, she said, "Women looked at Corso and the other Beats and asked, 'If these men can free themselves from constricted gender roles—getting married, working for a corporation and so on—why can't we?'" The poet and rock singer Patti Smith, eulogizing Corso in the *Village Voice,* said, "All who have stories, real or embellished, of Gregory's legendary mischief and chaotic indiscretions must also have stories of his beauty, his remorse, and his generosity." She added, "He has left us two legacies: a body of work that will endure for its beauty, discipline, and influential energy, and his human qualities. He was part Pete Rose, part Percy Bysshe Shelley."

The connection to Shelley continued in death as it had in life. Massimo De Feo and Corine

Young reported from Rome (for the May 11 *Woodstock Journal*, a literary review) on the fate of Corso's ashes:

> Around two hundred people were present in the so-called "English Cemetery" in Rome, Italy, on Saturday morning, May 5, to pay their last respects to Gregory Corso. The poet's ashes were buried in a tomb precisely in front of the grave of his great colleague Shelley, and not far from the one of John Keats.

The epitaph carved on his gravestone is from a verse of Corso's own work:

> Spirit
> is Life
> It flows thru
> the death of me
> endlessly
> like a river
> unafraid
> of becoming
> the sea

At the final ceremony in Rome, said the *Woodstock Journal*, "Mozart flowed through the air from loudspeakers, and the notes of an 'independent' clarinet played old Spanish revolutionary songs." That music, like Corso's own poetry, created a blend of the revolutionary and the classical, a hymn to life even in death.

Selected Bibliography

WORKS OF GREGORY CORSO

POETRY

The Vestal Lady on Brattle and Other Poems. Cambridge, Mass.: Richard Brukenfeld, 1955.

Bomb. San Francisco: City Lights, 1958. (Broadside.)

Gasoline. San Francisco: City Lights, 1958.

The Happy Birthday of Death. New York: New Directions, 1960.

Minutes to Go. With Sinclair Beiles, William S. Burroughs, and Brion Gysin. Paris: Two Cities Press, 1960; San Francisco: Beach Press, 1968.

Long Live Man. Norfolk, Conn.: New Directions, 1962.

Selected Poems. London: Eyre and Spottiswoode Press, 1962.

Elegaic Feelings American. New York: New Directions, 1970.

"Gasoline" and "The Vestal Lady on Brattle." San Francisco: City Lights, 1976. (Reprint of both books in one volume.)

Herald of the Autochthonic Spirit. New York: New Directions, 1981.

Mindfield: New and Selected Poems. New York: Thunder's Mouth Press, 1989.

OTHER WORKS

The American Express. Paris: Olympia Press, 1961.

"Berlin Impressions." *Evergreen Review* 5, no. 16:69–83 (January–February 1961). (Essay.)

In This Hung-up Age. In *New Directions in Prose and Poetry.* Vol. 18. Edited by James Laughlin. New York: New Directions, 1964. Pp. 149–161. (Play.)

JOURNALS, CORRESPONDENCE, AND MANUSCRIPTS

Principal manuscript collections are held at the Department of Special Collections, Green Library, Stanford University; Thomas J. Dodd Research Center, University of Connecticut; Harry Ransom Humanities Center, University of Texas, Austin; Lilly Library, Indiana University.

CRITICAL AND BIOGRAPHICAL STUDIES

Andre, Michael. "Interview." In Gregory Corso, *Writings from Unmuzzled Ox Magazine.* New York: Bookslinger, 1981. Pp. 123–158. (Interview from 1972.)

Birnbaum, Henry. *"The Happy Birthday of Death."* *Poetry* 97, no. 2:119–120 (November 1960). (Review.)

Campbell, James. *This Is the Beat Generation.* Berkeley: University of California Press, 2001.

Cherkovski, Neeli. "Revolutionary of the Spirit: Gregory Corso." In his *Whitman's Wild Children:*

Portraits of Twelve Poets. Venice, Calif.: Lapis Press, 1988. Pp. 225–252.

Cocchi, Raffaele. "Gregory Corso: Poetic Vision and Memory as a Child of Italian Origin on the Streets and Roads of Omerica [*sic*]." *Rivista di studi anglo-americani* 3, nos. 4–5:342–352 (1984–1985).

Cook, Bruce. "An Urchin Shelley." In his *The Beat Generation*. New York: Scribner, 1971. Pp. 133–149.

Creeley, Robert. "Gregory Corso 1930–2001." *Woodstock Journal* 7, no. 3 (www.woodstockjournal.com/corso.html), February 2–16, 2001.

Denney, Reuel. "Invitations to the Listener: Nine Young Poets and Their Audiences." *Poetry* 89, no. 1:45–53 (1956).

De Feo, Massimo, and Corine Young. "Gregory Corso Arrives in Rome." *Woodstock Journal* (http://www.woodstockjournal.com/corso7-10.html).

Ehrenpreis, Irvin. "Recent Poetry." *Minnesota Review* 1, no. 3:369 (spring 1961). (Review of *The Happy Birthday of Death*.)

Foster, Edward Halsey. *Understanding the Beats*. Columbia: University of South Carolina Press, 1992.

Fraser, G. S. "Plug Project Repeat." *Partisan Review* 27, no. 4:746–747 (fall 1960). (Review of *The Happy Birthday of Death*.)

French, Warren. *The San Francisco Poetry Renaissance, 1955–1960*. Boston: Twayne, 1991.

Gaiser, Carolyn. "Gregory Corso: A Poet the Beat Way." In *A Casebook on the Beat*. Edited by Thomas Parkinson. New York: Crowell, 1961. Pp. 266–275.

Gooch, Brad. *City Poet: The Life and Times of Frank O'Hara*. New York: Knopf, 1993.

Grunes, Dennis. "The Mythifying Memory: Corso's *Elegaic Feelings American*." *Contemporary Poetry* 2, no. 3:51–61 (1977).

Harney, Steve. "Ethnos and the Beat Poets." *Journal of American Studies* 25, no. 3:363–380 (1991).

Hartman, Geoffrey. "No Marvelous Boys." *Kenyon Review* 25, no. 2:374–375 (spring 1963). (Review of *Long Live Man*.)

Howard, Richard. "Gregory Corso." In his *Alone with America: Essays on the Art of Poetry in the United States since 1950*. New York: Atheneum, 1969. Enl. ed., 1980. Pp. 76–83.

Levine, Rosalind. "Six Young Poets." *Poetry* 93, no. 3:183–184 (December 1958). (Review of *Gasoline*.)

McClanahan, Thomas. "Gregory Corso." In *Dictionary of Literary Biography*. Vol. 5, *American Poets since World War II*. Edited by Donald J. Greiner. Detroit: Gale, 1980. Pp. 142–148.

McKenzie, James. "New Directions: On First Looking into Corso's *The Happy Birthday of Death*." *North Dakota Quarterly* 50, no. 2:85–93 (1982).

McNeil, Helen. "The Archaeology of Gender in the Beat Movement." In *The Beat Generation Writers*. Edited by A. Robert Lee. London: Pluto Press, 1996. Pp. 178–199.

Miles, Barry. *The Beat Hotel*. New York: Grove, 2000.

Philip, Jim. "Journeys in the Mindfield: Gregory Corso Reconsidered." In *The Beat Generation Writers*. Edited by A. Robert Lee. London: Pluto Press, 1996. Pp. 61–73.

Sayre, Nora. "The Poet's Theater." *Grand Street* 3, no. 3:92–105 (spring 1984).

Schwartz, Marilyn. "Gregory Corso." In *Dictionary of Literary Biography*. Vol. 16, *The Beats: Literary Bohemians in Postwar America*. Edited by Ann Charters. Detroit: Gale, 1983. Pp. 117–140.

Seigel, Catherine. "Corso, Kinnell, and the Bomb." *University of Dayton Review* 18, no. 3:95–103 (summer 1987).

Simpson, Louis. "Poetry Chronicle." *Hudson Review* 16, no. 1:130–140 (spring 1963). (Review of *Long Live Man*.)

Skau, Michael. *A Clown in a Grave: Complexities and Tensions in the Works of Gregory Corso*. Carbondale: Southern Illinois University Press, 1999.

Stephenson, Gregory. *Exiled Angel: A Study of the Work of Gregory Corso*. London: Hearing Eye Press, 1989.

Trilling, Diana. "The Other Night at Columbia." *Partisan Review* 26:214–230 (spring 1959).

—*JONATHAN N. BARRON*

Stephen Dixon

1936–

STEPHEN DIXON'S LITERARY career spans the age in which fiction writers faced a problem handled much earlier in the twentieth century by practitioners of other arts, including music, painting, sculpture, and photography. The challenge posed by modernism was that a work of art not be *about* something but *be* that something itself. For composers, this meant departing from the concept of program music, the romantic disposition that had claimed a one-to-one correspondence between emotions, ideas, or narrative themes and specific ways of arranging sound. For painters, the result was abstraction, most dramatically so in the style of action painting in which the canvas became not a surface upon which to represent but an area within which to act. Photographers would seem to have faced the toughest problem in practicing this new aesthetic, as their cameras focused almost inevitably on the real world; yet by using light as a subject and textures as tonality, they joined the movement toward self-apparency.

When Dixon's first short story, "The Chess House," appeared in the spring 1963 issue of the *Paris Review,* fiction writers had yet to successfully engage the issue of moving beyond representation. Even when his first collection of short fiction, *No Relief,* was published in 1976, followed the next year by his first novel, *Work,* the matter was still being debated. Could fiction in any way escape the duty of depicting persons, places, and things such as they are in the real world? Given that its tools were not musical notes, daubs of paint, or even impressions of light as captured by a lens, but rather words, the task seemed impossible. As linguistic signifiers, words necessarily refer. Such referentiality can

be complicated, as modernist writers such as James Joyce and Gertrude Stein had shown, but never completely escaped. In the thirteen years between his initial story publication and first collection, Dixon witnessed Richard Brautigan use metaphors and similes so outrageously that they became a subject in themselves (*Trout Fishing in America,* 1967); Ronald Sukenick write a novel whose subject is a writer named Ronald Sukenick writing a novel with the same themes and characters (*Up,* 1968); and Kurt Vonnegut wrestle with the matter of silence, facing the problem that there is nothing intelligent to say about a massacre like the firebombing of Dresden (*Slaughterhouse-Five,* 1969).

Even as Dixon took his place among the serious novelists of his day, Gilbert Sorrentino was signaling a virtual surrender to the anti-representational challenge by making a parody of it in *Mulligan Stew* (1979). The growing prominence of a new style of writing, minimalism, as practiced by Ann Beattie and Raymond Carver, suggested that the best a writer could do was to trim down depictions to an absolute sparseness. Carver's *What We Talk about When We Talk about Love* (1981) and *Cathedral* (1983) exemplify this trend, of which Stephen Dixon appears to be a participant. Yet his fiction has plenty of representational detail. The difference is what motivated the use of such material, and how—once introduced—it took on a fictively generative life of its own.

Beginning with the stories collected in *No Relief* and continuing with short fiction and novels published into the twenty-first century, the fiction of Stephen Dixon does seem to be less about something than being that something itself. Yet he is neither metafictive, using a reflexivity of action in order to portray the act of writing, nor minimalistic, paring down descriptions until the bare bones of attitude would carry the narrative by its own stark insistence. Most obviously, he refuses to tease his readers with anything abstract or obscure. Dixon's novels and short stories are clear as a bell, with no question at all about what is going on. His characters are familiar to the point of banality, and their actions never reach beyond the scope of what can happen to any American city dweller at just about any time. The difference is that these happenings are not reported by observing the outside world but are generated internally by the key elements set in place at the narrative's beginning.

Social mannerists such as John Cheever and John Updike ask readers to believe not just in their characters but in the larger world they inhabit; the fortunes of these characters will be to interact with the sign system that is commonly shared, legible to all and accepted as the real world. A protagonist introduced on the first page, for example, may not come into sharp focus until page fifteen or fifty, when he or she interacts with something like a product taken down from a supermarket shelf or a recognizable sociopolitical attitude. A Dixon story or novel is quite different from this because what happens within its confines is predicated entirely by what is squarely before the reader on page one. Whatever follows must be created by the interaction of those elements fully apparent from the start. There can be variations, however: in the novel *Interstate* (1995) the author tells his story eight times, each version working out the initial set of details differently, not from contrasting perspectives but according to varying possibilities of outcome.

Dixon's genius in this and other works is his generating so much action from so little beginning material. Whereas a conventional realist would demand a literacy of the entire world,

Dixon asks only that readers accept the flat statement of his work's first sentence. From there forward, narrative momentum carries on as if by itself. Such an approach rules out a focus on subject, whether it be moral statements or visual representations, which in traditional fiction can sometimes support a resolution independent of the writing's texture. Dixon gives readers the texture itself, something that will not translate into attitudes already formed by reactions to the real world. What happens in a Dixon story happens on the page, developing on its own terms from materials offered at the start as factors for what will follow. In this sense the author follows the practice of Samuel Beckett, whose own minimalism is less of a paring down than it is an exercise in the genius of combination, showing how many such permutations can be generated from so few original elements. Yet Dixon's work is very much of his own time and place, suggesting that American urban culture of the late twentieth and early twenty-first centuries may indeed be reflective of such practice. Therefore if his stories and novels are about something, it is this methodology itself as an example of the world today.

CHILDHOOD, EDUCATION, AND EARLY OCCUPATIONS

Stephen Dixon's family name is Ditchik. The child of Abraham (a dentist) and Florence (an interior decorator and designer), he was born on June 6, 1936, in Brooklyn, New York. At age one he moved with his family to the Upper West Side of Manhattan, where the typical brownstone in which Stephen was raised also housed his father's dental practice. When his elementary education began, his parents changed his last name to Dixon but kept their own as Ditchik. The author remembers this event as being more pertinent to his life at school than at home because he had to adjust to the rigors of education at the same time his associates were calling him by a new name. Throughout his life Dixon has remained close to his family; he was the sibling who stayed at home to help nurse his ailing father and the son who kept in closest contact with his mother, who lived well into her nineties. Their block in the west seventies, between Columbus Avenue and Central Park West, is a frequent location in his fiction. Most Americans know the area as the starting point for the Macy's Thanksgiving Day Parade, and in "The Parade," a chapter from his novel *I.* (2002), Dixon writes affectionately of how this event was experienced from his family's unique perspective. While some familiar urban themes, such as anonymity and a general sense of danger, appear elsewhere in the author's work, the sense of nurture and stability he derived from his "street" (as he calls it in "Ann From the Street") serves as an enduring strength in Dixon's life and writing.

Intending to join his father in the practice of dentistry, Dixon began an undergraduate program in 1954 at the City College of New York with an emphasis in the sciences. When this proved unsuited to his talents, he changed his major to international relations, preparing for a career in radio news. His first assignment was with News Associates and Radio Press in Washington, D.C., where among other duties he conducted interviews with major political figures of the time. In 1961 he returned to New York City and took a position as an editor for CBS news, working with Hughes Rudd (then a promising fiction writer, who would go on to fame as a news commentator with CBS television). Dixon's first professional work with literature began about this same time: editing a pair of detective magazines for Fawcett Publications, a firm then marketing another relatively unknown author, Kurt Vonnegut, as a spy novelist (*Mother Night,* 1961). Having published his first short fiction in the *Paris Review* and more in several other of the more prestigious venues of the time, Dixon won a Wallace Stegner Fel-

lowship in creative writing, and spent the 1964–1965 academic year at Stanford University in California.

Returning to New York, the author continued publishing short stories in a wide range of magazines that included popular monthlies as well as academic quarterlies. To support himself he worked in a number of odd jobs, passing from retail salesperson at Macy's department store to bartender, waiter, and substitute teacher. Irregular work such as this bought him time to write and also to draw. Dixon spent part of one year sketching in Paris, and his artwork appears on the covers of his collections *14 Stories* (1980) and *Man on Stage* (1996), his novel *Tisch* (1999), and his chapbook *The Switch* (1999), as well as throughout the pages of *Man on Stage.* The title of his second novel, *Work,* suggests that performing a job is something Dixon takes seriously. It is a factor of life that provides a structuring element as well as thematic interest. Not until fall of 1980 did his regular academic career begin, with an assistant professorship in the Writing Seminars at Johns Hopkins University in Baltimore. Here he would marry Anne Frydman, a translator, scholar, and professor of Russian literature, in 1983, and have two daughters, Sophia and Antonia. By not settling into a regular profession until age forty-four and not beginning a family until several years later, Stephen Dixon was in a position to savor such details of life as might be routine for others. While his early fiction often features protagonists in problematic jobs and volatile personal relationships, his later work is no less tensive, for even a happy marriage and responsible, rewarding parenthood can never be things taken for granted.

As professor of fiction at Johns Hopkins University and having served for a time as the creative writing program's chair, Dixon has become a widely respected author of serious fiction, winning awards from the American Academy of Arts and Letters and being a frequent finalist for the National Book Award. While maintaining the family home in a suburb of Baltimore, Dixon and his wife for many years kept an apartment in New York City where they would spend occasional weekends, holidays, and part of each summer, the balance of their academic vacation months devoted to summer cottage life in coastal Maine. Maryland and Maine are regular locations in his fiction, but Stephen Dixon's most characteristic work is set in the urban geographies and demographies of Manhattan, where the sometimes stressful rhythms of life in the big city give his stories and novels an unmistakable energy, a power that is able to turn the least of things into a compulsive narrative-making situation.

A FICTION OF RELATIONSHIPS

Appearing under the small press imprint of Street Fiction (Ann Arbor, Michigan) in 1976, *No Relief* draws just five stories from the scores Stephen Dixon had already published in order to present a style of writing that draws its life from the energy of relationships. Whether dealing with feuding lovers or a son tending to a terminally ill father or the business that transpires among neighbors or between co-workers, these early narratives establish a principle the author will hold to for the length of his career. Nothing in life is so small that, when combined with just one other small element, it cannot expand into almost infinite proportions. Such combinations not only draw on complex aspects of the participants, bringing out characteristics that might not otherwise be known, even to themselves, but also threaten to take on a life of their own that is well beyond the power of any single person to control.

"Mac in Love" begins with what will become a typical Dixon ploy, using as a story's first line a sentence that readers might typically expect to be its last: "She said 'You're crazy, Mac,' and shut the door." A statement like this might well be the conclusion to a detailed narrative comprising all the reasons why the protagonist is indeed crazy, but as an opener it leaves the resolution in doubt. Or at least in doubt as far as Mac is concerned because for the next eleven pages he does everything he can to fight the statement's sense of closure. He rings the bell, kicks the door, and when begged not to annoy the neighbors across the hall resorts to sending up a message with the woman's friend, who arrives just as he leaves the building. He watches from the street and imagines the two women talking about him, filling in the details of his annoying behavior. He breaks into what he presumes is happening by shouting from the street. Soon a neighbor in another apartment is involved. As the police are called, Mac frets through his memories of the relationship, which appears to have had more downs than ups to it. Even the police call is problematic, with Mac trying to keep the lovers' conversation going even as he is subdued and hauled away.

Is Mac crazy? To start with, readers have only the other person's word for it. But by the end a friend, a neighbor, and a pair of New York City policemen would be ready to agree—and all solely from the final words of an unseen, unheard confrontation, one that the protagonist will not let end until the physical force of the law intervenes. His lover may have thought she was ending things on the first line of the first page. But this is a Stephen Dixon story, where, like in the classic example of chaos theory, the fluttering of a butterfly's wings in China may lead to a hurricane days later on the other side of the world. If chaos theory seems too intellectually abstruse, Dixon's own feeling for the dynamics of a relationship acknowledges the immense power involved, power that, once erupted, is extremely hard to contain.

The four other stories selected for *No Relief* support this same belief. In the most exceptional of their occurrences, a neighbor shoots himself in despair over a note the protagonist has received by mistake, and sorting out psychological responsibility takes ten times as long as the event itself. The longest piece, "Last May," involves the death of a father and the self-sustaining routine of hospital life, a world in itself that breeds new relationships within its functioning. In the title story a protagonist reverses the situation of "Mac in Love" and calls for a breakup himself; for a few pages he feels good about it, but in trying to find someone to tell about it and failing to articulate his feelings he winds up struggling to put the affair back in order. "Good couples are basically good opposites," he learns this night, and he finds that he cannot live comfortably without the creative tension such a situation engenders.

Work (1977), also with Street Fiction Press, is Dixon's first published novel (although unpublished novels preceding it would appear later in his career). Its premise is a simple one, clearly stated in the book's first lines, yet it contains the seeds for almost two hundred pages of complex action. "I'm looking for work," the narrator begins. "I'm an actor so I take all kinds of jobs when I can't find enough work on stage or in television, movies or commercials to live on." The fill-in job he finds, then, will be something for which he is professionally unsuited, guaranteeing that there will be problems. The problems, though, are less important to the novel's composition than are the simple practices involved in working for a bar and restaurant chain. From the narrator's perspective, the myriad rules and regulations are as complicated as the most obscure Egyptology. Yet they function as the parameters of a world devoted to the serving of food and drink and the making of very real money, some of which the narrator needs to survive. Just as a typical Dixon protagonist draws energy from the persistence necessary to make a relationship of opposites function, the character struggling with the problems of working as a bartender finds

more than ample narrative material in what should be the most simple aspects of the job.

With his second novel, *Too Late* (1978), Stephen Dixon breaks into the major leagues of publishing with a contract from Harper & Row. Its plot involves both features of his early fiction: the power of a relationship and the complexities of an institution's routine. The protagonist and the woman with whom he lives attend a movie. She finds it too violent and so leaves early. He agrees to meet her later and stays to the ending. When she never returns home, a long involvement with the police begins. Here is where the author's talent for the propulsive effect of compulsive narrative shows most effectively. Like the character in "Mac in Love," he refuses to give up, hounding everyone from the detective on the case to his neighbors, whose unresponsiveness prompts tirades like this:

Did anyone tear up that note I wrote saying Donna's been missing since late Thursday night? It's true. I was in a movie with her. Theater. The Coliseum. This Thursday night. Last. She left early. I'm sorry if I've awakened any of you or am keeping you from going to sleep but I have to go on. Donna didn't like the movie. Hello? I thought I heard someone, a door opening, did I? Well she left early and said she'd see me home. She never got home. Or maybe she did but she wasn't home when I got there about an hour later. The police are looking for her now. They think foul play. I don't know what to think. I'm almost too panicked to think. I'm scared as hell for her that's for sure and I'll do anything to get her back short of putting her life in more danger if that's what it's in. This is nothing my yelling upstairs at this hour waking or keeping everyone up as much as it must be to most of you. Nothing compared to what I might do such as knocking on your doors at all hours tonight if I think that's necessary to see if you know anything about where she might be. So answer me now, please, to avoid my having to knock on your doors tonight or worse, did anyone see Donna get home? That's all the note's about.

This is just an excerpt of a single paragraph running two pages long, urged forward by the incessant present-tense narrative that Dixon employs as his characteristic mode of storytelling. Although the occasions for it will develop and change throughout the novel's action, its intensity never lets up, just as the protagonist himself remains so persistent as to exhaust the world around him. In the end this intensity is all that is left to his life, the loss of his lover having turned into a compulsion that feeds on its own manic energy. The narrative is not so much about this compulsion as it is an example of it. From the initial issue of violence in the film to the protagonist's foreboding walk home and growing paranoia, every element that occurs in the novel's action contributes to a chilling effect. Yet there is nothing mechanical or artificial about the process. The protagonist is a fully drawn character, and readers get the idea that he would like nothing more than to get back to the regular aspects of his life. But by taking one wrong step—letting his partner leave the movie early, without him—he has allowed alien, even occult forces to assume control of existence. In struggling with them he defines himself in a way routine business might not allow.

Quite Contrary: The Mary and Newt Story (1979) is Dixon's second book with Harper & Row. Like *No Relief* it is extremely selective in the short stories it collects. All eleven are interconnected stories relating to the urban love story that the two characters of the subtitle live. The greatest point of consistency in the larger narrative is that they are forever breaking up and then getting back together again. There is a great emotional energy to these incidents, to the point that readers might suspect the only reason they resume the relationship is so that they can have the pleasure of once again ending it. As a narrative device this particular trait is simple yet inventive. Its most important function is to keep the overall set of stories going while other aspects of character become apparent. Newt is a writer, and he involves his relationship with Mary (and with others) in his work—sometimes metafictively, taking self-conscious care as he crafts an explanation for the page, other times directly, as a story will consist of his letters, false starts, first drafts, and all. As happens in *Too Late,* a strong sense of living in the city prevails, although the opportunity of so many smaller narratives allows for a broader perspective. Yet *Quite Contrary* is not slice-of-life realism, for the characters' lives are seen in the context of their relationship and with a focus that roves through the experiences they share, from interest in the arts to involvement with their families.

Stephen Dixon's four books from the late 1970s are drawn from a much greater body of work. By 1979 he had published one hundred and twenty-five stories and had written two other novels that did not come into print until much later in his career. The selectivity of what he does present to a readership in this period makes for a coherence not always found in the work of a new writer. The two novels and pair of story collections have New York City for their common scene. This choice is not accidental, as the pressures of urban life are felt at almost every moment, influencing both action and character. Lovers cannot have an animated conversation without attracting attention; even at home, apartment walls are thin, and there is always the communal stage of hallway, lobby, or street. If the people in these fictions seem compulsive, they are only fitting in with their surroundings, living in rhythm with the sometimes frantic mood of Manhattan. In such circumstances personal relationships in little neighborhood pockets take on added significance, and attention is as concentrated here as it might be on a life raft at sea.

The devices Dixon uses to stimulate his narrative action are similarly coherent. Although every one of them is extremely simple in terms of theory, all emerge naturally from the circumstances of city life. Struggling actors need to find work; couples must balance their commitment to each other with the complex demands of careers and other interests; and whether it be a vague but persistent threat of violence or a promise of bountiful social experience, the city is always present as an opportunity, influencing what Dixon's characters do. New York offers millions of chances at any one moment. Open a door and an entirely new world is presented, such as the bar and restaurant chain of *Work.* But close the door and it is over—until another and totally different opportunity arises. Such is the narrative promise of Stephen Dixon's world.

A FICTION OF STRUCTURES

Narrative promise for Dixon can be so rich that it quite literally cries out for structuring. Such is the disposition of his works from the 1980s, a period when his career as a creative writing teacher was firmly established and his fiction found a home in the very best of specialist literary presses. Johns Hopkins University Press published the first of several collections, *14 Stories,* that signaled a fresh concern with organizational technique. A typical story would begin with a problem, one to which its protagonist would apply structuring talents in an attempt to find a solution. Not that these structuring talents help, of course. As might be expected from the author of *Work* and *Quite Contrary,* this structuring quickly builds momentum and proceeds by an energy of its own, sometimes leaving the original problem forgotten, other times compounding it.

Typical of *14 Stories* is "Streets," a narrative told in the Dixon style of jerky, almost breathless present tense. "Two people stand on the street corner," it begins. "Or rather she stands on the corner," it continues, immediately compromising any presumption of authority. "He's gone into the corner store. She looks up. A jet plane passes. She waves at the plane and

laughs." Is the plane important? Who knows? In phenomenological fashion the story is letting itself be formed by whatever is observed, with the relative value of events something to be decided later after all the data is in. But given that this is Stephen Dixon's New York City, data quickly threatens to overwhelm narrative sense. By the bottom of the story's first page a scuffle takes place among three people the narrator has been observing. Passersby turn to him as if he knows what is going on. He does not. But as all three are lying on the ground injured, something must be done.

For the next ten pages great blocks of unbroken description alternate with page-long exchanges of quick conversation with only a few words to each line. A rhythm is thus established that makes comprehension easier, at least for the reader: as successive details accumulate, bystanders react, with the alternating bulk and thinness of the story's typesetting indicating the action's ebb and flow. At its center, though, a resolution is slow in coming. Because the narrator has witnessed the incident's beginning, he is expected to take charge. But he has no idea of how to proceed. Information is either incomplete or contradictory, and any initiative he takes is immediately challenged. Simply sending a little girl to phone the police leads to a page of debate: is she old enough to be responsible, what is the age of responsibility, anyway, and how much does a call cost at a pay phone? For three victims, should two ambulances (that hold two victims each) be summoned, or three, given that the trio has been fighting among themselves. The narrator even debates with himself, formulating a style of moral triage in which he would decide who among the three deserves to be helped first.

After all these attempts at categorization come to nothing, Dixon's protagonist decides to leave and telephone for help himself. He enters a store and at once finds himself part of an argument between a man and woman. Intervening, he is attacked himself and crawls out into the street as the couple inflict further injuries on each other. A crowd forms. A debate begins on the proper way to get help. With the beginning of his story replicated with himself now at the center, the narrator despairs of anything worthwhile getting done and closes his eyes—and there the story ends in the only way it could given how everything that is seen leads to further complicating developments. It is the structuring impulse of "Streets" rather than any reported action that gives the story its reason for being.

From this same collection, "The Signing" indicates that something can be made out of nothing. In his simple refusal to sign some hospital papers this narrator generates a genuine catastrophe involving a real threat to his own life, yet this catastrophe brings him nowhere except back to the same hospital room, where in the process of being treated for his own injuries he is coaxed into signing the papers. Specifically, he lets his hand be guided through the act. Only by going limp can he let the riot of structuring impulses end, from the medical facility's rules to its security guard's limits of authority and the procedures by which a bus driver can or cannot get involved in the incident.

Can Dixon's protagonists never get a straight answer? A theme of *14 Stories* is that attempting to structure existence so that it becomes accountable to reason is a good way of creating endless complications. The title piece is a good example. "Eugene Randall held the gun in front of his mouth and fired," it begins—again a logical enough line to end a story, but a real problem for starting one. In his sad desire to end it all, the man has only set in motion a number of other beginnings, none of which are resolved in a proper sense. For one thing, he misses, only wounding himself. His garbled call to the hotel's switchboard operator gets mistaken as sexual harassment, heavy breathing and all. The bullet from his gun breaks a windowpane through which his suicide note blows away—only to be found by a pair of young lovers who misinterpret it as a sign to them from heaven. A block away the bullet hits a brownstone roof, causing the boy who is playing there to reason in his fright that somebody is trying to kill him.

A phone call, a note, a bullet—all are messages. And "14 Stories" proceeds by means of all these messages being misinterpreted. But whether it is another hotel guest thinking that the shot he has heard is from a television program, or the floor maid who resents having to clean up—"Why me?" she wonders—everyone involved reveals much about themselves. Of course none of these events would have happened if Eugene Randall had not tried to end things. But then nothing is as it seems, including the fourteen stories of the title. Although Mr. Randall is registered in Room 1403, he is really on the thirteenth floor, but that number has been superstitiously skipped. If readers then think that the collection's title refers to the number of stories it contains, they are wrong again: there are only thirteen. Once more Dixon has shown how the tendency to categorize is universal, a typically rational attempt to make sense of doings that are in fact random or chaotic.

14 Stories presents movingly human portraits as well, such as that of the teacher in "The Sub" who lives his life in an endless grammar of subjunctives and optatives, a shoulda-woulda-coulda life that he prefers to keep on that level. Or like Dave, the lonely narrator of "Ann from the Street," who, by imagining himself Ann's husband and her coming home to him, makes his own isolation all the more poignant. To his credit Dixon avoids sentimentality by letting the event happen in language, the narrator's sentence structure breaking apart when Ann walks away but coming back into focus when she gets home and performs her role in Dave's imagination. "Later she might say or before we get to bed that she met someone I know on the street," he fantasizes. "I'd say 'Who?' and she'd say 'You. I said I'd give you your regards. No, you said to give your best and I said I'd tell you I saw you on the street,'" a convolution as complex as anything in the magical realism of such South American writers as Jorge Luis Borges or Gabriel García Márquez and yet as moving as hopeless loneliness can be.

Dixon's other collections of this period demonstrate a growing interest in character, yet never in a static way. For him persons reveal their most telling traits in the ways they try to organize existence or, at the very least, by responding to conditions that have characters of their own. As has become customary in the author's work, city life has a personality of its own. Step out the door and onto the street and something vexing is almost guaranteed to happen. At the very least the constant hum of urban activity reminds one that there is a presence out there, ready at any time to intrude. More often Dixon's protagonists happen onto things, such as the panhandling episode described in "The Watch" from Dixon's debut volume with North Point Press in San Francisco, *Movies* (1983). In trying to shake off a beggar the narrator gives what he thinks is a half dollar but, he realizes too late, is actually his expensive pocket watch. Trying to get it back generates a narrative that says much about the narrator's persistence, ingenuity, and—ultimately—desperation. By the end when, after a week's involvements, the watch is returned, the narrator can only accuse the culprit of being what the reader has known him to be all along (as Dixon's character should have known from the beginning): a bum.

The title story from *Time to Go* (1984), published by Johns Hopkins University Press, anticipates a deeper emotion that will be explored in much later works. Its fifteen pages are divided into six sections, all of them episodes in the narrator's engagement and marriage. In the first he is shopping for an engagement present and being hectored at every step by his father. Readers wonder at the embarrassment as sales clerks offer merchandise and the old man counsels everything from frugality to dickering. In another section, as the narrator and his fiancée pick out wedding rings, the father is once more butting in, offering advice and trying to manage the whole event. Even if the narrator is not mortified, it seems his fiancée should be uncomfortable with the awkwardness of this interference. At this point readers notice something about the father's comments: only the son is hearing them. Like the voice of conscience he need not be physically present in order to guide his son's actions. The final section confirms what readers may now suspect. At the wedding reception the narrator, now a proud groom, searches for his father. When found the old man is crying. But nothing is wrong—he is just happy for his son. As the narrator reaches to embrace him, he disappears, turning back into the creature of memory he has been since his death.

Novels of this period—*Fall & Rise* in 1985 with North Point, *Garbage* in 1988 with the Cane Hill Press of New York City—are as concentrated in effect as a short story. *Fall & Rise* goes to extraordinary lengths to highlight the achievement of such concentration, having 245 closely set pages, some of them with paragraphs running twenty pages (eight thousand words) long, all centered on the events of one evening and a morning following, as a narrator meets a woman at a party and tries to make contact again afterward. Within these limits the author expands possibilities of both character and action, showing that even the most minimal occasions (as were those in the narratives of *14 Stories*) are not inhibitions but rather invitations to write—and write and write. Dixon's motive for composition in *Fall & Rise* breathes a universe of life into the smallest of situations. "I meet her at a party," his narrator begins, and from the ongoing present tense evolves a seemingly endless story packed with episodic adventures that all take place within the six or seven hours during which he meets the woman, spends most of the night walking the streets wondering how to see her again, and eventually seeks shelter at her apartment for what remains of the night. She allows him to stay on the couch until breakfast, and that is all. No relationship develops; for all the novel's bulk and packed action, there is no time.

But, as has become so typical of Stephen Dixon's method, a thorough portrait of the protagonist has been drawn, complete with the context of New York, where he lives and breathes and thinks. At the party his plans for getting to talk with the woman in question exceed by several thousand the few words he eventually manages to exchange with her because he insists on evaluating each according to all of its linguistic permutations (say and do nothing, say nothing but do something, or vice versa, and so forth). At a few points in the narrative the woman's consciousness gets the opportunity to express itself, multiplying the possibilities. Even after he has won himself a place on her couch for the night, his narrative continues with a bad dream, from which she wakes him. The novel can end only when she feeds him, dresses him in borrowed clothes, and sends him off with his mission accomplished: making contact, his motive since the novel's first line.

While spread across a greater span of time and comprising less than half the length of *Fall & Rise, Garbage* achieves an equally concentrated effect thanks to its focus on a very specific problem: a narrator being threatened by gangsters who want to take over the trash disposal contract for his bar and extort confiscatory payment. It all starts with the most routine of occurrences as two men come in and order beers. Their pressure to get his garbage haulage is at first subtle and then becomes relentless. Every Dixon narrative has one form of compulsion or another, and here two of them meet as the bar owner resists and the mobsters keep pushing in. Their methods are those of organized crime, including threats, intimidation, and slowly escalating violence. Against this the narrator poses his own stubborn refusal. By the end his bar is in shambles and his life in ruins.

What is remarkable is how he gets into this position. From event to event the narrative has never taken a big, dramatic step. Everything is slow and easy, even though over several dozen pages the reader will have noted an increase in the level of intensity to both the thugs' pressure and the bar owner's resistance. It is inevitable that something must eventually break; as with *Fall & Rise,* Dixon signals its inevitability with how the second and third lines of the novel follow so inexorably from the first. This syntactic necessity makes the author's fiction cohere on a soundly structural level, giving him the chance to depict a character and describe an action that would otherwise take much more time and space. Nothing that happens in a Dixon narrative is anything less than totally convincing, no matter how preposterous the event may appear out of context. Compulsion is all.

A FICTION OF ASPECTS

In the late 1980s and early 1990s Stephen Dixon began consolidating his techniques and preparing to apply them to massively sustained works. By the end he would be poised to produce a body of fiction unrivaled in the century's last decade.

Between 1988 and 1990 he would publish four collections with as many publishers: *The Play and Other Stories* (1988) with Coffee House Press, *Love and Will* (1989) with British American Publishing/Paris Review Editions, *All Gone* (1990) with Johns Hopkins University Press, and *Friends: More Will and Magna Stories* (1990) with Greg Boyd's small press in Santa Maria, California, Asylum Arts. By this time Dixon had placed over three hundred stories in magazines, thrice the number that had been gathered in his nine collections. Although most of these volumes would center on new work, he had the advantage of looking back at three decades of productive writing in order to build support for new directions. Dixon's canon develops in such a coherent way because of his great store of materials and talent for finding new strengths in what may have been, when first written, exploratory attempts that would not become main currents until many years later.

His four collections of this period show different specific interests at work. *The Play* selects stories that address special challenges: writing a book review (when the protagonist has never done one), struggling against despondency in a way that makes one's situation only worse (and thereby explaining how this emotional state may have come about in the first place), and even such simple acts as crossing a bridge and following a road. The pieces in *All Gone* feature narratives prompted by false information or data that cannot be believed. There are misunderstandings, genuine and deliberate, and uncertainties of memory that lead to further complications. Highlighting this state of affairs are the contexts for these problems: court documents, medical records, criminal investigations. In the title story the narrator searches for a pair of young hoodlums who have killed his friend on the subway, beating him to death and, for extra measure, throwing his body on the tracks. But, rather than acquire information or pursue a method of detection, he simply replicates his friend's activity that got him in trouble with the hoods. He is never threatened, but he loses himself in the act of trying to recreate his friend's murder (during which he intends to scream for help and get his attackers arrested, a typically Dixonesque confusion of means and ends). The conclusion comes only because the murderers are caught, but completely independent of the narrator's action. That they are released for lack of witnesses only confirms the

story's theme that any search for information runs the risk of being sidetracked by personal issues.

The multiform aspects of character are displayed in the two specially organized collections *Love and Will* and *Friends: More Will and Magna Stories*. Will Taub is the first of Dixon's several figures who are dealt with serially in the many facets of their existence. Each character appears in several books, and within each novel or story collection is seen in various guises, sometimes with apparent contradiction. Then, when the author feels he has done as much as he can with the character, attention moves on to another individual. From different versions of history to contrasts in the genre used to treat them, Dixon's protagonists are larger than any single view of them. It becomes fiction's task to contain these multiplicities—as it must, because the author emphatically insists on a single identity of character, no matter how many different things happen to that character and how variously he reacts.

Relating to women is always a challenge for Dixon's men, not because of any deficiencies of their own but because they make so much of the structures of relationships themselves. Dixon makes this point in "Said," a story from the *Love and Will* connection that takes the characters' identities for granted. What is important is how they relate, and this can be shown in a manner that is almost schematic:

He said, she said.
    She left the room, he followed her.
    He said, she said.
    She locked herself in the bathroom, he slammed the door with his fists.
    He said.
    She said nothing.
    He said.
    He slammed the door with his fists, kicked the door bottom.
    She said, he said, she said.

He batted the door with his shoulder, went into the kitchen, got a screwdriver, returned and started unscrewing the bathroom doorknob.

She said.

He said nothing, unscrewed the doorknob, pulled the doorknob out of the door, but the door stayed locked. He threw the doorknob against the door, picked it up and threw it down the hall, banged the door with the screwdriver handle, wedged the screwdriver blade between the door and jamb and tried forcing the door open. The blade broke, the door stayed locked.

He said, she said, he said.

From this first page "Said" continues for three and a half more, giving named identities only to the police and medical personnel who eventually become involved. No lines of dialogue appear and no statements follow. Why should they? Any reader knows the predictable content of the lovers' quarrel (probably over nothing) and its messy aftermath (so much trouble over what should have stayed nothing much at all). But from this episode readers learn how powerful such relationships are. The same sense of compulsion drives Will through nineteen other short narratives. Shorter than most Dixon stories, they are the fits and starts of an existence, the alternating moods that together form a life. *Love and Will* displays the wide range of Will's experience, while *Friends* centers on the relationship he shares with Magna. Will writes, and struggles with existence. Magna is more directly concerned with womanhood, serving as Dixon's first extended work with a female character. Together Will and Magna provide a good example of how, in the wake of worldly conditions proven to be so weighty by a writer like Samuel Beckett, people can indeed continue to face the mundane trials of life. "I can't go on," the typical Beckett protagonist says—but, by saying it, goes on. Will and Magna continue within a language whose very snares would restrain them. A typical moment in their lives is captured at the start of "Only the Cat Escapes":

Magna comes into the room. "Oh, Will, you're reading in bed. That's what I had decided to do. Would you mind if I joined you?"

"Come ahead."

She lies beside me on the bed and opens her book. I return to my book. She says after about a minute "Suppose I told you I don't want to read right now?"

"Let's say you just told me."

"That's what I meant. Suppose I did. What would you say?"

"I'd say, 'What do you mean you don't want to read right now?'"

"And suppose I answered that I don't want to read right now because I have something else in mind?"

"Then I'd ask what that is."

"Let's say you have asked."

"Let's say I have."

"And let's say I then said I'd like to sleep with you right now."

"So?"

"Well, what's your reply?"

"My reply?" I put my book down and think. "My reply?" She puts her book on top of my book between us. Her cat jumps on the bed and lies on my feet. I say "Do you think your cat should be on the bed at a time like this?"

"What time is that?"

"A time when I'm about to say that I think it's a pretty good idea if we do sleep together right now."

"If you did say that then I'd say it probably isn't a good time for my cat to be on the bed."

"All right, let's say I said it."

"Then I suppose I should tell the cat to get off the bed."

"Why don't you."

"I will."

Just then the cat jumps off the bed and runs underneath it.

As the story's title states, only the cat escapes this linguistic tangle so suggestive of a typical Vladimir and Estragon exchange in Beckett's

Waiting for Godot. Yet this is no bare stage of absurdist drama, but rather just the type of dialogue a couple might have on the way to making love. Why don't they just get to it and begin the act? Because, as Dixon shows, people live their lives within language and are to some extent creatures of it. Certainly there is no way to escape its grammatical net. To get something done together—to get anything done at all—they must negotiate a delicate web of syntactic constructions, any one of which might falter and send their relationship tumbling into an abyss. And so Will and Magna continue, struggling to exist in the same language Stephen Dixon's stories use to describe them. Once again his fiction is not *about* something but *is* that something itself—yet in a totally accessible way that suggests the actual lives of real people.

Frog (1991), also with British American Publishing, is Dixon's most complete and exhaustive treatment of the many aspects of character. Its protagonist, Howard Tetch, is given no less than 769 pages in which to have everything about him revealed. Like the Will and Magna stories, *Frog* contains a cycle, one of genre itself in addition to the common subject. The volume begins with fourteen stories ("Frog in Prague," "Frog Remembers," "Frog's Nanny," "Frog Dances," "Frog Fears," and so forth), which are followed by a novella ("Frog Dies," a completely hypothetical plot), two more stories, a full-length novel centered on Frog's mother, another novella ("Frog's Sister"), a novel's length of materials called "Frog Fragments" that gather up anything and everything about him not already covered. To end the book Dixon offers a last short story, "Frog," in which the recurrent appellation is identified by source: not just the nickname the text has given to Howard Tetch (no person in the narrative has ever used it), but its genesis in the name of the family's pet turtle that Howard, in his most fulfilling moment, saves from dehydration, an act that undoes the tendencies toward all of his

worst features and allows him to end the book as an admirable (if ever beleaguered) human being.

The massive impact of a work like *Frog,* so huge and encompassing yet so relentlessly centered, has brought Steven Dixon his greatest public and critical attention so far. As Steven Moore reported in the *Washington Post Book World,* the author has here produced a work to match the dimensions of fiction enlarged by James Joyce in *Finnegans Wake* (1939). "Dixon is called an 'experimental realist,'" Moore allowed, "but readers who are scared off by the e-word (or by evocations of *Finnegans Wake*) can rest assured that *Frog* is easy reading, too easy maybe, often requiring no more effort than would be needed listening to a voluble stranger in a bar telling a long story about how he met his wife, or sitting on the couch with an aged aunt turning the pages of a photo album and telling the stories behind each picture."

To this sense of narrative Dixon adds a very telling sense of fragility. In one of the stories, "Frog Dances," Howard Tetch as a middle-aging but still single man passes an open window, through which he sees a new father dancing with his infant child. He thinks it is wonderful and is encouraged to make a family life for himself. Resolving to get his life on track, he improves his career, seeks to meet a nice woman, and does. They fall in love, marry, and have a child. Helping bring the baby home from the hospital, he is seized with joy and begins dancing with it. Just then he sees a stranger staring in through the window and quickly shuts the curtain, so his happiness cannot be seen, thereby perhaps denying the life-changing inspiration to someone else. He himself could have lost out just as easily, as this and other narratives in *Frog* suggest. What does not happen in his life is almost as important as what does, and the multifaceted aspect of the volume allows all such aspects to be treated.

Long Made Short (1994) rounds out Dixon's experiments with multiple aspects. In these stories he subtracts elements so that more is done with less. Memories are richer for all the childhood friends who have been lost; what could have happened supplements, in *Frog* fashion, what does, making the inevitability of the protagonist's own mortality all the more substantial. Even coming back to the house after a full day away makes those events seem richer. Each act of subtraction throws into higher profile the rhythm of a particular experience, and from that rhythm Dixon generates a narrative in a Beckettian fashion that other writers, even the closest realists, might miss.

A FICTION OF DIMENSIONS

In 1994 Stephen Dixon began a period in which he published with Henry Holt, Thomas Pynchon's publisher of the time. With Holt, Dixon produced a body of work whose expansiveness rivals Pynchon and exceeds what so many other "meganovelists" or "novelists of excess" (in the critic Tom LeClair's terms) had been offering. LeClair's favorites include Thomas Pynchon, of course, and also Robert Coover, William H. Gass, and Don DeLillo. All of them practice a deliberate overkill of information, responding to the enormity of existence with an encyclopedic attempt to take in everything. For his part Dixon remains selective, letting the pace of his narrative either pick up or discard items according to how they either do or do not advance the action. Yet he becomes a meganovelist of all by enlarging his sense of dimension. In his three Holt novels, *Interstate, Gould* (1997), and *30: Pieces of a Novel* (1999), he creates a fiction of dimensions—no longer aspects of a character or event, but actual replays of events with different permutations, sometimes even complete opposites, in order to give them the fullest imaginative attention.

At the same time, the great wealth of the author's canon becomes evident with Holt's publication of *The Stories of Stephen Dixon* (1994), a collection of sixty pieces, massive in itself (642 pages) yet representing less than a quarter of his total output. Covering three full decades of his writing career, it lets readers see the development his work has taken, from an emphasis on relationships and structures to an understanding that the most complete narratives involve a working with aspects and dimensions. Yet from start to finish these sixty stories, first published between 1963 and 1993, show a consistency of voice that has become unmistakably Dixon, stressed with the rhythms of an existence that is forever under examination and being put to the most rigorous test.

Interstate has its roots in a theme Dixon first develops as part of *Frog,* specifically the story "Frog Takes a Swim" in which a parent's worst nightmare happens when his child disappears and, despite efforts which come to dominate the protagonist's life, cannot be found. This application of Dixonesque compulsion to such a basic human fear is worthy of a novel—and not just a novel, but eight of them. In this new work the author tells a story of some senseless road-rage reaction by two strangers that leaves one of his daughters shot and dying, if not already dead. He then retells it seven times. The major effect of such dimensionality, of course, is to make the experience seem like a terrible dream. That it may be is suggested by the eighth version, a reward to the reader (who has had to digest some truly terrifying and unnerving material) that allows the father's car trip with his daughters to come off without a hitch, all of them arriving safe and sound, with the little girls put to bed with a comfort that the readers will feel as their own. But there is no obvious reductiveness to the last version. Its sense of closure comes largely from the fact that just about every other permutation of events has been exercised; there has been so much *bad* that the only possibility remaining is *good.* Only in this way, with all the dimensions of the experience fully explored, does the author feel privileged to end things nicely. Or to end at all, given the compulsion to treat the event in its full, terrible amplitude.

Gould is subtitled "a novel in two novels," but it is in fact much more than that. Its first part, somewhat more than half of the book, is called "Abortions" and consists of six episodes (one extremely long paragraph each) in the protagonist's life that involved a lover's abortion. Each relationship has lacked very deep involvement, and for most there has been a specific alienating element. Hence ending with an abortion is not out of character, though each prompts a serious self-examination. To fully understand the character of his protagonist, Gould Bookbinder, Dixon marshals several of his techniques, including the concentration of lengthy paragraphs from *Fall & Rise,* the multiple versions of *Interstate,* the multiple genres of *Frog,* and the dynamics of a couple's relationship from *Quite Contrary.* Some of these incidents begin where other writers would find an ending, and still more of them are propelled by an urgency entirely of the protagonist's making, well beyond any rational promptings. Thus the author draws on his greatest strengths for this most difficult of topics, a woman's abortion and the extent to which her decision involves her partner, Gould.

These six episodes add up to a convincing novel. But as in *Frog,* Dixon wants to try his theme in another genre as well, and so the second part of *Gould* follows as "Evangeline," a narrative with a single focus, rather than six, that constitutes another novel—or, more properly, a novella, as it runs to about thirty thousand words. Its most obvious difference is that while centering on another of Gould's romantic relationships, this one uniquely fails to end with an abortion. As such, the novella invites comparison and contrast with "Abortions," adding dimensionality to the six earlier aspects of Gould's affairs. All of the things that drove Gould and his earlier lovers apart seem small, even picky, compared to the dissatisfactions he tolerates in his relationship with Evangeline.

What was selfish on his part in the novel's six events becomes selfless in the novella. As if his character must escape the episodic nature of a longer narrative, Dixon provides the novella as a form in which Gould can more readily show his better nature, a nature that can withstand a specific and sustained test. As opposed to the diachronic nature of "Abortions" in which the half dozen instances appear in strictly chronological order with each time period discrete, "Evangeline" is narrated in a fully synchronic manner with elements from different points in time mixed together and drawn on not in the service of history but in order to develop character and theme. Neither Gould himself nor his experiences with partners' abortions, it turns out, are best understood in terms of time's progression. Instead readers can see how emotion powers each experience in a way that narrative dimensionality can best express.

30 is devoted to Gould Bookbinder as well. First written as drafts after "Abortions" had been completed but before "Evangeline" was conceived, these pieces grew into a novel when the author decided to conclude with a complete picture. The typographic symbol "-30-" is what journalists used to put at the bottom of a page of copy when their story was done, signaling the end. Dixon's book consists of twenty-nine pieces, most of them about ten pages each, followed by a thirtieth called "Ends," which has fifteen subsections and runs from page 394 to page 672. In all Dixon produced a hefty work well over a quarter million words long, less of a meganovel or novel of excess than the postmodern equivalent of a tome by Dostoevsky or Tolstoy. Those writers too used dimensionality to capture the imaginative space of their world.

Stephen Dixon does it in a way that invites readers to participate in the form as well as in the content so that readers themselves accumulate sketches of Gould Bookbinder in the same way his creator gathers such materials. This is why some pieces contain contradictory information (in terms of small details); such specifics are always a matter for eventual sorting out, deciding which contribute best to the intended effect—and that effect cannot be measured until the very end, the "-30-" alerting the reader that the story is done.

In a conventional work such conflicting pieces of information about a character would never fit together; in this multidimensional novel, there is room for all of them, an expansive sense of inclusion that again recalls the nineteenth century Russian masters. Dixon knows that if readers are to comprehend experience it has to be in a way that lets various facets retain their own integrity. He offers no phony summations and none of the forced naturalisms that postmodern times have proven to be so false. Totalization is not this author's goal, for no one on earth is going to have a life that adds up neatly in round, equally divisible numbers. There is always something off the scale, escaping limits of the chart. And those are the elements Dixon finds most useful in adding sense to the fragments of existence. In giving life to its central character, *30* recovers lost time from the past while projecting an infinity of hypotheticals for the future. Within both directions a very real Gould Bookbinder can be located recalling an event from his childhood, celebrating a success yet worried about a possible failure, or glorying in a moment's happiness while fretting over sadnesses he may have caused.

How convincing is Dixon's method? In one piece, "The Bed," he lets Gould tell the story of his mother's death, a simple six-word statement that to make sense must be expanded into a 13,000-word narrative. These words in turn regret, remember, and only at the very end dramatize in the full sense what may have been lost had their sentiments been placed up front. In this manner Dixon makes a narrative of storytelling itself, letting readers come to understand Gould Bookbinder as he himself has worked to see him.

Stephen Dixon's short fiction from this period shows the same tendency toward dimensionality, though the author takes advantage of the shorter form to accomplish other tasks as well. *Man on Stage: Play Stories,* published in Davis, California, by Hi Jinx Press (with the involvement once more of Greg Boyd), presents four pieces in which the characters are on the dramatic floorboards: literally in "Portrait" and figuratively elsewhere when in "Toscana" a couple dine alfresco in a trendy upper Manhattan restaurant. *Sleep* (1999), with Coffee House Press in Minneapolis, gathers twenty-two stories, some dating back twenty years or more, with everything from straightforward narratives to more typically Dixonesque tales in which characters systematically undo themselves even as they try to construct an action. There are even a pair of metafictive tricks: "The Elevator," in which narrative duration is tested against the time in which an elevator door can be reasonably held open, and "Tails," an almost maddeningly self-reflexive critique of self-reflection.

Most selections, however, have a more subtle dimensionality to them, such as the spatial dimensions of time (as a father meets his daughter at the school bus stop and realizes how maturity will soon end the reality of this treasured practice) and the many facets of a simple object (such as a kitchen knife put to other purposes). Personalities themselves are subject to metamorphosis in these stories, whether by subtractions and absences ("My Life Up Till Now") or actual transformation (of a cat into a dog and of a human into a combination of these two in "The Dat"). Although told in a realistic manner, these narratives depend for their effect on the author's work with language as he plies it like a painter works with the texture of oils or a composer blends the tonalities of sound. "On a Windy Night" shows three generations of father and daughters doing just this, reworking the language of memory until the object so cherished has been transformed into something completely different yet equally important. Even impossible futures become imaginatively workable thanks to the English language's subjunctive and optative moods. Given the dimensionality of language, anything is possible, and so Dixon is always sure to ground his materials on this linguistic base.

A FICTION OF PRESENCE

At the turn of the twenty-first century Stephen Dixon's canon of work is not only firmly established but also growing in both directions. He continues to produce new fiction—the Red Hen Press (of Palmdale, California) has published *Tisch* (1999), the author's first completed but never before issued novel (worked on between 1963 and 1969)—and has plans to make available another previously unpublished work from the years just afterward, *The Story of a Story and Other Stories: A Novel.* Because Dixon has also written a dramatically new novel, *I.* (2002), with McSweeny's Books of Brooklyn and San Francisco, it is possible to examine each end of his career at once. Such examination finds a fiction of presence, an emphatic need to get the integrity of existence firmly on the page and to convince readers that the author is providing a persuasive account. In *Tisch* the protagonist is every bit as compelling as is the character "I." who alternately narrates or is told about in *I*. The difference is that Richard Tisch is presented without full benefit of the many techniques Stephen Dixon has developed over the intervening years. Tisch's story is one of relationships struggling to be formed, structures working to be built, aspects

crying to be seen, and dimensions waiting to be worked in all their composite fullness. By the time of *I.*, all these techniques and more are put to good service in portraying another story eager to be told, this one occupying the page with a strong sense of narrative presence.

Richard Tisch is a man trying desperately to establish a sense of presence in his own life. At the novel's start, he is lying in bed, tangled up in the covers and loath to get up, for two reasons: last night has been a waste of drinking, and he has been dreaming of a similar time in the army when his sergeant had to rouse him. For the next 175 pages Tisch tries to proceed with his life but in spirit never gets very far. Even to step outside demands a style of cheerleading that at least shows he is alive. As he tells himself:

> Get out in the world. Leave your stuffy flat. Enjoy this gorgeous city. Don't be a morbid geek all your life. Love, cope, meet, relate, love, be merry, see people, spend money, have fun, eat steaks, drink du Pape, test yourself, see how far your perimeters lie, put some weight on your arms, color in your cheeks, sunshine in your mind. So go—vamoose, I said get the heck out of here.

Yet Tisch's problems turn out to be much like a novelist's; he must find a way to turn all those imperatives into effective actions. Imperatives alone will only propel him through a Beckett-like routine of rummaging through the closet, struggling into his parka, and careening downstairs to face the outside world.

Once there he makes a disaster of it. Whether dealing with a neighbor about her barking dog or getting involved in the altercation of another couple, he is not able to connect with the world's ongoing narrative in any useful way. Lacking the talents to relate, to structure, and to deal with life in its many aspects and multidimensionality, he nevertheless has the compulsive power to go on. As such he is Dixon's most stripped-down character—not quite a Beckettian figure because the world he collides with is fully realized and quite recognizable, but a very spare creature in his drives (which at times seem manic) and habits (which are too often alcoholic). What can be made of such a person? For now, pure forward motion. In *Tisch,* narrative energy serves as its own subject with everything else in the novel just glancing off it as Tisch makes his impact on persons, places, and things. Like any human being he would like to have a reason for being, a sense of presence that is secure among the doings of this world. But in Stephen Dixon's canon that presence is still a long way off.

I. most certainly finds it. The nineteen pieces that form the novel are put together in typical Dixon fashion, eighteen of them working much like short stories (ten to twenty pages each, with the same central character put through variations of familiar action) while the last, running eighty-eight pages, takes everything readers have learned about the protagonist (and his wife, a frequent figure in many of the earlier narratives) and lets it inform a more expansive action only a novella can decently express. Although there are elements of Howard Tetch and Gould Bookbinder to his character, I. himself seems much like the general Dixon protagonist, like the narrator of *Interstate* whose nervous attempts to deal with the world and its threats only seem to court the hardest aspects of existence.

His name bears study. It is not used in every story, and it first appears a little more than one-third through the book in a story told in the third person but slanted to the point of view of a nameless "he." Its appearance prompts some narrative comment: "But what's he going on about. I. isn't his initial ('I am not I.' he's tempted to say, but that's not the person he's writing this in)." As a narrative technique it lets Dixon assume the strong presence of a first-person storyteller in situations where the author still wants the Jamesian benefit of detachment within a sense of psychological involvement.

Such a technique is appropriate given the special role he plays. The novel's first two chapters—the first set in Paris during I.'s earlier days, the second taking place more recently in America, where he drives his daughters to school—are predicated on a sense of "what if." What if a friend took him to the expensive restaurant in his modest Parisian hotel; what if his hurried shortcut through the school's parking lot had injured another student's mother? Therefore readers know that I., like so many Dixon protagonists (and especially the protagonist of *Interstate*), is a person who lives as much in the realms of possibility as of fact. Indeed his life is so much larger because of this that it becomes that much harder to live. The third piece, "The Switch," introduces something else about his existence: that it is shared with a wife who is seriously ill and demands a great amount of care from him. Giving it is rewarding. He is a good husband, but the physically and emotionally taxing nature of it all weighs upon his feelings. To exorcise the bad thoughts, as it were, he undertakes a switch, something a fiction writer might do, and imagines that he is the invalid and his wife is the put-upon caregiver. In this world, posited as it is by the conditional mode, Dixon is able to have his characters act and express feelings in ways that the normal limits of narrative would not allow. Do they really exist? Perhaps they really do, but as unspeakable irritations and inexpressible thoughts. "The Switch" lets them appear on the page, taking their place so early in this novel that they will enhance the reader's sense of this protagonist's presence.

With its eighteen short narratives and one long one, *I.* allows plenty of room for development. There are scenes trying to the hero's life, but also rewarding ones, such as his memories of the Macy's Thanksgiving Day Parade beginning just a block away from his home in the west seventies of Manhattan. Yet even here there is a presence that asserts itself, as at the very end he makes a visit home and asks his mother why she never took off time from cooking the holiday dinner to have a look at the event staged in so much splendor at the end of their street. He has figured that she never wanted to. Now, so many years later, he learns to his great surprise that she did. "I've always wanted to see it from the parade route," she confesses, now so late in her life that she cannot be assured of being alive for the next one. "And when I finally had the chance after you kids were out of the house and my turkey dinners and responsibilities got much smaller, it was always one thing or another that prevented me, and I also didn't feel very comfortable going to it alone." And so for her the parade of this chapter's title has been an absence, one that will never be filled, even though its presence has been made so real in the memories preceding this revelation. The revelation, in fact, reinforces this strong presence of details, for it is not something everyone can share, not even someone so much a part of the source.

The worries that run through so many of these pieces are resolved in the novella, "Again," that concludes the book. It begins somewhat like *Fall & Rise* as the protagonist sees a woman at a party and strives to make contact with her. This time he does, but at the price of a fresh complication: learning that she is sitting not in a chair but in a wheelchair. In a narrative that gives a sense of resolution and happy closure to so many of the anxieties regarding their relationship that runs through this book, the protagonist worries if her debility makes her a person to avoid. Through many scenes he wrestles with the problem, and only after seeing it from all aspects in a multiplicity of dimensions does he arrive at the decision that has let the novel about his life come to be. As the woman has done herself, he will learn to live with it.

Including such a longer work at the end of so many shorter facets of his characters' lives has become something Stephen Dixon finds neces-

sary—not so much to extend or expand his work as to show his themes at their fullest. Even though it proceeds by gathering up so many fragments, his fiction now develops until it can resolve itself with a feeling of ease and a fulfilling sense of amplitude. If a subject presents itself, it must be addressed in all its aspects, all its possibilities. Having done such, Dixon can feel he has treated it with the full powers of fiction, letting his writing be a worthwhile object in itself.

Selected Bibliography

WORKS OF STEPHEN DIXON

NOVELS

Work. Ann Arbor, Mich.: Street Fiction Press, 1977.

Too Late. New York: Harper & Row, 1978.

Fall & Rise. San Francisco: North Point Press, 1985.

Garbage. New York: Cane Hill Press, 1988.

Interstate. New York: Henry Holt, 1995.

Gould: A Novel in Two Novels. New York: Henry Holt, 1997.

30: Pieces of a Novel. New York: Henry Holt, 1999.

Tisch. Palmdale, Calif.: Red Hen Press, 1999. (Early novel.)

I. Brooklyn and San Francisco: McSweeny's Books, 2002.

The Story of a Story and Other Stories: A Novel. Palmdale, Calif.: Red Hen Press, in preparation. (Early novel.)

SHORT STORY COLLECTIONS

No Relief. Ann Arbor, Mich.: Street Fiction Press, 1976.

Quite Contrary: The Mary and Newt Story. New York: Harper & Row, 1979. (Related stories.)

14 Stories. Baltimore: Johns Hopkins University Press, 1980.

Movies: Seventeen Stories. San Francisco: North Point Press, 1983.

Time to Go. Baltimore: Johns Hopkins University Press, 1984.

The Play and Other Stories. Minneapolis: Coffee House Press, 1988.

Love and Will: Twenty Stories. A Paris Review Edition. Latham, N.Y.: British American Publishing, 1989. (Related stories.)

All Gone. Baltimore: Johns Hopkins University Press, 1990.

Friends: More Will and Magna Stories. Santa Maria, Calif.: Asylum Arts Publishing, 1990.

Long Made Short. Baltimore: Johns Hopkins University Press, 1994.

The Stories of Stephen Dixon. New York: Henry Holt, 1994. (Includes "The Chess House.")

Man on Stage: Play Stories. Davis, Calif.: Hi Jinx Press, 1996.

Sleep: Stories. Minneapolis: Coffee House Press, 1999.

OTHER WORKS

"The New Era," "Ray," "Grace Calls," and "Making a Break." In *Making a Break.* Edited by Robert Bonazzi and Rochelle Bonazzi. Austin, Tex.: Latitudes Press, 1975. Pp. 193–243. (Stories.)

Frog. New York: British American Publishing, 1991. (Novel, novellas, stories.)

The Switch. Minneapolis: Rain Taxi, 1999. (Chapbook, story.)

CRITICAL STUDIES

Boyd, Greg. "The Story's Story: A Letter to Stephen Dixon." In his *Balzac's Dolls and Other Essays, Studies, and Literary Sketches.* Daphne, Ala.: Légèreté Press, 1987. Pp. 131–138.

Chénetier, Marc. *Beyond Suspicion: New American Fiction Since 1960.* Philadelphia: University of Pennsylvania Press, 1966.

Cummins, Walter. "Story Worlds." *Literary Review* 17:462–472 (winter 1982).

Everding, Kelly, and Eric Lorberger. "Stephen Dixon." *Rain Taxi Review of Books* 1:10–17 (fall 1996).

Kelly, John. "Writing as an Art without Compromise." *Baltimore Sun,* July 22, 1984, pp. 1F, 8F–9F.

Klinkowitz, Jerome. *The Self-Apparent Word: Fiction as Language/Language as Fiction.* Carbondale: Southern Illinois University Press, 1984.

———. *Structuring the Void: The Struggle for Subject in Contemporary American Fiction.* Durham, N.C.: Duke University Press, 1992.

———. *You've Got to Be Carefully Taught: Learning and Relearning Literature.* Carbondale: Southern Illinois University Press, 2001.

LeClair, Tom. *The Art of Excess: Mastery in Contemporary American Fiction.* Urbana: University of Illinois Press, 1989.

Mandelbaum, Paul. "Dangerous Obsessions." *Johns Hopkins Magazine* 61:6–7, 15 (August 1987).

Martin, Richard. "The Critic as Entertainer: Ten Digressions and a Diversion on Stereotypes and Innovations." *Amerikastudien/American Studies* (Munich) 30:425–428 (1985).

Moore, Steven. "Frog." *Washington Post Book World,* January 19, 1992, pp. 5–6.

Saltzman, Arthur M. *The Novel in the Balance.* Columbia: University of South Carolina Press, 1993.

—JEROME KLINKOWITZ

Leslie Epstein

1938–

THE JEWISH AMERICAN writer Leslie Epstein falls uneasily between an older, more established figure such as Saul Bellow and a younger writer such as Allegra Goodman. His yoking of the farcical with the morally serious is often seen as problematic. He has, in short, not managed to attract the sustained critical attention that would lead to a wide readership. But Epstein is an important writer nonetheless, not only because he takes on themes of wide cultural significance but also because the shape and ring of his paragraphs are so delightful.

Even Epstein's harshest critics do not deny his talent or intelligence, but many feel that his thickly textured plotting is as excessive as is his habit of pulling readers in quite opposite directions. In the eighteenth century, Dr. Samuel Johnson, arguably the principal tastemaker of his day, dismissed the work of seventeenth-century metaphysical poets such as John Donne and Andrew Marvell because they did not conform to the dictates of literary classicism. Johnson was put off by the surface incongruity of metaphysical conceits, which, he complained, "yoked heterogeneous elements by violence." In the twentieth century, T. S. Eliot, the preeminent tastemaker of his day, rescued the Metaphysical conceit from Dr. Johnson's displeasure and helped to make the muscular imagery of John Donne and Andrew Marvell a building block of modernist poetry.

With a nip here, a tuck there, something of the same scenario might be applied Leslie Epstein's fiction. As Katha Politt points out in a review of *The Steinway Quintet* (1976) that appeared in the *New York Times Book Review,* "If writers got gold stars for the risks they took,

Leslie Epstein would get a handful." Epstein's work is replete with risks, with efforts to combine high and low, slapstick and seriousness, the unexpected with the conventional. His typical protagonist wants to save the world, or at least to keep evil at bay, but comic disruptions always lurk around the corner.

In an essay for the Contemporary Authors Autobiography Series, Epstein talks about how the word "Jew," "especially in the mouth of a Gentile," has remained "highly charged" and personally troubling for him—troubling because (at least for the first decade of his life) Epstein doubts whether he ever heard the word "Jew" mentioned within his family. Given the fact that he was born in Los Angeles (May 4, 1938), at a time when Germans were beginning to send Jews to Dachau, and, more important, that he was the son of Lillian Targen and Philip Epstein, the latter who together with his twin brother, Julius, was a Hollywood screenwriter (among their many credits was *Casablanca*), one would think it impossible for Epstein to have avoided "Jewishness" of some sort as he grew up. Not so, for the Hollywood community of that time was not only secular but also so deracinated and so frightened of the way that many equated Jews with communists that Epstein became "Jewish American" only after a long struggle to find out who he was in the context of a world that had systematically exterminated six million of his coreligionists.

In all of this, it is important to remember that the dumb luck of geography spared Epstein's life. Had he been born in Poland, it is highly unlikely that he would have survived the night and fog of the Holocaust. To understand what this means in the fullest sense of historical consequence, one first has to have a Jewish consciousness, something that Epstein only acquired relatively late in his life as the result of sustained reading and thought. He worked hard to be identified as a Jewish American writer, just as an older generation (one thinks of Bernard Malamud, Philip Roth, and Saul Bellow) kept insisting that they were "American" writers who happened to be Jewish.

At the time when Epstein watched—usually from an upstairs vantage point and in pajamas—Hollywood stars such as his neighbors Joseph Cotton and Gregory Peck parade through his parents' living room, there was an unwritten code that Jews could command studios, direct films, write screenplays, but not flaunt their Jewishness in front of the camera. Louis B. Mayer believed that "if you bring out a Jew in film, you're in trouble," and Jack Warner once told John Garfield (Julie Garfinkle) that "people are gonna find out you're a Jew sooner or later, but better later."

Still, some aspects of Jewishness that surfaced later were hardwired into Epstein's genes. The Holocaust is one; a Jewish sensibility is another. As Epstein puts it in his autobiographical essay:

> From childhood I might have been born with an innate grasp of the fate of the Jews. What a person learns later, the facts of physics, the formulas about the mass of objects and the square of their distance, only confirms what he carries within like the weight of his bones. Hints, hushings, inflections, a glance: these pass from Jew to Jew, and from child to child, by a kind of psychic osmosis. So it was that history passed molecule by molecule through the membrane that held me apart from my fellows, and apart from a world long denied.

To feel oneself being "held apart" is perhaps the central condition of what an earlier generation of Jewish American intellectuals called "alienation." Granted, in the case of writers such as Irving Howe or Isaac Rosenfeld, what they meant was a sense that they no longer fit into the parochial immigrant Jewish world they came from, nor did they quite fit into the mainstream culture that, all too often, made it clear that Jews were unwelcome. Epstein is hardly an example of this brand of alienation; rather, he grew up in a community where Jews were prominent members of the dream factory called Hollywood, however much that they preferred not to call attention to their Jewishness.

What is remarkable about Epstein's life is the way that a boy raised on Christmas trees rather than Hanukkah lights and on Easter egg hunts rather than Passover seders should turn into the writer he became. Part of that arithmetic began in 1953, a year after the United States exploded a hydrogen bomb on the western Pacific atoll of Eniwetok and the Russians replied in kind. He belonged to a generation of schoolchildren that learned how to "duck and cover" during classroom drills and to see the world as a place that could explode at any moment: "The very air," Epstein writes, "might catch fire."

What so haunted Epstein about the cold war and its threats of mass destruction ultimately became fused in his imagination with the technologies of death that the Nazis introduced during the Holocaust. How should a writer react to such material? In Epstein's case, his first novel, *P. D. Kimerakov* (1975), took the form of spoof, albeit with a serious underbelly, and his subsequent work maintained the posture of a person with a long history of being a wisecracker. For example, Epstein admits in his autobiographical essay that he made a habit of testing limits and of being in hot water. He was banished (for three days) from the Webb School, where he had been sent two years after his father's death; he was, temporarily, expelled from Yale, and he had his share of troubles at Oxford.

Perhaps some of Epstein's against-the-grain streak was inherited from his father and uncle. During the late 1940s, Jack Warner, the head of Warner Brothers Studio, was asked to appear before the House Un-American Activities Committee, where he provided a long list of "subversives," largely people with whom he had had contractual disputes. Among these were the Epstein brothers—Roosevelt Democrats and perennial champions of the underdog. When they received a questionnaire asking them (a) Have you ever been a member of a subversive organization? And (b) What was it? the Epsteins replied "yes" to the first part, and "Warner Brothers" to the second. Their son and nephew was cut from the same cloth, but, despite his various scrapes with school authorities, he managed not only to secure a B.A. degree from Yale in 1960 but also a Rhodes scholarship to Oxford in 1962 and an M.A. degree from the University of California, Los Angeles, in 1963.

Epstein spent ten years as a professor of English at Queens College (1965–1975) and then moved to Boston University, where he is the director of its prestigious Creative Writing Program. In addition to his Rhodes scholarship, he has received several grants from the National Endowment for the Arts, been named a Fellow of the Guggenheim Foundation and the Rockefeller Institute at Bellagio, Italy, been cited by the National Critics Circle and the American Library Association for his 1979 novel *King of the Jews,* and was a finalist for the National Jewish Book Award for the 1997 book *Pandaemonium.* He regularly contributes stories, essays, and reviews to periodicals such as *Atlantic Monthly, Esquire, The Nation,* and others. Particularly notable is his memoir of a trip to Germany, "Pictures at an Extermination," that appeared in *Harper's* in September 2000.

Epstein tried his hand at a short story when he was fourteen years old, but he did not return to the form for many years. However, during his last year at Yale, he came to the decision that "when I was ready to write, it would be as a Jew; or, better, when I was a Jew, I would be ready to write." In his case, however, the old Yiddish expression *Shver tu zein a Yid* ("It's

hard to be a Jew") proved to be all too true. What writing as a Jew required was a sense of history, and a way of coming to grips with the greatest imaginative leap of all—"that of comprehending, out of nothingness, an empty whirlwind, the glare of a burning bush, the 'I am that I am.'" It would take years before Epstein's aspirations and his accomplishments as a writer began to fuse.

Things started to fall into place for Epstein the young writer during his second year at Oxford. He devoured everything he could read about the Holocaust—this at a time when the Berlin Wall kept reminding him of the historical walls that had been erected around the Jewish ghettos. At one point in his reading he came across Gerald Reitlinger's *The Final Solution,* a study of the Holocaust published in 1953, and a stray sentence about an odd character named Chaim Rumkowski set into motion an obsession that, years later, caused him to spend considerable time at New York City's YIVO Institute for Jewish Research poring over accounts of Rumkowski's life. Eventually, the research—and his inventive rendering of the Lodz ghetto *Judenrat,* or Jewish Council—ended in *King of the Jews,* his best-known and most controversial novel.

Two related factors figure prominently in Epstein's style: one is his penchant for seeing fiction in "scenic units," something that he learned as a theater student, and the other is his willingness to give himself over to a compelling "voice," whether it is the narrator of *King of the Jews* or Leib Goldkorn, perhaps his most delightful character. Style is, of course, only part of what makes Epstein's fiction tick; there is also his effort to reconfigure how we see both the Holocaust and contemporary history, with its ongoing battle between what Evil means and what Good consists of. Whatever else he might be, Epstein is no pietist, and perhaps this accounts for the guarded reception his books have encountered. American literature is filled with writers who were not fully recognized during their lifetimes (a comparison with Herman Melville—essentially rediscovered during the 1920s—comes to mind). Behind the slapstick and high jinks—the broad comedy and sheer excess—of Epstein's novels, there is a moral gravitas that pulses underneath.

P. D. KIMERAKOV

P. D. Kimerakov, the title character of Epstein's first novel, is a Russian scientist doing secret research about the aging problem that affects Russian astronauts as they travel through space. Kimerakov is sent to America to attend a gerontolists' convention, and this sets into motion a dizzying array of Russian and American agents who pop in and out of scenes wearing a wide variety of disguises. Thus is the premise set for a spoof on the outpouring of Russian spy spoofs that proliferated in the 1970s—everything from the James Bond series of books (and then films) to *The Man from U.N.C.L.E.* television series. Writing for the *Best Sellers,* the reviewer Anne Marie Stamford described *P. D. Kimerakov* as resembling "a Woody Allen movie with a screenplay by Kurt Vonnegut." The problem for Stamford, however, was that "Mr. Epstein lacks the Vonnegut wit and the spontaneity of Woody Allen to pull it off."

Perhaps Epstein's debut novel was overburdened with verbal farce, or perhaps his verbal farce would have worked better as a screenplay. The novel is narrated by an enigmatic, never fully identified Russian who peppers his unstinting praise of Communism with off-the-wall aphorisms such as "A pig wearing trousers will roll in the mud." The voice is just right for the absurdist flavor of the novel itself, but as Anne Marie Stamford saw it, even though the book is funny, it is "simply not interesting."

Writing in the *New York Times Book Review,* David Bromwich felt differently. Despite some excess in the way, for example, Kimerakov falls in love with an American dancing girl (managed by a fun-loving, altogether implausible CIA agent named L. T. Kapp), the novel also offers an honesty he admires: Epstein "cannot hide the essential grimness of this particular corner of history, and he knows that pathos will be at war with buffoonery throughout his story." Indeed: "pathos at war with buffoonery" is the trademark not only of *P. D. Kimerakov* but also of the novels that followed.

Another benchmark of Epstein's work is a style that deserves the adjective "elegant." For instance, Epstein writes, Kimerakov "walked a bit like water, smoothly, balancing instead of dishes a delicate heart." Kimerakov's story is rendered warmly, as he tries to invent all manner of religious truths (like other Epstein characters, he is a comically sincere seeker); and when Kimerakov fixes on the aging process of spiders, Epstein provides pages of precisely turned detail.

What worried many critics, however, was the often abrupt shift of gears that sent the novel's plotline off into several directions. Yes, many of the novel's scenes were hilarious, and, yes, it was abundantly clear that Epstein had a lyrical gift, but Bromwich, for example, wondered if the novel would not have been much improved "if only Epstein had let the story carry him where it would, and not decided, as he must have, to make a try at broad comedy under the oddest of handicaps." First novels generally carry with them more promises, more sheer ambition, than they do accomplishment. That is the case with *P. D. Kimerakov,* a work that made it clear readers would be hearing from Epstein in future books.

THE SERIOCOMIC SAGA OF LEIB GOLDKORN

Leib Goldkorn makes his first appearance in "The Steinway Quintet"—the title novella of Epstein's 1976 collection *The Steinway Quintet Plus Four*—which centers on a group of eastern

European musicians working at the Steinway Restaurant on New York's Lower East Side. The story is another example of Epstein's fondness for the screwball comedies that were part of the Hollywood scene when he was growing up, and an example of his habit of intertwining outlandish plot elements with an underbelly of moral seriousness. Goldkorn is as out of place and outmoded as is the Steinway Restaurant where he performs. Once a favorite haunt of Sarah Bernhardt and Albert Einstein, the restaurant has fallen on hard times, and the neighborhood no longer cares about the cultural life that once flourished there. Goldkorn's Old World ways are equally passé. He has been systematically reduced to society's margins, but even so, his comic spirit continues to beat on. And if the story's premise is something of a stretch—two local hoodlums take the restaurant's aged waiters, patrons, and orchestra members hostage, demanding a huge ransom and a plane to China—it serves to enforce the conflict between Goldkorn's genteel world and the havoc of modern-day life. Culture is on one end of the continuum, violence on the other.

Goldkorn is rendered with great affection but without sentimentality. He is wide-eyed, playful, and most of all, an inveterate optimist, but he is not simply a lovable schnook with a Yiddish accent. Far more important to Goldkorn's character are the ways in which Epstein explores the tension between the belief in rational thought (which characterized many Jews of Goldkorn's vintage) and the sober recognition that rational thought was of little value to Jews when confronted with Hitler. Epstein's comedy arises from the gap between puny reason and knife-wielding thugs. The result includes a patron with a passion for Freudian analysis who asks, "What is the cause of this fear of death?" and then goes on to answer his poser this way: "Let us think of it in a rational manner. Is it not in reality the childish fear of losing the penis? Of being cut off from this source of guilty pleasure? Notice how when we recognize the source of our anxiety it at once disappears. Now we feel truly joyful." Katha Pollitt rightly calls the speech so much nonsense, but there is a nub of truth hidden inside the Freudian mumbo-jumbo, for *truly* recognizing the source of our troubles—and Epstein would argue that comedy is the best path toward this truth—is a way that art, rather than Freud, can help to liberate us. That is precisely where the unsinkable Leib Goldkorn comes in. As the quintet plays its last concert for its audience of captives and captors, he suddenly feels himself swept up by what can only be called a transcendental vision: Goldkorn is

> no longer the separate citizen, but also a part of that ocean, like a grain of salt, no different from those other grains . . . yes, even—do not be alarmed by what I now say—even the two murderers, for they were a part of that ocean, too. That ocean. That darkness, friends. We know what it is, do we not?

Pollitt suggests that what we know that we know is "our common humanity," that which explains more than does the patron spouting rehashed Freud. In the case of "The Steinway Quintet"—and even more so in *Goldkorn Tales* (1985)—music speaks both to the imagination and the heart. Goldkorn's speeches are meant to be witty, and they are, but they also speak to the best that a European Jewish consciousness can bring to the anarchy of contemporary America.

Epstein's novella takes up most of the space in this collection, and it is important for bringing Goldkorn into the world of letters, but there are other, shorter stories as well: "Lessons," "Tell Me My Fortune," "The Disciple of Bacon," and "Memory." Each charts out a complex situation and then follows it to an intellectual, perhaps *too* intellectual, conclusion. One story—"The Disciple of Bacon," about a Romanian exile who (mis)spent his life trying to prove that Mozart was a Jew—is notable because it was written early in Epstein's career, at a time when he was just beginning to find his voice as a professional writer. However, it would be the novel and novella, rather than the short story, that provided Epstein with the space he needed to accommodate his inventiveness and energy. As for Goldkorn, he remains the "voice" that Epstein enjoys the most and the one to whom he returned in two later volumes.

In the opening lines of *Goldkorn Tales,* a book composed of three novellas about Goldkorn's comic life as a would-be musician, the mood is still comic but tempered by uneasiness and tinges of darkness:

> Good evening, my name is Leib Goldkorn and my specialty is woodwind instruments, with emphasis on the flute. However, in 1963, on the Avenue Amsterdam, my instrument was stolen from me by an unknown person and has not in spite of strong efforts been to this day returned. This is the reason I play at the Steinway Restaurant the Bechstein piano and not the Rudall & Rose–model flute, with which my career began at the Imperial Royal Hof-Operntheater Orchester.

Goldkorn's tortured English syntax could easily have been *too* wrong, he easily could have become a total clown instead of a partial one, but Epstein keeps the balance between his character's comedic flourishes and his moral center in a proper aesthetic balance.

Goldkorn's years at the Steinway Restaurant are a study in fortune spiraling ever downward. He ends up working inside the restaurant as a shoeshine boy and outside it as a street musician, waving his highly trained musician's hands over water glasses. All the while, he is tending to his sickly wife, Clara. As Epstein points out in an interview with Dan Cryer for *Newsday,* music is the driving force in *Goldkorn Tales,* but in *Ice Fire Water: A Leib Goldkorn Cocktail* (1999), "it's the unsublimated Goldkorn, and his phallus has taken the place of his flute. It's really a clinging to life through his sexuality."

What remains in *Ice Fire Water*—when virtually everything that had mattered to Goldkorn was stripped away—is his voice, one seasoned by sorrow and able to turn quotidian woe into bursts of language and dashes of poetry:

> Waking? I had not once through the long night of anticipation closed my eyes. I heard, from my corner of the Posturepedic, the snores of my wife. In a glass, formerly containing seedless jelly, her dentures lay like a mollusk under inches of water. On the pillow, her wig. From her nightdress a breast protruded. This was reminiscent of the Zeppelin IV I had seen in my youth: length 140 meters, filled with inflammable gas. Even if this exposure had provoked in me a modicum of libertinism, the fact that Clara and I had not exchanged any but the most essential of words—*insulin, sweetheart? A potty perhaps?*—since the debacle with Father Fingerhut [Clara's affair] would have driven from my mind any entertainment of erotics.

Ice Fire Water alternates between memory and desire. The novel's sans-serif portions hark back to the Hitler era and Goldkorn's seriocomic effort to produce what he regards as his masterpiece: the opera, "Esther: A Jewish Girl at the Persian Court." The ambitious work, Goldkorn insists, might yet "change history's course. Surely the subtle French, so wise in the ways of the world, would understand the association of Haman with Hitler. Both begin with the letter H. *Formez vos bataillons!*" As with *Pandaemonium,* the shoot-'em-up Hollywood Western that serves as an allegory for the Holocaust, the Esther saga continues Epstein's career-long habit of linking high seriousness with farce. Epstein does this because he believes, as he put it in the *Newsday* interview, that "Farce at its very highest has great insights into life. [Samuel Beckett's] *Waiting for Godot* is a wonderful example. It's no accident that Bert Lahr played that part. It's a kind of vaudeville and existential tragedy of man at the edge." That Goldkorn, a graduate of Vienna's Akademie fur Musik, Philosophie, und darsteliende Kunst, is destined to endure comic disappointments and oversized misadventures should not be surprising. The three novellas collected in *Goldkorn Tales* (an expanded version of "The Steinway Quintet"; "Music of the Spheres," about an outlandish, oversized production of *Othello;* and "The Magic Flute," about a plot to assassinate the restaurant's owner, suspected of being a Nazi) provide the template from which *Ice Fire Water* was struck.

The difference, however, is that the Goldkorn we have come to love is now surrounded by a richer, more mature texture. B-list Hollywood actresses mingle with a bulging cast of fictional extras. On one hand, the result is playfulness of a high and delightful order; on the other, the high jinks sometimes make for a complicated, unwieldy read. In each case, Hitler or his agents make cameo appearances as Sonja Henie finds herself at the mercy of Hollywood's Darryl Zanuck or as Esther Williams gazes at the bubbling cauldron that a group of cannibals have prepared for her death, and their dinner.

Epstein gives Hollywood melodrama the comic send-up it deserves and in the process turns the altogether predictable into high art. This is so partly because he renders his characters with just the right tight-lipped, ironic treatment and partly because he hides tragedy under the guise of an ever-darkening comedy. Only Goldkorn is immune to Epstein's ironic commentary, and this is because he holds fast to his belief that music constitutes what slim hope for redemption one has. For Epstein, the question, possibly the only one that matters, is how to limn the twentieth century and the oceans of blood it has occasioned. In the service of this project, Epstein seems never to have met a pratfall, pun, or misplaced preposition he did not love. These entities attach themselves to the hapless Goldkorn as do bananas to unsuspecting shoes. In this sense, Epstein's protagonist seems less a variation of Saul Bellow's aging, increasingly disgruntled Artur Sammler than an avatar of James Joyce's bumbling Leopold Bloom. Like Bloom's, Goldkorn's stream of consciousness is awash in misinformation. In "Ice," for instance, here is how he leaps over the obvious facts about the *New York Times* book critic Michiko Kakutani, who (in real life) favorably reviewed Goldkorn's memoir, *Goldkorn Tales:* "Kakutani? Kakutani? Michiko? What kind of name is that? Javanese? Japanese? Like the place mat weaver, Marimekko, perhaps a Finn? A person with such insight is not likely American born. Naturally I wrote a brief note of appreciation, suggesting a small luncheon." Thus is the scene set for a series of crossed purposes and missed directions as Goldkorn, expecting to lunch with a Finn, fails to recognize the Japanese woman staring at him through the glass partition at the Plaza Hotel's Court of Palms restaurant.

Or consider this moment from "Ice," as a famished Goldkorn devours the artificial fruits that comprise the singer Carmen Miranda's trademark headdress:

What was this? Delusion? Fantasy? Trick of the light? It seemed that someone—one of the crewmen perhaps, or an officer, or else a worker from the kitchen—had left on the nearby deck boards what looked to be a basket of mouth-waterng fruits. Ah, magnanimous Marxist! To each according to his needs. . . . As a leopard leaps from its limb, Leib fell upon the compote. Real! It was real! I stuffed an orange, a pear, and a tangelo all at once, peels included, into my mouth. . . . "*Caramba!*" That was a woman's scream—the very same woman who, pale of skin, with black eyelashes and full painted lips—balanced these edibles on top of her head. "*Idiota! Cretino!*" she cried, with undeniable justification. I had devoured the better part of her hat.

Ice Fire Water brings the Goldkorn saga to a spectacular finish. He has never been wilder, never funnier, and Epstein never more confident about the possibilities of postmodernism as he continues to explore the horrific darkness just beneath Goldkorn's individual troubles. The result is a "Goldkorn cocktail" that successfully mixes "real" character with imagined ones, the beautiful with the ugly, and aspects of goodness with unspeakable evil. In old age (Goldkorn is now in his nineties), he remains the same clown, the same schlemiel, he always was, but his insights now seem both wiser and aesthetically earned.

KING OF THE JEWS

Given the furor that arose in the wake of the 2002 Jewish Museum exhibit "Mirroring Evil: Nazi Images/Recent Art," the outcry that greeted Leslie Epstein's 1979 novel, *King of the Jews*—which has ultimately attained status as a classic of Holocaust literature—now seems minor. His impious depiction of the Lodz ghetto is no match for the bad taste of a Lego block concentration camp or the many other pieces of postmodernist art that rightly infuriated so many. However, as Ellen Handler Spitz, the catalog essayist for the controversial exhibit, tried to explain in a letter to the *New York Times* (February 5, 2002), "The Holocaust is a subject that cannot be treated without risk of offense; yet it must be treated and in new ways as years go by." That prediction (some would call it a frightening omen) suggests that artists will find ever-new ways of putting the Holocaust to artistic use and that those who prefer a respectful silence will find themselves offended.

Epstein's novel about the systematic destruction of Poland's Lodz ghetto was a pioneering effort to write a novel of the Holocaust. Its fictional portrayal of the ghetto's *Judenrat* (Jewish Council) in general and Chaim Rumkowski, its flamboyant leader, in particular touched on sensitive nerves that had already been inflamed by the publication of Hannah Arendt's controversial historical study *Eichmann in Jerusalem* (1963). Arendt's assault on those Jewish elders who cooperated with their Nazi captors in enforcing the restrictions on

Jews and ultimately sending Jews to the death camps—who thus were, in her view, accountable for the lack of resistance by those trapped inside the Nazi juggernaut—created violent divisions in the already combative world of New York intellectuals. Animosity aroused by the book lasted for at least two decades after Arendt's accounts of the Adolf Eichmann trial first began appearing in *The New Yorker* magazine. In a retrospective look at the controversy titled "Eichmann in New York: The New York Intellectuals and the Hannah Arendt Controversy" (*Princeton University Library Chronicle* 63, nos. 1–2 [2001–2002]), Anson Rabinbach writes:

> What united Arendt's New York critics was above all the apparent moral superciliousness of her famous contention that the "recognized Jewish leaders . . . almost without exception, cooperated in one way or another, for one reason or another, with the Nazis," and that this cooperation was the "very cornerstone" of Nazi anti-Jewish policy. Her reviewers, most notably [Lionel] Abel, contrasted that judgment with what was perceived as her excessive charity toward the trial defendant. She had applied an exalted standard of judgment to the Jewish leaders, while applying no comparable yardstick to the likes of Eichmann, who, in Abel's words, "comes off better in her book than do her victims." The "line" of the New York intellectuals, wrote [Dwight] Macdonald glibly, was that Arendt's book was "soft on Eichmann, hard on the Jews."

Because Lodz's *Judenrat* figures so prominently in Epstein's novel, and because he had spent so much time researching its activity, it is hardly surprising that Epstein would also have strong views about this matter. In his autobiographical essay, he sides with Arendt in her judgment on the elders' failure of leadership, but in ways that speak to how he conceives the role of a novelist:

> What so angered her critics—her claim that the Jewish leadership in Europe had been so compro-

mised, so woeful, that the Jews themselves would have been better if they had had no self-government at all, and had merely run—seemed to me then, as it does now, so obvious as to be almost a truism. How on earth could thing have been worse? The second half of her thesis, concerning the banality of the *Obersturmbannfuehrer,* and of evil in general, was not welcome news either. Clearly her readers, Jews and Gentiles, were more comfortable thinking of Eichmann and Himmler and Goebbels and the rest as either subhuman, or superhuman, monsters, beasts, psychopaths, and not as human beings much like themselves. What struck me most about her argument—that evil was a kind of thoughtlessness, a shallowness, an inability to realize what one is doing, a remoteness from reality, and, above all, a denial of one's connectedness to others—was how much radical wickedness resembled a defect, and perhaps a disease, of imagination.

The stunned silence about the Holocaust that was pervasive during the 1950s and 1960s could only be healed by writers whose plain responsibility was, in Epstein's words, "to show the world what those plain men had done." Moreover, only those who have the imagination to recognize, "what they share with the force of evil—in her [Arendt's] words, 'the shame of being human . . . the inescapable guilt of the human race'—can fight against it." Epstein clearly sides with Arendt and the few others who concluded that a capacity to imagine evil within ourselves as well as the enemy was not only necessary but also the only way to, as Epstein puts it, "give meaning to the suffering of the Jewish people."

Given such large sentiments and high purpose, Epstein must have been shocked by the harsh reception that *King of the Jews* received. Writing in the pages of *Commentary,* Ruth Wisse argues that "the book bears the same relation to the Holocaust as *M*A*S*H* does to the Korean War. Its flat caricatures, cabaret style of narration, and stylized theatrical staging for all the main events of the plot belong to the category of farce." Other reviews also have commented

on the apparent "disconnect" between farce and tragedy, between low laughs and high moral purpose. The charges of incongruity in his narrative tone and content had been leveled against Epstein in his earlier books; the difference is that *King of the Jews* dares to speak about the unspeakable—and to do this in what many readers saw as an inappropriate, wisecracking way. As Neal Ascherson puts it, "The plunge attempted by Leslie Epstein in *King of the Jews* required not merely courage but a degree of self-confidence approaching the suicidal." By contrast, Robert Alter, writing for the *New York Times Book Review,* admires the narrative structure of Epstein's novel; pointing to the inherent difficulties of writing Holocaust fiction, he summarized Epstein's novel as a "grim moral fable."

For many readers, however, the issue that disturbed them was simpler: Epstein lacked the proper credentials to write about the Holocaust. He was not a witness to the disaster, not even European. Instead, Epstein was American-born and, worse, raised in southern California as the son of a Hollywood scriptwriter. He knew about movies but lacked the temperament necessary to confront something as dark, as unexplainable, as the Holocaust. For these reasons, some readers feel he had no right to this material, no right to be a witness through the imagination. Jane Larkin Crain, writing in *Saturday Review,* worries about Epstein's effort to blanket the realities of the Lodz ghetto in "pseudomythology": "It is as if 6,000,000 Jews hadn't really suffered and died at a particular time and place at all, but had merely been conjured up by Leslie Epstein as background for his fanciful exploration of the Eternal Enigma of the Jew."

The issue of Holocaust piety hung over the book's reception as well. Epstein is a firm believer that the worst sin a writer can commit is sentimentality—and writing about the Holocaust is no exception. *King of the Jews* is filled with black comedy of the sort that made Joseph

Heller's *Catch-22* such a distinctive—and disturbing—novel. However, Heller places his long catalog of absurdities at the end of World War II, when the war no longer meant fighting with an enemy but, rather, dealing with thick-headed officers out to kill soldiers caught in the grip of comically insane rules. His protagonist, John Yossarian, struck many as a very "Jewish" character, but Heller takes some pains to insist that he is an Assyrian, even more the "outsider" than a Jewish protagonist might have been.

By contrast, Epstein relies on an overriding dramatic irony—namely, that readers know the fate of the Lodz ghetto in ways that those caught in the Nazi death machine do not. That is partly what makes Epstein's rendering of day-to-day life in the Lodz ghetto so unsettling. His un-named narrator is at once jaunty and somebody who provides the necessary aesthetic distance (what Epstein calls a "psychic shutter") between himself and the ghetto's horrible fate. Some critics liken this narrator to Franz Kafka. Other critics feel that the novel's narrative voice—and many of its other narrative resonances—evoked an older tradition of Yiddish storytelling, such as that of Sholem Aleichem. Epstein himself cannot quite account for the voice that begins with "In the winter of 1918–1919, on a day when the wind was blowing, I. C. Trumpelman arrived in our town." He had wanted "high seriousness—not high spirits," but Epstein soon found himself captivated by this homey "voice" and gave himself over to it.

The manner of telling does not, in fact, obscure the seriousness of the novel's central dilemma: that the Jewish Council is given the chance to organize the ghetto in ways that might spare many at the price of a few. Should there be no Council of Elders, the reader clearly comes to understand, the Nazis would attend to business in ways that would be far worse. Enter the real-life Chaim Rumkowksi, or as he is called in Epstein's novel, Isaiah Chaim Trumpelman. Epstein's Trumpelman is a kaleidoscopic character: turn him one way and he is a con man, a doctor who practices medicine without a license; a quarter-turn later, he is a consummate healer and a man who nearly earns his reputation as a "savior." The facts of Rumkowski's excess become even more excessive as Epstein limns Trumpelman into a character readers love to hate.

Epstein's research on Holocaust history at YIVO put him in an imaginative contact with the larger-than-life Rumkowski, a man who had ghetto currency and stamps adorned with his picture and who rode down the ghetto streets on a white stallion. He cuts a strange figure, one as glamorous as it was ultimately pathetic. *Judenrat* leaders in other doomed Polish cities committed suicide when the fate of their Jews became clear. Not so Rumkowski. He hung on to his dream of saving a remnant of Jews even as that "remnant" systematically dwindled. Here, according to Wisse, is where Epstein's novel should have done much more:

> To dramatize this moral plight of the Jews, the book is studded with relevant debates. . . . There is even a debate . . . on whether children being deported to their death should be lulled with bright dreams or told that "Oswiecim is the homeland of the Jews." . . . But the debates, which include many classical ghetto arguments culled from various Holocaust anthologies, are phrased in snappy one-liners that make the "excruciating moral dilemma" of the Jews sound like entries on a multiple-choice exam.

Jane Larkin Crain is even harsher:

> "There is something in history that makes all men act the same!" cries one of the characters toward the novel's close, implying that the "persecuted" and the "persecutor" are as one. Somewhere else, Trumpelman himself exclaims: "This is what a Jew is. . . . A Jew is a shit like everyone else." It is in the service of this sort of vulgar perversity that the author has felt free to trivialize the Nazi Holocaust.

Behind such harsh assessments is a sense that Epstein had "danced on the graves of the Jews," to quote one of Epstein's own characters who expresses outrage that the ghetto is mounting a production of *Macbeth*. What place, if any, does humor have in Holocaust fiction? As he was writing *Everything Is Illuminated* (2002), the young writer Jonathan Safran Foer—a third-generation child of survivors—asked himself the same question and then went on to write a thick novel filled with the comic history of his grandfather's shtetl and the mangled English of his Ukrainian guide. In Foer's case, the comedy works because it leads, inevitably, to a chilling account of destruction and systematic death. One could say that *King of the Jews* did the same thing, but much earlier.

In Epstein's comic hands, the Lodz *Judenrat* often becomes the gang that could not shoot straight, either given over to protecting individual fiefdoms or to quarreling about petty matters as the angel of death hovers overhead. The result makes for a devastating portrait, all the more so because of Trumpelman's mythic stature as the savior of the Jews. At the same time, however, Epstein took upon himself the task of giving the Lodz ghetto a sense of life as the arc of its doom moved ever closer. His cast of characters runs into the hundreds, as he explores the Jewish tendency to organize—and, yes, to *over*organize—life. There are numerous unions and guilds, not to mention the Jewish police, firefighters, and political factions. Dozens of very minor characters—including a Leib Goldkorn, who may, or may not, be the character met earlier at the Steinway Restaurant—thicken the texture of Epstein's vibrantly imagined world.

Over all of them, Trumpelman not only cuts a heroic figure, but his stories—particularly those told in the orphan's asylum, bring elements of "romance" to those youngsters he cares about most. Trumpelman is a master storyteller, and

Epstein gives him free rein. "My dear children," one typical Trumpelman story begins,

> from my earliest days I have suffered from a wanderlust that has taken me to many places, in many lands. Only now, at the end of my life, have struck roots—here, with you, in your town. One day, many years ago, I arrived at the port of Memel and for no reason, on an impulse, boarded the steamer *Morgenstern*, which was tied up at the piers. . . . I knew that this little steamer . . . was meant to travel along the Baltic coasts. But then, the many passengers, the coal, the coal piles on the docks—this could only mean an open-sea journey, across the earth perhaps, perhaps to America!

Trumpelman then launches into a full-scale adventure of the sort found in romantic fictions, and the orphans under his care are mesmerized. *King of the Jews* is packed with such storytelling and with tales within tales. But it also has moments filled with dark dramatic ironies as people put a positive spin on events that crack the heart:

> In the great wave of optimism that swept the Ghetto even the most disturbing news was seen in a favorable light. When the patients were suddenly removed from the hospital, when the prisoners disappeared from the Tsarnecka Street jail, everyone accepted the explanation that the former were being transported to rest homes, the latter to work on the unfinished dikes. Then all the clothes came back, but not the people inside them.

Or consider these directives posted by "the Conquerers," one of Epstein's many euphemisms for the Nazis: "*It is strictly forbidden to interfere with any Jew who is attempting suicide,*" reads one regulation posted atop a tall bridge, together with a companion regulation stipulating that "*Jews wishing to commit suicide are requested to make certain they have proper identification cards in their pockets.*" Those who were quick to criticize Epstein for tastelessness or for yoking farce with moral gravitas apparently were not aware of the gallows humor that flourished in the Jewish ghettos and concentration camps. Epstein's literary approach to imagining the Holocaust—which is, one must remember, the work of a man who went from a largely secular childhood to become a self-consciously Jewish writer—has also brought down the wrath of those who felt, and who still feel, that "Holocaust literature" is a contradiction in terms. Why, they wonder, did Epstein fashion a world in which words such as "Nazi" or even "German" do not appear, and Hitler himself is disturbingly recast in the novel as "Horowitz"? Part of the answer no doubt lies in Epstein's effort to allegorize the Lodz ghetto; part may have to do with the demands of fiction itself. Yet another explanation, however, is that Epstein used "storytelling" as a way of keeping the horror simultaneously at arm's length and yet close at hand. In the years since its publication in 1979, *King of the Jews* has stood the test of time; its energy and its heartrending humor seem less to be irreverent and more to demonstrate clearly that there is a place for an imaginative literature of the Holocaust.

REGINA

During the long genesis of his 1990 novel *Pinto and Sons,* Epstein took time out to write *Goldkorn Tales* and *Regina* (1982), a novel about a middle-aged woman suffering through a crisis of the soul and one that most fully exploited his interest in drama. As Susan Lydon points out in the *Village Voice,* despite the countless thousands of words written about versions of male menopause, Jewish women in a similar condition have been largely "invisible." Lydon's assessment may or may not be true, but Epstein took on a certain amount of risk by attempting to bring a character such as Regina Glassman alive on the page.

In large measure, Epstein succeeds. As with, say, Edna Pontellier in Kate Chopin's *The Awakening,* Regina has lived too much of her life in a somnambulistic stupor, but she comes to full consciousness in Epstein's account of her search for selfhood. Caught between her unlikable teenaged sons and the blind selfishness of her mother's senility, Regina has had neither the time nor the conditions that make spiritual growth possible. She is, nonetheless, determined to try.

Epstein not only wraps Regina in a blanket of literary allusions—to the heroines of Anton Chekhov, Gustave Flaubert, and Leo Tolstoy—but also tells her story in a style that harks back to his long-standing admiration for Saul Bellow. For some readers, the weighty texture seems excessive, a charge that has been raised against his previous novels. But Epstein's careful dismantling of a healer's "miracles" and Regina's movement toward a more genuine version of transcendence grounded in the ordinary gives his protagonist a centered reality of her own.

There was a time in contemporary American literature when male authors were warned about trying to inhabit a female consciousness. Such objections are clearly dubious when viewed in the light of Flaubert's portrayal of Madame Bovary or Tolstoy's tragic narrative of Anna Karenina. Epstein himself knows that the test of a novel is how convincing its characters, male or female, are. There are no doubt dozens of ways that *Regina* could have been a disaster. The novel avoids them. In its exploration of a woman's consciousness, the novel successfully illuminates Regina's condition as well as ours.

Regina nonetheless seems atypical of Epstein's work, not only because of its female protagonist but also because it lacks the narrative range and high-energy gusto of his other books. As a character remarks at the end, "Lots of things, in my opinion, have got to be a secret." Epstein does not provide *all* the answers to Regina's questions, much less to her dilemma, but by the end of the book she is at least on the right track. In addition, and importantly, *Regina* kept Epstein at the writing desk—a good thing—and the book he produced as he struggled with *Pinto and Sons* is both worthy and *good*.

PINTO AND SONS

Epstein struggled with *Pinto and Sons* for the better part of a decade, trying to give the story of Adolph Pinto the range and ambition it deserved. Written under the shadow of the success—and controversy—that *King of the Jews* had generated, he was well aware that his next thick book would be judged against that watermark. As Epstein puts it in his autobiographical essay,

> The attention given to *King of the Jews* would now be refocused on me. My next large book had to be as good as the one that had come before. I was self-conscious, self-critical, in a way I had not yet experienced. But this is a happy hurdle, really, and one that any real writer (that is, an author who has more than one good book in him, just as a genius is someone with two great ideas) is only too eager to jump.

Adolph Pinto, a Hungarian Jew, comes to America in 1840 to study medicine, and in a series of bizarre, picaresque adventures learns bitter lessons about the paradise he imagined America was. Pinto is, above all else, an idealist, someone who, as Michiko Kakutani points out in a review for the *New York Times,* believes "wholeheartedly in the credo of science and progress." Imagine his fascination when he and some Harvard medical school friends witness the first demonstration of anesthesia. For Pinto, "life without pain" now seems possible.

Unfortunately, when Pinto and two friends botch an amputation of a man's leg, Pinto is thrown out of medical school and finds himself wandering from one farcical misadventure to another. Pinto ends up in California, where he is swept up by the gold-rush fever of that time and place. He quickly learns that, for many Americans, the goal is not knowledge or life without pain, but wealth.

Pinto's picaresque adventures continue on the western prairies as he and his mule, Neptune, become a parodic version of Don Quixote and his horse, Rocinante. Ultimately, Pinto finds himself bonding with a tribe of Indians in ways that remind us of the ways that certain Jewish American writers (e.g., Bernard Malamud in "The People") have speculated about Native Americans as members of the Lost Tribe of Israel. Other allusions include touches of Thomas Berger's parodic Western, *Little Big Man,* in the mix.

At one point, Pinto rescues an Indian woman's baby, names him General George, and adopts him as his own son. He also starts educating the young Modoc Indians who live nearby (shades of I. C. Trumpelman at the orphanage), using the poetry of Robert Burns and the principles of mathematics to instill in them a love of knowledge. What the white men have abandoned, the Indians will now have—at least if Pinto has anything to say about it. Soon his band of youth scholars (Pinto calls them "the Children of the Enlightenment" and gives them absurd new names: Newton Mike, Kepler Jim, Bacon Jack, and Paracelsus Max) are speaking fluent English, albeit with a Scottish accent. The result is the sort of free-spirited brio that had become Epstein's thumbprint.

Plot complications—invariably oversized and comic—continue when his old medical school friend, Mike Townsend, builds the world's largest gold mine and employs hundreds of Indians at slave wages. Meanwhile Pinto has a new obsession: finding a cure for rabies. Both fixations lead to disaster—a mine explosion kills dozens of Indian workers, and Pinto's experiments lead to the death of his son, General George. The rumblings of war between whites and Indians quickly follow, with Pinto caught in the middle as he tries to use scientific knowledge to come up with a solution.

As Kakutani points out,

Mr. Epstein wants to use his hero's dilemmas to examine large historical and moral questions. In this case, the failure of reason and science to solve such intractable problems as illness, racial conflict and death; the tendency of large, man-made schemes (whether noble or selfish in motive) to go awry; and the limitations attached to the promises of the frontier and the American Dream.

Unfortunately, *Pinto and Sons* is an instance where large ambitions do not end with solid accomplishment. The roller-coaster ride of grisly incident piled atop grisly incident mutes the moral seriousness that is ultimately the novel's purpose. As Richard Elder observes in a review for the *Los Angeles Times,* "*Pinto and Sons* sprawls, and not in a way that favors it. The various narratives—ether experiments, the Gold Rush, peddling among the Indians, the rabies and machine gun discoveries, the mine-building and mine disaster, the Indian war, don't always connect."

Pinto ends his days working for a prosperous department store, no longer the picaresque bumbler he once was. When he learns of Louis Pasteur's rabies cure, he goes out to Alcatraz (where the captives of the Indian war have been imprisoned) and shouts the news up to the walls—in the unlikely event that any of his Indians, his "sons," are still alive. He remains the same would-be but ineffectual "healer" he always was, although his idealism has surely been shaken and even he must realize that it did not much matter which side he was on when the machine gun laboriously fashioned by the Indians found itself up against the mortars and machine guns the army brought to the battle.

PANDAEMONIUM

In his 1997 novel, *Pandaemonium,* a thick novel that deserves more attention than it has thus far received, Epstein marvelously fuses the low and high themes that have preoccupied him throughout his career—Hollywood, movie Westerns, and the Holocaust. Hollywood is the world's dream factory, a place where myths are manufactured and the imagination often seems to outstrip reality itself, and Leslie Epstein knows this milieu with an intimacy few contemporary writers can match, for he grew up a stone's throw from the backlots and could count Tinseltown celebrities as family friends. Moreover, Epstein's *King of the Jews* made it clear that he had a flair for historically anchored fiction and for writing about the Holocaust in provocative, controversial ways.

The year is 1938, and Peter Lorre, the Hungarian Jewish actor, is *Pandaemonium*'s nervous narrator. What he sees—and what makes him skittish—is a world on the brink of war and a studio system that seems always on the edge of implosion. He is making a trip to Chancellor Hitler's Germany very much against his will, even as he worries that his Mr. Moto series, a knockoff of the popular Charlie Chan mysteries, is about to be cancelled. Meanwhile, grandiose visions—of a new production of *Antigone* or, later, of a shoot-'em-up Western that bears more than a few prophetic resemblances to the Holocaust—swirl around Lorre as the novel's cast of minor characters (e.g., Adolf Hitler, Josef Goebbels, a fictional German director named Rudolph Von Beckmann) and dizzying plot complications raise dark questions about film, the imagination, and the cunning of history.

Pandaemonium brings to mind D. H. Lawrence's definition of the modern novel as a "loose baggy monster," one that takes on the sprawling, chaotic nature of the society it tries to describe. Or perhaps, because this is a fictional account of filmmaking, the work of Federico Fellini offers a useful comparison with *Pandaemonium;* Epstein's mixture of social realism with the surreal and hallucinatory suggests the effect one feels when watching a Fellini film such as *The Clowns.*

Epstein's imaginary world, however, places the Holocaust at its center, albeit by indirection and parable. At one point Maestro Von Beckmann insists that he wants nothing to do with Hollywood (where "from the top to the bottom, you would find only Jews") and then goes on to explain why:

> How they cling to the world, these people! They affirm it with all five senses. But the world beyond those senses—*that* they have no regard for, no belief in, no way of knowing. It leaves them mystified. . . . And this indifference, of course, affects their art. If one does not believe—as Antigone believes, to take one instance—in the reality of the other world, the afterlife, the land of the gods, then one's art turns toward the subjective. The mark of the Jew is that confronted by the existence of a world beyond his five senses, he adds a sixth: the psyche, which turns the unknowable world into an illusion.

Ultimately, Von Beckmann finds his way to Hollywood, but the tragic results unroll as systematically as they do when the well-intentioned Oedipus sets out to find the murderer who is, ironically enough, himself or when one realizes that the essence of tragedy is an understanding that that which cannot be, must be; and that that which must be, cannot be.

Epstein peppers his atmospheric novel with speeches that ache to be underlined, but he also knows how to give local color and comic relief their due. For example, readers are treated to large swathes of the *Chatterbox,* a Hollywood insider gossip column modeled on those penned by Louella Parsons:

> Maybe, as Mr. Hearst always says, we should try a little of Herr Hitler's elbow grease in the good old U.S. of A. One person who won't be raising a stein of beer is Peter Lorre, who is also on his way to join Von Beckmann's Salzburg premiere. He changed his name from Laszlo Loewenstein for a good reason, though his fans know him as Mr. I. A. Moto. I have heard that Granite [Studio] is planning a whole new series of adventures for the slant-eyed sleuth. . . .

"Pandaemonium" means "a place of disorder"; in Milton's *Paradise Lost,* Satan erected his palace there. For Epstein, it is not only the western town where a film is shot but also a lively emblem of Hollywood itself. Although Hollywood had already been pilloried by novels such as F. Scott Fitzgerald's uncompleted *The Last Tycoon* and Nathanael West's *The Day of the Locust,* even these extraordinary earlier works do not pack quite the same cinematic scope or depth of ideas that Epstein provides in his account of how passion and madness combine to turn the world into "pandaemonium."

"BONES" AND THE JACOBI FAMILY

"Bones," published in the *Princeton University Library Chronicle,* is short story that is part of a longer work in progress about the Jacobi family. Focused on a post–World War II trick-or-treat outing along San Remo Drive in Los Angeles, it contains many of the details found in Epstein's autobiographical essay: Hollywood stars who live in the neighborhood—Mary Astor, Virginia Bruce, Linda Darnell, and Gregory Peck (who passes out the goodies himself)—along with the likes of the writer and intellectual Thomas Mann; the pampered circumstance of children being chauffeurred from place to place as maids answer the doors; and a child's first exposure to anti-Semitism in the form of the word "kike."

Hollywood is never far from Epstein's consciousness. The same can also be said for his realization that Jewishness and history's mortal pang are inextricably tangled. If it is true that he uses comedy, often of a dark hue, to investigate the circumstances of his past, it is equally true that he has carved out a distinctive style. Excess is part of his method, just as moral passion is part of his consciousness. The story "Bones," written in what might be viewed as the latter stages of Epstein's mid-career, suggests a return to the *Judenrein* world that Epstein knew as a child, the Jewish soul he developed as an adult, and his place as a full-fledged Jewish American writer.

Selected Bibliography

WORKS BY LESLIE EPSTEIN

NOVELS
P. D. Kimerakov. Boston: Little, Brown, 1975.

King of the Jews. New York: Coward, McCann, and Geoghegan, 1979.

Regina. New York: Coward, McCann, and Geoghegan, 1982.

Pinto and Sons. Boston: Houghton Mifflin, 1990.

Pandaemonium. New York: St. Martin's Press, 1997.

SHORT STORIES
The Steinway Quintet Plus Four. Boston: Little, Brown, 1976.

Goldkorn Tales. New York: Dutton, 1985. (Three novellas.)

Ice Fire Water: A Leib Goldkorn Cocktail. New York: Norton, 1999. (Three novellas.)

"Bones." *Princeton University Library Chronicle* 63, nos. 1–2:75–84 (2001–2002).

MANUSCRIPT COLLECTIONS
Leslie Epstein's papers are housed at Middlebury College, Middlebury, Vermont.

OTHER WORKS
"Leslie Epstein, 1938–." In *Contemporary Authors Autobiography Series.* Vol. 12. Detroit: Gale, 1990.

"Pictures at an Extermination." *Harper's,* September 2000, pp. 53–64.

BOOK REVIEWS

Alter, Robert. "A Fable of Power." *New York Times Book Review,* February 4, 1979, p. 1. (Review of *King of the Jews.*)

Ascherson, Neal. "The Damned." *New York Review of Books,* April 5, 1979, pp. 27–29. (Review of *King of the Jews.*)

Bromwich, David. Review of *P. D. Kimerakov. New York Times Book Review,* August 10, 1975, p. 6.

Crain, Jane Larkin. "Books in Brief: *King of the Jews.*" *Saturday Review,* March 31, 1979, p. 53.

Elder, Richard. Review of *Pinto and Sons. Los Angeles Times,* November 22, 1990, p. E14.

Kakutani, Michiko. Review of *Pinto and Sons. New York Times,* November 16, 1990, p. C36.

Lydon, Susan. Review of *Regina. Village Voice,* January 18, 1983, p. 37.

Pollitt, Katha. Review of *The Steinway Quintet Plus Four. New York Times Book Review,* December 12, 1976, p. 7.

Stamford, Anne Marie. Review of *P. D. Kimerakov. Best Sellers,* September 1975, p. 162.

Wisse, Ruth. "Fairy Tale." *Commentary* 67, no. 5:76–78 (May 1979). (Review of *King of the Jews.*)

INTERVIEW

Cryer, Dan. "Talking with Leslie Epstein." *Newsday,* December 10, 1999, p. B11.

—*SANFORD PINSKER*

Albert Goldbarth

1948–

*I*N GENERAL, CONTEMPORARY American poetry is an art of compression, of saying the most in the least amount of words, but from the start of his career, Albert Goldbarth has swum against this current. In Goldbarth's poetry, people, things, and places join across all boundaries: temporal, social, economic, and cultural. In his work, best defined as a poetry of collage effects, multiple narratives compete for attention; most poems weave at least three distinct stories together. Writing in *Poetry* magazine in 1987, David Shapiro surmised that "Goldbarth's poetry is no doubt a kind of maximalist rebuke" to contemporary poetry's pieties of plain language, short lyrics, and few allusions and references. Echoing this sentiment, Ben Downing, in *Parnassus,* viewed Goldbarth's talent for finding connections among the most disparate phenomena as so unusual that he declared him "a one man -ism." The poet and editor David Baker called Goldbarth "a sort of cultural phenomenon" because "his is a vast, inclusive, electric, rambunctious, frequently zany, even downright messy poetic vision."

Goldbarth published more than twenty books of poems and four books of essays in the years between 1973 and 2001. A distinguished professor of the humanities at Wichita State University in Kansas, he has held numerous visiting appointments at colleges and universities and, in 2002, he won, for the second time, the National Book Critics Circle Award.

EARLY YEARS AND FIRST BOOKS

Goldbarth published his first book in 1973, when he was still in his twenties. From that time, he published a new book almost every year. Born on January 31, 1948, to Fannie Seligman Goldbarth and Irving Goldbarth, an underwriter for an insurance firm, he grew up in a close family that included a younger sister, Olivia, and the constant presence of his grandparents. His childhood and youth in Chicago proved to be a seedbed for future poems. As he says in "Before" (from the 1981 collection *Faith*),

> . . . I'd come
> from History, and before that
> from a lineage of ragpickers,
> songpluckers, kettlemenders, renderers
> of humpfat of the candles, masters of
> disputation over a nuance of scripture,
> debtors, diddlers, elegiasts and jewelers

Goldbarth's 1990 essay "Threshold" (collected in *A Sympathy of Souls,* 1990) describes where he grew up in Chicago, on Washtenaw Avenue: "The neighborhood was lower middle-class, and I suppose its wants were." He adds, "what I remember mainly, though, is . . . just a daily kind of frantic male-workforce and female-housework treadmill-run to stay in place."

When Goldbarth was a young boy his paternal grandmother, the Grandma Nettie of so many poems, lived with the family; her death was his first experience of intense grief. He writes about the event with both sadness and irony in his poem "What I Call What They Call Onanism" (from *Faith*):

> And I remember
> their praying for Grandma, once
> the diabetes had carried her off, praying
> hard for her life in Heaven. Not that
> praying hard for her life on Earth had helped.

In "Sayings/For Luck" (also from *Faith)* he recalls other images from his childhood:

> We lived in a wood house.
> Grandpa drank tea through a sugar cube. Sweet
> tit in his lips. The walls were wood and
> the stairs were wood, and sang. Grandma always
>   said
> *Not with your hands.* Daddy left but
> came back.

In an essay from *Dark Waves and Light Matter* (1999) Goldbarth recalls his father "always down at that desk, embattled by numbers, the spiral of tape from the adding machine having frozen his pose." The household itself, for all of its secular interests, was nonetheless religious. Although he now describes himself as a nonobservant Jew, Goldbarth grew up in a kosher home where Yiddish was frequently spoken. He attended Sunday school and the synagogue and had his bar mitzvah at age thirteen. In "Duo Tried Killing Man with Bacon" (from the 1999 collection *Troubled Lovers in History*) he recalls the religious milieu of his childhood, describing his father as a man imbued with earnest spiritual valor, who

> set my weekend curfew, and heeded the vast
>   refusals of the kosher laws,
> etc., sternly certain that these self-set limits saved
>   us from the limitless
> predations of the universe. . . .

In other poems he recalls his father's more secular heroism: "this man helped search for bodies in the flooded mine, and helped patrol from plunderers after the gang war." His combined portraits ultimately create a complex picture of a father who proved to be a central force in Albert Goldbarth's future development both as a poet and as a man. Attempting to summarize this relationship with an appropriately mathematical metaphor, Goldbarth writes of his father (in *Dark Waves and Light Matter*): "He was no coward, he was simply a man who

understood: we're x in a universal equation that's always looking to preface us with a minus sign."

Literature played almost no role in the house where he was raised, nor was Goldbarth especially literary as a youth, but even as a boy, he took his fantasy as seriously as his reality. In "Grove" (from *Faith*) he writes, "There in the house on Washtenaw Avenue, I'd hug myself under the covers and squint, and populate the whorls of the planks in the walls with a squadron of heroes—Flash Gordon, Roy Rogers, some guy who could breathe like a fish." Comic books provided Goldbarth with imaginative solace and adventure that served as an antidote to the dull fiscal realities of actuary tables, hard work, and an otherwise overly burdened adult realm of hard pragmatism. (In *A Sympathy of Souls* he recalls accompanying his father on his insurance rounds: "I was only eight, but already it was clear to me: the fiscal wasn't my world.") And, in a witty essay from *Dark Waves and Light Matter,* Goldbarth reprints his first published work, which begins, "Dear Editor: I think *Green Lantern* is one of the most exciting and different action magazines on the market today." This letter published in an early issue (number 3) of *Green Lantern,* a comic book, encapsulates just what sort of poet Goldbarth would become. For although it appears in a comic book, it is a critical reaction taking the story seriously; in the letter's conclusion the future poet chastises the editors for not adhering to their audience's knowledge of previous issues. This same wonderful combination of fact and fancy eventually defined his poetic style.

This poetic style came rather early in Goldbarth's life. As the turmoil of the 1960s rocked the country, Goldbarth, in college, fell into writing. After graduating from the University of Illinois at Chicago in 1969, he was accepted into the prestigious Writers' Workshop at the University of Iowa. He graduated in 1971 with an M.F.A. in creative writing and returned to Chicago, where he taught at both Elgin Community College and Central YMCA Community College, Chicago, coordinated writers' workshops in area schools, and began publishing his poetry. In 1972 he received his first big break when the *Poetry Northwest* awarded him its prestigious Theodore Roethke prize. Goldbarth's first book, *Under Cover* (1973), was a chapbook of fifteen poems, dedicated to his parents and to "Syl," a woman who haunts much of his early poetry. This first book, although full of references to his friends, is also indicative of an already eclectic and wide-ranging intellect.

1973–1974: BIRTH OF A POET

In 1973 Goldbarth enrolled in the University of Utah's Ph.D. program, which at that time was one of the only programs in the United States to offer a doctorate in creative writing. By then he had already made a name for himself with publication in many literary magazines. This flurry of activity culminated in a personal annus mirabilis, when he published an 82-page collection, *Coprolites* (1973); a 69-page book-length poem, *Opticks* (1974); as well as a commercial, trade book collection, *Jan. 31* (1974). This 103-page collection, in turn, was nominated for a National Book Award.

This remarkable period, which put Goldbarth firmly on the map of American poetry, belonged to an era when that poetry was dominated by two styles. The first, "deep image poetry," transformed the idea of the short lyric into a domestic form of surrealism, whereas the second, "the voice poem," emphasized, in plain language and sharp imagery, personal anecdotes from the poet's own life. All three of Goldbarth's early books expanded on, exaggerated, and even questioned these lyric trends, and even the lyric itself. Instead of the short lyric, for example, Goldbarth's poetry consists of long narrative poems spanning many pages (indeed, the volume *Opticks* is but one long poem). And, in

an era emphasizing the spoken sound of regular folk, Goldbarth mixed the language of conversation with the arcane vocabularies of archeology, science, and the literary past. In these collections one finds not just the story of the poet's life but also a rich texture of historical, scientific, literary, and popular cultural knowledge. His own life and experience remains hermetic, sealed, only barely alluded to while the worlds of science, history, and the like are brought into the surface texture of the poem. As a result, these early poems ask to be read as transhistorical, universal sparks in a centuries-old poetic fire.

The first collection published during this period, *Coprolites,* derives its title from the word for fossilized excrement. Archeologists examine human coprolites for clues to the past. In the back of Goldbarth's first book, *Under Cover,* the publishers announced that the next book would be called "The Feces Fruit." The name was changed to "coprolites" perhaps to reflect a more learned approach to even this earthiest of subjects that Goldbarth had chosen to explore in his poetry. Many readers felt that the display of such obscure knowledge and vocabulary was, in effect, Goldbarth's way of thumbing his nose at a poetry scene deficient in such obviously learned references. Michael Heffernan, reviewing the collection in the *Midwest Quarterly,* read the book's dedication, "to my contemporaries," as a challenge rather than as an acknowledgment. Even the poetic forms were unusual—despite the book's standard eighty-two pages, it contained only sixteen, mostly long, poems. In turn, these were divided into five sections that travel the course of human history and traverse a variety of landscapes. The title poem, for example, begins in prehistory—"Cooking-smoke scents the sky"— and concludes, "Let me pass my ancestor's seed / to a new generation. Amen. Amen." In the second poem, "Throat," Goldbarth cites Chester S. Chard's 1969 book *Man in Prehistory,* which asserts that the human personality has more in common with the character of the wolf than it does with the character of other primates. From that observation, Goldbarth constructs a love poem that speaks of desire in decidedly animal-istic, wolfish terms: "The Kiss; and The Curse; and The Voice of the Wolf / howling once a month / for its own kind."

In the book's second section each of the four poems weaves two dramatic monologues in and out of each other. Each poem contains two stories, two characters. The crosscutting tech-nique allows each poem to create a dialogue across numerous boundaries—geographic, temporal, and linguistic. In "Dialogue: William Harvey; Joan of Arc" the Englishman who discovered the circulation of blood speaks in stanzas alternating with the voice of the French martyr. In the other "dialogues" Goldbarth actu-ally invents some of the personae. One meets "Alkest (54–74), a Pompeiian slave," whose voice alternates with that of the very real alchemist Nicolas Flamel. Similarly, the voice of the invented Joseph Busch (1858–1948), an "elderly German art restorer," alternates with the voice of the very real Johann Joachim Winckelmann, the discoverer of Pompeii and the father of archeology. All of these poems reveal what Richard Hugo called Goldbarth's "rich verbal imagination," and their diction and intellectual range won much critical attention.

The second volume Goldbarth published dur-ing this period was *Opticks: A Poem in Seven Sections.* Dedicated (like *Under Cover*) to "Syl," Goldbarth adds that she is the one "who sees through me / who saw through me." The book then uses "seeing" as a trope. To do this Goldbarth creates a modernist collage of ideas, theories, scenes, anecdotes, and vignettes about glass, seeing, and the very idea of what we can know in order to explore the meaning of a particular love affair with Syl and of relation-ships more generally. Although the poetry says little about Sylvia and Goldbarth, the book itself

derives its emotional energy from this intimate relationship. Reviewers also praised this book, but some, like the poet Dave Smith (writing in the *Midwest Quarterly*), thought the "great vine of a poem" was "sadly etiolated by haste and demonstrative of Goldbarth's racy faults." As with *Coprolites,* this long poem reveled not only in excrement but also in explicit sexual scenes. Smith objected to the poetry's obsession with feces and genitalia and faulted Goldbarth's disregard of nouns and verbs in favor of a poet-ics of adjectives. Nonetheless, said Smith, he could not help but "applaud Goldbarth's energy, his willingness to challenge big tasks."

The second of Goldbarth's books published in 1974 was a collection named after his own birth date: *Jan. 31.* More than the previous three books, this collection marked Goldbarth's entry into the larger literary world; the volume even had back-cover blurbs from such well-established poets as David Wagoner and Richard Hugo. Unlike the previous two books, *Jan. 31* consists of fifty mostly shorter lyrics. Their brevity, however, is offset by the fact that, as Goldbarth says in a note to the reader, they are meant to be read as "a loosely organized sequence." Like his other poems, these too are at once openly personal and opaque and her-metic. The book, Goldbarth says on the dedica-tion page of the first edition hardback, is "meant as a diary of sorts kept through a metaphorical winter." The theme, he says, is "survival." As it turns out, the poems chart a love affair gone awry; they tell a tale of loss and aggravation in strong, often densely textured and symbolic language. Yet the particulars and details of the characters, even the specifics that lead to their breakup, are not provided. As with *Opticks,* numerous other stories from history and the like take the place of what would otherwise have been more personal information.

The title poem serves as an example. In the late 1960s and early 1970s the military draft was perhaps the central defining generational trauma. Goldbarth, as student and academic, did not enter the military, but many of his peers did. His poem "Jan. 31," a five-part, ten-page miniature epic, charts a feeling of deep anxiety as it folds Goldbarth's life, the Vietnam War, and the world of ancient Babylon into an exploration of loss, faith, and cyclical redemption. Read in the context of the book's "metaphorical winter," it is also an analogy to the pain of love gone sour. In the poem's first section the reader encounters a disgusting and brutal scene with graphic depictions of the torture and killing of innocents to please a Babylonian king. At the same time, a court astrologer is introduced. Only at the end of the section are readers told "In America it's winter." The metaphor resonates beyond the merely personal and applies to the Vietnam War, where others are being tortured for a new "king," the contemporary leader, the president.

The second section of "Jan. 31" refers to two lovers, Goldbarth and a woman, and announces the defeat of their love: "in the January night we wake, // radioing for help." By the third section of the poem, Goldbarth analyzes himself— "I'm the snowman"—and reports that his lover accuses him: "all the girls who left my bed / frostbitten." He then charts a fever of heat in the night but "It's not a happy fever." By the poem's end, he says, "History repeats itself." He then returns to the first section's scene of ancient Babylon. This time, the soldiers and even the king's servants upon his death willingly lie down to die and be buried with the king. Says Goldbarth, "Space curves / and returns upon itself. This is fact." In the short final section, titled "1973," the scene is a week during one of the many peace talks of the Vietnam War: "The Honorable Peace," Goldbarth announces, "today's my birthday." At midnight he suddenly finds himself thinking

of all the others, in Egypt, in Ur

who were also buried

alone in the unescapable overhanging of earth

when a ruler died.

He then offers what becomes a generational lament:

to be 25, and to trust
in the ancient myths of cycle and rebirth,

their small, sentimental proof, one tear
under Aquarius.

In these lines Goldbarth both welcomes a universal spirit of redemption and declares its obsolescence.

In the most sensitive review of this powerful poem and book, Jonathan Katz wrote that Goldbarth meant to "establish the idea that the natural order of things is cyclical and if, like space curving back on itself, history repeats its processes of human bondage and suffering, then it likewise regenerates knowledge and strength." Goldbarth, says Katz, "casts himself in the role of mythmaker." *Jan. 31* was nominated for the prestigious National Book Award, and it also brought Goldbarth a National Endowment for the Arts Fellowship and his first major academic appointment. In 1974 he became a visiting assistant professor in creative writing at Cornell University.

A MORE PERSONAL POETRY

While at Cornell, Goldbarth published *Keeping* (1975), a significant poetic departure. The book jacket itself announced that his poetry was turning to a more self-revelatory set of themes: the front cover reproduced a picture of Goldbarth as a child and had his signature on the photograph, whereas on the back cover readers saw a contemporary photograph of the smiling poet. The book, however, at fifty pages, was not a collection of lyrics but rather a sequence of just two long poems: "What We Came Through" and "The Small Vision." In the first poem Goldbarth returns to his relationship with Sylvia:

> Here, my darling,
> from me to you, cut open inscribed
> What We Came Through.

This long poem in fourteen sections, a kind of super-sonnet, charts his cross-country trips from Utah to New York, where he had begun teaching at Cornell. As is traditional for sonnets, the poem charts a love affair, the "human energy, Albert and Sylvia." It is by far Goldbarth's most personal early work. In the second poem, by contrast, Goldbarth creates a collage out of stories of John Milton, Galileo, and his own love affairs, finding ever-newer connections between his life and the lives of others.

In 1976 Goldbarth left Cornell and spent a year teaching at Syracuse University. That year he also published *A Year of Happy* (1976). David Starkey has speculated that the dearth of criticism concerning *Keeping* and *A Year of Happy,* given the poet's notoriety following the success of *Jan. 31,* was due to the fact that "there was simply too much poetry available from Goldbarth." Critics did assess the new poetry when Goldbarth published *Comings Back* (1976), a major book from a major press, Doubleday. Like *Jan. 31,* this book is a sequence. At 141 pages it is even more expansive than any of his earlier books and contains many long poems. The personal turn continues as well. The poems refer to Sylvia ("Some Poems around Some Lights" and "Refrains/Remains/Reminders") and to another woman, Ellen, who first appears in *Keeping* ("The Chariots/The Gods") and to whom *A Year of Happy* is dedicated. Also returning in this book are references to friends seen in his first book, *Under Cover.* Readers now encounter such friends as Tony ("Letter to Tony"), Michael, Richard, and Ginnie. The book also reflects more earnestly on Goldbarth's own family, particularly his father, and even invokes the Jewish tradition by offering a kaddish, or prayer for the dead, in honor of his uncle.

Despite this more personal turn, however, the basic theme established in *Coprolites* that things, people, places, and historical moments are not disparate but rather intimately connected is maintained. The poems and even the title, meanwhile, further develop Goldbarth's governing metaphor, first established in *Jan. 31,* that such interconnections can best be understood through the figure of "the curve." This figure depicts for Goldbarth the confluence of space and time and the irrelevance of any notion of linear history. In the first section of *Comings Back* he moves from the prehistory of humanity to his own relationship with Sylvia. The second section's poems chart moments in time from the year 1000 to the year 2075. The book then concludes with the poem, "Refrains/Remains/Reminders," a kind of metaphysical autobiography based on the idea of a cyclical return:

>   ... For I
> have come east, never having been east
> before: I've come back, come
> home.

Referring to his move east to Ithaca, New York, this poem, inevitably, given Goldbarth's historical imagination, turns to the classical Ithaka, to his family, his friends, and ultimately to a larger mythic time. At one point, the poem meditates on Heinrich Schliemann and his nineteenth-century exploration of Ithaka. Goldbarth writes:

>   ... This
> Is it. It's 1878, and Schliemann
>
> scrapes dirt from his first validating wedge of ancient
>   Ithaka.

Then in section seven of this poem:

> It's central New York. In
> and out, now
> clear, now unclouded, two
> thrushes stitch gray sky.

The reviews of this collection were mixed in their reaction to Goldbarth's attempt to fuse his own life with that of larger topics. The poet Mary Kinzie thought the book's references to friends and family smacked of a smug "coterie attitude" pertinent only to "the sensitive, disaffected cronies," and Lorrie Goldensohn felt "all the poems feel the same in touch and tone, their bonhomie forced." Victor Contoski, however, appreciated how the "poet discovers relationships between the most unlikely objects" and so created an "intellectual excitement" worthy of praise.

Out of all this publishing activity, Goldbarth's academic career continued to rise. In 1977 he was appointed to the faculty of the University of Texas at Austin as a professor of creative writing. After ten years in Texas he left in 1987 to become distinguished professor of humanities at Wichita State University in Wichita, Kansas.

AN EXPLOSION OF POETRY

Between 1976 and 1982 Goldbarth published nine books: a long poem in a chapbook, *Curve* (1977); a book-length poem, *Different Fleshes* (1979); three chapbook collections, *Ink, Blood, Semen* (1980), *The Smuggler's Handbook* (1980), and *I Am a Sonnet* (1980); another long poem, *Eurekas* (1981); a remarkable, if little noticed, collection, *Faith* (1981); a book consisting of three long poems, *Who Gathered and Whispered behind Me* (1981); and a chapbook, *Goldbarth's Book of Occult Phenomena* (1982). In addition to these books, in 1979 he also edited an anthology of long poems titled *Every Pleasure,* introducing his favored genre to a wider literary public. He capped this prodigious period of his career with the publication of *Original Light* (1983), a collection of new and selected poems.

David Starkey, in his overview of the poet, has pointed out that given all this activity, "a new book by Goldbarth could hardly be seen as a literary event." Surprisingly, however, many of these books did receive critical attention. And those that did not, like *Curve,* were nonetheless noteworthy departures from Goldbarth's earlier work. In that long poem, published as a chapbook, Goldbarth returns to the metaphor of the curve, beginning the poem in India with a man: "He sits on the steps of Benares / stinking in its heat." The man meditates about killing a fly, and the poem then recalls instances of torture: in ancient Babylon, in a German concentration camp. Ultimately, everything in the poem curves back to the poet, who, as in "Refrains/Remains/Reminders," draws his readers into the poem's concerns and reproduces his own signature as part of the poem.

> Here, I sign my name to this page
> And place it in your cornea
> In the nourishing flow of blood
> That carries back through the eye's round jellies

The poet then reproduces his actual signature.

By contrast, *Different Fleshes,* subtitled "a novel-poem," tells its tale of connectivity through the lives of others. When he reprinted the poem in *Across the Layers* (1993), Goldbarth wrote that the poem, "an alternation of prose and poetry, narrative and lyricism," is "about the idea that the journey to remake one's self can be an outward travel (for instance, expatriatism) or inward, psychic pilgrimage; and that these equal but 'different fleshes' can find a link of conjoining." As one reviewer, Charley Shively, put it, the poem "plays a wide panoply of macho he-men in Texas and Paris against an extraordinary drag queen, Barbette nee Vander Clyde." Simply summarized, the poem tells the tale of a historical figure, Vander Clyde, born in 1897 in Round Rock, Texas. Vander Clyde transformed himself from a ranch hand into an internationally famous acrobat and drag queen known as Barbette, the toast of

Paris. Perhaps because he came from a town close to Goldbarth's new Texas home, the poet felt some connection to this alienated soul who reinvented everything about himself including his gender. Whatever the psychological connection may be, in the poem Vander Clyde does become a foil for Goldbarth's further explorations of his own life and its interconnection to others. In the poem Goldbarth weaves a tale of a local strip club in Austin with the tale of Vander Clyde. Throughout the poem Goldbarth makes numerous remarkable leaps: "I speak of Diderot and Vander Clyde by way, through wide blurred trial, of focusing on a glass decanter of bordeaux late 1923." In the end this poem, as with so much of his work, becomes a hymn to friendship, a poem of personal love and desire.

The poem's breadth and craziness provoked the first sustained critical essay on Goldbarth's work in *American Poetry Review.* There, Michael King summarized Goldbarth's unique style as "musing, self-mocking yet fundamentally serious, sensual, one metaphorical idea leaping or tailing into another, long contemplative passages brought short by comic rhetorical questions, and sudden bursts of arcane knowledge borrowed or invented from an obscure text." King praised the style as well as its use in this long poem. Other critics, however, felt that the poem's ethics were suspect. Charley Shively argued that Goldbarth had erased the sexuality at the heart of Barbette's tale, and he criticized the poet for creating a poetry that dealt in only white or black. Harping on Goldbarth's inability to see gray in that universe ("Goldbarth cannot give up his polarities, contrasts, copulations"), Shively concludes that the poet's "failure to give more voice to Barbette is a crime—both literary and moral."

In 1981 Goldbarth published two books whose poetry turned decidedly toward his Jewish heritage: a collection of three long poems, *Who Gathered and Whispered behind Me,* that takes its title from the autobiography *Ma Vie* by the Jewish artist Marc Chagall; and *Faith.* In reviewing *Who Gathered,* the critic John Addiego compared Goldbarth to Allen Ginsberg, saying that Goldbarth, like Ginsberg (the author of the poem "Kaddish"), had begun to discover a wealth of poetry in the mines of the Jewish tradition. One poem, "The Window Is an Almanach," focuses almost entirely on Chagall's stained glass windows in Jerusalem as well as on Goldbarth's grandmother, Rose Seligman. Addiego points to the way that poem in particular shows Goldbarth's fundamental connection to Judaism: "using the grandmother's voice in intermittent passages, Goldbarth enlarges her thematic messages about Light and Dark, particularly her renditions of tales from a thirteenth-century book of esoteric Jewish mysticism."

Who Gathered and Whispered behind Me was a dress rehearsal for a 108-page production, *Faith,* that same year, in which Goldbarth's poems more fully enter the new terrain (for him) of Jewish life both secular and spiritual. Especially notable is the fact that this book turns to the mystery of religious faith, what Goldbarth ultimately calls the "beyond" of spiritual phenomena.

In these poems Goldbarth tells the story of his immediate family and its relationship to Jewish religious and cultural traditions. The book explores his heritage, Judaism; his home, Chicago; and his family, the Goldbarths (his father's family) and the Seligmans (his mother's family). David Starkey praises the poem "35,000 Feet—The Lanterns" as one of the "most affectionate poems in the book." Starkey admires its daring because it imagines the poet's grandfather and grandmother making love and creating the possibility of his own birth. The book is divided into two sections, and the first section continues Goldbarth's autobiographical explorations. It includes three poems to his father and three to his mother, one of which, "First Ride and First Walk," imagines Goldbarth's own birth: "They lifted me from the glass case / in my week-old sleek pink skin." There are also three poems for himself and three for his sister.

The poems in the book's second section are less immediately personal, and, says Starkey, "Though not conventionally religious, Goldbarth nonetheless religiously celebrates the mystery of the cosmos." The second section's concluding poem, "Carrell/Klee/and Cosmos's Groom," invokes the Jewish belief that the Sabbath is a mystical version of the marriage bed where heaven and earth join. Given the racy, earthy interests of Goldbarth's poetry to this point in his career, the realization that his own heritage condones such intense sexuality allows him to conclude, "Not that I deny the body. I love the body." In the poem's final lines he writes, "tonight the groom will carry the threshold / across the bride. *Tonight forever.*"

Although almost entirely ignored by the literary press, the book is the first to realize the dramatic, imaginative, and emotional potential of his own life and family. None of his other books had been so explicit or detailed about such personal material.

ORIGINAL LIGHT

So much work published in so short a time and covering such a wide stylistic, thematic, and emotional range all but demanded the publication of an edition of selected poems. In *Original Light* (1983) Goldbarth chose to draw only from six of his earlier works. And, rather than offer a chronological tour of his poetry, he instead mixed his newest work with older work in order to create a completely new narrative sequence. This blend of old and new, although unusual for a typical edition of selected poems, reflected Goldbarth's belief that, because all things are related, and because time curves in on itself, chronology as a measure of development and meaning is fundamentally a false way to measure a poetic career. Only the story counts.

To make the case for his unusual notion of story, time, and narrative development, the book begins with a new poem, "The Importance of Artists' Biographies." This poem connects the past to the present by showing how art never has been nor ever will be beholden to the chains of linear time. From this introductory poem there follow three sections. Of them, the third, "Chronologues," consisting of the dramatic monologues and dialogues that Goldbarth had first published in *Coprolites,* received the most critical attention.

Of the book's poems, even many of the "old" poems were new to readers because they came from limited and hard-to-find small press publications like the fourteen-page *Ink, Blood, Semen.* Of that chapbook's nine poems, six were reprinted in the selected poems. Other poems, like "Mnemonic Devices," first printed in *The Smuggler's Handbook,* exemplify Goldbarth's new concerns of family and heritage as part of his ongoing interest in the multilayered reality of time:

My
Sister and I become an acronym for: all
of Central Europe, its soups, its partidye cloths,
the coins on its eyelids.

In the lyrics of the new poems, meanwhile, readers learn, as they would have from the book's dedication, that Goldbarth had recently married. The book was dedicated to his new wife and includes a number of poems to her, including "The Form and Function of the Novel." Other new poems depict the lower depths of love, such as "Worlds," where Goldbarth describes a breakup by connecting events from the year 1120 to the time 11:20:

. . . your leaving

is always a watchface
held halted in its own two hands. . . .

In "Semiotics/The Doctor's Doll" Goldbarth makes this same point by reflecting on his own name and allowing that reflection to spiral outward into the idea of "naming" as a tribal, ritualistic prehistorical human event:

>   —An old name, Albert, my
> grandfather's name and then mine. So now I'm
> his
> ambassador, from a world
> of ghetto donkeycarts, fat Sabbath candles, soup-
> steam
> foggling the windows, and a voice in blessing
> hovering
> like God's own special hummingbird over the
> wine . . .
> —Or older, a clan-name, a cave-name,
> Runs-With-The-Bears, Old-Trout-Mouth,
> a beast-name, a bird-name.

Strong reviews followed the publication of this edition of selected poems. Michael Simms, in *Southwest Review,* explained that the prefatory poem "introduces the recurrent themes of the book: our conceptions of time and distance, the self-consciousness of the artist, the 'wise-ass jokes' that history plays." Reviewers like Robert Cording uncovered a central aesthetic structure in Goldbarth's poems: "[they] depend almost entirely on two conditions: the accumulation of random ideas which, at some point, suddenly 'click' into a pattern; and a shift in tone which usually accompanies that 'click.'" Referring to "The Importance of Artists' Biographies," Cording highlights Goldbarth's central governing metaphor of "the curve": "If all light returns because the universe curves, then too, perhaps all that we imagine forms a kind of galactic gallery where nothing we've seen 'can be lost.'"

The poet Diane Wakoski thought the very idea of a thirty-five-year-old poet publishing a collection of selected poems was absurd. "Goldbarth's best poetry evolves a study of being, using ideas from physics and philosophy about time, distance, motion and light," she granted, but she was particularly angered by the poetry in "Chronologues," calling it just so much "armchair voyeurism." Poets, she declared

after reading those poems, should always and only write out of "personal experiences and miseries (or joys)." By contrast, the poet William Logan felt that "Chronologues" were among the best poems of Goldbarth's career because, in them, Goldbarth "stops being Goldbarth for a moment."

Perhaps the most influential review was Philip Lopate's in the *New York Times Book Review.* "In a typical performance," Lopate said, "[Goldbarth] will juggle many different ideas and images, not only keeping them all in the air but establishing surprising connections among them that yield a large general meaning." He singled out as "a fine long poem, 'A Sanguinary,' which keeps wading further and further outward to embrace its subject, blood, in all its negative and positive aspects." He did, however, also echo Wakoski's complaint: "Reading some of these dialogues is as wearying as being locked in a room with a maniacal medievalist graduate student who won't shut up. And that is puzzling, because Mr. Goldbarth's poetry can be quiet and observant and caring off and on." Altogether, these selected poems present readers with Goldbarth's best work. They offer a taste of his multifaceted interests, including divergent genres from the long poem to the lyric, and a wide array of themes from autobiography to philosophical and historical exploration and meditation. Throughout, readers are treated to Goldbarth's humor, his delightful juxtapositions, and bizarre wit.

A FULLY FORMED POETICS AND A TURN TO THE ESSAY

Following his selected poems, Goldbarth did not publish a book for three years: in his terms, an eternity. When, in 1986, he published *Arts and Sciences,* the polarized title announced the interests that had long been his central obsession. This collection of poetry also demonstrates a newly emergent style that sets the stage for the books that follow. The poems in this and all of Goldbarth's future collections relate to one another, making each book a single super-poem. Each poem depends on Goldbarth's now fully developed style of collage effects: multiple narratives mixed with high and low diction; high and low art mixed with science and science fiction; the occult traditions mixed with normative religious faith.

The book is divided into sections; the first, "Some Science," engages physics, astronomy, geology, and the like. Still rooted in autobiography, these poems insist on pushing the autobiographical references into scientific terrain. As one example, a poem concerning the birth of his niece, "Problem Solving," refers not just to the birth but also to engineering—to bridge building—and to artist engineers ranging from Leonardo da Vinci to the poet's sister. Other poems—for instance, "Vestigal"—meditate on evolution.

In the section "Some Art" Goldbarth reflects on his own life but only as a way to turn outward and find his connection to such painters as Pieter Brueghel, Paolo Uccello, Rembrandt, and Albrecht Dürer. Even the simple objects on his desk are taken up in his ongoing search for connection. For all of their wide-ranging references, however, these poems maintain their personal, self-reflective atmosphere—most movingly, in "A Window Seat," a poem about the death of his wife Morgan's sister.

Continuing to develop his interest in the long poem, in "Knees/Dura-Europos" Goldbarth meditates on archeology, another familiar metaphor in his work. In this poem the once-lost town of Dura-Europos and its history of cruelties becomes a bitter example of Goldbarth's general theory of human history: "the basic bonework's always there: some good times, / then pain, then abandonment." In another long poem, "The Praises," Goldbarth imagines what the six alleged illegitimate children of the poet Walt Whitman would say if they could speak as adults: the poem, written in their voices, recalls the triumphs of "Chrono-logues." Of all the long poems in this book, however, "Cathay" was most often singled out for praise. In its collage of stories one reads of Goldbarth's Chicago neighborhood and a neighbor boy's mugging; of the poet's father; of a Chinese artist; and, throughout, of Christopher Columbus.

Writing in *Poetry* magazine, the poet David Shapiro said all of these poems are "an affirmation of a many-layered allegory whose meanings cannot be simply plucked or pierced." While he had much to praise he also sounded a note of caution that plagued Goldbarth in future reviews: "The disadvantage is that the strategy of strangeness and deviation will itself become a norm. And, as a matter of fact, Goldbarth's largesse does become a kind of familiar music, with its most likely tactics of dislocation and discontinuity." What was an original style of collage and radical juxtaposition, Shapiro felt, was at risk of turning into a mannerism, a stylistic cliché.

In the *New York Times Book Review* the poet Emily Grosholz sounded yet another warning: for all of his learning, Goldbarth "missed an important function of science, and discursive thought generally, which is to make discriminations when and where they are needed." She concluded, "If, without compromising his own sense of reality's ambiguous richness, Mr. Goldbarth could make his poems more orderly and spare, they would more often be greater than the sum of their parts."

These critiques of Goldbarth's style, however, should not detract from the central importance of this collection. Despite these poems' meandering poetics, their many voices and wide variety of topics ultimately work together and create distinct unified poetic wholes. Each poem establishes a web of connection between its many seemingly disparate parts and, amazingly, each poem often connects to the others in the book. Altogether, this book is a triumph of connection, of what the Romantic poets called "organic unity."

At one point in "Cathay," Goldbarth asks, "Those who came before—how close do we feel to them, do we *really* feel to them?" This question drives his next collection of poems, *Popular Culture* (1990), which won the prestigious Ohio State University Press/*The Journal* Poetry Award and began Goldbarth's long association with Ohio State University Press. In the collection Goldbarth brings to the fore his longtime interest in popular culture: comic books and their characters, such as Little Orphan Annie and Donald Duck; radio shows, such as *Captain Midnight;* old movies, such as *Frankenstein;* detective stories about Sherlock Holmes; and even 1960s girl bands like the Shangri-Las.

For all of its surface humor and pop references, however, *Popular Culture* is, fundamentally, a book of pain and suffering. Poems address the death of Goldbarth's sister-in-law ("Donald Duck in Danish"), the death of his father ("Shangri-La"), and the divorce from his wife, Morgan ("The Gulf"). One poem, "Qebehseneuf," is a sort-of prayer dedicated to his mother, sick in the hospital with colon cancer. Another moving poem, titled "Again," addresses both the death of his father and his divorce.

In the *New York Times Book Review* Stan Friedman said, "Frivolity and disposable culture collide and meld with loss, childhood and love as if all were set loose inside a particle accelerator." Friedman found Goldbarth's poetic style annoying: "Line breaks are haphazard, rhyme is witty but random. And if sometimes the wordplay is too coy, the sentiment too sentimental, a page-long stanza in need of a haircut, well, the reader must understand. 'The words we save / are the words we save everything else in.' The man is desperate."

Whether or not such critiques provoked Goldbarth or not is unknown; but shortly after *Popular Culture,* the poet published *A Sympathy of Souls.* These eight essays maintained the Goldbarth style of crosscutting narratives and linking cultures, time zones, and continents with stunning mental leaps embracing science, art, popular culture, and personal experience. But their nature as essays also meant they no longer had to adhere to the formal requirements of poetry such as stanza, line break, meter, rhyme, and the like. Frank Allen, writing in *Library Journal,* offered the best summary of their eclectic concerns: "episodes in the lives of family and friends; Hasidic legends; natural history; . . . fictionalized biographies of chemist Marie Curie and dancer Loie Fuller" as well as popular culture from comic books to toy shows.

In one of the collection's more affecting essays, "After Yitzl," Goldbarth imagines a counterlife, a counterself, Yitzl, who exists in a parallel universe. His story weaves in and out of Goldbarth's own story. At one point, during the Jewish ceremony of unveiling his father's tombstone a full year after the death, Goldbarth, at the grave, looks around and observes, "In back, my father's father's grave, the man I'm named for. Staring hard and lost at the chiseling, ALBERT GOLDBARTH. My name. His dates." In the way they make the idea of linear time, or the distinction between the mundane and the cosmic, seem irrelevant, these essays continue Goldbarth's self-exploration across all boundaries temporal and cultural.

In these essays Goldbarth also lets readers into his private life, alluding not only to his divorce but also to his second marriage, to Skyler Lovelace. In a particularly poignant essay, "Wind up Sushi," Goldbarth reflects on the strict, almost spartan, certainly rule-bound youth of his second wife. Comparing that childhood to his own family's indulgent acceptance of his love of comic books, Goldbarth turns his thought to his father's spirit: "It makes me crazy to knock at my father's stone, and rouse him from worms, from seraphs" in order to say "thank you." Only in this present moment, says Goldbarth, does he realize that such an acknowledgement has been "so long delayed in the saying."

Goldbarth published a chapbook, *Delft: An Essay-Poem,* in 1990 as well. This disquisition on fleas and seventeenth-century Dutch painting, among other things, was eventually incorporated in a second collection of essays, *Great Topics of the World* (1994). Whatever the generic contours of *Delft,* clearly, as of 1990, Goldbarth was going to work in prose as well as poetry. Both genres enabled him to continue his ongoing project of finding connections, toying with time.

HEAVEN AND EARTH

In 1991 Goldbarth's collection *Heaven and Earth: A Cosmology* won the National Book Critics Circle Award. Reporting on the NBCC awards ceremony in New York, the reporter for the *San Francisco Chronicle* said, "The real fun occurred . . . when poetry winner Albert Goldbarth, author of *Heaven and Earth: A Cosmology,* admonished the audience and the NBCC board members behind him to raise their right hands and repeat after him, 'I promise to read more poetry, not to read so much fiction and nonfiction. . . .'"

In their citation for the prize the NBCC said Goldbarth was like "manna in the desert, a cure for what ails our poetry." By 1991, in other words, Goldbarth's refusal to write a more conventionally autobiographical or more conventionally lyrical poetry had, at last, won acceptance by the literary community. In addition to this prize, Goldbarth also received a substantial critical boost in 1991 when the eminent Harvard literature professor Helen Vendler wrote admiringly of his work in *The New Yorker.* Declaring Goldbarth to be one of the great

contemporary American poets of the imagination, she argued that his imagination had two principle interests. The first was popular culture: "the earliest source of the rich multiplicity that appeases the collector in him." The other, she said, had not "found its adequate embodiment" but is "what is usually called religious, and it leans toward New Age superstitions," such as an interest in past lives, a collective unconscious, and the mystical rather than rabbinic traditions of Judaism. She added, "Goldbarth's tenderness toward the mystical does not, however, vitiate his enormous curiosity, or the momentum of his zest, or his sympathy of souls with the historical personages he resuscitates." Unlike many other critics, Vendler had little but praise to offer with regard to his stylistic techniques: "The typical procedure of a Goldbarth poem . . . is to keep two or three stories in mind at once, each of them somehow an analogue or a contradiction of another." Far from finding his style exasperating, she found such an eclectic collage oddly, even wonderfully, stimulating to the reader's imagination.

In *Heaven and Earth* Goldbarth characteristically fuses his interest in science with his knowledge of history and culture and with references to his own family and friends. The exploration of his family and his past, particularly the world of his grandparents, is especially notable in such poems as "Coin" and "Steerage." In "The History of Buttons" he also returns to his favorite metaphor of the curve:

> But the light of physics goes on
> unthinkably, it curves time, it
> goes all the way to where there's God or no God
> then loops back and doesn't
> care what it holds and it holds everything
> *Across the Layers*

By 1993, it had been ten years since Goldbarth's last edition of selected poems. The success of *Heaven and Earth* created a timely opportunity for the publication of *Across the Layers: Poems*

Old and New (1993). Like *Original Light,* this book brings old poems into a new sequential order and so transforms their collective story as it mixes them with new poems. Read in this new sequence the poems tell a tale of a son's relationship to his father. They depict the death of that father and explore the relationship both to the man, to memory, and to death itself.

Aside from that new sequence, the book also includes two other sections. In the first section Goldbarth reprinted *Different Fleshes* (1979) in its entirety, and in the third and final section he prints a new poem, a long collage "essay-poem" titled "Dual." Like *Delft* it was eventually incorporated into a book of essays (*Many Circles,* 2001), but in this collection it concludes a 217-page volume of poetry that proves just how far from the days of his first book Goldbarth has moved from a strictly lyric poetry.

The new poems included in *Across the Layers* stand out for their imaginative reach. In "Gallery" Goldbarth imagines his grandfather's immigration as a scene out of Pierre-Auguste Renoir's painting *The Boating Party:*

When my grandfather stepped from the boat
they gave him a choice of paintings to enter.
 "This one,"
he said by a nod of his head. Why not?

And in the thirty-three sonnet-length stanzas of "Radio Pope" Goldbarth tells the story of a woman paleontologist whose work is "constructing museum diorama models." As her tale unfolds, readers learn that she is the abused daughter of a fanatic collector of old radios. The poem is actually a dual narrative of the father and the daughter. Connecting both characters to the airwaves, to the past, to family, the poem explores the very idea of connection itself. By the end, its main character believes her father's spirit has actually come to her as if in a mysterious radio wave: "but if I concentrated, I could tune it / clearer. Lost it . . . (concentrating) . . . Here it comes. . . . "

Having tuned in to her father's frequency, she says,

He said he was waiting—not "him," not "waiting," exactly. More
like a joining—an organization, a worldwide organization, and
one day I'd join too, he said. There wasn't any rush though.

The final section of this book, the long concluding poem "Dual," ostensibly a meditation on the life and work of the photographer Diane Arbus, continues this same interest in finding connections between the spiritual and the real. In "Dual" Goldbarth defines the history of the Western world as a polarized contest between a once-dominant holistic monism, a unified philosophy, and a now-dominant Cartesian dualism that "separates mind from body; objective worlds from subjective." Goldbarth places his faith in that earlier, monist sensibility, using his vast knowledge of contemporary science to make the case for its defense. He says of the new physics that it "posits a 'layerverse' of endless contiguous universes; the ones most near us, horribly boringly like us; and the farther we move in any direction . . . the stronger the malleability." Goldbarth finds in the new science an endorsement of his central metaphor, the curve.

Commenting on "Dual," David Barber praised its dramatization of "existential doubleness and blurring boundaries between forbidden knowledge and higher wisdom." He declared the poem to be "a bracing excursus on the morally vexed proposition that 'nothing is safe from merging into its elseness.'" Turning to Goldbarth's poetry more generally, Barber wrote, "Albert is American poetry's consummate showman. With their whirlwind energies and combustible enthusiasms, their zany encyclopedic lore, chromatic lingo, and sheer chutzpah, Goldbarth's poems are bravura extravaganzas." He concluded, "What makes Goldbarth's best poems irresistibly memorable is not their dizzying profusion but their heroic efforts on behalf of memory itself."

Following Helen Vendler's insight that collecting was also a central metaphor to Goldbarth's poetry, the reviewer in the *Chicago Review,* Andrew Winston, argued that "Goldbarth has latched on to a central truth of the material age: our collections define us as we define our collections. He tries to see under and through these quirky passions, for collecting is a curious obsession—the holding, the finding and treasuring of the odd and oblique, as Goldbarth does in his poetry." Winston also thought the prominence of the poet's father in this collection had a deeper metaphorical significance for the poetry as a whole: "To find meaning, to make appropriate homage to the passing of Irving Goldbarth, is to connect it both to the cosmic passage of light and to the temporal and the physical moment of knowledge. To understand anything, one must take the long view."

Altogether, this second volume of selected poems put a cap on two full decades of work in a singular thematic terrain combing popular culture, autobiography, and contemporary science in a unique and recognizable style.

A SPIRITUAL TURN TO THE BEYOND

Within a year after publishing *Across the Layers,* Goldbarth released three new books: *The Gods* (1993), *Great Topics of the World: Essays* (1994), and *Marriage and Other Science Fiction* (1994). Of these, the collection of essays attracted the most attention. Of that book's four essays, "Delft," earlier published as a chapbook, garnered the most praise in the reviews. Another remarkable essay from the book, "Worlds," tells the story of his grandfather, his namesake. It connects that relative to the famous Boston Lowells—to the astronomer Percival, who argued there were canals on Mars, and to his sister the imagist poet, Amy Lowell. Inserting his grandfather—a Yiddish-speaking immigrant—into this milieu of a lesbian poet and a wild-haired astronomer, and adding for good measure the cartoonist inventor of the wacky character Krazy Kat, George Herriman, was little short of a surreal imaginative triumph. Reviewers were impressed. Ben Downing wrote in *Parnassus* that "the mere act of bringing [these disparate characters] together in Arizona (!!) . . . hoists a defiant middle finger to the universe and its red-tape casualties; just because such and such didn't happen, Goldbarth reasons, doesn't mean it couldn't have."

Writing in the *Los Angeles Times,* Richard Eder said,

> *Worlds* is a beguiling dream of simultaneities. Amy Lowell, Percival's corpulent, cigar-smoking poet sister, arrives with her deep devotion to Keats and her shared cult of the moon. Flagstaff, Ariz., becomes a focusing-glass of times and cultures: the Navajos and their spirits, the eccentric Bostonian Brahmanisms of Percival the scientist and the artist Amy, Krazy Kat's grass-roots American version of moonbeams, and the resourceful blend of Polish-Jewish meditative practicalities. Goldbarth has taken time and bent it into a rainbow.

William Ferguson, in the *New York Times Book Review,* was similarly enthusiastic, commenting that Goldbarth's "difficult but rewarding essays . . . have much in common with poetry: density of expression, verbal beauty, an artful joining of disparate entities into something new that illuminates as it entertains." Richard Eder, too, made this point: "All four [of the essays] are about time, art, science, and the feel and awkward fit of humanity's skin upon humanity's back. And the first, 'Delft,' although it reserves important places for Vermeer's paintings, the Dutch microscope-maker Antony van Leeuwenhoek, and the workings of young lust, is held together by fleas and the exuberant literary tricks that Goldbarth—a poet and you know it—gets them to perform."

The attention given to the essays, published only a short year after the selected poems, all but ensured a general dearth of criticism would accompany Goldbarth's next two collections of poetry, *The Gods* and *Marriage, and Other Science Fiction.* Stylistically, these books, both from Ohio State University Press, do not pave any new ground. Nor do they necessarily explore new terrain in their themes. They do, however, pick up a thread announced by the new poetry of *Across the Layers:* the idea of transcendence and of a mystical realm, or connecting current.

In a poem from *The Gods* titled "A Refuge," for example, the poet describes himself as

> . . . half-blind
> with Kansas sun outside
> and Goldbarth darkness inside

This dichotomy of light and dark, of the outside world and the inner psychic realm, becomes a refrain for the book. In another section, "The Mythic Adventures of Louie and Rosie," he returns to the story of his grandparents with seven poems. Perhaps the most outlandish of them is "The Jewish Poets of Arabic Spain, (10th to 13th Centuries), with Chinese Poets Piping Out of Clouds (and Once an Irishman)." Another section of the book, a sequence of eight twenty-line stanzas, "The Books/P,L,E," tells a story of a woman who finds on the beach a board stamped with the letters "PLE." She tries to connect those letters to some meaning, some story: "apples," "spleen," "nipples," "pleasure," "plexus," "please," "splendid journey," and the poem's last word, "complete," all compete for her attention. The book's longest poem, a seven-section mock epic, "The Book of Speedy," is also perhaps its most bizarre. The poem turns some Alka Seltzer into a deity and attempts to prove that one can find holiness in even the most crass commercialism; Goldbarth means to prove that sublimity exists even in stomach acid.

Marriage and Other Science Fiction, meanwhile, stands out as the first of Goldbarth's

books in more than a decade to consist almost entirely of shorter lyrics. As with his other work, the poems in this book join the personal to the metaphysical—often through bizarre pop-cultural unions of science and science fiction. Yet, as in *Popular Culture,* the veneer of lighthearted wonderment actually hides painful depths. Returning to a familiar scene of past sin, the poet writes, "I could see my father's / heart break, in his face." In this poem, "The Emergence of Flight from Aristotle's Mud," Goldbarth recalls the moment when, at age thirteen, he refused to participate in the Passover seder. In the terrifying poem "Fang" Goldbarth accounts for the domestic cruelties that plague ordinary lives, while in the title poem he returns again to the experience of his first wife's sister's death. This book has its share of delightful, less intense moments as well, such as a poem where the poet and his wife read on their porch: she reads a history of Western civilization, he a comic book.

THE SHIFT TO DRAMA

In 1996 Ben Downing wrote the first and still the only substantial critical essay reading Goldbarth's poetry and the prose together. To Downing, the two genres are but twin poles of the same phenomenon, in which Goldbarth's singular theme was "thou shalt forge links." Attempting to categorize the poet's central influences and themes, Downing first points to Goldbarth's bawdy, overtly sexual, always explicit subject matter. Downing places Goldbarth in the tradition of Philip Roth's great sexual adolescent character Alexander Portnoy and points out that Portnoy himself, like Goldbarth, derives from "a boisterous pack led by the likes of Rabelais, Swift, and the archrake Lord Rochester." This erotic, sexual, and most striking aspect of Goldbarth's work joins with a cluster of other themes derived from the work of Walt Whitman. Downing views Goldbarth's work as sharing Whitman's "enthusiasms for long lines, the kosmos, concupiscent fluids, and most of all themselves." Added to this mix of Eros and Whitman, Downing also finds a debt to James Joyce because, like Joyce, Goldbarth loves to coin new words and to exalt and revel in language itself. Like Joyce, Goldbarth's "jocular lyricism" lovingly admires even the most disgusting of items. A final theme and influence, says Downing, is humor, particularly the legacy of Jewish American humor.

Turning to Goldbarth's poetic technique, his prosody, however, Downing is less generous than Vendler. The poet's line breaks, he says, are mostly "rude, sudden jerky enjambments." In the end Downing privileges the essayist over the poet, saying the essays in *Great Topics of the World* make it "alarmingly close to being a perfect book, each essay a little world made cunningly, each sentence a just-so sweep of the compass." Indeed, claims Downing, "So ductile is Goldbarth in *Great Topics* that the bland term 'essay' hardly delimits his hothouse transmutations."

Goldbarth published two more collections in 1996: *Adventures in Ancient Egypt* and *A Lineage of Ragpickers, Songpluckers, Elegiasts, and Jewelers: Selected Poems of Jewish Family Life, 1973–1995*. The second of these is mostly a thematically based collection of selected poems culled from earlier volumes, but the poems in *Adventures in Ancient Egypt* are new. Their most striking formal feature is the turn to drama, whereas their most striking thematic revelation is a turn to a more vulnerable, self-reflexive poetry.

In general, however, *Adventures in Ancient Egypt* continues to develop Goldbarth's ongoing interest in connection. In "The Saga of Stupidity and Wonder" he writes, "The history of the world could be written / in anything's history." But its new willingness to explore the poet's vulnerable and private self led many to see it as a particularly impressive development in

Goldbarth's career. This increased willingness to be weak, wrong, confessional—in short, vulnerable—is apparent in the opening poem, "In the X-Ray of the Sarcophagus of Ta-pero":

> You ask me:
> what do *I* know of ancient Egypt?—
>
> almost nothing. A couple of coffee-table books.
> A couple of lecture series with slides.

This admission does not prevent Goldbarth from alluding to what knowledge he does have of the subject in order to make metaphorical use of it. It simply makes the charge of intellectual hubris harder to sustain. This opening poem is followed by what David Baker calls "five sequential poems." The first of these, a twelve-stanza unrhymed sonnet sequence with the general heading "Ancient Stories," connects the lives of two individuals to the world of prehistory and ancient Egypt. After that sequence there follows another sequence of prose poems (originally published as a chapbook, *Ancient Musics,* in 1995). This second sequence brings together the artifacts of ancient Egypt with scenes and anecdotes from Goldbarth's own life. In a third sequence of twelve poems that connect time zones often in striking ways, one reads a particularly exciting and fresh poem: "The Lives of the—Wha'?" This poem marks a rare moment when Goldbarth turns his satire on his own stylistic innovations and techniques. Recalling his well-known poem "The Importance of Artists' Biographies," this new poem depicts Goldbarth entering into the world of Uccello and Rosa Bonheur. In the fifth stanza one reads "—huh? My wife steps into this poem now, / asking me why I always sneak off in disguise to a secret place in my head." From this turn to self-criticism, the poem then reaches back outward and becomes a beautiful love lyric to his wife.

The final two of the five sequences are, for Baker, the most moving poetry in the book. The three-part "Ancient Semitic Rituals for the

Dead," a mix of prose poetry and lyrics, includes Goldbarth's first drama, a scene depicting his meeting with the ghost of his father. In that scene the painful moment when Goldbarth refused to adhere to the Jewish traditions during a Passover seder is again recalled. In the book's final sequence Goldbarth creates a kaddish for his mother, recently dead of colon cancer. That final sequence, "Ancient Egypt/Fannie Goldbarth," says Baker, is an especially apt metaphor: "Who better to emulate than the Egyptians, with their remarkable successes of preservation . . . in order to preserve the memory of one's loved ones."

Taken as a whole, this book, says Baker, is "explicit, stark, and beautifully disturbing." He goes so far as to say that it is among Goldbarth's most important because "even with all of the variety of forms . . . no poems, no sections, seem weak or out of place. The book reads like a single narrative, a life-history of the poet, his family and mother, as well as a life-history of language."

FIVE NEW BOOKS

After *Adventures in Ancient Egypt,* Goldbarth entered another prolific phase, publishing three collections of poetry—*Beyond* (1998), *Troubled Lovers in History* (1999), and *Saving Lives* (2001)—and two books of essays—*Dark Waves and Light Matter* (1999) and *Many Circles* (2001; his first volume of selected essays). In retrospect, each of these books merely highlights what Baker had first noticed in *Adventures in Ancient Egypt:* Goldbarth's writing both in prose and poetry is far more willing to expose the poet's more vulnerable aspects; it is more openly self-critical even as it becomes more and more spiritual in its concerns.

In *Beyond,* for example, Goldbarth's willingness to confront his own foibles leads to a remarkably loose poetry of speech rhythms and dialogue (particularly in "Roses and Skulls" and

"Because It Happened," in which the Yiddish rhythms of his relatives seamlessly merge with the jargon of a "hoity-toity rib joint"). For all of its conversational easy tones, however, this book is tightly constructed. Each of its poems belongs to a sequence. Collectively, they develop a central theme of transcendence. In the first poem the woman from "Radio Pope" returns, thinking again of the beyond in five sonnet-length stanzas. The seventeen poems that follow that sequence each pursue an aspect of the beyond. Then, in the book's final section, "The Two Domains," Goldbarth creates another poetic drama forty-four pages long. (Before publication in this collection "The Two Domains" was performed at Beloit College under the auspices of the *Beloit Poetry Review.* Beloit also published the poem as a chapbook.)

"The Two Domains" tells the story of two lovers from 1888 who are killed just before they can consummate their affair. That tale is juxtaposed with the story of a twentieth-century woman owner of a mail-order catalog company. She discovers that her warehouse is haunted: its objects are continually flying about at top speed. To solve the problem she calls a man who bills himself as a ghostbuster. Eventually, to stop the objects from their crazy flights, she has sex with the man and "the air was calm, and I was calm. // Untenanted by restless spirits." To tell the story, Goldbarth weaves together lyric, dramatic monologue, catalog entries, diary entries, and many other forms of writing. This formal collage joins with the narrative collage of three couples: the twentieth-century lovers, Goldbarth and his wife, and the lovers of the 1880s.

In his next book, *Troubled Lovers in History,* relationships (the central issue of "The Two Domains") become the governing interest of the book. The poem "Complete with Starry Night and Bourbon Shots" recalls his difficult relationship with his first wife's father, his former father-in-law, Bob Potts, in order to write a moving elegy. In the poem "In" one encounters a crazy mix of people and time zones as the poem meditates on the strange confluence of the invisible and visible universe, using X rays as the major metaphor.

Another poem, "***The Battle of the Century!!!***" describes Goldbarth at his parents' grave site. While there he hears two voices, one saying "Look down" and another saying "Look up." In both cases he does as commanded, proving to himself that he is equally drawn both to the beyond above—the metaphysical, spiritual world of transcendence—and to the here and now below—to dirt, worms, and tangible physical sensation. The poem brings together early-nineteenth-century sideshow wrestlers and 1930s comic-book superheroes: these characters, said Jeffrey Schotts, "engage in hyperbolic battle, revealing the conflicts against death engaged by Goldbarth's inevitably dying mother and even by 'two sixteen-year-old lovers / screwing madly, for the contrast, on top of a grave.'" At the end of this poem, Goldbarth thinks of the two obsessions pulling at him: "Each, beseeching allegiance / Earth and Air."

In general, positive reviews lauded this book. Graham Christian in *Library Journal* compared Goldbarth's technique to that of an avant-garde filmmaker with "the verbal-aesthetic equivalents of jump-cut editing and the hand-held camera." In *Poetry* David Yezzi wrote, "There's enough fizz in an Albert Goldbarth poem to charge a seltzer bottle." Yezzi meant to praise Goldbarth's style, not criticize his substance, and, in his April 2000 review he offered an astute analysis of Goldbarth's poetic technique. After a close reading of "Against," he noted that the form consists of three sonnet-length stanzas, in which each stanza depicts a scene of struggle between people—an old married couple, schoolchildren, the inhabitants of two medieval towns: "In a neat mimetic effect, the poem itself finds a formal opposition between the rangy movements of the argument and the tidy sonnet-like paragraphs that contain them."

Jeffrey Schotts, meanwhile, praised the introspective, self-critical tone of this collection: "The collection, despite its ambivalence toward autobiography and its insistence on creating fiction disguised as truth, has an exceedingly personal depth."

CONCLUSION

Three books followed within two years of *Troubled Lovers in History:* an essay collection titled *Dark Waves and Light Matter;* a collection of poetry, *Saving Lives;* and a volume of selected essays, *Many Circles.* Of these, the poetry collection, *Saving Lives,* put Goldbarth again in the national limelight. It won the National Book Critics Circle Award for 2002, making Goldbarth the first poet since 1981 to win that honor twice. In an interview for National Public Radio's *All Things Considered* (March 12, 2002), Susan Stamberg asked the poet a question she said all poets surely hate: "What are your poems about?" Goldbarth responded: "The human condition."

From his first collection, *Under Cover,* in 1973 to the 2001 collection *Saving Lives,* the human condition has been the core concern of this most generous and expansive poet. And for all his interest in connectivity, unity, and a multilayered idea of history, his work is also, finally, an exploration of the self and of that self's relation to time. In his early work Goldbarth explored the connection between art and its double, life; between the popular and the serious; between science and the mysteries; over time his work has come to explore the connection between the visible and invisible worlds. Read as an ongoing "layerverse," to use his term, Goldbarth's poetry and prose is a work of ongoing revelation, seeking out the hidden, exposing the "beyond," forging links, and insisting that all things connect. As the title of his selected essays of 2001 declared, his work is indeed a set of many circles.

Selected Bibliography

WORKS OF ALBERT GOLDBARTH

POETRY

Coprolites. New York: New Rivers, 1973.

Under Cover. Crete, Nebr.: Best Cellar, 1973.

Jan. 31. Garden City, N.Y.: Doubleday, 1974.

Opticks: A Poem in Seven Sections. New York: Seven Woods, 1974.

Keeping. Ithaca, N.Y.: Ithaca House, 1975.

Comings Back. Garden City, N.Y.: Doubleday, 1976.

A Year of Happy. Raleigh: North Carolina Review Press, 1976.

Curve: Overlapping Narratives. New York: New Rivers, 1977.

Different Fleshes: A Novel-Poem. Geneva, N.Y.: Hobart and William Smith Colleges Press, 1979.

I Am a Sonnet. New York: Seven Woods Press, 1980.

Ink, Blood, Semen. Cleveland: Bits Press, Department of English, Case Western Reserve University, 1980.

The Smuggler's Handbook. Wollaston, Mass.: Chowder Chapbooks, 1980.

Eurekas. Memphis, Tenn.: Raccoon Press, 1981.

Faith. St. Paul, Minn.: New Rivers, 1981.

Who Gathered and Whispered behind Me. Seattle: L'Epervier, 1981.

Goldbarth's Book of Occult Phenomena. Des Moines, Iowa: Blue Buildings, 1982.

Original Light: New and Selected Poems, 1973–1983. Princeton, N.J.: Ontario Review Press, 1983.

Albert's Horoscope Almanac. Minneapolis, Minn.: Bieler Press, 1986.

Arts and Sciences. Princeton, N.J.: Ontario Review Press, 1986.

Delft: An Essay-Poem. Maryville, Mo.: GreenTower Press, 1990.

Popular Culture. Columbus: Ohio State University Press, 1990.

Heaven and Earth: A Cosmology. Athens: University of Georgia Press, 1991.

Across the Layers: Poems Old and New. Athens: University of Georgia Press, 1993.

The Gods. Columbus: Ohio State University Press, 1993.

Marriage and Other Science Fiction. Columbus: Ohio State University Press, 1994.

Ancient Musics: A Poetry Sequence. Kansas City, Mo.: Helicon Nine Editions, 1995.

Adventures in Ancient Egypt. Columbus: Ohio State University Press, 1996.

A Lineage of Ragpickers, Songpluckers, Elegiasts, and Jewelers: Selected Poems of Jewish Family Life, 1973–1995. St. Louis, Mo.: Time Being Books, 1996.

Beyond. Boston: David R. Godine, 1998.

Troubled Lovers in History. Columbus: Ohio State University Press, 1999.

Saving Lives. Columbus: Ohio State University Press, 2001.

COLLECTED ESSAYS

A Sympathy of Souls. Minneapolis, Minn.: Coffee House Press, 1990.

Great Topics of the World: Essays. Boston: David R. Godine, 1994; New York: Picador, 1996.

Dark Waves and Light Matter. Athens: University of Georgia Press, 1999.

Many Circles: New and Selected Essays. St. Paul, Minn.: Graywolf Press, 2001.

CRITICAL AND BIOGRAPHICAL STUDIES

Addiego, John. Review of *Who Gathered and Whispered behind Me. Northwest Review* 20, no. 1:136–140 (1982).

Allen, Frank. Review of *Sympathy of Souls. Library Journal* 115, no. 11:113 (1990).

Baker, David. Review of *Popular Culture. Poetry* 158 (June 1991): 158.

———. "Hieroglyphs of Erasure." *Kenyon Review* 19:173–179 (summer–fall 1997). (Review of *Adventures in Ancient Egypt.*)

Barber, David. "Life Studies." *Poetry* 166, no. 1:46–51 (April 1995). (Review of *Across the Layers.*)

Christian, Graham. Review of *Troubled Lovers in History. Library Journal* 124, no. 5:82 (March 15, 1999).

Contoski, Victor. "Late Returns." *Prairie Schooner* 51, no. 4:419–421 (1977–1978). (Review of *Comings Back.*)

Cording, Robert. Review of *Original Light. Carolina Quarterly* 36, no. 2:91–95 (winter 1984).

Downing, Ben. "The Wizard of Wichita." *Parnassus* 21, nos. 1–2:277ff. (1996). (Reviews of *Across the Layers* and *Great Topics of the World.*)

Eder, Richard. "Tales of Time, Science, and the Awkward Feel of Humanity." *Los Angeles Times,* December 16, 1994, p. E9. (Review of *Great Topics of the World.*)

Ferguson, William. Review of *Great Topics of the World. New York Times Book Review,* December 25, 1994, p. 11.

Friedman, Stan. Review of *Popular Culture. New York Times Book Review,* September 23, 1990, p. 48.

Goldensohn, Lorrie. "Loading the Rifts." *Parnassus* 7, no. 2:124–140 (1979). (Review of *Comings Back.*)

Grosholz, Emily. "The Importance of Being Learned." *New York Times Book Review,* January 4, 1987, p. 22. (Review of *Arts and Sciences.*)

Heffernan, Michael. "Good Manure." *Midwest Quarterly* 16, no. 1:221–226 (winter 1975). (Review of *Coprolites.*)

Holt, Patricia. "Schmoozing at the Critics Awards." *San Francisco Chronicle Sunday Review,* March 29, 1992, p. 2.

Johnston, Dillon. Review of *Coprolites. Shenandoah* 26, no. 2:96–97 (winter 1975).

Kaganoff, Peggy. Review of *Arts and Sciences. Publishers Weekly,* September 19, 1986, p. 139.

———. Review of *Popular Culture. Publishers Weekly,* October 6, 1989, p. 94.

Katz, Jonathan. "Sing Goddamm." *Midwest Quarterly* 16, no. 1:230–234 (winter 1975). (Review of *Jan. 31.*)

King, Michael. "*Different Fleshes:* The Poetry of Albert Goldbarth." *American Poetry Review* 9, no. 2:5–6 (1980).

Kinzie, Mary. "How Could Fools Get Tired!" *Poetry* 132, no. 1:31–52 (April 1978). (Review of *Comings Back.*)

Logan, William. Review of *Original Light. Poetry* 145, no. 2:103–105 (November 1984).

Lopate, Philip. "A Way to Live While Waiting." *New York Times Book Review,* October 2, 1983, pp. 15, 30. (Review of *Original Light.*)

Oliphant, Dave. "Goldbarth's Vocabulary Banquet and Treatise of Sand." *Margins,* December 1974, pp. 37, 58.

Publishers Weekly. Review of *A Sympathy of Souls.* May 4, 1990, p. 65.

Schotts, Jeffrey. Review of *Troubled Lovers in History. Raintaxi* 4 (summer 1999) (http://www.raintaxi.com/online/1999summer/goldbarth.shtml).

Shapiro, David. Review of *Arts and Sciences. Poetry* 150:38 (April 1987).

Shively, Charley. Review of *Different Fleshes. American Book Review* 4, no. 3:11 (1982).

Simms, Michael. "The Same River Twice." *Southwest Review* 69, no. 3:344–346 (1984). (Review of *Original Light.*)

Smith, Dave. "Drit [*sic*] under Glass." *Midwest Quarterly* 16 no. 1:227–229 (winter 1975). (Review of *Opticks.*)

Starkey, David. "Albert Goldbarth." In *Dictionary of Literary Biography.* Vol. 120, *American Poets since World War II,* 2d series. Edited by R. S. Gwynn. Detroit: Gale, 1992. Pp. 90–95.

Vendler, Helen. "Imagination Pressing Back: Frank Bidart, Albert Goldbarth, and Amy Clampitt." *The New Yorker* 67:103–111 (June 10, 1991). Reprinted in her *Soul Says: On Recent Poetry.* Cambridge, Mass.: Harvard University Press, Belknap Press, 1995. pp. 71–91.

Wakoski. Diane. "The Life of Albert Goldbarth." *American Poetry Review* 6, no. 4:8 (1984). (Review of *Original Light.*)

Winston, Andrew. Review of *Across the Layers. Chicago Review* 40, nos. 2–3:177–181 (1994).

Yezzi, David. Review of *Troubled Lovers in History. Poetry* 176, no. 1:40 (April 2000).

—*JONATHAN N. BARRON*

John Haines

1924–

JOHN HAINES POSSESSES a sensibility and awareness that may soon be lost to American letters. Initially trained in sculpture and painting, Haines eventually found his art in words, in poetry and nonfiction prose. However, unlike most contemporary writers, Haines discovered and nurtured his poetic voice during twenty-five years living, hunting, trapping, and writing in the Alaska wilderness near Richardson. Many people have written about the wilderness experience in North America, fewer have lived it, and fewer still, far fewer, have experienced it and have the voice of a poet to express that experience. In this sense much of Haines's work is a gift, a song about a way of living that is arguably no longer available.

Haines is a far-reaching poet and essayist, and not all of his work is about the wilderness. His writing engages art, politics, and the everyday lives and tasks of American people. Ranging from the Arctic Circle to Manhattan to the suburbs of California, all of his work seeks a commitment to the land and to the people and at the same time voices a resistance to the governmental, economic, and social exploitation of all environments, human and nonhuman. The voice often modulates from indignation, to elegy, to wonder and celebration.

Born on June 29, 1924, in Norfolk, Virginia, Haines is the son of John Meade Haines, who was an officer at the Naval Training Station in Norfolk. His mother was Helen M. Donaldson, and although she seems to have enjoyed the life of a naval officer's wife, she was impatient with the military caste system of officers and enlisted men, possessed of a democratic spirit Haines seems to have inherited. She also disliked the constant uprooting. Shortly after Haines's birth, the family moved to Vallejo, California, where Haines's brother Robert was born in 1926. The family spent many of the Great Depression years at the old naval gun factory—known as the Yard—in Washington, D.C., where Haines and his brother experienced much of their adolescence in the industrial landscape of the Yard and along the polluted Anacostia estuary. However, he also spent many fine days fishing with his father in Virginia and upper Maryland.

As military families will, the Haines family moved all over the United States. Perhaps this lack of rootedness helps explain Haines's later ferocious attachment to a particular place. But he also enjoyed positive influences during his childhood, one in particular that may have subtly pointed him on his way to becoming a writer. Haines mentions in the opening essay of *Fables and Distances: New and Selected Essays* (1996), "Within the Words: An Apprenticeship," that one of the finest things his father did for him as a child was to read to him aloud, and the effect of his father's voice awakened in him the awareness "that in that echo of a voice, of the words within the voice and the voice within the words, comes our earliest and most lasting sense of the language, its traditions and its possibilities." Also his high school teacher Roy Burge played a record of a British scholar reciting Chaucer's "Prologue" to *The Canterbury Tales* in Middle English, and Haines carried the echo of this voice with him aboard ship during World War II and, one suspects, long afterward.

Though he is reticent about his experiences in World War II, Haines saw active duty with both the Atlantic and Pacific Fleets from 1943 to

1946 and earned several battle stars. After the war, aided by the GI Bill, Haines attended the National Art School in Washington, D.C., but before his first year was out he decided to seek a different kind of adventure in Alaska. There, about seventy miles southeast of Fairbanks, he built a small house, stocked up on firewood, and filed a claim for the homestead at Richardson. In 2002 the homestead was nominated as a historic site to be placed on the National Register as the John M. Haines Homestead Historic District. Haines dates his birth as a poet from his move to Alaska.

That first winter, confronted with the raw power of the Alaska landscape, with masses of snow, mountains, frozen rivers, and especially the strange quality of light—and the sheer paucity of it—Haines knew he had found a place that spoke deeply to him. He also soon realized that he would not be able to capture in paint or charcoal the landscape that came to dominate his imagination. His inability to express the wonder the landscape provoked in him left him downcast, and he began to write. Though the landscape itself seemed to demand an aesthetic response from Haines, that response remained inadequate without the inclusion of the people who had long inhabited the region. It follows that Haines's most important teachers may have been the inhabitants of Richardson, who lived a life close to the land, who taught Haines how to survive in the harsh landscape by hunting and trapping, and who taught him the value—both practical and aesthetic—of everyday physical work with the hands, with animals, and with the materials of the earth.

After that first winter and the following summer, Haines returned to Washington, D.C., where he again attended art school from 1948 to 1949, this time at American University. There he knew Caresse Crosby of Black Sun Press and attended a reading at Charles Olson's house. He was employed for a time as a draftsman in the Department of the Navy before he moved to

New York City to attend the Hans Hofmann School of Fine Arts, where he studied from 1950 to 1952. He also continued to write poetry, having "simply caught fire with the written word." In New York he lived near the East River and the Williamsburg Bridge. The cityscape affected him—though not nearly as intensely—in much the same way as the Alaska landscape did, and the city too demanded from him a response that Haines once again sensed would not be met with clay or paint. One aspect of his response to the city and the East River was an intense engagement with Hart Crane's work, and Crane figures as one of Haines's early influences—along with T. S. Eliot, William Carlos Williams, and William Butler Yeats among the modernist poets—in Haines's turn toward poetry.

While in New York, Haines moved with such figures of the art and literary world as Weldon Kees, David Smith, Franz Kline, Willem de Kooning, and Jack Tworkov, and he published his first poem during this time. He lived in near poverty, although he is careful to point out that at that time many in his circle lived a kind of bohemian lifestyle in which poverty and the experience of the just-ended war were a common bond. This bond became particularly strong in one instance, when after vacating a cockroach-infested room in a fleabag rooming house, Haines was offered a place to stay in a loft shared by three female students at the Hofmann School, one of whom, Peggy Davis, he married in the following year, 1951. Still mentally struggling with whether to pursue writing and poetry, visual art, or both, Haines suffered from migraine headaches. One morning on his walk to the Hofmann School from the Lower East Side toward West Eighth Street in the Village, he paused on a street corner, acutely aware that he must make a decision, and he opted for the life of a poet. This decision he calls, in a letter, a "foolhardy business" though still—after all these years—with the assurance that he had, foolhardy or not, done the right thing. Although he was unaware of their cause at the time, his headaches never recurred.

Leaving the city for good in 1952, Haines returned via California to the homestead in Richardson, where he remained until 1969, eking out a living hunting, trapping, and working occasionally as a carpenter. Haines writes in another essay from *Fables and Distances,* "Notes from an Interrupted Journal," that "My affection for this landscape has been among the oldest and deepest things in my life. This is where I was born, improbably at the age of twenty-three." Although this time was financially meager, it has been a rich source of poetry and prose, and during this time Haines began publishing more of his poems. He was awarded a Guggenheim Foundation Fellowship in 1965, which brought him some financial relief, and in the following year his landmark first book of poems, *Winter News,* was published by Wesleyan University Press. But before considering Haines's poetry, it seems appropriate to engage his prose. This goes far out of the chronological order of the published work but returns thematically to the period leading up to *Winter News.* With the publication in 1989 of his memoir *The Stars, the Snow, the Fire: Twenty-five Years in the Northern Wilderness,* Haines articulated in splendid, evocative prose what those years in Alaska meant to him as a human being and as a poet. Alaska and his life there have been the most important influences on his prose and poetry.

In the essay "The Writer as Alaskan" from his 1981 book *Living off the Country: Essays on Poetry and Place,* Haines writes:

> Why I chose that particular place rather than another probably can't be answered completely. I might have gone elsewhere and become a very different poet and person. But there was, most likely, no other region where I might have had that original experience of the North American wilderness. Unlike other "wilderness" areas,

> Alaska in those days seemed open-ended. I could walk north from my homestead at Richardson all the way to the Arctic Ocean and never cross a road nor encounter a village. This kind of freedom may no longer be available, but at that time it gave to the country a limitlessness and mystery hard to find now on this planet.

He chose a way of living and writing that he saw as productive of a viable human participation in the ecological community, and in the process he also questioned the current ways of living in North America. His manner of writing cannot be separated from his way of living, and the reference to open-endedness suggests an ongoing experience, left off in Alaska and picked up in the writing and reading of his prose and poetry.

THE STARS, THE SNOW, THE FIRE

Already recognized as a fine poet, Haines, with the publication of *The Stars, the Snow, the Fire,* emerged as a major voice in contemporary American nature writing. Though profoundly moved by the idea and the experience of wilderness, Haines focuses more on what it means for a human being to live in close contact with the physical world than on external nature. The aesthetic value in this book is lodged in a particular way of inhabiting a particular place. The book discloses that Richardson, Alaska, was at one time more populated than it was at the time of Haines's residency and that the landscape has been altered by miners, trappers, and pipeline crews. It is a wild place certainly, but it is also deeply inscribed with human presence. In this way the land becomes an important nexus of nature and culture.

Full of ice, blood, bone, fur, death, hardship, and especially silence, Haines's depiction of his world is not an idyllic paean to the pristine wild. It is the engagement of an ecosystem, and this engagement requires a recognition of interrelationships. Haines's prose accesses these interrelationships in the moments when he is most intensely in close contact with neighbors, animals, and the physical world; these moments are then tapped in instants of intense reflection and made available by their retelling. Telling stories is one of the ways the community of Richardson is sustained, and Haines writes about long winter hours around the roadhouse table telling stories and drinking coffee spiked with rum:

A chronicle of the wise, the foolish and the lucky—it will be resumed one evening when we are here again, to renew the playful innocence of an early day when men could stand in wonder at a beast, to marvel at a world abundant with things that walked and flew and swam and seemed possessed of understanding, to speak at times almost like men themselves.

The act of renewal includes a retrieval of a time when humans felt wonder and respect for the world, its abundance, and the animals that inhabit it along with human beings. Again the element of wonder is introduced, growing out of a perception of shared human existence as it interrelates with the landscape and the rest of creation. Haines, through sharing his experience of proximity to the physical and storied land, involves readers in a shared ecological perception of community and world in which the cultural and the natural emerge as inseparable.

In his preface to *The Stars, the Snow, the Fire,* Haines writes, "In reliving parts of the narrative, I seem to have wandered through a number of historical periods, geological epochs, and states of mind, always returning to a source, a country that is both specific and ideal." The country is ideal in that it can provide him with a potential way of perceiving the world and his relation to it. It is also a source of the creative imagination. It is specific in that it is the physical placc in which Haines lived and worked with the full intensity of experience understood in his work as an interpenetration of individual and environment. In the most forthright language, Haines sees the ecology of his watershed as a living entity: "Like all young rivers, the Tanana does strange and unpredictable things." The river has agency, it "does" things, and the landscape around Richardson participates in Haines's experience.

Agency is foregrounded by Haines's attempt to present experience in an ecological way that includes human beings and artistic endeavor in natural ecosystems. He sets his characters in relationships to the physical world in a manner that makes their agency unmistakable. In an interview with Robert Hedin in *Northwest Review,* Haines comments:

I suppose that what you see . . . in my own writing owes much to my having lived for so long in circumstances that more or less compelled me to see human activity on a background of such elemental scale that even today, with all the changes that have occurred, earth and the weather tend to overshadow nearly everything else. Yet it takes very little human interference to change things: one word spoken in an absolute stillness, one shout, one rifle shot, means more, changes more, than a thousand people marching in a city where noise is the first element.

Living in circumstances where one is acutely aware of one's place in a world not drowned out with human noise and activity brings one to the awareness that each and every action has ramifications in the world, that, as Haines claims in *The Stars, the Snow, the Fire,* "before knowledge, there was wisdom, grounded in the shadows of a dimly lit age." Silence prompts this awareness, and this silence establishes a context for all that happens in *The Stars, the Snow, the Fire.*

Even the silence of a tiny animal like a bat can heighten an awareness of what Haines terms "being." "Being" is less a state of isolate existence than an existence within a state of interrelationships, an existence in which relations to others—to both human and nonhuman, both animate and inanimate nature—is the defining characteristic. These relationships seem to precede language, and awareness of such a quality of being in the world results in Haines's attempt to articulate silence:

> And to think, from this long vista of empty light and deepening shade, that so small and refined a creature could fill an uncertain niche in the world; and that its absence would leave not just a momentary gap in nature, but a lack in one's own existence, one less possibility of being.

These glimpses of "Empty light," "deepening shade," "absence," "gap," "lack," and a pause of uncertainty all suggest silence without explicitly naming or knowing it. Seen in such a long vista of light and silence, both human and animal, right down to the smallest individual creature, have intricate meaning in the larger context of "being." "Being" implies openness to ecological possibility, to the possibility that the nonhuman creatures of the world enrich human existence. The key to fully experiencing "being" might, in the simplest terms, entail that one pause and listen, be quiet for once.

His attempt to articulate ecological "being" is largely successful in *The Stars, the Snow, the Fire,* and Haines grounds his essays on a period of years that were experienced in a real place, but which of course have been altered by memory:

> It is true also that certain experiences, states of mind, and ways of life, cannot be willed back. That intuitive relation to the world we shared with animals, with everything that exists, once outgrown, rarely returns in all its convincing power. Observation, studies in the field, no matter how acute and exhaustive, cannot replace it, for the experience cannot be reduced to abstractions, formulas, and explanations. It is rank, it smells of blood and killed meat, is compounded of fear, of danger and delight in unequal measure. To the extent that it can even be called "experience" and not by some other, forgotten name, it requires a surrender few of us now are willing to make. Yet, in the brief clarity and intensity of an encounter

with nature, in the act of love, and (since we are concerned with a book) in the recalling and retelling of a few elemental episodes, certain key moments in that experience can be regained. On these depends the one vitality of life without which no art, no spiritual definition, no true relation to the world is possible.

In this passage are condensed the ingredients for a "true relation" to the world. It is helpful simply to list them: "intuitive relation," "experience," "fear," "danger," "delight," "surrender," "clarity," "intensity," "love," "recalling," "retelling," "regained." In a nutshell these words could be used as descriptors for a state of consciousness requisite for an ecological perception of the world. Haines suggests that without the moments of insight that meld these responses, no art is possible, so for him both being and art depend upon this "true relation to the world." This relation requires, to take the title of a Haines essay, "A Certain Attention to the World" that results in "delight, that sense of delight in discovery that renews everything and keeps the world fresh. Without it, poetry dies, art dies; the heart and the spirit die, and in the end we die."

WINTER NEWS, THE STONE HARP, TWENTY POEMS

In 1966, at age forty-two, Haines published his first book of poems, *Winter News,* dedicated to Jo Ella Hussey, to whom he was married from 1960 to 1970. (His first marriage had ended in divorce in 1957.) He subsequently published steadily, with fifteen books of poetry and five of prose to his credit. Haines's ferocious attachment to place has been mentioned, and the poems in *Winter News* are imbedded in the Alaska landscape in which Haines lived and worked. An intense attention to place remains central in his early books, and although he rightfully resists the limiting label of "Alaskan poet," in these poems Alaska is an overwhelming presence. However, it is a common misjudgment to consider poems that engage a particular land-scape as somehow decorative and therefore more limited in their cultural value than poems that address, say, a twentieth-century wasteland.

In *Winter News* (as in all of Haines's work) place is never simply visually compelling acre-age. For Haines place is imbued with spirit, with fear, danger, and delight. Place participates in the spirituality of the human being. The at-tachment to place or, better, to the interrelation-ship among ecosystems, human beings, and the aesthetic expression of the human being, becomes the nexus of place, community, and culture. For a poet like Haines, culture grows narrow and hollow without this attachment to the places and ecosystems human beings inhabit. Wendell Berry, one of the most eloquent advocates of place, acknowledges his debt and gratitude to Haines in the only full-length criti-cal treatment of Haines's work, *The Wilderness of Vision: On the Poetry of John Haines* (1996), edited by Kevin Bezner and Kevin Walzer. Recalling a 1969 reading by Haines at the Stan-ford University library, Berry also comments on the poems, many of which were from *Winter News:*

> Mr. Haines's poems, as I heard them that evening, told that they were the work of a mind that had taught itself to be quiet for a long time. His lines were qualified unremittingly by a silence that they came from and were going toward, that they for a moment broke.

This quietness and attentiveness toward silence indicate also a mind that has taught itself to listen, and this ability to listen to the silent world—and to articulate that silence so that relationships between that world and human expression be heard—provides the connection that for artists like Haines and Berry is the key to a renewed human relationship to both culture and the physical world.

The poems in *Winter News* are mostly spare, intensely imagistic lyrics that are intimately related to the life Haines led in Alaska, but there is little evidence of the confessional poet in Haines. The speaker of the poems often seems to disappear into the image, and perhaps this accounts for the many commentators who have made so much of Haines's early debt to Robert Bly, James Wright, and other deep image poets. To be sure Haines was strongly influenced by their work and by the German poet Georg Trakl's use of the image, but Haines clearly claims that the work of Bly and Wright—and of Bly's magazine *The Fifties*—primarily provided him with a sense that he was indeed connected to a larger writing culture than he felt himself to be in Alaska. Bly and other contemporary poets helped Haines find his own voice, as Haines explained in an interview with David Stark and Robert Hedin: "It was remarkable and exciting, and for me especially so far off there in the woods, to feel that at last I was beginning to do something that was my own."

The typical movement in a Bly poem from the same period, for instance, moves from the landscape to an image that is deeply lodged in the poet's consciousness, one that arises from his personal depths and that is intensely personal and at times impenetrable. Haines, however, reins his images in to a greater degree. In "Poem of the Forgotten," there is a specific link between image and place:

> Well quit of the world,
> I framed a house of moss and timber,
> called it a home,
> and sat in the warm evenings
> singing to myself as a man sings
> when he knows there is
> no one to hear.
>
> I made my bed under the shadow
> of leaves, and awoke
> in the first snow of autumn,
> filled with silence.

The unrhymed lines are tightly controlled with subtle assonance and consonance that cause words like "moss," "timber," and "home" to resonate with "warm," "man," "knows," "shadows," and "awoke." The final pair of lines links two images of central importance to this book, snow and silence. Both the snow and the speaker are "filled with silence," and the silence connects the speaker to both the shadow of leaves and the snow. So the physical acts of building a house and singing result in an intimate linkage of the poet to the dominant characteristics of the northern landscape, snow and silence, and this linkage is voiced only in the poem's quiet moment.

Houses and cabins also figure prominently in these poems, and in "The House of the Injured," the speaker "found a house in the forest, / small, windowless, and dark." Within the house is an injured bird:

> the beak was half eaten away,
> and its heart beat wildly
> under the rumpled feathers.
>
> I sank to my knees—
> a man shown the face of God.

A deserted cabin in an isolated forest houses not only an image of an injured animal but also, for Haines, an intimation of deity in the suffering and vibrant urge for life of an animal. The passive construction of "a man shown" suggests that this vision is a kind of gift bestowed upon the speaker in a particular place and time.

Cabins also house less abstract images, images of the real people Haines knew when he lived at the homestead in Richardson. In "Deserted Cabin," Haines envisions his friend Campbell, now gone, still living at his cabin:

> The bitterness of a soul
> that wanted only to walk
> in the sun and pick
> the ripening berries.

The poem addresses Campbell's poverty, which caused his bitterness; it also subtly indicts a culture that devalues a life based on simplicity and the intense desire to perform the most basic of human activities. This book suggests, though rarely overtly, a threat lurking in the North, the sense that a life more primal and close to the natural world poses a potential menace to the way most people have come to live in the United States. The absence of a near relationship between people and place bodes ill for cultural health.

Haines's poems often grow from actual incidents in his life in Alaska. One night upon returning home, Haines found a visitor who had seen the light of his cabin and come seeking warmth and rest during his long walk to Fairbanks. Haines and his wife gave the stranger, an Eskimo, food and the loan of a coat and gloves, and they sat in the light of a kerosene lamp talking of their differences and commonalities living in the northern woods. The stranger went on his way, and Haines recalls standing and listening to the sound of the man's boot soles crunching the snow. In "Poems and Places," in *Living off the Country,* Haines recalls the incident:

> I thought for a long time of his visit, his presence in the room of the cabin, and the sound of his footsteps. There seemed to be so much resonance there, so much possibility in that figure of a man of his race walking on that road, the old route between Asia and America.

In Haines's poem "The Traveler," this simple act of human decency and connection reverberates across epochs and cultures. The poem moves from specifics of incident,

> I remember an Eskimo
> from Holy Cross, walking one evening
> on the road to Fairbanks,

to a specific setting, Haines's cabin, in which "A lamp full of shadows burned / on the table before us." Again the figures of cabin and shadows predominate, but then comes an important shift in the poem. Haines writes, "Thousands of years passed," and he goes on to create a counterintuitive image of traditional native life—"a red memory against whiteness"— that seems to grow from the far past, not as it does from thousands of years in the future. Haines then returns to the present:

> The footsteps of a man walking alone
> on the frozen road from Asia
> crunched in the darkness
> and were gone.

The implications of a poem like this are powerful. There is a sense that a way of life thought long passed will reemerge in the future, and that way of life is shrouded in mystery and shadows. There is an ominous tone to the poem that suggests that the cultures displaced and colonized by Euro-Americans still lurk powerfully in human consciousness, certainly in the past, and likely in the future. Prehistoric travel on the road between Asia and North America has not ceased but cycles in a continuum of time, and the poem forbids one to think Americans have safely shut away the native populations whose cultures and traditional lands have been damaged or destroyed. All of these ideas are lodged in a concrete engagement with a real person in a specific place.

Haines's next two volumes, *The Stone Harp* (1971) and *Twenty Poems* (1971), further engage the North, but they differ from *Winter News* in important ways. *The Stone Harp* is divided into three titled sections, "In Nature," "America," and "Signs." *The Stone Harp* is also evocative and ecologically focused, but especially the section "America" has an apocalyptic and revolutionary tone. Some of the poems are overtly political, for example, "Lies," in which Haines writes that "The Man from Texas / is a coarse and wrinkled spider," clearly suggesting former president Lyndon Johnson, and "Each time he pulls at a thread / one of his listeners dies." More subtly executed, the poem "The

Legend of Paper Plates" uses the figure of paper plates as a metaphor for the throwaway culture of the United States, and the poem is less locked in to its historical moment. "The Legend of Paper Plates" begins:

> They trace their ancestry
> back to the forest.
> There all the family stood
> proud, bushy and strong.

The family represents of course the trees of the great North American forests, and Haines then links the trees to human beings, "the young people cut down / and sold to the mills." Brought into the present, the trees are bleached and crushed, and "You see them at any picnic." Finally the plates, like the people,

> are thin and pliable,
> porous and identical.
> They are made to be thrown away.

Subsequent poems in the sequence are titled "Dream of the Cardboard Lover," "The Dollhouse," and "A Poem Like a Grenade."

The movement is from the demeaning effects of a culture that Haines sees, through its most mundane material artifacts, as homogenizing and destructive of the dignity of both people and ecologies. For Haines and many writers of the Vietnam era, this degradation of culture at home and abroad demanded a clear response. Although he does not advocate throwing grenades, he does call for action to dislodge a government many saw as hopelessly corrupt and dangerous. Haines's weapon of choice, however, is a poem. With the country mired in Vietnam, racial tension, ecological destruction, and social unrest, Haines saw little reason for optimism at the turn of the decade, and this collection ends on a note of deep pessimism in "The Flight":

> and our life like a refugee cart
> overturned in the road,
> a wheel slowly spinning . . .

Twenty Poems is a slim, hand-printed, handsome book of which 485 copies were made. This elegant collection of poems again gathers Haines's Alaskan experience into the world of general experience. The tone is tempered from the one in *The Stone Harp,* though a powerful protest against the ecological exploitation of the North still exerts significant force in these poems. "The Invaders" begins:

> It was the country I loved,
> and they came over the hills
> at daybreak.

The invaders here are military and industrial interests, who condone stripping forests and "bruising the snows" in endless pursuit of economic and political gain. The line "bruising the snows" is especially poignant because, as shown, the snow is one of Haines's prominent images for the North. His way of life in the North represents in both real and figurative ways an antidote to modes of living that exact a too-great toll on the ecosystems and communities that sustain humans.

Importantly Haines has remained consistent on this issue. In a 2001 compilation entitled *Arctic Refuge: A Circle of Testimony,* Haines's declaration reads:

> There must be, I feel, certain places on this planet that remain undisturbed, for what they are and what they represent in terms of a society's ultimate values. If we are to say, and demonstrate, that nothing finally is sacred, and that everything must remain open to exploitation, then it seems to me that America must relinquish all claims to a moral leadership in this world. We do not govern simply through laws and force, but by example—by what we reveal of our basic values in relation to Nature and a resident people.

It is clear from this poem and this statement that the North has remained for Haines (and for others) not only a place to which he is personally attached but also a place that functions as a ground upon which basic American values and morality are continually tested. In this vast, thinly settled area, the conflicting American urges to revere the natural world and to exploit it are shown forward as if lit by the midnight sun.

For Haines, in 1971 as well as in 2001, the insatiable demand for exploitation endangers the basic moral values that Americans feel are the framework of the country itself. The fact that the urge to exploit seems to be consistently on the upswing also accounts for the sense of urgency in much of Haines's work. Many, Haines among them, feel that in the exploitation of the physical world lurks not only the surrender of cherished American values but also the quickened demise of the human race. To knowingly strip away our ecological base is a form of species-specific mass suicide.

But many of these poems are much quieter ones, and it seems that part of the antidote to human rapacity toward the natural world and other human beings is to learn to appreciate the beauty of where one finds oneself and of the other people one finds there. Again, although the voice in many of Haines's poems is that of the solitary human being confronted with the vastness of the physical world, the most tender, and most important moments in Haines's work, as in "The Hermitage," arrive in company of other humans:

> And once in a strange silence
> I felt quite close
> the beating of a human heart.

The poems are not declarations but often movements of the mind from imposed isolation to the intuition of love, love extended to another human, to the dead, to the ecosystem and all it contains. So those who were close and are now gone are also gathered together in Haines's verse. Haines has claimed, in "Notes from an Uninterrupted Journal," that his knowledge of the Alaska wilderness and the people who live there "goes back over thirty years; farther back than that, if I include what I know of it from the recalled memory of older and vanished neighbors." He states in his poem "The Dance," written for the Kayak Press editor George Hitchcock, "the dance / gathers everything / into a haunted forest."

In the dance of *Twenty Poems,* however, the figures of other artists also surface more prominently than in the earlier work. Haines of course never relinquished his interest in visual art, and *The Stone Harp* includes a poem that references Albrecht Dürer. In *Twenty Poems* three poems that directly address artists have an important place toward the end of the book. This is a foreshadowing of things to come, when in *New Poems: 1980–88* (1990) Haines addresses the importance of the art world to his work more thoroughly. This gathering of landscape, people, and art into his poetry illustrates that, in the ecology of Haines's poetics, a neat separation of individual, landscape, and culture is no longer tenable. In this resides also a major portion of Haines's important contribution to contemporary letters. Poems—all cultural artifacts—exist in an ecological matrix that includes both the physical and the social worlds. Haines, as shown, understood that his life began in Alaska, and his realization that the Alaska wilderness was intricately involved in both Western and native cultures takes his work to a new level.

CICADA, NEWS FROM THE GLACIER, NEW POEMS

After serving as poet in residence at the University of Alaska in 1972 and 1973, Haines published a small volume of poems entitled *Leaves and Ashes* in 1974, the same year of his divorce from Jane McWhorter, whom he had married in 1970. *Leaves and Ashes* was followed by *In Five Years Time* in 1976. That same year Haines was awarded the Amy Lowell Scholarship to

travel in England and Scotland, and *Cicada* appeared in 1977, containing many revised poems from *Leaves and Ashes* along with new poems. During his stay in England, Haines also gained enough distance to begin gathering ideas for his memoir, which eventually took form in *The Stars, the Snow, the Fire.*

Cicada marks a significant shift for Haines. The poems are often longer, and they are populated by more people, who are often presented in domestic circumstances, reflecting the time Haines spent during the early 1970s with a household of stepchildren. By the time Haines married again, in 1978, he was no longer living exclusively in Alaska but had served as a visiting professor at the University of Washington and as a visiting lecturer at the University of Montana. Unlike the majority of contemporary poets, Haines never landed permanently at a university teaching post, and this too enabled him to maintain a certain distance from which to view the contemporary poetry scene. There is in *Cicada* also a distance from the Alaska landscape, although its effect never entirely disappears from Haines's work. Certainly the revolutionary tone of *The Stone Harp* has been tempered further, though the poet's dismay with contemporary culture never vanishes entirely.

The metaphors in *Cicada* are more elaborate, and the poems are more discursive, though the dominant figures of dreams, trees, and shadows consistently remain. "Skagway" (titled "The Skagway Houses" in *Leaves and Ashes*) conjures up the Alaska coastal town that begins in promise but like so many American cities declines: "I traced in the gravel of Main Street / a map of my fading country . . . ," and the lines ending in ellipses seem to warn of an ongoing process. Perhaps the standout poem of the collection, "The Stone Bear" is a meditation on a crumbling grave marker in the form of a rearing bear. Moving from the stone figure of the bear, the poem in the next section imagines an earthly bear's existence, and in the third section, the poet reenters, contemplating both the promise of the life before him and the possibility of his art and him freezing into stone, the threat of his work guarding a little-visited grave. From this fear, however, the closing poem of the first section, "There Are No Such Trees in Alpine California," moves toward qualified promise, "the stilled heart come home / through smoke and falling leaves."

The four sections that comprise the collection enact a movement from the threat of death and stagnation to a new birth. A cycle of poems in the third section is addressed to women, often to young girls. There is a focus on a girl's transformation into a woman, as in "For Anne, at a Little Distance," and the poems are in large part rooted in domestic life. The major figure surfacing in these poems, however, is Daphne, invoked with all her connotations of the nymph pursued by Apollo, the god of poetry and eloquence. She is also a figure of metamorphosis, having been transformed into the laurel tree. Because the image of trees is a dominant one in these poems and the laurel is the tree of the poet, this figure of transformation bears much weight in the context of this collection. It seems clear that Haines is beginning to move away from the focus on Alaska that he worked through in his first three books. There is a change in the work, and one senses a change in the poet.

However, with all due respect, it is a fine thing that Haines never completely worked through this focus. Though not always the controlling force in the later poems, Alaska never recedes completely. And this book, with its added dimension of the domestic sphere, ends on a significantly different note from *The Stone Harp,* which leaves readers with the image of a refugee cart upturned in the road, wheel spinning in the air. *Cicada* closes with the image of, again, tribal wanderings that seem to be juxtaposed from the past to the future, but this time readers arrive at "awakening eastern

streets." Of course the title of the collection itself implies metamorphosis, but some cicada nymphs live in the ground for fifteen years before they emerge fully grown to live only about a week. So there may be an ironic underside to even the qualified optimism in this collection.

In 1977 Haines published *In a Dusty Light,* another hand-printed and hand-sewn edition, of which one thousand were sewn in paper and sixty-two in boards. Gue Walker illustrated the volume. Two poems from *Cicada* have been reprinted in this small, elegant book, "Driving through Oregon" and "Things." This group of poems travels down into the plains and mountains of the lower forty-eight states, and it contains a magnificent cycle of poems that move through Glacier Park from the west and then down the eastern side of the park into Missoula, where Haines resides. In 1981 he published *Living off the Country: Essays on Poetry and Place,* which collects personal essays, criticism, and reviews written in the late 1960s and the 1970s. Most of *In a Dusty Light* is included in *News from the Glacier: Selected Poems 1960–1980,* which appeared in 1982, the same year his fourth marriage ended. Also in 1982 Haines received an Honorary Doctor of Letters from the University of Alaska, Fairbanks and the Alaska Governor's Award in the Arts for his life contribution to the arts in Alaska.

At this juncture Haines's methods of composition deserve discussion. Although of course the method of composition is never the same for any two poems, it is reasonable to make a couple of generalizations based on Haines's own comments in *Fables and Distances* about a poem, "The Eye in the Rock," included in both *In a Dusty Light* and *News from the Glacier.* All poems are a form of meditation, but there are many ways to meditate. For Haines some poems, and particularly those in *Winter News,* are the result of something "brooded upon" for perhaps years by the poet, and his brooding is expressed in a short and concentrated poem. Other poems enact meditation in process, and a longer, more discursive poem results. These more discursive poems arrive in full force a bit later in Haines's career, but "The Eye of the Rock" is a good example of a poem that has qualities of both the immediate and the discursive.

The poem grows from a late morning, during which Haines and a few companions explored a painted rock on the western shore of Flathead Lake near Kalispell, Montana. Native people painted the rock around one thousand years ago, and the figures of animals, geometric shapes, and a human eye, though fascinating, seemed random. Haines photographed the scene, and only after long study of the photographs did a pattern emerge in which the eye matched the natural configuration of the rock, forming a human face. The poem begins in immediacy, confronting the reader with the east-facing rock, and in the third stanza with the thought that

> It is only rock, blue or green,
> cloudy with lichen,
> changing in the waterlight.

This impression leads to a meditative voice that says "no" to the preceding stanza and reflects: "Yet blood moves in this rock." No longer an inanimate thing, "only a rock," the rock becomes a living, bleeding entity. This movement between immediate and discursive is incorporated into the structure of the poem with three-line, impressionistic stanzas alternating with longer stanzas that enact the process of meditation spurred on by the shorter stanzas. In its fullness the poem insists that everyday, common sense assumptions that landforms are dead things and that the expression of past cultures are inert relics no longer suffice. The landscape is a living thing, and though access to the ways and thoughts of peoples who lived in a culture that recognized the land as alive no longer exists, maybe in some deep memory one can catch a glimpse of their ways of understanding and then perhaps present it in a poem.

Haines perceives that the rock can live, and this perception expressed is what Haines thinks of as the gift of poetry. He writes in his essay "The Eye in the Rock," in *Fables and Distances:*

> I do not believe in using the world as a source of egotistical aggrandizement—in going through the world looking for things and events to set a poem in motion. This is a trick that can be learned, but to me it is the literary equivalent of the material exploitation that in one way or another is wasting so much of the life of this planet.

For Haines poetry has a deep responsibility to both human culture and the realm of nonhuman existence, and in this sense Haines taps into a much older understanding of what poetry is. He retains the belief that poetry can help change the world, can make the world a better place to live, can even perhaps stir people to action.

His sustained belief in the face of high odds that poetry can still perform such a socially valuable function is also evident in the time Haines spends with many of his poems. Some of them require years to come to fruition, and even then they undergo revision. *Winter News* was revised and reissued in 1983, and some of the poems in *News from the Glacier* have been reworked from their original form. For instance, the poem "At White River" in *Cicada* becomes "At Slim's River" in *News from the Glacier.* In the later printing the first stanza has been streamlined from five lines to three, drawing the reader more effectively into the poem's movement from the start. The lines from the earlier version:

> We drove south from Burwash Landing
> that blue and gusty day.
> Close by the White River delta
> we stopped to read a sign
> creaking on its chains in the wind

are compressed:

Past Burwash and the White River delta,
we stopped to read a sign
creaking on its chains in the wind.

The improvement in the lines is obvious, and Haines works tirelessly on his poems. It seems as if he never puts any aside for any length of time.

Haines never seems at a loss for a project, and in 1984 he was awarded his second Guggenheim Fellowship in poetry. In 1985 Haines received the Alice Fay di Castagnola Prize from the Poetry Society of America and an Ingram Merrill Foundation Grant. He also collaborated in 1984 with the composer John Luther Adams on *Forest without Leaves,* a cantata for chorus and orchestra, which was first performed on November 11, 1984, in Fairbanks. *Forest without Leaves*—performed by the Arctic Chamber Orchestra and Choir, conducted by Byron McGilvray—was recorded by Owl Recordings in 1987, and one of the sequences in Haines's award-winning volume *New Poems: 1980–88* is a revised and reorganized version of the haunting libretto.

The chronological trajectory of this essay arrives now back at 1989, the year *The Stars, the Snow, the Fire* appeared and put Haines on the map as a prominent voice in contemporary nature writing. Haines also served as visiting professor at Ohio University from 1989 through 1990 and in 1990 *New Poems: 1980–88* arrived to much acclaim. *New Poems* won the Western Arts Federation Award and the Lenore Marshall/ *The Nation* Award, and Haines shared the Poets Prize with Mark Jarman. The citation for the Western Arts Award, written by Jorie Graham, Elizabeth Hardwick, William Kittredge, and N. Scott Momaday, reads:

John Haines is a man of character in the most American sense—solitary; strong. He has spent much of his life in wild country, and he has written of the wilderness with profound wonder, perception, and thanksgiving. He has given us an indispensable sense of our country, our continent, and our earth in his poems. His work, his whole work, enriches us.

New Poems marks another departure for Haines, and it does indeed "enrich us." The book retains its touch on the life Haines led in Alaska, though Haines now travels far beyond that landscape. In his introduction to *New Poems,* Dana Gioia writes, "If one views Haines's poetic development as a journey from the specific geography of the Alaskan wilderness to the uncharted places of the spirit, then that journey is now complete." The book consists primarily of seven sequences. The poems are generally longer compared to the short, concentrated lyrics of the earlier work, though Haines often combines short, intense lyrics to form a larger sequence. Only one sequence refers specifically to Haines's life in Alaska. The pieces are far more allusive than his earlier work.

Haines has often said that he believes a poet can aspire to a kind of vision, and perhaps it is his search for vision that leads him to figures like Edward Hopper, Pablo Picasso, Vincent van Gogh, Auguste Rodin, Hieronymus Bosch, and Dante. Most of the poems and sequences focus on or allude to the creative process or the process of meditation Haines began to develop in "The Eye in the Rock." For instance, a short poem, "Tenderfoot" is dated 1962–1982, twenty years in the process. The opening poem "Little Cosmic Dust Poem" sets the context of *New Poems* "In the radiant field of Orion," though the poem comes to ground in "This arm, this hand / my voice, your face, this love." In line with a point Haines has routinely made, "Little Cosmic Dust Poem" expands the concept of nature to include the solar system itself. The implications of this insistence are grand. To say humans can destroy nature—or fix it for that matter—is arrogantly absurd if nature includes Orion and the Crab Nebula. But more than that, within the universe the most important and poignant acts possible are hands touching, voices sounding, and simple gestures of love. Although these poems are far different from the earlier poems, in this "Little Cosmic Dust Poem" one senses a resonance across twenty years from "The Traveler" of *Winter News,* where the simple sharing of warmth leads to a meditation upon eons of human existence.

A stellar performance, the sequence "Days of Edward Hopper" is a fine example of Haines's achievement in this book of poems. The sequence of poems is not to be read as a treatment of Hopper's paintings. Haines claims that Hopper's subject matter—houses, city streets, the everyday life of Americans—helped him recall meaningful scenes from his youth. Some of the primary concerns of Hopper's art, however, belong also to Haines. Haines is deeply influenced by modernist American poets, yet he often resists modernist abstraction in favor of a more objective presentation of his material. It is often the juxtaposition of images clearly drawn from everyday life that becomes compelling in Haines's poetry. Just so, during the great influx of modernist art from Europe in the 1920s, Hopper remained committed to the American landscape and the attempt to paint a representational art based on American life. Hopper too relied heavily on observation and memory, so it is understandable why Haines finds a deep attraction to his work, which goes far beyond evoking childhood memory.

In the first poem of the sequence, Haines recalls the houses so often painted by Hopper. The houses are worn, do not quite seem to fit their environment, and

Brick dust was their pigment,
mortar and the grit of brownstone
ground underfoot, plaster
flaked to the purity of snow.

It is interesting here that the crumbling houses are linked to the purity Haines has so often found in the snow, and the images in these new poems brush against the resonant images of the northern landscape from the earlier work. In this sense the poems are not necessarily something brand new but new things built from both fresh and tested images. One of the most impressive aspects of this book is that Haines no longer lodges his work primarily in the northern landscape. He has evolved into a poet who finds the source of poetry not only in the landscape but more fully in the juncture between environment, his own vision, and art. *New Poems* is also a return for Haines because he has to a large degree revisited painting and sculpture but this time as master of his own medium.

Even though Haines is moving away from Alaska aesthetically, it would be remiss not to address the sequence in *New Poems* that returns to the Alaskan environment. The "Rain Country" sequence is a recollection of the places and people Haines loved in Richardson, the places and people now gone. It is a poignant poem about memory. The poet remains alone, "Remembering, fitting names / to a rain-soaked map." All is forgotten except for the retelling, and the people and places inhabiting memory rely on the poet to keep them speaking. He writes "in the brown ink of leaves," asking that

The names, and the voices
within them, speak now
for the slow rust of things
that are muttered in sleep.

This collection of poems is an attempt at salvation through memory of people, places, and art, its salvatory vision most clearly evoked at the end of the book, where "one tree, one leaf, / gives us plenty of light." *New Poems* deeply rewards sustained attention.

LATER WORK

In the years following *New Poems,* Haines served as visiting writer at George Washington University (1991), chair of poetry at the University of Cincinnati (1992), and chair of Excellence in the Arts at Austin Peay State University (1993), and he received the Lifetime Achievement Award from the Alaska Center for the Book in 1994. Subsequently he received the Lifetime Achievement Award from the Library of Congress and the Academy Award in Literature from the American Academy of Arts and Letters (1994), and in 1997 he was named a fellow by the American Academy of Poets. More important to Haines than any of these awards, on his seventieth birthday he married Joy De Stefano at his homestead in Richardson.

Although Haines was teaching and collecting honors during this time, he remained busy publishing books. *The Owl in the Mask of the Dreamer: Collected Poems* appeared in 1993, followed by *Where the Twilight Never Ends* in 1994. *Where the Twilight Never Ends* prints previously uncollected poems from the 1960s, and an expanded paperback version of *The Owl in the Mask of the Dreamer* was published in 1996. This version adds many of the poems from *Where the Twilight Never Ends*. *Fables and Distances: New and Selected Essays* also arrived in 1996, and it is a key source for Haines's views on everything from poetry to ecology to his own childhood. He shows himself again to be not only an important American poet but also a premier essayist. The following year Haines gathered up his earliest poems from 1948 through 1954 and published them in *At the End of This Summer: Poems 1948–1954*. It seemed that with this book scholars, critics, and devotees of Haines would be able to take a long, leisurely look at the trajectory of his work from its beginning to its maturity.

However, never one to lie idle, in 2001—three years short of eighty years old—Haines brought out a new book of poems, *For the Century's End: Poems 1990–1999*. In it Haines produced another forceful collection of poems that investigates the landscape and its relationship to the individual mind, the relationship

between poetry and the other arts, and the political relationship of poetry to the *socia*. In his preface to the collection Haines speaks straight up about addressing political issues, and one hears a distant murmur from *The Stone Harp*. But these new poems are the meditations of a poet and thinker who has reached full maturity. The close of the century seems to evoke a similar indignity to that of the poet of thirty years previous. Written before the catastrophic events of September 11, 2001, there is an uncanny prescience at work in these poems. Although, for a poet like Haines, so finely attuned to the cyclical nature of all life, it is not surprising that he sensed a recurring ill wind.

Reaching back to one of the most powerful iconic images of the Vietnam era, the poem "Kent State, May 1970" opens with the word "Premonitory." It then puts in play John Filo's famous photograph of Mary Ann Vechio leaning terror-stricken over the body of Jeffrey Miller, one of four Kent State students slain by Ohio National Guard rifle fire on May 4, 1970. Haines asks:

> How often has that image returned,
> to fade and reappear, then fade again?
> In Rwanda, in Grozny, Oklahoma . . .
> Kabul, city of rubble and orphans.

Tragically the terror conveyed by the image has returned home in a way none imagined, in part spawned from the rubble of Kabul. Haines asks how long before the body in the photograph rises up, how long before her cry awakens us. The poem is both a moving tribute to the dead and a call to awaken from complacency to the realization that the images that seem frozen in time are living and bear a warning.

Haines also reaches a bit further in time to the photographs of August Sander, who is best known for his pictures of Cologne before World War II. In "The Unemployed, Disabled, and Insane," Haines again picks for his central image a photograph, this time of two blind children holding hands, and it is unnecessary for the reader to be familiar with Sander's photograph to be moved by this poem (though it helps). The children stare blindly out of 1929 Germany, from a culture on the cusp of committing the gravest crimes of the twentieth century. The poem shifts to the refugees inhabiting the late twentieth century, ready "to cross the border / into that same still-haunted age." Readers are reminded that the events of the past have not vanished. Haines's poems seek to replenish the power of these images to awaken people to a shared history, and this arousal from cultural slumber is a deeply political act.

"For the Century's End" consists of both short poems and longer sequences, and in a strange and moving sequence, Haines treats an unusual art form. He revisits several trips to wax museums in Victoria, British Columbia, San Francisco, and Seattle. His observations of wax figures ranges historically from Henry VIII, to Bismark, to Richard Nixon. Clearly these are not the personages most people admire, and Haines uses the wax figures as a way into a meditation on history and the abuse of power. Another long sequence returns to a history of a different sort, and Haines rekindles his interest in the cave art and petroglyphs of North American Indians.

"In the Cave at Lone Tree Meadow" ties this book—with its concerned treatment of late-century politics—to the whole body of Haines's work. In a characteristic movement the poem retrieves a past culture:

> A long time gone, a quiet hunter
> carved in this smoky wall
> an image of the thing he followed.

The image of the hunter/artist resonates with Haines's own life and with his earlier subject matter. Haines of course used to hunt for animals, and he still hunts actively for images. He examines the images on the walls, and he recognizes one, the sign of a bear, as akin to another "a long way north / in the sand at Glacier Crossing." Recollecting his own experience of the hunt, he finds his quarry strangely "changed to stone." The reference is to the image of a bear on a stone wall, but it is difficult not to think of Haines's earlier work here, especially "The Stone Bear" from *Cicada,* and its mediation on art, life, and death. Haines continues:

> I have lived a long time,
> Followed the stone track of things,
> The snail-trace and watermark
> Of our troubled passage.

The poet follows the most difficult and ephemeral of trails across solid rock and across the watermark on the page—across physical nature and art—in search "of our troubled passage." In "The Stone Bear" Haines followed a "chosen path, / carrying in myself an aging strength." Twenty-four years later Haines remained steady on that path, as eagerly as ever attempting to renew human relationships to their primal past, to their historical past, and to the ecologies in which all human culture is embedded.

This book of poems presents work that both touches on images that have fascinated Haines from the beginning of his career and attempts new angles from which to engage a common humanity. Many of the sturdy images are here, mist, shadow, and forest, but perhaps the most powerful of all Haines's images resurfaces in this collection, the silent power of the snow— "the cold logic of the snow" ("The Ghost Towns"). In one of the final poems, "Snow," Haines uses the snow to think back, through the "snow gone black / with coal dust in Ohio," through the snow covering Alaska, all the way back to the snows of his childhood, sledding in the Yard in Washington, D.C. The final scene of the book, "To the End," returns to "the fleeting image of a vacant house, / a dust of snow on the steps—" coming full circle to the silence of snow and the vision of a house. That image is as fleeting as "being," and perhaps Haines's work, as Novallis said of philosophy, reflects his attempt and by extension the culture's attempt to go back home, to find a way to live in and with the world, with and not against one another. For Haines—as for all of us—in the end, we have but one home—the earth on which we stand and to which we return.

Selected Bibliography

WORKS OF JOHN HAINES

POETRY

Winter News: Poems. Middletown, Conn.: Wesleyan University Press, 1966. Rev. ed., 1983.

The Stone Harp. Middletown, Conn.: Wesleyan University Press, 1971.

Twenty Poems. Santa Barbara, Calif.: Unicorn Press, 1971.

Leaves and Ashes: Poems. Santa Cruz, Calif.: Kayak Press, 1974.

In Five Years Time. Missoula, Mont.: Smokeroot Press, 1976.

Cicada. Middletown, Conn.: Wesleyan University Press, 1977.

In a Dusty Light. Port Townsend, Wash.: Graywolf Press, 1977.

News from the Glacier: Selected Poems 1960–1980. Middletown, Conn.: Wesleyan University Press, 1982.

Meditation on a Skull Carved in Crystal. Waldron Island, Wash.: Brooding Heron Press, 1989.

New Poems: 1980–88. Brownsville, Oreg.: Story Line Press, 1990.

Rain Country. Richmond, Mass.: Mad River Press, 1990.

The Owl in the Mask of the Dreamer: Collected Poems. St. Paul, Minn.: Graywolf Press, 1993. (Revised and expanded in a paperback edition in 1996.)

Where the Twilight Never Ends. Boise, Idaho: Limberlost Press, 1994.

At the End of This Summer: Poems, 1948–1954. Port Townsend, Wash.: Copper Canyon Press, 1997.

For the Century's End: Poems, 1990–1999. Seattle: University of Washington Press, 2001.

PROSE

Living off the Country: Essays on Poetry and Place. Ann Arbor: University of Michigan Press, 1981.

Of Traps and Snares. Delta Junction, Alaska: Dragon Press, 1981.

Other Days: Selections from a Work in Progress. Port Townsend, Wash.: Graywolf Press, 1982.

The Stars, the Snow, the Fire: Twenty-five Years in the Northern Wilderness. St. Paul, Minn.: Graywolf Press, 1989. (Paperback edition, New York: Washington Square Press, 1991. Reissued in paperback by Graywolf in 2000.)

Fables and Distances: New and Selected Essays. St. Paul, Minn.: Graywolf Press, 1996.

SOUND RECORDINGS

Forest without Leaves. Music composed by John Luther Adams. Text by John Haines. Performed by the Arctic Chamber Orchestra and Choir, Byron McGilvray, Conductor. Boulder, Colo.: Owl Recordings, 1987.

MANUSCRIPTS

John Haines's papers and manuscripts are held at Ohio University, at the University of Alaska at Fairbanks, in the John Haines Collection at the University of Alaska at Anchorage, and in the Berg Collection at the New York Public Library.

CRITICAL AND BIOGRAPHICAL STUDIES

Bezner, Kevin. "John Haines." In *Updating the Literary West.* Western Literature Association. Fort Worth: Texas Christian University Press, 1997. Pp. 274–277.

Bezner, Kevin, and Kevin Walzer, eds. *The Wilderness of Vision: On the Poetry of John Haines.* Brownsville, Oreg.: Story Line Press, 1996.

Cohen, Marty. "Memoirs from Dreamtime." *Parnassus: Poetry in Review* 16:143–159 (fall 1991).

Lentfer, Hank, and Carolyn Servid, comps. *Arctic*

Refuge: A Circle of Testimony. Minneapolis, Minn.: Milkweed Editions, 2001.

Levertov, Denise. "Some Affinities of Content." *New and Selected Essays.* New York: New Directions, 1992. Pp. 1–21.

McGovern, Martin. "John Haines." In *Contemporary Poetry.* Edited by Tracy Cevalier. Chicago: St. James Press, 1991. Pp. 370–372.

McPherson, Sandra. "The Working Line." In *A Field Guide to Contemporary Poetry and Poetics.* Edited by Stuart Friebert and David Young. New York: Longman, 1980. Pp. 57–64.

Metzger, Linda, ed. *Contemporary Authors, New Revision Series.* Vol. 13. Detroit: Gale, 1984. Pp. 238–239.

Perkins, David. *A History of Modern Poetry.* Vol. 2, *Modernism and After.* Cambridge, Mass.: Harvard University Press, Belknap Press, 1987.

Rogers, Steven B., ed. *A Gradual Twilight: An Appreciation of John Haines.* Fort Lee, N.J.: CavanKerry Press, 2002.

Stafford, William. "John Haines." In *Contemporary Poets.* 3d ed. Edited by James Vinson. New York: St. Martin's Press, 1980. Pp. 621–623.

Wild, Peter. *John Haines.* Western Writers Series. Boise, Idaho: Boise State University, 1985.

Wilson, James R. "Relentless Self-Scrutiny: The Poetry of John Haines." *Alaska Review* 3, no. 7:16–27 (1969).

INTERVIEWS

Bezner, Kevin. "An Interview with John Haines." *Green Mountains Review* 6, no. 2:9–15 (1993).

Coffin, Arthur. "An Interview with John Haines." *Jeffers Studies* 2, no. 4:47–56 (1998).

Cooperman, Matthew. "Wilderness and Witness: An Interview with John Haines." *Quarter after Eight* 3:111–127 (1996).

Hedin, Robert. "An Interview with John Haines." *Northwest Review* 27, no. 2:62–76 (1989).

Hedin, Robert, and David Stark. "An Interview with John Haines." *New England Review and Bread Loaf Quarterly* 4, no. 1:104–124 (autumn 1991).

—*CORNELIUS BROWNE*

Joy Harjo

1951–

A GIFTED ARTIST, Joy Harjo has been a painter, dancer, screenwriter, musician, and children's author, but she is primarily known as a Native American poet. She is not a full-blooded American Indian but a mixture of Creek, Cherokee, French, Irish, and African American ancestry, and she was raised in a city, not on a reservation. However, she strongly identifies with her native heritage and frequently employs themes in her poetry that are common to Native American writers—love of the natural world, the interrelatedness of all life, survival, continuance, the power of memory, and transcendence.

When she writes, Harjo believes that "there is an old Creek within me that often participates." Although her primary inspiration originates from her Creek roots, she also draws on sacred images and stories from other tribes and cultures, creating through her poetry what Jim Rupert calls "mythic space." For Harjo, myth is more than legend. It is, as she told Donelle R. Ruwe (1994), "an alive, interactive event that is present in the everyday." Because Harjo views the world through the lens of myth, her poetry takes on a mystical quality. Borders between the ordinary and extraordinary dissolve, boundaries between past and present blur, and the real and the supernatural coexist on the same plane. In Native American cultures myth is also closely related to visionary experiences and ritual. The visions of sages and shamans who actively seek guidance from the spirit world are given to the people to empower and guide them, ultimately forming the basis for ceremonies. Many of Harjo's poems reflect the relationship between myth and ritual, including her signature poem, "She Had Some Horses." In a sense, she is a modern-day sage or prophet who gives her poems as a gift to humanity.

From Harjo's point of view, myth is closely related to memory, which can either be individual or collective. She told Angels Carabi in *The Spiral of Memory: Interviews* (1996), "*Memory* for me becomes a big word; it's like saying 'world.'"

> Memory is the nucleus of every cell; it's what runs; it's the gravity, the gravity of the Earth. In a way, it's like the stories themselves, the origin of the stories, and the continuance of all the stories. It's this great pool, this mythic pool of knowledge and history that we live inside.

Memory plays a large role in forming a cohesive ethnic identity, which contributes to keeping a culture alive. The stories handed down through oral tradition have continually reaffirmed the validity of Native American traditions and have served as a unifying factor within the community. Memory can also serve as a crucial factor in the survival of the individual. Harjo constantly draws on personal memories as well as images from modern life to dramatize the contemporary concerns of American Indians. By using poetry to interpret those experiences, Harjo taps the power of memory to heal and transform.

Because of the long history of oral tradition in American Indian culture, native people have a great respect for the power of language. Harjo shares this respect, although she is ambivalent about writing in English because she views it as "the enemy's language." During the process of colonization, use of tribal languages was prohibited in Indian schools, which resulted in the inability of many native people to speak their own language. Yet to be able to speak well is still revered in the Native American culture. Because Harjo does not speak Creek, poetry became for her a "sacred language within the English language." This sacred language gives Harjo and other Native American writers creative power over the pain and fear caused by the brutality of colonization. By naming their pain, they confront it, and in confronting it, they are freed from its influence over their lives.

Gloria Bird, coeditor with Harjo of *Reinventing the Enemy's Language: Contemporary Native Women's Writing of North America* (1997), notes that using the "colonizer's tongue" to reflect back to the Euro-American culture the horrors of colonization politicizes the language. When Carabi asked about the political aspect of her work, Harjo replied: "I don't think that a poet can separate herself or himself from the world. . . .The poet is charged with being the truth teller of the culture, of the times. . . . Poetry . . . demands the truth, and you cannot separate the poem from your political reality." Much of Harjo's work reflects her interest in social and political concerns, especially women's issues, although she says she is not actively involved in women's organizations. In an interview with Laura Coltelli, Harjo denied being a feminist in the same way white middle-class women are feminists because "the word 'feminism' doesn't carry over to the tribal world, but a concept mirroring similar meanings would. Let's see what would it then be called—empowerment, some kind of empowerment." Yet many of Harjo's poems deal with the issues concerning minority women who have been abused and marginalized. "I Am a Dangerous Woman," the Noni Daylight series, and "The Woman Hanging from the Thirteenth Floor Window" are only a few examples of poems that portray the powerless and in doing so empower them.

Myth, memory, history, and language are all related to landscape in Harjo's work. As a child, she remembers digging in the "dark, rich earth" by her house in Oklahoma. "I would dig piles of earth with a stick, smell it, form it," she writes in "Biopoetics Sketch for *Greenfield Review*" (1981–1982). "It had sound. Maybe that's when I first learned to write poetry." This experience provided her with a physical connection to both past and present. With the coming of the Europeans, the landscape became scarred by the violent history of colonization and the oppression of native people and other minority cultures. It has been further blighted by urban development, the embodiment of Western "civilization." However, the land has also been blessed by the spirits of the native people who once inhabited it, their history, and the sacred stories that sprang from their relationship with and respect for the land.

Harjo not only writes about the physical landscape of Oklahoma and the Southwest, she also explores the interior landscape of the mind, heart, and spirit. Many of her poems deal with the effects of pain, fear, and abuse, which native people have suffered as a result of their minority status. By writing about the psychological effects of marginalization, Harjo seeks healing and transformation through the power of words. Harjo's largely autobiographical work has become a survival technique: "In a strange kind of sense [writing] frees me to believe in myself, to be able to speak, to have a voice. Because it is my survival."

THE LIFE

Throughout Harjo's childhood and early adulthood, survival was a constant concern. Born Joy Foster in Tulsa, Oklahoma, on May 9, 1951, the daughter of Allen W. Foster, a sheetmetal worker, and Wynema Baker Foster, a waitress, Harjo was the first of four children. Her father was a from a prominent Creek family, and his great-grandfather Monahwee led the Creeks in the Redstick War against Andrew Jackson in the 1800s. Monahwee subsequently died on the Trail of Tears during the tribe's removal from Alabama to Oklahoma. Monahwee's daughter Katie married Henry Marsie Harjo, who was a Baptist minister and half African American. When oil was discovered on Marsie Harjo's land, the family became rich. The two daughters, Naomi, Harjo's grandmother, and Lois, Harjo's great-aunt, went to college to study art. Joy Foster identified strongly with the artists on her father's side of the family. As a child she loved to draw, and in college she studied painting. When she reached the age of nineteen, she enrolled as a full member in the Mvskoke branch of the Creek tribe, taking the surname "Harjo" in honor of her paternal grandmother. "Harjo" or "Hadjo" is a common name among the Creeks and means "courage."

Harjo's mother was of mixed Cherokee, Irish, and French descent. Her marriage to Allen Foster deteriorated because of his drinking and his physical and emotional abuse. He frequently became violent when he was drunk, brought home a succession of lovers, and was sometimes jailed because of his brutal behavior. Harjo recalls that she and her siblings would often hide in terror when he came home from work. After Harjo's parents finally divorced, Harjo's mother married a man who hated Indians and who also abused the family verbally and emotionally. The cruelty of her stepfather affected Harjo's life outside the home. "As a child, I had a very difficult time speaking," Harjo told Bill Moyers. "I remember the teachers at school threatening to write my parents because I was not speaking in class, but I was terrified. Painting was a way for me to do what I felt it was given to me to do."

Painting was not only a way for Harjo to express herself, it also opened up educational opportunities. After her stepfather threw her out of the house when she was sixteen, Harjo enrolled in the fine arts program at the Institute of American Indian Arts in Santa Fe, New Mexico. The education was inferior, and she remembers the teachers humiliated the students. Harjo, like many of her classmates from other tribes, turned to drugs, alcohol, and self-mutilation to express her anger and fear. However, despite its drawbacks, the school did help Harjo stretch herself creatively. Also during this time she married a fellow student, Phil Wilmon, and became pregnant with her first child, a son she named Phil Dayn. She writes about his birth in "Warrior Road," an essay published in *Reinventing the Enemy's Language*. Harjo and Wilmon later divorced.

After she graduated from high school, Harjo enrolled in the University of New Mexico as a premed student and then switched her major to art. She finally became a creative writing major after attending poetry readings by Leslie Marmon Silko, Simon Ortiz, and other Native American writers. She was also influenced by writers from other backgrounds, including Pablo Neruda, June Jordan, William Butler Yeats, Anne Sexton, and Sylvia Plath. Ortiz was not only Harjo's mentor, he also was the father of her daughter, Rainy Dawn. Ortiz and Harjo separated soon after their child was born.

Harjo did not begin to write poetry until she was twenty-two, which is considered a relatively late start for a poet. As a single mother of two children, a student, and a part-time worker, she was under stress and stood on the edge of an emotional breakdown. Painting had helped Harjo weather the trauma of her early childhood and adolescence; poetry took her one step further, and the woman who was afraid to speak as a child found her voice as a poet.

She graduated in 1976 and was accepted into the M.F.A. creative writing program at the University of Iowa. There she was exposed to James Wright, Meridel Le Sueur, Adrienne Rich, Audre Lorde, and other poets who influenced her work. After receiving her graduate degree in

1978, she attended classes at the Anthropology Film Center in Santa Fe, where she learned the art of filmmaking. She also taught at several schools, including the Institute of American Indian Arts in Santa Fe (1978–1979, 1983–1984); Arizona State University in Tempe (1980–1981); the University of Colorado in Boulder (1985–1988); the University of Arizona in Tucson (1988–1990); and the University of New Mexico in Albuquerque (1991–1995). Her publications include two chapbooks, seven poetry collections, an anthology of Native American women writers, and a children's book. In 1986 she learned to play the saxophone and created her first jazz band, Poetic Justice, with whom she recorded albums of her poetry set to music. She resides in Hawaii and travels with her second band, The Real Revolution.

WHAT MOON DROVE ME TO THIS?

Harjo published *What Moon Drove Me to This?* her first full collection of poems, in 1979. Included in this collection are ten poems that first appeared in *The Last Song,* a chapbook published in 1975. Harjo acknowledges that her early poems "were written during a difficult period in my life. You could see the beginnings of something, but it wasn't quite cooked." The short, one-page poems consisting of lyrics based on her personal experience do, indeed, prefigure the images, themes, and subjects of her later work, including the primacy of nature, the encroachment of cities, the blurring of borders between material and spiritual reality, the significance of American Indian myth and culture, her preoccupation with survival, and her interest in feminist concerns and the power of language. Many of the poems lack punctuation and capitalization, which may be due to the influence of poets whose work Harjo was reading at the time, including Ortiz and Barney Bush. Her early style may also be a conscious

protest against the grammatical rules of the language of the colonizer.

The "moon" in the title relates to Harjo's frequent use of this image throughout the collection and is indicative of her growing feminism. As Patricia Clark Smith and Paula Gunn Allen note, the moon is a symbol of "a full, intelligent female person." However, Harjo also frequently uses it as a symbol of self-destruction. In "Swimming," for example, the moon "is about to do herself in," and "dangles" like a sickle above the speaker's bed. In "Going towards Pojoaque, A December Full Moon / 72," the unearthly glow of the full moon "was so bright / I could see the bones / in my hands." The moon can also represent "mythic space" where wholeness and enlightenment are found. Sometimes self-destructive impulses and the search for entrance into mythic space are linked. In "Looking Back" the Chinese court poet Li Po (701–762) embraces the moon and follows it "into the universe of a Chinese river," just as the speaker pursues the full moon by driving "90 miles an hour / into its yellow shoulder." The attainment of spiritual enlightenment and meaning far outweighs the risk of physical death.

Self-destruction and the search for meaning also characterize the Noni Daylight series of four persona poems. Juxtaposing images from the natural world and urban life, this series highlights the social and psychological alienation to which native women are often subject. Noni Daylight is a 1970s urban, mixed-blood Native American woman, a single mother, an alcoholic, and a drug abuser. She is constantly on the move, not only traveling between the urban and natural landscapes but also crossing the borders between mythic space and mundane reality and between tribal and nontribal lifestyles in search of herself. In a sense she is Harjo's alter ego. In an interview with Joseph Bruchac, Harjo said, "In the beginning she became another way for me to speak." Noni speaks through her actions, communicating her torment and confusion. In "The First Noni Daylight" Noni lies in a hospital bed after attempting suicide in order to manipulate her lover into remaining with her. In "Origin" and "Evidence" Noni drives away from the city, fleeing from the hopelessness of her life by seeking a spiritual connection to the land of her ancestors. She seems to find it in "Origin":

> Noni heard
> that the Hopi say that the Grand Canyon
> is the birthplace of their people. But
> she thinks most of the world
> must have originated
> from that point.

In both "Origin" and "Evidence" the key word "edge" is used to show that Noni is poised on the brink between two conflicting cultures, between survival and self-destruction and between material and mythic reality. Edge and cliff imagery are predominant in "Watching Crow, Looking toward the Manzano Mountains," "Kansas City Coyote," "Out," "Red Horse Wind over Albuquerque," and other poems, suggesting the precarious position Native Americans occupy within the dominant culture.

"Edges" and "sharp ridges" also appear in "I Am a Dangerous Woman," but the speaker seems more assertive and in control than Noni Daylight. The scene is a modern airport surrounded by the foothills of the Sandia Mountains. The contrast between the natural landscape and the human-constructed airport illustrates the clash between the native and Euro-American cultures. The woman is asked by the security guards to step into their "guncatcher machine," which is set off by her metal belt. She is conscious of her seductive femininity as she removes her belt "so easy / that it catches the glance / of a man standing nearby." The refrain "I am a dangerous woman," repeated three times, once as the title and twice in the poem itself, not only emphasizes her feminine power

but also mocks the men and their high-tech machine. The poem ends:

> i am a dangerous woman
> but the weapon is not visible
> security will never find it
> they can't hear the clicking
> of the gun
>   inside my head

The woman's anger is more powerful than any weapon. Although she complies with the requests of the airport security guards, her strength of identity—I am a dangerous woman—prevents her from being cowed by male domination or the trappings of white culture.

In contrast to the independence of the narrator of "I Am a Dangerous Woman," Noni Daylight in "Someone Talking" is still dependent on male attention and love. Sitting on a front porch in Iowa next to one of her lovers, and with the aid of "a little wine," she remembers another night she spent with a different man in Oklahoma and searches for the words to reconstruct her experience:

> Where is the word for a warm night
> and how it continues to here,
> a thousand miles from that time?
> Milky Way.
> And there are other words
> in other languages. Always
> in movement.

Here words express more than thoughts and feelings. They are dynamic, forming a continuum that transcends time and links the past to the present moment. Although words are basic tools of communication, their meanings may be ambiguous so the speaker and the listener perceive differently what is being said, as in the following lines:

> Maybe the man of words speaks
> like the cricket.

Noni Daylight
hears him that way.

Thus, language has the power to confuse as well as clarify and to divide as well as to connect people to each other.

Harjo's frequent merger of images from the natural world and human characters in her poems is another way she connects past and present. Based on Navaho myth, the horses in "Four Horse Songs" are each of a different color—white, red, gray, and yellow—and correspond to the four directions. Although the horse is traditionally a symbol of power and strength, Harjo views the horse as "vulnerable." The Native American figures represented by the white, red, and gray horses are lost in despair, victims of white culture and alcoholism. Only the yellow horse has hope. As he

gallops home near Tsaile
the sun is low and almost gone
but he has faith
in its returning.

This image of the horse galloping off into the sunset, trusting that the darkness will not always prevail, is a powerful symbol of the belief of Native Americans that their culture will not only survive but someday flourish again. Appearing frequently in the next collection, the horse archetype is developed further and takes on a variety of meanings.

SHE HAD SOME HORSES

Moving beyond the short haiku-like lyrics of *What Moon Drove Me to This?* the poems in *She Had Some Horses* (1983) are longer, and the themes and images are more complex. The book is divided into four sections—"Survivors," "What I Should Have Said," "She Had Some Horses," and "I Give You Back." "Survivors" includes twenty-five poems, while the number of poems in the other sections decrease, with the final section containing only one work. Beginning and ending with poems about fear, the cyclical arrangement of the works represents a journey toward wholeness and healing. On a more universal scale, the poems reflect Harjo's growing poetic sophistication in expressing her thoughts on Native American and feminist issues.

An ardent admirer of the black poet and social activist Audre Lorde, Harjo begins her collection with two poems that allude to Lorde's "A Litany for Survival." Lorde's poem explores the effect fear and oppression have had on minority women and calls on them to speak out against their subjugation by white patriarchal culture. Continuing the "edge" imagery of *What Moon Drove Me to This?* and echoing the phrase "constant edges" in Lorde's poem, Harjo uses "edge" five times in the first poem, "Call It Fear." The repetition of "edge" coupled with the recurrence of "backwards" conveys an urgent sense of psychological crisis and confusion. Controlling the speaker completely, fear manifests itself physically in the heart that beats against the ribs like "horses in their galloping flight," through the perceptions where language becomes unintelligible ("talking backwards"), and in the internal landscape of the speaker ("there is this edge within me"). Yet as the speaker struggles with her fear, her perception begins to change, and the "edge" becomes "a string of shadow horses kicking / and pulling me out of my belly." This powerful image of spiritual rebirth emerging from psychic death foreshadows the evolution from fear to freedom that shapes the book as a whole.

"Anchorage," the second poem in the collection, also reflects the influence of "A Litany for Survival." Dedicated to Lorde, the poem presents a distinctly Native American, multilayered view of the world. The poem was inspired by Harjo's visit in the early 1980s to Anchorage, Alaska, where she conducted writing workshops for prison inmates, most of whom were Native Americans and African Americans. Past and present coexist in the city that was carved by the ice of glaciers then nearly destroyed when "a storm of boiling earth cracked open / the streets" during the devastating earthquake on Good Friday, March 27, 1964. The mythic realm interacts with the natural world as spirits of ancestors cavort above Anchorage in an "air / which is another ocean." The deleterious effects of colonization are still at work, embodied in an "Athabascan / grandmother, folded up, smelling like 200 years / of blood and piss," and in Henry, a prison inmate, who was shot at eight times outside a liquor store but miraculously was unharmed. Both Native Americans and African Americans have been victims of urban violence and racism. By telling Henry's story and dedicating the poem to Lorde, Harjo crosses ethnic boundaries to connect the histories of Native Americans and African Americans by stressing the injustices both groups have suffered as a result of white colonization. The concluding lines of "Anchorage" echo the last lines of Lorde's poem, "So it is better to speak remembering we were never meant to survive." Harjo's poem ends:

> Everyone laughed at the impossibility of it,
> but also the truth. Because who would believe
> the fantastic and terrible story of all of our
>   survival
> those who were never meant
>   to survive?

For Native Americans, survival is linked to a strong community where the individual is valued and respected. However, the marginalized status of urban Native Americans often isolates them from themselves and their culture, putting their survival in jeopardy. Henry and the Athabascan grandmother are examples of Native Americans who have survived but who nonetheless remain trapped by poverty, alcoholism, crime, and urban violence. Sometimes suicide seems like the only way out. "The

Woman Hanging from the Thirteenth Floor Window" on the east side of Chicago tells the story of a woman who "thinks she will be set free" of her hopeless situation by taking her own life. Although she is "not alone" and has three children, her life is fractured in "several pieces because of the two husbands / she has had." That she is hanging from the thirteenth floor is significant. Many buildings do not have a thirteenth floor because of the superstition associated with the number thirteen. Hanging between life and death, good and bad luck, she is a liminal figure who is separated from her children, her neighbors, and the Native American community where she was raised. No longer nurtured by her own people, she

> is the woman hanging from the 13th floor
>   window,
> and she knows she is hanging by her own fingers,
>   her
> own skin, her own thread of indecision.

Lamenting "the lost beauty" of her life, she desires to speak, but her "teeth break off at the edges" and she cannot articulate her despair. Her attempted suicide speaks for her. The climax of the drama never achieves a resolution. Instead:

> She thinks she remembers listening to her own
>   life
> break loose, as she falls from the 13th floor
> window on the east side of Chicago, or as she
> climbs back up to claim herself again.

The ambiguous ending offers hope that, in the in-between state of indecision, the woman made a conscious choice to survive and assert her selfhood. However, the possibility also remains that she let go, leaving the reader to wonder whether the woman chose survival or whether she followed through on her initial self-destructive impulses.

In a second series of persona poems, Noni Daylight continues to struggle with her own self-destructive feelings. In "Heartbeat" she cuts "acid into tiny squares" because she "wants out" of her desperate existence. However, in "Kansas City" she seems to find some sort of peace. Although she is older and nearly spent, "a dishrag wrung out over bones," she has chosen to stay in Kansas City to "raise the children she had by different men, all colors." She has no regrets, and if she could live her life over again, she would still choose to have liaisons with the men who fathered her children because each taught her something about herself. Her traveling days seem to be over as she stands

> . . . near the tracks
> waving
> at the last train to leave
> Kansas City.

In "She Remembers the Future" Noni speaks to her "otherself" about her self-destructive tendencies and chooses survival:

> She asks,
> "Should I dream you afraid
> so that you are forced to save
> yourself?
>
> Or should you ride colored horses
> into the cutting edge of the sky
> to know
>
> that we're alive
> we are alive."

Noni may be a survivor, but she does not appear in Harjo's work again. Instead, she moves off the pages of Harjo's books into the poetry of another Native American writer, Barney Bush. Harjo laughingly told Coltelli, "I never saw her again. She never came back!"

The theme of survival is again presented in the title poem of the collection. The speaker of the poem is searching for a way to reconcile conflicting areas of her personality in order to shape her identity as a modern Native American woman. The poem is written in the form of an American Indian chant. "She had some horses" and "she had horses" are repeated throughout the poem, giving the piece a rhythmic, songlike quality. This repetition not only reinforces the speaker's Native American identity in the face of living in an alien Euro-American culture but also evokes the healing power of ritual. The purpose of ceremonial repetition is, as Paula Gunn Allen points out, "to integrate: to fuse the individual with his or her fellows, the community of people with that of the other kingdoms, and this larger communal group with the worlds beyond this one."

The speaker's psychic landscape has been deeply fragmented by fear and anger and is exacerbated by her marginal status as a mixed-blood American Indian. The spiritual, psychological, and cultural conflicts at war in the speaker's subconscious mind are expressed in a series of images personified by the horse. In the first stanza, the woman acknowledges that her life is connected to the earth ("She had horses who were skins of ocean water. / . . . / She had horses who were splintered red cliff"). In the second stanza, the sensuality of images like "She had horses with full, brown thighs" clash with violent descriptions like "She had horses who licked razor blades." The speaker's fear is apparent in the third stanza, when she acknowledges that "She had horses who were much too shy, and kept quiet / in stalls of their own making." The speaker is engaged in a naming ritual that, by the end of the poem, gives her power over her spiritual, cultural, and physical life. Her attainment of healing and wholeness brought about by the ceremonial naming leads the speaker to the realization that

> She had some horses she loved.
> She had some horses she hated.
>
> These were the same horses.

This fusion of opposites leads the poet to the final ceremony of letting go in the last poem of the collection.

The speaker in "I Give You Back" uses apostrophe and chant in a ceremony to cast off the "beautiful, terrible fear" that controls her. In addressing fear, the repetition of "I release you" and "I am not afraid to" allow the speaker to formally confront fear and repudiate it:

> I take myself back, fear.
> You are not my shadow any longer.
> I won't hold you in my hands.
> You can't live in my eyes, my ears, my voice
> my belly, or in my heart my heart
> my heart   my heart

This ritualistic exorcism liberates her, and by overcoming fear, the speaker is reborn and transformed into a new person. In Harjo's subsequent work, the theme of transformation becomes more prominent.

"She Had Some Horses" and "I Give You Back" are two of ten tracks included on *Letter from the End of the Twentieth Century,* a compact disc released by Harjo and her band Poetic Justice in 1997. Harjo's rhythmic verbal chant in both pieces is enhanced by a synthesis of Native American and jazz background music. For example, the phrase "my heart my heart / my heart my heart" is set to the beat of a Native American powwow drum, mimicking the beating of a human heart. The fusion of music and poetry is natural given that song was an important component of the oral tradition. In her next publication, Harjo again crosses artistic boundaries by blending the visual with the poetic.

SECRETS FROM THE CENTER OF THE WORLD

The Southwest landscape is a major presence in Harjo's poetry, providing her with a wealth of images and poetic insight. In *Secrets from the Center of the World* (1989), the desert landscape photographs of the astronomer Stephen Strom complement Harjo's visionary verse in what is for her a first-time collaboration. Strom, an amateur photographer, began to take pictures of Navajo country when he was a professor at Navaho Community College in Tsaile, Arizona. Instead of trying to capture the vastness of the western landscape in one photograph, Strom concentrates on smaller sections of land, which brings out remarkable depth and detail. Harjo's prose poem coupled with Strom's thirty color photographs offer a unique perspective on the relationship among the land and the creatures that have occupied it in the past and those who inhabit it now. Harjo notes in her introduction that "the photographs are not separate from the land, or larger than it. Rather they gracefully and respectfully exist inside it. Breathe with it. The world is not static but inside a field that vibrates. The whole earth vibrates."

Harjo responds to the physical details of the landscape in the pictures and interprets them poetically and mythically, often moving beyond the borders of the photographs to present a cosmic vision. The land does indeed speak to Harjo of creation, evolution, memory, and continuance. For the golden, sand-swept area known as Moencopi Rise, she writes:

> Moencopi Rise stuns me into perfect relationship, as I feed a skinny black dog the rest of my crackers, drink coffee, contemplate the frozen memory of stones. Nearby are the footprints of dinosaurs, climbing toward the next century.

Strom's photographs, though taken of particular landscapes, cause Harjo to reflect on the larger creation. The mud hills near Nazlini prompt her, figuratively speaking, to see eternity in a grain of sand:

> I can hear the sizzle of newborn stars, and know anything of meaning, of the fierce magic emerging here. I am witness to flexible eternity, the evolving past, and I know we will live forever, as dust or breath in the face of stars, in the shifting pattern of winds.

It is not surprising that Harjo alludes to cosmology given the fact that her collaborator is an astronomer. Her poetic vision often penetrates the shell of material reality to expose transcendence just as the telescope of an astronomer reveals the mysteries of the universe. However, she realizes that her visionary language can never adequately express the magnificence of nature:

> This land is a poem of ochre and burnt sand I could never write, unless paper were the sacrament of sky, and ink the broken line of wild horses staggering the horizon several miles away. Even then, does anything written ever matter to the earth, wind, and sky?

Compared to the poet's words, the elements of nature are eternal. Yet regardless of the limitations of language, the poet still strives to uncover the many dimensions or "secrets" of life.

Where is the center of the world? Harjo seems to be saying that the center is a mystical and psychic construct originating within the individual as he or she interacts with the environment. At the beginning of the collection, she writes, "My house is the red earth; it could be the center of the world." The center can also be elusive, hidden by the "radio waves" of daily life. For Harjo, like many mystics, it is necessary to retreat from the world for a while in order to see clearly and truly.

IN MAD LOVE AND WAR

Returning from her desert pilgrimage in *Secrets from the Center of the World,* Harjo reenters the urban landscape with fresh vision in her fourth collection, *In Mad Love and War* (1990), which won the William Carlos Williams Award from the Poetry Society of America and the Delmore Schwartz Award Memorial Prize from New York University. Myth, autobiography, political and social witness, music, and spirituality ap-

pear once again in her work but are used more expansively as she broadens her scope to address not only the plight of Native Americans but the dispossession of African Americans and Central Americans by Euro-American culture. Her multicultural concerns, touched upon in *She Had Some Horses,* are explored more in-depth in poems that include "Strange Fruit," "Resurrection," and "The Real Revolution Is Love."

The collection opens with a single poem, "Grace," and closes with a prayer, "Eagle Poem." The free verse and prose poems of the two main sections, "The Wars" and "Mad Love," return to the quest for wholeness that was presented in *She Had Some Horses* but with a difference. Where the central word in the first two collections was "edge," the key word—and theme—in *In Mad Love and War* is "transformation." The conflicts in the first section, whether they be personal, cultural, societal, or international, are transformed by "the epic search for grace," leading toward a more complete vision of healing and regeneration.

While the horse appears as the central archetypal image in *What Moon Drove Me to This?* and *She Had Some Horses,* the deer inspires three poems in *In Mad Love and War.* "Deer Dancer," the second poem in "The Wars," tells the story of a young woman who dances naked in a "bar of broken survivors." The patrons project their longing for their lost tribal heritage onto the woman, who becomes for them "the end of beauty." When the woman begins to dance on a tabletop, sensuality merges with myth, and the woman is transformed into Deer Woman:

> She was the myth slipped down through dreamtime. The promise of feast we all knew was coming. The deer who crossed through knots of a curse to find us. She was no slouch, and neither were we, watching.

> The music ended. And so does the story. I wasn't there. But I imagined her like this, not a stained

red dress with tape on her heels but the deer who entered our dream in white dawn, breathed mist into pine trees, her fawn a blessing of meat, the ancestors who never left.

The dancer offers hope to the onlookers that their lives also may be transformed through her "deer magic," saving them from alcoholism and "poison by culture." Through her, they suddenly are aware of the possibility that there is "something larger than the memory of a dispossessed people," as Harjo says in "Grace," freeing them to see beyond their broken lives.

"Deer Ghost" and "Song for Myself and the Deer to Return On" begin the "Mad Love" section. As in "Deer Dancer," the speakers in both poems are trying to return "home" to the mythic space of their ancestors in order to find healing in "something larger" than themselves. The reality of the spirit world connects the narrators with their heritage, providing a way "to get us all back" to traditional native values before the culture becomes swallowed up by Euro-American society.

The cultural impact of racism is explored in "For Anna Mae Pictou Aquash, Whose Spirit Is Present Here and in the Dappled Stars (for we remember the story and must tell it again so we may all live)" and "Strange Fruit," poems of witness that deal with the murders of two women, one Native American and one African American. The first tells the story of Anna Mae Pictou Aquash, a Micmac Indian and a member of the radical American Indian Movement who was found killed on the Pine Ridge Reservation in South Dakota in 1976. Initially it was assumed that she died of exposure, but later it was discovered that she had died of a bullet fired in the back of her head at close range. Harjo memorializes her as

the shimmering young woman
                    who found her
  voice,
when you were warned to be silent, or have your

body cut away
from you like an elegant weed.

The second poem, "Strange Fruit," recounts the story of Jacqueline Peters, a black activist who was hanged in California by the Ku Klux Klan in 1986 after attempting to organize a local chapter of the National Association for the Advancement of Colored People (NAACP) in response to the lynching of a young black man. The title is taken from a song by Billie Holiday, and the poem is an eerie dramatic monologue spoken by Peters during the last few moments of her life as "her feet dance away from this killing tree." Both of these poems illustrate the power of storytelling to keep memory alive. In recounting the martyrdoms of Anna Mae Pictou Aquash and Jacqueline Peters, Harjo honors them as warriors, exposes the evil that caused their deaths, and empowers others in the fight against injustice so the horrors of oppression are not repeated.

Closing "The Wars" section, "The Real Revolution Is Love" also deals with oppression and survival, this time in Nicaragua. Invited to participate in the 1986 International Poetry Festival in Managua hosted by the liberationist theologian and poet Ernesto Cardinale, Harjo and a small group of poets gather for an early morning party on the patio of the hotel. The people are all from indigenous backgrounds, including American Indian, Puerto Rican, and Central American. As Harjo observes their erotic interactions, she also alludes to their shared experience as victims of colonization:

I argue with Roberto, and laugh across the continent to Diane, who is on the other side of the flat, round table whose surface ships would fall off if they sailed to the other side. *We are Anishnabe and Creek. We have wars of our own.* Knowing this we laugh and laugh, until she disappears into the poinsettia forest with Pedro, who is still arriving from Puerto Rico.

The erotic love of the partygoers and the "furious love" of the speaker in the face of ongoing political oppression point to the transcendent love that can resolve hatreds and that links the poems in the next section, "Mad Love." "Transformations" is the most powerful example of this transcendence. The prose poem begins, "This is a letter to you," an allusion to Emily Dickinson's poem #441, which begins "This is my letter to the World." Writing in a stream of consciousness style, the speaker begins by talking about hatred and cautioning the reader about its dangerous effects:

> This poem is a letter to tell you that I have smelled the hatred you have tried to find me with; you would like to destroy me. Bone splintered in the eye of one you choose to name your enemy won't make it better for you to see.

The limitations of language come into play as she searches for the words to communicate her message. "I don't know what that has to do with what I am trying to tell you," "What I mean is," and "That's what I mean to tell you" indicate a process by which the speaker seeks to transform her thoughts and feelings into a meaningful message. "You can turn a poem into something else" and "hatred can be turned into something else, if you have the right words" imply a ritualistic incantation that has the power to transform a negative into a positive. The last line of the poem, however, ends in a paradox, "This is your hatred back. She loves you," implying that language, whether written or spoken, can go only so far in helping to bring about the love and grace that will eventually result in resolution to conflict.

Yet if we learn how to interpret the languages of the natural and spiritual worlds, we may be able to gain access to a power that is not limited by verbal constructs. In "Eagle Poem" the speaker suggests that to pray you must

> open your whole self
> To sky, to earth, to sun, to moon

> To one whole voice that is you.
> And know there is more
> That you can't see, can't hear,
> Can't know except in moments
> Steadily growing . . .

The journey toward transformation begins with the understanding of the spoken and written word. But to continue the process, one must accept that "there is more / That you can't see, can't hear" and take the next step by bringing one's total awareness into mystical communication with the sacred that sustains and permeates the physical world.

THE WOMAN WHO FELL FROM THE SKY

Transformation as articulated through Native American creation myths continues to be a central theme in *The Woman Who Fell from the Sky* (1994). The title of the collection is taken from an Iroquois story in which a beautiful young woman becomes the bride of the sun. When he discovers that she is pregnant, he accuses her of adultery, angrily rips the tree of life out of the ground, and hurls his wife down the opening. As she falls from the sky, a flock of ducks gently supports her and delivers her safely to the earth.

Two sections of Harjo's book, "Tribal Memory" and "The World Ends Here," parallel this myth. The first represents the Native American descent into destruction as a result of colonization. The second, in spite of its rather gloomy title, offers the hope of healing and regeneration. Throughout the book, Harjo continues to address issues such as the limitations of language, the destruction of native culture and its survival, the importance of storytelling and myth, and the pernicious effects of urban life on the lives of native people. Most of the pieces are prose poems, reflecting Harjo's calling as a storyteller as well as a poet. Each poem is accompanied by an italicized commentary that provides background information on the piece. Readers new to Harjo's poetry no doubt will find these notes helpful in understanding her work.

The title poem is a long prose poem modeled on the Iroquois myth. It tells the story of two Native Americans who undergo transformation through love: Johnny, a homeless, alcoholic Vietnam War veteran who renames himself "Saint Coincidence" after getting lucky at pitching pennies, and Lila, a girl he meets while attending Indian boarding school. After graduation, Johnny enters the army. Lila marries, works at a Dairy Queen, and after giving birth to three children, enters "a place her husband had warned her was too sacred for women." Paralleling the Iroquois creation myth, Lila "looked into the forbidden place and leaped," implying that she engaged in an adulterous relationship. Her fall from grace leads to love and renewal as she and Johnny meet again in front of a convenience store, where he is begging for change. In the commentary that follows the poem, Harjo tells about one of her mystical visions in which she traveled far above the earth and then looked down to see the earth covered with "an elastic web of light." She credits her vision with giving her a "different perspective" on the power of love to transform: "I understood love to be the very gravity holding each leaf, each cell, this earthly star together."

"A Postcolonial Tale" also juxtaposes images from Native American creation myth and those from contemporary life but is more of a commentary than a story. The first line—"Every day is a reenactment of the creation story"—is filled with promise, but as the poem progresses, the promise is derailed by the imposition of Western culture onto the native population by the mass media.

Once we abandoned ourselves for television, the box that separates the dreamer from the dreaming. It was as if we were stolen, put into a bag and carried on the back of a whiteman who pretends to own the earth and sky.

This falling away from a traditional way of life brings native culture to "somewhere near the diminishing point of civilization, not far from the trickster's bag of tricks." A creative as well as a destructive force in Native American cosmology, the trickster often rescues native populations from the brink of destruction. In contrast to the white man's bag that cuts off Indian people from their traditions and traps them through assimilation, the trickster's bag contains "the tools" to free them to survive and re-create themselves through collective imagination and storytelling.

As in her other collections, storytelling provides a constructive way for Harjo to address and deal with the harsh realities of modern urban life. In "Letter from the End of the Twentieth Century" she tells about a conversation with a Chicago taxicab driver from Nigeria named Rammi. They discuss the senseless murder of one of Rammi's Nigerian friends, who was shot in the back of the head as he filled his gas tank. Harjo imagines the dead man's spirit wandering the streets of Chicago, looking for his killer in order to "settle the story of his murder before joining his ancestors or he will come back a ghost." When the spirit finally finds the man in a jail cell, he realizes that, if he killed the man, the police would assume it was suicide. Instead he chooses to forgive him. His redemptive action transforms his murderer from a disgraced youth into a repentant young man who "learns to love himself as he never could, because his enemy, who has every reason to destroy him, loves him."

In spite of the apocalyptic overtones reflected in the title "The World Ends Here," the poems in the second section offer the possibility of healing and renewal even in the face of personal, urban, and cultural violence. Death and loss in pieces like "Witness" and "Fishing" are balanced by hope and affirmation in "The Promise of Blue Horses" and "Sonata for the Invisible." The title of the final poem, "Perhaps the World Ends Here," suggests the possibility that the ominous prophecy reflected in the section title could be avoided. However, the future of the world may not be decided in seats of governmental power but rather around the perimeter of a common piece of household furniture, the kitchen table. Harjo writes:

> It is here that children are given instructions on what it means to be human. We make men at it, we make women. . . .

> Wars have begun and ended at this table. It is a place to hide in the shadow of terror. A place to celebrate the terrible victory.

> We have given birth on this table, and have prepared our parents for burial here.

The center of the home becomes the center of the world, taking on cosmic significance as birth meets death, joy meets sorrow, and war meets peace. The kitchen table also symbolizes continuance and blessing in spite of life's sufferings and acts as a unifying force, linking together all members of the human family.

A MAP TO THE NEXT WORLD: POEMS AND TALES

Seeking new direction as she stands at the brink of the twenty-first century, Harjo surveys the totality of her experience thus far in *A Map to the Next World: Poems and Tales* (2000). Although personal in tone and subject, this collection continues to address larger issues, such as the power of love, the brutal aftereffects of colonization on indigenous people, the importance of keeping native traditions and values alive, the central role family history plays in the life of the individual, and the power of memory to shape one's experiences into a meaningful

whole. Now living in Hawaii, Harjo weaves both American Indian and Hawaiian myths, particularly creation myths, with personal experience to "map" the individual's journey from fragmentation to wholeness. The use of the myths of the two indigenous cultures also connects the history of the tribes of the Sandwich Islands to that of their North American brothers and sisters.

The book is divided into four parts: "Songline of Dawn," "Returning from the Enemy," "This Is My Heart; It Is a Good Heart," and "In the Beautiful Perfume and Stink of the World." The title poem of the collection appears in the first section and is dedicated to one of Harjo's granddaughters, Desiray Kierra Chee. It is based on a Navaho emergence myth that tells about the first people who emerged from the fourth world, where all was barren, into the fifth, a new place of promise and possibilities. In an initiation ceremony of sorts, Harjo takes her granddaughter on a journey through the "fourth world" of the late twentieth century. It is a place where "supermarkets and malls, the altars of money . . . best describe the detour from grace," where "monsters are born of nuclear anger" and where pollution leaves "a trail of paper, diapers, needles and wasted blood." Moving through mythic time, Harjo recalls the period before the white man came, when Indians once "knew everything in this lush promise," and grieves for the lost culture that taught native people how to speak to birds "by their personal names." She acknowledges that Native Americans "were never perfect" and have fallen from grace partly because they embraced Western culture and abandoned their ancestors "for science." Her life as a mixed-blood Indian has affected her own vision, and she claims that she can draw only "an imperfect map," which will guide her granddaughter no farther than the border of the fourth world. As the child matures into a woman, she will step into the "fifth world" of adulthood, where she must draw her own map to help her find her way as a native person living in an alien society in the twenty-first century.

Harjo explores more deeply the wounds inflicted upon her family by that alien society in three works that deal with her troubled relationship with her father. "Twins meet up with monsters in the glittering city," a prose piece closing the "Songline of Dawn" section, recounts a conversation Harjo had with her fellow writer Greg Sarris before they were mugged on a Hollywood, California, street. Harjo introduces the reader to her father, "a Mvskoke Creek . . . a mechanic whose sensual charisma made him attractive to danger." She attributes his "unpredictable, rough" nature to the loss of his mother when he was a baby, the violence of his father, and "the confusion of being Indian in a society in which his existence was shameful." His cultural alienation often resulted in outrageous behavior. In "ceremony" she recalls that, when she was a child and sick with pneumonia, her father stole into the room where she and her brothers and sister slept and occupied a cot with one of his girlfriends. In spite of the fact that her father abandoned the family when Harjo was eight, she remembers the times when he was able to express his love, even though it was "flawed." Both "twins meet up with monsters in the glittering city" and "ceremony" are precursors to the title poem of the second section and prepare Harjo to confront and work out the relationship between her and her father.

Twenty-eight pages long, "Returning from the Enemy" is the centerpiece of the book. Although her earlier work dealt with alcoholism, domestic violence, and broken families, Harjo writes for the first time specifically about the effects colonization had on her father and her relationship with him. Given that this collection represents an evaluation of her life at its midpoint, it is necessary for Harjo finally to face a deeply painful relationship that has been the root of her fear and self-hatred so she can

move on. When questioned by Janice Gould about the reasons for the poem's length and prominence in the collection, Harjo remarked:

> In some ways I had to come up against the father paradigm, the male paradigm, see it in myself, become it, allow myself to be controlled by it, nearly destroyed by it over and over again in relationships until I was able to walk through it, until it had no hold on me anymore.

In writing the poem, Harjo was influenced by the poetry of Adrienne Rich and Sharon Olds as well as Hawaiian chants and Creek stomp dance songs.

Harjo begins her purification ritual with resolution and determination: "It's time to begin. I know it and have dreaded the knot of memory as it unwinds in my gut." Autobiographical narrative on the left-hand page alternates with poetic interpretation on the facing page. The narrative chronicles the events that affected the love-hate relationship Harjo had with her father during her difficult childhood and adolescence, while the poetry is a commentary on the destructive effects colonization had on Indian culture. The painful realization that "you can't change history" is played out through the generations as fear, anger, and despair is passed down from parent to child, resulting in an unbroken chain of dysfunctional families and personal relationships. In one of the narratives, she comments:

> In mythic stories a child can be born of a liaison between the sun and a woman. And then the child is born and the next day the child is no longer a child but a full-grown human. It all happens that fast. And you think you won't repeat anything you judged them for, but there you are picking your own children up from the babysitter after the bars are closed, the same leather jacket as your father, your own perfume instead of your mother's and you stumble a little as you carry them out to the truck.

Harjo paints a bleak picture of her early life, but myth again guides her in her quest for meaning and healing. Water is a central but ambivalent image in "Returning from the Enemy" and takes on several meanings. The story of the watermonster, a creature in Native American legend associated with destruction, informs the story of her father who "loved the water" just as "the water loved him." His affair with another woman, whom Harjo bitterly identifies as "the daughter of the watermonster," broke up her family. In an ironic twist, water becomes an agent of revenge instead of a force associated with the destruction of her family when, in her anger, she imagines the colonizer disappearing "into the deep." Although water can destroy, it can also cleanse and is critical to Harjo's transformation. At the end of her psychological and spiritual purification, Harjo writes:

Our paths make luminous threads in the web of
  gravel and water.
The shimmer varies according to emotional tenor,
to the ability to make songs out of the debris of
  destruction
as we climb from the watery gut to the stars.

She finally makes peace with her dead father's memory, but the ritual in "Returning from the Enemy" is actually a preparation for another, more recent challenge. Harjo told Gould that, while she was writing the poem, she also

began untangling from a relationship that had many of the same tones as the relationship with my father. This relationship contained the same silencing, the same need for control, the same struggle with colonization, and there was an ongoing love that often appeared to disappear in the terrible waves of fear.

The process of disentangling herself from controlling love that began in "ceremony" culminates in "The Ceremony," the opening poem of "This Is My Heart; It Is a Good Heart." As Harjo prepares to move out of the home she shared with her lover, she "makes a ceremony for leaving," walking through each room of the house she and her companion had "built together from scraps of earth and tenderness, through the aftermath of loving," and saying good-bye to those things that "would be no longer intimate" to her.

Leaving behind relationships that are killing her emotionally and spiritually is essential to Harjo's survival and growth as an artist. Death, whether it is psychological or spiritual, often shadows the shimmering images in her poetry. However, there is no death without rebirth, and the cycle of life reflected in nature is mirrored throughout the body of Harjo's work. Emerging from the purgation rituals in "ceremony," "Returning from the Enemy," and "The Ceremony," Harjo experiences a renewed sense of self in "This Is My Heart." In contrast to Noni Daylight's feelings of resignation and loss portrayed in "Kansas City," "This Is My Heart" reflects the perspective of a middle-aged woman who has survived pain and fear and is now thriving. Each of four strophes begins with a statement of affirmation and satisfaction—"This is my heart. It is a good heart"; "My head is a good head"; "This is my soul. It is a good soul"; and "This is my song. It is a good song." The recurrence of "It is a good" is reminiscent of the Genesis myth in which God pronounces each stage of creation "good." In a sense, Harjo is emerging from her personal "fourth world" of darkness and suffering into a fifth world, where continued growth is now possible. She is living out her own perpetual creation myth, constantly dying and being reborn, as she develops as an artist and a human being.

HOW WE BECAME HUMAN: NEW AND SELECTED POEMS

Up to this point, Harjo has published an impressive body of original poetry and prose. However, continued growth cannot take place without stopping for periods of reflection. In *How We Became Human: New and Selected Poems*

(2002), Harjo compiles prose and poetry from her first chapbook and six preceding collections, offering a unique view of her evolution as an artist as well as her personal and spiritual development. In addition to the older poems, which are arranged according to publication title, an eighth section titled "New Poems, 1999–2001" includes thirteen previously uncollected works. "New Poems" treat many of the same feminist and social issues found in her previous work, but her perspective has matured. Also the Hawaiian landscape predominates as Harjo responds to her environment, and she draws more frequently on native Hawaiian myth, blending it with the Native American.

A few examples will illustrate these observations. "I'm Not Ready to Die Yet" is a meditation on the end of life. While her death "peers at the world through a plumeria tree" and eternity "blooms / With delectable mangoes, bananas," her instinct for survival and enjoyment of life staves off death's advances for the present. Yet she cannot avoid reflecting on the inevitable. As she imagines her ashes being scattered on the water, she envisions that

> the city will go on shining
> At the edge of the water . . . Someone will be
>   hammering
> Someone will be frying fish
> The workmen will go home
> To eat poi, pork, and rice,

and realizes the rhythm of life will continue without her. "Morning Prayers," in which she says "good-bye to the girl / with her urgent prayers for redemption," is a poignant lament for the lost idealism of youth and a moving reminder that middle age is often marked by uncertainty, loss of vision, and disillusionment.

The section closes with "When the World Ended as We Knew It," a scathing revision of "Perhaps the World Ends Here" in *The Woman Who Fell from the Sky*. In an apparent reference to the terrorist attacks on the twin towers of the World Trade Center on September 11, 2001, Harjo speaks for the Indian community when she claims that "we knew it was coming." Apocalyptic references to

> two towers . . . from the east island of commerce
>   . . .
> Swallowed
> by a fire dragon, by oil and fear.
> Eaten whole

and to "those who would steal to be president / to be king or emperor" amount to a bitter attack on the Euro-American social, economic, and political structures that have oppressed poor and dispossessed populations through the centuries and into the modern era. The comforting image of the kitchen table as a symbol of stability and continuance is gone, replaced by images of war and destruction. Nevertheless, hope remains a possibility.

> The kick beneath the skin of the earth
> we felt there, beneath us
> a warm animal
> a song being born between the legs of her,
> a poem

underscores the power of language and the transcendence of nature to heal the wounds human beings inflict on one another and on the planet.

From the simple autobiographical lyrics of *What Moon Drove Me to This?* to the complex constructions and political commentary of *She Had Some Horses* and *In Mad Love and War* and finally to the luminous images and hard-won insights of *A Map to the Next World* and *How We Became Human*, Harjo has constantly strived to communicate growth, transcendence, and renewal. Her quest for self-definition and affirmation expressed through images from everyday life and Native American myth is not confined to her own people but is typical of the whole of humanity. As Harjo continues to mature as a poet and as a human being, her vision will no doubt become even more expansive as she seeks to perceive the mystery that underlies physical reality. "I am still on that journey," she writes. "The stuff I need for singing by whatever means is garnered from every thought, every heart that ever pounded the earth, the intelligence that directs the stars. . . . I take it from there, write or play through the heartbreak of the tenderness of being until I am the sky, the earth, the song and the singer."

Selected Bibliography

WORKS OF JOY HARJO

POETRY

The Last Song. Las Cruces, N.Mex.: Puerto Del Sol, 1975. (Chapbook.)

What Moon Drove Me to This? New York: I. Reed Books, 1979.

She Had Some Horses. New York: Thunder's Mouth Press, 1983.

Secrets from the Center of the World. Photographs by Stephen Strom. Tucson: Sun Tracks and University of Arizona Press, 1989.

In Mad Love and War. Middletown, Conn.: Wesleyan University Press, 1990.

Fishing. Browerville, Minn.: Ox Head, 1992. (Miniature fine press.)

The Woman Who Fell from the Sky. New York: Norton, 1994.

A Map to the Next World: Poems and Tales. New York: Norton, 2000.

How We Became Human: New and Selected Poems. New York: Norton, 2002.

SHORT STORIES

"The Flood." *Grand Street* 9, no. 4:77–79 (summer 1990).

"Boston." *Ploughshares* 17, nos. 2–3:183–184 (fall 1991).

OTHER WORKS

"Biopoetics Sketch for *Greenfield Review.*" *Greenfield Review* 9:8–9 (winter 1981–1982).

"Oklahoma: The Prairie of Woods." In *The Remembered Earth: An Anthology of Contemporary Native American Literature.* Edited by Geary Hobson. Albuquerque: University of New Mexico Press, 1981. Pp. 43–44.

The Woman Who Fell from the Sky. New York: Norton, 1994. (Audiocassette.)

"Joy Harjo." In *The Poet's Notebook.* Edited by Stephen Kuusisto, Deborah Tall, and David Weiss. New York: Norton, 1995. Pp. 80–93.

"My Sister, Myself: Two Paths to Survival." *Ms.* 6:70–73 (September–October, 1995).

Harjo, Joy, and Gloria Bird, eds. *Reinventing the Enemy's Language: Contemporary Native Women's Writing of North America.* New York: Norton, 1997.

Letter from the End of the Twentieth Century. With Poetic Justice. Boulder, Colo.: Silver Wave Records, 1997. (Compact disc.)

"Finding the Groove." In *Sleeping with One Eye Open: Women Writers and the Art of Survival.* Edited by Marilyn Kallet and Judith Ortiz Cofer. Athens, Ga.: University of Georgia Press, 1999. Pp. 151–152.

The Good Luck Cat. Illustrated by Paul Lee. San Diego: Harcourt, 2000. (Children's fiction.)

CRITICAL AND BIOGRAPHICAL STUDIES

Adamson, Joni. "And the Ground Spoke: Joy Harjo and the Struggle for a Land-Based Language." In her *American Indian Literature, Environmental Justice, and Ecocriticism: The Middle Place.* Tucson: University of Arizona Press, 2001. Pp. 116–127.

Allen, Paula Gunn. *The Sacred Hoop: Recovering the Feminine in American Indian Traditions.* Boston: Beacon, 1992.

Andrews, Jennifer. "In the Belly of a Laughing God: Reading Humor and Irony in the Poetry of Joy Harjo." *American Indian Quarterly* 24, no. 2:200–218 (spring 2000).

Arant, T. J. "Varieties of 'Grace': A Native American Poem." *English Journal* 82, no. 5:99–103 (September 1993).

Bezner, Kevin. "'A Song to Call the Deer in Creek': The Creek Indian Heritage in Joy Harjo's Poetry." *Eclectic Literary Forum* 5, no. 3:44–46 (fall 1995).

Bloom, Harold, ed. "Joy Harjo." In *Native American Women Writers*. Philadelphia: Chelsea House, 1998. Pp. 38–49.

Donovan, Kathleen M. "Dark Continent/Dark Woman: Hélène Cixous and Joy Harjo." In her *Feminist Readings of Native American Literature: Coming to Voice*. Tucson: University of Arizona Press, 1998. Pp. 139–159.

Goodman, Jenny. "Politics and the Personal Lyric in the Poetry of Joy Harjo and C. D. Wright." *MELUS* 19, no. 2:35–55 (summer 1994).

Holmes, Kristine. "'This Woman Can Cross Any Line': Feminist Tricksters in the Works of Nora Naranjo-Morse and Joy Harjo." *Studies in American Indian Literatures* 7, no. 1:45–63 (spring 1995).

Hussain, Azfar. "Joy Harjo and Her Poetics as Praxis." *Wicazo Sa Review* 15, no. 2:27–62 (fall 2000).

Jahner, Elaine A. "Knowing All the Way Down to Fire." In *Feminist Measures: Soundings in Poetry and Theory*. Edited by Lynn Keller and Cristanne Miller. Ann Arbor: University of Michigan Press, 1994. Pp. 163–183.

Johnson, Robert. "Inspired Lines: Reading Joy Harjo's Prose Poems." *American Indian Quarterly* 23, no. 3–4:13–23 (summer–fall 1999).

Keyes, Claire. "Between Ruin and Celebration: Joy Harjo's *In Mad Love and War.*" *Borderlines: Studies in American Culture* 3, no. 4:389–395 (1996).

Lang, Nancy. "'Twin Gods Bending Over': Joy Harjo and Poetic Memory." *MELUS* 18, no. 3:41–49 (fall 1993).

Leen, Mary. "An Art of Saying: Joy Harjo's Poetry and the Survival of Storytelling." *American Indian Quarterly* 19, no. 1:1–16 (winter 1995).

Lobo, Susan, and Kurt Peters, eds. *American Indians and the Urban Experience*. Walnut Creek, Calif.: Altamira Press, 2001.

Ludlow, Jeannie. "Working (In) the In-Between: Poetry, Criticism, Interrogation, and Interruption." *American Indian Literatures* 6, no. 1:24–42 (spring 1994).

Luna, Christopher. "Joy Harjo." *Current Biography* 62, no. 8:50–55 (August 2001).

McAdams, Janet. "Casting for a (New) New World: The Poetry of Joy Harjo." In *Women Poets of the Americas: Toward a Pan-American Gathering.*

Edited by Jacqueline Vaught Brogan and Cordelia Chàvez Candelaria. Notre Dame, Ind.: University of Notre Dame Press, 1999. Pp. 210–232.

Martin, Joel W. *Sacred Revolt: The Muskogees' Struggle for a New World*. Boston: Beacon, 1991.

Pettit, Rhonda. *Joy Harjo*. Boise, Idaho: Boise State University, 1998.

Rupert, Jim. "Paula Gunn Allen and Joy Harjo: Closing the Distance between Personal and Mythic Space." *American Indian Quarterly* 7, no. 1:27–40 (spring 1983).

Scarry, John. "Representing Real Worlds: The Evolving Poetry of Joy Harjo." *World Literature Today* 66, no. 2:286–291 (spring 1992).

Smith, Patricia Clark, and Paula Gunn Allen. "Earthly Relations, Carnal Knowledge: Southwestern American Indian Women Writers and Landscape." In *The Desert Is No Lady: Southwestern Landscapes in Women's Writing and Art*. Edited by Vera Norwood and Janice Monk. New Haven, Conn.: Yale University Press, 1987. Pp. 174–196.

Wickman, Patricia Riles. *The Tree That Bends: Discourse, Power, and the Survival of the Maskókî People*. Tuscaloosa: University of Alabama Press, 1999.

Wiget, Andrew. "Nightriding with Noni Daylight: The Many Horse Songs of Joy Harjo." *Forum* 1:185–196 (1989).

Wilson, Norma C. "The Ground Speaks: The Poetry of Joy Harjo." In her *The Nature of Native American Poetry*. Albuquerque: University of New Mexico Press, 2001. Pp. 109–122.

INTERVIEWS

Coltelli, Laura, ed. *Winged Words: American Indian Writers Speak*. Lincoln: University of Nebraska Press, 1990. Pp. 55–68.

———. *The Spiral of Memory: Interviews*. Ann Arbor: University of Michigan Press, 1996.

Crawford, John, and Patricia Clark Smith. "Interview with Joy Harjo." In *This Is about Vision: Interviews with Southwestern Writers*. Edited by William Balassi, John F. Crawford, and Annie O. Eysturoy. Albuquerque: University of New Mexico Press, 1990. Pp. 171–179.

Gould, Janice. "An Interview with Joy Harjo." *Western American Literature* 35, no. 2:131–142 (summer 2000).

Moyers, Bill. "Joy Harjo." In *The Language of Life: A Festival of Poets.* Edited by James Haba. New York: Doubleday, 1995. Pp. 156–172.

Ruwe, Donelle R. "Weaving Stories for Food: An Interview with Joy Harjo." *Religion and Literature* 26, no. 1:57–64 (spring 1994).

Smith, Stephanie Izarek. "An Interview with Joy Harjo." *Poets and Writers* 21, no. 4:22–27 (July–August 1993).

—PEGGE BOCHYNSKI

John Knowles

1926–2001

JOHN KNOWLES WAS born on September 16, 1926, in Fairmont, West Virginia. He was the third of four children born to James Myron Knowles, who worked in the booming coal industry, and Mary Beatrice (Shea) Knowles. There are no biographical or autobiographical writings that would indicate that the first fourteen years of Knowles's life were anything but ordinary. No traumatic event—parental suicide, loss of family fortune, near-death experiences—appears to have played a part in his early formative years. His mother and father were both originally from Massachusetts and held the belief that the best education was to be found in New England. Whatever position Knowles's father held in the coal business, he had the financial means to send his eldest son to Mercersburg Academy in Pennsylvania and then to Dartmouth College in New Hampshire. It was expected that Knowles would follow in his brother's footsteps, but he found a catalog from Phillips Exeter Academy in the family home and mailed in the preliminary application. The results of his entrance examinations revealed that the high school Knowles attended in Fairmont had ill prepared him for the rigorous academic demands of Exeter. He knew little Latin and even less math, but his English essay on *Jane Eyre* showed a potential for writing and he was approved for admission to the fall term of 1942.

"When I entered Exeter in the fall of 1942, I didn't know that it had one of the most rigorous secondary curriculums in the country. I thought I was fairly bright, but no one at Exeter shared this view," he wrote years later in the essay "A Naturally Superior School" (1956). Because of his poor scholastic preparation, Knowles was put back one year when he entered Exeter, and he was required to start Latin all over again despite two previous years of Latin study. It appeared that he would not remain at the school long after the first grading period, in which he posted a 27 in mathematics and a 14 in physics, but nonetheless he had fallen in love with the place: he directed all his energies toward his coursework, and soon he was passing every subject easily and was awarded a one-hundred-dollar grant by the school. Far from being an exclusive academic factory that catered to what Knowles called "spoiled little would-be aristocrats fenced off from American life" he found it to be "a matter-of-fact school where democratic diversity was taken for granted." He remembered in particular the blending of the several differently accented voices: the Harvard Yard diction of a boy from Boston, the slow, syrup-like voice of a young Floridian, the crisp Vermont speech pattern, the gruff, grunt-like sounds of a boy from Arizona. To these he added his own West Virginia mountain drawl. There were no obvious indicators of a student's family's affluence, he wrote approvingly:

> This is why the atmosphere of Exeter is more democratic than that of many public high schools. No one is permitted to have a car, so that avenue of conspicuous consumption is cut. There is little variation in clothes; slacks or khaki pants and a sports jacket are standard. Wealthy parents are not encouraged to send their sons large amounts of money; it would simply create the problem of where to spend it.

After the first year, Knowles returned to Exeter for the summer session of 1943 and managed to catch up the year he had been put back.

Knowles remembered that summer of 1943 as the happiest time of his life. It was a time of relaxed rules and relaxed teachers, a time of peace as war raged in other parts of the world. And it was from the memories of that time that Knowles created his masterpiece. Boys from other schools came to Exeter that summer. One of them was David Hackett, who came from Milton Academy in Massachusetts. Hackett roomed across the hall from Knowles for the six-week summer session and the two became close lifelong friends. They were among the founding members of a club at Exeter whose very name is redolent of the charming innocence of Mark Twain's tales of boyhood: the Super Suicide Society of the Summer Session. Boys who sought membership in the society were required to jump from a branch of a tall tree into the river below; no easy feat since during the summer the river was shallow and it took a prodigious leap to land in a spot that would not cause serious injury.

When Knowles returned to Exeter for the fall 1943 session, he found it to be a very different place. The war was making itself felt even in this isolated and idyllic school. Most of the younger teachers had disappeared one way or another into the war effort. Suddenly every activity at Exeter was "for the war." The boys harvested apples, cleared railroads and an old railroad yard, and organized countless collection drives. In moments of relaxation they were shown patriotic movies. The academic standards did not waiver, although older, more remote teachers taught the boys. In the essay "A Special Time, a Special School" (1995) Knowles fondly remembered one in particular, Mr. Galbraith, who taught Latin.

A finer, more inspiring teacher I never encountered. By the time he was through with me, I thoroughly understood the nature and structure of a language, and he had crucially influenced both my thinking and the way I expressed it in words. I am the writer I am because of him.

The war continued to claim staff and students and by 1944 Knowles was the only pupil in his senior English class.

POSTWAR YEARS

Knowles graduated from Exeter in August of 1944, and that fall he enrolled at Yale University. Before beginning his studies at Yale he enlisted in the U.S. Army Air Force Cadet Program. He spent eight months in the air force program, training in Texas and Illinois, and qualified as a pilot; by then, however, the war had ended. After his discharge, he returned to Yale. Knowles found the prestigious university disappointing after Exeter. The teachers at Yale, he felt, were not there primarily for the sake of the students' education. He endured listening to timeworn lectures given in auditorium-sized classrooms and attending small group sessions led by professors who were preoccupied with the reputations they had gained outside of the university.

During his senior year at Yale, Knowles began work on a novel titled "Descent into Proselito," which he continued to work on after receiving his B.A. degree in English, in 1949. He served briefly as assistant editor of the *Yale Alumni* magazine, and then in 1950 he took a job as a reporter and drama critic with the *Hartford Courant*. He left the newspaper in 1952 and traveled through Italy and southern France, supporting himself by writing an occasional freelance piece.

During this time, Knowles made the acquaintance of America's eminent man of letters Thornton Wilder—the author of such masterpieces of fiction as *The Cabala* (1926), *The Bridge of San Luis Rey* (1927), and the magnificent stage play *Our Town* (1938)—who became an important friend and mentor to the aspiring young writer. Wilder, a 1920 Yale graduate nearly thirty years Knowles's senior, had returned to his alma mater in 1950 to give an address at the thirtieth reunion of his class. Knowles covered the event for the alumni magazine. Shortly thereafter, Knowles presented himself at the door of Wilder's home in Hamden, Connecticut, on the pretext of asking the great man to proofread his article and make such corrections as he deemed necessary before publication. Knowles also just happened to have brought with him the manuscript of his novel "Descent into Proselito."

Wilder read a portion of the work and wrote to Knowles,

> Now I am at page 151. It is agreeable, fluent but I cannot read further—because it is hard to read a work in which the author is not deeply engaged. Now you have many a qualification for writing, and perhaps for writing a novel, but the qualifications rest in you really unactivated until you find a subject which you are deeply moved about, very much absorbed in.

Knowles took Wilder's advice (a long-winded variation on Hemingway's dictum to "write what you know") and for the rest of his writing career he mined that which he was "deeply moved about" to produce his works. Wilder was so impressed by the potential he saw in Knowles that he read and critiqued everything Knowles sent him for the next several years.

FIRST STORIES AND *HOLIDAY*

In 1953 *Story* magazine published a short story by Knowles titled "A Turn with the Sun." It was the first work of fiction by Knowles to find its way into print and it laid the foundation for all of Knowles's work to come. In it the reader is introduced to the prototype of Knowles's prep school boy who is anxious to find his place among his peers, Lawrence Stewart. As the story begins, Lawrence and his teammates are returning from the junior varsity playing fields of Devon School, where they, the Red team, have defeated the Blues thanks to Lawrence's game-winning goal. He is briefly elevated by the status his skill at lacrosse has given him. However, before even reaching the bridge that separates the junior varsity field from the varsity field, he sinks again into the understanding that after seven months he has not yet settled into the school as his teammate Bead has.

> He merely inhabited the nether world of the unregarded, where no one bothered him or bothered about him. Why, after all, should they? He had entered in fourth-form year, when the class was already clearly stratified, he arrived knowing only one person in the school, he came from a small Virginia town which no one had ever heard of, he was unremarkable athletically, his clothes were wrong, his vocabulary was wrong, and when he talked at all it was about the wrong things.

As he crosses the bridge, Lawrence remembers an event that had taken place there last September on his fourth day at school. Several boys had been diving from the railing into the icy river twenty-five feet below. Lawrence had climbed the railing and had executed a remarkable two-and-a-half somersault dive to the amazement of all those who witnessed it. Afterward, he had visited the school's gymnasium and trophy room. There amid the cups, medals, and banners, he felt he had found the heart of Devon; the sacred chapel devoted to the scholar-athlete. At the far end of the room stood the Holy Grail of Devon, the James Harvey Fullerton Cup, which was awarded each year to the senior who best exemplified the highest traditions of the school.

Lawrence's diving feat had earned him a dinner invitation from Ging Powers, a senior from Lawrence's hometown, and that evening Lawrence met Ging and two other seniors, Vinnie James and Charles Morrell, at the sedate Devon Inn. During the meal it became apparent that he was clearly out of his league in the company of the older boys, and in his eagerness to impress he succeeded only in widening the gulf between them. By dinner's end he had made a complete and utter fool of himself. In the weeks that followed, his attempts to become "one of the boys" had been defeated or ignored. Frustrated, he had charted a new course: "He would turn his back upon the school and the way things went there; he would no longer be embroiled in Devon's cheap competition for importance." He called upon his capacity for self-discipline to aid him in becoming the school's greatest scholar-athlete: "The greatest, and the most inaccessible." He studied hard and gained the favorable attention of several of his teachers. He exhibited great ability in swimming and made the junior varsity team. All this caused his classmates to reevaluate him and seek his friendship. However, "he had divorced himself from them so successfully that now he didn't care."

This new attitude did not confine itself to the school. On a trip home to Virginia during spring vacation, Lawrence had a fight with his girlfriend, Janine. "You're changed and I hate you," she cried at the end of the argument, and then, indignantly, "Who do you think you are, anyhow? I hate you!" When he returned to Devon in mid-April, winter had passed; the Northern Hemisphere had "turned once again toward the sun" and fresh air drifted through the open windows in Lawrence's room. Something had changed in Lawrence, too; his icy rigidity began to thaw out. He neglected his studies and showed small signs that he might be open to friendly companionship.

Now at the bridge with his teammates after his game-winning goal, he asks Bead if he is going to the movie that night. It is painfully clear that Lawrence hopes more than anything that the boy will say that he is and suggest that they go together; instead Bead hedges, saying that his friend Bruce had said something about

going. Although Bead suggests that they get together in the Butt Room for a smoke after dinner, Lawrence feels that his painful attempt to reach out has been completely rejected. "Lawrence sensed once again that he was helplessly sliding back, slowly but inexorably into the foggy social bottomland where unacceptable first-year boys dwell." He returns to his room to shower and change out of his athletic gear and then revisits the trophy room. The coming of spring has brought about a change in the way Lawrence sees the hallowed spot. For him it is no longer a sacred chapel but a crypt—a repository of forgotten names and forgotten feats. He steps out of its darkness into the warm sunshine, certain that it is going to be a good summer and that, in the passage of time, the earth turning around the sun, all will eventually be well.

After dinner, Lawrence joins Bead and Bruce in the Butt Room and then tags along with them to take the first swim of the spring season in the river. He climbs the railing of the bridge and executes a perfect dive as he had the previous September. This time however, after rising to the surface, he suddenly turns over on his back and sinks to the bottom. The efforts of his companions to revive him are futile. A conference is held two days later. The school officials are anxious to determine Lawrence's state of mind at the time of his dive. After some perfunctory questioning of Bead and Bruce, everyone agrees that it was an accidental death, but the reader senses that they are not as sure of that as they appear to be. Ironically, it is through this event, over which he seemingly had no control, that Lawrence reaches the pantheon of Devon demigods. An enlarged photograph of him in his junior varsity swimming suit is hung in the trophy room.

In 1956 *Cosmopolitan* magazine published Knowles's second short story that used Devon School as its setting, "Phineas." In this story Knowles makes a stylistic change, switching from the third-person narrative of "A Turn with the Sun" to a first-person narrative. The story begins with the unnamed protagonist approaching the door of a fine home in a Massachusetts town. As he prepares himself to knock on the door, he tells the reader about the events that began three months earlier and have now led him to this place. He remembers another door, the door to the room he occupied during Devon's summer session. Opening it, he got his first look at his roommate, Phineas, or Finny as everyone calls him. The first thing the narrator noticed about Finny was his carelessness regarding his clothes, which he pulled out of his suitcase in a startlingly haphazard manner. He was even more surprised when Finny began to express his beliefs about subjects ranging from God to sex. Speaking of Finny's beliefs, the narrator tells us, "I didn't like them much; they had an eccentric, first-hand originality which cut straight across everything I had been told to believe." Finny exhibited a joyousness that the narrator found as disarming as Finny's penchant for wearing a brilliant pink shirt. When Finny asked him about his sexual conquests, the narrator put him off with what he thought was "a cool, rebuffing tone." Although the narrator was intrigued by Finny's outgoing, good-natured personality, he kept his distance. "I wasn't going to be opened up like that suitcase, to have him yank out all my thoughts and feelings and scatter them around underfoot."

The narrator goes on to tell us that Finny was a natural athlete who could have excelled in the more prestigious games such as football but preferred to participate in those games that allowed the player some degree of individual creativity: lacrosse, hockey, and soccer. Finny was not boastful about his prowess. Indeed, he believed that one's success in any endeavor was the result of some natural, effortless ability within the person. He lacked a natural, effortless ability in academics, however, and found reason for celebration if he should be lucky enough to score a C on his schoolwork. The narrator was Finny's opposite, a fair athlete but an outstanding scholar. When his grades began to slip—that is, when he received a B on a paper—he began to suspect that Finny was jealous of his classroom excellence and was deliberately trying to undermine him.

> And then I realized, with relief, that we were equals. He wasn't so unlike me, so peacefully himself, unconscious of conflict and rivalry, after all. He was as vulnerable and treacherous as everybody else. I began to feel more comfortable with him; I almost even liked him.

As the summer session dragged on, all the students seemed bored. All, that is, except Finny. He convinced the boys to join him by the river at a tall tree that the seniors used to simulate jumping from a torpedoed troopship into the water. A few of the boys—Bobby Zane, Chet Douglass, and Elwin "Leper" Lepellier—followed the narrator and Finny to the tree. Finny stripped off his clothes and climbed the wooden rungs nailed into the tree's trunk, edged his way out onto the high limb, and jumped. Although he rapidly surfaced and praised the experience as the most fun he had had all week, the others were reluctant to follow his lead. The narrator, however, hated Finny for putting him in a situation where he must choose either to risk his life or, backing down, risk a life not worth living. He made the jump. Finny was delighted and promptly drew up a charter for a club that he called the Super Suicide Society of the Summer Session, naming himself and the narrator charter members and Bobby, Chet, and Leper trainees. Advancement in the club was dependent upon the difficulty of each member's jump. As the weeks went by the club met almost every evening. It began to interfere with the narrator's study time. Just before an important French exam, Finny burst into their room and told the narrator to put his books away and come see Leper make his first jump. The narrator, who had been trying hard to study, slammed his French book shut and shouted, "Okay, we go watch little lily-livered Lepellier not jump from the tree, and I ruin my grade." Finny was clearly surprised; he had believed that the narrator's academic success came naturally. He explained that he had not known that the narrator needed to study and insisted that he stay behind. The revelation that Finny had not been jealous of him and had not been trying to undermine his academic achievement was unbearable: Finny's quality of character was shown as something the narrator could never attain. Finny's very presence was a reminder of the narrator's shortcomings. He followed the others to the tree and, when he and Finny were on the limb preparing to make a double jump, he caused Finny to lose his balance and fall to the ground.

Several days later, the narrator visited Finny in the school's infirmary. One of Finny's legs had been shattered in the fall from the tree and, although he would eventually be able to walk, he would never again participate in any sports. The narrator had been overwhelmed by guilt and was frightened that Finny might suspect that his fall was not an accident. He approached Finny's bed and tried to discover Finny's thoughts about what had happened. "'How did you fall, how could you fall off like that?' 'I just fell.' His eyes looked vaguely into my face. 'Something jiggled and I fell over.'" Finny said he remembered thinking of reaching out to the narrator before he fell, and the narrator accused him of wanting to drag him down with him. Finny answered that he wanted to get hold of him so that he could maintain his balance and not fall. The narrator continued to press him to remember what made him fall.

> His eyes continued their roaming across my face. "I don't know. I must have lost my balance. It must have been that. I did have the feeling that when you were standing there beside me, y—I don't know. I must have been delirious—so I just have to forget it. I just fell, that's all." He turned

away to grope for something among the pillows. "I'm sorry about that feeling I had."

The narrator saw this refusal to accuse a friend of some heinous act, based on a mere feeling, as Finny's finest victory. Before he could tell Finny the truth, the nurse and Dr. Stanpole came in and he returned to his dormitory.

> I walked down the corridor of elms descending from the infirmary to the dormitories, and at every tree I seemed to leave something I had envied Finny—his popularity, his skill at sports, his background, his ease. It was none of these I had wanted from him. It was the honesty of his every move and his every thought.

Dr. Stanpole decided that Finny was not strong enough to have any more visitors, and when the summer session came to an end, Finny was sent home by ambulance. The narrator went home for a month's vacation before the start of the fall term. He took a detour on his return trip to Devon School and at the story's end he is standing at the door of Finny's home rehearsing what he will say.

In December 1956 *Holiday,* a popular travel magazine, published an essay by Knowles titled "A Naturally Superior School." The piece contains valuable autobiographical material relating to Knowles's education and it is also a good example of Knowles's developing prose style. What could have been a dreary article about a prestigious New England prep school written by a nostalgic alumnus is instead a splendid presentation of times past and present thanks in large part to Knowles's descriptive abilities. When writing about a boy he interviewed for the piece, Knowles shows us a type of overreaching nihilist commonly found on most campuses.

> Yet inevitably there is an Exeter "type." I met him one day last winter while talking to a group of students at the school.
>
> "Oh, I don't think anyone's typical here, certainly I'm not," he said quietly, giving the first

definite clue that he was. "As a matter of fact, I'm fairly nego about the school."

"Nego" is the new word for the Exeter attitude; it means negative, indifferent. This boy, whose first name was Barney, had the nego manner, a slightly satirical unconcern, which he manifested whenever he wasn't occupied as a varsity soccer player, member of the student council, tenor in the glee club and choir, varsity lacrosse player and secretary of the class. The rest of the time, except for his eighteen hours of classes every week, and the study hours to prepare for them, he was nego.

In describing the principal's office Knowles creates a hospitable environment in very few words.

From his office, a large room with green walls and an active fireplace, he can look out on the central quadrangle of the school. Flurries of large-flaked snow were rapidly whitening this quadrangle one morning last winter when Principal Saltonstall mentioned his view of Exeter's present and future.

Throughout the essay glimpses of Knowles the budding novelist can be seen. Indeed, the last four paragraphs comprise a poetic description of the seasonal changes at Exeter that is worthy of Robert Frost or Galway Kinnell. "At night the outside lamps shine on a white, silent world of cold elegance. The narrow white houses with their green shutters belong in this frozen landscape, the small windows letting little of the inner warmth escape outdoors."

Holiday offered Knowles the post of associate editor in 1957. Knowles accepted, leaving the apartment he shared with the actor Bradford Dillman in the Hell's Kitchen section of New York and moving to Philadelphia where the *Holiday* offices were located. For the next three years Knowles contributed pieces for the magazine's "Lively Arts" section. In addition to "A Naturally Superior School," *Holiday* printed one other signed piece by Knowles, an essay on an emerging sport for which he had developed a passion while vacationing on the French Rivi-

era in the early 1950s. The piece was titled "A Cold Plunge into Skin Diving." In 1958, during a return visit to the Cape d'Antibes, Knowles had the pleasure of meeting and receiving diving tips from the inventor of the self-contained underwater breathing apparatus (SCUBA), Jacques Cousteau.

In addition to the mysteries of the deep, Knowles continued to explore the mysteries of male adolescence through his writing. In 1959 he gave a manuscript to a literary agent who dutifully presented it to eleven of the best publishing houses in the United States. They all declined to accept it for publication. However, the London publisher Secker and Warburg bought the rights and published a British edition. The *Times Literary Supplement* called it "a novel of altogether exceptional power and distinction," saying, "There is no gush. There is no smut. If this is Mr. Knowles's first novel it shows an astonishingly firm grip of the right end of the stick." Simon Raven, writing for the *Spectator,* said the book, "modest as it is in tone, is likely to leave you thinking." Although Maurice Richardson's review in the *New Statesman* was less favorable, he admitted that this "short, thoughtful, ambitious American study of a fatal relationship between two upper-class schoolboys in late adolescence during the war" contained "several abrupt and pleasing variations from conventional American attitudes." These and other positive reviews caught the attention of American editors, and in 1960 the Macmillan Company in New York published what is considered Knowles's finest work, *A Separate Peace.*

A SEPARATE PEACE

The title of Knowles's classic comes from another American classic, Ernest Hemingway's *A Farewell to Arms.* In the second chapter of the fourth book of that novel, published thirty-one years earlier, Hemingway's protagonist, Lt.

Frederick Henry, is riding on a train from Milan to Stresa. He has chosen to escape from the madness he has endured as a volunteer ambulance driver on the Italian front during World War I. In borrowed civilian clothes he sits and watches the Lombard countryside go past his compartment window. "I had the paper," he says, "but I did not read it because I did not want to read about the war. I was going to forget the war. I had made a separate peace." Another quotation from Hemingway's novel is of significance to the story Knowles tells. Lt. Henry, enjoying a moment of sanctuary with his beloved English nurse, Catherine Barkley, reflects on their fate:

> If people bring so much courage to this world the world has to kill them to break them, so of course it kills them. The world breaks every one and afterward many are strong at the broken places. But those that will not break it kills. It kills the very good and the very gentle and the brave impartially. If you are none of these you can be sure it will kill you too but there will be no special hurry.

The truth of Hemingway's prophecy finds its way into the lives of Knowles's characters and changes them forever.

Knowles retains the first-person narrative of "Phineas" and gives the narrator a name: Gene Forrester. As in the short story, the novel begins with a return of the protagonist. Knowles, however, has lengthened the period of absence considerably, and now the reader will learn of the fatal events at Devon School through the memory of an adult. Gene returns to the preparatory school he had attended fifteen years earlier. Now in his thirties and possessing "more money and success and 'security,'" Gene has come to face a fearful event that took place when he was a student there and that has haunted him ever since.

It is an early afternoon in late November when Gene arrives in Devon, New Hampshire. A raw, wet wind moans through the stripped trees. The houses he passes are described as "forbidding." He remembers, "I had rarely seen anyone go into one of them, or anyone playing on a lawn, or even an open window." The streets of the town and the grounds of his old school are deserted. Gene surmises that everyone was "at sports." He walks through this surreal atmosphere undisturbed by any other person, alone with his memories of fear. "Looking back now across fifteen years, I could see with great clarity the fear I had lived in, which must mean that in the interval I had succeeded in a very important undertaking: I must have made my escape from it." Nevertheless, Gene feels that peace will come to him only after he visits two sites, both described as "fearful."

The first site is located in the school's First Academy Building. Gene enters through the building's swinging doors and stands in the marble foyer looking at a long, white marble stairway. He notices that although the steps have endured decades of hurrying feet upon their surfaces, they show little wear. Gene reflects that the marble must be unusually hard and thinks to himself, "It was surprising that I had overlooked that, that crucial fact."

Gene leaves the building and crosses some distance through soggy fields to a grove of trees beside a river. In the worsening weather he seeks the other site that has drawn him back to Devon, a tree. At first he is surprised to find several trees on the riverbank, "Any one of them might have been the one I was looking for. Unbelievable that there were other trees which looked like it here. It had loomed in my memory as a huge lone spike dominating the riverbank, forbidding as an artillery piece, high as a beanstalk." However, Gene is able to identify the tree of his quest by some small scars on its trunk and by a large limb reaching over the river and a smaller limb growing close to it. Standing there gazing up into it, Gene sees that the tree is no longer the giant monster of his childhood fears. Indeed, it now appears to him "shrunken, weary from age, enfeebled, dry." Gene is glad he has made the treacherous trek through inhospitable weather to see this tree. He has found that, "Nothing endures, not a tree, not love, not even a death by violence." Now, with Gene returning home a changed man, Knowles at last begins the story of the hard marble stairway and the mysterious tree and what role they played for the boys of Devon School during the summer of 1942.

At this point the narrative perspective changes somewhat; it becomes lighter, younger, as if the adult Gene were reciting his story to a psychiatrist who has put him under a hypnotic trance. A close reading reveals occasions when the voices mingle; the boy recounting and the man interpreting. An example of this is found at the end of the second chapter; Finny has just kept Gene from falling to certain injury and possible death. The "boy" Gene is breathlessly grateful; "If Finny hadn't come up right behind me . . . if he hadn't been there . . . I could have fallen on the bank and broken my back! if I had fallen awkwardly enough I could have been killed. Finny had practically saved my life." The "man" Gene begins the third chapter bitterly resentful; "Yes, he had practically saved my life. He had also practically lost it for me. I wouldn't have been on that damn limb except for him. I wouldn't have turned around, and so lost my balance, if he hadn't been there. I didn't need to feel any tremendous rush of gratitude toward Phineas." Notice also how "Finny" becomes "Phineas" depending on the point of view.

The first four and a half chapters of *A Separate Peace* recall the events in "Phineas" with some additions and some cosmetic changes. For instance, the war in Europe is much more of a threatening and mysterious presence. Members of the senior class are being prepared during this summer session for their eventual military service. "The class above, seniors, draft-bait, practically soldiers, rushed ahead of us toward the war. They were caught up in accelerated courses and first-aid programs and a physical hardening regimen." There is a change in Finny as well. He is not just the self-appointed leader of a small group of boys as portrayed in the short story; indeed, he is positively gregarious, a favorite of all the boys in the junior class and the teachers as well. Early in the book Gene reflects, "Finny could shine with everyone, he attracted everyone he met. I was glad of that too. Naturally. He was my roommate and my best friend." Flashy in dress, inventive in games, and charming in adult company, Finny is a "Peter Pan" to whom the "Lost Boys" of Devon School, those who have not yet developed such a strong sense of self, are naturally drawn.

Like the Finny of "Phineas," he is an accomplished athlete, but unlike the short story character he participates in the "more prestigious games" such as football, a game he abhorred in the short story. He has won several sports awards, but the recognitions bestowed have been as much for qualities of his character as for his physical prowess: "the Winslow Galbraith Memorial Football Trophy for having brought the most Christian sportsmanship to the game during the 1941–1942 season, the Margaret Duke Bonaventura ribbon and prize for the student who conducted himself at hockey most like the way her son had done." His flamboyant pink shirt is still part of his wardrobe, and he adds another sartorial oddity to his appearance: the wearing of the Devon School tie as a belt.

In addition to the Super Suicide Society of the Summer Session, Finny invents another activity, an essentially teamless game called Blitzball. Finny is oblivious to the amount of time these entertainments consume, but Gene is beginning to resent their demands. One afternoon, Finny and Gene are alone in the pool area reading a bronze plaque that displays the records set in various swimming events. Finny is surprised that the record for the one-hundred yards freestyle, fifty-three seconds, has stood unbroken for more than two years. He has a feeling that he can beat that time and, with Gene as his starter and timer, proceeds to do so, beating the standing record by more than half a second. Gene is amazed and wants the feat repeated in front of witnesses but Finny refuses. "No, I just wanted to see if I could do it. Now I know." Gene is puzzled by his friend and begins to see him in another light; "You are too good to be true," he tells him.

Finny insists that Gene keep the news of his record-breaking swim to himself. He dismisses the whole thing by saying that swimming in a pool is not really swimming at all. He persuades Gene to break school rules and take a three-hour bicycle trip with him to the seashore, where he can show him some real swimming. The ocean proves too powerful for Gene, and he spends the afternoon on the sand watching Finny glide through the rough surf. They have dinner at a hot dog stand and sleep among the sand dunes. Finny tells Gene that he is his best pal, and Gene almost returns the feeling. "But something held me back. Perhaps I was stopped by that level of feeling, deeper than thought, which contains the truth." At dawn, Gene is anxious to get back to school. It is nearly seven o'clock and it will take three hours to get there—just in time for Gene's important trigonometry test. Finny, however, is in no hurry and takes a morning swim. They arrive back at Devon unnoticed. Gene fails the test, the first test he has ever failed, and he suspects that Finny is deliberately luring him away from his studies. Here the reader begins to understand that Gene, unlike Finny, is far from being at peace with himself or anyone else, and it clouds his perceptions just as that morning the "strange gray thing, like sunshine seen through burlap" has distorted the first dawn he had ever seen.

Gene makes the self-serving mistake of projecting his own personality onto Finny. He decides that his seemingly perfect roommate is really no better than he is, that Finny is every bit as filled with jealousy, envy, and enmity as

Gene. This distorted perception gives Gene some feelings of satisfaction and relief. He can dismiss the notion that he could learn something of value, something that could enrich his life, from Finny. This corresponds to his attitude toward learning in general. He considers himself a good student although, he adds, "I wasn't really interested and excited by learning itself, the way Chet Douglass was." Chet is Gene's academic rival, but Gene feels that he has an advantage because Chet, according to Gene, "was weakened by the very genuineness of his interest in learning."

In the weeks leading up to final exams, Gene redoubles his efforts to be named head of the class. For a while he also continues to take part in the nightly activities of the suicide society, until they finally become too intrusive on his studies. On the night before a crucial French exam, an exam for which he does not feel prepared, Gene is interrupted in his review work by Finny. The scenes that follow are taken almost word for word from "Phineas": Gene explodes in anger, Finny is surprised that Gene has to study hard to achieve good grades, and Gene is forced to see the darkness of his own heart. The realization that Finny has never harbored feelings of enmity, jealousy, or competition against him is more than Gene can bear. "Now I knew that there never was and never could have been any rivalry between us. I was not of the same quality as he. I couldn't stand this." The following scene at the tree and Finny's injury is also taken directly from "Phineas."

With Finny in the infirmary, Gene spends all the time he can alone in their dorm room waiting to be called to account for the unspeakable act he has committed. Days pass and nothing happens; again he misreads Finny's goodness and assumes that Finny is just biding his time until he can attack Gene face to face. One evening, in a desperate attempt to escape himself, Gene dresses in Finny's clothes. In

Finny's pink shirt he looks in the mirror and sees himself transformed into Finny, complete with the trademark humorous, optimistic expression. The sight gives Gene intense relief; by becoming Finny he feels he "would never stumble through the confusions of my own character again." Feeling safely transformed, Gene enjoys the first good night's sleep he has had in a long time. The dawn, however, brings with it the reality of who he is and what he has done. As in the short story, Gene's attempt to make a clean breast of his crime is interrupted in the infirmary, and Finny is sent home to heal and recover. Gene goes home for a short summer vacation, and on his return to Devon he makes a detour to Finny's home and knocks on the door. Now all those who read "Phineas" and wondered, "What happened next?" have their question answered.

A cleaning lady leads Gene into a room where Finny is propped up by pillows in a large armchair by the fireplace. After some small talk, Gene finally confesses that he caused Finny to fall. Finny, however, refuses to believe it and their exchange becomes heated. Finny tells Gene to shut up and go away. This uncharacteristic outburst makes Gene realize that he is causing Finny a deeper injury than that inflicted by the fall. Gene tries to back out of his confession and wonders if he really did cause the accident: "Had I really and definitely and knowingly done it to him after all? I couldn't remember, I couldn't think. However it was, it was worse for him to know it. I had to take it back." The two boys sit silently for a while, then Gene wearily blames his behavior on the effects of his long train trip and lack of sleep. Finny accepts this and the two part peacefully; Finny expects that he will be fit enough to return to school by Thanksgiving.

The Devon School to which Gene returns is quite different from the idyllic place he knew in the summer. A new seriousness and sternness is imposed upon the boys, and the message conveyed in the first day of school's sermon is that if you break the rules you will be broken. As Gene tells us, "Peace had deserted Devon." Gene occupies the same dorm room he had during the summer, and he is pleased that he has not been assigned a new roommate. There have been some dormitory reassignments, and Brinker Hadley now occupies the room across from Gene's. Brinker provides the second unpleasant event of Gene's first day back, the first being a fight with an obnoxious student named Cliff Quackenbush that resulted in both boys falling in the river and Gene receiving a severe reprimand from Mr. Ludsbury, the director of the dormitory. Brinker, a character based on Knowles's classmate and longtime friend, Gore Vidal, is a master of sarcastic accusations, and he accuses Gene of causing Finny's injury so that he can have the dorm room all to himself. Gene tries to redirect the conversation by suggesting they go to the Butt Room for a smoke. Once there, however, Brinker presents Gene to the ten boys gathered there as his prisoner and proceeds to conduct a trial. Gene manages to deflect their taunts with a bluff sarcastic swagger, but in fact he is shaken to learn that some in the school suspect that he deliberately caused Finny's fall.

By winter, the war in Europe asserts itself deeper into the lives of the boys at Devon. Like Knowles's class at Exeter, the boys are called upon to help in the war effort on the home front. After an unusually early and heavy snowfall, several of the boys volunteer to shovel snow off the train tracks. They spend a long day shoveling the wet, heavy snow, and by late afternoon the line is cleared enough to allow a train to come through. It is a troop train filled with new recruits who are not much older than the Devon boys. A cheer goes up from the soldiers and the boys respond in kind. After the train has passed, Brinker is filled with enthusiasm and announces that he will enlist first thing tomorrow. The idea appeals to Gene, who sees in it the chance to divest himself of himself and be molded by other forces. He reveals a remarkable bit of insight: "The war would be deadly, all right. But I was used to finding something deadly in things that attracted me; there was always something deadly lurking in anything I wanted, anything I loved. And if it wasn't there, as for example with Phineas, then I put it there myself."

Gene returns to his dormitory filled with excitement; his future is decided and his redemption is assured. But, as he opens the door to his room, "Everything that had happened throughout the day faded like that first false snowfall of the winter. Phineas was back." Except for the cast on his leg and the crutches he requires now, nothing has changed in Finny, and with his return Gene feels again the peace he had enjoyed during the summer. He abandons his decision to enlist and devotes himself to helping the cast-encumbered Finny in any way he can. Finny, on the other hand, has decided that since he can no longer take part in sports, he will train Gene, developing him into an athlete able to compete in the 1944 Olympics. Of course, with the world at war there will be no 1944 Olympics, but Finny refuses to believe in the reality of the war. He is certain that it is a fraud concocted by a group of fat old men to keep the young in their place. Gene buys into Finny's vision of peace until he sees the true horror of the war's existence in the person of Elwin "Leper" Lepellier. Leper, the introverted, nature-loving pacifist, is impressed by a recruitment film shown to the boys. A week later he enlists in the ski troops and is gone. Leper becomes legendary among the boys, who imagine him participating in the thick of battle. However, soon after Leper's departure Gene receives a telegram from him. In it Leper tells Gene that he has "escaped" from the army and begs Gene to come visit him at his mother's home. Gene arrives in Vermont to find his formerly mild-mannered classmate in a barely controllable state of psychosis. Leper never made it to the war; the rigors of basic training proved enough to make his mind snap. Before the army could declare him mentally unfit and give him a Section 8 discharge, a disgrace that would follow him the rest of his life, Leper ran away.

Leper's return is pivotal to the story in two ways: first, he is an example to Gene and the others of what the war is capable of doing to them; second, he makes it clear to Gene that he knows the truth about what caused Finny to fall and he knows of the savage who lurks beneath Gene's friendly demeanor. As if to prove Leper right, Gene knocks the boy out of his chair in a fit of rage. Gene flees back to Devon, away from the truth Leper represents, just as Leper had fled home to Vermont, away from the truth of the war. However, the safety and security Gene finds with Finny is short-lived. Late one night Brinker and three of his friends burst into Gene and Finny's room. "His friends half-lifted us half-roughly, and we were hustled down the stairs." They are taken across campus to the First Academy Building and forced up the marble staircase to the Assembly Room. There in the gloom await several senior boys dressed in their black graduation gowns and sitting in chairs on a platform. Finny and Gene think that this is some sort of schoolboy prank until Brinker makes it clear that it is instead an investigation of what really caused Finny's injury. Finny is contemptuous of the proceedings and, as he always has, refuses to believe that Gene had anything to do with the accident. As the questions and answers fly around the room, however, he begins to see that Gene's involvement is a possibility. Hoping to clear the matter up, Finny tells Brinker that the other person who witnessed the event, Leper, has been lurking about the school and might be in one of the rooms. He is found and brought to the Assembly Room, where his testimony makes it clear that Gene was on the limb with Finny and deliberately caused the limb to bounce, displacing Finny. Finny has had enough. Teary-eyed, he rises to leave and tells Gene, "I just don't care. Never mind." After a brief, heated exchange with Brinker, he rushes from the room. The next sound the boys hear is that of Finny's body falling down the hard marble steps.

Finny is carried to Dr. Stanpole's car and driven to the infirmary. Gene follows at a distance, feeling that he is the last person Finny would want beside him right now. He lingers outside the infirmary until all is quiet and he tries to talk to Finny through a window he has managed to open. Finny is unnaturally furious with Gene: "You want to break something else in me! Is that why you're here!" After thrashing wildly to get out of his hospital bed and get his hands on Gene, Finny gives up, exhausted, and collapses. Gene repeats that he is sorry several times before leaving the window. He spends the night wandering the campus and finally falls asleep sheltered by a ramp under the stadium. When he returns to his room the next morning, he finds a note from Dr. Stanpole asking him to bring some of Finny's things to the infirmary. There, Gene stands in the middle of Finny's room wanting to say something but unable to do so as Finny calmly and quietly goes through the items Gene has brought. When Gene notices that Finny's hands are trembling, he feels free to speak.

Gene reminds Finny that he had tried to tell him the truth about what had happened on the tree limb. Finny says he remembers that Gene had indeed tried and then directs the conversation in an unexpected direction; he claims that he had been trying all winter to enlist in an army, any army—Canadian, Chinese—but none would accept him because of his broken leg. Gene manages a bit of humor by telling Finny that he would not be any good to any army even if his leg were whole, that he would find some way to involve the opposing sides in some sort of friendly game such as baseball; "You'd make

a mess, a terrible mess, Finny, out of the war." Finny again does something unexpected; he bursts into tears and begs to know that what Gene had done had not been a malicious attack against him personally, that it had been some uncontrollable impulse and not hatred. Gene pleads with Finny to believe him: "Tell me how to show you. It was just some ignorance inside me, some crazy thing inside me, something blind, that's all it was." Finny closes his eyes and nods his head; he tells Gene that he believes him.

Gene spends the rest of the day anxiously awaiting the time when he can revisit his friend. Dr. Stanpole has told him that Finny's bone would be reset that afternoon and that by five o'clock he should be coming out of his anesthesia. Knowles suspensefully takes the reader through each hour that passes and each activity Gene finds to fill the time. Finally, Gene arrives at the infirmary and is stunned to learn from Dr. Stanpole that Finny has died during the operation. Stanpole believes that some marrow had escaped from Finny's broken bone and found its way through the bloodstream to his heart, stopping it instantly. Gene attends Finny's funeral in Boston and tells the reader that he did not cry then or ever about Finny. He feels like it is he himself who has died and one does not cry at one's own funeral.

This could have, perhaps should have, been the end of the story, but Knowles includes one more chapter. In it he endears himself to the members of the growing antiwar protests of the 1960s, and, perhaps, young people for all times, by taking a swipe at the older generation. After Finny's burial, the plot jumps ahead to graduation and the day the first troops arrive to use Devon School as a base. Recruitment officers from all branches of military service are on campus, and the seniors are deciding which one would suit them best. Brinker's father is introduced at this point to represent the prowar mentality. He is a veteran of World War I who fought as an infantryman in the foxholes of France. He admonishes his son and Gene that they should work hard in the service to earn respectable war records. His patriotic bluster is lost on the two boys, who answer that they have decided to choose cleaner duty that is less likely to include combat: Gene has enlisted in the navy and Brinker the coast guard. Brinker's father does little to conceal his disappointment and leaves to rejoin his wife. Brinker apologizes to Gene for his father's behavior, and Gene says it is understandable since the old man is probably feeling jealous and left out. Brinker responds with the words that, in one form or another, became a rallying cry for Vietnam War protesters: "Left out! He and his crowd are responsible for it! And *we're* going to fight it!" Gene, however, is unconcerned. Before even donning a uniform, he knows he has fought his war and destroyed his true enemy. By burying himself in Finny's grave and resurrecting and placing onto his new self (much like the pink shirt) that which made Finny the embodiment of peace, Gene has already killed his two-headed monster, fear and hate.

> During the time I was with him, Phineas created an atmosphere in which I continued now to live, a way of sizing up the world with erratic and entirely personal reservations, letting its rocklike facts sift through and be accepted only a little at a time, only as much as he could assimilate without a sense of chaos and loss.

Gene has achieved a peace separate from those who build defensive walls to protect themselves from enemies, real or imagined.

THE PEACE THAT FOLLOWED

A Separate Peace was an instant commercial and critical success. Knowles has written that he knew it was a good book but that he felt it would attract only a limited audience. He expected sales to reach perhaps three thousand copies. When the first printing of seven thousand sold quickly and the book was also picked up by a paperback publisher, he was pleasantly surprised. In an article for *Esquire* commemorating the twenty-fifth anniversary of the publication of *A Separate Peace* he wrote,

> Then it was as though a wave, a very large wave, were gathering force in the distance and moving toward me. There was a far-off rumbling coming nearer; letters, then more letters, began to arrive from readers; then teachers took the book up by the thousands, and the sales climbed and climbed.
>
> For all these years it has sold between 250,000 and four hundred thousand copies every year, and then of course there is the money. *A Separate Peace* is my annuity, the faithful offspring who will keep me in my old age. It brings me sometimes $30,000 and once $90,000 a year, year in and year out for a quarter of a century, never less.

In addition to being regularly assigned by high school English teachers who are delighted to have a less controversial alternative to the perennial favorite of adolescents, *The Catcher in the Rye* by J. D. Salinger, *A Separate Peace* enjoys a separate life as a classic of gay fiction. Gay readers are drawn to Knowles's story by its honest depiction of the sexual tensions that thrive in boys' prep schools. The novel also earned Knowles the Rosenthal Award from the National Institute of Arts and Letters and the William Faulkner Award for the most promising first novel of 1960, and it was nominated for the National Book Award. This sudden fame and fortune allowed Knowles to leave his job at *Holiday* and to travel where he pleased and write what he pleased. This freedom from financial concerns may also have had a destructive impact on his future literary efforts. Indeed, although he continued to work within the motif of the individual trying to create an identity separate from the external forces that have molded him, nothing he wrote afterward came close to reaching the heights of acclaim and reward of *A Separate Peace*.

In the 1960s Knowles traveled throughout the Middle East and served as writer in residence at the University of North Carolina at Chapel Hill (1963–1964) and at Princeton University (1968–1969). Knowles's second novel, *Morning in Antibes* (1962), lacked the structural soundness and psychological insight of *A Separate Peace.* It was followed by a travelogue of his European and Middle Eastern journeys, *Double Vision: American Thoughts Abroad* (1964); another novel, *Indian Summer* (1966); and a collection of short stories, *Phineas: Six Stories* (1968).

Knowles took up more or less permanent residence in Southampton, Long Island, in 1970. Here he developed a close friendship with the deeply troubled and often troublesome author Truman Capote. None of Capote's brilliance found its way into Knowles's writing, however, and his three novels of the 1970s, *The Paragon* (1971), *Spreading Fires* (1974), and *A Vein of Riches* (1978) were ignored by critics and the reading public.

In what may have been an attempt to remind the book world of what he had once been capable of achieving through his writing, Knowles published *Peace Breaks Out* (1981). The novel is sometimes referred to as a companion piece or sequel to *A Separate Peace,* but in fact they only share a common setting, Devon School. The boys of the first novel do not reappear nor are they even mentioned. Pete Hallam, Devon class of 1937, returns to teach history after serving in World War II. Here he encounters the frustrations of a class of boys who had been prepared to wage war but who must now find a place for themselves in a world at peace. The title is borrowed from Bertolt Brecht's 1941 play set during the Thirty Years War, *Mother Courage and Her Children.* The play's title character suffers a reversal of fortune when peace is declared, and exclaims, "Don't tell me peace has broken out—when I've just gone and bought all these supplies!"

Postwar America, finding itself without an enemy, became suspicious of its former allies, particularly the Soviet Union, and began an attack on the imagined enemy within: those Americans who held political and philosophical opinions thought to be destructive to the "American way of life." Knowles takes this nationwide paranoia and places it on the campus of Devon School, where two of Hallam's students, Wexford and Hochschwender, play out their personal prejudices to a tragic end. Unlike *A Separate Peace,* which ends rather optimistically, *Peace Breaks Out* offers the reader a vision of hopelessness regarding the American character—a character prone to savagery, stupidity, and violence. Again, critics and readers were disappointed.

A Stolen Past (1983) begins with the familiar motif of a man returning to his alma mater after a long period of time. Allan Preiston, a successful novelist, has come back to Yale after a thirty-year absence to deliver a lecture. Through Preiston, Knowles reflects on his own changing opinions of himself and his role as a writer.

Knowles's last novel, *The Private Life of Axie Reed* (1986), is almost a parody of Hemingway's "The Snows of Kilimanjaro." A fifty-year-old movie star, Alexandra Reed, has suffered a near-fatal fall. Her doctor tells her that he has done everything he can for her and it is now up to her to find the strength to live. As she drifts in and out of consciousness she tells us the story of her life. At times, her cousin, Nick Reed, who is her official biographer, takes up her story. Critics and readers found the work clichéd and lacking every element that made Knowles's first novel unforgettable.

In 1986 Knowles moved to Fort Lauderdale, Florida. There he taught creative writing at Florida Atlantic University and worked on his autobiography. That work was left unfinished when he was moved to a nursing home in late October 2001. John Knowles died there after a short illness on Thursday, November 29, 2001, at the age of seventy-five. Although the majority of his work can be described, as Granville Hicks wrote of *Indian Summer,* in *Saturday Review,* as "something that Knowles just tossed off—and might better have tossed away," *A Separate Peace* earned Knowles a secure place among the most respected American writers.

Selected Bibliography

WORKS OF JOHN KNOWLES

NOVELS AND SHORT STORIES

A Separate Peace. New York: Macmillan, 1960.

Morning in Antibes. New York: Macmillan, 1962.

Indian Summer. New York: Random House, 1966.

Phineas: Six Stories. New York: Random House, 1968. (Contains "A Turn with the Sun," "Summer Street," "The Peeping Tom," "Martin the Fisherman," "Phineas," and "The Reading of the Will.")

The Paragon. New York: Random House, 1971.

Spreading Fires. New York: Random House, 1974.

A Vein of Riches. Boston: Little, Brown, 1978.

Peace Breaks Out. New York: Holt, Rinehart, and Winston, 1981.

A Stolen Past. New York: Holt, Rinehart, and Winston, 1983.

The Private Life of Axie Reed. New York: Dutton, 1986.

NONFICTION

"A Naturally Superior School." *Holiday* 20, no. 6:70ff. (December 1956).

"A Cold Plunge into Skin Diving." *Holiday* 25, no. 3:78–85 (June 1959).

Double Vision: American Thoughts Abroad. New York: Macmillan, 1964.

"My Separate Peace." *Esquire,* March 1985, pp. 107–109.

"A Special Time, A Special School." *Exeter Bulletin* (http://library.exeter.edu/dept/separate_peace/article.html), summer 1995.

CRITICAL AND BIOGRAPHICAL STUDIES

Bryant, Hallman Bell. *A Separate Peace: The War Within.* New York: Twayne, 1990. (Contains a helpful chronology of Knowles's life and works through 1988, but it fails to include *A Stolen Past.*)

Carragher, Bernard. "There Really Was a Super Suicide Society." *New York Times,* October 8, 1972, section 2, pp. 2, 7, 17.

Clarke, Gerald. *Capote: A Biography.* New York: Simon & Schuster, 1988. (Contains some interesting recollections of Knowles's friendship with Capote.)

Ellis, James. "*A Separate Peace:* The Fall from Innocence." *English Journal* 53, no. 5:313–318 (May 1964).

Halio, Jay L. "John Knowles's Short Novels." *Studies in Short Fiction* 1, no. 2:107–112 (winter 1964).

Harrison, Gilbert A. *The Enthusiast: A Life of Thorton Wilder.* New Haven, Conn.: Ticknor & Fields, 1983. (Briefly touches on how Knowles met Wilder and the advice Wilder gave to the young author.)

Hicks, Granville. "Blandishments of Wealth." *Saturday Review,* August 13, 1966, pp. 23–24.

McDonald, James L. "The Novels of John Knowles." *Arizona Quarterly* 23, no. 4:335–342 (winter 1967).

Nelson, Robert M. "John Knowles." *Dictionary of Literary Biography.* Vol. 6, *American Novelists since World War II,* 2d series. Detroit: Gale, 1980. Pp. 167–177.

Raven, Simon. "No Time for War." *Spectator,* May 1, 1959, p. 630.

Richardson, Maurice. "*A Separate Peace.*" *New Statesman,* May 2, 1959, p. 618.

Sarotte, George-Michael. *Like a Brother, Like a Lover: Male Homosexuality in the American Novel and Theater from Herman Melville to James Baldwin.* Garden City, N.Y.: Doubleday, 1978.

"School Reports." *Times Literary Supplement,* May 1, 1959, p. 262.

Weber, Ronald. "Narrative Method in *A Separate Peace.*" *Studies in Short Fiction* 3, no. 1:63–72 (fall 1965).

Witherington, Paul. "*A Separate Peace:* A Study in Structural Ambiguity." *English Journal* 54, no. 9:795–800 (December 1965).

Wolfe, Peter. "The Impact of Knowles's *A Separate Peace.*" *University Review* (University of Missouri) 36, no. 3:189–198 (March 1970).

FILM BASED ON A WORK BY
JOHN KNOWLES

A Separate Peace. Screenplay by Fred Segal. Directed by Larry Peerce. Paramount, 1972.

—CHARLES R. BAKER

J. D. McClatchy

1945–

JOSEPH D. MCCLATCHY Jr., born August 12, 1945, in Bryn Mawr, Pennsylvania, is the eldest of four children and the only son of Joseph Donald and Mary Jane Hayden McClatchy. He was called "Sandy" as a child and is known only by that name. He attended Catholic schools in suburban Philadelphia and then Georgetown University, from which he was graduated summa cum laude with a B.A. degree in classics and English in 1967. Although a longtime lapsed Catholic, he credits his Jesuit education with giving him a rigorous, serious training in linguistic and literary studies. He entered the doctoral program in English at Yale, but his graduate career was interrupted by the Vietnam War. He spent 1968 through 1971 as an English instructor at LaSalle College in Philadelphia before returning to New Haven to complete his doctorate, under the supervision of Geoffrey Hartman, in 1974. Interestingly for a poet who has come to be thought of as an "aesthetic," indeed a formalist writer, his dissertation, "The Tradition of Contemporary Confessional Poetry," served as the basis of his first critical book, *Anne Sexton: The Artist and Her Critics* (1978). From the beginning, in other words, McClatchy proved himself a writer of varying tastes and temperaments, comfortable with the flamboyant, often histrionic work of Sexton and other melodramatic poets of the 1960s and 1970s as well as with the more tempered measures of poets such as James Merrill, Anthony Hecht, and Richard Wilbur, all of whom might be said to have descended from the school of W. H. Auden or to have at least brought forward Auden's legacy into the post–World War II American poetry scene.

McClatchy taught for seven years at Yale (1974–1981), and for the following twenty years he lived a somewhat peripatetic academic life, holding temporary teaching posts at Princeton, Rutgers, Columbia, the University of California at Los Angeles, and Johns Hopkins. He returned to Yale as editor of the distinguished quarterly *The Yale Review* in 1991 and assumed a position as a permanent member of the faculty in 2002.

McClatchy has made a career as a man of letters in the old-fashioned sense. Educated in the classics and in possession of a working knowledge of the great traditions of Western art and literature, he has produced a body of work that includes not only five books of poetry but also books of criticism and translation, editions of other poets, and beginning in 1989, opera libretti for the composers William Schuman, Francis Thorne, Bruce Saylor, and Tobias Picker. *White Paper on Contemporary American Poetry* (1989), a collection of assorted literary criticism, was awarded the Melville Cane Award by the Poetry Society of America. In 1996 he became a chancellor of the Academy of American Poets. Two years later he was elected a fellow of the American Academy of Arts and Sciences, and the following year he became a member of the American Academy of Arts and Letters.

McClatchy cultivated relationships with American poets starting in graduate school. Over the years many of these blossomed into friendships as the senior writers came to take their junior colleague as an equal. Robert Lowell invited McClatchy to visit him in Cambridge after he read McClatchy's review of *The*

Dolphin (1973). McClatchy also met Sexton at the same time that he was getting to know other poets who came through New Haven or who lived there, notably Robert Penn Warren, Richard Howard, Mark Strand, and John Hollander. He wrote a fan letter to James Merrill in 1972, from which developed an increasingly intimate friendship that lasted until Merrill's death in 1995. McClatchy, along with the poet-critic Stephen Yenser, is Merrill's literary executor.

At the same time—during the decade of the seventies, as he was approaching his thirtieth birthday—McClatchy was adjusting to his homosexuality. He discusses his fling with psychotherapy in various pages of *Twenty Questions: (Posed by Poems)* (1998), especially in the essay "My Fountain Pen." The relationship between his lived life and his poetic styles is something he discusses in an interview with Lorin Stein in *Poets and Writers Magazine*. As a Catholic child he liked to devise evasive names for his sins. Confession, secrecy, and evasion are established modes in Catholicism of course, and complementing a religious regime with the secular confessionals of psychotherapy enabled the young McClatchy to come to grips with himself and to become "truer" in his writing. "Truth," however, must not be mistaken for facts, since McClatchy (like Merrill before him) admits to having invented some details in his prose and poetry that are imaginatively if not actually true: "Over the years, I've tried to learn more and loosen up. I've tried to write more openly of my life, but I have felt free to lie in order to make the facts into a truth." Meanwhile, right after his fiftieth birthday, McClatchy met the young and talented book designer Chip Kidd, with whom he came to share his life and residences in Manhattan and Stonington, Connecticut, the charming seaside village to which he moved in part because of his friendship with Merrill, who lived there from the mid-1950s until his death.

When McClatchy was given an Award in Literature by the American Academy and Institute of Arts and Letters in 1991, his citation read in part:

> J. D. McClatchy is a poet who has emerged into highly distinctive achievement in his third collection, *The Rest of the Way*. Formally a master, with enormous technical skills, McClatchy writes with an authentic blend of cognitive force and a savage emotional intensity, brilliantly restrained by his care for firm rhetorical control. His increasingly complex sense of our historical overdeterminations is complemented by his concern for adjusting the balance between his own poems and tradition. It may be that no more eloquent poet will emerge in his American generation.

What turns out to be most surprising about McClatchy's poetic development is precisely his gradual unleashing of the "savage emotional intensity" noted above. Whereas many poets begin their careers with the force, energy, and unbridled passions associated with youth and then modulate into greater degrees of reasonableness or moderation, McClatchy began carefully, sedulously imitating his teachers. A natural expert in verse technique from the beginning (again like Merrill), McClatchy came gradually both to loosen his forms and his diction and to take on more serious, indeed deeply moral and historical issues. He began as a poet of the "scenic" or "aesthetic" mode, which was in part a program of self-containment. As he became more open about his life (and more comfortable with and open about his homosexuality in a way that resembles the gradual comings out of Merrill and Adrienne Rich from a previous generation), McClatchy also alighted upon a genuine and affecting personal voice.

It might have been possible at the start of McClatchy's career to predict some of his future successes. It would not have been possible, however, to mark out the paths he forged as his poetry and prose opened to encompass a greater, more mature and capacious imaginative vision.

One truism about contemporary American poetry holds that writers often have a "breakthrough" volume, a book after one or more apprentice works in which the writer finds what John Keats called his or her "true voice of feeling." For Robert Lowell the volume was the 1959 *Life Studies;* for Adrienne Rich, the 1963 *Snapshots of a Daughter-in-Law.* In the case of McClatchy, *The Rest of the Way* (1990), his fifth volume, marks an increase in independence; it prepares the way for the startling originality of the subsequent two books of poems.

EARLY WORKS

Scenes from Another Life (1981) comes with a title redolent of the work of James Merrill. The very idea that one's life is a drama, replete with stage-worthy or at least memorable events, and that one's past is another country or a version of Arthur Rimbaud's famous dictum that "I *is* another" (*Je est un autre*) marks McClatchy as a poet sensitive to "scenes" and to his own life as merely a version of a work in progress. The title seems to announce either "this is what I used to be, but I have now passed beyond it," or "although you may think these are autobiographical poems, they are not really about the actual Sandy McClatchy, who, like Walt Whitman, is always above and behind rather than in front of you." In other words: "Reader, Beware." In jacket notices, Robert Penn Warren praises the poems for their wit, formal variety, and elaborate syntax, and John Hollander commends them as discursive, moving, and witty. Richard Howard, probably the most important "dramatic" American poet of the second half of the twentieth century (his deeply plumbed monologues of other characters, real or imagined, suggest the appeal he might have had for a younger gay poet trying on different versions of the self by exploring other people's lives), wrote an introduction. He says clearly that the other life comes from loss and sorrow and that the life one imagines is not the life one lives but a compensation for it: "To acknowledge an alien eloquence is indeed to be cut off (or relieved?) from the messy me." Commending McClatchy for "a mind as active as phosphorous," Howard reminds the reader that active curiosity is a prerequisite for imaginative maneuvers, especially in a young poet for whom the world is or ought to be fresh, enticing, perilous, and beautiful.

In an interview in the *Paris Review,* McClatchy looks back on his early work with some embarrassed hesitation:

> I thought poetry was merely language. I thought poems don't mean; they *be* [He is alluding to the famous dictum of Archibald MacLeish]. I thought that a suitably snazzy poetic diction and a complicated syntax would somehow conjure the poem's occasion. I was trying for . . . a weary sophistication? a haughty *symboliste* perch? the revolving disco ball of Stevensian abstraction? In any case, I was writing to show off what I knew—a sure sign of uncertainty, no?

Certainly this is a just estimation of the book's title poem, the most imitative but also one of the book's most successful ones. The young speaker sounds old and tired, wistful, regretful, a kind of James Merrill in the making. Whether the love affair he recounts is real or imagined is irrelevant. From the opening lines readers know they are dealing with a poet whose life and love need to be shared and for whom time and love are the conditions as well as the subjects of poetry:

> I read today through that Book of Ours—
> A night breeze must have paged it back
> Past the empty days since to entries
> With a script as dark as last night's
> Dream of you. Back to the Letter Scene . . .

For the young man love and letters, life and letters, time and togetherness (the clear pun in "Ours/Hours") are interwoven into a complex but elegant fabric.

Many of the poems here, like "Fetish," the first one in the book, deal with objects—as symbols or talismans—or with tourist scenes ("The Pleasure of Ruins"), in which a mysterious "you" often mingles with an uncertain "I." In other words, places, scenes, words, things—all externals—replace or reflect internal states of feeling. Sturm und Drang is repressed, deflected, subdued. The poems overwhelm with both their politeness and their technical mastery. Even young McClatchy, dipping into a suitcase of poetic forms, could write terza rima and rhymed quatrains. It is no wonder that as an impressionable graduate student he was excited by Anne Sexton and her outrageous behavior. The main feelings in his poems seem to be desire and regret; the first line of "From a Balcony" is "I'm out for one last look at something else," as though the tourist is building up a repertory suitable for memory and nostalgia. Occasionally the verbal wit and verbal infatuation undo the propriety of a sentence, as when the mixed metaphor of "Frozen warp, / fired weft of the seasons' / Loom" ("Poplars") peculiarly combines pottery and weaving as ways of seeing an external natural scene.

In his *Paris Review* interview McClatchy acknowledges a fondness only for the book's longest poem (the last to be composed), "The Tears of the Pilgrims," a narrative reminiscence loosely woven around episodes in a theme-and-variations format that he came to prefer for many later, stronger poems. Here are both McClatchy's youthful pretensions (what is one to make of the unspecified scenes, persons, story?) and signs of his future strengths (his characteristic mixture of religion, love, travel, landscape, and introspection builds a complex picture of the relation of self and world).

Stars Principal (1986) begins and ends with two strong, representative McClatchy poems, discussed below. Both deal with the writer and his life, and both suggest the ways in which a literary life is a kind of performance. In between

are more conventional poems about works of art, a garden bestiary entitled "North Country Sketches" (concerning a summer house in Vermont that McClatchy shared with the poet Alfred Corn), and a continuation of the theme-and-variations format entitled "First Steps," in which the literal and figurative first steps of the young, then adolescent, then mature Sandy Mc-Clatchy are complemented by a section in the persona of Walt Whitman, America's first and greatest gay poet. Once again the making of a composite self demands the making of a poetic medley. And as McClatchy confirms in his interviews, what passes for "facts" in autobiography may be true although fictional, in the same way that one constantly threads past selves as well as invented and imagined ones into any present idea of what one is. At the poem's end the speaker opens the pages of his dog-eared copy of the selected poems of W. H. Auden (who becomes a kind of household god in McClatchy's world). He gives a clear indication—literal and figurative—of the intermingling of life and letters:

And between the pages, pressed to that wound
He'd sent his letter to, a wildflower
Itself now paper-thin, a splayed sun-bow—
Covenant with what memory it was meant
To recall? The boy I was? Or the figure
Of the youth I am in this poem? The future
Sometimes seems former lives, or stages
Of a life, drawing them out of the past,
The flashing moment's hasp snapped up.

McClatchy's tones intermingle with those of James Merrill, who in his own chronicles of love and loss details the growth of the artist through time and an exploration of erotic and verbal energies. Always the sedulous student, McClatchy has written a moving poem but still something of an exercise in another writer's style.

Clarity and relaxation are the new notes sounded in the book. "At a Reading," the first poem, broaches a real and important issue about speech and performance. In lambent iambic pentameter it describes a poetry reading during which the speaker sees a young man talking to a young woman. He realizes only after a while that she is deaf and her friend is repeating the poem to her, one line after Anthony Hecht (the performer) has uttered it. He now understands that what he mistook for rudeness is really a version, almost an allegory, of artistic transmission and responsiveness. (It is for this reason that he places the poem first in the volume. It prepares us for all the lessons that follow.) What began as a mere episode of observation ends with a sense of artistic ventriloquism and of our shared humanity:

> . . . And like the girl, I found myself
> Looking at the boy, your voice suddenly
> Thrown into him, as he echoed the woman's
> Final rendering, a voice that drove upward
> Onto the lampblack twigs just beyond her view
> To look back on her body there, on its page
> Of monologue. The words, as they came—
> Came from you, from the woman, from the voice
> In the trees—were his then, the poem come
> From someone else's lips, as it can.

The importance of this poem's position is matched by that of "Ovid's Farewell," the volume's conclusion. Here the Roman poet Ovid (43 B.C.E.–18 C.E.) writes a letter to his beloved wife Fabia on the eve of his departure for exile to the bleak settlement at Tomis on the Black Sea, in the far reaches of the Roman Empire. Taking on the persona of another poet, McClatchy relates a story of universal power. What does or should a poet do? How does he assume the character of other people? Ovid writes:

> We all live someone
> Else's story, so we may know how
> It turns out.

In elegant syllabic stanzas (composed of lines containing 11-9-5-9-9-11 syllables apiece) McClatchy synthesizes his classical education, his continuing explorations of selfhood, his interest in narrative, and his thematic concern with growth, passion, and exile (themes he shares with Ovid). The poem marks his commitment to change (as did "First Steps") as well as to the kind of art poem dealing with static objects he had been writing from the start of his career. As in Ovid's *Metamorphoses*, the more things change the more they either stay the same or become more truly themselves. Ovid's infamous but unknown *error* (the Latin word does not really contain modern notions of criminality) for which he was exiled seems to have been compounded, in McClatchy's poem, of equal parts of lived life and literary efforts. The poem begins:

> What was my fault? A book, and something I
>   saw.
>   The one he never read, the other
>   He was author of.
>   Not his daughter—her adulteries
>   Were with boys from other men's beds, mine
> Merely with women from other men's poems—
>
> But his empire.

Augustus has exiled the poet for both something he may have witnessed and something he may have written. In either case, McClatchy's Ovid makes a confession that hides as much as it reveals. What it asserts is one of the facts that we do know about the poet's life; that a beloved older brother died when young. And it places the brother among the "stars" of the volume's title (borrowed from Gerard Manly Hopkins), the resting place of many of the final figures in the *Metamorphoses* as well. Life leads to stellification through the making of myths and poems. The poem ends:

> Exile—a boy into death, the bit of life
>   Stranded in a song, or its singer—
>   Is the end of our
>   Belief. It comes to pass, the last change
>   As the first, from a stream of star-shot

Wonderment that falls down to our home on
  earth.

It is "our home on earth" that McClatchy, a
thoroughly secular poet, comes to focus upon in
his succeeding volumes.

THE REST OF THE WAY

McClatchy has always been an experimental
poet, not in the more vulgar or misused sense
of that word but in the more accurate and
historically attuned one. That is, he constantly
reaches to find the proper form for any poem
and opens himself to new formal experimentations. In his interview with the poet Daniel Hall
for *Paris Review,* he admits: "I *am* drawn to the
power of tradition. I *do* work in 'conventional'
ways. I prefer formal techniques, and use sonnets and rhyme, any manner of scheme to give
a shape and order—of feeling as well as argument—to a poem." Having learned his craft
while young (Auden said this is the greatest lesson a young poet can claim) and having proved
himself capable of sestinas, pantoums, syllabics,
as well as more garden variety verse forms in
both baroque and straightforward or conversational syntax, McClatchy settles down a bit in
The Rest of the Way, which contains two
important poetic series, each in a different mode.
"Kilim" is a fifteen-part sonnet sequence (each
of the sonnets taking a slightly different form)
that uses a virtuoso style appropriate to the pattern of the titular carpet and also to the interwoven themes of grief, transformation, and history
itself. Originally published in a small edition,
"Kilim" was hailed by Richard Wilbur as "a
remarkable performance, a rich sustained
meditation on the making of order and meaning." The sequence shows—as some of
McClatchy's earlier, artful poems did not—a
perfect wedding of style and vision. The intricacies of the carpet match those of the sonnet,
which is itself capable of multiple combina-

tions. In this sequence the last line of each sonnet becomes the first of the succeeding one, as
though the author were trying to provide an
equivalent to the thread woven into and thereby
becoming the design of a fabric. In the third
sonnet McClatchy cites the similarity between
molecular genetics and artistic production or
between complexities at the micro and macro
levels:

> Nietzsche said the poem is a dance
> In chains. Molecular life enchained by chance?
> The bonds of atoms formulas distill
> Are strains that resonate, the elements
> Held both far together and close apart.

Later, in the ninth sonnet, issues of complicity
extend to a human life and to all of human history:

> When seen and heard as one, a page of text
>   And an urgent voice make up a history—
> Matter, pattern, sources a poem selects.
>   The carpet, too, is a complicity.

Mature artistry requires more than mere flam-
boyance. "Kilim" proves that McClatchy's
poetry has reached a new level.

More impressive than McClatchy's effort at
"complicity" (a well-chosen word for the carpet,
the poetic sequence, and all historical and scenic
intersections) is his other sequence here, "An
Essay on Friendship," done in the easy colloquial mode inherited from the Roman poet
Horace (65–8 B.C.E.). In nine sections composed
of tercets (a form associated with Wallace
Stevens), the poem unfolds from a French
epigram used as a subtitle: "Friendship is love
without wings." Friendship, the most secular
and social of virtues, is also the quality least
discussed by poets. Verse, especially lyric
poetry, is associated with the passions of love,
the chains of Eros with amorous as well as
artistic flights of fancy. McClatchy composed

this poem in fact in the aftermath of the breakup of a love affair. Rather than moan over that, however, he turns to the complex and subtle gratification offered by a different kind of human relationship. Friendship is more grounded, less glamorous than love and consequently more rather than less interesting a subject. The poem interweaves casual observation with personal reminiscence, and it is also a series of responses to Jean Renoir's great tragicomic prewar film *The Rules of the Game,* concerning human relations at an aristocratic country estate during a weekend house party. The comedy of manners, albeit with a tragic, accidental death at its climax, is Mozartean in the expansiveness of its vision and of its sense (voiced by the servant Octave, played by the director himself) that "the one terrible thing / Is that everyone has his own good reasons." McClatchy's poem celebrates tolerance and charity, the virtues promoted by the film, as the touchstones of friendship. He asks a question that readers probably have never before considered:

> Is there such a thing as unrequited
> Friendship? I doubt it. Even what's about
> The house, as ordinary, as humble as habit—
>
> The mutt, the TV, the rusted window tray
> Of African violets in their tinfoil ruffs—
> Returns our affection with a loyalty
>
> Two parts pluck and the third a bright instinct
> To please. (Our habits too are friends, of course.
> The sloppy and aggressive ones as well
>
> Seem pleas for attention from puberty's
> Imaginary comrade or the Job's comforters
> Of middle age.)

The disciplines and pleasures of friendship are therefore appropriate to middle age or at least are most likely recognized by middle-aged persons. (McClatchy was forty-nine when the volume was published.) In friendship one recognizes "different registers" of oneself and one's relationships with others. Each friend reflects a different aspect of one's own "self."

The poem ends "when at last the lights come up" as two friends stumble out of a theater showing Renoir's film, which they have seen countless times before. Like Stevens' "interior paramour," McClatchy's addressee is probably not a real person but a composite figure, superior to the "younger self" who first saw the film:

> He's a friend too. But not so close as you.
>
> He hasn't the taste for flaws that you and I
> Share, and wants to believe in vice and genius,
> The sort of steam that vanishes now above one
>
> Last cup of tea—though I could sit here forever
> Passing the life and times back and forth
> Across the table with you, my ideal friend.

The tones in this poem—subtle, polished, colloquial—represent a perfection of the "middle voice," neither low and coarse nor inflated, hyperbolic, and impassioned, which has become a standard for poetry in the post–World War II generation. McClatchy handles these as well his secular subjects with considerably more finesse than most of his contemporaries.

McCLATCHY AS CRITIC

The generosity of spirit evident in this poem is an equally important constituent of McClatchy's work as a reviewer and critic. Both *White Paper on Contemporary American Poetry* (1989) and *Twenty Questions: (Posed by Poems)* (1998) are more than collections of miscellaneous, fugitive pieces; they illustrate the workings of a literary imagination in the process of defining and making an artist's life. Like all first-rate critics, McClatchy has independent, often unpredictable tastes, which he enjoys asserting in part for their shock value. (He prefers, he says, Mendelssohn to Beethoven, Vuillard to Picasso). Tired of masterpieces for their own sake, he expresses a judgment in favor of more modest artists and tastes. He writes a chiseled prose; he is charitable and clear-sighted at the same time. His tastes are if not catholic at least far-ranging, and he is always deferential to his subjects, never flaunting his own intellect but putting his critical intelligence at the service of his subjects. (This quality has enabled him to do exemplary work as a literary editor of Henry Wadsworth Longfellow as well as Anne Sexton.) He has the appealingly paradoxical quality of a person with self-sureness who can nevertheless transform himself as he writes on behalf of other artists. McClatchy is a subtle, careful reader (witness the two different essays on Alexander Pope and Ben Belitt in *Twenty Questions*); he also provides deft summary appraisals of such underpraised poets as Jean Garrigue and astute criticism of the art of Stephen Sondheim. The standard for all poet-critics in the last half of the twentieth century is Randall Jarrell. If not quite as prescient or hardheaded as Jarrell, McClatchy has a quick, precise touch (and a feeling for the mot juste) that makes readers willing and eager to reread his reviews to register his take on the subject. His prose naturally reflects his own sensibility.

White Paper contains significant reappraisals of Robert Penn Warren, Elizabeth Bishop, Robert Lowell, James Merrill, and others. In all of these essays McClatchy attends to the relationship of a poet's stylistic choices to what might be termed the development of his or her self. As the formal intricacies of the sonnets and the carpet in "Kilim" signified a version of the historical or political world, so the critic's reflections on a poet's work allow him to understand both the writer's inner life and the culture from which he or she emerges. McClatchy can see the contemporary also in terms of literary history. Citing Aristotle's ancient distinction, he says of John Hollander's *In Time*

and Place, a book composed of sections in prose and verse, that rhetoric is the natural counterpart to poetry.

> Freed from the figurative and rhythmical strictures of verse, from everything that we mean by "time" in verse, Hollander can ply the rhetorical (i.e., dramatic and psychological) strategies of formal speech to render more exactly the give-and-take of the mind's serious play in thinking about its problems, both artificial and real. Prose—its format and flow—allows the poet to deal with experience abstracted to his ideas about it, whether those ideas be theories or memories. It is, finally, the mother tongue of parables.

Such elegant summation of complex ideas suggests how lightly McClatchy wears his own learning.

Twenty Questions builds from autobiography and anecdote, through literary analysis and homages to masters, and concludes with a translation of Horace's *Ars Poetica,* that important early chapter in Western aesthetics. The whole constitutes a remarkable coming together of the personal and the scholarly; it evinces the wholeness of a life given to grappling with aesthetic questions. McClatchy relates his own development as a poet, which he here traces in a charming piece entitled "My Fountain Pen," in which "pen" and "penis" turn out to have more than a coincidental verbal resemblance. This autobiography also contains the seeds of its own "ars poetica," since McClatchy clarifies the relationship between his adolescent secrecies (that is, his reluctance to reveal his homosexuality to his parents until such time that they already knew about it) and the inevitable secrecies of any good poem:

> I dream about the three men whom I have loved most, love still, the men whom at the start I kept secret from others because they had so changed my life. Each of these men I have disguised in—or really, transformed into—poems in order to keep hold of them. Like some minor god in an old myth, I've changed them back into secrets. A

poem needs disguises. It needs secrets. It thrives on the tension between what is said and not said; it prefers the oblique, the implied, the ironic, the suggestive; when it speaks, it wants you to lean forward a little to overhear; it wants you to understand things only years later.

A poem both is and is not a piece of autobiography. McClatchy separates himself neatly from the overt theatricality of the confessional poets, at the same time acknowledging the way a poet uses materials from his or her life and hammers them into poems. But since a poem is also a work of art, it is by definition something that demands that readers tease meanings out of it, the best of which may be available only on second or third readings. Readers hear as well, in the remarks above, McClatchy's allegiance to classical aesthetics and also to the norms of politeness associated with well-bred persons; he never equates the "poem" with the "poet" himself or herself, preferring to give the poem a volition and a mind of its own. The poem, not the poet, speaks; the poem, not the poet, asks readers to respond to it. Like so many contemporary poets (both Merrill and John Ashbery come to mind as well as the more politically engaged Adrienne Rich), McClatchy revels in the multiplicity as well as the depth of the human self. And he uses the patterns of his poems as a means of discovering and of making patterns of his own self. In his *Paris Review* interview, he observes:

> The details of one's life should provide the scaffolding beneath which some larger myth is abuilding. I'm after patterns. Nabokov once said that the pattern of the thing precedes the thing. That's what I'm after. The best way for me to speculate about *the self*—about the isolation and anxieties and desires of selfhood—is to start with what I know, myself. But my own life is merely the means towards a different story. In fact, I rarely think of my past as "myself." I can't even remember much of my past: the film is now just a set of unrelated stills. In an odd sense, my younger self is my ghost. I write about what haunts me.

One's past is the basis for one's present (this is what Wordsworth meant when he said "the child is father of the man") and a different country altogether. One both is and is not the same, as one moves through life. A poet owes it to himself or herself and to his or her audience to build a version of his or her self that may include but ultimately transcend mere factuality as it reaches toward the truth of "a larger myth." No good poem retains a one-to-one correspondence with the details of the poet's lived life.

McClatchy's tastes are far-ranging and often surprising. He continues with reminiscences of Anne Sexton and Harold Bloom, his exemplary teacher at Yale. There are two pieces on James Merrill, the first of which ("Encountering the Sublime") nimbly introduces the complexities of this fin de siècle epic to novice readers, and the second, "Braving the Elements" (the title of one of Merrill's own books), is a moving memorial that originally appeared in *The New Yorker* one month after the poet's death. Once again McClatchy's prose tells as much about him as about his nominal subject, not only in its autobiographical reminiscence about their friendship but also in the cultural values and methods that the two poets shared. At the start of his career McClatchy often sounded as though he were imitating Merrill, with his elaborate forms, baroque syntax, world-weary tones, slightly evasive narrative maneuvers, and a fondness for "artful" subjects. The two men clearly shared similarities in upbringing, education, and tastes. But McClatchy takes the measure of his subject carefully, with both fondness and objectivity. Just as in his poetry, he has gradually proved himself no slavish imitator of the master, so in his appraisal of Merrill's life and work he is able to see his subject steadily and whole. What he says of Merrill's first poems applies equally to his own: "The aloof, lapidary glamour of his poems, their dissolves and emblems, were meant both to disguise feelings only dimly known and to declare his allegiance to a line of poets that could be traced from Wallace Stevens back to the Symbolistes." Like Merrill, McClatchy had from the start a syntax that (as he writes of his friend's) "darts and capers."

The translation of Horace ("The Art of Poetry") with which this volume ends brings together McClatchy's training in classics, his appetite for translation and adaptation, his preference for aesthetic principles rooted in common sense and moderation, and his own poetic sensibility. Consider the following simile from the poem's ending:

> Ut mala quem scabies aut morbus regius urget
> aut fanaticus error and iracunda Diana,
> vesanum tetigisse timent fugientque poetam
> qui sapiunt; agitant pueri incautique sequuntur.

> [As when a dreadful itch or jaundice, the illness
>   of monarchs, or
> a frenzied fit or lunacy, Diana's anger, curses a
>   man, so people
> who are wise fear to touch, and run away from, a
>   mad poet; rash
> children tease and follow him.] (My prose
>   translation)

McClatchy captures the epigrammatic sleight of hand that a literal prose translation inevitably misses:

> Sensible men will flee and fear to touch
> The frenzied poet, as if he were infectious—
> Mangy, jaundiced, rabid, even possessed.
> Only children tag along behind to tease him.

The series of adjectives in the penultimate line ("mangy, jaundiced, rabid . . . possessed") replicates the immediacy and concision of the original. More important than the actual success of the translation is the inevitable and perhaps unconscious revelation of the translator's own tastes. It has already been shown how McClatchy as a poet is attracted to both smaller, tighter, more elegant forms and larger, baggier,

or at least more various ones. One may sense his affinity with his Roman forebear when he remarks:

> It may seem odd that a poem praising classical design, and insisting on proportion and unity, should itself resemble a hodgepodge. Coleridge called the poem an "unmethodical miscellany." But that is part of its point, or at least of its fiction. The tone and drift of the poem derive from its being a verse letter. Personality rather than philosophy dominates. It is not a treatise, like Aristotle's.

TEN COMMANDMENTS

In his translation of Horace, as in "An Essay on Friendship," McClatchy implicitly pledges his allegiance to one aspect of the common inheritance from the ancient world, the idea of moderation and the middle voice, one he shares as well with his most important Anglo-American forebear, W. H. Auden. One might find in this a sign of the resignations of middle age. Certainly such resignation is one note—but not the primary one—in McClatchy's fourth book of poems, *Ten Commandments* (1998), which ends with his version (hardly a translation) of Horace's Ode (IV. 1) that begins "Intermissa, Venus, diu / rursus bella moves? Parce, precor, precor." In "Late Night Ode," a poem of flagrant weariness, McClatchy is true to the spirit if not the letter of Horace:

> It's over, love. Look at me pushing fifty now,
> Hair like grave-grass growing in both ears,
> The piles and boggy prostate, the crooked penis,
> The sour taste of each day's first lie . . .

The middle-aged man looks back enviously at his younger self and even succumbs to the temptations of Eros, at least in dreams. He covets his younger self and all the fury of his youth.

Such covetousness, however, is wasteful, indeed sinful. The wisdom of critical hindsight cannot really explain the direction McClatchy has followed in his fourth volume. It comes as a surprise to discover, in someone whose primary temperament has been decidedly and proudly secular, a serious turn toward the Decalogue, the foundational rock of Judeo-Christian ethics. This is not to say that these poems are orthodox or even conventionally religious; instead, they are allegories, sometimes explicit and sometimes covert, of the ethical and moral demands made by a secular man upon himself and his society. The volume possesses a tight organization, although the individual poems exhibit the characteristic variety and occasional looseness of means that McClatchy has always favored. Each of the ten sections—one for each commandment—starts off with a brief, sometimes allegorical introductory epigraph and continues with three poems in different forms or modes, all connected, sometimes opaquely, to the specific rules and prohibitions of the appropriate commandment. Without abandoning his earlier styles and subjects, and maintaining the technical variety he mastered as a young poet, McClatchy achieves in his fourth book a commanding ethical presence.

Here, for example, is the epigraphic opening of section 1 ("Thou Shalt Have None Other Gods But Me"):

"God spoke one and I heard two."
That is, he heard himself as well.
Can what I say be also true?
Shaky grounds on which to dwell.
I'd say that angels still rebel
Against authority. And you?

The initial tone is one of irony, doubt, and duplicity. The first full poem, "Dervish," experiments with doubleness and even tripleness. Composed in the hemistiches associated with Anglo-Saxon verse, "Dervish" depicts the movement of the Turkish mystics in their whirling religious dances as, back and forth, opposites coalesce. Around the rim of the mosque,

a "golden whiplash script" reminds one of writing, movement, the biblical prohibition of graven images, the nature of textuality, and even of Percy Bysshe Shelley's "life, like a dome of many-coloured glass" ("Adonais"). The poem ends:

It is time now to come back
            to the work of creation.
High over the planets
            a golden whiplash script
around the inmost rim
            of today's great dome
calls down: God
            is the light of the heavens,
a niche wherein is a lamp.
            The lamp is in glass.
The glass is a high,
            brightening, constant
star.

McClatchy has arranged a way of presenting unity in multeity and stasis in movement. The Judeo-Christian tradition of the Ten Commandments is supplemented here by the third great religion—Islam—but all are seen as part of a single motive, just as the whirling of the dervishes results in the semblance of dazzling stillness. As an appropriate piece of connection, the second poem in this section ("My Old Idols") is a trio of sonnets, each concerning a different kind of idol or worship from the speaker's past: an older boy, Maria Callas, and Father Moan, the Greek instructor whom the adolescent McClatchy longed to please in class.

Within the strict confines of his chosen subject—the commandments—McClatchy offers various forms, subjects, and speakers. In his first two books of poems he seemed confident, bored, eager, and nervous in equal measure. Here he has at last grown into himself and become a different kind of poet. He retains the technical mastery present from the start and even an easy autobiographical pretense, as in the five-sonnet sequence "My Mammogram," which comes in section 2 (as an example of graven images in the external world or of narcissism in the interior one). Any person, especially when confronting the mortality of the flesh, must ask of himself or herself if the body is the human self or merely one of its several disguises. Throughout the volume McClatchy sometimes offers literal examples of his subjects and sometimes metaphorical ones. In "Thou Shalt Not Steal," for example, "After Ovid: Apollo and Hyacinthus" updates Ovid's homoerotic myth by describing an old poet in love with a beautiful young waiter, who literally steals a pair of cuff links from him, thereby betraying his love:

> To have stolen from one who would give
> Anything: what better pretext
> To put an end to "an arrangement"?

And this is followed by a list of metaphorical "Stolen Hours," twelve epigrammatic haikus:

> Two chapters at night.
> A movie during the day.
> Oh, the sex between!

and then by a haunted homage entitled "After Magritte," a *ghazal* (a Persian form) in which a hallucinatory single-word refrain provides an elegantly surreal touch:

> The sill is clammy to the touch, and the view familiar.
> But doesn't that moon seem a little *too* familiar?
> His severed hand had been in someone's pocket.
> The stars hang perilously above Rue Familiar.
> The whore's pigeons seemed safe under his bowler,
> But when he spotted an opening, the banker grew familiar.

The whole point of the eleven couplets is to borrow (or steal) the obvious and thereby to defamiliarize what is commonplace. The poem is not only an homage to Magritte's weird familiarities but also an allegory of artistic indebtedness.

Because so many of McClatchy's poems deal at one level or another with an artist's life and methods, it is significant that the most capacious poem in the volume is "Auden's OED," whose position in section 9 ("Thou Shalt Not Bear False Witness") is initially hard to fathom. At the heart of this memoir (written in elegiac couplets, alternating lines of eleven and nine syllables) comes a recollection of the speaker's meeting with the man whose work he had long admired. The young McClatchy, sitting literally at the poet's "feet" during a poetry reading in New Haven, approaches him after the event, with an unread copy of his works to sign:

> Suddenly speechless, I counted on a lie
> and told him I knew his work by heart
> and would he autograph my unread copy.
> He reached in his jacket for a pen
> and at last looked distractedly up at me.
> A pause. "Turn around and bend over,"
> he ordered in a voice vexed with impatience
> I at once mistook for genuine
> interest—almost a proposition . . .

But what Auden wants instead is merely to make of the young man a desk upon which to write; years later McClatchy realizes that "he'd been writing / on me ever since that encounter."

Auden's complete set of the *Oxford English Dictionary* indeed passed from him to his lover Chester Kallman, to James Merrill, and then to McClatchy himself. Along with it came an artist's sacred belief in the truth-telling capacities of language. The thematic center of this poem is a version of an age-old truism concerning poetry and veracity. Reaffirming the opinion of Sir Philip Sidney (in his *Apology for Poetry*), McClatchy reminds readers that poetry "never lies because it never affirms," that is, it creates worlds and statements that are parallel to, not identical with, those of our "lived" lives. Likewise,

           the dictionary
  has no morality other than
definition itself. . . .

For a believer in words—in their efficacy and the human ability to misuse them—the dictionary is a Bible. Sitting on it, composing with it, relying on its laws and definitions, a poet finds in the dictionary a mission, a source, and a guide:

    Here is that faraway something else,
here between the crowded lines of scholarship.
    Here is the first rapture and final
dread of being found out by words, terms,
 phrases
    for what is unknown, unfelt, unloved.
Here in the end is the language of a life.

The poem ends with a prayer to Auden (as a kind of patron saint or intercessor) to keep the poet honest, committed to the joint acts of truth telling and truth making:

    Protect me, St. Wiz, protect us all
from this century by your true example.
    With what our language has come to know
about us, protect us still from both how much
    and how little we can understand
ourselves, from the unutterable blank page
    of soul, from the echoing silence
moments after the heavy book is slammed shut.

In this poem McClatchy clarifies his true religion. Whatever his actual reliance on the Decalogue, as a secular poet at the end of a millennium he is conscious of the demands of his artistic vocation.

HAZMAT

Those perilous demands incur increasingly high costs in *Hazmat* (2002), whose title (in spite of what sounds like an Arabic derivation) is an American abbreviation for "hazardous materials." Once again readers find a remarkable blending of autobiographical reminiscence and formal experimentation along with a heightened effort to broach complex moral and historical issues. Once again there's a sense of formality and playfulness that extends all the way from the title of the book to the titles of individual poems. All of them are two-syllable words (mostly trochaic, a few iambic: that is, part 1 has eleven poems, entitled "Fado," "Glanum," "Largesse," "Tankas," "Jihad," "Orchid," "Cancer," "Elbows," "Penis," "Feces," and "Tattoos"; part 2 has "Pibroch," "Aden," "Ouija," and a twenty-part section entitled "Motets"). The volume is divided into two sections. The consistency of the whole suggests the rhythm of a heartbeat—systole/diastole—or countless other dichotomies (on/off, body/soul, yes/no). The book has the heft of both a miscellany (which most books of lyric poems tend to be— accumulated as they often are for the publisher from a writer's work at hand from a certain period) and a unified whole. The rhythm of the individual titles is merely a surface indication of the depth of the poems' wholeness. *Hazmat* is McClatchy's most controlled, schematic collection.

The hazardous materials in the volume include matters of the heart, of the body, and of the creative spirit. In the first poem, "Fado" (a Portuguese equivalent of a blues song), the speaker holds his heart out to someone else and discovers in such action a dangerous enterprise. McClatchy's Catholic heritage, as well as his early fascination with the melodramatic and colloquial work of the "confessional" poets, is evident in his almost baroque image of a bleeding heart:

Suppose you could watch it burn,
A jagged crown of flames
Above the empty rooms
        Where counterclaims

Of air and anger feed
The fire's quickening flush

And into whose remorse
> Excuses rush.

The gift of a heart is never safe or simple. Love has the potential for destruction. The motif of destruction in fact is threaded throughout the volume. The following poem, "Glanum," contemplates the ruins of a Roman town in southern France in an easy trimeter rhythm that McClatchy has inherited from William Butler Yeats and Auden, poets who handled exactly the same theme. After an opening physical description of the scene and an effort to imagine the human activities that took place here, the poet turns away and into some easy conversational reflections:

> We call it ordinary
> Life—banal, wary,
> Able to withdraw
> From chaos or the law,
> Intent on the body's tides
> And the mysteries disguised
> At the bedside or the hearth,
> Where all things come apart.

The archaeological scene interests the poet primarily as a way of getting back into the lives of the original inhabitants. The poem performs an act of imaginative reparation. It also updates an age-old genre (favored by Lord Byron, among others): the contemplation of the ruins of empire. At the end it connects the natural setting, the beauty of the French afternoon and the light falling on the debris, to the relationship between the speaker and his lover:

> How closely it all comes to seem
> Like details on the table between
> Us at dinner yesterday,
> Our slab of sandstone laid
> With emblems for a meal.
> Knife and fork. A deal.
> Thistle-prick. Hollow bone.
> The olive's flesh and stone.

The poem's means—light trimeter couplets, easy diction, a characteristic tone combining accurate observation and airy wonder—achieve a more complex end. The ruins of empire become the occasion and setting for a delicate reconsideration of a human relationship; individual details (knife and fork, olive) turn into "emblems" of the life and decay of love.

The formal variety of these poems is dazzling but, by now in McClatchy's career, somewhat expected. "Tankas" uses the extended form of haiku to comment upon differences between twentieth-century Japan and its more exotic past. (The sequence is itself another example of the dualisms the book investigates.) "Jihad" is a three-sonnet sequence. "Feces" is written in syllabics (4-8-6-4 syllables per quatrain), "Penis" in elegiac couplets. In addition to constant variety in their verse forms, the poems also exhibit McClatchy's far-ranging intellectual curiosity and his ability to shift registers within a poem. The three-part "Cancer," for example, begins with a scientifically accurate description of physical danger (cancer itself as one of the hazardous materials signaled by his title). Its second section expands upon the idea of an individual body by contemplating the plague that decimated fifth-century Athens, and in the third the speaker recounts his reminiscence of his grandmother's death (from cancer) when he was ten. Appropriately the three parts are all sonnets with an ingenious rhyme scheme: the first lines of all three poems rhyme with one another, as do the second ones, and so on.

The three most impressive poems in the first section of the book are "Penis," "Feces," and "Tattoos," all concerned with what are often taken to be secret, shameful, embarrassing, or otherwise unmentionable bodily parts and practices. In the first, McClatchy's typically insouciant wit proves to be not a defense against but a sensible response to the entire range of cultural and psychological anxieties long associated with the male sexual organ. The penis becomes a character in its own right as well as a part of the human body. This is an example of the rhetorical device known as synecdoche, whereby a part stands for the whole. The penis has a will and a life of its own. It awakens with one every day:

> . . . Each man's member every morning
> May be gingerly held and juggled
> Inside his Jockey shorts or lazily scratched
> Through silk pajamas—in any case,
> *Fondled,* its puckered, sweat-sticky, fetid skin
> Lifted off the scrotal water-bed
> And hand-dried as if in a tumbler of air.
> Later, tucked behind the clerk's apron
> Or the financier's pin-stripes or the rapper's
> Baggy jeans, our meek little Clark Kent
> Daydreams at his desk of last night's heroics,
> Hounded by a double life black-mailed
> By grainy color shots of summer-cabin
> Or back-seat exploits that had won praise
> From their pliant, cooing co-conspirators.

(With regard to the relationship of part to whole, it is a nice detail in the passage above that McClatchy uses a plethora of double-barreled words—"sweat-sticky," "hand-dried," "back-seat," and so forth—to maintain the doubleness of the titular figure itself.) Just as McClatchy's other long poems extend the reach of his initial inquiries into a scene, an object, or an event, so too here the poem ends with a symbolic and cultural evaluation of the penis (or with what, as the poet wittily puts it, "it stands for"). All men, whether "small men with big ones" or

> big men with small,
> Lead lives of quiet compensation, power
> Surging up from or meekly mizzling
> Down to the trouser snake in their paradise.

The implicit allusion to Henry David Thoreau's famous remark that the majority of men "lead lives of quiet desperation" extends phallic dreams to larger existential dilemmas, but it is characteristic of McClatchy's style and tone that he never becomes heavy-handed or oppressive in making such connections or indeed in forc-

ing his allusive learning upon readers. The poem ends with a shocking historical detail. When asked why, in the face of mounting casualties, the United States remained in Vietnam, President Lyndon Johnson

> . . . unzipped
> His fly and slapped it on the table.
> "Gentlemen, this is why," he barked. "This is
> why."

LBJ's hawkish macho swagger is on display here, and so is McClatchy's less aggressive but pungent wit. The "it" slapped on the table is, in one way, grammatically uncertain in the sentence above, but in another the reference is absolutely clear: "it" is the sum total of all libidinal aggressions or what Sigmund Freud, using the proper Latin pronoun, would call simply the id.

"Penis" deals with power, "Feces" with creativity. The debts to Freud and Auden are equally clear in this poem. "The nurturing nothingness" that the body becomes is both something and nothing, the site and the evidence of making and unmaking (another sign, in the volume, of pairings). Feces give evidence of past selves, and they are relics to hoard and to worship (as the young McClatchy says he once did, when at nine he saved and stored his in an attic closet, "the clutter now become a shrine / for my little monstrance"). As Freud long ago recognized, they are like money, worthless in themselves but signs of getting and spending, parts of one's natural economies of absorption and gain, followed by expulsion and loss. They are symbols of conversion. The young Sandy hides his droppings but is discovered. The "closet" even becomes a symbol of other (sexual) secrets hidden but predicted and known all along:

> Nothing was lost.
> Within a week the mess had dried
> into a brick the size
> of an idea

arried around
ever since. Capitalism
 thrives on needs satisfied,
  losses thwarted,

  its retentive,
delirious claim to matter.
  Mine was in the closet.
   Discovery

   followed, of course,
and punishment, and worried looks.
  Already she knew what
   I would become.

He would become a gay man but also a compulsive hoarder and recycler of his own physical and psychic energies, in other words, an artist. Bodily parts and awareness of them, followed by the ways one exercises and employs them, open one up to the possibilities of mental, indeed spiritual activities. Through the lightness of his verse (and even in the shapeliness of his little stanzas for this poem) McClatchy broaches complex issues.

The three-part poem "Tattoos" uses two imagined scenes of bodily decoration (the first in Chicago, 1969, when three navy swabs have themselves decorated before heading to Vietnam, the second in New Zealand, circa 1890, when a local prince undergoes the rituals of bodily inscription that signify his ascent to tribal manhood) to surround a discursive middle section that meditates on the uses and history of tattooing. Not only does tattooing distinguish humans from the gods, on one side, and the animals, on the other, but "ornament / Is particularity." An attention to discrete particulars is one of the hallmarks of McClatchy's poetry, and one might also take his mastery of different verse techniques as a version of ornamentation in his work, a means of marking himself as a unique artist. Like a poetic "form," a tattoo signifies individuality and a kind of mask:

Any arrangement elaborates
A desire to mask that part of the world
One's body is.

Like James Merrill and Oscar Wilde before him, McClatchy—as gay man and aesthete—knows that wearing a mask or having an inscription that marks as well as hides is the surest way of telling a truth. To mark oneself indicates a desire to belong to a group (of navy buddies, of any tribe bonded by ritual) and to assert distinctiveness. (Here is another dichotomy in a volume filled with them.) The urge to decorate one's body signifies a need

. . . to fix a moment,
Some port of call, a hot one-night stand,
A rush of mother-love or Satan worship.

In other words, one commemorates a time, a place, a feeling, something that otherwise would vanish except in memory. A tattoo does what a poem also does: it allows one to feel, momentarily, that one has evaded death by rendering at least one part of one's temporal experience immortal. A body changes; a tattoo does not. "But whether encoded or flaunted, there's death / At the bottom of every tattoo" just as death is the final inscription in the writing of one's own life. All of one's energies come to naught, as the moving last lines of this section both assert and combat:

My gifts are never packaged, never
Teasingly postponed by the need to undo
The puzzled perfections of surface.
All over I am open to whatever
 You may make of me, and death soon will,
Its unmarked grave the shape of things to come,
 The page there was no time to write on.

Just as animals mark territory, wearers of tattoos stake out their own claims for uniqueness, and poets inscribe marks not on their bodies but on the blank surfaces of pieces of paper. Eventually mortality catches up with all of them.

The second part of *Hazmat* is a different sort of miscellany. In addition to three individual poems (concluding with an homage to James

Merrill, "Ouija"), the bulk of this section consists of a series of shorter poems grouped under the heading "Motets," most of which concern pain, disease, physical ailments, in other words the "hazmat" of bodily life itself. Each poem is a little scene or vignette that includes a revelation, a small epiphany, an experience of self-enlightenment. The very form of a "motet" (the word is a diminutive of the French "mot") is appropriate to McClatchy's energies here. Usually sacred, a motet is a polyphonic composition sung without accompaniment. So these poems, each individuated, add up to a group containing many voices. The one and the many come together in different keys. Again a sense of polarities controls many of the poems. For example, in "The News," set in Mexico, one finds a newsstand with pornographic comic books:

> Up and down. In and out.
> That old scandal. The flesh corrupted
> with pleasure and punished with more.

It is a nice detail that the last motet, "Two Men," ends with a rhymed couplet (only one other poem in the series, "Hotel Bar," has a similar ending) concerning the years of a couple's relationship:

> May ours together
> fill a future that will have come out right,
> each of us, both of us, brought at last to light.

Hazmat ends with a tribute to James Merrill, whose bizarre semi–science fiction epic *The Changing Light at Sandover* (1982) has been a puzzlement and an irritant since its individual parts began appearing in 1976. For a younger poet like McClatchy, *The Changing Light* is a source of both inspiration and frustration. Many poets have tried to imitate Merrill's tones and verse mastery, and some have even resorted to the Ouija board, which provided Merrill with a gimcrack mechanism in his epic to get in touch with spirits from other worlds and to attempt to plumb the mysteries of the universe at both the microscopic and cosmic levels. Although the style of "Ouija" is often more Merrill's than McClatchy's, the final address to the dead poet, mentor, and friend is one of this volume's most moving sections, as it acknowledges many kinds of hazardous materials—playing with fire by imitating other poets or trying to contact the dead. By extension any contacts with the living may prove equally hazardous.

Thirteen eleven-line stanzas recount the experiment with the Ouija board played by McClatchy and three friends at the master's Stonington house one weekend after Merrill had been called away on a family emergency. The poem concludes with a direct address to the absent (now in two senses of the word) host. JM (Merrill's initials refer to him as a character in his own poem) has "become a voice, letters on a page." He has merged into the characters of the common alphabet. McClatchy has always deferred to mentors—this must be one legacy of his Catholic boyhood—and in "Ouija" he pays homage to an important poetic precursor and close friend. The poems about W. H. Auden and Anthony Hecht seem preparatory exercises for the testimony to Merrill's ongoing influence, even after his untimely death:

> Why will words cohere and dissolve on this
>   blank
> And not their darker meanings, an unspoken grief
> I've reached for and felt sliding as if over
> Poster board smoothed by years of being used
> To giving back the bright presence drawn
>
> Up from within yourself, your starry heart
> So empty, so large, too filled with others
> Not to fear an unworthiness indwelling.
> You took everything on faith but death,
> An old friend's or the breathless lining
> Of any new encounter, so that fresh acolytes,
> Once back home, would remark with wonder
> On your otherworldliness.

Being "filled with others" is one way to deepen an empathetic imagination capable of creating a starry cast of characters, as Merrill has done in his epic and as McClatchy has begun himself to do. In the first part of *The Changing Light,* "The Book of Ephraim," Merrill asks a question that resounds through McClatchy's work as well as his own: "Young chameleon, I used to / Ask how on earth one got sufficiently / Imbued with otherness." Just as one develops a "self" by becoming imbued with otherness, "otherworld-liness" turns out to be the best way of being at home in this world as well. Even after death—or perhaps especially after death—Merrill continues to inspire McClatchy, who says he "*can hear your voice from the other side, / That king-dom-come memory makes of the past.*" Merrill's letters from faraway places, filled with "anec-dotes of love—no, antidotes," prove that stories (or any created art) provide the safest refuge from or cure for the aches and diseases of spirit and body, all the hazardous materials of lived life.

In midcareer McClatchy has never wholly abandoned his status as an acolyte to the masters who meant the most to him when he was still a young man; Auden and Merrill, among the poets, are tutelary deities. But he has also suc-cessfully emerged from the shadows or from under the wings of these precursors to develop his own voice, to express his own concerns, and to navigate the straits of life with control and expertise.

Selected Bibliography

WORKS OF J. D. McCLATCHY

POETRY
Scenes from Another Life: Poems. New York: Bra-ziller, 1981; London: Secker & Warburg, 1983.

Lantskip, Platan, Creatures Ramp'd. Parenthèse Signatures, 1983.

Stars Principal: Poems. New York: Collier, 1986; London: Collier Macmillan, 1986.

Kilim. New York: Sea Cliff Press, 1987.

The Rest of the Way: Poems. New York: Knopf, 1990.

Ten Commandments: Poems. New York: Knopf, 1998.

Divison of Spoils. London: Arc Publications, 2002.

Hazmat. New York: Knopf, 2002.

CRITICISM
Anne Sexton: The Artist and Her Critics. Blooming-ton: Indiana University Press, 1978. (Edited by McClatchy.)

White Paper on Contemporary American Poetry. New York: Columbia University Press, 1989.

Twenty Questions: (Posed by Poems). New York: Columbia University Press, 1998.

OPERA LIBRETTI
A Question of Taste. Music by William Schuman. 1989.

Mario and the Magician. Music by Francis Thorne. 1994.

Orpheus Descending. Music by Bruce Saylor. 1994.

Emmeline: An Opera. Music by Tobias Picker. 1996.

INTERVIEWS
Hall, Daniel. "The Art of Poetry." *Paris Review,* forthcoming.

Stein, Lorin. "Confessions of a Poet: A Profile of J. D. McClatchy." *Poets and Writers Magazine,* January/February 1998, pp. 1–6.

—*WILLARD SPIEGELMAN*

Frank McCourt

1930–

THE FRANK MCCOURT who won fame, accolades, and a 1997 Pulitzer Prize for his best-selling memoir *Angela's Ashes* (1996) was a far cry from the four-year-old Brooklyn-born boy dumped into poverty in the lanes of Limerick in the 1930s. After McCourt, a retired Stuyvesant High School teacher, roared across the best-seller list, he found himself interviewed on ABC, CBS, NBC, NPR, and Fox News by Katie Couric, Ed Bradley, and Charles Osgood. He was sought out for appearances on *The Rosie O'Donnell Show* and *Late Night with Conan O'Brien,* and he spoke at the White House. According to Maura McCay, tickets for McCourt's talk at the 1998 Vancouver International Writers Festival sold in six minutes flat. On McCourt's 1999 book tour for his follow-up best-seller, *'Tis* (1999), one doctor was so resolved to attend a Connecticut book signing by McCourt that, according to the *Publishers Weekly* author Daisy Maryles, the doctor offered "to bribe a bookstore employee with medical service for her child for life in hopes of securing a seat." Years before in Limerick, the McCourt children, at best, would have waited hours at the dispensary merely to procure a docket to see a doctor. Such an irony might have come from the pen of McCourt himself. Yet the seeds of his success—a hunger for betterment and a passion for words—germinate in Frank McCourt's two best-selling memoirs, *Angela's Ashes* and *'Tis.*

Born on August 19, 1930, in Brooklyn, New York, to Irish immigrants Malachy McCourt and Angela Sheehan, Frank McCourt moved to Limerick, Ireland, with his parents and three brothers in the mid-1930s. At age nineteen, McCourt returned to New York City, where he worked emptying ashtrays in the Palm Court lobby of the Biltmore Hotel until he was drafted during the Korean War. Following his army service in Germany, McCourt returned to New York, where he worked in a variety of jobs before using the GI Bill to attend New York University (NYU). McCourt received a teaching degree from NYU and began a successful career as a high school English teacher. After his retirement from Stuyvesant High School in Manhattan, McCourt fulfilled his dream of becoming a writer, first with *Angela's Ashes* and then with his follow-up best-selling memoir *'Tis,* which describes his early years working and teaching in New York City.

ANGELA'S ASHES

Frank McCourt's breakthrough book, *Angela's Ashes,* disarms readers from the start. Before readers have read a paragraph or two, McCourt raises the stereotype of the "miserable, Irish childhood," describes the drunken, "loquacious father" and the moaning mother, and ironizes them. McCourt's tale looks back to how things should have been in his life and contrasts them with how his family really lived in the 1930s and 1940s. The book begins with acknowledgment of his parents' departure from New York, "My father and mother should have stayed in New York where they met and married and where I was born," a departure that seems much like Adam and Eve's expulsion from Paradise. After the wistful nod to what might have been, McCourt chronicles the demons and the hell that followed that expulsion.

Although the memoir begins in regret for children dead, opportunities lost, and places gone, it ends in hope and return. In a CNBC interview with Tim Russert, McCourt explained that he had planned to end his first book with the 1981 death of his mother Angela in New York and the subsequent scattering of her ashes in Limerick (hence the title *Angela's Ashes*), but Nan Graham, his editor at Scribner, advised him to end his book with his return to America and to save the rest of his material for another book (which became *'Tis*). *Angela's Ashes,* then, reverses the cliché of the Irish-born son who leaves for America, dreams of Ireland, and at last returns home to his native Ireland. "Instead"—a word McCourt uses—his first book begins and ends with its hero in America. McCourt's leaving and returning to New York frame the story while his longing for America suffuses it. Within this memoir, the Brooklyn-born son encloses his fifteen years of childhood and young adulthood in Ireland, a time he spent watching James Cagney movies at the Lyric Cinema, living a nightmare of "a miserable, Irish Catholic childhood" in Limerick, and dreaming of returning to America.

Throughout the memoir, McCourt uses deliberate, almost chanting, repetition to intensify both sorrow and humor. For example, in the brief second paragraph of *Angela's Ashes,* he repeats "worse" and "Irish" twice, "miserable" four times, and "childhood" six times. McCourt enhances each rhythmic repetition by layering new ideas or adjectives into the mix. He defuses the sentimentality and confronts the cliché of his own litany of Irish sorrows, "the shiftless loquacious alcoholic father; the pious defeated mother moaning by the fire . . . the English and the terrible things they did to us for eight hundred long years" with anticlimax and irony. "Above all—we were wet."

When young Frank describes his introduction to Leamy's National School in Limerick, McCourt again uses repetition to lace his story with humor:

One master will hit you if you don't know that Eamon DeValera is the greatest man that ever lived. Another master will hit you if you don't know that Michael Collins was the greatest man that ever lived. Mr. Benson hates America and you have to remember to hate America or he'll hit you. Mr. O'Dea hates England and you have to remember to hate England or he'll hit you. If you say anything good about Oliver Cromwell they'll all hit you.

After a brief exposition of his mother's history (it is, after all, Angela's ashes) from her birth to his, McCourt finds his narrator's voice, the voice of a child, and readers see and hear vignettes of the young McCourt's life from ages three to nineteen. Through the wonder of young Frankie's eyes, the reader hears the tale of hunger as the child might have experienced these pitiable moments in his life. Carolyn Hughes, in an interview with McCourt published in *Poets and Writers,* argues that McCourt's device of using the child as narrator "works to soften the tragedy." She explains that the child's "innocent, even lighthearted perspective, without judgment . . . makes room for . . . poignancy and humor." In the same article, Hughes implies that McCourt achieved this perspective by waiting to write his memoir. She quotes McCourt as saying, "It couldn't have happened earlier because I didn't have any kind of balance. . . . If I had written this book thirty years ago, it would have been an indictment, a condemnation—humorless." Thankfully, McCourt's humor makes the tale of his tragic past almost bearable, and readers find themselves laughing with him at his misery. It is no wonder McCourt took half a lifetime to find the voice with which to write *Angela's Ashes.*

If the memoir begins with an expulsion from Paradise, the child's narrative begins with a Cain and Abel story. "I'm in a playground on Classon Avenue in Brooklyn with my brother Malachy. He's two. I'm three. We're on the seesaw. Up, Down, up, down. Malachy goes up. I get off. Malachy goes down." When Frank stands up suddenly from the seesaw, his two-year-old brother Malachy bites his tongue, bleeds, and gets whisked off to the hospital by a pregnant Angela. Young Malachy has golden hair, blue eyes, and pink cheeks, and his mother describes him as "the happiest child in the world." She describes the black-haired, brown-eyed Frankie as having "the odd manner like his father," a description that sets Frank apart from his brothers and haunts him throughout his childhood.

Frank connects his brother's blood to that of a dying dog hit by a car. "Why did the dog die?" he asks his father's friend, Mr. MacAdorey. But the answer, "It was his time, Francis," marks a sharp contrast to the narrator's implication that his sister Maggie and brothers Eugene and Oliver die before their time, victims of poverty and ignorance. After the death of three McCourt children and the miscarriage of another, Dr. Troy in Limerick asks why baby Oliver had not been brought to a hospital. The child narrator recalls: "Dad said he didn't know and Mam said she didn't know and Dr. Troy said that's why children die. People don't know." Frank's complicity in Malachy's injury heightens the sense that the deaths of baby Maggie in Brooklyn and the twins Eugene and Oliver in Limerick were preventable, avoidable, not because it was their "time."

The voice of the child narrator proves particularly effective when McCourt describes his childlike reaction to the deaths of the twins Eugene and Oliver. When the carriage and horse bear the coffin of Oliver to the graveyard, young Frank directs his anger at a jackdaw perched on Oliver's grave. After his father warns him not to throw rocks at the jackdaw "because it might be somebody's soul," Frank thinks when he is a man he will come back and "leave the graveyard littered with dead jackdaws." In the weeks that follow Oliver's death, Frank and his brother Malachy try to amuse the remaining twin,

Eugene, who pines for his brother "Ollie," but six months later Eugene also dies.

In portraying his reaction to Eugene's death, McCourt follows a short staccato paragraph, "He died anyway," with almost a three-page paragraph, which describes the night before Eugene's burial. Mixed together in this child's-eye view, Uncle Pat Sheehan (who had been dropped on his head as a child) sings nonsense words to his song "The Road to Rasheen." Uncle Pa Keating tells stories about being gassed by the Germans and how the gas in his system lit fires in the trenches to boil water for tea during the Great War. After these comic touches, Uncle Pat carefully lowers the baby's body into a small casket. The effect of this short and long paragraph in quick succession works like a high-pitched cry followed by a long, low moan for the dead. The day of the burial, when Frank goes to South's pub to find his father, the image of Eugene's small white coffin with "two black pints" resting on it completes the intertwining of the tragic and comic aspects of this scene.

HUNGERS

More ample than sorrow, death, and even comic irony in McCourt's memoir are depictions of both wonder and hunger. Throughout his narrative, Frank, ever looking for direction, always wonders what to do and rarely gets answers that satisfy him. He speculates, "If you ask a question they tell you it's a mystery, you'll understand when you grow up." In Brooklyn, he does not know what to do when the twins are hungry or when his mother speaks to him sharply after his sister Margaret dies. In Ireland, he wonders about chamber pots and where sheep and cows go at night. He wonders why people say "there, there" to his brother Malachy when he cries. He wonders what to do when a drunken woman in a Dublin cell offers him a piece of butterscotch from her mouth. In his grandmother's house in

Limerick, he looks at a picture of the Sacred Heart of Jesus and wonders why the man's heart is on fire. In the middle of the night, when his mother is sick and his Aunt Aggie says the child is lost, fetch an ambulance, he wonders, "what child is lost because we're all here not a lost child anywhere." Despite his continual wondering, he does not wonder when Mr. Coffey and Mr. Kane, who distribute charity through the Dispensary, question and shame his mother while his father is working in England. After the men make fun of the McCourt name and tease Angela that her husband has taken up with a Piccadilly tart, Frank recalls, "We're all very quiet, even the baby Alphie, because we know what Mr. Kane did to our mother."

Most dramatically, however, McCourt portrays the child's physical hunger for food as well as his emotional hunger for love and attention. Starting from the day of Malachy's accident on the seesaw, Frank remembers his own physical hunger. "I wish I had something to eat," he recalls, "but there's nothing in the icebox but cabbage leaves floating in the melted ice." Frank's early memories are riddled with his own hunger, his brother Malachy's hunger, and the hungry cries of the twins Eugene and Oliver. Years later in Limerick, when he has his first job carrying the dinner pail of his grandmother's border Bill Galvin, Frank is so hungry from the smell of potatoes, boiled bacon, and cabbage that he begins to sample the contents of the dinner pail. His grandmother's punishment for this consists of his carrying the dinner pail for Galvin for two weeks without pay and forcing him to watch Galvin devour his dinner.

In both Brooklyn and Limerick, Frank occasionally even feels compelled to steal to feed his brothers. On the playground in Brooklyn, when Malachy and Frank can no longer distract the twins from their hunger by making funny faces and dropping things off their heads, Frank steals a bunch of bananas from the Italian grocery man. Frank's quandary about how to explain the twins' banana-smeared faces is solved when the grocery man appears at the playground gate with a bag of fruit for the boys. "Gotta bag o' fruit. I don' give id to you. I trow it out. . . . Give them twins a banana. Shud 'em up. I hear 'em all the way across the street." Years later in Limerick, with their father working in England (but not sending any money home) and their mother ill in bed with pneumonia, Frank and his brothers steal lemonade, bread, and marmalade from the big houses of the rich. Malachy tells Frank he has only done "what Robin Hood would have done, rob the rich and give to the poor."

Sometimes when his father has work, his mother cooks "mashed potatoes, peas and ham, and a trifle . . . [with] layers of fruit and warm delicious custard on a cake soaked in sherry," but more often, whether his father works in New York, Limerick, or Coventry, money goes for alcohol, not food. His father's rapacity for "the pint" across two continents keeps the Guinness family in business and impoverishes the McCourts.

In New York, only the charity of the Italian vegetable man, Mrs. Leibowitz, and Minnie MacAdorey keeps the children from starvation. After the death of baby Margaret, with Frank's mother unable to rouse herself and Frank's father drinking in bars up and down Flatbush and Atlantic Avenue, Mrs. Leibowitz brings pea and lentil soup, and Frank wonders why she cannot be his mother. When Minnie MacAdorey arrives with clean diapers and mashed potatoes with butter and salt, Frank wishes that "Minnie could be my mother so that I could eat like this all the time." Later in Limerick, the dole, the Saint Vincent De Paul Society, mounting credit from Kathleen O'Connell's shop, occasional family handouts, and begging for scraps from the priest's dinner feed the children when their father drinks his wages or the dole.

The alcoholism of Malachy McCourt Sr. darkens the lives of the remaining McCourt children and shadows them into adulthood. He holds jobs for only a few weeks, until he drinks his wages, and comes home with whiskey breath singing "Kevin Barry" and "Roddy McCorley," sad songs about fallen Irish heroes. He wakes his sons and urges them to promise to die for Ireland: "Up, boys, up, Francis, Malachy, Oliver, Eugene, The Red Branch Knights, The Fenian Men, the IRA, Up, up." Beverly J. Matiko, in her article "Ritual and the Rhetoric of Repetition in *Angela's Ashes*" (2000), documents seven or more similar recurrences of this event in the memoir and finds at least thirty references to Frank's father's drinking in the first chapter of the book alone. Matiko skillfully delves into the "powerful rhetorical impact" of these repeated nighttime events. She argues for their "status of ritual" in the McCourt family by noting the sameness of the activity, the similarity of the hour of occurrence, the repetition of language and songs.

Repeated rituals should bind families, tribes, or organizations, but Malachy McCourt's disruptive nocturnal ritual wakes the children from sleep and leaves Angela on the side, weeping and complaining. Matiko notes the significance of the breaking of the ritual when Malachy Sr. appears before Easter with a candle, "not as his family's savior but rather as the voice of chaos, perhaps even an antiChrist." For Matiko, the illumination provided by the candle helps break the ritual and allows Malachy's sons to see him with new eyes. Perhaps, even before he lights the candle, Malachy's calling from below changes the ritual. Instead of "Up, boys, up," he calls, "Francis, Malachy, come down here boys, I have the Friday Penny for you." As Angela sobs "with the coat over her mouth," his father's namesake, young Malachy, breaks the ritual. "I don't want his old Friday Penny. He can keep it," young Malachy retorts. The ruckus wakes baby Michael. The young Fenian

Knights Eugene and Oliver, like Kevin Barry and Roddy McCorley before them, have already gone to their graves. Frank tells his father, "I don't want it [the Friday Penny], either," and the ritual is broken.

Despite the breaking of this ritual, Frank cannot completely reject his father, for he loves the moments when Malachy is not in the clutch of alcoholism. He loves most being with his father early in the morning, when the rest of the house is asleep. "In the morning we have the world to ourselves and he never tells me to die for Ireland." Over the fire his father has lit, they drink tea, and Malachy tells him of the old days in Ireland, when masters roamed from ditch to ditch educating children in secret. On nights when he has not been drinking, Malachy tells the children stories he makes up out of his head. Frank has his own special stories his father tells him of Cuchulain, the great Irish warrior from the North, and of the Angel on the Seventh Step who brings babies.

In thinking about these differences in his father, young Frank concludes:

> I think my father is like the Holy Trinity with three people in him, the one in the morning with the paper, the one at night with the stories and the prayers, and then the one who does the bad thing and comes home with the smell of whiskey and wants us to die for Ireland.

Torn between his love for his father and his loyalty to his long-suffering mother, Frank, when his mother sends him to find his father in the pubs after baby Alphie is born, cannot betray his father, even though his father has drunk the five pounds his family sent from the North for the new baby. Instead, he returns home, knowing that "a man that drinks the money for a new baby is gone beyond the beyonds." When the Americans enter World War II, Malachy Sr. leaves to find work in England. Once there, he rarely sends money home (further impoverishing his family because they cannot go on the dole), only occasionally returns to Ireland, and eventually abandons his family completely.

SEARCHING FOR A FATHER

Even before his father leaves for England, Frank searches for other father figures to emulate. With his father gone completely, he looks to the other men in his life to discover what it means to be a man. At age nine, he begins on Friday nights to help his Uncle Pat sell newspapers and deliver *The Limerick Leader*. He makes a princely sixpence hauling papers, but more important, he makes the acquaintance of Mr. Timoney, a blind man who lost his sight as a result of years of service in the English army in India.

Frank earns sixpence reading Jonathan Swift's *A Modest Proposal* to Mr. Timoney on Saturday mornings and forms a special connection to him. "Mr. Timoney is an old man but he talks to me like a friend and I can say what I feel." Frank tells Mr. Timoney his troubles and cherishes his time with him. Before they can read *Gulliver's Travels* together, Mr. Timoney is taken to the City Home. Armed with *Gulliver's Travels,* Frank tries, in vain, to follow Mr. Timoney there to continue reading to him, but when Frank is turned away at the gate, he mourns the loss of both the reading and the man. A few years later, when Frank is in the hospital for badly infected eyes, he meets Mr. Timoney again and offers to read to him once more. Timoney gently declines. "I'm beyond reading," he tells Frank. "I was smart enough to put things in my head in my youth and now I have a library in my head." Out of sight of Mr. Timoney, Frank weeps, but his mother admonishes him. "He's not even your father," she says.

After his own father has left for England, Frank becomes the man of the house and in time gains the opportunity to be a man in his own eyes by having an after-school job. When the McCourt's neighbor Mr. Hannon, who drives the coal float, needs a helper, Frank as-

sists him on the coal float by lugging the heavy bags of coal. Reins and whip in his hands, driving the float horse, Frank flushes full of pride as he passes his classmates after school. When his badly infected eyes worsen with the coal dust and his mother forces him to quit the job with Mr. Hannon, Frank feels he has lost his chance to be a man. He pleads, "I want the job. I want to bring home the shilling. I want to be a man." If Mr. Timoney enforces in Frank the love of reading, Mr. Hannon teaches him pride in his work. During the time they share together, Mr. Hannon becomes as attached to Frank as Frank becomes to him. When Mrs. Hannon confides in Frank that he gave Mr. Hannon "the feeling of a son," Frank's eyes burn, and he does not know why he is crying.

Another father figure, Mr. O'Halloran, the headmaster in Leamy's National School, recognizes talent in Frank and tries to open doors to enable him to continue his education. Unlike the other masters, Mr. O'Halloran seeks to inspire his young charges with a love of learning. "Stock your minds and you can move through the world resplendent," he tells his class. Maura McCay, who heard McCourt give the Duthie Memorial Lecture at the Vancouver International Writers Festival, noted McCourt recalled that O'Halloran, the only teacher who ever encouraged him, thought he had "promise as a writer." Recognizing Frank's cleverness, Mr. O'Halloran urges Angela to send Frank to the Christian Brothers for secondary school, but the teachers there claim they have no room for him and shut the door in his face.

Frank, who at fourteen prefers to start his first job as a man, is relieved, but Angela is furious and warns him not to let a door close in his face again. Aunt Aggie buys him his clothes for his new job in the telegraph office, where he makes a pound his first week. Now playing the role of father himself, Frank takes his younger brother Michael to see *Yankee Doodle Dandy* at the Savoy Theatre and for fish and chips and lemonade at the Coliseum Café. Although after his first week of work he seeks to gratify himself and treat his brother, he soon realizes his need to take a longer view of his future, and he decides he has to begin to save his money to return to America.

An ever-present father substitute, Uncle Pa Keating represents to Frank all that is independent in man. Having served in the Great War, Uncle Pa is confident in his manhood and does not give a "fiddler's fart" about others' opinions. He is able to go to the pub and have just one pint, he keeps his steady job in the gas works, and he manages to coexist fairly amicably with Frank's fractious Aunt Aggie. The night before Frank's sixteenth birthday, Uncle Pa takes Frank's father's place and buys him his first pint. "I know 'tis not the same without your father," he tells him. "'Tis what I'd do if I had a son." Pa Keating also warns Frank not to take the exam to become a permanent telegram boy. Instead he tells Frank he should get out of Limerick and go to America. Because of Uncle Pa, Frank seeks out a different job and increases his resolve to save money to leave Ireland for America. Through his kindness and no nonsense approach to life, Uncle Pa is instrumental in helping Frank realize his dream.

In one of his infrequent letters from England, Malachy Sr. writes to say he will be home for Christmas. The children trudge to the railroad station with Angela and wait for train after train until long after midnight. When the man in the signal tower offers the children sandwiches and cocoa, Frank wishes he had a father like that. From all these father figures Frank learns to break his father's ritual. Through these different father substitutes, Frank can imagine other ways to live and be a man.

The most positive trait Frank takes from his father is his love of words, and *Angela's Ashes* is awash with songs, poems, movies, plays, and books of every kind. Frank cherishes memories of his father telling stories and helping the children with their assignments. His father makes up stories about people they know in the lanes and places them in foreign lands with exotic animals. And however painful may be the memory, he recalls his father's many sad songs about dying for Ireland. He also remembers that people came from all over the lanes to have his father write letters for them.

Frank also remembers his mother's singing "Any one can see that I wanted your kiss" when his father has a job and brings home his wages. And he recalls her singing "The Nights of the Kerry Dancing" to her old friend Dennis Clohessy, sick in bed with consumption. When Frank recovers from typhoid fever in the hospital, he exchanges poems and songs with a dying diphtheria patient, Patricia Madigan, who recites most of the poem "The Highwayman" for him one verse at a time. She lends him a book about English history that he devours, but the nuns move him to another floor before Patricia can finish reciting the poem to him. She dies before he learns the end of the poem and the outcome for Bess, the landlord's daughter.

From the English history book Patricia gave him, Frank memorizes two lines of Shakespeare: "I do believe, induced by potent circumstances / That thou art my enemy." For the sheer love and beauty of the words, he repeats the two lines over and over to himself like a mantra. Reciting Shakespeare, Frank thinks, is "like having jewels in my mouth." Seamus, one of the attendants at the Fever Hospital, promises to discover the end of "The Highwayman" for Frank. Although he never learned to read, Seamus learns the final verses of the poem from a man in a pub, memorizes them, and recites them for McCourt. Frank encounters Seamus again when he returns to the hospital with sore eyes. Then Seamus recites "The Owl and the Pussy Cat" for him, a poem that Frank had not wanted to hear from Patricia Madigan but that he welcomes after her death as a way of feeling close to her again. Another hospital attendant finds more books for Frank, and feasting on words, Frank reads his way through *Tom Brown's School Days, The Amazing Quest of Mr. Ernest Bliss,* and the works of P. G. Wodehouse.

After months in the Fever Hospital, Frank at first is not allowed to move up to the sixth grade in school. Instead, he must stay in the class with his former master, Mr. O'Dea. But Frank's own way with words saves him from the embarrassment of spending another year in fifth grade, in his younger brother Malachy's class. To taunt Frank, his teacher tells him to write a composition showing how much he learned the year before. When O'Dea assigns him to write about what would have happened if Jesus Christ had been born in Limerick, Frank composes his story "Jesus and the Weather." In this story Frank argues that Jesus would not have wanted to have been born in Limerick with the River Shannon that kills because "he'd catch consumption and be dead in a month and there wouldn't be any Catholic Church." At first, O'Dea quizzes Frank, repeatedly asking him if his father has written the assignment, but Frank tells him no. Overwhelmed by the poignancy of the young McCourt's composition, O'Dea quickly moves Frank into the sixth grade.

Frank further deepens his love for Shakespeare and other playwrights when his grandmother's blind neighbor Mrs. Purcell receives a government radio. He sits outside Mrs. Purcell's window on Sunday nights listening to plays on the BBC. When Mrs. Purcell's daughter invites Frank inside their house, she and her mother listen with Frank to Shakespeare, George Bernard Shaw, Sean O'Casey, and Henrik Ibsen, as Frank gets an education in dramatic literature. He loves all the playwrights, but his favorite remains Shakespeare. For Frank, "Shakespeare is like mashed potatoes, you can never get enough of him." After they hear the plays, Frank and the Purcells listen to news of

the world. On the American Armed Forces Radio, they hear Duke Ellington and Billie Holiday, and Frank dreams again of returning to America.

A dark period in Frank's life, his family's move to his mother's cousin Laman Griffin's, is relieved only by Frank's access to the library. Laman sends Frank off to walk the two miles to the library with his library card and a letter asking the librarian to allow Frank into the adult part of the library. One rainy day, Miss O'Riordan, the librarian, invites Frank to stay inside and read *Butler's Lives of the Saints.* Intrigued and titillated by harrowing accounts of virgin martyrs, Frank rushes back and forth between the dictionary and the *Lives of the Saints* as he tries to decode sexual mysteries. Unaware of the reason for Frank's sudden interest in saints, Miss O'Riordan writes to Angela praising Frank's interest in saintly matters. He revels in his reading for months, until Miss O'Riordan catches him with an inappropriate book. Realizing Frank's true interest, Miss O'Riordan confiscates Laman Griffin's library card, and Frank's library days are over in Limerick.

Frank discovers that, like his father, he has talents as a letter writer. Mrs. Finucane, who lends money to people in the lanes to make purchases in stores, hires Frank to send threatening letters to the poor people who owe her money. Frank makes his first money as a writer by writing powerful letters with impressive words like "inasmuch." The letters frighten people into paying their bills, Mrs. Finucane continues to pay Frank, and he begins to seriously save money in his post office savings account to buy passage on a ship to America.

When Frank is sixteen, following his Uncle Pa's advice, he leaves his job delivering telegrams. Answering an advertisement for "A smart boy wanted," he goes to work for Easons Ltd., where he helps distribute newspapers and magazines. As he rises in the ranks at Easons, he has time to read *The Irish Times, The Times of London,* and other Irish and American newspapers and magazines. Although he never had the opportunity to attend secondary school, he stores his head with knowledge as he keeps dreaming of America. Living mostly on his love for words, McCourt somehow survives the child's hunger for food and love; the adolescent's hunger for respect, dignity (and perhaps a little sex); and the man's hunger for work, opportunity, and a little "peace ease and comfort."

By age nineteen, Frank has finally saved (and pilfered) enough money to book his passage on the *Irish Oak,* sailing from Cork to New York. The night before he leaves the songs, poems, and stories of Ireland behind, his mother Angela throws him a "bit of a party." In a rhythmic litany of sorrow and laughter, Uncle Pat sings his nonsense song "The Road to Rasheen," Angela tearfully sings "A Mother's Love Is a Blessing," and Aunt Aggie claims that the lunar eclipse, predicting the end of the world, is a bad omen for Frank's going. "Oh, end of the world my arse, says Uncle Pa," who always puts things into perspective. "'Tis the beginning for Frankie McCourt." Within days the Brooklyn-born son with the Irish tongue sails into New York Harbor to claim his dreams.

After its publication in 1996, *Angela's Ashes* in its hardback and paperback forms remained on best-seller lists for over three years. It received the Pulitzer Prize for biography, the National Book Critics Circle Award, the *Boston Book Review*'s Non-Fiction prize, the Abbey Award, and the *Los Angeles Times* Book Award. *Time* and *Newsweek* magazines both named it the best book of the year, and it became available in eighteen countries. In 1999 a major motion picture of the memoir, directed by Alan Parker and starring Emily Watson and Robert Carlisle, was released.

'TIS

The nineteen-year-old Frank McCourt depicted at the end of *Angela's Ashes* sustained himself on dreams of America. Following a night of sexual freedom in Poughkeepsie and flush with hope, the young McCourt stands on the deck of the *Irish Oak* with the ship's wireless officer. Together they look out at the lights of America, and when the officer asks, "Isn't this a great country altogether?" McCourt's answer, "'Tis," becomes both the final chapter of *Angela's Ashes* and the title of his second memoir. Of course, McCourt had planned and dreamed of sailing into New York Harbor rather than into Albany, so the realization of his long-held dream begins with a disappointment. Even though the outcome of *'Tis* implies that this is a "great country altogether" right from its opening pages, McCourt's second memoir reveals the tension between the dream of America and its reality.

Although *'Tis* did not receive the same effusive critical acclaim as *Angela's Ashes,* it was well received and spent considerable time gracing best-seller lists. Instead of the present tense of the child narrator in *Angela's Ashes,* McCourt's adult narrator uses a combination of past and present tenses. This technique carries forward the immediacy of *Angela's Ashes* but adds a retrospective feeling of longing and regret. As McCourt narrates his picaresque journey of maturing adulthood across two continents, the faults and missteps are his own rather than his father's. At times, the sad and comic adventures he experiences and the vivid characters he encounters seem random and disparate, but they are all, in fact, linked by the gap between the dream of America and its reality, the clash between competing cultures, Frank's continued search for father substitutes, and his quest for self-fulfillment in reading, teaching, and finally writing.

Despite the disappointments Frank encounters in America (like his sailing into Albany), he begins his entry into U.S. culture and life wide open to American delights and experiences. In Albany, where Frank's boat docks, the Irish priest Frank meets on the boat takes him for lemon meringue pie and coffee. It is Frank's first taste of lemon meringue pie, his first taste of America, and he loves it. On the train to New York City, he sees college students, and by the time Frank arrives in Grand Central Station, he is already dreaming of becoming a "student somewhere in America, in a college like the ones in films." In his struggle to become one of these students, he spends years overcoming obstacles.

PURSUING THE DREAM

Because he is Irish, Frank receives a job through the Democratic Party on the recommendation of the priest he met on his trip to America. Frank's first job emptying ashtrays and cleaning up in the lobby in the Palm Court of the Biltmore Hotel is considered a prestigious plum for a new immigrant. But the Palm Court is full of college students his own age, and Frank is ashamed of his houseman's uniform, dustpan, and broom. Andrew O'Hehir, in his *Salon* review, describes *'Tis* as a "painful immigrant's journey of loss and reinvention." He sums up the theme of McCourt's second memoir as "adulthood, and especially manhood, isn't all it's cracked up to be." O'Hehir compares McCourt's experience as a new immigrant, "lonely and uncertain, he works at menial jobs and lives in rooming houses," to that of his own Dublin-born father. In fact, McCourt's immigrant experience resonated with thousands of readers.

While working at the Biltmore Hotel, McCourt experiences another crack in his American dream when he becomes aware of racial prejudice and class consciousness. If he ranks below the college students and even the Palm Court waiters, the Puerto Rican workers in the kitchen of the Biltmore Hotel, who wear aprons and wash dishes, rank well below him. They give him leftover food from the kitchen and offer to teach him Spanish, and Frank admires their spirit. He knows, however, that he has "opportunities for advancement" they do not share and that he makes $2.50 more a week than they do merely because he is Irish and because a priest recommended him to a Democratic Party boss.

Despite his Irish American job, Frank finds it hard to get by financially in New York City. His job at the Biltmore pays $10 a week. He keeps $5 for himself and sends $5 to his mother in Ireland. He undergoes personal privations to send money home to his mother, but he has some comfort in knowing the money he sends home to Ireland allows his mother and brothers to have a goose rather than a pig's head for Christmas. After a while, he makes another $10 a week and gets his breakfast free for cleaning out toilets for the Greek owner of a diner on Third Avenue. The owner cannot understand why Frank, who can speak English, is not pursuing an education, but a flare-up of Frank's old eye infection puts him in arrears $2 for special soap, $2 for a haircut, and $10 for ointment. Left with almost no money for himself, Frank receives mounting requests from Angela to send additional money home to Ireland.

Even though many obstacles block McCourt's path, father figures in America continue to support and encourage his desire for learning and education. During his first weekend in New York, before his Biltmore Hotel job begins, Frank saunters into Costello's, an Irish bar. The proprietor, Tim Costello, sends Frank off to the New York Public Library and tells him not to come back until he has read Dr. Johnson. "Read your Johnson, read your Pope. . . . Don't come back here till you've read *The Lives of the English Poets*." At the library, Frank goes "weak at the knees" when he sees the "miles of shelves" and knows he can stay there and read as long as he wants. Later he goes back to the bar with his library books, but Costello tells him, "You don't have them in your head so go home and read," and he does.

Frank's love of reading and for the written word, his longing for an education, and finally, his desire to write himself, all remain constant as he navigates the tricky shoals of American life. Even on the boat from Ireland, he begins to read Fyodor Dostoyevsky's *Crime and Punishment* rather than introduce himself to rich American travelers. The only book he brings with him from Ireland is the *Complete Works of Shakespeare,* which he bought in Limerick with half his weekly wages from his job delivering telegrams. His love of Shakespeare, however, involves him in a Charlie Chaplinesque misadventure.

Despite his dreams or, perhaps, because of his overeagerness to see them come true, Frank fumbles and often does not know how to act or what to do as he tries to pursue his life in America. In a memorable comic sequence in *'Tis,* Frank tries to realize too many aspects of his dreams at one time. When he notices that Laurence Olivier's film of Shakespeare's *Hamlet* is playing at the Sixty-eighth Street Playhouse, he decides to have a memorable evening enjoying his favorite Shakespeare on screen, drinking ginger ale, and eating his favorite American food, lemon meringue pie. Unlike the audience at the Lyric Cinema in Limerick, patrons of the Sixty-eighth Street Playhouse must not bring their own food into the theater, so Frank smuggles his pie and ginger ale in under his black raincoat.

Inside the theater, his carefully planned evening begins to unravel. First, another man tries to molest him in the theater, so he leaves to go to the men's room. There he has difficulty opening the ginger ale bottle without a church key. Trying to open the ginger ale, he breaks the bottle in the men's room and cuts himself. During this confusion, a man rushing into the men's room smashes Frank's pie box. Finally,

an usher arrives, complains that Frank is getting blood all over the men's room, notices the raincoat, insinuates he is a molester, and forces Frank to leave the theater and miss the movie. Like a greedy child, he wants all of his delights at one time, and he ends up missing them all. He wonders "why America is so hard and complicated that I have trouble going to see *Hamlet* with a lemon meringue pie and a bottle of ginger ale."

Wherever he travels in New York, Frank still longingly watches college students with books under their arms. In his boardinghouse lodgings, he reads as long as light is available. When his landlady make him put his light out, he closes his eyes and uses his imagination to picture his past life in Limerick. Only being drafted during the Korean War saves Frank from the Biltmore Hotel and the boardinghouses. He continues to help his mother and brothers by signing over his army allotment to Angela, and the American GI Bill eventually enables him to get a college education.

Through all the places he travels with the army, Frank continues to seek out good literature to read. He finds a copy of *Crime and Punishment* in an army hospital and finally completes the book he began on his crossing to America. Posted to Germany, he learns more about American ways by mingling with Italian American and Jewish American enlisted men. Sent on laundry detail to Dachau, McCourt is haunted by the atrocities committed there by the Nazis during World War II. He touches the ovens, says a prayer for those who perished there, and finds himself, for once, unable to eat. "I take my tray with the bowl of Hungarian goulash and bread to the table by the window . . . but when I look out there are the ovens and I'm not much in the mood for Hungarian goulash anymore and this is the first time in my life I ever pushed food away."

Being stationed in Germany enables Frank to visit his mother in Limerick for the first time since his departure. When he goes back to Ireland, he wears his corporal's uniform, feels good about himself, and wants to be admired as a Yank. He expects his mother to be in the new house he has provided for her with his military allotment, but she is still living in the lanes in her mother's house with his Uncle Pat. Unable to understand her attachment to her old life, he quarrels with her, checks into the National Hotel, and feels ashamed. Finally, he convinces her to move into the new house with electricity and hot and cold running water. "The minute she steps into the hall the paleness goes from her face and the sharpness from her nose," and she offers him a nice cup of tea.

Although he reconciles with Angela, Frank is still plagued by past demons and resentments toward both his parents. Angela urges Frank to visit his father and his father's aging mother in the North. When he arrives in Belfast, Frank, at first, is happy that his father and grandmother think he looks "grand" in his uniform. Soon, though, he cannot stand the way the father who abandoned his family puts on the "air of one in the grip of sanctifying grace." And he cannot stand the way his grandmother speaks ill of his mother for living with her cousin Laman Griffin after she was evicted for nonpayment of rent from the rooms she had shared with Malachy. Though years have passed, Frank still blames his father for abandoning his family. Angry and bitter and unhappy about his own anger and bitterness, Frank quarrels with his grandmother, hitches a ride, and returns to his mother in Limerick before heading back to Germany. There he consoles himself until his discharge by reading Herman Melville's *Pierre, or the Ambiguities* in the army hospital and by reading books by Zane Grey and Mark Twain from the army base library.

Discharged from the army, Frank moves into a boardinghouse with other Irish Americans, puts his desire for an education on hold, and pursues the American dream by making "good money" unloading trucks at a warehouse. In his search for a father figure, Frank is drawn to Horace, a black man who at lunch "sits away from the rest of us" and "smiles once in a while and says nothing because that's the way it is." A Jamaican dockworker, Horace is a positive father figure for Frank, just as Uncle Pa and other men before him were. When Frank and a friend go out for a beer with Horace, they discover that Horace is not welcome in some bars just because of his color. Frank admires the man and hates the racial prejudice of their ignorant coworkers. Frank does not understand why Horace takes their abuse, but the older man has higher goals. His son is in college in Canada, and Horace sacrifices and works for his son's future and success. The Jamaican also urges Frank to use his GI Bill to go on in school and to make something of himself. Going to school becomes Frank's renewed dream, just as going to America had been his old dream, a dream that had not solved all his problems. At this point, however, attending college remains only a vague dream fluttering in the corners of his mind, a dream he seems incapable of making tangible.

Merely making money at the warehouse neither contents nor fulfills Frank, and he becomes restless "because there's nothing in my head but confusion and darkness." In an attempt to improve himself, he accepts a white-collar job as a Blue Cross trainee (where he lies that he has a high school education), but he is not satisfied with life in an office either. Returning to the warehouse, he makes $75 a week until he is laid off and takes a job hauling meat at Merchants Refrigerating. There his platform boss, Peter McNamee, another father figure, also tells him he should be going to school and using his GI Bill, but he feels trapped without a high school diploma. One day when work is slow, the workers at Merchants Refrigerating are allowed to go home early, and Frank wanders into the White Horse Tavern on Hudson Street. He has "read in the paper it's a favorite place of poets, especially the wild man, Dylan Thomas." Disgusted with himself, Frank reconsiders his life, finds it wanting, walks out of the bar, and keeps on walking until he finds himself at the admissions office at NYU.

Impressed by his knowledge of literature, the kindly dean of admissions allows Frank to enroll in two classes, Introduction to Literature and History of Education, despite his lack of a high school degree. Frank is alternately praised and humiliated by his professors. His Introduction to Literature professor praises his love of Jonathan Swift but criticizes his "simplistic approach to literature." When he first enrolled in NYU and bought his textbooks, Frank eagerly covered them with NYU's purple book covers, but now he puts his books away in his bag because, he thinks, "I make a fool of myself in my first literature class and I wonder why I left Limerick at all." Though discouraged, Frank continues reading, persists in looking up words like "existentialism" in the dictionary, and searches the *Encyclopedia Britannica* for information about famous Irish writers like William Butler Yeats and John Millington Synge.

During the summers, while attending NYU, Frank works in the Bakers and Williams Warehouse, and one day he runs into the dockworker Horace again at lunchtime. They sit together side by side outside on the piers, and Frank promises himself that he will never forget the day they shared a ham and cheese hero sandwich and a quart of Rheingold. Frank urges Horace to fight the prejudice of the men he works with, but Horace tells Frank that he chooses his fights. When Horace calls Frank "son," Frank tears up as he did over Mr. Hannon and Mr. Timoney in *Angela's Ashes.* "Tears are dropping on the sandwich and I don't know why, can't explain it to Horace or myself." When Horace gives Frank his large white handkerchief, Frank knows he will keep it forever. To Frank, Horace

is often "the father I'd like to have even if he's black and I'm white."

Throughout his own struggles, Frank continues to see to the needs of his family in Ireland. Years before, Frank had sent money to bring his brother Malachy to America. Like Frank, Malachy had joined the service and provided Angela with his allotment. With Malachy sending his air force allotment to keep Angela "comfortable in Limerick," Frank can, at last, afford to send money to bring his brother Michael to America. In Limerick, Frank's younger brother Alphie attends the Christian Brothers School, where he will be the first in the family to have the opportunity to complete his high school education and where "he can have an egg every day if he likes." After his arrival in New York, Michael works until Malachy leaves the service. When Michael enlists and signs his allotment over to Angela, Frank has three years in which to focus his energy on providing for himself and completing his education at NYU.

After his initial struggles, Frank makes strides at NYU, receives praise from his English Composition lecturer Mr. Calitri for a composition about his bed in Limerick, and falls in love with Alberta (Mike) Small with her "blonde hair, blue eyes, luscious lips, a bosom that is an occasion of sin." Alberta represents everything in America he is not and has not had—the high school prom date, regular meals, little white window curtains, and Protestant ways. She finds his Irish accent "cute," and he is hopelessly smitten with her. With Alberta, Frank is torn between his mother's admonition to stick to your own kind and his desire for her American beauty and all it represents.

Everything in her that is different from him alternately excites and repels him. Mostly, he does not really understand her and her family and their ways. For these reasons, their relationship is almost always in conflict. When she takes him to her father's apartment, for example, he cannot understand their lack of hospitality.

Her father and grandmother ignore him, do not ask him to sit down or offer him a cup of tea. He does not understand, either, why she does not seem to protect him in this environment, why she leaves him standing alone in the room with her grandmother and her father. He thinks his "mother in Limerick would never leave anyone standing in the middle of the room like this . . . because in the lanes of Limerick it's a bad thing to ignore anyone and even worse to forget the cup of tea."

Frank and Alberta continue to clash over their cultural differences, and they have a horrible falling out when he will not wear a tie to a cocktail party. He wants to go downtown to the Village and talk where "men with beards and women with long hair and beads are reading poetry in coffee houses and bars." She prefers to go uptown to cocktail parties with people who "join the country club, play golf and drink martinis." She tells him that "all the men will be wearing ties. You're in America now." He cannot bend to her will, so she hails a taxi and goes on to the party without him. Separated from her, all he can think of is "Mike Small, blonde, blue-eyed, delicious, sailing through life in her easy Episcopalian way." He is intrigued by her otherness, but she worries that he has too much wildness and disorder in him to be caged in a neat little life. Eventually, they reconcile, marry, and have a child, but their cultural clashes inevitably draw them apart. Years later, when his marriage disintegrates completely, Frank thinks of his mother's advice to stick to his own kind.

TEACHING WRITING

When Frank finally completes his degree at NYU, he wants to teach English, but his accent and appearance prevent him from getting a teaching job in the suburbs. When a teacher retires suddenly midterm, he begins his teaching career in a vocational high school. His life as a teacher seems not only different from that of the masters in Leamy's National School but also different from all his expectations. He is not prepared for the students' lack of respect for teachers, and he does not expect the cynicism of the experienced teachers. He does not count on either lunchroom duty or the amount of bureaucracy he must deal with on a daily basis. While he makes a measly salary as a teacher, Malachy and Michael are living the high life uptown in Manhattan running bars.

After all Frank has suffered to get his education, his brothers' success, making more money tending bar and living carefree lives, tempts him to turn his back on teaching, its low pay, and its difficulties. He does not, though, because he thinks that after a night of "serving drinks and amusing the customers" he would accuse himself of "taking the easy way" out. His vocational students resist all his efforts to educate them until, in the back cupboard of his classroom, he finds his teaching salvation, old stories by former students. The essays written by his current students' fathers and uncles and mothers and aunts—some of whom died in World War II—intrigue his students. He gives them back their history, and he learns to teach from his students.

With his teacher's salary and the money he makes working for a finance company in the summer, Frank can afford to visit his mother in Ireland again. In the airplane he can see that "the river gleams silver and the fields rolling away are somber shades of green except where the sun shines and emeralds the land." Living in a boardinghouse when he first arrived in New York, Frank closed his eyes and dreamed of Limerick, but now Limerick has changed. Many people he knew have died or emigrated. There is less poverty. "No barefoot children. No women in shawls." He feels like a visitor to Limerick, a man who belongs neither in America nor in Ireland, still an outsider.

Becoming a father connects Frank to the world. After his daughter Maggie is born, he visits Ireland once more and feels comfortable there, inside his own skin again. He even visits Belfast and wants to walk the streets as the troubles burst around him. He loves his mornings with Maggie, just as he loved his mornings with his own father. He loves to hear her "talking dream talk" and asking him questions. He wants to be a Kodak Dad, documenting every American moment of Maggie's life, but his marriage crumbles. He still cherishes walking Maggie to school, but when she is almost eight, she wants to walk to school with her friends. Frank separates from his wife, and Maggie, like Frank McCourt himself, grows up without a father in the house.

Despite difficulties in his personal life, Frank experiences success as a teacher. He is offered an opportunity to teach night classes to adult paraprofessional women getting two-year associate degrees at New York Technical College in Brooklyn. For these African American and Hispanic women, education is the "only road to sanity." Their stories and determination inspire McCourt, and he approaches teaching with renewed vigor. Before long, he lands a job teaching creative writing at the prestigious Stuyvesant High School. He uses the students' own mythologies of cartoons and nursery rhymes to excite them about writing, and his comparison of Bugs Bunny to Odysseus inspires lively discussions.

Even though he is successful as a teacher, McCourt covets a space on the wall at the Lion's Head, where the framed book jackets of writers hang. "At the Lion's Head you had to prove yourself in ink or be quiet. There was no place here for teachers and I went on looking at the wall, envious." In her *New York Times* review of *'Tis,* Maureen Howard comments, "If the Lion's Head still faced the tail end of Sheridan Square, its walls would be papered

with . . . McCourt's memoir. . . . Here's the fellow who can prove himself in ink."

McCourt's mother's death in New York in 1981 and his father's death in Ireland in 1985 begin to settle old scores. Flying to his father's funeral in Belfast, he remains conflicted between "the life of misfortune" his father inflicted on his mother and the mornings like "pearls" he shared with his father. After his retirement from teaching, McCourt begins his life as a writer. Writing *Angela's Ashes,* he told Carolyn Hughes, finally got "that toxic stuff out." *'Tis* ends as he had first planned for *Angela's Ashes* to end, with the scattering of Angela McCourt's ashes in Limerick.

WRITING AND THE MEMOIR

The writer Jonathan Greenberg, a former student of McCourt, recalls that McCourt in the Stuyvesant classroom followed no "fixed format," but his class on any day might include "his ride on the subway that morning, the purpose of life or his lamentable salary." His first comment on Greenberg's high school story, "too slick and glib," was followed by "awkward, trite, irrelevant conclusion. You dragged it by the ears" and "Do you keep a notebook?" McCourt kept inspiring Greenberg and the other students to dig inside for material, and Greenberg was finally rewarded with "excellent last line. Skillful narrative, energetic, lively." Greenberg sums up his experience of McCourt's class: "I became a writer that year, and have remained one ever since." McCourt has attracted a wider audience for his advice about writing. Keep scribbling, he tells audiences. Write down lists.

Describing his writing process to Hughes, McCourt said he kept journals for years before he began writing in earnest. "All the time I was a writer not writing, just jotting things down in notebooks." Composing in longhand on one side of a notebook, he wrote *Angela's Ashes* in less than a year. Following the advice he gave his classes, he kept the left side for comments about "what he needed to dig deeper into."

McCourt's choice of the memoir form was deliberate. In "Frank about Memoirs," Brendan O'Neill quotes McCourt describing the difference between autobiography and memoir: "An autobiography is an attempt to bring up all the facts, and to stick to them, faithfully and chronologically. But a memoir is an *impression* of your life. If an autobiography is like a photograph, then a memoir is like a painting." Four months before the publication of *Angela's Ashes,* the *New York Times* devoted its entire magazine section to the literary memoir. In his introduction to that issue, Jame Atlas proclaimed that the "triumph of memoir is now established fact." Great Britain had seen a glut of memoirs in that country after the publication of Nick Hornby's *Fever Pitch* (1992). Memoirs of presidents and all the presidents' men (and women), sports figures, major and minor celebrities and their hangers-on are certainly not new. What sets McCourt's memoirs apart, and sent grandmothers scurrying to the attic to find their dusty diaries, is that millions of people have read his memoirs not because of *who* he is but because of the powerful story he tells and the magic of his telling it. Living in Rome, Frank McCourt is at work on his third memoir.

Selected Bibliography

WORKS BY FRANK McCOURT

BOOKS
Angela's Ashes: A Memoir. New York: Scribner, 1996.
'Tis: A Memoir. New York: Scribner, 1999.

OTHER WORKS
A Couple of Blaguards. New York, 1977. (Two-man, two-act cabaret act, coauthored with Malachy McCourt, and also acted with Malachy.)

The Irish . . . and How They Got That Way. Produced by the Irish Repertory Theatre, New York, 1997. (Musical review. Early version, *Irish Stew,* performed as one-man show, Minneapolis, 1992.)
"Introduction." In Tony Hendra, *Brotherhood.* New York: Sterling Publishing, 2001.

CRITICAL AND BIOGRAPHICAL STUDIES
Atlas, James. "Confessing for Voyeurs: The Age of the Literary Memoir Is Now." *New York Times Magazine,* May 12, 1996, section 6, p. 25.
Bing, Jonathan. "Mass-marketing Memories: Publishing Memoir's Mania." *Writer's Digest* 77, no. 10:48 (1997).
"Fighting Irish." *National Review,* October 26, 1998, p. 40.
Gingher, Robert Sterling. "Out of the Ashes: The Voice of a Child in Limerick Returns Transformed into That of a Young Man Finding His Place in New York City." *World and I* 14, no. 4:255ff. (April 2000).
Greenberg, Jonathan. "Reflections on Creative Writing Class: The Taught." *New York Times,* April 14, 2002, section 4A, Education Life Supplement, pp. 23–24.
Howard, Maureen. "McCourt's New World." *New York Times Book Review,* September 19, 1999, section 7, p. 1.
"Irish Books: Angela's Offspring." *The Economist,* February 27, 1999, p. 83.
Kirtz, Bill. "Out of the Mouths of . . . (Memoirist Frank McCourt's Child's Voice)." *The Quill* 86, no. 3:8 (1998).
McCay, Maura. "Living His Wildest Dreams McCourt Rises from the Ashes." Celtic Connection (www.celtic-connection/lit/mccourt-12-98.html), December 1998.
Matiko, Beverly J. "Ritual and Rhetoric of Repetition in *Angela's Ashes.*" *Michigan Academician* 32, no. 3:289ff. (2000).
Maryles, Daisy, and Dick Donahue. "McCourt Leads the Court." *Publishers Weekly,* October 4, 1999, p. 19.
O'IIehir, Andrew. "America the Brutal." *Salon* (http://www.salon.com/books/feature/1999/08/31/tis), August 31, 1999.

O'Neill, Brendan. "Frank about Memoirs." *Spiked* (http://www.spiked-online.com/Articles/0000 0002D136.htm), June 21, 2001.

Ottaway, Celine. "Frank McCourt, Memoir Mania." *Albany Times Union,* March 6, 1999.

Smith, Patrick. "What Memoir Forgets." *The Nation,* July 27, 1998, p. 30.

INTERVIEWS

Hughes, Carolyn T. "Looking Forward to the Past." *Poets and Writers* 27, no. 5:22–29 (September–October 1999).

Mosle, Sara. "Talking to the Teacher." *New York Times Magazine,* September 12, 1999, p. 57.

Russert, Tim. "McCourt Discusses His Book *Angela's Ashes* and Events of His Life." CNBC. Lexis-Nexis, March 16, 1997.

FILM BASED ON A WORK OF FRANK McCOURT

Angela's Ashes. Directed by Alan Parker. Paramount, 1999.

—MARY ELLEN BERTOLINI

Sue Miller

1943–

*I*N THE YEARS after the publication in 1986 of her first novel, *The Good Mother,* Sue Miller has established herself as one of America's premier writers of realistic fiction. To have published one's first novel at age forty-three surely figures as a late start; Miller's career is impressive in that she followed up *The Good Mother* with several more strong novels and a collection of short stories. All her books take the family as their central subject, invariably experienced and analyzed through the eyes and voice of a woman, more often than not a divorced parent. In itself this choice of subject and protagonist is unexceptional, even potentially narrowing and constricting. But Miller has triumphed over such limitations by creating and exploiting a remarkably flexible narrative voice, so that *listening* to her fiction is an essential component in apprehending it. She has also taken care to avoid adopting a solemn or overly pious attitude toward her subjects; she eludes the trap of solemnity by remaining alert to ironies, to the possibility of humor in even the gravest of situations. The narrative presence stays alert, probing, restless, rather than settling into one or another affirmation. A similarly restless and explorative spirit can be felt in her familiarity with American places, the cities and small towns—real and imagined—where her stories play themselves out. Cambridge and Boston, Chicago and San Francisco, along with small towns and summer places in Vermont and Maine, are among the territories she writes about with love and knowledge. When a character gets to go to Paris it is very much an exception to the general rule.

Along with these qualities informing her "family" realism is a stylistic conservatism that is likely, for some readers at least, to seem as much a liability as an asset. That is, coming late in the twentieth century, she writes as if both modernism and postmodernism, vague as those terms are, simply were not to the point of her project, perhaps did not even exist. The experiments and verbal audacities of James Joyce, Marcel Proust, William Faulkner, or Virginia Woolf seem to have held no more attraction, as styles for her to emulate, than the exertions of contemporary fabulists like Thomas Pynchon, John Barth, and Toni Morrison or laid-back minimalists like Raymond Carver and his progeny. (Some of the stories in her single collection do have affiliations with the deadpan minimalist impulse to say little and say it tonelessly.) Although her prose sometimes rises to "poetic" intensities of expression, it almost never resists our intelligences by attempting to be difficult—to strain against the limits of language by way of hinting at truths beyond words. If you can't say it, you can't whistle it either, it was said apropos of Ludwig Wittgenstein; something like this commitment to intelligible though complex statement is the lifebone of Miller's enterprise.

Nor do her novels, even as they frequently move among generations and different time periods, exhibit the willful narrative disruptions of a writer she admires, Alice Munro. Munro is primarily a writer of stories, but one has the impression that the difficulties, waywardnesses, and confusions those stories present are significant in constituting—at least to some readers—something deeper and more serious than Miller's relatively direct presentation. Munro's narratives, like those of other contemporaries—Maureen Howard and Marilyn Robinson come to mind—are sometimes oblique and make more critical work for the reader than do Miller's lucid continuities. There is as well the possibility that the success of her novels, especially *The Good Mother* and *While I Was Gone* (the latter, published in 1999, was selected by Oprah Winfrey's book club), may have influenced reviewers to moderate their praise, figuring that anyone this readable must have artistic limitations that keep her out of the top drawer. If such condescension exists, it is misguided and the result of not thinking hard enough about how Miller's stories make their distinctively satisfying imprint. Her very lucidity, that is, presents a challenge to the critic of fiction.

SOME BIOGRAPHICAL FACTS

Sue Miller was born on November 29, 1943, and grew up in Chicago as Susan Nichols, the second child of four born to James Hastings Nichols, an ordained minister who taught church history at the University of Chicago and Princeton Theological Seminary, and Judith Beach Nichols, a homemaker. Her father and both her grandfathers were Protestant ministers, and the generally ecclesiastical cast of this heritage helped instill in her what she has spoken of as "strong ideas of right and wrong"—of life as consisting significantly of "moral patterns." A bookish adolescent, Miller got good grades, skipped her senior year in high school, and at age sixteen entered Radcliffe College (now Harvard). She majored in English (she took a single course in creative writing) and graduated with a B.A. degree in 1964 but has said she was overwhelmed by college and learned little. Her years at Radcliffe coincided with the opening up of new possibilities for expression and disruption in both the life and art of the later

1960s, and this period would figure significantly in her novels.

Soon after graduation she married a medical student and in 1971 gave birth to a son, three years after whose birth she was divorced. During her marriage Miller worked to supplement her husband's medical school expenses: among her jobs were teaching high school, waitressing, modeling, and doing laboratory work for research on the behavior of rats in mazes (*The Good Mother*'s heroine has such a job). After divorcing, she worked for eight years as a teacher in day-care centers and parent cooperatives, and she earned a master's degree from Harvard in early childhood care. (She also earned M.A. degrees from Boston University in creative writing and from Wesleyan University in teaching.) In 1979 she was awarded a fellowship in creative writing from Boston University, and her first published stories—in *Ploughshares,* the *North American Review,* and the *Atlantic Monthly*—followed soon after. It would be wrong, however, to assume that her decision to become a writer was an abrupt one, since she had been writing all along—stories, as well as a couple of discarded novels. An honorable mention from Pushcart Press in 1984 for her stories, and a Bunting Institute Fellowship from Radcliffe during the period 1983–1984, led to the publication of *The Good Mother*. In 1984 she married the novelist Douglas Bauer (they later divorced) and lived with him in Boston while teaching at various academic institutions—Boston University, Massachusetts Institute of Technology, Tufts. But the years beginning in 1986 have been mainly characterized by the steady work that produced those books to which we now turn.

THE GOOD MOTHER

Miller's first novel was an enormous success, remaining for weeks on the best-seller list. (Its eventual sales in paperback would exceed one million copies.) She was fortunate in working with Harper & Row's canny editor Ted Solotaroff, who was assiduous in getting prepublication copies of the book into the hands of experienced reviewers. She herself recalls being "startled" by the book's success: "It changed my life quite literally," she says in an interview with Ron Fletcher. "It was like what getting tenure used to mean: Now that you're safe do something brave." Although she refers here to the freedom to experiment she felt in writing *Family Pictures,* the 1990 novel that would succeed *The Good Mother,* it should be said that her first novel is also a brave book that has not lost its power to compel.

Throughout her career Miller has been willing, even eager, to discuss her writing in interviews, as if the chance to respond to questions helped her think about what she had done as a novelist. She called her first novel a "corrective" to her previous (unpublished) ones, in that it had a plot: and there is no doubt that *The Good Mother* proceeds in an orderly fashion with its events causally linked, its transitions from one moment to the next clear and apparent. But many novels fulfill such "plot" demands while exhibiting little of Miller's capacity to engage the reader. As for the novel's content, it seems to have developed out of a principled idea: she had become dissatisfied with "a number of postfeminist novels which suggested that all you need to do is shed your husband and then you enter this glorious new life of accomplishment and ease," she told *Publishers Weekly.* One may presume that in her own life, "shedding" her first husband did not automatically issue in a glorious life; but more to the point is her reference to unnamed novels by women that appeared in the 1970s, which were written to illustrate such a liberation. The decade was one in which divorce in America became more common, doubtless helped along by the formation of women's groups dedicated to exploring possibilities for female life other than being a good spouse and mother. Miller went on in *PW* to comment almost disapprovingly on the assumptions of her novel's heroine, Anna Dunlap, "a person who thought she could make her life like someone else's, who thought she could be in control of her life." For Miller this seemed "a false thing to believe in this world."

From the beginning of the novel, this thematic idea is fully apparent, indeed flatly named in the narrative. Thinking about the future, after she and her husband, Brian, have filed for divorce, Anna feels happy:

> The divorce seemed to me a fine, brave thing to do. I had a sense, a drunken irresponsible sense, of being about to begin my life, of moving beyond the claims of my own family, of Brian, into a passionate experiment, a claim on myself. Somehow, in this vision, I romanticized Molly into a sidekick, a companion, Robin to my Batman.

This is of course a vision ripe for comeuppance, and its characterization by the first-person narrator as irresponsible romanticization is forthright and unambiguous. The events of the novel are, if anything, all too confirming of the heroine's irresponsibility. Anna's taking on a lover, Leo Cutter, with whom she discovers passionate sex, leads to the careless if almost inadvertent exposure of her daughter to such matters and to the husband's bringing suit against Anna for custody of Molly. In the resultant court battle, which Anna loses, her belief that "she could be in control of her life" is revealed as dangerous blindness. If anything, the novelist runs the risk of a too self-righteous and punitive disposal of her heroine.

In fact the novel does not feel that way because—and this will be the case as well in Miller's later books—the first-person voice is an expansive and hospitable one, inviting us not only to listen carefully to its rhythms and tonal inflections but also to try them on, try them out, as one might inhabit the voice of a speaker in a lyric poem. The beginning of chapter 4, describing Anna and her daughter settling comfortably into their Cambridge apartment and neighborhood, may suggest the easy range and resourcefulness of narrative presentation:

> Now began a period of real ease for us, of finally moving into our new life in Cambridge with some sense of ownership. It was the ugliest time of year for the part of town we lived in—winter. The few lindens on our street stood black and hopeless once their leaves had fallen, their brutally pruned limbs exposed in awkward V shapes around the looping telephone wires. The snow fell and stayed and turned black with car exhaust, carbuncled with dog shit. The vast potholed parking lot at the Porter Square shopping center grew dirty mountains of plowed snow at its periphery, down which the tough kids of the neighborhood slid on stolen garbage can lids or plastic trashbags.

She and Molly take long walks together, stopping in various stores on Massachusetts Avenue that, in their ugliness, their "very lack of distinction appealed to me, comforted me, just as my shabby furniture did." In such passages readers are interested less in what Anna is feeling and how it fits into the developing story than in the authority of Miller's writing as it presents, unerringly, the particular look of a Cambridge locale—in this case Porter, not Harvard or Central, Square. In other words the novelist asks us to care about things other than the moral state of her protagonist.

We also care about, indeed are amused by, Anna's capacity for pointed observation, given the shape of humorous formulation by Miller's neatly crafted sentences. As a novelist she has never been praised for her humor, and admittedly she does not go in for comic scenes. But her observations are often sharply ironic, as seen in two moments from Anna's career as a piano teacher (along with running rats at the laboratory, she gives lessons to seven students). One of her students is Mr. Nakagawa, who "played every piece very slowly and precisely in a dynamic range stretching from forte to

mezzo forte. But every week, on his own terms, he mastered whatever I assigned him and played it soberly, loudly, exactly as he'd played whatever piece I'd assigned him the week before." This satire is so quietly effective as to be virtually unobtrusive—one need only know that the dynamic range from forte to mezzo forte is a narrow one. Or there is Ursula Hoffman, who becomes Anna's friend and shares with Anna the trials of her chaotic sexual life. During one piano lesson, after Ursula has confided an episode involving oral sex with her latest lover, she turns back to the keyboard: "With the first note struck, her foot slammed down on the loud pedal, and there it stayed, taking an occasional ill-timed breather, until the piece was over. The air swam with blurry notes." When Anna tactfully suggests she play the passage without pedal, Ursula replies "Oh, that fucking pedal. . . . Did I have it down the whole time?" Granted these moments occur relatively early in the novel and act as comic relief from the increasingly somber story in which Anna finds herself featured. But aside from demonstrating musical savvy on Miller's part, they exhibit her credentials as an ironic spirit who every so often enlivens the steadier, more self-concerned tone of the narrative. Like the local observations of Cambridge life, such moments deflect from and qualify the potentially melodramatic strain of a life that is moving from proud self-sufficiency to painful dependence.

Of course what made the novel a best-seller was something rather different than its command of place and ironic voice. There is, for example, the terrifying scene early in the book, when Anna leaves Molly in the car, is detained on her errand, and comes back to find her daughter shuddering and exhausted. Then there are two moments in her sexual relationship with Leo, one presented as it happens, the other emerging only later on. In the first of these, Anna allows Molly to come into bed when she and Leo have just finished making love; in the second, which Anna learns about from Leo only after her husband has begun legal proceedings, Molly questions Leo (who has just showered) about his penis, asks if she may touch it, and is allowed to do so. These two mistakes in judgment, as Anna later admits they were, are the crucial factors in the judge's decision to award custody of the daughter to her father; they are also crucial in turning Anna away from her lover, "betraying" him insofar as she agrees to the court not to see Leo again if her daughter is given back to her.

Such relatively sensationalistic details drive a plot that focuses on the anguished mind of the heroine. They also invite critics of the book to direct their commentary too exclusively at Anna's character as it survives both the loss of her child and her lover, and as she embraces the difficult role of being a "good mother" when visitations rather than daily proximity become the conditions of her life with Molly. One of these critics, Roberta White, concludes her essay on the novel with the following formulation: "Even though Anna loses custody of her child, her sad history affirms the value of private over public values, of love over law. Inwardly, she recoups some of her loss, at least to the extent that she retains a rich sensibility and is not embittered." There is nothing really mistaken in talking this way except that it ignores aspects of the novel that make it larger and more interesting than the record of a struggling individual sensibility. Miller herself, while being properly grateful for the book's enormous success, said in an interview with Shirley Nelson that she worried about being typecast forever as a "domestic" writer when in fact her books also contained "explorations of legal, medical, and political ideas about the self— about ourselves and how we conduct ourselves." These "broader concerns" she felt had not received as much attention as they deserved.

Apropos of such concerns, Miller in her acknowledgments to the novel says she con-

sulted books on custody cases, expert witnesses, and family law. This research bears fruit in Anna's remarkably telling conversations with her lawyer, Muth; with the psychologist Dr. Payne (brought in by Muth as an expert witness); and in the trial tactics of her husband's lawyer. Although quotation cannot bring out the gathering impact of these institutional vocabularies (the law, the medical, the sociological) as they impinge upon the good mother's good intentions, they demonstrate Miller's curiosity about the way things work in the larger world. These ways are often (inevitably?) not in accord with the moral idealism of the protagonist, and they will be further explored in the novels following *The Good Mother.*

The other way of moving beyond narrative claustrophobia—made use of by Miller in all her books—is to situate the protagonist in a larger, generational story. So *The Good Mother* begins with Anna and Molly on a short vacation in a New Hampshire backwater that reminds Anna of her grandparents' house in Maine. Over the course of the novel she will make three trips to that house, the last of which is to borrow money for the expenses of her trial. And even before the main action of the book begins—the love affair with Leo and its consequences— Anna's adolescent life with her parents, and her summer visits to two very different sets of grandparents, have grounded her in a history, solidly specified.

The Good Mother is reluctant to conclude itself and probably goes on a bit too long as, after the decision goes against Anna, she first engages in a potentially suicidal car journey (she has procured Leo's gun and buries it in the sands of Newburyport, Massachusetts), then in a move to Washington to be closer to Molly (whose father and stepmother have moved there), then in a return to Boston, where Anna's story ends in a modified acceptance of the diminished future. But the book has essentially concluded itself with the judge's adverse decision—the real work of the novel is accomplished. And that work is the joint effort of novelist and reader, so when, on the back cover of a paperback edition of *The Good Mother,* it is hailed as "one of those rare novels you live more than you read," we may remind ourselves that this is an illusion. It is Miller's achievement rather, in this fine first novel, to make us forget, at least part of the time, that we are reading words on a page artfully arranged to bring us up against life.

SHORT FICTION: *INVENTING THE ABBOTTS*

Published the year after *The Good Mother,* Miller's first and only collection of stories solidified, if it did not much extend, her talents and reputation. *Inventing the Abbotts* (1987) consists of eleven stories, of which the title story is by far the longest as well as the most interesting. (It was originally published in *Mademoiselle,* although its protagonist is male.) The ten years or so previous to Miller's short story collection had seen the emergence of such practitioners in the mode as Ann Beattie (*Distortions,* 1976), Raymond Carver (*Would You Please Be Quiet, Please?* 1976), and Bobbie Ann Mason (*Shiloh,* 1982). For all their differences, these writers were concerned with rendering the lives of unremarkable, often rather inarticulate and aimless people with less-than-heroic careers and problems. The characters are presented in an unjudgmental, deadpan way that results—especially in Beattie's case—in a mannered feel to the prose. A few of Miller's opening sentences from stories in *Inventing the Abbotts* may suggest similarities with such literary presentation, as well as the expectations readers are invited to entertain about characters: "Tyler loved women. He was in love with women" ("Tyler and Brina"); "There were seven slides, and Georgia was naked in all of them" ("Slides"); "Charlie Kelly was her eighth lover since the divorce" ("Expensive Gifts"); "Alan watched Jody bending down to get something out of the refrigerator" ("The Quality of Life"). The stories are populated with single parents, spouses who have remarried, confused children—with unheroic people destined for anything but a tragic fate. In the main, however, Miller refrains from making her characters the butts of critical, satiric humor; she does not, as do Beattie and Carver on occasions—create her people only to demolish them.

But carefully observed and skillfully put together as these stories are, it is only the title one that is likely to endure as a rereadable piece of fiction. This may be due merely to the fact that its length—thirty pages, rather than the usual ten of the other stories—gives Miller room to expatiate and muse on things in a manner close to that of her novels. "Inventing the Abbotts" is also to be distinguished, in its narrative presence, from Miller's other fiction in that Doug, the first-person speaker, is male, his subject the behavior of his older brother, Jacey, as it plays out in relation to each of the three daughters of the Abbott family. Within the upper-middle-class world shared by the narrator's family and the Abbotts there is an important difference as laid out in the opening paragraph:

> Lloyd Abbott wasn't the richest man in our town, but he had, in his daughters, a vehicle for displaying his wealth that some of the richer men didn't have. And, more unusual in our midwestern community, he had the inclination to do so. And so, at least twice a year, passing by the Abbotts' house on the way to school, we boys would see the striped fabric of a tent stretched out over their grand backyard, and we'd know there was going to be another occasion for social anxiety. One of the Abbott girls was having a birthday, or graduating, or coming out, or going away to college. "Or getting her period," I once said to my brother, but he didn't like that. He didn't much like me at that time, either.

The midwestern milieu, later to be contrasted with the east (the narrator goes off to Harvard), recalls F. Scott Fitzgerald, and it may even be that Miller, in creating the friendly, informal, and expansive voice heard here, wrote with an eye toward that predecessor. Closer to home is the presence of John Cheever, whose work Miller admires and whose story "Goodbye, My Brother" has affinities, both in subject and style, with hers.

In many ways "Inventing the Abbotts" is an anomaly in her work and not just because of its male protagonist. The leisurely, controlled, slightly detached and amused atmosphere generated by the recollecting narrative voice in no way suggests the more intensely pitched, "psychological" style of *The Good Mother* and of Miller's later books—although parts of *Family Pictures* are comparable. That she ceased to write stories probably had to do with nothing more than how busily she was getting on with the job of being a novelist, and we need not regret the scarcity in her work of the kind of shrewd, agreeable observation that comprises this short tale: the kind of accomplished fiction represented by the title story—and in less expansive, more detached ways by others in the collection—added little of originality to what was occurring in the work of her predecessors and contemporaries. (Russell Banks's 1986 collection, *Success Stories,* is a book into which "Inventing the Abbotts" would have fitted neatly.) At any rate, by the time *Inventing the Abbotts* was published, Miller had launched herself into the writing of her longest novel, *Family Pictures,* a book that took her four years to complete.

FAMILY PICTURES

Although she toyed with two other titles—"The Cure" and "Perfection"—for this "family" novel into which she wanted to get everything, the eventual title was the right one. Nina Eberhardt, the fourth child of six in an affluent family in Chicago, is a photographer and, by virtue of the narrative pages spoken through her, is the Eberhardt family member we get to know best. But inasmuch as the real photographer is Sue Miller, her title well suits a novel that, unlike *The Good Mother,* is not the least plot-driven, with a narrative quite unlike the intensely focused story that is Anna Dunlap's. The pictorial metaphor bids to impart coherence to a sprawling book about a big family. Miller set out, she told the interviewer Don Lee, to write "a kind of plotless, shapeless book that was a speculation on the meaning of suffering and the twentieth-century explanations for it—religion and psychiatry—and the floundering we do with those traditions." With seventeen chapters in all, *Family Pictures* is divided into two parts; its span of years ranges from 1954 to 1979, with three undated chapters (including the opening and closing ones) occurring in Nina's present imagination. Instead of following an orderly progression, the novel jumps back and forth within the twenty-five years treated and also moves between third- and first-person narration.

The book begins cleverly and arrestingly with Nina recalling to us a moment in time—her brother Mack's fourteenth birthday—when her other brother Randall (later revealed to be autistic) utters, as if out of nowhere, the words "Happy Birthday, dear Mackie." Nina's sister Liddie, eldest of the children, is enthusiastic at Randall's contribution but is quickly cautioned by their father David, a psychiatrist, that she need not get excited since "that's about his annual quota of words, isn't it?" Lainey, David's wife, then makes a face that reflects her sadness at this deflationary comment. This is the way it happened, yes? But no: Nina's mother later tells her that Randall never spoke after the age of four and that the memory is Liddie's, appropriated by Nina who at the time was only an infant. Yet, Nina tells us, "it seems as clear as a picture I might have taken. I could swear this is exactly what happened." She proceeds to generalize:

But that's the way it is in a family isn't it? The stories get passed around, polished, embellished. Liddie's version or Mack's version changes as it becomes my version. And when I tell them, it's not just that the events are different but that they all mean something different too. Something I want them to mean.

With fine economy we are introduced to the eight members of the family (Nina's two younger sisters, Mary and Sarah, were not yet born when Randall uttered his words about Mackie) and to conflicting tones of voice: David's ironic medical-professional debunking; Lainey's wordless vulnerability; the articulate and rebellious Mack and Nina; and at the center of things the silent Randall, whose influence on the family is the pivot on which the book turns.

David wants to put Randall in some sort of institutional setting with the possibility of curing him (in the 1950s Bruno Bettelheim ran such an "orthogenic" school), whereas Lainie wants to and succeeds in keeping him at home. In an attempt somehow to atone or compensate for her "fault" in bearing the autistic Randall, Lainey has three more children while David increasingly detaches himself from her and begins to have affairs, eventually leaving the household. He returns when Randall physically assaults his mother (Randall is then, finally, sent away) but leaves again for good when the children are more or less grown up. The adolescent lives, replete with much "acting out," of Mack and Nina are featured, with a good deal of accurately stated details from the late 1960s scene in Chicago—as in this passage describing how Mack hangs around blues clubs in the black ghetto and smokes marijuana with his friends:

For a while their smoking had an exciting quality to it, had seemed wonderfully dangerous and alien just because of its association with those places, those rhythms. The first long hit of the stale-tasting smoke would call up for Mack the dim, cigarette-clouded interior of Pepper's and that new music—pickup a cappella groups, visiting pros, bands full

of old men with Delta accents so thick Mack just waited for their laughter to cue his own, helpless to understand them.

The passage is typical in its density of specification—Miller's trademark—that makes her family pictures so pictorial. The novelist knows whereof she speaks and knows what places look like and voices sound like. When Nina fears she is pregnant, she leaves home, takes a bus to Columbus where her lover is teaching at Ohio State, and registers the impact of a new city:

Later Columbus began, and was reassuringly like Chicago in its outer stretches—the black neighborhoods, the sturdy, squat houses and apartment buildings. But then she was shocked by the downtown area, which was shuttered and deserted. Blocks of storefront windows were blank, or backed with ripped paper, or soaped. Here and there was a spot of neon, a bar. But there were no restaurants, no hotels, none of the life Nina thought she could step into.

The year is 1970; the downtowns have departed.

From a novel with many strong and memorable scenes, one might single out a chapter titled "The Party," at the end of which David leaves home. The year is 1963, with a social atmosphere reminiscent of John Updike's *Couples* in which the young marrieds-with-children entertain one another with food, drink, parties, and the sexual connections that flower from these activities. In "The Party" an Updike-like event is presented through the eyes of Nina and her sisters who, in their pajamas, are allowed to observe the flirtations and disappointments from the vantage point of the top of the stairs. There is also a powerful and painful chapter in which Mackie, having dropped out of Harvard, argues with David about his future— the Vietnam War making such a decision more than usually important. And in a scene that touches the tragicomic note, Nina goes out on the town with Mack and his friends, smokes pot, then comes back with them to strip the wallpaper from Randall's empty room (he has by then been institutionalized), finally to be discovered by David, whose psychoanalytic cool is put to the test by this aggression.

Family Pictures lives in such scenes and perhaps lives at the expense, over the longer run, of narrative continuity and accumulated power. A mainly sympathetic reviewer of the book complained nevertheless about a "mechanical" feel to it; there was too much "explaining," wrote Crystal Gromer: "Reading *Family Pictures* is a little like sitting around the Thanksgiving Day table, too full, listening to the endless stories that are supposed to enable you to catch up on what other family members are doing." This seems a fair complaint to register: do we need a flashback to David's parents and how he grew up in southern New Hampshire? Do we want, late in the book, to be given full details of Mack's unhappy marriage? There is a related too-muchness at certain moments in Nina's first-person narrative, when fifteen pages before the novel concludes we find her contemplating her face in the mirror in these terms: "My face was pretty, I think, but not with that open, eager expression a girl has. There was something sad in it. I saw that I'd changed, in spite of the way I had thought of myself, in spite of everything I'd done to stay safe from time." Yet a reader who finds Miller's language here simply not inventive or hard-working enough to pass muster might recall that any narrative of a certain length, as Randall Jarrell observed, is going to have something wrong with it, and we should remember that Dryden pointed out the existence of "flats," passages that "creep along" in Milton's *Paradise Lost*. That said, Miller's second novel should be admired as an impressive effort to fill a large canvas with pictures of a family. The novelist Jane Smiley, whose *Ordinary Love; and Good Will* (1989) invites comparison with Miller's novel, wrote that *Family Pictures* depicted

domestic spaces in a manner "as spacious and encompassing as any respected American novel, a work whose cumulative insight blossoms into wisdom and whose steady focus on a single family reveals much of what there is to know about the American middle class in the middle of our century."

FOR LOVE

At one interesting moment in Miller's third novel, *For Love* (1993), its heroine, Lottie Gardner, remembers back to the time she was a young mother and "religiously followed the soaps." Having picked up her son Ryan from his baby-sitter, she would put him down after lunch for his nap, then lie down herself next to her "tiny, blurry TV . . . and watch the self-destructive affairs, the bitter rivalries, the medical and legal ferments, as they played themselves out incrementally." Now she finds a similar "eager fascination" in her sometime-friend Elizabeth's "slow-moving narrative, her tedious piling up of mundane and yet—to Lottie—compelling detail." Revealing here is the fact that such affairs, rivalries, and ferments are the stuff of Miller's own fiction; also that an unconvinced reader of her first two novels—and of *For Love,* which runs to four hundred or so pages—might object to their overdetailed, too deliberately paced narratives. In fact one reviewer of *Family Pictures,* Wendy Lesser, began her review with as condescending a first sentence as can be imagined, confiding in us that "Sue Miller's novels always surprise me by being less bad than I expect them to be." Lesser went on to complain about the topicality of her "unpromising" subjects, subjects that Miller's "restrained" prose only partially managed to lift into "less bad" dimensions. This sort of sniffy holding off at arm's length of the writer and her too-soap-opera-like materials simply refuses to consider the more interesting question of how it is that Miller's narratives, with their plebeian subjects forthrightly handled, attain the subtlety of art.

Both the characters and circumstances of *For Love* are wholly familiar to readers of her earlier work. Questioned once as to why she always wrote about the family, she replied with a question herself—"Why did Conrad always write about sailing?"—and answered it by saying, "It's a way to write about life." In *For Love* the protagonist and the story's exclusive focus is middle-aged Charlotte (Lottie) Gardner, married rather uneasily (her second marriage) to a Chicago oncologist whose wife has recently died of cancer. Lottie is asked by her brother Cameron, who runs a bookstore in Boston, to come back east and dismantle their mother's house in Cambridge. (Their mother is now immobilized in a nursing home.) Lottie and her teenage son Ryan take on the task that will extend for some weeks in the summer. By novelistic coincidence, an old school friend of Lottie's, Elizabeth, is also spending the summer in Cambridge, vacationing from her own rocky marriage by visiting her mother who lives down the street from Lottie's mother's house. Cameron and Elizabeth revive a childhood passion and commence an affair, which is brought to a bad end by the inadvertent death of Elizabeth's baby-sitter Jessica. Elizabeth has sent the sitter outside to warn Cameron to stay away because her husband Lawrence has returned. Cameron—who by appearing is already disobeying a previous warning from Elizabeth to stay away—drives into the driveway and Jessica, slightly drunk, fails to get out of the way of his car. The happenings leading up to this event, and its ramifications—all this that somehow happened "for love"—are the novel's substance.

But most interesting is what Lottie makes of it all. She is not only a concerned party but also a writer of essays about medical issues who is currently assaying a complicated and nebulous topic—the nature of love in contemporary times. By the end of the novel, restored to her marriage back in Chicago, she gives up the essay after deciding that only a novel can be adequate to the story she wants to tell. So *For Love* is Miller's contribution to Lottie's education, and throughout the book the writer's closeness to her heroine is patent, even more so than in *The Good Mother.* Part of this closeness, potentially claustrophobic, is a matter of Miller's employing third-person present tense for those sections of the novel that are to be understood as taking place in the present. By the time *For Love* appeared, the third-person present mode, as used by writers like Bobbie Ann Mason and Ann Beattie, had become a commonplace feature of fictional narrative. Three decades earlier, when John Updike used it to narrate *Rabbit, Run* and his subsequent Rabbit novels, it was—to Updike's sense at least—fairly rare. For Miller, as for Updike, third-person present provides an edgy, immediate, on-the-move style useful for vigorously unrolling the protagonist's stream of thoughts. Perhaps the most memorable sequence in *Rabbit, Run*—the hero's abortive car trip south in the attempt to run away from home—is echoed by a chapter near the end of *For Love* in which Lottie drives the wrong way on the Wilbur Cross Parkway in Connecticut (away from rather than toward Cambridge) and ends up many hours later back home in Chicago.

The novel's pace is more deliberate, less flurried, when Miller uses the third-person past tense to render the events leading up to the deadly accident. There is a good deal of speculation on Lottie's part about what she and her fellow human creatures will do "for love," and since she's been reading, among others, literary "authorities" on the subject, it's appropriate that they enter the book from time to time, elevating things to a contemplative perspective. This is of course what the dogged simplicities of soap-opera narrative cannot afford: the only time a character on the soaps is allowed to pick up a book is when it will be immediately replaced by a piece of action, the book thankfully put aside. In Lottie's narrative, writers such as Shakespeare, Donne, Stendahl, Turgenev, Tolstoy are present, often through their particular words. (For example, lines from Donne's "Air and Angels"—"For, nor in nothing, nor in things / Extreme and scatt'ring bright, can love inhere"—prompt a meditation on the extremities of love.) But a more unlikely writer on the subject of love than any of these—Mark Twain—appears in perhaps the most affecting and beautifully wrought of these reflective moments. Lottie has just driven her visiting husband to his plane back to Chicago, after a weekend of intense lovemaking and equally intense quarreling (she is unsure when she will join him in Chicago or whether she will join him at all). Instead of returning to her Cambridge house she parks in Boston and, from her vantage point in the Public Gardens, observes a wedding party from the Ritz-Carlton entering the park. It is a party of Japanese, and they pose for wedding pictures in "various versions of perfection":

> Their uniformity to her eye gave them a nearly emblematic quality; they reminded her of the little bride and groom statues on the top of a wedding cake. . . .
>
> Lottie thought suddenly of a quote from Twain; not a quote she'd read for this new essay, the one on love; but the one about grief. He was talking about marriage and death. He called marriage the supreme "felicity"—the word had struck Lottie—and also the supreme tragedy. The deeper the love, he said, the surer the tragedy and the more painful when it came. Felicitations, she thought, looking at the doll-like couple; and get ready.

These perfectly disposed sentences, the final one in particular, might be said to contain all that Lottie and her creator have to "say" about love, certainly about married love. But emerging suddenly, as the formulation does, it takes us with surprise and with the sad pleasure of a truth as imagined by a novelist.

THE DISTINGUISHED GUEST

The titles of Miller's novels always have a twist to them: how "good" is the good mother; how reassuringly homey are the family pictures; what is to be done for love? Her fourth novel, *The Distinguished Guest* (1995), about a woman dying of Parkinson's disease who lives for some weeks at her son's house while she waits for her new apartment to be ready—and decides instead to put an end to her life—is no exception to the rule. Lily Maynard has written a highly successful memoir and published some stories. She is "distinguished" in a way, but her real story and that of her family's is only mockingly suggested in the chilly formality of the book's title. In a way it is Miller's most experimental novel in that, compared to the intense focus on a woman's complicated trouble that fuels the energies of *The Good Mother* and *For Love* as well as parts of *Family Pictures, The Distinguished Guest* is more elliptical in its approach and in its tone of presentation.

It is the only novel of hers that received relatively unenthusiastic reviews—Michiko Kakutani in the *New York Times* called it "surprisingly disappointing"; it is also, like the novels that would follow it, relatively compressed at 282 pages. Its main focus is, even more than on Lily Maynard, on her son Alan, an architect who finds his mother's presence in his house unsettling to say the least. But a number of other characters receive more than perfunctory attention, especially Alan's wife, Gaby; their older son, Thomas; and Linnett Baird, a journalist writing a piece about Lily for *The New Yorker,* who comes to interview her and perhaps help her with the writing of a new story. None of these characters is allowed a privileged point of view; their understandings are partial, often confused, unsatisfactory, and never endorsed by the novelist. When Harper-Collins (which ceased to be Miller's publisher after this novel) needed a summary line for *The Distinguished Guest,* they settled on, Miller told

Suzanne L. MacLachlan, "At the heart of every family lies the unspoken truth." Unexceptional enough, but also not true enough, and in reducing the book to "a pithy, two-sentence thing," Miller added, "they were doing the exact opposite of what a writer is trying to do—to make it utterly irreducible." It is possible that in avoiding the reducible, in writing a novel from which it is extremely difficult to extract any moral or memorable bit of wisdom, that Miller necessarily missed the popular success achieved by her previous books.

Those books succeeded in incorporating kinds of public vocabularies (medical, legal) into stories of individual and familial struggle. In *The Distinguished Guest* the notable vocabularies are architectural—employed to make credible Alan's professional life—and sociological-racial—by way of establishing Lily's and her deceased (and divorced) husband's commitment to and disagreement about the civil rights movement. Lily's political passion lies deep in Alan's resentment at his mother for putting such things first: when as a boy he was beaten up by some black teenagers, his mother seemed less concerned with that fact than with the possibility Alan would resent an entire race. This conflict is brought out when Lily is interviewed by a young black woman writing her Ph.D. dissertation on black-white interaction in the 1950s and 1960s, who questions Lily's idealization of the Chicago group of racially mixed women of which she was a member. The scene in which Lily defends her version of things against the young woman's questioning, while the journalist Linnett tapes the proceedings and Alan gives his version of what happened back then, is one of the best in the book—perhaps the most complexly orchestrated, many-sided conversation Miller had yet produced. Although this aspect of the novel did not please Kakutani (who complained that the novel was diluted with "lots of extraneous talk about race relations"), it should be seen rather as Miller's

determination to move beyond and above the subject vision of a closed-in consciousness.

To speak of orchestration is to invoke the musical metaphor, fittingly: Miller's ear and intelligence in alluding to music is impressive. (She studied the piano and clearly has done a lot of listening to serious music—and not only to "serious" music: in *For Love,* Lottie has a good ear for an early Billie Holiday recording, one of her best, titled "Miss Brown to You.") At one important moment in *The Distinguished Guest* a bit of musical performance moves what has turned into a painful family moment onto another level. At dinner, with great effort and with Linnett's spoken assistance, Lily asserts that there is no surer road to heartbreak than having high expectations for your children. The remark makes Alan angry, and he is tempted to respond harshly. His wife cautions him with a look while the journalist is ashamed of being made the vehicle for Lily's wounding charge. Then abruptly Thomas, the son who is studying piano at the conservatory and who has been playing "Tea for Two" until stopping to hear his grandmother's quoted remark, now begins again to play, this time the third movement of Robert Schumann's Fantasy. It is, especially for Alan, a transcendent moment, and Miller describes its effect this way:

> The music moved forward, the voices in it somewhat gradually merging into a triumphant, yet grave, song, which burst forth once and then retreated; and then came forward again, insisting on the possibility of a joy made deeper by sorrow, offering, somehow, a vision, musically, of a boundlessly wide and painful beauty.

Such grandly expressive writing seemed to one reviewer, Laura Shapiro, too much, and she called it "so conscientiously beautiful that it brings the narrative to a dead halt." Shapiro may be answered by pointing out that this moment ends a chapter—halting the narrative, but only briefly—and, more important, that Miller's sentence about the Schumann movement is not just "conscientiously beautiful," as if she is trying too hard for effect, but truly conscientious in that it is responsive to the contours and movement of Schumann's wonderfully grave and magnanimous piece. In her sentence, Miller's own writing through its syntactical hesitations and suspensions pays deference to the advance and retreat one hears in the Schumann.

The novel's tour de force is the chapter in which Lily, relieved for a morning of her usual debilitations from Parkinson's, carries out the suicide for which she has laid up preparations. A hurricane is about to hit the area, and Alan and Gaby's house is close to the predicted center. While they hurriedly try to arrange for Lily's transportation someplace else, as they attend to Alan's other threatened house projects, the distinguished guest manages through manipulative half-truths and some lies to arrange to be alone in the house, thus released into the routine of pills and vodka that will end her life. In her final moment she feels the world's stillness—"as still and deep as a lost meadow"—and hears her mother's voice calling her as she "rose from the sunstruck field she sat in. 'Coming,' she thought she said. 'Coming.'" In some ways this feels like the true ending of the novel since what follows is less telling. Paragraphs from Lily's last story are quoted (Miller is not very successful in the interpolated bits of her memoir and fiction in making Lily more interesting or credible to us), and a too-extended review is provided, once more, of Alan's feelings about his mother. But these are defects—if defects they are—in a novel notable for its disinterested and patient play among a varied and strongly drawn cast of characters, and for its reach out beyond them to a period in America's racial and religious culture.

WHILE I WAS GONE

After publishing *The Distinguished Guest,* Miller changed course by beginning a book about her father's death from Alzheimer's disease. The book floundered and she dropped it (but only temporarily—*The Story of My Father: A Memoir* will appear in 2003) and turned to writing *While I Was Gone.* In this 1999 novel she resumes the first-person singular mode she so successfully made use of in *The Good Mother.* Compared to Anna Dunlap's voice in that novel, Jo Becker's in *While I Was Gone* is even more presuming and informal in its address to us: "I'm a veterinarian," she tells us in the opening chapter, "and the crises among animals are less complex, more manageable, than those of humans." Or, looking at herself in the mirror, she sees "a nice-looking middle-aged person, someone you wouldn't look at twice if you passed her on the street." She has never been beautiful, she tells us, but was once "attractive, tall and blond and strong-looking," with "a notable kind of energy, and people—men—were drawn to it." This directness is a considered strategy on the novelist's part to embrace, almost eagerly, the limitations, the "blinkered vision" (as Miller put it in an interview with Michelle Huneven) of a character whom the novel will show to have made a very large mistake about herself.

Jo's present life is a fulfilled one: married to Daniel Becker, a hardworking minister, she is mother to three grown daughters (the youngest still in college) and devoted to her work. (As usual, Miller has mastered the technical vocabulary of the animal doctor.) Yet, perhaps inevitably, her happiness has its underside, a feeling of dislocation from her past, from the person she was as a young woman in the late 1960s. Memory's claims are disturbing ones, and the book's first chapter devotes itself to creating a feeling of suspension between present and past, the moment "when you're poised exactly between the things in life you want to do and those you need to do, and it seems for a few blessed seconds that they are all going to be the same." But since this is the beginning of a novel, those things will be shown to be not at all the same.

What Jo "needs" to do, it turns out, is revisit her past, a journey prompted by the discovery that Eli Mayhew, one of the members of a Cambridge communal house where Jo lived in 1968, is also now living in the western Massachusetts town Miller calls Adams Mills. His wife brings in Eli's sick dog for treatment, and when the dog has to be put down, Eli himself enters the novel and reencounters Jo. Miller takes us back to 1968 when Jo, under the alias Licia Stead (she has left her husband and taken on a pseudonym), becomes caught up in the excitements of communal living, a life that ends with the brutal murder of Dana Jablonski, a housemate who was a particularly vivid presence for Jo. It is assumed the murderer was unknown, someone looking for money; the commune breaks up, and Jo goes on to meet her minister husband-to-be.

The novel proceeds in the present with richly done family pictures of the Beckers' quotidian existence: a Thanksgiving visit from their three daughters; an evening out listening to the eldest, Cassie, singing in her rock group; a convincing sermon preached by Daniel (Miller spent her childhood listening to sermons, she has reminded us) that fills Jo with renewed love for him. But the claims of fantasy assert themselves as alternative: first the Beckers entertain Eli and his wife; then Jo gets together with him for coffee; finally, and at her suggestion, they arrange to meet for a drink at the Ritz in Boston. Jo contemplates taking a room there (she has invented a fictitious reason for the trip to Boston) should things blossom into an affair. The actual meeting and its disastrous outcome—Eli confesses that it was he who, in a jealous rage, murdered Dana—is the substance of the novel's most compelling chapter. While Jo has been imagining a sexual possibility for her and Eli, he has been leading up to unburdening himself of his secret to what he imagines will

be a sympathetic ear. After all, he tells Jo, think how agonized he was by Dana's death; think of the subsequent good he has tried to do as a scientist. He asks her to help him to put all this behind him. Appalled, Jo asks him what he expects *her* to do with this revelation; Eli replies, "Well, I don't expect you to turn me into the police." Abruptly she leaves the table, manages to elude him as he follows her, and drives home in a state of shock to make a confession of her own to Daniel that she had spent the afternoon in Boston with another man.

The remainder of *While I Was Gone* consists of Jo's attempt to reconcile with her husband, who is devastated by this betrayal of trust even though, as Jo puts it, she hadn't really "done" anything. She does go to the police with Eli's confession, to no avail because when questioned he denies having made it (and denies the murder), suggesting that Jo's accusation was inspired by jealousy, a reaction to a sexual advance spurned. As Jo admits to herself, something like that did happen. Miller's own comment in the interview with Huneven on the climactic Boston chapter could also be applied to the chapters that follow: Jo and Eli's conversation at the Ritz demonstrates "a complete misunderstanding on both sides working to push the whole conversation further and further." She added that it was also "very pleasurable to write." Such pleasure is exactly what her heroine does not feel, which is why the distinction between the suffering patient and the novelistic agent is a crucial one.

It is only when Miller lets up on her heroine and permits her the too wisely expansive voice of one who has *learned,* that we may become uneasy. On the book's final page, Jo speculates on what it has all meant:

Perhaps it's best to live with the possibility that around any corner, at any time, may come the person who reminds you of your own capacity to surprise yourself, to put at risk everything that's dear to you. Who reminds you of the distances we have to bridge to begin to know anything about one another. Who reminds you that what seems to be—even about yourself—may not be. That like him, you need to be forgiven.

One may recall Jane Eyre's triumphant voice at the end of Charlotte Brontë's novel, Jane's first-person singular having reduced all other voices to silence. Jo Becker's voice isn't triumphant in that way, but the swell of repetitions in which she doles out her achieved wisdom is not something from which Miller succeeds in maintaining a healthy distance. We might guess that this resonant conclusion did the novel no harm when Oprah Winfrey's team certified it with their approval—but *While I Was Gone* is more satisfyingly complicated than the message with which it concludes.

THE WORLD BELOW

The World Below, published in 2001, is in many ways Miller's best novel yet—certainly her most shapely and assured. Its themes and characters are cut from the same cloth as her earlier books, but the note of hectic urgency, as heard from time to time in the central figures of *The Good Mother, For Love,* and *While I Was Gone,* is absent, or at least muted. This is due partly to the fact that its heroine is a twice-divorced mother of three, fifty-two-year-old Catherine Hubbard, who is moving into the acceptances of middle age. More important, she is not the only "heroine" of the book but shares that role with her grandmother Georgia Holbrooke, in whose house in a rural Vermont village Catherine lived for a spell as a young girl—a house which she now goes to inhabit again after Georgia's death.

There she finds herself living in another world from her present-day one—as described in the novel's title, "the world below." A poem of Robert Frost's, "Carpe Diem," entertains the notion that one must seize the day, live in the present, but concludes wistfully but firmly that this is impossible. Frost's poem ends

> But bid life seize the present?
> It lives less in the present
> Than in the future always,
> And less in both together
> Than the past. The present
> Is too much for the senses,
> Too crowding, too confusing—
> Too present to imagine.

The World Below begins with an injunction— "Imagine it"—an urging that occurs more than once in the course of the narrative spanning— though not giving them all equal time—seven generations, beginning with the death of Georgia's mother and her grandmother's unsuccessful attempt to take over the rearing of her and her siblings, and ending with the birth of Catherine's granddaughter in a San Francisco hospital. To live in both the future and the past is a burden adopted by a woman whose present life of getting and spending seems to have stalled.

The World Below is the most symmetrical of Miller's books, divided down the middle into two parts with eight chapters in each. The narrative voice artfully varies between Catherine's first-person account and the third-person presentation of her grandmother, a presentation made possible by Catherine's discovery of a trove of diaries kept by Georgia. Even before discovering the diaries, Catherine bears a resemblance to earlier Miller heroines, in the way these women have strong attractions toward and preoccupations with grandparents, often in New England locales. She describes her feelings toward this other life, now recapturable only in imagination, as she takes an early-morning walk in the southern Vermont town where her grandmother lived and died:

> I could still feel it—the same charm, the same pull the town had for me when I'd come here before, something that had to do with the pull of

my grandparents' lives too, the promise of some ordered and old-fashioned way of living that I knew full well I sentimentalized: a world I had created in my imagination, where words like "lilac" and "fidelity" had a similar weight and power.

Aware of her own idealizing and sentimentalizing tendencies, she refuses to discard the pull or promise of another way of living that is unlike the "messier and more ambiguous world" of her San Francisco present. Yet as she reads her grandmother's diaries and registers the affecting story of Georgia's stay, as a young woman, in the Maine sanatorium where she was being treated for tuberculosis, Catherine's picture of her grandmother complicates itself. For at the sanatorium Georgia became the lover of another patient, a mortally ill young man who left the sanatorium only to die. In her concealment of the affair from the man she would marry (Catherine's grandfather, the doctor who treated Georgia), Georgia's life is shown to be not without its own ambiguities and complications that refuse to be smoothed away by the idealizings of her granddaughter.

Although Catherine is tempted to remain in Vermont, perhaps to marry an older man she meets there, she decides against giving in to the pull of the past when she is forcefully drawn back to San Francisco by the premature birth of a granddaughter ("her little bruised face, her lashless lids," as observed in the ventilator). Talking to her daughter's husband, who asks her about Vermont, Catherine now finds it to be "light-years away. It's as though one world sort of negates the other." For all the imaginative identification she has been enabled to make with the lives of a previous generation, that imagining must also take into account and respect "the sense of difference, of distance, between my grandparent's world and my own." In the metaphorical terms of the novel, patiently worked out as they are, it is like looking—as she once did with her grandfather—over the side of a boat and seeing the outlines of a building submerged in the lake,

> the way the buildings had looked through the shifting mirror of the water, the way the world below was there and then not there and then there again, and the way I felt that day looking down into it, dizzy with my sense of yearning and loss for what was gone, and somehow for all that would ever be gone, in my life.

It would be rash to attempt to read Miller's entire career in terms dictated by a single passage from one of her novels, yet these words do seem a true gloss, and a poetic one, on much of the fiction's energies, giving expression to them in a voice and style her readers have come to treasure.

Selected Bibliography

WORKS OF SUE MILLER

NOVELS AND SHORT STORIES

The Good Mother. New York: Harper & Row, 1986.

Inventing the Abbotts, and Other Stories. New York: Harper & Row, 1987.

Family Pictures. New York: Harper & Row, 1990.

For Love. New York: HarperCollins, 1993.

The Distinguished Guest. New York: HarperCollins, 1995.

While I Was Gone. New York: Knopf, 1999.

The World Below. New York: Knopf, 2001.

ESSAYS AND MEMOIR

Introduction to *The Passage of Time. Ploughshares* 19, nos. 2–3:5–9 (fall 1993). (Special edition edited by Miller.)

"Virtual Reality: The Perils of Seeking a Novelist's Facts in Her Fiction." *New York Times*, April 12, 1999, p. E1.

The Story of My Father: A Memoir. New York: Knopf, 2003.

CRITICAL AND BIOGRAPHICAL STUDIES

Caldwell, Gail. "Stretching for Love." *Boston Globe,* March 28, 1993, p. B38.

Daly, Brenda, and Susan L. Woods. "Sue Miller." In *Dictionary of Literary Biography.* Vol. 143, *American Novelists since World War II,* 3d series. Detroit: Gale, 1994. Pp. 151–158.

Gromer, Crystal. "Another Unhappy Family." *Commonweal,* October 12, 1990, p. 589. (Review of *Family Pictures.*)

Kakutani, Michiko. "Books of the Times." *New York Times,* April 23, 1986, p. C20. (Review of *The Good Mother.*)

———. "Summing Up a Life, with Outside Help." *New York Times,* April 21, 1995, p. C32. (Review of *The Distinguished Guest.*)

Lee, Don. "About Sue Miller." *Ploughshares* 19, nos. 2–3:235–240 (fall 1993).

Lehmann-Haupt, Christopher. "Books of the Times; If Romance Confronts Domesticity." *New York Times,* April 5, 1993, p. C18. (Review of *For Love.*)

Lesser, Wendy. "Sue Miller's Tangled Family Web." *Washington Post,* May 15, 1990, p. C3. (Review of *Family Pictures.*)

Parini, Jay. "The Good Wife." *New York Times Book Review,* February 21, 1999, p. 10. (Review of *While I Was Gone.*)

Pritchard, William H. "Generation Gaps." *New York Times Book Review,* October 7, 2001, p. 10. (Review of *The World Below.*)

Shapiro, Laura. Review of *The Distinguished Guest. Newsweek,* April 24, 1995, p. 62.

Smiley, Jane. Review of *Family Pictures. New York Times Book Review,* April 22, 1990, p. 1.

White, Roberta. "Anna's Quotidian Love: Sue Miller's *The Good Mother.*" In *Mother Puzzles: Daughters and Mothers in Contemporary American Literature.* Edited by Mickey Pearlman. New York: Greenwood Press, 1989. Pp. 11–22.

INTERVIEWS

Fletcher, Ron. "Where Heart Meets Hearth: A Conversation with Sue Miller." *Bookpage* (www.http://www.bookpage.com/9902bp/sue_miller.html), February 1999.

Herbert, Rosemary. "*PW* Interviews: Susan Miller." *Publishers Weekly,* May 2, 1986, pp. 60–61.

Huneven, Michelle. "A Conversation with Sue Miller." In *While I Was Gone.* New York: Ballantine Books, 2000.

MacLachlan, Suzanne L. "Conversation with Sue Miller." *Christian Science Monitor,* May 9, 1995, p. 13.

Nelson, Shirley. "A Conversation with Sue Miller." *Image: A Journal of the Arts and Religion* 16:53–61 (summer 1997).

Pearlman, Mickey. "Sue Miller." In her *Listen to Their Voices: Twenty Interviews with Women Who Write.* New York: Norton, 1993. Pp. 162–171.

—*WILLIAM H. PRITCHARD*

Ann Patchett

1963–

AFTER AN APPRENTICESHIP writing articles, short stories, and book reviews for popular magazines and newspapers during her twenties, Ann Patchett published four acclaimed novels within ten years. Her inventive plots and fluid prose have garnered literary awards, admiration from critics and fellow authors, and an ever-growing audience of devoted readers. A resident of Nashville, Tennessee, since childhood, Patchett is sometimes viewed as a southern writer because several early stories and her first two books take place mainly in the South; but her settings have also included California, Nebraska, and South America.

Patchett's characters are as varied as her settings. From an assembly of unwed mothers to a houseful of rural terrorists and elite hostages, unique communities develop in each book. Sometimes compared to Anne Tyler for her interest in surrogate families, Patchett acknowledges a variety of literary influences, including the great Russian novelists of the nineteenth century and the South American masters of magical realism. An enthusiastic reader, she says her work has benefited from Raymond Chandler's expert plotting, Anton Chekhov's character development, and Joan Didion's apt descriptions. Patchett treats her readers as collaborators who bring their own imagination to her novels.

Patchett has told several interviewers that isolation is one of her major themes. Physically, the households in *The Patron Saint of Liars* (1992), *Taft* (1994), *The Magician's Assistant* (1997), and *Bel Canto* (2001) are separate from the larger society, but her characters find ways to break through the barriers that divide them from others, even when those barriers are of class, race, and national origin. Despite references to child abuse, AIDS, authoritarian rulers, and teenage pregnancy, Patchett's fiction is more concerned with personal relationships than with social problems. Deep relationships can develop in surprising environments, yet these human bonds are liable to strain and even destruction, a vulnerability that is underscored by the books' many references to childhood.

From a stillborn baby in *The Patron Saint of Liars* to a murdered ten-year-old boy in *Bel Canto,* children embody life's fragility in Patchett's fiction. Transience and death are as familiar to Patchett's novels as they are to Robert Frost's poems, and like Frost, Patchett compensates for life's losses with tokens of beauty, glints of humor, and quests for communion. But Patchett's characters often cross great distances before they find their soulmates and their own true selves. The mythic quality of these journeys is enhanced by elemental events like childbirth, as well as ritualistic scenes like weddings. Allusions to saints' lives, Arthurian legend, and opera scenarios further infuse the contemporary plots with an otherworldly dimension. A few reviewers have objected when events and characters seem unrealistic or unlikely, but most of Patchett's readers are intrigued by the strong imaginative quality of her fiction. Critical reaction to Patchett's four novels published between 1992 and 2001 was almost universally positive, with *The Magician's Assistant* and *Bel Canto* achieving exceptional popularity. Alex Clark of the Manchester *Guardian* applauds Patchett's "bravura confidence and inventiveness" in *Bel Canto,* but she could be describing each of the previous volumes in adding that "the novel's sensibilities extend from the sly wit of observational humour to subtle, mournful insights into the nature of yearning and desire."

BIOGRAPHY

Ann Patchett was born in Los Angeles, California, on December 2, 1963, the daughter of Frank Patchett, a police officer, and Jeanne Wilkinson Ray, a nurse and the author of *Julie and Romeo* (2000), a best-selling novel. Patchett's parents divorced when she was five, and she and her older sister moved with their mother to Nashville. Patchett has maintained ties to the West Coast, frequently traveling there to visit her father and her extended family, and she considers her father one of the most interesting people she knows. During his thirty-five years in law enforcement, he was involved in such high-profile cases as the Charles Manson murders and the Robert F. Kennedy assassination. (At one point, Ann Patchett began to write a nonfiction book about the Los Angeles Police Department, but she set aside the project to write *The Magician's Assistant,* which opens at the city's Cedars-Sinai Hospital.)

Throughout Patchett's childhood in Tennessee, she exchanged long letters with her father in California. "I made a habit of storing up my life and writing it down for him. I write because of my father's strong, clear handwriting," she says in her 1998 essay "Writing and a Life Lived Well." Her mother's "wonderful" but unpublished poems were another stimulus to Patchett's early interest in a writing career. A less positive factor was the criticism of a teacher who seemed to delight in her struggles with spelling, punctuation, and handwriting. In defense and revenge, she produced homework that was unusually clever and humorous; and after the grade-schooler was badly injured in a car accident, she decided that, with her new

chance at life, she would become an author. Years later, the attention that her high school friends at Nashville's St. Bernard Academy gave to dates and dancing, Patchett invested in writing.

Patchett has commented on the importance of spending many years in female company, not only with the Sisters of Mercy and the girls at St. Bernard's but also at home with her mother, sister, and grandmother. After their mother remarried, Patchett and her sister shared a bedroom with two stepsisters on long summer visits. A female atmosphere was pervasive at Camp Sycamore in rural Tennessee, where Patchett first encountered *Ms.* magazine, and later at Sarah Lawrence College in New York. From small details such as singing Carole King songs in elementary school and larger influences such as reading Edith Wharton and Sylvia Plath as a teenager, the voices and ideas of women shaped Patchett's childhood, and she has said that she never felt inferior to men. In a September 2001 essay titled "Women among Women" (for the *New York Times Magazine*'s "Women and Power" issue), she concludes: "This is how I define myself: before I am a citizen, a Catholic, a writer, a member of my family, I am a woman. The group is where my loyalty lies."

At fourteen, Ann Patchett loved T. S. Eliot, and poetry was her first creative writing course at Sarah Lawrence; however, she claims she has never written a poem worth publishing. Her second college writing class, a two-semester workshop taught by Allan Gurganus, pointed her instead in the direction of short stories and then novels. Patchett says that the grueling discipline of completing a weekly story taught her 90 percent of what she knows about writing fiction. Gurganus assigned Isaac Babel's collected stories as the course text, filled the margins of students' manuscripts with advice in brown ink, led them on a field trip to the

Cloisters museum of medieval art and architecture, and read aloud to them from Raymond Carver, Vladimir Nabokov, and even Joan Crawford.

With additional instruction from Russell Banks and Grace Paley, Patchett continued to develop her skills at prose. When she was a sophomore, she wrote "All Little Colored Children Should Play the Harmonica," winner of a Henfield Foundation/*Transatlantic Review* Award in 1983. On her twenty-first birthday, the piece became her first published fiction with its appearance in the *Paris Review*. Narrated by Grover T. Smiley, a talented harmonica player who declines his teacher's offer of a less "bucolic" instrument, Patchett's story—which was later adapted into a play—was the first of several she wrote about young African American characters in the South. These included "Why I Like Laurel" for *Seventeen* (in April 1990) and "Heaven" for the *Southern Review* (in July 1989), both set in small-town Tennessee during the 1940s and related in the present tense by Delia Smiley, presumably Grover T.'s sister. Such protagonists resemble the sensitive and poignantly amusing children in the fiction of Carson McCullers, an author whom Patchett much admires.

Patchett thought she might develop enough pieces about the Smiley family to publish a collection, but she was not satisfied with her efforts. She quit writing short fiction when she was twenty-five, and although she says that her stories are best forgotten, she earned the Editor's Choice awards for fiction from the *Iowa Journal of Literary Studies* in 1986 and from *Columbia: A Magazine of Poetry and Prose* in 1987. Other early honors included residential fellowships at two prestigious writers' colonies, Yaddo and the Millay Colony, as well as the James A. Michener/Copernicus Award from the University of Iowa for a first novel in progress, all in 1989.

In the decade after Patchett earned a master's degree from the Iowa Writers Workshop in 1987, she became a prolific freelance writer. The fresh perceptions and occasional whimsicality that characterized her short fiction informed her nonfiction as well, whether her topic was thank-you notes or the chemistry of romance. Patchett has observed that *Seventeen* magazine, her first regular outlet, helped her become a disciplined writer. She humorously explains that the staff rejected so many of her early submissions that she soon lost her ego and gained the ability to write effortlessly in many different voices.

Patchett has said that two of the subjects that sold best to the magazine market were the two she had the most trouble with in her own life: the teenaged years and marriage. This flippant allusion does not suggest the heartache Patchett exposes in her 1995 essay "The Sacrament of Divorce." Describing the one year she spent as a wife, she states simply: "These are the facts: I married him when I should not have and later on I left." Patchett took a plane back to Nashville from Pennsylvania, where she had lived with her husband while teaching as writer in residence at Allegheny College in the 1989–1990 academic year. Recalling her depression and feelings of guilt, Patchett describes the broken sleep, the experience of shampooing her hair "again and again" some mornings because she could not remember if she had washed it yet, and the awful sensation of getting lost more than once on her four-mile drive from the family home to her new job at a T.G.I. Friday's restaurant. Like her childhood car accident, however, divorce was not only traumatic but clarifying, a presage of new possibilities. Having survived, Patchett says in "Sacrament," she was convinced she could give up anything if necessary, including writing, "which was my joy and greatest source of self-definition." After many years in the closed world of academe, temporary work as a waitress seemed refreshing; yet Patchett held on to her dream of writing books.

Outside support came in the form of a fellowship from the Fine Arts Work Center in Provincetown, Massachusetts, where she wrote the whole text of her first novel, *The Patron Saint of Liars* (1992), during a seven-month residency. Patchett has returned to college campuses for short terms as a creative writing teacher, but she has not sought a permanent university affiliation. She was a visiting assistant professor at Murray State University in 1992 and the Tennessee Williams Fellow in Creative Writing at the University of the South in 1997, as well as the 1999 Zale Writer in Residence at Newcomb College Center for Research for Women on the Tulane University campus in New Orleans. Throughout the 1990s, her articles and book reviews appeared in an unusual range of media, from *Bridal Guide* and the *Village Voice* to *Gourmet* and the *Chicago Tribune*. After she quit writing for *Seventeen* in 1994, she became a frequent contributor to *Vogue* and *GQ*.

Although by the late 1990s Patchett cut back drastically on magazine and newspaper writing in order to work almost full-time on her novels, she accepted special assignments, such as writing about a trip to Italy to take in the opera (for *Gourmet,* in June 2001) and an article comparing Dale Earnhardt and Eudora Welty as southern icons (for the *New York Times Magazine*'s December 30, 2001, issue on deaths of 2001). In an essay for the *New York Times Magazine* in July 2000, "As Is the Daughter, So Is Her Mother," Patchett pays tribute to her mother for publishing a late-life best-seller and compares Jeanne Ray's novel *Julie and Romeo* to a locomotive rushing at full speed: "My mother's book roars, whereas one of my novels makes a sound like a cricket being set down in the lawn." The enthusiasm of writers and reviewers for each of Patchett's books belies this modest imagery, however; and her six-part tour journal for HarperCollins's author website describes warm welcomes at bookstores throughout the country during her travels in summer 2001 with

Bel Canto. Critical recognition in the 1990s included the Tennessee Writer of the Year award, a Guggenheim Fellowship, the Janet Heidinger Kafka Prize for fiction, a Bunting Institute Fellowship at Radcliffe College, and a place on the short list for the United Kingdom's Orange Prize for Fiction. *Bel Canto* won the 2002 PEN/Faulkner Award, America's largest peer-juried prize for fiction.

When Patchett is not on book tours or research trips, she spends most mornings composing at the computer in her Nashville home. Her dog, Rose, is her subject in articles for *Vogue* and *Bark,* and Patchett's visits with her elderly grandmother are an important part of her day. This quiet routine reminds Patchett of Eudora Welty's life as writer and companion to her aging mother in Jackson, Mississippi. A great admirer of Welty's fiction, she numbers many other authors among her favorites, including Gurganus, Cormac McCarthy, Jane Austen, Nabokov, Thomas Mann, William Faulkner, Nathanael West, Leo Tolstoy, Phillip Roth, Gabriel García Márquez, Alice Munro, Toni Morrison, Saul Bellow, John Updike, and her personal friends Lucy Grealy and Elizabeth McCracken, to both of whom she dedicated her third novel, *The Magician's Assistant.* McCracken's literary advice has been indispensable ever since she and Patchett were fellows during the same period at the Fine Arts Work Center on Cape Cod more than a decade ago. Patchett says they have exchanged manuscripts so often that they can internalize each other's responses.

One of Patchett's most unusual excursions from Nashville was a trip to the Badlands and Yellowstone for *Outside* magazine with her close friend Karl VanDevender sharing the driving in a rented twenty-nine-foot Winnebago. "For all of my bone-deep distrust of motor homes, they do combine two of my favorite pastimes: compulsive driving and occasional napping," says Patchett in the June 1998 essay "My Road to Hell Was Paved." In November

2001 she wrote for the *New York Times Magazine* about her long road trip from New York to Nashville in the aftermath of the September 11, 2001, terrorist attacks. Characterizing America as "a restless nation" and reflecting on the appeal of road trips through America's open spaces, Patchett observes, "We have been saddling horses and driving down railroad spikes ever since our ancestors got off their ships. The only thing that even came close to the thrill of the trip was the pleasure of arriving."

For many of Patchett's characters, the trip is highly charged, but pleasure is not always the dominant emotion. Yet travel they must, covering hundreds, sometimes thousands, of miles in all four novels. Ann Patchett says she loves traveling in her imagination, and she thinks she would still vary the settings of her books if she had been born in the South instead of spending her first five years a long journey away in California. Even more imaginative than her geographic range, however, is the aura of mystery that marks the novels in small and sometimes major ways. When the novelist Alice McDermott reviewed *The Patron Saint of Liars* for the *New York Times Book Review* in 1992, the headline proclaimed "A Sense of the Miraculous," an anticipation too of the three books that followed.

THE PATRON SAINT OF LIARS

Houghton Mifflin's press kit for Patchett's first novel introduced the author as a Tennessee native currently living in Kentucky. Several of Patchett's early short stories had been set in the South, and her publisher apparently chose to market her work as southern fiction in the vein of Bobbie Ann Mason, Josephine Humphreys, Kaye Gibbons, Lee Smith, and other women novelists who had won acclaim during the 1980s. Patchett lived in Kentucky only temporarily as a visiting assistant professor at Murray State, but Mason's short stories and her best-selling novel *In Country* (1985) had placed Kentucky on the contemporary literary map. The great popularity of Nashville as a musical center, especially in the wake of Robert Altman's award-winning 1975 film *Nashville,* likewise created a mystique for the false statement on the dust jacket of *The Patron Saint of Liars* that Patchett was born in that city.

Patchett says she worked out a plot with an unwed mothers' home, a Kentucky town, and a runaway woman while she was waiting on tables at the Nashville T.G.I. Friday's, the job she took after she left her own unhappy marriage and returned to the South. In this first novel, however, the South's regional identity is less important than the South's remoteness from California, the state that the protagonist, Rose Clinton, flees for Kentucky. The loose model for the story's residence for unwed mothers was actually Saint Ann's Home in Los Angeles.

Protective of her young characters, Patchett has said she believed that "everything would be so much simpler and safer for them if they were in west Kentucky instead of east L.A." Moving letters from her pregnant sister in Alaska influenced Patchett's depiction of Rose Clinton, and she incorporated several lines from those letters into her story. The tenderness toward the innocent that Patchett reveals in such authorial decisions remains a constant in her four novels. Loved ones die or disappear, and survivors grieve for them. Blood is shed, almost ritualistically, before each novel ends. Yet somehow, despite the wrenching losses and the bursts of violence, innocence—tempered by new knowledge—is preserved.

The May 1 publication of *The Patron Saint of Liars* was probably scheduled as a Mother's Day tie-in. Mothers and surrogate mothers abound at Saint Elizabeth's Home, where aging Catholic nuns provide shelter for successive groups of unmarried girls and for the runaway Rose, who narrates the first of the book's three main divisions. Rose lies to the stern Mother

Corinne that her husband died in a car accident, not suspecting how familiar the tragedy would sound to the sister superior. "Everybody says they had a really great husband but he died, in a car crash or something," her unmarried roommate Angie giggles, adding that a land mine in Vietnam is the death weapon in some current versions of the cover story. The central action of *The Patron Saint of Liars* begins in 1968, and Angie's passing reference to war in Vietnam, along with the novel's later allusions to World War II, underscores the contrasting peacefulness of the female domestic sphere at Saint Elizabeth's, where girls sip iced tea on the porch on summer afternoons; but neither the nuns nor their guests are strangers to suffering. When Angie advises that the best attitude for newcomers to the home is to "just look down at your hands and act all sad and penitent," Rose's sardonic "Great" conceals her true sorrow and penitence. And, consistent with the many other intense child-parent bonds in Patchett's novels, Rose's feelings have more to do with the beloved mother she left in San Diego than with the husband she abandoned in Marina del Rey.

The day the gynecologist congratulated her on her pregnancy, Rose suddenly realized that her nearly three-year marriage had lacked joy from the start because she did not love the twenty-six-year-old Thomas. Before they met, she had coolly rejected boyfriends who were more articulate and more aggressive sexually than he was; but the religiously devout Rose misread her own throbbing response to the shy Thomas as a sign from God when it was simply "the plainest form of nineteen-year-old sexual desire on a dark beach of the Pacific Ocean in southern California in May." Rose seeks temporary relief from her marriage on solitary drives up and down the Pacific Coast Highway, but the fact of her pregnancy precipitates a more defiant escape. Like characters in Patchett's later novels, Rose takes extreme measures to redefine herself, breaking drastically with her past.

Without telling Thomas she is pregnant, she drops him off at the high school where he teaches math, then leaves a formal good-bye note that warns him not to look for her.

Safe haven is sacred in Patchett's fiction, and Rose's parish priest arranges the pastoral sanctuary in Kentucky, but he begs that she at least speak with her mother before making the journey. Father O'Donnell resembles the elderly Catholic clerics in Mary Gordon's novels who uncomfortably balance an opposition to divorce with a sensitivity to women's distress; and, like Gordon's dutiful Catholic daughters, Rose carries a heavy burden of guilt. Father O'Donnell knows that Rose's beautiful mother, Helen, widowed in her twenties, loved her dead young husband and their only daughter so much that she did not consider marrying again until Rose had a home of her own. Helen used to watch the teenaged Rose apply makeup before a date, trying to see her "harshly" as a stranger might so she could "prepare me somehow for what was to come." The reality of the child's vulnerability deepens the love between the two, a dynamic that also appears in Patchett's treatment of fatherhood, both in *The Patron Saint of Liars* and in her second novel, *Taft*. When Rose tells the shocked Father O'Donnell, "I'll give her up," she believes that, if she surrenders what matters most to her, "then maybe God would respect my desperation." Rose has to pull over to the side of the road twice before she crosses the California line because her tears for her mother are blinding, and for years afterward she wakes up sobbing from dreams of Helen.

The excruciating nature of their separation influences the surprising events that follow in Kentucky. Even though residents apply to Saint Elizabeth's Home with the understanding that their children will be adopted at birth, Rose becomes set upon keeping her baby as the due date approaches. Without divorcing Thomas, she accepts a marriage proposal from Son Abbott, the home's lonely handyman, who assumes she is an unwed mother and who loved her at first sight. After a rushed ceremony at a nearby justice of the peace's home, Rose's narrative ends abruptly with her determination to call the unborn child Cecilia, the name on Son's tattooed arm. When he pleads that she reconsider, the reader suddenly realizes that Rose is not the only character with secrets from the past.

Much as Faulkner reveals the secrets of the Compsons and the Bundrens through a succession of viewpoints in *The Sound and the Fury* and *As I Lay Dying,* Ann Patchett shifts from Rose's perspective to Son's and finally to young Cecilia's. Like Caddy Compson and Addie Bundren before her, Rose Clinton is the focus of her family's confused love and thus the unifying force of the whole book; but Patchett's fiction has a supernatural dimension that is foreign to the Yoknapatawpha saga. Beginning with a prologue narrated in a folksy but unidentified voice, *The Patron Saint of Liars* makes a down-to-earth case for the existence of miracles.

Like the seeping of amniotic fluid before a birth, a healing spring trickles to the surface in the novel's first lines: "Two o'clock in the morning, a Thursday morning, the first bit of water broke through the ground of George Clatterbuck's back pasture in Habit, Kentucky, and not a living soul saw it. Spring didn't care." The farmer, stumbling across the new stream on a rabbit hunt in 1906, thinks the sulfurous smell is "a bad sign"; but he is no more adept than the nineteen-year-old Rose at reading nature's signals. Before long, however, he observes the curative impact of the mineral waters on his diseased livestock. More dramatically, his little girl June recovers from a serious disease after Clatterbuck makes her drink a jarful of the foul-tasting water. Many others are healed in the years after George feels "the call to witness," and the wealthy husband of one cured woman builds the Hotel Louisa in the Clatterbucks' field during the era when hot-springs hotels are flourishing in nearby states. The stock market crash of 1929 and the drying up of the restorative stream shut down the grand resort, but the hotel has two subsequent lives: first, as a retirement house for a religious order from Ohio, and later as the nuns' refuge for unwed mothers.

Homey images of birth and healing mingle with allusions to the divine throughout the prologue, setting the scene not only for the pregnant Rose's arrival at Saint Elizabeth's in 1968 but also for Son Abbott's account of his providential arrival as a teenaged hitchhiker in 1944. Discharged from the military after he was accidentally shot during basic training, and guilt-stricken that he did not rescue his fiancée Cecilia from drowning in a Tennessee quarry, Son bears scars of the body and the spirit. But Sister Evangeline, the most unusual nun at Saint Elizabeth's, startles him by reading his mind as he washes dinner dishes that first night in her kitchen. She observes that some "bad thing" turned him into a traveler, but it had nothing to do with the war or his wound, nor was it his fault. Recollecting the nun's gesture of comfort, Son could almost be describing a baptism: "And then she put her hands down in the water and held my hands." The cleansing water and the ritualistic laying on of hands signal Son's absolution and also his initiation into the women's world at Saint Elizabeth's.

Throughout her years at the home, as mother superior and then as cook, Sister Evangeline has a talent for placing her sympathetic hands over the wombs of Saint Elizabeth's girls to tell them, with infallible accuracy, their baby's sex. A wise crone figure, Sister Evangeline foresees that the infant daughter of Rose's friend Angie will die, but her special vision is limited. Although she knows Rose and Son will marry, she does not know that Rose has left a husband in California, nor that Rose will suddenly drive away from Habit, Kentucky, fifteen years later when Thomas sends a letter to say he is on his way. He tracks Rose from the postmarks on cards she recently sent her mother, and he wants to see her in person to soften the news that Helen has died; but Rose cannot bear the thought of a reunion with Thomas. Her evasive farewell note, addressed to "Everyone" at Saint Elizabeth's, is no comfort at all to her daughter, Cecilia, who doubts that the secretive Rose ever really loved her and Son.

"Cecilia," the final section of *The Patron Saint of Liars,* is related by the feisty teenager; but Sissy (as Son always calls her) knows hardly any of the family history recorded in the "Rose" and "Son" narratives, and Patchett skillfully depicts the girl's anger, confusion, and curiosity during the period of Rose's flight and Thomas' visit. Shortly before Rose leaves, Sissy saves Son from probable death by getting him to the hospital after he sustains a serious head injury from an accident at home. The shock of meeting Thomas a few days after Rose's departure deals Son an equally harsh emotional blow. Like Son's deep cut, a mysterious wound on Sister Evangeline's hand embodies the pain Rose both inflicts and shares. The special powers the nun displays in all three narratives—Rose's, Son's, and then Cecilia's—imply that she bears the stigmata, a miraculous mark of great holiness and a remembrance of Christ's crucifixion. Son's head injury and his very name further signify themes of sacrificial suffering and ultimate redemption.

With her arcane knowledge of saints' lives, Sister Evangeline is the patron saint of liars for Saint Elizabeth's Home, guarding the household's many secrets, including the new revelations about Rose's past. As surrogate family members, she and Son shield the young Cecilia from realizing that Thomas is her biological father. Sissy, who comforts her sad elders after Rose's flight, receives comfort herself from an unexpected source near the end of the novel. Finally admitting her love for her mother, she gazes hungrily at Thomas' photographs of the young Rose, beautiful visions that "seemed to make up for everything, secrets and lost time."

A CBS television adaptation of *The Patron Saint of Liars,* released in 1998 and starring Dana Delany as Rose, transformed Patchett's subdued conclusion by adding scenes that portray Rose's return to Saint Elizabeth's and a parallel return of the curative spring. Good-natured about such tampering, Patchett says she was well compensated for the film rights and did not worry about the revisions. In an essay for *GQ,* she comically described her part as a film extra in the role of an unwed mother.

The Patron Saint of Liars was the only first novel selected by the American Library Association's Notable Books Council as an outstanding fictional work of 1992, and the *New York Times* designated it a Notable Book. That same year Patchett was a featured new novelist at the fourth annual Eudora Welty Writers' Symposium held by the Mississippi University for Women in Columbus. The conference theme for 1992, "Infinite Variety: The Many Modes of Southern Writing," is an apt title for the body of writing that Patchett would produce over the decade that followed. Even though such traditionally southern concerns as family, the past, and storytelling remain constant in her four novels, each book takes a new direction, eventually leading Patchett so far from Habit, Kentucky, that southern voices disappear completely.

TAFT

In *The Patron Saint of Liars,* Rose Clinton calls Saint Elizabeth's Home "a country unto itself." Muddy's bar in *Taft,* Patchett's second novel, is another such microcosm but with a broader constituency. Staff and customers at the Beale Street establishment comprise a small world of men and women, black and white, young and old. Analogous to the physical and figurative distances between California and Kentucky in the earlier book is the contrast between urban Memphis and east Tennessee in *Taft. The Companion to Southern Literature* (2002) includes the book in an entry on literature set in Memphis; and, superficially, Patchett's story is southern fiction, with its mention of Elvis and Graceland, W. C. Handy Park, the blues, Shiloh, Cherokee Indians, and the Mississippi River. For all the regional allusions, however, the South is no more central to *Taft*—which Patchett wrote in Wyoming and Montana—than it was to *The Patron Saint of Liars*.

Muddy's bar is significant not because it is situated on the most famous street in the major city of the mid-South but because it provides a surrogate home for a surrogate family. The British writer Henry Green supplies Patchett's epigraph: "Home seemed a heaven and that we were cast out"; the rhythm is Miltonic, and so is the notion of displacement from an innocent Eden. The displaced include the novel's three main characters: the African American narrator John Nickel, who dreams of a permanent home with his girlfriend, Marion, and their son Franklin; and the two fatherless Caucasian teenagers, Fay and Carl Taft, who feel more at home in the bar Nickel manages than they do in the house of their wealthy Memphis relatives. Like the young women at Saint Elizabeth's Home in *The Patron Saint of Liars*, the sister and brother from Coalfield, Tennessee, are so desperate for emotional shelter that they lie to gain admittance. Fay pretends to be twenty so John Nickel will hire her, and then she conceals her job from her mother, aunt, and uncle; Carl, a year younger than his sister, tries to hide his drug habit. "Everything hinged on the dead father," Nickel reflects not long after meeting the siblings.

Taft's impact on Fay and Carl is not surprising; but he exerts an unusual influence on John Nickel, a man who never met him and who is his opposite in many ways. The force that binds them is a love of children—their own children, most specifically, but other men's children as well. Nickel seems to know all the street kids on Beale. Eddie, a young back flip artist, makes him think of his nine-year-old son Franklin, and Nickel is angry that Eddie's father lets him skip school in order to support the two of them by "tossing himself up in the air so fast and so often that I got sick to my stomach just watching him." In a parallel vignette, Taft is kind to the son of an African American coworker at the Royal Hill Carpet plant in Coalfield. When young Tommy knocks at the door to sell candy for a school fundraiser, Taft buys four expensive bars and gives the boy advice for improving sales in an all-white neighborhood.

Separated by white space from John Nickel's first-person narrative, and related in the third person and the present tense, the Taft section seems to be a spliced flashback, independent of the central action. But the dialogue between Taft and Tommy, like the other Taft scenes in the book, is generated by John Nickel. Presumably Nickel's visualizations evolve from anecdotes that Fay and Carl share with him; yet the teenagers' most casual remarks can shape the Taft scenes in startling ways. Three pages after Fay tells John Nickel she would name a son Levon if she ever had one, the bar manager pictures a late-night encounter in which Taft's wife calls him Levon. Nickel soon becomes so absorbed in picturing his counterpart that some of the Taft episodes fill several pages, the sheer degree of detail suggesting that the interpolated scenes could be quite remote from Taft's actual experiences.

In an interview with the novelist Elizabeth McCracken, Ann Patchett compares her selection of Nickel as narrator to a casting call. Having assembled the characters for a story about a black family and a white family meeting in the contemporary South, she began writing from several viewpoints, the same approach she had employed in *The Patron Saint of Liars*. But John Nickel emerged as her most "reliable" character, so she followed his strong voice to create the narrative structure. Patchett does not comment on Nickel's standard English usage, a noteworthy contrast to the inflections and diction contemporary authors often employ to suggest a distinctively African American, or even a distinctively southern, voice. Nor does Taft sound like a boy who grew up poor in the shadow of the Smoky Mountains.

Patchett told McCracken that John Nickel acts a writer's part in creating the Taft scenes in order to answer his questions about Taft's children and also to reflect upon the condition of fatherhood. Alternating between Nickel's autobiographical narrative and his invented biography of Taft, the author felt she was "working in a hall of mirrors: I imagine a character who imagines a character." As an experiment in narrative technique, *Taft* is often surreal in its impact, not unlike the metafiction of John Barth or the magic realism of Jorge Luis Borges and Gabriel García Márquez—authors famous for their self-reflexive storytellers and contending plotlines.

Nickel's growing fascination with Taft coincides with his own deepening involvement in the lives of Fay and Carl, an involvement that spirals into a romance, unconsummated but intense, between John Nickel and Fay. Each fills a terrible void in the other's life. If the thirty-four-year-old man is a father figure and fantasy lover for Fay, she becomes—in the absence of Franklin and Marion—both Nickel's child and an object of his desire. Fay makes the first overture the night she tells John Nickel about her father's death. After he drives her and the stoned Carl to their uncle's house, Nickel carries the semiconscious boy through the dark rooms in a harrowing scene that recalls Richard Wright's *Native Son*. On a similar rescue mission, Bigger Thomas feared discovery in Wright's novel; and John Nickel imagines being shot by the teenagers' uncle, who would convince the police that he had good cause to kill an intruding black man.

Nickel is not caught, however, and Fay begs to go home with him. "My whole body heard her," he says. But, by association, John Nickel thinks of Marion, who loved him when he was a twenty-five-year-old drummer and she was as young as Fay: "I should have asked Marion to marry me, the second she told me she was pregnant. That was the mistake." Even though Marion hates Nickel for ignoring her phone call when she was in labor with Franklin, he was so moved by his first view of the baby that, ever since, he has been trying to make up for his early carelessness. Marion refused his belated marriage proposals; and, after brief periods of living with him, she took a nursing job in Florida and left Memphis with their son. Even before his imagination becomes preoccupied with Taft, John Nickel displays a knack for invention. When Marion phones from Miami near the beginning of the book, crying that Franklin needed stitches after he fell while playing, Nickel pictures a whole scenario of rough boys in pursuit of his child.

The vision of Franklin's accident displays motifs of threat and vulnerability that are central to the whole novel. Nickel becomes nauseous at imagining the blood dripping into the boy's eye, so he focuses his mind instead on the girl who just asked for a bar job. The link between Franklin and Fay is obvious in his worried thought: "I wondered who was looking out for her." Nickel's subsequent attempts to safeguard both of Taft's children almost get him killed near the end of the story. Shot in the neck by Carl when the boy tries to rob Muddy's, Nickel does not let his assistant manager call the police. Because Marion has come back to town to visit her family, Nickel is able to get help from a physician friend who won't report the shooting. John Nickel pictures Taft struck down by a corresponding pain, and the tales of two fathers intersect dramatically as he writes himself into a Taft scene for the first and only time. In his imagination, Nickel takes Carl's place at Taft's side while the frantic boy runs to his Coalfield neighbors for help, and when Taft dies of a heart attack, Nickel awakens from a feverish sleep at Marion's family home, where she has taken him to recover from the assault at the bar.

Like Sister Evangeline in *The Patron Saint of Liars,* Marion's mother is a wise woman and sympathetic confessor who helps bring about a new order of life in the closing pages of *Taft.* In a long talk with Fay, Mrs. Woodmoore persuades the girl not to visit the convalescent John Nickel; she later reports the conversation to John to remind him about his family responsibilities. Soon afterward Nickel decides: "Pick one job and do it right. I was picking Franklin." Marion is a comforting presence at his bedside, and it becomes clear that she has not attempted to alienate the affectionate little boy from his father. Nor has Marion discouraged Franklin's precocious talent for drumming, even though she long ago pressured Nickel to give up his band for a more conventional job. The lilac bush John Nickel sees outside the window is yet another hopeful sign, a sturdy promise of spring after the cold February weeks and the dark nights that dominate the novel.

Most hopeful of all, however, is one last Taft episode, a scene of innocence regained and mortality staved off. Nickel imagines Taft at twenty-six on an outing with his children. Amazed that Fay is almost five, Taft warns her to keep Carl away from a creek that can abruptly flood in springtime, but he is confident he can protect the two small figures: "His hair hasn't started to thin and his hearing hasn't been damaged by the noise of the machines in the carpet factory and he hasn't had that partial bridge yet." Taft, as John Nickel last envisions him, is "still fast enough to outrun any sort of trouble," sure he can grab Carl before he has a chance to fall—in a way that Nickel was unable to keep his own son from falling in the main plot. By concluding *Taft* with this touching view of a much younger Carl and Fay, Patchett has Nickel relinquish his claims on the pair while also paying homage to a fellow father-protector.

Patchett has commented that Taft was, in fact, powerless to keep his grown children safe and that John Nickel's determination to shield Frank- lin will be similarly threatened. Thus, she considers her conclusion both hopeful and hopeless.

Ann Patchett retains a special affection for her second novel, which was never as popular with readers as her other books. In the late 1990s Morgan Freeman bought the film rights, and Patchett completed a screenplay for a proposed feature film, so it seemed *Taft* might gain a second life and a much larger audience. Freeman saw himself playing the role of a somewhat older John Nickel, and Winona Ryder had been proposed for the part of a twenty-something Fay.

THE MAGICIAN'S ASSISTANT

Coastal California is as attractive in *The Magician's Assistant* as it is in Rose Clinton's section of *The Patron Saint of Liars.* Rather than retrace the journey from urban West to rural South, however, Patchett develops a more drastic contrast in her story about a secretive man born into a dysfunctional family in Alliance, Nebraska. Guy Fetters reinvents himself as Parsifal, a celebrity magician and dealer in fine rugs who finds a truer family in vibrant Los Angeles. There he meets his gay Vietnamese lover, Phan, who is a computer genius, and his beautiful Jewish assistant, Sabine, who builds architectural models (and who becomes Parsifal's wife after Phan dies). Patchett suggests that the setting and the happy life the three talented and creative friends share are equally miraculous: "They lived in the magnificence of a well-watered desert where things that could not possibly exist, thrived. They lived on the edge of a country that would not have cared for them anyway, and they were loved. They were home." As Diana Postlethwaite says in her *New York Times* review of *Taft,* Patchett portrays "loving communities formed in unexpected places." Phan even buys adjoining plots in luxurious Forest Lawn cemetery because, he tells Sabine, the three should never be separated unless she chooses to be buried somewhere else.

Almost as unusual as the Los Angeles household is the surrogate family of women and children that Sabine discovers in Nebraska after Phan dies of AIDS and Parsifal suffers a fatal stroke months later. Dividing *The Magician's Assistant* into two large sections, Patchett headlines the contrasts between the two worlds with the titles "At the Intersection of George Burns and Gracie Allen" and "Nebraska." Sabine first learns about the Nebraska relatives from Parsifal's will, and because he had said so little about his past, she speculates that the Fetterses cruelly rejected him at an early age for his homosexuality. At the same time, however, she finds that the few early memories Parsifal shared with her are pure fiction: his family is not rich, they are not from Connecticut, and, far from dying in a fiery car wreck, they have been living in the same house Guy left forever as a teenager. Elizabeth Bernstein calls Sabine's reluctant trip to frigid Nebraska a "journey of redemption" in which Sabine, her mother-in-law, and her two sisters-in-law are each "finally able to understand the past—and to discover something of her own desires and potential." Not only does Sabine adjust to her new role as an in-law and an aunt, but she digs an old magic set out of Parsifal's childhood closet and brings her fascinated nephews closer to the uncle they never met.

In response to critics who deem it unlikely that Sabine would marry a gay magician after twenty years as his assistant, Patchett told interviewer Jennifer Bojorquez that the essential element of the relationship was that the couple loved each other, adding, "Sex is great, but it's not the heart of the matter." Sabine responds similarly to Dot Fetters when Parsifal's mother tries to understand the marriage: "I really

believe he loved me, but there are a lot of different ways to love someone." Indeed, while in Nebraska, Sabine comes to love the members of Parsifal's family in unexpected ways, most notably developing a romantic love for Parsifal's unhappily married sister Kitty that takes them both by surprise. Given the emotion each woman has invested in Parsifal, their mutual attraction might seem to be a desperate act of substitution. Yet Patchett implies that, in Kitty, Sabine has finally found the real passion of her life: "This was the thing that everyone had told her about, the thing that she had given up for Parsifal before she really understood what it was." Sabine's relationship with Kitty is no more unlikely than her relationship with Parsifal and no more incredible than the true magic Sabine works at the end of the book, when she performs an impossible card trick she has learned from Parsifal in a dream.

Sabine's debut as a magician occurs at the reception celebrating her sister-in-law Bertie's marriage, a day of festivity and hope that offsets earlier scenes of grief and violence. The girl who serves as magician's assistant is the only guest who realizes Sabine's performance is truly marvelous, but both Bertie and Kitty describe the act as "wonderful"; and Patchett further emphasizes the concluding mood of awe by having Sabine reflect "how wonderful it was to have the bride bring you your cake, the bride who looked so much like a cake herself, shining white and in every way decorated." This mood of brightness and elation is anticipated early in the "Nebraska" section of the book when Sabine lands in the midst of a blizzard after a nerve-racking flight in a small plane. At the airport, Bertie and Mrs. Fetters "called her name with a kind of joyful wonder that she had never heard in the word Sabine before. They threw themselves together onto her neck. What was lost is now found." The ceremonial welcome, with its biblical echo of the beloved's return, does not immediately lift the depressing impact of Parsifal's death, however. For the Fetters women, Sabine's presence helps to compensate for Guy's absence; but Sabine is convinced that "without magicians, the assistants were lost." Only after weeks of delving into his family past is she able to redefine herself and face the future, an act of reconstruction that consumes her sleeping hours as well as the waking ones.

With increasing emphasis, Patchett's first three books display the power of the imagination to transcend the most stubborn obstacles to understanding; and, like the Taft scenes in her second novel, Sabine's dreams of Phan and Parsifal are central to the structure and the meaning of *The Magician's Assistant.* Parsifal's talent for professional illusions and private mysteries is no more impressive than the imaginative capability Sabine demonstrates in fitting together the reported pieces of his life as meticulously as she builds architectural models in Los Angeles. The high value her clients place on these intricate creations affirms that Sabine's sleight of hand is not limited to her performances as Parsifal's assistant. Her greatest tour de force of all, however, is neither her legerdemain on stage nor her architectural work but her dream work.

During the fourteen months after Phan's agonizing death, Sabine humored Parsifal when he related his dreams about a refreshed and beautiful Phan lounging by a gorgeous swimming pool: "She put no stock in dreams. To her they were just a television left on in another room." Because Sabine has no memory of her own dreams at the beginning of the novel, the vivid scenes that come to her after Parsifal's death are especially remarkable. While Parsifal's dreams were consolatory in function, Sabine's are visionary, prophesying future events and illuminating the past. In her most shocking reverie, she understands that Phan intervened from the afterlife to grant her desperate wish that Parsifal be spared a drawn-out death from AIDS. Although Sabine's subconscious could be producing outrageous answers to her urgent questions, these visions seem more like authentic apparitions or visitations than dreams. Moreover, near the end of the novel, Kitty—who has never met Phan—tells Sabine that she too dreams about both men, "all the time."

The novelist Robert Olen Butler says (on the book's dustcover) that "reading *The Magician's Assistant* is like watching a master illusionist at work. Ann Patchett fills her readers with wonder, delight, and a new sense of possibility." At the same time Patchett is a magician, Parsifal—like John Nickel in *Taft*—is an author. For those who love him, he is a treasured text as well. According to Kitty, her brother "rewrote his whole life history. He could be his own father"; and Sabine is consoled by the prospect of learning at last about his first eighteen years, "forgotten volumes of her favorite work." Borrowing the name of the Arthurian knight who found the Grail despite all the odds against him, Parsifal refashioned himself so thoroughly that he nearly managed to erase the bleak plot and the forbidding patriarch of his youth. He even revised the story behind the neat scar on his face: a hockey injury at Dartmouth, he tells Sabine. Yet he never went to Dartmouth, and Dot Fetters later tells her that seven-year-old Guy fell while running with the lawn shears and an emergency room doctor had to put Guy in a laundry bag to stitch his deep cut after he refused medical treatment.

Much more terrible is the confrontation between the teenaged Guy and his abusive father that Kitty describes to the shocked Sabine. Intervening when Albert Fetters kicked the pregnant Dot Fetters on the kitchen floor, the boy hit the enraged man, accidentally killing him. When Guy's sister Bertie was born, Guy was in the state reformatory; and he saw the family only briefly on his release three years later, before he became Parsifal, a quintessential Californian and a splendid guest on the Johnny Carson show. The point of magic, Sabine reflects, is "to take people in, make them forget what was real and possible"; and Parsifal's fictions serve the same powerful purpose.

Distracted by the improbabilities Patchett herself conjures up, the reviewer Suzanne Berne says the main attraction of *The Magician's Assistant* lies in the countless little means by which Parsifal's loved ones console each other and strengthen the bonds among them. Yet Berne also allows that "a struggle with credulity" could be integral to Patchett's theme of love's transformative magic: "Improbable relationships can flourish; strange havens do exist. Becoming accustomed to sad endings may be more naïve than believing, now and then, in happily ever after." In fact, Patchett's endings have less in common with fairy tales than they do with Shakespeare's tragicomedies or Stephen Sondheim's dark musicals. A new order is established but it is tentative, and the survivors' scars are impossible to ignore, even in wedding regalia.

BEL CANTO

Creative writing instructors usually advise students to write about what they know and to avoid melodrama, Ann Patchett notes; but she has always been attracted to the unfamiliar, and she decided that *Bel Canto* would follow her melodramatic urge to its limits. In contrast to the domestic emergencies in *The Patron Saint of Liars, Taft,* and *The Magician's Assistant,* the plot of her 2001 novel was linked to an actual and very public crisis. Gripped by the news coverage of the terrorist takeover at the Japanese embassy in Lima, Peru, in 1996, Patchett was imagining characters for her fourth novel even before the three-month siege ended. Media reports on hostages and captors who played soccer and chess together, ordered pizzas, and watched soap operas fascinated the author with their ironies and incongruities.

Although Patchett sets her action in an unnamed South American country and fills the vice president's mansion with an international cast, she sees connections between *Bel Canto* and her previous work. In an article for the *BookPage* website, she says that the Lima tragedy "had all the elements I was interested in: the construction of family, the displacement from home, a life that was at once dangerous and completely benign." If the danger in this book is on a scale unprecedented in her earlier stories, so is the tender air of benignity. *Bel Canto* was published early in summer 2001, when the Peruvian assault had faded in the collective memory; but, in the aftermath of the September 11, 2001, terrorist attacks, the novelist Robb Forman Dew believed Americans might take comfort from Patchett's book because of its ultimate hopefulness.

Three protagonists—the international lyric soprano Roxane Coss, the famous electronics executive Katsumi Hosokawa, and the brilliant translator Gen Watanabe—embody the hopes and longings of this largest, most unusual of Patchett's fictional communities. As a performance artist, Roxane Coss is even more charismatic and more spectacular than Parsifal of *The Magician's Assistant.* Engaged at a large sum to be the centerpiece of a single evening's festivities, she is flown to the remote Spanish-speaking nation for commercial rather than artistic ends. Hoping to lure a major Japanese firm to boost the economy, the government persuades Hosokawa to celebrate his fifty-third birthday at an exclusive presentation by the woman whose voice he prizes above that of Maria Callas. Opera has been Hosokawa's obsession since 1954, when his father accompanied him to *Rigoletto* as a gift on his eleventh birthday: "Tiny people, insects, really, slipped out from behind the curtains, opened their mouths, and with their voices gilded the walls with their yearning, their grief, their boundless, reckless love that would lead each one to separate ruin." Patchett's reference to 1954 makes it clear that *Bel Canto* is set in 1996, the year of the guerrilla takeover in Peru, a country she visited in the course of her research for the novel. Yet the soul of the novel is not politics but beautiful singing, as the title implies; and Patchett's most extensive preparation for writing was her immersion in opera.

Patchett says she created the character of the soprano from Chicago because the real-life takeover was a situation suited to opera. Her model for Roxane Coss's magnetic personality was Karol Bennett, the only opera singer Patchett knows personally. Although they were fellows together at the Bunting Institute at Radcliffe College during 1990–1991, Patchett had no recordings of Bennett's performances, and to imagine Roxane's voice she listened especially to recordings by Rene Fleming. Fred Plotkin's *Opera 101* was Patchett's valuable guidebook, and reading the libretto before hearing each new opera helped her to prize a musical genre that had never appealed to her. Now an opera lover, Patchett feels as if she has learned a new language.

Because Mr. Hosokawa (as the narrator respectfully calls him) has loved Roxane Coss's voice for years before meeting her, and because music embodies life for him, it is not surprising that the Japanese pilgrim falls in love with the woman herself. More unexpected, however, is the degree of devotion she inspires among hostages and terrorists alike. After her Swedish accompanist dies of a diabetic attack and the three terrorist generals release most of the mansion's guests and staff members, Roxane is the sole woman of the forty captives who remain. The best musician among them replaces the Swede at the piano for Roxane's daily singing, but each of the others is, in a sense, the soprano's assistant. As the Russian Fyodorov passionately declares, "It is a kind of talent in itself, to be an audience."

Before many weeks pass, Roxane's companions adjust so thoroughly to their new existence that it becomes difficult to imagine a world beyond the walls surrounding the landscaped grounds. Unusual friendships and skills flourish; most miraculous, perhaps, is the emergence of Cesar, a teenaged terrorist, as a musical prodigy who can imitate Roxane's soprano voice with uncanny precision. Patchett compares her enclosed universe to the confined stage on which Thomas Mann developed the action of *The Magic Mountain,* and she joked to Dave Weich that another "artistic influence" was the adventure film *The Poseidon Adventure:* "You're going along, it's fine, then everything turns upside down, people band together, sacrifices are made, there's passion, there's loss, there's a journey, and at the end you cut a hole in the boat and you come out into the light." All that her novel lacks, she says, is the emergence from the dark.

A seasonal mist named the *garua* dims the light considerably in *Bel Canto,* but of course Patchett has the book's dark climax in mind. Before the end of the first chapter, the narrator remarks that "in fact it was the terrorists who would not survive the ordeal," a brief statement that is easily forgotten in the course of the dramatic plot. During the months of the siege, several young terrorists are transfixed by a television soap opera that tells a parallel story of terrorism, captivity, and romance; and Patchett's readers are tempted to imagine a correspondingly happy finale for the book. On the advice of her novelist friend Elizabeth Mc-Cracken, Patchett eliminated a prologue that would have given readers more clues to the violent outcome. Instead of a prologue, Patchett provides an epilogue; and it is set not in South America but in Italy, where Roxane Coss has just married a fellow survivor, Gen Watanabe. Roxane's music is now as necessary to Gen as it had been to Mr. Hosokawa, the only hostage killed in the government's counterattack—shot to death while protecting the terrorist Carmen, whom Gen had loved. Like each of Patchett's previous novels, *Bel Canto* concludes with a tenuous recovery from great losses. The newly-weds will establish a new life together, not in Roxane's America or Gen's Japan, but in the country where, according to the bridegroom, all opera singers should live. Their fellow survivor Simon Thibault is sure that the couple married for love: "the love of each other and the love of all the people they remembered."

Love is, in fact, Ann Patchett's leitmotiv, from *The Patron Saint of Liars* through *Bel Canto;* and, as Sabine tells Dot Fetters in *The Magician's Assistant,* there are many ways of showing love. Because Patchett refuses to repeat herself, each of the four novels develops a highly distinctive set of circumstances and characters, as well as a different mode of story-telling. She believes the greatest achievement of *Bel Canto* is her invention of a truly omniscient third-person narrator, capable of gliding into every corner of Patchett's literary microcosm. Without claiming to match Tolstoy's virtuosity, she says that big nineteenth-century novels like *Anna Karenina* were her exemplars. Patchett's narrator pays homage to another epic novelist in observing that one of the hostages is reading García Márquez's *One Hundred Years of Solitude.* As the 2002 selection of the PEN/Faulkner Foundation, *Bel Canto* places the author in the company of such outstanding American authors as Peter Taylor, John Edgar Wideman, Richard Ford, Ha Jin, and Philip Roth.

Bel Canto is Patchett's most direct statement on the astonishing power of art to arrest time and set it into motion. Roxane Coss wields this power, but so does the novelist. She places her characters in a suspended moment, and they realize the inadequacy of clocks to measure their confusing experience. In a gesture reminiscent of Welty's wise old Solomon in the story "Liv-vie," Gen gives his watch to a young terrorist because the hours are no longer under his control. The narrator meditates, sometimes wryly, on the relativity of time, offering similes to convey the captives' new perceptions. It is, for example, "as if the world had become a giant train station in which everything was delayed until further notice." Patchett's fifth novel promised to be as unique as its predecessors, but the occasional philosophizing in *Bel Canto* anticipated issues to come. Loosely structured on Fyodor Dostoevsky's *The Brothers Karamazov,* the author's work in progress in 2002 concerns the intersection between science and faith. Readers might speculate that, at the point of juncture, Patchett would position an uncommon family, threatened at the heart, yet open—once again—to signs and wonders.

Selected Bibliography

WORKS OF ANN PATCHETT

NOVELS
The Patron Saint of Liars. Boston: Houghton Mifflin, 1992.
Taft. Boston: Houghton Mifflin, 1994.
The Magician's Assistant. New York: Harcourt Brace, 1997.
Bel Canto. New York: HarperCollins, 2001.

ESSAYS
"The Sacrament of Divorce." In *Women on Divorce: A Bedside Companion.* Edited by Penny Kaganoff and Susan Spano. New York: Harcourt Brace, 1995. Pp. 1–13. (With reference to her own experience, Patchett speaks of the pain involved in failed marriages, as well as the second chances offered by divorce.)
"Snake Bite." In *Joyful Noise: The New Testament Revisited.* Edited by Rick Moody and Darcey Steinke. Boston: Little, Brown, 1997. Pp. 145–151. (Citing the biblical sources for snake handling, Patchett comments on the tradition in the Church of the Holiness Faith in the South.)
"My Road to Hell Was Paved." *Outside* (http://www.outsidemag.com/magazine/0698/9806

rv.html), June 1998. (A comic narrative of Patchett's conversion to life on the road in a twenty-nine-foot recreational vehicle named Minnie.)

"Writing and a Life Lived Well: Notes on Allan Gurganus." In *Why I Write: Thoughts on the Craft of Fiction.* Edited by Will Blythe. Boston: Little, Brown, 1998. Pp. 61–68. (Patchett discusses her early decision to become a writer and the impact of the novelist Allan Gurganus, her first college fiction teacher.)

"As Is the Daughter, So Is Her Mother." *New York Times Magazine,* July 23, 2000, p. 66. (Patchett pays tribute to her mother for publishing a late-life first novel, the best-selling love story *Julie and Romeo.*)

"An Affair to Remember." *Gourmet,* June 2001, pp. 83, 86–87. (Patchett's humorous account of her trip to Italy for the opera, this essay refers to her novel *Bel Canto.*)

"Women among Women." *New York Times Magazine,* September 9, 2001, pp. 97, 103. (In her essay for the "Women and Power" issue, Patchett reflects on the lifelong pleasure and comfort of female company.)

"The Long Drive Home." *New York Times Magazine,* November 25, 2001, pp. 21–22. (Patchett describes the personal and national appeal of road trips through America's open spaces, but in the aftermath of the September 2001 terrorist attacks she calls for conservation of fuel resources as a patriotic measure.)

"Ann Patchett: Turning a News Story into a Novel." *BookPage* (http://www.bookpage.com/0106bp/ann_patchett.html). (Patchett's commentary on the writing of *Bel Canto.*)

"Southern Comforts." *New York Times Magazine,* December 30, 2001, p. 40. (Comparing the writer Eudora Welty and the NASCAR celebrity Dale Earnhardt after their deaths in 2001, Patchett notes the persistence of southern identity.)

SHORT STORIES

"All Little Colored Children Should Play the Harmonica." *Paris Review* 26:180–192 (winter 1984).

"Heaven." *Southern Review* 25, no. 3:734–741 (July 1989).

"Why I Like Laurel." *Seventeen,* April 1990, pp. 244–245, 248–251.

CRITICAL AND BIOGRAPHICAL STUDIES

Berne, Suzanne. "Sleight of Hand." *New York Times Book Review,* November 16, 1997, p. 17. (Review of *The Magician's Assistant.*)

Clark, Alex. "Danger Arias." *The Guardian* (Manchester, U.K.), July 14, 2001. (http://books.guardian.co.uk/reviews/generalfiction/0,6121,521254,00.html). (Review of *Bel Canto.*)

Dew, Robb Forman. "Comfort Books: Nourishing the Spirit." *Washington Post Book World,* December 2, 2001, p. 3. (One of twelve writers and scholars invited to recommend books for stressful times, Dew selects *Bel Canto.*)

McDermott, Alice. "A Sense of the Miraculous." *New York Times Book Review,* July 26, 1992, p. 6. (Review of *The Patron Saint of Liars.*)

"Patchett, Ann 1963–." In *Contemporary Authors, New Revision Series.* Vol. 64. Detroit: Gale, 1998. Pp. 310–311. (This concise survey of the works through *The Magician's Assistant* includes a bibliography of periodical reviews.)

Postlethwaite, Diana. "Memphis Blues Again." *New York Times Book Review,* October 16, 1994, p. 11. (Review of *Taft.*)

Stelzmann, Rainulf A. "Das Problem der Heiligkeit in unserer Zeit: Die Romane Anne Tylers und Ann Patchetts." *Stimmen der Zeit* 211, no. 7:489–500 (July 1993). (This early response to Patchett's fiction by a German scholar compares her to Anne Tyler for their portrayals of the American middle class.)

Vogrin, Valerie. "Patchett, Ann." In *American Women Writers: A Critical Reference Guide from Colonial Times to the Present,* 2d ed. Vol. 3. Edited by Taryn Benbow-Pfalzgraf. Detroit: St. James Press, 2000. P. 258. (The bibliographical note for this brief overview of Patchett's career lists several reviews of her first three novels.)

INTERVIEWS

Bernstein, Elizabeth. "*PW* Interview: Ann Patchett: The Novelist as Magician." *Publishers Weekly,* October 13, 1997, pp. 52–53. (An excellent brief introduction to Patchett's life, personality, and the works through *The Magician's Assistant.*)

Bojorquez, Jennifer. "The Magic Touch: Ann Patchett Learns a Few Tricks of Her Own While Writing *The Magician's Assistant,* A Magical Love Story." *Sacramento Bee,* October 15, 1998, p. E1. (This West Coast interviewer cites several responses to the earlier novels and asks Patchett about her home life and her research for *The Magician's Assistant.*)

Hall, Joan Wylie. "Ann Patchett's 'Imagination Travel.'" *Southern Register,* winter 2002, pp. 13–14. (Patchett comments on southern authors and audiences, Morgan Freeman's interest in *Taft,* and her research on opera for *Bel Canto.*)

McCracken, Elizabeth. "Author Interview." In "Reader's Guide to *Taft.*" *ReadingGroupGuides.com* (http://www.readinggroupguides.com/guides/taft-author.html#interview). (The best source on the writing of Patchett's second novel, this interview with her friend McCracken discusses the characters, point of view, and sense of danger in *Taft.*)

Moonshower, Candace B. "One on One with Anne [*sic*] Patchett." *Pif Magazine,* January 2001 (http://www.pifmagazine.com/2001/01/i_a_patchett1.php3). (A good source of biographical information, especially on the early roots of her writing career, this long interview refers to Patchett's themes, settings, the women in her novels, and several of her favorite authors.)

Weich, Dave. "Ann Patchett Hits All the Right Notes." Powells online bookstore (http://www.powells.com/authors/patchett.html), June 27, 2001. (This lengthy conversation with Patchett focuses on *Bel Canto,* with additional material on the author's life, her early freelance writing, and the themes of her fiction.)

Weisgall, Deborah. "Summer Reading 2001: The Magic Opera." *Radcliffe Quarterly* (summer 2001) (http://www.radcliffe.edu/quarterly/200103/summer8a.html). (In this brief but substantial discussion of *Bel Canto,* Patchett sees the protagonist Roxane Coss as a redemptive force and views Messner, the Red Cross negotiator, as a tragic Cassandra figure.)

FILM BASED ON A WORK OF ANN PATCHETT

The Patron Saint of Liars. Screenplay by Lynn Roth. Directed by Stephen Gyllenhaal. CBS television, 1998.

—JOAN WYLIE HALL

Richard Russo

1949–

PLACE GIVES RISE to character in the work of Richard Russo. He is known mainly for five novels that blend comic character studies with a deep sense of the dignity of the working class in vivid small-town American locations. Despite his own postgraduate education, Russo consistently exhibits ambivalence about the world of academia; his works clearly value the pragmatism, stoicism, humor, and determination associated with working people rather than the heady abstractions linked with the life of the mind. His work also betrays a passionate but unsentimental attachment to the fading towns of the industrial Northeast and respect for the hardworking men and women who populate them. Russo's deft comic sense, which he has characterized as "a kind of spiritual optimism," nevertheless allows amusing interludes that run the gamut from black humor to slapstick.

In Russo's fictional world, characters' fates are inextricably linked, and everything can be seen from more than one perspective. His commitment to showing the web of connections among characters, however, proceeds in an apparently desultory way, through episodic and occasionally rambling narratives that situate Russo's work squarely in the realist tradition. His fiction is informed by a comic spirit of generosity that often allows for reconciliation even among characters who are avowed enemies. Perhaps this is why this realistic writer has also been called, by Mel Gussow for the *New York Times,* "an alchemist, transforming the quotidian—everyday people and seemingly ordinary events—into the quintessential." Russo has also written short stories, television movies, and several screenplays.

BIOGRAPHY

Richard Russo was born on July 15, 1949, in the small industrial town of Gloversville, New York, to working-class parents. His father, James Russo, was a manual laborer who preferred the company of his drinking companions to that of his young son, and the two only became close when Russo grew old enough to occupy a nearby barstool and enjoy his father's stories. His mother, Jean Findlay, indulged her son's passion for reading and found money to buy the books he craved even when times were tight. Russo's maternal grandfather had instilled in his daughter a desire for the college education he himself could never afford. When her education was cut short by her marriage, Russo's mother passed the ambition along to her son. He has credited his mother with making him a writer.

Russo attended Bishop Burke High School, where, he has said, he preferred to read anything that was not assigned over whatever was in the school curriculum. After graduation he put as much distance as he could between himself and the depressed upstate town in which he had grown up. He received a bachelor's degree from the University of Arizona, earning money to pay for his education by doing manual labor on road crews in New York State, occasionally working alongside his father. He continued his studies, earning a Ph.D. in American literature from Arizona in 1980 and an M.F.A. in 1981.

Shortly before he completed his doctorate, Russo strayed into creative writing classes. A professor who read a draft of a first novel identified one chapter, a flashback occurring among blue-collar workers in New York State, as the only bit worth saving and encouraged Russo to expand that section. It turned out to be good advice. Russo found his natural subject by writing about the place and people he knew best. All of his novels are set in the industrial Northeast, largely among the working classes. Though James Russo died of lung cancer before his son's first novel appeared in print, Richard Russo has repeatedly written with insight about the relation between charismatic but difficult fathers and sons.

Russo published his first novels while teaching at Southern Illinois University at Carbondale, at Pennsylvania State University at Altoona, and at Colby College in Maine. The sale of the film rights to his third novel, *Nobody's Fool* (1993), in the mid-1990s enabled Russo to leave his teaching career and pursue writing full-time. Russo lives with his family (his wife, Barbara, and his daughters, Kate and Emily) in coastal Maine, where he writes every day in a local delicatessen amid the regular clientele. He was awarded the Pulitzer Prize for fiction in 2002 for his fifth novel, *Empire Falls* (2001).

MOHAWK

"The town of Mohawk, like its residents, is located in the author's imagination." This brief disclaimer is found on the title page of *Mohawk* (1986), Russo's first novel and the first of two to take place in this fading small town in upstate New York. Once a center for leather tanning, Mohawk is limping along. Years of chemical dumping are taking their toll on its residents, who are dying at unprecedented rates from cancer and related diseases. But Mohawk is a toxic environment in more ways than one. It is also a place where long-held secrets and failures from the past come back; where no ghost is ever, it seems, entirely buried.

Two locations are especially important and will recur in Russo's novels. One is the tavern where men gather at the end of a working day:

> Greenie's seldom did any real business, except for roughly one hour a day. During that hour it did the best business in town. At a few minutes before five, men from the tannery and surrounding glove shops began to drop in for a quick schooner on the way home to dinner. Between five and six, the bartender didn't bother to turn off the tap, and just ran his tapered glasses beneath the wide open spigot. The second busiest man in Greenie's was Untemeyer, the bookie, who went through three tablets of paper slips, one hundred sheets each, looking up from his task only long enough to see whose name to write down next.

Gambling is a preoccupation for Russo's characters in this and later novels. Yet when one man's number finally hits, he is so stunned that he gives the money away. Nowhere in his calculation of odds does winning actually seem possible, given Mohawk's hard-luck history.

The second location where everyone gathers is the Mohawk Grill. Its proprietor, the laconic Harry Saunders, feeds everyone in town, including Mohawk's strangest resident, a near-silent, shaggy man in his thirties. "Wild Bill" Gaffney would be homeless without Harry, and he is, albeit unwittingly, at the center of the novel's most important actions. Taunted by a gang of tough local teenage boys, Wild Bill hurts one of them badly when he intervenes to stop a fight in which Randall Younger is being beaten. Later Randall repays the debt by rescuing Wild Bill, almost magically, from a hospital being demolished. It is a feat that goes down in town lore. Randall's grandfather Mather Grouse marvels:

> The boy was responsible. Facing annihilation, he had entered the collapsing building even as the very roof and walls were giving way . . . . *Just think of it.* No man could have done it. Only a boy. But just the same. The boy calmly stepping

through the chaos . . . calmly climbing through the rubble, in through one of the broken windows on the ground floor, bricks and wiring and wood falling all around, the walls shuddering under the impact of the [wrecking] ball, the air too thick to breathe.

A few people in town, however, are not pleased to see Wild Bill walk away. His sadistic father, Rory, a petty criminal with the next score on his mind, does not like being reminded of his son's existence. But his uncle Walt, the local cop, is tormented by the sight of Wild Bill. Officer Gaffney is oppressed by a memory he cannot banish. Years earlier Wild Bill was a normal if rebellious teenager, and Rory beat his son savagely, injuring him to the point of brain damage. Fearful of his cruel brother, Walt has carried the secret of his own failure to intervene ever since. Now just the sight of Wild Bill shambling down the street makes him angry and ashamed. "For some time now, the policeman has understood that [when he hesitated] he'd made the choice of his life, though he hadn't suspected it at the time. Or even for years afterward." Walt's inability to turn his brother Rory over to the authorities has paid dividends in shame and guilt over the years and issues in a violent confrontation that leaves all three men dead at the end of the novel.

Though it builds to a melodramatic conclusion, *Mohawk* proceeds in an apparently desultory way, moving back and forth among the characters and shifting forward six years to follow Randall Younger, now a college dropout, returning to town. Anxious to avoid the Vietnam draft and unsure what he should do next, Randall must also figure out how to negotiate the competing claims of his divorced parents, his frustrated mother and his unreliable, alcoholic father. In characteristic fashion Russo develops all these characters equally. Randall's mother, Anne, is herself a dutiful daughter who has returned to Mohawk to tend her aging parents after years in New York City. This move also brings Anne nearer to the one man she has ever really loved, Dan Wood, who has been in a wheelchair since an automobile accident years ago but is still married to Anne's cousin and best friend. Life in Mohawk is not easy for Anne. Her mother is losing her grip on reality (in a memorable scene the elderly woman digs up the front lawn at dawn to get rid of all the earthworms), and Anne's proud, stern father is dying slowly of emphysema, his oxygen tank a battlefield between his controlling wife and adult daughter. Starved for air as he is, the sick Mather Grouse enjoys his only full breath when he is tugging on a forbidden cigarette. Mather, too, is haunted by the claims of the past. He has a secret that plagues him and is being taunted by Rory Gaffney, the one man in town who suspects it.

But Anne's former husband, Dallas Younger, who has never left Mohawk and who has done little with his life since his athletic stardom in high school, is in some ways Russo's central character. Dallas is the feckless, generous, irresponsible figure who recurs throughout Russo's novels and who is clearly modeled on Russo's own father. Dallas has never known how to be a father to Randall; he drinks too much, lives precariously from paycheck to insufficient paycheck, and is still mourning the death of his brother without knowing how to acknowledge his loss directly. Instead he turns up at odd hours at his brother's house to visit the widow and her young daughter, making drunken, rambling offers of help, which he promptly forgets. He means well but is completely unable to make good on his promises:

> Dallas said he was sorry, and he was, too, though in much the same way he was sorry about a rainy day or something else he had no control over. When he drank too much, he nearly always blacked out and had to depend on people to tell him what he'd been up to, and because he was often told that he became sentimental at such times, he supposed it must be true, though he couldn't say for sure.

Dallas, like the characters who follow him in later novels, exerts an unexpectedly important influence on the adolescent son from whose life he has been largely absent. In *Mohawk,* Randall turns out to be both his parents' child. Given the opportunity and means to act honorably in a final confrontation with the Gaffney brothers, he acquits his mother's side of the family well and even (after a fashion) avenges the harm done to old Mather Grouse by the Gaffneys. But Randall also acts shrewdly. He has enough of his father in him to leave jail (where he has been wrongly detained) through the bathroom window, thus escaping the military police who are waiting outside to take him to his draft board for military service.

Mohawk is a complexly plotted, episodic novel that concludes by tracing each of its many characters' fates. The author won praise for his skill at rendering the rhythms of life in a small town, for devising an immensely readable narrative, and for creating sympathetic characters. Even in his first book, Russo prizes a spirit of forgiveness that is remarkable given the damage his characters do to each other. The image of Wild Bill struggling to carry the body of his abusive father toward the long-demolished hospital for help is one the reader will not easily forget. For Russo sometimes the most apparently damaged characters have hearts that are whole.

THE RISK POOL

Russo's second novel is also set in Mohawk, and the narrative is divided into four sections corresponding to the four "seasons" in the depressed town: "Fourth of July," "Mohawk Fair," "Eat the Bird," and "Winter." As *The Risk Pool* (1988) opens, the narrator, Ned Hall, explains how his father had to be dragged at gunpoint from a poker game while his mother gave birth to Ned. The action is largely directed in fact by the narrator's intermittent but memo-

rable contacts with his ne'er-do-well father. Sam Hall arrives at Ned's schoolyard in a dirty white convertible one afternoon in 1953, offering the first-grader a ride and putting the lie to the story the boy has told, that his father is dead. He materializes in the backyard one day shortly afterward, watching as his timid son contemplates jumping from one tree branch to the next highest one.

> I knew when I saw him standing there that I had never intended to jump. "Well?" he said. And that one word was all it took. I don't remember jumping. Suddenly, I just had a hold of the limb with both hands, then had a knee over, then with a heave, I was up. The rest of the way would be easy, I knew, and I didn't care about it. I could do it any day.

A week later, "he kidnapped me," Ned recalls. Sam takes Ned fishing, and in the chaotic excitement of his father's orbit, the boy forgets the orderly, protected world his mother has made for him. They return to face his mother's wrath. The normally placid woman pulls out her father's old service revolver and fires six rounds into the car before Sam disappears again, leaving his puzzled son dreaming of his father's return.

Russo has said, "The deepest feelings of *The Risk Pool* are traceable to me and my father." His parents divorced when he was in high school, as he explained to Mel Gussow: "My father wasn't good at enforceable obligations, like husband to wife. As soon as you told him he had to do something, that was the end of that." However, Russo grew closer to his father as the years passed; his fictional characters bear witness to a boy's continuing attempts to puzzle out his charismatic but elusive parent. In *The Risk Pool* the narrator offers Sam's point of view, presumably as his son eventually comes to understand it:

> He had intended the kidnapping—an idea he thought of and acted upon in the same instant—to

demonstrate that a boy *needed* a father. Instead, everything had turned out badly. . . . He had snatched a clean, happy, reasonably well-adjusted boy and was returning less than twenty-four hours later a dirty little vagabond in wet sneakers and a torn t-shirt, whose poison-ivied legs and arms were raked raw, whose eyes were nearly swollen shut.

As another character observes, Sam Hall "should have been issued with a warning label."

In the absence of his father, Ned's home life is considerably quieter. His mother, who calms down from her ordeal with the help first of Librium and then of the Catholic Church, forms an attachment to a young priest. Ned, an altar boy, spends his summer days at the rectory with Father Michaels while his mother is at work. One morning he sees Father Michaels, sans collar, at the breakfast table. Even more puzzling is the priest's refusal to give Ned's radiant mother Communion when she approaches the altar rail the next Sunday morning. Though his mother looks "softer, lovelier, almost younger" that morning at Mass, she quits going to church "cold turkey" when Father Michaels leaves the altar abruptly. Ned's mother descends into a withering depression, losing her job and refusing to leave the house.

Almost magically Sam Hall reappears. Shocked by his wife's disintegration, Sam brings Ned to live in his cavernous, almost empty apartment above Klein's department store in downtown Mohawk. The town has seen better days; most of the stately old buildings have been vacated, condemned, or razed. Sam gets Ned a job sweeping up the beauty salon across the hall, and the boy learns both to hide his savings from his improvident father and to shoplift by letting himself into Klein's after hours. He also meets his father's friends, men who move restlessly from bar to bar, stopping often to place bets, argue about the handicapping of horses, or have a bite at the Mohawk Grill. (Several characters from *Mohawk* reappear,

though they are relegated to minor roles.) Ned lives more in his father's world than one populated by his peers. Though he spends many happy afternoons ensconced in the public library, there is virtually no mention of school hours or childhood friends. Sam's buddies treat the boy with the same benign disregard his father offers, but not to worry: "Lest it seem that I was neglected, I should point out that once I became known to the Mohawk Grill crowd, it was like having about two dozen more or less negligent fathers whose slender attentions and vague goodwill nevertheless added up."

Ned also meets Sam's longtime girlfriend, Eileen Littler, and observes firsthand the war of wills between Sam and Eileen's muscle-bound teenage son, Drew: "A meal at the Littlers' was a feast of tension." Sam, at best inattentive toward his own son, becomes murderously angry at Drew's laziness and lack of respect for his mother. Their hostilities veer into violence, eventually estranging Eileen from Sam. Drew's mother has never revealed the name of her son's father, and the boy's twin obsessions are his motorcycle (on which he is killed before the novel ends) and his anger at the "Money People," especially Jack Ward, whose beautiful home Drew vows he will own one day. Only when Jack Ward dies unexpectedly does the meaning of Drew's ambition become clear to Ned: Drew believes Ward is his father. This is neither confirmed nor denied; the author is more interested in the stories people tell themselves than in their veracity. At the same time *The Risk Pool* is a novel about the power of paternity; his lack of a father makes Drew angry, confused, and recklessly self-destructive.

Money is crucial in a Russo novel; here too a father's power to teach is clear. Folks in rundown Mohawk live close to the bone, and thrifty Ned works first cleaning the beauty parlor, then salvaging lost golf balls from the country club pond and reselling them to golfers. But when

Sam goes to jail briefly, he helps himself to Ned's carefully concealed savings account, and the boy learns that money is not something to get steamed up over: "[Sam] figured if you had money and somebody needed some, you gave it to him, at least if the guy was all right and would do the same for you. Later on, if you needed it and he had it you could call on him. In the meantime, if you didn't need it, you left him alone." Of his own father, Russo told Gussow, "He was one of the most generous men I've ever known about any kind of unenforceable obligation." Ned also comes to understand his own career as a shoplifter when he ponders the thievery he sees at Jack Ward's house during the man's wake: "Most people who stole weren't taking what they believed to be others' property. They were taking what they themselves deserved, all the things they'd been cheated out of. That, now that I thought about it, was why I'd raided Klein's. It had been an act of revenge, not avarice."

So bifurcated is Ned's upbringing that at one point the boy suspects his mother, hospitalized after her breakdown, has died and no one will tell him. When after two years his mother recovers her health enough to provide a home for Ned, he returns to "clean sheets, freshly pressed shirts, dinners eaten at a table in the house where I lived." He does not see his father again for ten years, he reports, "nor did I ever hear a word concerning his whereabouts. Not a letter, not a Christmas card." The novel accordingly skips any account of these years, picking up the narrative only when Sam Hall reenters.

A decade later Ned is a compulsive gambler in Arizona who has just lost his graduate school tuition money. The autobiographical link is clear: Russo himself received a doctorate in American literature from the University of Arizona. He returned home to do construction work alongside his father in New York State each summer, as he told Wendy Smith for *Publishers Weekly:*

My life has become easier through education, but I know what real work is. That sense of these people and their lives trails behind me and is always a factor in my imagination. As a younger man, I equated success with putting that world behind me. In terms of my writing, in terms of my heart, it took me a long time to discover that it meant more than anything else.

To the critic Edward Hower he has said, "We'll never know any place better than the place we grew up, and no place, I suspect, will ever be more important to us, at least in terms of our imaginative lives."

While Ned is trying to figure out how to recover from his financial tailspin, he is called back to Mohawk. His father's drinking, casual for years, has gotten out of control. The remaining two sections of the novel feature Ned's return to Mohawk after a time away. Both times Ned is summoned by his father's friends to attend to Sam's failing health; both times the reluctant patient instead restores his son. This "cure" involves immersion in Sam's chaotic, unruly life. Ned takes a job tending bar (ostensibly as research for his anthropology thesis) and replaces gambling with serious drinking, falling effortlessly into step with his father. Russo describes a typical evening out with Sam and his friends:

With a blue baseball game tilting down from the corner above the bar, we tended to the business of being men, brown sweating bottles of beer lined up in phalanxes, bought not as needed but in rounds, the real drinkers setting a pace, like the lead runners in a road race, finding a stride, feeling instinctively the race's length, its rhythms. Our collective composition always changing, as somebody heard somebody was somewhere and went to find him, get that ten-spot he was owed, somebody else slipping into the vacated space at the bar, ensuring welcome by buying a round or promising to get the next one. Sometimes loud— all of us shouting at once, pointing at the replay on the blue screen—sometimes hushed, conspiratorial, can I take twenty till Monday, I wouldn't ask, but . . . It was all rhythm and stride and knowing when to move, what it would take to get you from where you were to another spot just like it a hundred yards down the street where they had two pool tables instead of the one. . . . When you understood the rhythms, the subtleties made sense.

Ned also accepts a commission from the widowed Mrs. Ward to edit her father's dense history of Mohawk County. Mrs. Ward is, like Ned's own mother, a remote woman who lives in a world dominated by memories of her powerful father. Ned enjoys working on the manuscript but is not blind to the ironies attending its eventual publication: "The editor . . . restored to the original every one of the thousand or so . . . changes I made, offering to the book-reading public of Mohawk County, [Mrs. Ward's] father's vision, complete, unmolested, faithful, and, trust me, utterly unreadable." Ned falls uneasily in love with the Wards' beautiful (if bland) daughter Tria and reflects on his ambivalence toward her as if it is unavoidable:

My father and [his friends] were Mohawk men, which meant that somewhere along the line each had turned his back on a woman. Many had turned their back on more than one. Most now realized that in doing so they'd fucked up. Some would even admit it when they were drunk enough. A few . . . would try to return thirty years after the fact, to women who didn't even exist anymore, who had gone evil or horny or crazy with waiting and raising kids, or had just dried up from working two hard jobs.

When it comes to relations with women, Ned fears that he too may be a "Mohawk man."

The novel's brief final episode brings Ned back to Mohawk (this time from New York City), after another decade, for his father's last days. Sam is reduced by cancer but still stubborn and full of more life than most healthy people enjoy. Ned is awaiting the birth of his own first child, which comes directly after his father's wake at a Mohawk bar. A younger Ned had declared that he regretted the two years spent "under my father's dubious spell" and

claimed that Sam had "always considered me a bit slow, permanently impaired by my mother's ethics and my early days as an altar boy." But the Ned of the novel's conclusion clearly shares the sentiment voiced at Sam's "send-off" party by one of his cronies: "I don't know who'll lead us astray now." Ned returns home to his newborn son voluntarily, not at gunpoint; his business in Mohawk is finished. Ned is ready to begin the important work of being a father himself.

The Risk Pool was widely praised for its closely observed details and, according to Jack Sullivan, its "blackly funny . . . brilliant, deadpan writing." Its meandering structure was also noted by Sullivan: "In line with [his characters'] boozy stoicism, Mr. Russo has designed an ingenious narrative method in which events seem to be building toward resolutions or epiphanies only to keep crashing in on themselves and lurching forward again, leaving eerie gaps in the story that resemble blackouts. . . . Yet seemingly random images and subplots do ultimately coalesce."

NOBODY'S FOOL

In *Nobody's Fool* (1993) Russo again sets in motion a large cast of characters who live in a small, run-down town in upstate New York. Unlike Mohawk, however, North Bath has seen better days. It was a vacation destination in the nineteenth century until its mineral springs suddenly went dry. Rival Schuyler Springs picked up the town's tourist trade, and North Bath's long decline began. Now the oldest elm trees are dying, and once-stately Victorian homes shelter the last survivors of the large families of yore. Russo's characters seldom look back though. They are too busy making ends meet to wax nostalgic about the old days. Characters beat a well-worn path from the diners, betting offices, and bars they frequent to each others' apartments and work sites, reliably reencountering each other as they do so.

Work—finding it and avoiding it—is central to the concerns of the book. The main character Sully is a likable, tough guy pushing sixty whose fall off a ladder has left him unable to do the demanding physical labor he knows. His lawyer and drinking friend Wirf thinks they have a pretty good workmen's compensation case. Wirf just wishes Sully would do his time in the community college philosophy course his disability agreement has consigned him to and stop taking jobs on the side. Sully knows better; the law is never going to give him any version of a free ride. He is just not lucky enough. Even worse, he thinks he may be at the beginning of a "stupid streak." The novel's events occur during a week and a half around Thanksgiving and trace the contours of Sully's bad luck until it turns into something surprising and wonderful.

Sully may lose the apartment he rents upstairs from Beryl Peoples, a retired eighth-grade teacher and his unlikely friend. Miss Beryl is also worried these days. She has decided this is the year God is going to "lower the boom" on her, and she only hopes she will know when the time is right to give up her independence. She fears depending on her son, Clive Jr., a banker who is pressing Miss Beryl to relinquish her large and comfortable Victorian house or at the very least to evict her unreliable tenant. Clive Jr. (whom Sully calls "The Bank") believes North Bath is about to experience a boom coincident with the building of "The Ultimate Escape Fun Park" on the outskirts of town. Clive insists North Bath will soon be the "Gold Coast," though many longtime residents are more dubious. The cemetery is next door to the proposed site, and "already the juxtaposition of the two 'ultimate escapes' had become a dark local joke." Much to his chagrin, Clive Jr. realizes, "There would always be at least two skeptics in Bath, at least as long as his mother and Sully were on the scene." Sully and Miss Beryl have a bond that Clive Jr. can neither fathom nor undo. Miss Beryl views Sully, her amiable, forgetful upstairs neighbor, as her ally, a word she is not at all sure applies to her own son. She recognizes in herself the "near total collapse of any natural maternal instinct to accord one's children more credit than they are due."

Beyond the threat of eviction, Sully is even lower than usual on money, and he needs a new truck. His bad knee makes itself known whether he is sitting, standing, or resting, and Sully is becoming more reliant on the free samples his personal pharmacist dispenses from the glove compartment of his car. When Sully is lucky, he has "ambient soreness," but lately his knee, "which always hummed dully, was singing full throat." "The sight of the grotesque swelling, the deep discoloration, the skin stretched so tightly that it glistened, was something Sully himself had grown accustomed to. It was the look on other people's faces that scared him." Sully has a high pain threshold, something he acquired from taking his father's drunken beatings as a boy and on which he prides himself. However, this pain has a new relentlessness.

But a man must work, and most of Sully's work is supplied, off the books, by Carl Roebuck, the one man in town Sully envies. At thirty-five Carl "was threatening to use up, singlehandedly, all the luck there was left in an unlucky town." Sully has a crush on Carl's beautiful wife, Toby. Carl, however, keeps giving Toby the sexually transmitted diseases he picks up during his many casual affairs, and she is pretty angry about it. Newly pregnant, Toby is more beautiful—and thus more tormenting—than ever. The two men have an ongoing battle about payment owed Sully for a past job. When Sully steals Carl's new snowblower as payment, Carl steals it back and secures it (or so he believes) by setting a vicious dog sentinel. Undeterred, Sully drugs the guard dog and reclaims the machine. Then the two men pass

Rasputin, whose drug-induced stroke has turned him into a drooling, affectionate—and wholly useless—beast, back and forth for the remainder of the novel.

Their comic exchanges do not hide the affectionate exasperation Sully feels for the younger man. Carl advises Sully to have surgery on his knee, noting his own improvement after a recent heart operation. "'I got news for you,' Sully said. 'They didn't fix your heart. They just made it so it wouldn't stop beating for a while. If they'd fixed it, you'd be faithful to your wife and pay your employees what you owe them.'" Sully always has the last word in their verbal sparring, which both men enjoy. Sully tells Carl:

> "In a town this size, there's only room for one lucky man, and you're him. The rest of us just have to do the best we can." Carl snorted. "You're the only man I know who believes in luck." Sully nodded. "I believed in intelligence and hard work until I met you. Only luck explains you."

The novel sparkles with Sully's pleasure in his wisecracks and quick retorts. No one is exempt. Sully is an equal-opportunity harasser, though he prefers those who cannot see it coming. "'I hope you don't ever catch fire and have me standing nearby with a hose,' the policeman said to Sully's retreating form. 'That's where you'd be, all right,' Sully said over his shoulder. 'Off at a safe distance, holding your hose.'" "Dialogue is what Mr. Russo does best," wrote the reviewer Francine Prose. "The novel's tone has the same low-key, smart-alecky intelligence as its characters," who are "capable of combining hard labor with metaphysical speculation."

Sully has a partner of sorts, the smelly and dull-witted Rub Squeers, who has several virtues to offset his many failings. Rub is no complainer: he "could stand hip deep in the overflow of a ruptured septic tank as pleasantly as if he were in the middle of a field of daisies. This made him invaluable to Sully who, not overly fastidious, could distinguish between the smell of shit and that of daisies." Rub tolerates others' mistakes. When Sully loads a truck so full of concrete blocks that it sinks irretrievably in the mud, he need not fear Rub's derision: "Other people's stupidity elicited only sympathy in Rub, who identified so strongly and immediately with dumbness that he lost all advantage." In fact Sully considers Rub

> the perfect dance partner, always content to let [others] . . . lead. The beauty of Rub was that he had no agenda of his own. If Sully was in a hurry or had somewhere to go, another job to do when this one was finished, hauling ass was fine with Rub. If for some reason—like they were being paid by the hour—they needed to go slow, then Rub was even more of a marvel the way he was able to stay in motion without accomplishing anything. Rub was a perfect laborer.

The novel repeatedly outlines Rub's humble ambitions and desires. He passes his workdays wishing aloud for small things: to be invisible for a day in order to watch Toby Roebuck in the shower, to get a job paying twenty dollars an hour in a nearby resort hotel, that a favorite soft drink will come back on the market. Sully, half listening to Rub's litany, is constantly "amazed by the modesty of Rub's fantasies":

> Often there was a curious wisdom about Rub's imaginings, as if he'd learned about life that nothing ever comes to you clean but instead with caveats and provisos that could render the gifts worthless or leave you hungry for more. It was as if somewhere in the back of Rub's mind he knew that he was better off without whatever it was he wished for.

Rub fears his wife, Bootsie (who is furnishing their apartment with goods she shoplifts from her job at Woolworth's), and is fanatically loyal to Sully, whom he considers his best friend. But with the return of Sully's son Peter to North Bath, Rub feels his position is endangered. This gets worse when Peter, turned down for tenure by the college where he teaches and deserted by his unhappy wife, comes to work with Sully. More than anything else, Rub wishes it was just him and Sully again.

Sully is also on the outs with his longtime married lover, Ruth, a woman who has waited for Sully too long. They have been together off and on for years, as everyone in town but Ruth's clueless husband knows. But this time it looks like their period of "being good" may be permanent. Tired from working the day shift as a cashier at the IGA and evenings waiting tables at a local restaurant, Ruth is tired, too, of Sully's predictable unpredictability. When Sully, surprised that Ruth knows where he has been one afternoon, accuses her of ESP, Ruth responds wearily that "nobody needed any extra senses to figure Sully out."

However, "to Sully, the deepest of life's mysteries were the mysteries of his own behavior," and his shifting relationship with his son Peter and his grandson Will absorb much of his attention during the week that passes in the novel. Sully was at best an absentee father when Peter was young; his former wife Vera's "most nagging fear when Peter was growing up was that Sully might one day wake up and take an interest in their son." There is little likelihood of this: "Given half a chance, [Sully] gravitated naturally to the easy camaraderie of the lunchroom, the barroom, the company of men, of another man's wife." But, when Peter's wife decamps with the couple's other children, Sully's response to the extremely timid six-year-old boy who remains behind in North Bath with Peter takes him by surprise, "as if some natural, biological affection were coming to him late, after skipping a generation."

Will likes his grandpa, even though he believes he is not supposed to; their time together makes him less timorous. Time with Will in turn helps Sully understand his own son's boyhood:

> Peter had been the same way, an almost comatose kid. . . . If you didn't tell him to open a door, he'd just stand in front of it. At the time it had not occurred to Sully that the reason might be fear. The fear of doing the wrong thing. It seemed obvious now.

However, their growing camaraderie is offset for Sully by ambivalence: "Every time he laid eyes on Peter he felt in the pit of his stomach the vague, monstrous debt a man owes. . . . A grandson simply extended the debt, let you know that you still owed it, that the interest is compounded."

Part of the difficulty for Sully is that remembering Peter's childhood and participating in Will's reminds him bitterly of his own father. Big Jim Sullivan was a man who fooled others. Charming until he had too much to drink, he was brutal to his wife and sons in an era when domestic violence was nobody's business. The novel features harrowing descriptions of his rage. One time Big Jim frightened a young boy poking around a building he was guarding, and the boy fell to his death, impaled on a wrought iron fence spike. Sully had vowed never to forgive Big Jim, who forgave himself too easily: "Watching his own father's house decay and fall apart had been deeply satisfying" to Sully. Self-defeating practices like this cause his friends to consider Sully "the uncontested master of the futile gesture." Only when Peter and Sully begin salvaging building materials from the old Sullivan house, literally ripping the place to shreds, does Sully confront the ghost of his father.

Before Sully's "stupid streak" ends, he punches out the cop he has been needling for weeks and briefly goes to jail. Peter and Toby Roebuck fall in love; lawyer Wirf is diagnosed with cancer; Ruth's daughter and granddaughter, on the run from violence in their home, appeal to Miss Beryl and Sully for protection; and Clive Jr. runs off with the backers' money for "The Ultimate Escape" when his own escape from North Bath and his awful fiancée beckons. Russo enjoys tying the loose strands of the narrative together and giving a final report on even peripheral characters. Miss Beryl, thinking over her years of friendship with Sully and her son's long-standing resentment of that bond, asserts it decisively by paying the back taxes on the Sullivan house, giving Sully a home. Peter and Will decide to stay on in North Bath, strengthening the new bonds of family. And Sully's lucky number, on which he has placed countless bets, finally wins, paying enough money for him to buy a new truck and helping father and son get on their feet again. But the magic of the novel's last pages is that Sully comes to feel the truth of one of the "cockamamie theories" his philosophy professor had explained:

> According to him, everybody, all the people in the world, were linked by invisible strings, and when you moved you were really exerting influence on other people. Even if you couldn't see the strings pulling, they were there just the same. At the time Sully had considered the idea bullshit. After all, he'd been lurching through life for pretty close to sixty years without having any noticeable effect on anybody but himself. . . . But all this had been before Thanksgiving, before Peter showed up needing things and bringing his own needy little boy with him, before Janey had come looking for him when she needed a place to hide, before he learned of Ralph and Vera's troubles and that Wirf was sick. Maybe there were strings. Maybe you caused things even when you tried hard not to.

This notion is central to Russo's practice as a novelist. Like Charles Dickens and George Eliot before him, he creates a vibrant set of characters whose fortunes will be more intertwined than seems apparent or likely. What the characters make of these connections is far more important than the events that reveal them. A fundamental generosity of spirit and an easygoing ability to accept what comes are key to Sully's persona. When he at last relinquishes the anger he has carried toward his own father since childhood, Sully grows up. That the surprising love he feels has skipped a generation matters less than that he embraces it now, in time for his grandson.

Partway through *Nobody's Fool,* Carl Roebuck salutes Sully, calling him "Thief of Snowblowers, Poisoner of Dogs, Flipper of Pancakes, Secret Father and Grandfather," and ending with his classic epithet for Sully, "Jack-Off, All Trades." This irreverent catalog, however, captures only a few traits of the complex central character of *Nobody's Fool.*

Critics and readers alike embraced this novel, though its length and digressiveness elicited a few complaints. The sprawling quality of *Nobody's Fool,* however, makes sense given Russo's fascination with novelists like Dickens and Eliot, whom he cited to Wendy Smith as the strongest influences on his own work "because of their ambition, their wanting to see more of the world, their desire not just to look at the interior workings of a single character and situation." He claims he would rather have written *Middlemarch,* Eliot's classic study of the interlocked destinies of the residents in a provincial Victorian town, than any other book. In 1994 *Nobody's Fool* was made into a popular film starring Paul Newman and Jessica Tandy. It was directed by Robert Benton, who collaborated with Russo on the screenplay for *Twilight* (1998).

STRAIGHT MAN

Straight Man (1997), Russo's fourth novel, is an academic satire. Again the milieu is familiar. Russo taught for more than twenty-five years before leaving teaching to pursue writing full-time. He is quick to point out, however, that the financially stressed, third-rate state college that provides the setting for *Straight Man* is a composite rather than a portrait of any one institution. The protagonist, Professor William Henry "Hank" Devereaux Jr., is mired in a midlife crisis, stuck in his tenured position. In an interview with Lewis Burke Frumkes, for *The Writer,* Russo characterizes Hank as "willing to do almost anything to stir things up."

Surrounded by colleagues whose foibles he knows all too well and whose expertise he derides, Hank believes himself the last honest man. Never one to resist a wisecrack when the opportunity arises, Hank irritates his colleagues and exasperates his long-suffering wife, Lily. Before she leaves town for the weekend, Lily asks Hank to take care of himself: "I have this fear. I can't decide where you're going to be when I get home. In the hospital or in jail." Over the next few days an escalating series of comic misadventures helps Hank make both predictions come true.

Word is going around the university that each department head has been asked to make a list of those professors whose services are expendable, and none of Hank's colleagues in the English department, which he chairs, believes Hank will refuse to make such a list. More fatally, each is worried that his or her name might be on the list Hank might be submitting. Their paranoia is not without justification. Among Hank's colleagues are the perennially drunk Billy Quigley, who is putting the last of his ten children through college and cannot afford to lose his job; Paul Rourke, who has been bitterly angry since Hank refused to sell him a piece of land on the desirable side of Allegheny Wells adjacent to Hank's own property, thus relegating Rourke to the crummy, treeless real estate on the lower side of the slope; and Gracie, who is so annoyed by Hank's taunts during a department meeting that she whacks him with her spiral notebook. Its barbed metal end hooks Hank in the nose, and when the novel opens, he is both bleeding and laughing.

Maybe the problem is that they have all known each other too long. One colleague, Finny, had a two-week interlude as a transvestite many years ago, and no one, least of all Hank, has forgotten it: "Never was a man dressed as a woman more full of joie de vivre than Finny off his meds. . . . Since then he's caused no problems, unless you considered his arrogant

incompetence and brain-scalding classroom tedium problematic." But Hank's younger colleagues seem just as ridiculous. Under the influence of cultural studies and feminist critical theory, one professor has declared he has no further use for literature and will not permit his students to write at all. "In department meetings, whenever a masculine pronoun was used, [he] corrected the speaker, saying 'Or she.' . . . Lately, everyone . . . had come to refer to him as Orshee." Orshee struggles against his privilege as a white male, privately informing Hank that he feels he ought to be first on the redundancy list and inviting Hank's derision. As Hank sees it, "In English departments the most serious competition is for the role of straight man."

Hank has a few allies among his department members, most notably Billy Quigley's daughter Meg, who is working as an adjunct instructor, and his own efficient secretary Rachel, who has been turning out masterful short stories on the side and with whom Hank is half in love. Another colleague and drinking buddy, Tony Coniglia, has been offering extracurricular sex instruction to his female students for years. The dean, Jacob Rose, is on his side too, but even Jacob has been warning Hank that he can only goad his colleagues so far. Finny, for one, "is threatening litigation if you don't stop harassing him about his degree from the Ventura Boulevard Burrito Palace and School for the Arts." The other department members are unimpressed by the satiric "Soul of the University" columns Devereaux has been writing for the local paper under the pseudonym "Lucky Hank," and they are threatening a recall of the chair. The very notion makes Hank chuckle: "Name one time in the last twenty years when that wasn't true." He knows, however, that his has been "rule by exasperation" and that he is "a rather vague pain in the collective ass."

Hank's health does not seem all that good, either. Worried about the trouble he is having urinating, Hank quickly becomes convinced a tumor is blocking his flow. He is also blocked creatively, unable to produce a sequel to the well-received novel he wrote years ago. Hank is self-medicating both problems with large doses of alcohol. Reeling between meetings, bars, and the creative writing workshops he leads, which are full of untalented, aggressively hostile students, Hank finds himself unexpectedly in the media limelight. The university's recalcitrant board of trustees has withheld departmental budgets, and tension is mounting. Hank, walking by the campus pond, mischievously threatens to kill a duck a day until he gets a budget. With a Groucho Marx fake nose covering his own damaged proboscis, Hank draws a crowd, and a local news crew happens to get the speech on videotape. Then geese start turning up dead, and everyone comes gunning for Hank, who wants only to hide. Much of his time in the novel is spent ducking into one location to avoid a colleague or neighbor and running immediately into another.

Hank needs time, moreover, to contemplate—or avoid—his own family problems. His daughter Julie's marriage is apparently unraveling, even as the couple is hopelessly mired in building a house that looks exactly like the one in which Julie was raised. Hank also comes to suspect that his wife is actually out of town with his best friend Jacob; in fact he keeps imagining Lily with other men. Reasonably enough, Hank sees this as a symptom of his own derangement: "Many of my male colleagues—married and divorced—regularly confess to sexual longings. They all want to get laid. But, to my knowledge, I'm the only one who regularly envisions my *wife* getting laid." Finally, Hank's long-estranged parents have reunited, and his father, himself a famous English professor and writer, has just arrived in Allegheny Wells.

Like other Russo novels, *Straight Man* explores the long shadow cast by an absent or difficult father, though Hank Sr. stays largely offstage. Hank's mother hectors her son into visiting the philandering husband who abandoned them both when Hank was a boy and who is now himself reduced by illness. Forgiving his father is something Hank finds difficult to do, though he is not unmindful of the fact that he has followed nearly in his father's scholarly footsteps while rejecting any pretense to the "high seriousness" toward which both parents encouraged him. By the time the meeting occurs, toward the end of the novel, the drama has gone out of whatever conflict the two men might have had. The elderly Hank Sr. is forgetful and more than preoccupied by his belief that he wronged Charles Dickens by undervaluing his work years ago. Hank is stunned by his father's continuing self-absorption; surely by this time the man might be expected to shift his priorities from the aesthetic to the familial. The realization that his father is unmoored from human ties nevertheless frees Hank to see how much he values his own connections, and he recognizes grace and forgiveness in the faces looking back at him:

> Only after we've done a thing do we know what we'll do, and by then whatever we've done has already begun to sever itself from clear significance, at least for the doer. Which is why we have spouses and children and parents and colleagues and friends, because someone has to know us better than we know ourselves. We need them to tell us. We need them to say, "I know you, Al. You're not the kind of man who."

Because this a comic novel, its dilemmas are happily resolved. Julie and her husband reconcile, the true duck killer is captured, and Hank's suspicions of his wife are unfounded. Russo also takes time for comic digressions, such as the story of how Lily's father landed in jail in Philadelphia or the ambitions of Missy Blaylock, the local news reporter, who frets that "breasts like hers are wasted in a small media market." He takes particular delight in chronicling the war zone that is Hank's writing classroom. Leo writes stories full of blood and murder. When he wonders if one gruesome sex scene is "overdone," Hank can only advise him, "Always understate necrophilia." Leo is pitted against Solange, a fellow student with black hair and "an angry streak of white—her mean streak." Hank is mesmerized by the unintentional humor on offer in student papers: "As a group they seem to believe that high moral indignation offsets and indeed outweighs all deficiencies of punctuation, spelling, grammar, logic, and style. In support of this notion there's only the entire culture." The class members' response to essays read aloud only deepens Hank's conviction that his students are unassailably ignorant: "The more outrageous, the more historically inaccurate and fallacious the analogies, the further the essays drift from the assigned topic, the more the authors are cheered." "Mediocrity," Hank concludes, "is a reasonable goal for our institution."

The scene toward which much of the novel is progressing, however, is the departmental vote, a masterpiece of slapstick comedy. After loudly professing indifference to his ouster, Hank suddenly finds himself caring more about the outcome than he expects, and he eavesdrops on the meeting from the crawlspace above the room's ceiling. Crouched in pitch blackness, covered in dust and his own urine (his blockage has given way to an unexpected flood just before the meeting begins), Hank tells himself: "Many inspired plans are hatched in darkness. And once dignity is surrendered, there are plenty of options." He launches anonymous missives about procedural errors down through the ceiling tiles and narrowly survives the vote. But the surprises keep coming. In the administrative shake-up that follows, Jacob is promoted to the role of campus executive officer and asks Hank to take his place as dean. Hank ruefully recalls: "When we were hired, we were *both* loose cannons. With this move, it's official: the revolution has become an institution."

His last shred of dignity evaporates, however, when (after a fall) Hank learns his blockage was nothing worse than "hysterical prostate, a phrase itself calculated to induce hysteria." Hank tries unsuccessfully to persuade his doctor that passing up the position of dean and relinquishing his tenure are "the symbolic equivalent of passing a stone." When he awakens in the hospital with a bad bump on the head, Lily has returned and is by his side. Hank muses on his luck: "Perhaps no man should possess the key to his wife's affections, what makes and keeps him worthy in her eyes. That would be like gaining unauthorized access to God's grace. We would not use such knowledge wisely." In his drugged relaxation, Hank realizes that Lily's predictions have come true:

> As I drift back into sleep, I can't help thinking that it's a wonderful thing to be right about the world. To weigh the evidence, always incomplete, and correctly intuit the whole, to see the world in a grain of sand, to recognize its beauty, its simplicity, its truth. It's as close as we get to God in this life, and we reside in the glow of such brief flashes of understanding, fully awake, sometimes, for two or three seconds, at peace with our existence. And then back to sleep we go.

Russo offers Hank's blissful and temporary sense of order as the fleeting but true intuition it is.

The epilogue, in typical Russo fashion, pulls all the pieces together by dispatching even the minor characters to their fates. We leave Hank on sabbatical, counting his blessings and observing the academic scene with a cheerfully dismayed acceptance of his place in its ritual chaos. Readers and critics again responded positively to *Straight Man,* which enjoyed the best notices of Russo's career. Tom De Haven for the *New York Times* called it "the funniest serious novel . . . since *Portnoy's Complaint,*" with "sadness and smothered panic" permeating the humor. In this briefer volume, reservations about Russo's rambling plotlines were diffused: "The novel's greatest pleasures derive not from any blazing impatience to see what happens next, but from pitch-perfect dialogue, persuasive characterization, and a rich progression of scenes, most of them crackling with an impudent, screwball energy." In a review for *World Literature Today,* Rita D. Jacobs praised Russo's "fine comic ear, split-second timing, and eye for the absurdity of everyday life." This novel too has been purchased with a screen adaptation in mind.

EMPIRE FALLS

With *Empire Falls* (2001), another novel named after a town, Russo returns to the dilapidated, small-town industrial setting that provides the milieu for most of his work. An omniscient narrator reveals another large cast of characters related by blood, work, or both. These ties go deeper and carry more import than the main characters at first realize, though in typical Russo fashion the narrator allows the reader to grasp or at least intuit these bonds quickly. This is another tale about the long reach of small-town ties: neither divorce nor death concludes a relationship or ends its consequences for the generations that follow.

This can be good or bad news, depending on the good or ill will of the characters involved. For the mild Miles Roby, it means he is tied to his confused wife, Janine, even as she believes a divorce from him will bring her quick relief. (She plans to marry Miles's main irritant, Walt, who goes by the nickname "The Silver Fox," as soon as possible.) Miles is tied to the wealthy Whiting family. The elderly Mrs. Whiting, who owns everything in the failing town, also owns Miles's business, the Empire Grill, and keeps him on a tight leash. Miles nurses twenty years' worth of guilt for his inability to love Cindy Whiting, the girl who was crippled in a hit-and-run accident as a child and who attempted suicide out of frustrated love for him when they were teenagers. What Miles does not know is that Cindy has recovered more fully than he thinks, while Mrs. Whiting is taking fuller and slower revenge for an offense he does not even comprehend.

At one time Miles imagined he would get away from Empire Falls. He has a mostly absent, mostly drunken father, whom his mother will not divorce (and who is a much less likeable character than his equivalent in Russo's earlier novels). Grace Roby manages to send Miles to college, hoping only that he will make his escape from the dead-end town. However, when his mother is struggling with the cancer that will kill her, Miles leaves school, takes over the Empire Grill, and settles in to become one of the town's most solid citizens. Grace dies angry that her son has been pulled back, partly through the intervention of her employer Mrs. Whiting, who makes Miles a long-term deal on the business. Francine Whiting and Grace Roby have a bond that links them in anger and frustrated love, and Mrs. Whiting is settling her score with Grace by ensuring that Miles stays stuck in Empire Falls.

Russo mingles mostly present-day omniscient narration with occasional chapters set a generation in the past to show the marriage of C. B. Whiting to Francine Robideaux, a penniless local girl with a sharp mind and a flinty determination to have her way. Later in life the unhappy C. B. observes "that he always had the last word in all differences of opinion with his wife, and that—two words, actually—was, 'Yes, dear.'" *Empire Falls* considers, in greater detail than earlier Russo novels, the relation between powerful families like the Whitings and the towns they transfigure. The opening of the novel describes in detail the unavailing effort of the Whitings some thirty years earlier to compensate for the poor situation of their new house. They have elected to build at the curve of the busy

Knox River, which offers a beautiful vista, protected from the wastes produced by their own textile mills. However, a foul smell quickly reveals a decaying moose stuck in the river bend. This is a spot where trash of all kinds builds up, defeating the family's efforts to stay above it all, insulated from the refuse their prosperity has generated. Their answer is to change the course of the river, and they duly blast a channel through the (aptly named) Robideaux Blight. An unexpected consequence of this change is that the river runs higher and faster during its periodic flood, with fatal (if long-delayed) consequences for the Whiting family heirs. This anecdote represents the arrogant class-consciousness of the Whiting family as handed down to the present day. It also carries a warning: this is a just universe, even if justice is slow in coming.

Flashbacks also eventually tell of C. B. Whiting's brief affair with Grace Roby, a disappointment that breaks Grace's heart and ruins her health. The nine-year-old Miles goes to Martha's Vineyard with his mother, escaping (he thinks) from his father's latest drunken rage. While staying in the cheapest cottage the Summer House resort offers, Miles has the feeling that his mother is waiting for someone or something. One night they meet a man who introduces himself as Charlie Mayne and who takes them on picnics and driving in his fancy sports car. His mother is radiant, though she is also mysteriously ill in the mornings. When they go back to Maine at the end of the week, however, his mother's bloom fades, and Miles's father eventually returns to plague Grace anew. It will be many years before Miles realizes that "Charlie Mayne" is none other than the richest married man in town. He sees then, too, that the special interest Mrs. Whiting has taken in his mother and him through the years is prompted by her jealous knowledge that her husband loved another woman better than herself. Miles comes in for his share of Mrs. Whiting's anger

as well, since C. B. would have abandoned his own daughter Cindy for Grace's child.

Russo's work frequently features family secrets, especially secrets of paternity or loss, though they are not usually as central as they are in *Empire Falls*. One of the best-kept secrets in town is that C. B. was driving the car that hit and disabled his daughter, an accident covered up to keep the family name clean. His guilt in turn disables him from loving Cindy, whom he has injured so grievously; he eventually commits suicide. Grace passes up her chance to escape Empire Falls with C. B. when she realizes he has no intention of taking Cindy with them. The child she is herself carrying, against all expectation, is not C. B.'s but her husband's, and David's birth ties Grace permanently down. The last nail in her coffin is the job she accepts as Mrs. Whiting's assistant when the mill closes and she loses her position there.

Another difference in *Empire Falls* is a more meditative tone. There is less narrative momentum in this settled and mostly content middle-aged man than there was in the loopy self-destructiveness of Russo's earlier protagonists. Miles Roby has fewer demons to battle than Sully in *Nobody's Fool* or Hank in *Straight Man,* and the novelist thus faces the challenge of making Miles as compelling as his rogues have been. He is, however, freer to concentrate on the long reach of the small town. Much of the novel is given to watching Miles figure out his complicated place in the history of Empire Falls, with a key piece of information revealed (appropriately) by a yellowed clipping from the local newspaper.

One thing completely familiar here is the setting. The Empire Grill is the nerve center of town, the place where everyone gathers—or at least passes through—several times a day. That this location recurs so frequently in Russo's books is perhaps unsurprising, given the author's work habits. He writes every morning at a deli on his own small town's main street before repairing in the afternoons to a local bar to revise his work. Thus the movements of his characters, the small circuits they travel through their hometowns, and the reliability with which they encounter both friend and nemesis are all features of Russo's chosen environment.

The Empire Grill is facing hard times and is struggling to attract the new clientele that can keep the family afloat. Miles's younger brother, David, is chef. As he recovers from the drunk driving incident that nearly killed him, he introduces ethnic cuisine alongside the more traditional meat loaf and potatoes that are the diner's normal fare. David is also nagging Miles to change venues entirely. He wants Miles to go into business with Francine's mother, Bea, who operates a local bar and whose liquor license would boost the brothers' revenue considerably. (The old-fashioned Mrs. Whiting will not let Miles make any changes to the Grill, and Miles is attacked by her deranged cat—a witch's familiar if there ever was one—every time he pays a call on his patron.)

Miles, however, is preoccupied with his moody, estranged wife, who has recently dropped fifty pounds and discovered sex—with another man. Janine's beau, Walt, has taken to hanging around the Grill and demanding that Miles arm wrestle him in what he clearly believes is a display of comradely affection. Miles is also uncomfortably aware of Charlene, the waitress with whom he has been half in love since adolescence but who prefers rough, dangerous men on motorcycles to Miles's more staid appeal. Charlene is untroubled by the Grill's new upscale clientele: "College professors tipped in the same fashion as other men—according to cup size." Miles is busy trying to help his friend Father Mark, the Catholic priest who is attempting to keep his flagging parish spiritually and financially afloat. It takes all both men can do to keep Father Tom, the irascible, senile former pastor, in line. (When Father Tom

and Miles's incorrigible father, Max, steal the rectory's car and head for Florida together, it is as though Russo's attention has flipped; now he shows what it feels like to be the responsible one left behind. Rather than going on the road with the anarchic pair, the novel stays home with Miles.) Miles is also preoccupied with Jimmy Minty, the town policeman who was his high school classmate and whom he dislikes intensely. Minty seems to be following Miles around town, and it makes Miles nervous. Most of all Miles is keeping an eye on his teenage daughter, Tick, who has an after-school job at the Grill but who never seems to eat a thing.

Empire Falls is the first of Russo's novels to explore teenage cruelties and uncertainties in depth. The writer has said his own daughter was the model for Tick. He also told Mel Gussow that "Writing this book I had a sense that my own truest destiny is as a father of my daughters." He captures the isolation and lightning-swift shifts of mood that characterize adolescence. Tick is enduring high school and the separation of her parents with remarkable grace. However, the idiocy of her teachers, the mind-numbing boredom of her classes, and the desperation of her classmates are almost too much to bear. Tick is trying to avoid her former boyfriend, Zack, the son of Jimmy Minty the cop and a bully in his own right. The isolation of losing all her other "friends," however, who dropped Tick when she dropped the football star, Zack, is telling on her. Zack will do anything he can to win Tick back, but his meanness and anger lead him to do exactly the wrong thing: he taunts the strange, silent classmate whom Tick has befriended. Miles has given the near-feral John Voss a job in the kitchen of the Grill, and the boy and Tick have begun a tentative friendship. But John Voss has been neglected too long. In a burst of violence unusual in a Russo novel, the boy eventually explodes, killing several schoolmates and precipitating Miles and Tick's departure from Empire Falls.

As tiresome and constraining as extended family ties can be, Russo depicts John Voss's murderous frenzy as the result of his mutilating solitude.

Empire Falls is unusual among Russo's novels for its more measured, less redemptive tenor. Though its main character is a Catholic who is actively practicing his faith, there are few moments of revelation and transcendence. When Miles carries his panicked daughter from the scene of the classroom slaughter, she is damaged. He takes Tick to Martha's Vineyard to recover and devotes himself entirely to her care. Although all five of Russo's novels are in some sense about the damage parents do, this is the first instance of a father present at the scene of the crime who is also willing and able to rescue his child. In keeping with the modest scale of the novel's faith, Miles's devotion to Tick is all he can offer, but it looks like it might be enough.

Before he leaves Empire Falls, however, Miles has a few scores to settle himself. He breaks Walt's arm in the long-demanded wrestling match and breaks Jimmy Minty's nose in a fistfight. The bigger and stronger policeman, however, sends Miles to the hospital before insisting on his arrest for assault. All this leads up to the most important confrontation, the one between Miles and Mrs. Whiting. When Miles gives the elderly woman his notice, she observes coolly, "Passionate decisions are seldom very sound." Miles challenges her:

> "When did you ever feel passion?" "Well, it's true I'm seldom swept away like those with more romantic temperaments," she concurred. "But we are what we are, and what can't be cured must be endured." "What can't be cured must be avenged," Miles said. "Isn't that what you mean?" She smiled appreciatively. "Payback is *how* we endure, dear boy."

Mrs. Whiting tells Miles sardonically that she believes herself "a model of Christian forbearance": "Did I not forgive your mother her trespass? Did I not welcome her into the very home she destroyed? Did I not offer her every opportunity for the expiation and redemption you Catholics are forever going on and on about?" When Miles again challenges her, calling it retribution instead of redemption, she replies smoothly, "Well, as I once explained to my husband, there was a little something in the relationship for each of us." This venomously precise argument has nothing of the good-natured wordplay that characterizes Russo's earlier novels.

In fact the last word is devoted to the revenge motif, through the spectacular flood that sweeps Mrs. Whiting off to her death in the river whose flow her husband had redirected. There is a story that all the male Whitings die cursing their inability to kill the wives they have grown to detest:

> C. B. Whiting died in the mistaken belief that like his forbears, he had failed to kill his wife. . . . Had he lived, it would have surprised and perhaps even cheered him to learn that he actually had sealed her doom the year he proposed to her, not long after the dead moose washed up on his bank.

The swollen river carries Mrs. Whiting along, and in a macabre twist:

> Astride the body, crouched at the shoulders of the dead woman, was a red-mouthed, howling cat. Together, dead woman and living cat bumped along the upstream edge of the straining dam, as if searching for a place to climb out and over. Bumping, nudging, seeking, until finally a small section of the structure gave way and they were gone.

The gruesome final image of the novel, which brings rough justice to the relentless Mrs. Whiting, is in keeping with the relative bleakness of *Empire Falls*. The rueful, laconic acceptance of human nature that ends Russo's earlier novels lends an upbeat (if bemused) tone to their final pages; the characters have a resilience and buoyancy that stay with the reader. However, the greater fragility of the characters and the more somber cast to *Empire Falls* perhaps indicates that the novelist's new work will follow a different, darker current.

Critics responded to what A. O. Scott for the *New York Times* called the "tongue-in-cheek portentousness" of the novel's title with pleasure, asserting that Russo was claiming new ground: "Russo may at last have joined his fellow northerners Russell Banks, Frederick Busch and Joyce Carol Oates in trying to rescue the proud, battered regional realist tradition from cuteness, eccentricity and sentimental condescension." The only danger is that Russo's "amiable, witty raconteur" persona may disguise the fact that he is also "one of the best novelists around." "People live more public lives in small settings," the critic Edward Hower added, situating Russo in a line of American writers from Mark Twain to Sherwood Anderson and Garrison Keillor. "Richard Russo's canvas may be small, but he has written a big book." The ambitious breadth and detail of his work, whether skewed to comic or tragic ends, also place Russo squarely in the tradition of the nineteenth century novelists whose work he prizes.

Selected Bibliography

WORKS OF RICHARD RUSSO

NOVELS AND SHORT STORIES
Mohawk. New York: Vintage, 1986.
The Risk Pool. New York: Random House, 1988.
Nobody's Fool. New York: Random House, 1993.
"Dog." *The New Yorker,* December 23, 1996, pp. 74–77.
Straight Man. New York: Random House, 1997.
"The Whore's Child." *Harper's,* February 1998, pp. 60–67.

Empire Falls. New York: Knopf, 2001.
The Whore's Child: And Other Stories. New York: Knopf, 2002.

OTHER WORKS
Twilight. Screenplay by Richard Russo and Robert Benton. Directed by Robert Benton. Paramount, 1998.
The Flamingo Rising. Screenplay by Richard Russo. Directed by Martha Coolidge. Hallmark Hall of Fame, 2001.

CRITICAL AND BIOGRAPHICAL STUDIES

Alleva, Richard E. "Paul Newman Performs." *Commonweal,* February 24, 1995, pp. 54–55.
Brzezinski, Steve. Review of *Straight Man. Antioch Review* 52, no. 1:173 (winter 1994).
Charles, Ron. "Pillorying Pretentious Professors." *Christian Science Monitor,* October 16, 1997, p. 14.
De Haven, Tom. "Screwball U." *New York Times Book Review,* July 6, 1997, p. 10. (Review of *Straight Man.*)
Gussow, Mel. "Writing a Novel in the Deli, Making Revisons in the Bar." *New York Times,* August 29, 2001, arts section, pp. 1–4.
Hower, Edward. "Small-Town Dreams." *The World and I* 16, no. 10:243–248 (October 2001). (Review of *Empire Falls.*)
Ingalls, Zoe. "A Novelist Finds Humor in Academic Woes." *Chronicle of Higher Education,* August 8, 1997, pp. B8–B9.
Jacobs, Rita D. Review of *Straight Man. World Literature Today* 72, no. 4:832–833 (autumn 1998).
Kaveney, Roz. "Bonds Men." *New Statesman,* July 7, 1993, pp. 39–40.
Koenig, Rhoda. Review of *Nobody's Fool. The New Yorker,* May 31, 1993, pp. 60–61.
Leader, Zachary. "Pretty, Green Graves." *Times Literary Supplement,* July 2, 1993, p. 23.
Prose, Francine. "Small-Town Smart Alecks." *New York Times Book Review,* June 20, 1993, pp. 13–14. (Review of *Nobody's Fool.*)

Purdum, Todd. "More Serious, More Funny." *New York Times Book Review,* December 18, 1988, p. 14.

Scott, A. O. "Townies." *New York Times Book Review,* June 24, 2001, p. 8. (Review of *Empire Falls.*)

Simon, John. "Two Cheers for Christmas." *National Review,* December 24, 1994, pp. 62–63.

Skow, John. "Boarded-up Glocca Morra." *Time,* May 3, 1993, pp. 66–68.

Steinberg, Sybil S. "Forecast: Fiction." *Publishers Weekly,* May 12, 1997, p. 56.

Sullivan, Jack. "'Things Get Bad,' Says Dad." *New York Times Book Review,* December 18, 1988, p. 14. (Review of *The Risk Pool.*)

INTERVIEWS

Frumkes, Lewis Burke. "A Conversation with Richard Russo." *The Writer* 113, no. 12:19–21 (December 2000).

Smith, Wendy. "Richard Russo: The Novelist Again Explores the Crucial Impact of Place on Individual Destinies." *Publishers Weekly,* June 7, 1993, pp. 43–44.

FILM BASED ON A WORK OF RICHARD RUSSO

Nobody's Fool. Directed by Robert Benton. Paramount, 1994.

—*TRICIA WELSCH*

Index

Arabic numbers printed in bold-face type refer to extended treatment of a subject.

"Beach Women, The" (Pinsky), **Supp. VI:** 241

"Beaded Pear, The" (Simpson), **Supp. IX:** 276

Beagle, Peter, **Supp. X:** 24

Beam, Jeffrey, **Supp. XII:** 98

Beaman, E. O., **Supp. IV Part 2:** 604

Bean, Michael, **Supp. V:** 203

Bean, Robert Bennett, **Supp. II Part 1:** 170

Bean Eaters, The (Brooks), **Supp. III Part 1:** 79–81

Be Angry at the Sun (Jeffers), **Supp. II Part 2:** 434

"Beanstalk Country, The" (T. Williams), **IV:** 383

Bean Trees, The (Kingsolver), **Supp. VII:** 197, 199–201, 202, 207, 209

"Bear" (Hogan), **Supp. IV Part 1:** 412

Bear, The (Faulkner), **Supp. VIII:** 184

"Bear, The" (Faulkner), **II:** 71–72, 73, 228; **IV:** 203; **Supp. IV Part 2:** 434; **Supp. IX:** 95; **Supp. X:** 30

"Bear, The" (Kinnell), **Supp. III Part 1:** 244

"Bear, The" (Momaday), **Supp. IV Part 2:** 480, 487

Bear and His Daughter: Stories (Stone), **Supp. V:** 295, 308

Beard, Charles, **I:** 214; **IV:** 429; **Supp. I Part 2:** 481, 490, 492, 632, 640, 643, 647

Beard, James, **I:** 341

Beard, Mary, **Supp. I Part 2:** 481

"Bearded Oaks" (Warren), **IV:** 240

Bearden, Romare, **Retro. Supp. I:** 209; **Supp. VIII:** 337, 342

Beardsley, Aubrey, **II:** 56; **IV:** 77

"Bears" (Rich), **Retro. Supp. II:** 280

"Beast" (Swenson), **Supp. IV Part 2:** 639

Beast God Forgot to Invent, The (Harrison), **Supp. VIII:** 37, 46, **51–52**

Beast in Me, The (Thurber), **Supp. I Part 2:** 615

"Beast in the Jungle, The" (James), **I:** 570; **II:** 335; **Retro. Supp. I:** 235; **Supp. V:** 103–104

Beast in View (Rukeyser), **Supp. VI:** 272, 273, 279, 280

"Beat! Beat! Drums!" (Whitman), **III:** 585

"Beatrice Palmato" (Wharton), **Retro. Supp. I:** 379

Beattie, Ann, **Supp. V:** 21–37; **Supp. XI:** 26; **Supp. XII:** 80, 139, 294

Beatty, General Sam, **I:** 193

Beaty, Jerome, **Supp. IV Part 1:** 331

Beaumont, Francis, **Supp. I Part 2:** 422

"Beauties of Santa Cruz, The" (Freneau), **Supp. II Part 1:** 260

Beautiful and Damned, The (Fitzgerald), **II:** 88, 89–91, 93, 263; **Retro. Supp. I:** **103–105**, 105, 106, 110; **Supp. IX:** 56, 57

Beautiful Changes, The (Wilbur), **Supp. III Part 2:** 544–550

"Beautiful Changes, The" (Wilbur), **Supp. III Part 2:** 549, 550

"Beautiful Child, A" (Capote), **Supp. III Part 1:** 113, 125

"Beautiful & Cruel" (Cisneros), **Supp. VII:** 63, 67

"Beautiful Woman Who Sings, The" (Gunn Allen), **Supp. IV Part 1:** 326

"Beauty" (Emerson), **II:** 2, 5

"Beauty" (Wylie), **Supp. I Part 2:** 710

"Beauty and the Beast" (Dove), **Supp. IV Part 1:** 245

"Beauty and the Beast" (fairy tale), **IV:** 266; **Supp. X:** 88

"Beauty and the Shoe Sluts" (Karr), **Supp. XI:** 250

Beauty of the Husband, The: A Fictional Essay in Twenty-Nine Tangos (Carson), **Supp. XII:** **113–114**

Beauty's Punishment (Rice), **Supp. VII:** 301

Beauty's Release: The Continued Erotic Adventures of Sleeping Beauty (Rice), **Supp. VII:** 301

Beauvoir, Simone de, **IV:** 477; **Retro. Supp. II:** 281; **Supp. I Part 1:** 51; **Supp. III Part 1:** 200–201, 208; **Supp. IV Part 1:** 360; **Supp. IX:** 4

"Because I could not stop for Death—" (Dickinson), **Retro. Supp. I:** **38–40**, 41, 43, 44

"Because It Happened" (Goldbarth), **Supp. XII:** 192

"Because You Mentioned the Spiritual Life" (Dunn), **Supp. XI:** 154

Bech: A Book (Updike), **IV:** 214; **Retro. Supp. I:** 329, 335

Beck, Dave, **I:** 493

Beck, Jack, **Supp. IV Part 2:** 560

Becker, Carl, **Supp. I Part 2:** 492, 493

Becker, Paula. *See* Modersohn, Mrs. Otto (Paula Becker)

Beckett, Samuel, **I:** 71, 91, 142, 298, 461; **III:** 387; **IV:** 95; **Retro. Supp. I:** 206; **Supp. IV Part 1:** 297, 368–369; **Supp. IV Part 2:** 424; **Supp. V:** 23, 53; **Supp. XI:** 104; **Supp. XII:** 21, 150–151

Beckett, Tom, **Supp. IV Part 2:** 419

Beckford, William, **I:** 204

Beckonings (Brooks), **Supp. III Part 1:** 85

"Becky" (Toomer), **Supp. III Part 2:** 481, 483; **Supp. IX:** 312

Becoming a Man: Half a Life Story (Monette), **Supp. X:** 146, 147, 149, 151, 152, **155–157**

"Becoming a Meadow" (Doty), **Supp. XI:** 124–125

"Becoming and Breaking: Poet and Poem" (Ríos), **Supp. IV Part 2:** 539

Becoming Canonical in American Poetry (Morris), **Retro. Supp. I:** 40

Becoming Light: New and Selected Poems (Jong), **Supp. V:** 115

"Bed, The" (Dixon), **Supp. XII:** 154

Beddoes, Thomas Lovell, **III:** 469; **Retro. Supp. I:** 285

Bedichek, Roy, **Supp. V:** 225

Bedient, Calvin, **Supp. IX:** 298; **Supp. XII:** 98

"Bed in the Sky, The" (Snyder), **Supp. VIII:** 300

Bednarik, Joseph, **Supp. VIII:** 39

"Bedrock" (Proulx), **Supp. VII:** 253

"Bee, The" (Lanier), **Supp. I Part 1:** 364

Beecher, Catharine, **Supp. I Part 2:** 581, 582–583, 584, 586, 588, 589, 591, 599; **Supp. X:** 103; **Supp. XI:** 193

Beecher, Charles, **Supp. I Part 2:** 588, 589

Beecher, Edward, **Supp. I Part 2:** 581, 582, 583, 584, 588, 591

Beecher, Harriet. *See* Stowe, Harriet Beecher

Beecher, Henry Ward, **II:** 275; **Supp. I Part 2:** 581; **Supp. XI:** 193

Beecher, Lyman, **Supp. I Part 2:** 580–581, 582, 583, 587, 588, 599; **Supp. XI:** 193

Beecher, Mrs. Lyman (Roxanna Foote), **Supp. I Part 2:** 580–581, 582, 588, 599

Beeching, Jack, **Supp. X:** 114, 117, 118, 123, 125, 126

"Beehive" (Toomer), **Supp. IX:** 317

"Bee Hunt, The" (Irving), **II:** 313

"Beekeeper's Daughter, The" (Plath), **Retro. Supp. II:** 246–247

"Bee Meeting, The" (Plath), **Retro. Supp. II:** 254–255

Bee Poems (Plath), **Retro. Supp. II:** 254–255

Beer, Thomas, **I:** 405

Beerbohm, Max, **III:** 472; **IV:** 436; **Supp. I Part 2:** 714

"Beer in the Sergeant Major's Hat, or The Sun Also Sneezes" (Chandler),

A Complete Listing of Authors in *American Writers*

Henry, O.   Supp. II
Hijuelos, Oscar   Supp. VIII
Hoffman, Alice   Supp. X
Hogan, Linda   Supp. IV
Holmes, Oliver Wendell   Supp. I
Howe, Irving   Supp. VI
Howe, Susan   Supp. IV
Howells, William Dean   Vol. II
Hughes, Langston   Supp. I
Hughes, Langston   Retro. Supp. I
Hugo, Richard   Supp. VI
Humphrey, William   Supp. IX
Hurston, Zora Neale   Supp. VI
Irving, John   Supp. VI
Irving, Washington   Vol. II
Jackson, Shirley   Supp. IX
James, Henry   Vol. II
James, Henry   Retro. Supp. I
James, William   Vol. II
Jarrell, Randall   Vol. II
Jeffers, Robinson   Supp. II
Jewett, Sarah Orne   Vol. II
Jewett, Sarah Orne   Retro. Supp. II
Johnson, Charles   Supp. VI
Jones, James   Supp. XI
Jong, Erica   Supp. V
Justice, Donald   Supp. VII
Karr, Mary   Supp. XI
Kazin, Alfred   Supp. VIII
Kennedy, William   Supp. VII
Kenyon, Jane   Supp. VII
Kerouac, Jack   Supp. III
Kincaid, Jamaica   Supp. VII
King, Stephen   Supp. V
Kingsolver, Barbara   Supp. VII
Kingston, Maxine Hong   Supp. V
Kinnell, Galway   Supp. III
Knowles, John   Supp. XII
Kosinski, Jerzy   Supp. VII
Kumin, Maxine   Supp. IV
Kunitz, Stanley   Supp. III
Kushner, Tony   Supp. IX
LaBastille, Anne   Supp. X
Lanier, Sidney   Supp. I

Lardner, Ring   Vol. II
Lee, Harper   Supp. VIII
Levertov, Denise   Supp. III
Levine, Philip   Supp. V
Levis, Larry   Supp. XI
Lewis, Sinclair   Vol. II
Lindsay, Vachel   Supp. I
London, Jack   Vol. II
Longfellow, Henry Wadsworth   Vol. II
Longfellow, Henry
    Wadsworth   Retro. Supp. II
Lowell, Amy   Vol. II
Lowell, James Russell   Supp. I
Lowell, Robert   Vol. II
Lowell, Robert   Retro. Supp. II
McCarthy, Cormac   Supp. VIII
McCarthy, Mary   Vol. II
McClatchy, J. D.   Supp. XII
McCourt, Frank   Supp. XII
McCullers, Carson   Vol. II
Macdonald, Ross   Supp. IV
McGrath, Thomas   Supp. X
McKay, Claude   Supp. X
MacLeish, Archibald   Vol. III
McMurty, Larry   Supp. V
McPhee, John   Supp. III
Mailer, Norman   Vol. III
Mailer, Norman   Retro. Supp. II
Malamud, Bernard   Supp. I
Marquand, John P.   Vol. III
Marshall, Paule   Supp. XI
Mason, Bobbie Ann   Supp. VIII
Masters, Edgar Lee   Supp. I
Mather, Cotton   Supp. II
Matthews, William   Supp. IX
Matthiessen, Peter   Supp. V
Maxwell, William   Supp. VIII
Melville, Herman   Vol. III
Melville, Herman   Retro. Supp. I
Mencken, H. L.   Vol. III
Merrill, James   Supp. III
Merton, Thomas   Supp. VIII
Merwin, W. S.   Supp. III
Millay, Edna St. Vincent   Vol. III

Sontag, Susan   Supp. III
Southern, Terry   Supp. XI
Stafford, William   Supp. XI
Stegner, Wallace   Supp. IV
Stein, Gertrude   Vol. IV
Steinbeck, John   Vol. IV
Stern, Gerald   Supp. IX
Stevens, Wallace   Vol. IV
Stevens, Wallace   Retro. Supp. I
Stone, Robert   Supp. V
Stowe, Harriet Beecher   Supp. I
Strand, Mark   Supp. IV
Styron, William   Vol. IV
Swenson, May   Supp. IV
Tan, Amy   Supp. X
Tate, Allen   Vol. IV
Taylor, Edward   Vol. IV
Taylor, Peter   Supp. V
Theroux, Paul   Supp. VIII
Thoreau, Henry David   Vol. IV
Thurber, James   Supp. I
Toomer, Jean   Supp. IX
Trilling, Lionel   Supp. III
Twain, Mark   Vol. IV
Tyler, Anne   Supp. IV
Updike, John   Vol. IV
Updike, John   Retro. Supp. I
Van Vechten, Carl   Supp. II
Veblen, Thorstein   Supp. I
Vidal, Gore   Supp. IV
Vonnegut, Kurt   Supp. II
Wagoner, David   Supp. IX

Walker, Alice   Supp. III
Wallace, David Foster   Supp. X
Warren, Robert Penn   Vol. IV
Welty, Eudora   Vol. IV
Welty, Eudora   Retro. Supp. I
West, Nathanael   Vol. IV
West, Nathanael   Retro. Supp. II
Wharton, Edith   Vol. IV
Wharton, Edith   Retro. Supp. I
White, E. B.   Supp. I
Whitman, Walt   Vol. IV
Whitman, Walt   Retro. Supp. I
Whittier, John Greenleaf   Supp. I
Wilbur, Richard   Supp. III
Wideman, John Edgar   Supp. X
Wilder, Thornton   Vol. IV
Williams, Tennessee   Vol. IV
Williams, William Carlos   Vol. IV
Williams, William Carlos   Retro. Supp. I
Wilson, August   Supp. VIII
Wilson, Edmund   Vol. IV
Winters, Yvor   Supp. II
Wolfe, Thomas   Vol. IV
Wolfe, Tom   Supp. III
Wolff, Tobias   Supp. VII
Wright, Charles   Supp. V
Wright, James   Supp. III
Wright, Richard   Vol. IV
Wylie, Elinor   Supp. I
Yates, Richard   Supp. XI
Zukofsky, Louis   Supp. III